LEADING INDICATORS AND BUSINESS CYCLE SURVEYS

Leading Indicators and Business Cycle Surveys

Papers presented at the 16th CIRET Conference Proceedings, Washington, D.C. 1983

edited by
KARL HEINRICH OPPENLÄNDER
and
GÜNTER POSER

St. Martin's Press New York

Printed in Great Britain
First published in the United States of America in 1984

ISBN 0-312-47645-0

Library of Congress Cataloging in Publication Data

CIRET Conference (16th : 1983 : Washington, D.C.)
Leading indicators and business cycle surveys.

Includes index.
1. Economic forecasting--Congresses. 2. Economic indicators--Congresses. 3. Business cycles--Congresses. 4. Economic surveys--Congresses. I. Oppenländer, Karl Heinrich, 1932- . II. Poser, Günter. III. Title.
HB3730.C535 1984 338.5'4 84-9981
ISBN 0-312-47645-0

Contents

Preface

This volume of proceedings contains the papers presented at the 16th CIRET Conference and summaries of the discussions of each session. Attached is a list of those papers that could not be discussed during the conference. These papers will be published in a forthcoming volume of CIRET Studies.

A workshop dealing with American business surveys, technical processing of survey results, and new survey activities was held the day before the conference began. It was chaired by Dr. G. Nerb, Ifo-Institute, Munich, and by G. Green, US Department of Commerce, Washington, D.C. A similar workshop will also be organized as part of the next conference that will take place in Vienna, Austria, in 1985.

During the conference the coordination committee decided to express special appreciation to Prof. Oskar Anderson, Prof. André Piatier, and Dr. Werner H. Strigel by declaring them to be honorary members of CIRET. We congratulate them on this honour.

This conference was the first CIRET Conference that took place in the United States of America. We thank the representatives of the following institutions for their financial contributions and organizational support: Atlantic Capital Corporation, New York, Dun & Bradstreet Corporation, New York, European Economic Commission, Brussels, German Marshall Fund, Washington D.C., National Federation of Independent Business, San Mateo, CA., and the US Bureau of Commerce, Washington, D.C.

We also thank all the participants who contributed to the success of the 16th CIRET Conference. We extend special thanks to Prof. V. Zarnowitz, University of Chicago, for his support in arranging the conference and to Mrs. Ziegler, the secretary of CIRET for her organizational efforts.

Munich, February 1984

Prof. Dr. Karl Heinrich Oppenländer
Prof. Dr. Günter Poser

First Session
Forecasting in Macro-economic Policy

Chairman:

G. Poser, Technische Hochschule Darmstadt

Darmstadt

The Use of Judgement in Econometric Forecasting

M.K. Evans
Evans Economics Inc.
Washington, D.C.

Introduction

Judgment has always been considered, and correctly so, to be part and parcel of any useful econometric forecast. In the short run, it has always been necessary to take into consideration various exogenous disturbances -- weather, strikes, shortages, etc. -- while in the long run the choice of estimates for monetary and fiscal policy certainly have an important bearing on the forecasts. Implicit in this approach was the belief that the structure of most econometric models was fundamentally sound; that if one only had accurate information about the exogenous variables, the forecasts would generally be close to the mark. This theory was given early support by the experience of the mid-1960's, when the success of econometric forecasters in gauging the effect of the Kennedy-Johnson tax cuts was followed by their inability to predict the sharp spurt in growth in late 1965 and early 1966, when the Johnson administration categorically lied about the size of the buildup in Vietnam.

Gradually, however, the veneer was stripped away from this approach. Several studies which examined the errors in econometric forecasts reached conclusions which directly contradicted this hypothesis. Early work by Haitovsky, Treyz, Su, and this author showed that in many cases, inserting the correct exogenous variables into the models resulted in worse forecasts than the ones which had actually been generated. Work by Ray Fair, in which he generated forecasts based on a model reestimated every quarter, but eschewed the use of any judgmental adjustments, gave far worse forecasts than those generated by any other reputable econometric model. In a lengthy series of papers, Stephen K. McNees has shown that no forecaster has been able to compile a significantly superior track record in spite of the fact that many different approaches are included in his comparisons. Finally, in recent work, Victor Zarnowitz has shown that the consensus forecasts have generated more accurate findings than individual predictions, and furthermore that those who have deviated the most from the consensus have had the worst forecasting record, even though their assumptions about policy were not greatly different. In spite of the old saw that the consensus is always wrong, those who have chosen to deviate from it have on balance been wrong even more often. Yet their exogenous <u>assumptions</u> on balance have been no worse.

Thus with the single exception of the Vietnam buildup, all the major forecasting errors which have been made by the profession since then have been the result of incorrect interpretation of exogenous events which were already known, rather than incorrect forecasts of these events.

- Economists generally forecasted that the 1968 tax surcharge would result in a slowdown in the economy -- particularly in consumer spending -- lower inflation, and a decline in interest rates. Instead, just the opposite happened. The personal savings rate declined from 7.9% to 6.3% in the very quarter of the surcharge, inflation increased from 4% to 6%, and the prime rate rose 2½% to a then-record 8½%.

- When the tax surcharge failed to slow inflation, the Nixon administration successful put on the brakes by suspending the investment tax credit, winding down the Vietnam War, and reducing money supply growth from 8% to 4%. While economists were generally in agreement that some slowdown in the economy would occur -- many were still keying off the previous year's tax increase -- they did not expect the recession to last very far into 1970. In fact, the decline accelerated when the surcharge was removed at midyear; forecasts that the unemployment rate would rise to 6% by the end of the year were widely maligned, although they turned out to be correct.

- The Nixon new game plan of August 1981 was a distinct surprise, and econometricians certainly cannot be faulted for failing to predict that a Republican President would impose wage and price controls, devalue the dollar, run the biggest full-employment peacetime deficit in history, and cause money supply growth to soar at a record rate. But in fact the forecasts for 1972, when all the surprising developments would have had their initial impact, were pretty good. What the econometricians completely failed to grasp was the inflationary impacts of these moves; they hence thought that inflation would increase 3% to 4% for 1973, whereas it rose more than 6% before the oil embargo occurred -- which brings us to our next point.

- Once again, few could be faulted for failing to predict that the price of imported oil would quadruple in 1974. However, it was after the oil increase had already occurred that the most serious forecasting errors began. Instead of the sharp decline in real GNP starting immediately, the economy managed to push ahead for almost another entire year until high interest rates and tight money caused a more serious recession than was expected. Both the timing and magnitude of the downturn then turned out to be misestimated.

- After the economy recovered, forecasters posted three fairly good years in a row by predicting continued growth for 1976, 1977, and 1978, but then generally predicted another recession in 1979. While real GNP did decline in one quarter, the economy quickly recovered and went forward until temporarily halted by the credit controls of spring 1980. The second energy crisis that hit late in 1978 once again served to postpone rather than accelerate the recession.

- Perhaps having been burned by predicting recessions too soon or too frequently, the profession then decided to predict that 1982 would be a good year, and continued to regurgitate this forecast even though the recession lasted through November. This error appeared to have been a clear case of ignoring the importance of tight money and high interest rates and overstating the effect of the tax cut.
- Finally, it was widely predicted that the upturn in 1983, particularly during the first half, would be quite anemic. However, the 9.2% growth rate in the second quarter puts this recovery right on track with previous upturns, although the second half of year may well turn out to be a disappointment.

In presenting this litany of errors, I do not mean to imply that my forecasts over the past 20 years have been any better than others, and I have shared in most if not all of the above mistakes. However, the record would appear to be quite clear on one point; errors have sprung, not from bad judgment or bad guesses about the principal exogenous variables, but apparently from the underlying structures of the model equations themselves. The models simply could not properly respond to changes in monetary policy, government spending, high interest rates, or inflationary expectations.

With some of the best minds in the economics profession focused on the estimation of econometric models, it remains for others, totally outside the profession, to suggest that economists generally and econometricians specifically are incompetent. Indeed, the weight of the evidence would seem to suggest instead that the econometricians did provide reasonable estimates of the equations for the sample periods in question. However, because economics remains very much a social science -- individuals, corporations, and institutions do change their mind about what are and are not important determinants of their future behavior -- the relationships often are unstable over time. Thus the true judgment of an econometrician depends not so much on his ability to forecast the levels and changes of key policy and exogenous variables correctly -- although that certainly helps -- but rather by the choice of variables to be included in the specific key equations of the model. It is the focus of this paper to examine how the specification of some of the key equations in typical macroeconomic models shift radically depending on what time period is chosen, and then to indicate how judgment is used in the crafting of the actual econometric model used for predicting the economy.

For this purpose we have selected six key equations of any model: consumption (represented here by the personal savings rate), capital spending, short-term interest rates, wage rates, the rate of inflation, and the overall stability of fiscal and monetary policy multipliers.

The sample period has been divided into four subgroups, which are as follows:

- 1955.1-1965.4, when monetary policy played a passive role.
- 1966.1-1972.4, when monetary policy was more active but inflation was generally thought to be under control.
- 1973.1-1979.2, when inflationary expectations became much more important and real interest rates were often negative.
- 1979.3-1983.2: The Volcker era, during which monetary policy played a primary role and fear of the government deficits became much more widespread and severe.

We have also examined these into longer time periods, including the entire 1955.1-1983.2 sample period. Before 1955, wartime controls invalidate most comparisons, so we have excluded the Korean War years and the recession immediately following the end of those hostilities.

In general we have tried to keep the equations relatively simple; the idea is not to improve the fits with dummy variables which do wonders for the sample period statistics but do not improve the forecasts at all. We have also used either ratios or percentage first differences in most cases; the idea is not to present imposing R^2 statistics which represent only common trends. Thus in many cases the equations explain only a relatively small proportion of the variance. But in our view that is really about how well these equations really do work. In any case, our emphasis is on the shift in what are usually believed to be stable parameters, not the goodness of fit statistics.

Consumption and Saving

Our approach to the consumption function is to assume that in the long run, the personal saving rate is correlated with the aftertax real rate of return, basically following the concepts of the permanent income hypothesis, and that short run fluctuations in the savings rate are due to changes in

Growth rate of personal income;

Money supply (M2);

Rate of inflation; and

Rate of unemployment.

The basic structure of the function is built around the idea that a faster than average growth rate in income will raise the saving rate, whereas a slower than average rate will reduce it. This viewpoint, of course, is consistent with the relative, permanent, and wealth-income hypotheses.

According to the permanent income hypothesis, the short-run marginal propensity to save (mps) ought to be different for wage and nonwage income, for income which is received steadily and that which varies greatly, income received by lower and upper-income recipients, and expected and unexpected changes in income. This would in turn suggest that the various components of disposable income -- wages and salaries, proprietors income, rental, interest and divident income, transfer payments, and taxes -- all be treated separately. Anyone who has estimated consumption or savings functions empirically realizes that it is not possible to jam all of these terms into the function and retain any structural stability.

We tried to compromise halfway on this issue by subdividing disposable income into (a) wages and salaries (b) all non-wage income, and (c) taxes, including personal contributions for social insurance. In other experiments we also tried grouping transfer payments with wages and salaries, on the grounds they had more in common with them than with rentier income. The derivation of the function (omitting for the moment all non-income terms) would thus have been:

$$S = a + bW + cR - dT \qquad a \cong 0 \text{ in long-run if no other terms}$$

$$\frac{S}{y} = a + b\,\frac{w}{y} + c\,\frac{R}{y} - d\,\frac{T}{y}$$

$$\frac{S}{y} \cong + b\left(\frac{\bar{y}\ \Delta\ W\ \bar{W}\ \Delta y}{\bar{y}\ 2}\right) + c\left(\frac{\bar{y}\ \Delta\ R\ \bar{R}\ \Delta y}{\bar{y}\ 2}\right) - d\left(\frac{\bar{y}\ \Delta\ T - \bar{T}\ \Delta y}{\bar{y}\ 2}\right)$$

$$\frac{S}{y} \cong b\left(\frac{\Delta W}{y} - \left(\frac{\bar{W}}{y}\right)\frac{\Delta y}{y}\right) + c\left(\frac{\Delta R}{y} - \left(\frac{\bar{R}}{y}\right)\frac{\Delta y}{y}\right) - d\left(\frac{\Delta T}{y} - \left(\frac{\bar{T}}{y}\right)\frac{\Delta y}{y}\right)$$

$$\frac{S}{y} \cong + b\ \frac{\Delta W}{y} + c\,\frac{\Delta R}{y} - d\,\frac{\Delta T}{y} - \frac{\Delta y}{y}\left[+ b\left(\frac{\bar{W}}{y}\right) + c\left(\frac{\bar{R}}{y}\right) - d\left(\frac{\bar{I}}{y}\right)\right]$$

If for example, b = 0.3, c = 0.6 and d = 0.5 then the reg. coefficients on $\frac{\Delta y}{y}$ would be approximately -0.4.

The W, R and T terms actually represent averages over several quarters, so the changes are also over several quarters.

As a matter of fact, the equations of this sort which we estimated for the entire sample period did have parameter estimates which corresponded more or less to the theoretical values indicated above. However, the stability completely broke down in the subsample period, and we decided to use a simpler approach, which was to take total personal income as one variable and taxes as the other, since the coefficients are significantly different for the tax variable.

One may question the use of a separate tax variable, and the much higher mps for taxes than other income. There would appear to be two reasons for this, one theoretical and the other empirical. On the theoretical side, changes in tax rates are generally "unexpected" and hence would probably have a higher marginal short-term mps than other types of income. On the empirical side, some of the changes in taxes are simply done with mirrors, such as when the Treasury changes the withholding rules without changing the tax rates. This occurred, for example, in 1972, when Nixon wanted to reduce the budget deficit in an election year and was willing to shift the burden of a higher deficit over to 1973. Hence personal income tax receipts rose an extra $20 billion in 1972. Since in fact tax rates had not risen, virtually the entire increase was reflected in a lower savings rate.

Another unusual feature of this savings rate function is that the lags of income are usually thought to be about three years, and most empirical consumption functions that do not rely on the easy way out of using lagged consumption incorporate this lag structure. We experimented with various lags on the components of disposable income up to 12 quarters, using assorted geometric lag distributions, but found that the significance tailed off quickly after one year.

We now turn briefly to the other variables included in the function. Money supply would be expected to have a negative sign; the faster money supply grows, the more consumers will spend for any given level of income, and hence the lower the savings rate. We have used M2, following the latest Friedman-Schwartz work; some experiments with M1 reveal that M2 is superior everywhere except for the pre-1960 period, when time and saving deposits accounted for only a small proportion of total money supply.

The aftertax real rate of return is calculated as:

$rr = (1 - t_{ms}) r_{AAA}$ - (average rate of inflation over the past four years

where

t_{ms} = marginal tax rate on savings

r_{AAA} = yield on Aaa-rated corporate bonds

Obviously we would expect that an increase in the rate of return would raise the personal savings rate.

The other two variables included in the function are attitudinal variables. A number of studies on consumer attitude indexes, which were widely thought to explain some of the fluctuations in consumer purchases, showed that these indexes could largely be explained by fluctuations in inflation and unemployment. During the 1950's and 1960's, it was widely believed that an increase in inflation and an increase in unemployment were both harmful to consumption; by worsening consumer attitudes, they resulted in a larger proportion of income being set aside for the rainy days that appeared ahead. Thus both of these variables would be positively correlated with the savings rate. Before running these regressions, it was our prior expectations that these would both have diminished in importance over time, since high inflation and high unemployment are now seen to be more akin to "normal" conditions, rather than the aberrations which they were seen as in the 1950's and 1960's. The actual equation used and the statistical results are given on the next two pages.

$$\frac{S}{y} = a_0 + a_1 \frac{4}{10} \sum_{i=0}^{3} (4 - i) \left(\frac{\Delta y}{y_{-1}} \right)_{-i} + a_2 \frac{4}{10} \sum_{i=0}^{3} (4 - i) \left(\frac{\Delta T}{y_{-1}} \right)_{-i}$$

$$+ a_3 \frac{4}{10} \sum_{i=0}^{3} (4 - i) \left(\frac{\Delta CPI}{CPI_{-1}} \right)_{-i} + a_4 \left(\frac{M2 - \overline{M2}}{\overline{M2}} \right)_{-2} + a_5 rr + a_6 \frac{1}{4} \sum_{i=1}^{4} UN_{-i}$$

Where

S = personal saving, billions of 1972 dollars

y = personal disposable income, 1972 dollars

T = personal income taxes and personal insurance contributions, billions of 1972 dollars

CPI = consumer price index, rental equivalency basis

M2 = money supply

UN - unemployment rate

rr = rate of return on personal saving $= r_{aaa}(1 - T_{ms}) - \frac{1}{4} \quad \frac{\overline{CPI} - \overline{CPI}_{-13}}{\overline{CPI}_{-13}}$

r_{aaa} = yield on Aaa-rated corporate bonds

T_{ms} = marginal tax rate on personal saving

In general $\overline{x} = \frac{1}{4} \sum_{i=1}^{4} x - i$

y,T and CPI terms are multiplied by $\frac{4}{10}$ to convert to annual rates

TABLE I

SAVINGS RATE

Sample Period	Y	T	CPI	M	RR	UN
1955.1-1965.4	0.39 (5.8)	0.07 (0.6)	0.76 (4.8)	-0.15 (-1.2)	-0.64 (-2.4)	-0.06 (-0.3)
1966.1-1972.4	0.02 (0.3)	-0.46 (-4.0)	-0.06 (-0.4)	-0.06 (-0.5)	0.73 (1.7)	0.43 (1.1)
1973.1-1979.2	-0.28 (-4.1)	-0.86 (-8.0)	0.15 (0.9)	0.18 (1.3)	1.90 (6.5)	1.70 (4.4)
1979.3-1983.2	0.47 (3.9)	-1.13 (-3.9)	-0.05 (-0.4)	-0.09 (-0.7)	-1.07 (-4.7)	-0.83 (-2.0)
1955.1-1972.4	0.18 (3.1)	-0.27 (-2.8)	0.21 (2.0)	-0.18 (-0.2)	-0.29 (-1.2)	-0.29 (-1.4)
1955.1-1979.2	0.06 (1.2)	-0.43 (-5.1)	0.23 (4.2)	0.08 (1.0)	0.13 (0.9)	-0.20 (-1.3)
1966.1-1983.2	-0.12 (-1.5)	0.10 (0.4)	-0.12 (-0.8)	-0.34 (-1.1)	-0.76 (-3.4)	-0.50 (-1.6)
1955.1-1983.2	0.08 (1.7)	-0.44 (-5.2)	0.13 (2.5)	0.12 (1.6)	0.06 (0.4)	-0.37 (-2.7)

The results in Table I exhibit a great degree of instability which supports no particular theory. During the first subperiod, the coefficient for changes in disposable income over the most recent four quarters is 0.39, which is roughly equivalent to the mps for the first year. This finding is in line with the estimates from large-scale macroeconomic models. The tax coefficient is not significant, which is surprising because the 1964 Kennedy-Johnson tax cut did in fact raise the savings rate substantially. However, the results are somewhat obscured by the fact that from 1963 to 1966, personal income taxes rose 23.5%, almost as great an increase as the 26.2% gain in personal income. The fact that taxes rose almost as much as income was caused by (a) very rapid growth rates during the period, and hence some bracket creep, (b) offsetting personal income tax increases, such as the end of the dividend credit, and (c) substantial increases in social security taxes. These factors gave rise to the quaint notion that the Kennedy-Johnson tax cut somehow "paid for itself," a phrase came back to haunt some of the Reagan Administration spokesmen.

The coefficient for inflation was highly significant in the 1955-65 period, indicating that a rise in inflation did raise the savings rate; however the unemployment term was nonsignificant and negative, which is the "wrong" sign according to prior expectations. The monetary variables had no influence in this period; the money supply was nonsignificantly negative, while the rate of return had the wrong sign. Even this function did not work entirely as expected, but it was for the most part a standard Keynesian function, with one attitudinal variable and no monetary influences.

This standard function rapidly fell apart in the next two subperiods, however. The income term first becomes insignificant and then actually turns negative, while the rate of return variable emerges as the most important variable in the equation. Clearly what happened during the 1975-79 period was the savings rate declined sharply, from 8.6% to 5.9%, even though real disposable income also grew at a slow rate. Some have suggested this was due to the fact that consumers got as much as $30 billion per year from capital gains in housing, which they then used for everyday consumer expenditures. Others have tied it to the sharp decline in the aftertax real rate of return which occurred as inflation accelerated. Whatever the reason, changes in saving did not correspond with changes in income. The significantly positive unemployment rate reflects the fact that the savings rate rose sharply in both the 1970 and the 1974-75 recessions. Elsewhere this has been attributed to the slowdown in money supply growth, but in general that variable was not significant in any of the subperiods and in fact had the wrong sign for the 1973-1979 subperiod.

On the basis of these results, it would not have been wildly illogical for an econometrician, estimating a savings function in 1979, to predict that the savings rate would rise sharply in the next few years because of the Reagan tax cuts and a tighter monetary policy which would significantly raise the real rate of interest. In fact, the real aftertax rate of return has moved from -3% in 1979 to slightly positive in mid-1983 -- but the personal saving rate continues to diminish and indeed in 1983.2 touched down a 33-year record low of 4.0%.

The results are thus unsatisfactory for all the standard theories of the consumption function. Income does not remain significant or even positive over the sample period. The attitudinal variables sometimes have the correct sign and other times the incorrect sign. In the sharpest turnaround of all, the rate of return variable appears to be strongly positive during the 1970's but then is as strongly negative during the 1980's.

From 1951 through 1976, the personal savings rate averaged about 7%, ranging as low as 5.4% and as high as 8.6%. Since then it has gradually declined to about 5%, where we expect it to remain for the next several quarters if not years. This has occurred in spite of a relatively high aftertax real rate of return, high unemployment, and fairly high inflation -- although it is temporarily low in 1983. Previously we would have expected all of these factors to raise the savings rate.

The complete collapse of what still remains the cornerstone of macroeconomic modeling calls into question the entire use of econometrics for forecasting. Of course one can point to various short-term aberrations occurring in the last four years which had not happened in the previous 25 years: the sudden imposition and then equally abrupt termination of the credit controls in mid-1980; the sustained level of double-digit inflation for almost a three-year period; the rise in the unemployment rate to a peak of 10.8% in late 1982; and the three year 25% across-the-board reduction in personal income tax rates which was nonetheless offset by tight monetary policy. Yet what we are in effect saying here is that judgment must be applied in each of these "special" cases; in essence, the judgment has overwhelmed econometrics.

Our judgment of the current state of the savings function would be as follows. During the past few years, the use of credit has become widespred, particularly with the use of bank credit cards. With new regulations basically eliminating all interest rate ceilings, both on the rates which customers can earn and the amount they can be charged, we would expect the use of credit to become an increasingly important determinant of consumer purchases. A recent Federal Reserve study has indicated that the increased use of credit cards may have raised consumer purchases by as much as 4%, which is approximately the amount the savings rate has fallen in the past eight years.

In addition, the two spasms of double-digit inflation during the past decade has left a sour taste about savings for many consumers. While the 3% rate of inflation is certainly an acceptable level, many consumers view it as strictly temporary -- and we would agree with them. Between easier availability of credit and the growing belief that saving doesn't pay, we think there has been a permanent shift in the savings function. The savings ethic, if not dead, has sorely diminished. It is this judgment -- as yet unsupported by econometric evidence -- that underlies our economic forecasts of consumption and saving for the next several years.

Capital Spending

Ever since Dale Jorgenson implemented the concept of the rental cost of capital into the investment function, the general structure of the equation has remained fairly stable, with most of the discussion revolving around the exact lag structure. The index of industrial production is used in our equation as the generalized output variable. Stock prices represent both the cost of equity capital and a measure of expected future profitability. Both of these are lagged over the previous year, with an average lag of two quarters. The index of capacity utilization, lagged one year, acts as a proxy variable for capital stock. The rental cost of capital term is included with an average lag of 1½ years, since financing decisions are generally made before the project is started; changes of plans in mid-course are usually affected only by unaffected fluctuations in sales or output.

For the first subperiod, this function works quite well, as shown in Table 2. The elasticity of the rental cost of capital variable taken at the sample period means is about 0.8, which is reasonably close to the theoretical value of unity. The elasticity of the output term is too low at about 0.4, but that is because industrial production is collinear with capacity utilization; if that is taken into account the output elasticity is slightly greater than unity.

$$Ip = b_0 + b_1 \frac{1}{10} \sum_{i=1}^{4} (5_{-i})\ XIP_{-i} + b_2 \frac{1}{10} \sum_{i=1}^{4} (5_{-i})\ SP_{-i}$$

$$+ b_3\ Cp_{-4} + b_4 \frac{1}{20} \sum_{i=1}^{8} w_i rcc_{-i-1}$$

where

Ip = nonresidential fixed investment, billions of 1972$

XIP = index of industrial production, 1967=100

SP = index of stock prices, Standard & Poor's 500

Cp = index of capacity utilization, %

rcc = rental cost of capital

$w_1 = 1,\ w_2 = 2,\ w_3 = 3,\ w_4 = 4,\ w_5 = 4,\ w_6 = 3,\ w_7 = 2,\ w_8 = 1$

$$rcc = \frac{2}{3}\ \frac{PIPE}{PPI}\ \frac{(r + \delta_e)\ (1 - uz_e - k)}{1 - u} + \frac{1}{3}\ \frac{PIPS}{PPI}\ \frac{(r + \delta_s)\ (1 - uz_s)}{1 - u}$$

where

PIPE = implicit deflator, producers durable equipment

PIPS = implicit deflator, nonresidential structures

PPI = producer price index, industrial commodities

r = yield on Aaa-rated corporate bonds

δe = economic rate of depreciation, equipment

δs = economic rate of depreciation, structures

k = rate of investment tax credit

u = marginal statutory Federal corporate income tax rate

ze = discounted value of depreciation for equipment

zs = discounted value of depreciation for structures

TABLE 2

CAPITAL SPENDING

Sample Period	XIP	SP	CP	rcc
1955.1-1965.4	0.43 (1.8)	0.18 (1.9)	0.78 (7.2)	-2.06 (-1.9)
1966.1-1972.4	0.78 (6.4)	0.05 (0.6)	0.72 (3.1)	+1.06 (2.5)
1973.1-1979.2	1.40 (8.7)	1.03 (2.3)	-0.94 (-1.2)	-0.98 (-2.1)
1979.3-1983.2	0.30 (0.6)	0.25 (1.6)	0.88 (1.5)	+0.65 (1.1)
1955.1-1972.4	0.93 (18.5)	0.13 (2.5)	0.67 (8.3)	0.36 (1.7)
1955.1-1979.2	1.08 (35.8)	-0.01 (-0.2)	0.84 (8.4)	0.37 (1.4)
1966.1-1983.2	1.15 (29.1)	0.45 (8.1)	0.13 (1.0)	-1.41 (-3.0)
1955.1-1983.2	1.02 (26.2)	0.18 (3.7)	0.32 (2.6)	0.60 (1.5)

However, once we leave the stability of the 1955-1965 era, the function begins to disintegrate rapidly; this pattern has previously been noted by those who have forecasted investment over the past 20 years. First, investment continued to increase in 1969 in spite of a sharp rise in interest rates and the imposition of a 10% corporate (as well as personal) income tax surcharge. Later, capital spending in real terms rose 12% and 13% in 1977 and 1978 in spite of the fact that interest rates were rising and stock prices were falling, the result of an increase in the capital gains tax rate to a maximum of 49.1%. On the other hand, a 50% reduction in depreciable lives of assets and other tax breaks for corporations in 1981 were followed by a 5% decline in real capital spending in 1982 and probably another 2% reduction in 1983. It appeared that investment was following changes in output but not the rental cost of capital.

Essentially, our subperiod regressions support this result. After a significant coefficient and relatively high elasticity for the cost of capital in the first period, this virtually disappears, turning positive in 1966-1972 and again in the 1979-1983 period. Indeed, for the entire sample period the coefficient is nonsignificantly positive -- although for the 1966-1983 subperiod, the coefficient is significantly negative, with an elasticity of about 0.25.

In this respect, we note with disappointment that the investment ratio for 1983 and 1984 will average about 10.2%, compared to the 9.6% ratio for the 1955-1964 decade -- before the myriad of tax incentives were implemented to spur capital formation. In fact, if one subtracts the incremental capital spending mandated by government regulation, the private sector investment ratio currently is slightly below the 1955-1964 average.

It is of course quite possible that the tax incentives have been offset by the dramatic rise in interest rates over the past 30 years. We tried to test this hypothesis by separating the bond yield from the tax components of the rental cost of capital, but the results were not only inconclusive but unstable among various subperiods, and are not summarized here.

From a judgmental point of view we continue to believe that higher interest rates hurt capital formation, and tax incentives help it. We would also argue that changes in output and expected future profitability are more important than interest rates, which are in turn more important than tax incentives. From a policy point of view, if some way could be found to provide sustained, balanced low inflationary growth with moderate real rates of interest, that would do more for investment than any imaginable tax incentives, including total abolition of the corporate income tax. From a forecasting point of view, we continue to predict values of the investment ratio which are historically at the low end of the scale so long as interest rates remain high, profit margins remain depressed, capacity utilization rates remain low, and real growth remains sluggish.

Interest Rates

The general theory of interest rate determination, as delineated by Friedman-Schwartz and Mundell, suggests the following four factors as the basic determinants of rates:

1. Level of economic activity. The faster the economy is growing, the higher the level of interest rates.

2. Level of saving. The higher the net national saving rate, the lower the level of interest rates.

3. Expected future rate of inflation and growth in the money supply. Since this is not known at the time of forecasting, some weighted average of past rates of inflation is generally used.

4. Monetary policy ease or tightness, generally measured by changes in reserve positions of the Fed, under the assumption of unchanged expectations of

growth in money or prices. According to Friedman-Schwartz, during the first year an increase in reserve availability lowers nominal interest rates; after that it has no effect on real rates, which means nominal rates rise by the rate of inflation.

In addition to this, policy targets are sometimes introduced into the equation. The Fed may actively try to push rates down if unemployment or the value of the dollar is too high, for example, or it may try to tighten if it thinks inflation is moving out of control even if it happens to be decreasing at the moment.

Several measures could be used for the level of economic activity. We could use one which is close to the financial markets, such as the change in loans; some broad-based measure, such as industrial production or even GNP itself; or some surrogate measure such as the rate of unemployment. The latter has some additional claim to legitimacy if the Fed also considers the level of unemployment to be a target variable.

Of these variables, GNP is actually the least appropriate, since it contains elements of both spending and saving, which have opposite effects on interest rates. Industrial production in current dollars (i.e., multiplied by the PPI) and loans give about the same results, largely because changes in production are dominated by inventory swings, which are closely tied to changes in loan demand. However, in the pre-Volcker era, the unemployment rate has the strongest negative sign, presumably because it was considered to be a target variable by the Fed.

On a theoretical basis, a dollar saved in the private sector ought to have the same effect on financial markets as a dollar saved by the Federal government. Yet much of the current discussion revolves around a discussion of the government deficit exclusively, as if the sharp decline in personal and corporate saving does not matter. While some of this emphasis is probably due to dislike of government deficits on philosophical grounds, there are two reasons why the government deficit might be more important. First, government borrowing demands are more inelastic. If interest rates rise too far, some private sector or municipal debt offerings may be postponed, thus limiting the upswing in interest rates; the Federal government of course has no such restraint. Second, government deficits are more visible and long-lasting. A net deficit situation on the part of private sector participants cannot continue indefinitely and hence to a certain extent contains seeds of its own correction, but obviously this is not so for the government deficit. Thus we have included both the total net saving rate and the government deficit ratio in this equation; if the latter is significant, that would indicate it has a proportionately greater effect.

The net instead of gross saving rate has been used because depreciation affects savings only inasmuch as it affects taxes. Consider a more or less typical firm with sales of \$100, payments for labor and materials of \$70, interest payments of \$10, and tax of \$5. It has 10 machines, each of which cost \$10 and each of which lasts 10 years. The money is borrowed at 10% and the firm uses straight-line depreciation.

Next year the tax laws change to permit DDB depreciation, so the firm pays no taxes. Net corporate saving has risen by \$5 billion, and this is so recorded in our calculations. However, to suggest that corporate saving went up by \$15 billion would be double counting.

We next turn to the question of inflation; the estimated equation is for the Federal funds rate, rather than a long-term rate, so the lags on inflation are much shorter. However, work we have done with long-term bond yields suggests that the same general comments are applicable, except with a 3 to 5 year lag for inflation.

In spite of the claims of the latter-day rational expectationalists, there is no empirical evidence whatsoever suggesting that future expectations are anything more or less than some weighted average of previous values of inflation. Indeed, whereas the consensus forecast has occasionally caught turning points in the real sector -- albeit more often the upturns than the downturns -- it has had no luck at all in catching major changes in the rate of inflation, particularly the decline in the past three years. We return to this point later.

The question of which deflator to choose has been made much easier by the recent revision of the CPI to exclude the cost of purchasing and financing a home. With these two components excluded and replaced by a rental equivalency index, the newly revised CPI stands as the best single measure of inflation. The implicit GNP deflator is a flawed measure because it excludes all direct effects of higher oil prices, and in addition quarterly changes in any implicit deflator contain a large random element.

The last variable, the change in reserve policy, can simply be measured as the change in the nonborrowed base, which is the variable which the Fed comes closest to controlling.

Based on these comments, we would then expect that changes in the Federal funds rate would be negatively related to unemployment, positively related to the change in the CPI, positively related to the net saving rate, negatively related to the government deficit ratio, and negatively related to changes in the nonborrowed base.

The empirical results, given in Table 3, however, show almost nothing of the sort. In the eight subperiods listed there, we find only one period -- 1966-1972 -- where all the variables have the "right" sign, and none where they are all significant.

$$r_{ff} = e_0 + e_1\, 4\, \frac{\Delta NMB}{NMB_{-1}} + e_2\, 2\left(\frac{CPI - CPI_{-2}}{CPI_{-2}}\right) + e_3 \frac{NSAV}{GNP}$$

$$+ e_4 \frac{DEF}{GNP} + e_5\, Un$$

where

r_{ff} = Federal funds rate, %

NMB = Nonborrowed monetary base, billions of $

CPI = Consumer price index, rental equivalency basis

NSAV = Net saving = personal saving + net corporate saving + government saving, all billions of $

GNP = Gross national product, billions of $

DEF = Federal government surplus or deficit, billions of $

Un = Unemployment rate, %

Factors of 4 and 2 are included to convert to annual rates.

TABLE 3

FEDERAL FUNDS RATE

Sample Period	NMB	CPI	Net Sav.	Gov't. DEF	UN
1955.1-1965.4	0.10 (2.5)	0.07 (0.7)	0.23 (1.0)	-0.13 (-0.6)	-0.27 (-0.9)
1966.1-1972.4	-0.13 (-2.0)	0.84 (4.8)	-0.50 (-1.6)	0.38 (1.4)	-0.26 (1.1)
1973.1-1979.2	-0.10 (1.3)	0.58 (5.0)	-0.25 (-0.7)	-0.41 (-1.1)	-1.61 (-2.4)
1979.3-1983.2	-1.04 (-5.3)	-0.16 (-1.5)	-1.58 (-2.2)	+3.90 (3.7)	+0.98 (0.9)
1955.1-1972.4	0.03 (0.8)	0.66 (6.7)	-0.26 (1.3)	0.12 (0.7)	-0.68 (3.2)
1955.1-1979.2	0.00 (0.0)	0.72 (17.2)	0.02 (0.1)	-0.08 (-0.6)	-0.60 (-4.2)
1966.1-1983.2	-0.29 (-2.6)	0.80 (5.9)	-0.57 (-1.8)	1.65 (3.7)	1.48 (3.4)
1955.1-1983.2	-0.05 (-0.6)	0.85 (12.8)	-0.33 (-1.3)	0.21 (0.7)	0.30 (1.0)

The most striking change is clearly the one between the 1955-1979.2 and 1979.3-1983.2 subperiods. Whereas in the earlier period the change in the CPI was highly significant with a coefficient of 0.72 and a t-ratio of 17.2, in the last period it was actually negative although not significantly so. In the earlier period the rate of unemployment was significantly negative and yet it became nonsignificantly positive in the late period. In addition, for the past four years both the net saving rate and the government deficit ratio have been significant with very large coefficients, whereas they were insignificant and generally had the wrong sign in the earlier periods. Perhaps most surprising, changes in the nonborrowed base were highly significant only in the last period, and in the earliest period even had a positive sign -- i.e., tightening the base would lower interest rates immediately. However, since monetary policy was used mainly in the breach during that earlier period, we probably have a simultaneous equation bias in which a decline in economic activity reduced both interest rates and the money supply, which meant that the nonborrowed base would fall in the absence of any specific policy change. Before 1966 the nonborrowed base and money supply were much more closely related, because financial disintermediation seldom occurred and few alternatives to bank accounts existed then.

In any case, it is not difficult to argue that a reasonably astute and diligent econometrician, faced with the evidence through mid-1979, would have argued that a sharp decline in the rate of inflation, coupled with an increase of 3% to 4% in the rate of unemployment, would have resulted in a plunge in the Federal funds rate and a real interest rate that was negative -- regardless of the posture of monetary and fiscal policy in the intermin. Yet with four additional years of data, real interest rates are near all-time peaks. Here it seems that judgment is primary; the empirical results are completely different depending on what sample period is chosen.

In our view, the negative relationship between the CPI and the funds rate is an aberration which will not be repeated. In the next several years, we expect that short-term rates will once again tend to follow the rate of inflation; in this sense, the elasticity of about 0.7 for that term seems likely to continue. The unemployment rate, or for that matter other measures of economic activity, will have a smaller but nonetheless significant effect; if the economy overheats, rates probably will rise even if the inflation rate does not budge, although faster growth would invariably be accompanied by higher inflation.

Net savings will continue to be important, although it is not clear whether the government deficit will continue to carry its recent premium. As a rough rule of thumb, we think that every 1% increase in the net saving rate would lower interest rates by ½%, and every 1% decrease in the deficit would lower rates by an additional ½%. This implies that returning the budget to balance would produce a real rate of interest of about -1%, which would be consistent with previous experience. This is not an unreasonable result, but may have been obtained by back-door reasoning, i.e., what elasticity would in fact produce a -1% real rate of interest with a balanced budget.

Finally, changes in reserve position will probably have a negligible effect on rates, partly because the Fed has in our opinion returned to a policy of targeting interest rates instead of money supply growth and partly because the deregulation of the banking sector means that reserves are less controllable than they used to be. But if the Fed were to change its policy again and start targeting money supply growth seriously, particularly M1 growth, the nonborrowed base would presumably regain its prior significance.

This is perhaps an extreme example of the breakdown of econometrics, and not as many functions are as unstable as those for interest rates. However, it does point up the degree to which judgment has assumed the primary role in prediction of at least one key variable of the overall economy.

Wage Rates

For many years, the relationship between wage rates and unemployment -- the so-called Phillips curve -- was one of the staples of econometrics. Recently, as inflation climbed to double-digit rates and returned to normal levels, it was found necessary to add the change in the CPI, lagged two quarters, as an additional determinant of the wage rate equation. However, this simply transforms the argument to read that the real wage rate is inversely correlated with the rate of unemployment. It was generally noted that wages, at least in the U.S., did not respond fully to changes in inflation, so the coefficient of this latter term is less than unity. In addition, the formulation was usually refined so that changes in wage rates were positively correlated with the inverse of unemployment. Using this nonlinear formulation means that a change in the unemployment rate from 5% to 4% would have about twice as much effect on wage rates as a change from 10% to 9%.

Even with all these modifications, however, the simple fact of the matter is that the real wage rate has not been negatively correlated with the unemployment rate ever since 1966. Since that date, wages have simply followed inflation and unemployment has not been a factor. This can be seen from the regression estimates given in Table 4. The regressions clearly show the diminishing power of the unemployment term. After a very strong coefficient in the first subperiod -- the coefficient indicates that a 1% change in unemployment near the average value of the subperiod, which would be about 5% -- would indeed change wage rates by about 1%, which is the traditional finding. However, in the latter three subperiods, the coefficient is not at all significant and sometimes has the wrong sign. Furthermore, one can also see the diminution in importance of the unemployment coefficient over time for the longer subperiods.

$$\frac{w - \overline{w}}{\overline{w}} = c_0 + c_1 \left(\frac{CPI - \overline{CPI}}{\overline{CPI}} \right)_{-2} + c_2 \cdot \frac{1}{\frac{1}{4} \sum_{i=1}^{4} Un_{-i}}$$

where

w = index of average hourly earnings, adjusted for overtime and interindustry mix

CPI = consumer price index, rental equivalency basis

Un = rate of unemployment, %

in general $\overline{x} = \frac{1}{4} \sum_{i=1}^{4} x_{-i}$

TABLE 4

WAGE RATES

Sample Period	CPI	UN
1955.1-1965.4	-0.03 (0.4)	0.130 (7.0)
1966.1-1972.4	0.75 (6.4)	-0.016 (-1.0)
1973.1-1979.2	0.31 (4.5)	0.009 (-0.4)
1979.3-1983.2	0.74 (7.5)	0.007 (0.2)
1955.1-1972.4	0.57 (7.1)	0.068 (3.8)
1955.1-1979.2	0.62 (17.1)	0.035 (2.6)
1966.1-1983.2	0.43 (11.3)	0.012 (1.0)
1955.1-1983.2	0.50 (21.0)	0.045 (3.8)

Hence the sole reason for smaller wage rate gains in the aggregate over the past two years was that inflation diminished. One can find a few examples, notably in the auto and steel industries, where not only real but nominal wage rates actually decreased. However, we would claim this was due more to the overvalued dollar and the loss of overseas markets -- which made workers realize they had priced themselves out of world markets -- rather than the total unemployment rate per se.

Our judgment would thus be that changes in unemployment are not likely to be a significant determinant of wage rates over the next several years. Wage earners will not only struggle to keep up with inflation, but will try to regain some of the losses that occurred in the 1979-1981 era of double-digit inflation, even if unemployment remains quite high.

Inflation

If one accepts this conclusion, however, it raises an even bigger question about the actual determinants of inflation within a complete model system, as opposed to the single-equation approach. By this we mean the following. Economists of all stripes readily acknowledge the very close correlation between changes in prices and unit labor costs. The standard error of using such an equation for "predicting" prices is only about 1%, as every surge in inflation in the postwar period has been accompanied by a similar surge in unit labor costs. Yet if in fact wage rates are related only to inflation and not to unemployment, than this close correlation degenerates into an ex post, rather than an ex ante, relationship. For if prices are a function of wages and wages a function of prices, we have explained nothing.

The consensus forecast made in mid-1981 -- after the back of inflation had already been broken -- claimed that the CPI would increase approximately 9% and

8% in 1982 and 1983 respectively. Actually, the CPI rose 6.1% last year and will rise about 3% this year (both figures on an annual average basis). These erroneous forecasts were based in large part on the fact that wage rates were rising at about a 9½% annual rate and the supposition that they would diminish very slowly; and the belief that productivity would not stage much of a comeback.

Thus to predict inflation, one should not start with a forecast of wage rates. That is the last step -- after inflation has been determined, then wage rates closely follow inflation with a lag of two quarters very closely. But this begs the question of what does determine inflation.

In our recent empirical work we have found that the principal determinations of inflation -- as measured by the newly revised CPI, which contains the rental equivalency index instead of the cost of buying and financing a home - are as follows:

1. Productivity
2. Money supply growth (M2) lagged two years
3. Value of the dollar
4. Energy prices
5. Food prices

Note in particular that this list does <u>not</u> contain the unemployment rate or capacity utilization, variables which have traditionally been considered pressure-of-demand factors affecting prices. The unemployment rate, as we have indicated, has long ceased to exert an independent influence on aggregate wage rate changes. Even lagging capacity utilization one year, and tying the rate of inflation to the level of capacity utilization -- in essence positing a nonlinear relationship in which inflation accelerates as the economy approaches full capacity -- does not generate the expected result.

The sub-sample period results are given in Table 5. It can be seen that the function starts off rather normally, with productivity and capacity utilization the two major variables determining changes in prices. Food and oil prices are also significant, but the money supply lagged two years is not. The value of the dollar has little effect because it was essentially stable over this period; any changes in the trade weighted average were due to small adjustments in European currency rates.

As the sample period advances, however,it becomes apparent that the money supply becomes more important -- in this sense the 1966.1-1983.2 regression is probably more reliable than the shorter subperiods, especially the last one, which really does not have enough independent observations to have any degrees of freedom left. The productivity term stays negative, and food and oil prices also become more important; the value of the dollar is negative but generally not significant. However, the index of capacity utilization for the 1966.1-1983.2 period is clearly negative, and with good reason: the double-digit bursts of inflation of 1974 and 1979-1981 were both accompanied by a sharp decline in utilization rates. Even lagging this variable one full year, which we have done in the regressions, does not obviate this negative correlation.

The rate of inflation, as measured by the new CPI, declined from 11% in 1980-81 to 3% in 1983. It might be useful to use the 1955.1-1979.2 equation to see how well such a function would have predicted the decline in inflation outside the sample period, knowing all the correct values of the exogenous variables, but without relying on any changes in wage rates, unemployment rates, or capacity utilization to generate this forecast.

$$\frac{CPI - CPI_{-4}}{CPI_{-4}} = d_0 + d_1 \frac{PROD - PROD_{-4}}{PROD_{-4}} + d_2 \left(\frac{M2 - M2_{-4}}{M2_{-4}} \right)_{-8}$$

$$+ d_3 \left(\frac{PPI_f - PPI_{f_{-4}}}{PPI_{f_{-4}}} \right)_{-2} + d_4 \left(\frac{PPI_0 - PPI_{0-4}}{PPI_{0-4}} \right)_{-2} + d_5 \ Cp_{-4}$$

$$+ d_6 \left(\frac{TWA\$ - TWA\$_{-4}}{TWA\$_{-4}} \right)_{-4}$$

where

CPI = consumer price index, rental equivalency basis

PROD = index of productivity, nonfarm private business sector

M2 = money supply

PPI_f = producer price index, food

PPI_o = producer price index, oil

Cp = index of capacity utilization

TWA$ = trade-weighted average of the U.S.$, calculated by EEI (weighted average of £, FFr, BFr, SFr, DFl, DM, ¥)

TABLE 5

RATE OF INFLATION (CPI)

Sample Period	PROD	M	Food	Oil	Value of Dollar	Cp
1955.1-1965.4	-0.25 (-2.8)	0.02 (0.3)	0.17 (5.6)	0.04 (1.7)	0.08 (0.5)	0.06 (1.8)
1966.1-1972.4	-0.31 (-4.1)	0.31 (3.8)	-0.02 (-0.8)	-0.10 (-2.0)	0.10 (1.4)	-0.23 (-5.3)
1973.1-1979.2	-0.44 (-3.8)	0.03 (0.3)	0.03 (1.6)	0.03 (3.5)	0.02 (0.5)	0.00 (0.0)
1979.3-1983.2	0.23 (1.0)	-0.03 (-0.3)	0.13 (2.8)	0.04 (4.9)	-0.02 (-1.0)	0.18 (2.3)
1955.1-1972.4	-0.27 (-3.0)	0.13 (2.0)	0.14 (4.1)	0.06 (2.0)	-0.23 (-2.2)	0.05 (1.2)
1955.1-1979.2	-0.26 (-2.6)	0.34 (5.4)	0.08 (3.2)	0.06 (5.9)	-0.01 (-0.1)	-0.04 (-1.0)
1966.1-1983.2	-0.40 (-4.0)	0.23 (3.2)	0.05 (2.0)	0.07 (9.8)	-0.03 (-1.2)	-0.16 (-4.4)
1955.1-1983.2	-0.38 (-3.9)	0.36 (6.1)	0.08 (3.3)	0.08 (9.1)	0.00 (0.1)	-0.10 (-2.6)

Productivity improved from -1% in 1979 and 1980 to +3% in 1983, which would have lowered inflation by about 1.0%, according to the coefficients of this equation. Money supply growth with a two year lag apparently slowed down about 2%, although it is difficult to measure this exactly because of all the changes in the banking regulations; that would have lowered inflation another 0.7%. The wholesale price of food dropped from about 15% to 0% currently, which would have reduced inflation by 1.2%. Oil price increases peaked at 75% (at the wholesale level) and were recently declining at about a 10% annual rate, so that is a shift of 5%, the single largest factor. Together, these variables account for a reduction of 7.9%, which is surprisingly close to the 8% reduction which has actually occurred. Recall this is <u>outside</u> the sample period.

That does not mean we necessarily believe it happened just that way; once again, some judgment must come to the fore. The productivity coefficient is probably understated; since this series is not empirically robust and contains c disproportionate amount of noise, it is more likely that a 1% change in the underlying rate of productivity eventually translates into a 1% change ir inflation. The money supply coefficient is probably understated in the sense that food and energy prices are not totally exogenous; they too are affected by change: in aggregate demand, particularly on a worldwide basis. Furthermore, monetar policy tightened by more than the 2% indicated by using M2, since the creation o money market mutual funds and money market deposit accounts have stripped th M's of their old meaning. Our judgment would be that of the 8% reduction i inflation, approximately 3% was due to the stabilization of OPEC policies an deregulation of domestic oil, 2% to 3% was due to the improvement i productivity, and 2% to 3% was due to slower growth in the money supply.

That still means that the independent effects of the decline in wage gain: the reduction in capacity utilization, and the increse in unemployment are zer

The impetus for lower inflation originated in this slower money supply growth, in the stabilization of oil policies, and in the improvement in productivity. The decline in wage gains followed, not led, this reduction in inflation.

Monetary and Fiscal Policy Multipliers

Throughout this paper we have noted the importance, or lack thereof, of monetary policy variables, but except for the separate use of tax receipts in the savings rate and some marginal importance of the rental cost of capital in the investment function, have said little about fiscal policy variables. Yet a sizable body of economic opinion still believes that fiscal policy multipliers are at least as important as monetary policy multipliers, even in spite of the current depressed level of the economy.

Keynesians generally argue that the increases in government spending or tax cuts do not have much of a stimulatory effect on the economy as long as the full-employment budget is close to balance, as it was in 1981 and the early part of 1982. However, as expenditures continued to grow 5% a year in real terms and the second and third stages of the personal income tax cut took effect, the full-employment deficit started to rise and has now reached a level of approximately 3%. Thus, for example, the Congressional Budget Office recently claimed that one of the major factors contributing to the impressive performance of the economy during the first half of 1983 was indeed the burgeoning full-employment deficit.

Regardless of one's political or economic beliefs, everyone presumably agrees that an increase in the full-employment budget deficit is stimulatory in the short run if in fact monetary policy is fully accommodative. Similarly, such an increase would have no effect if the Fed took specific countervailing measures to offset any stimulus through tighter monetary policy and higher interest rates. The question is which set of assumptions corresponds more closely to the real world.

The argument about whether monetary or fiscal policy multipliers are more stable was discussed at great length during the 1950's, and perhaps it is not the better part of valor to reopen old wounds where combatants on both sides of the argument are so sure of their position that they will admit no evidence from the other side. Yet in view of the reemerging belief that we are spending our way back into prosperity, some simple results may be appropriate nonetheless.

Using the raw data for government expenditures and receipts biases the results against the fiscal policy multipliers. During recessions, government expenditures increase faster because of automatic stabilizers, while at the same time tax receipts diminish because of slower growth or absolute declines in personal and corporate income. For this reason we have used the measures of full-employment government receipts and expenditures calculated by the Department of Commerce.

The lag structure was arrived at on an empirical basis, using the standard criteria of choosing the lags with the highest t-statistics for the total sample period. It is not much of a surprise that both money supply and fiscal variables begin with a lag of one quarter; after about a year, the individual terms once again begin to tail off rapidly, and while the lags could have been extended to six to eight quarters, they would have made no significant difference in the outcome.

The results, which are summarized in Table 6, will undoubtedly come as quite a surprise to those who would argue that the importance of monetary policy is a relatively recent development. Indeed, these results show that changes in the money supply have always had a significant positive relationship with changes in GNP, while the effects of taxes has been somewhat more problematical and those of expenditures quite insignificant. Only in one period -- the Vietnam War era -- did the increase and decline in government spending have a significant effect on real GNP.

TABLE 6

CONSISTENCY OF FISCAL AND MONETARY MULTIPLIERS

Sample Period	Percentage Change in: M2	FER	FEE
1955.1-1965.4	0.81	-0.23	-0.18
	(2.0)	(1.1)	(1.3)
1966.1-1972.4	0.51	-0.09	+0.19
	(3.0)	(1.0)	(1.5)
1973.1-1979.2	0.73	-0.43	+0.08
	(2.2)	(1.9)	(0.4)
1979.3-1983.2	1.60	+0.10	+0.11
	(1.2)	(0.3)	(0.2)
1955.1-1972.4	0.50	-0.20	-0.07
	(3.1)	(2.2)	(0.8)
1955.1-1979.2	0.50	-0.31	-0.03
	(4.0)	(4.3)	(0.5)
1966.1-1983.2	0.59	-0.18	0.12
	(3.5)	(2.1)	(1.0)
1955.1-1983.2	0.47	-0.26	-0.07
	(3.6)	(3.6)	(0.9)

Independent variable: $\frac{\Delta GNP}{GNP_{-1}}$, annual rates

$$\frac{\Delta GNPX}{GNPX_{-1}} = f_0 + f_1\left(\frac{M2 - M2_{-4}}{M2_{-4}}\right)_{-1} + f_2\left(\frac{FGFT - FGFT_{-4}}{FGFT_{-4}}\right)_{-1}$$

$$+ f_3\left(\frac{FGFE - FGFE_{-4}}{FGFE_{-4}}\right)_{-1}$$

where

GNPX = gross national product, billions of 1972$

N.B. % changes in GNP have been converted to annual rates

M2 = money supply

FGFT = Federal government full-employment tax receipts, billions of $

FGFE = Federal government full-employment expenditures, billions of $

The coefficients given in Table 6 are elasticities; to convert them to the traditional multiplier analysis, one would multiply by the inverse of the ratio of government spending (or taxes) to GNP. Since Federal government spending has traditionally been about 20% of GNP, these coefficients would be multiplied by about 5. For example, the total sample period regression shows a coefficient of -0.26 for taxes, which indicates a first-year cut multiplier of about 1.3, slightly smaller but not materially different from the figures obtained from complete Keynesian model systems.

The government expenditure multipliers, however, are negative over the sample period, although they are clearly not significant and the results suggest that the true value is probably around zero. Even during the Vietnam War period, the coefficient was only marginally significant, with an indicated multiplier of less than 0.8.

The coefficients for the money supply term indicate that over the entire sample period, a 1% change in M2 has resulted in about a ½% change in real GNP during the following year. However, it should be noted that this coefficient zoomed to 1.60 in the most recent subperiod, which corresponds to the Volcker era. In our view, this coefficient is likely to settle down at about 1.0, lower than the recent experience but somewhat higher than in the 1955-1979 era.

The conclusion to be drawn here, we believe, is that <u>fiscal policy serves at the pleasure of monetary policy</u>. In other words, if the authorities choose to make monetary policy accommodative, then increases in spending or decreases in tax rates will have the usual multipliers of 1 to 1½ for the first year. However, this happens less often than might generally be expected; in most periods, a reduction in money supply growth has been used to offset at least part of the fiscal policy expansion. Only during the period of the Vietnam War buildup and the beginning of the Great Society programs was monetary policy uncompromisingly hitched to greater fiscal expansion; in general it has served as a brake on larger full-employment deficits.

Thus the forecaster is required to judge the degree to which fiscal policy expansion will be offset by monetary stringency. Econometrics cannot answer this question and as the results from Table 6 show, it does vary substantially over the postwar period.

Monetary policy changed dramatically in mid-1982, when three years of almost unprecedented tightness suddenly gave way to double-digit money supply growth for the next nine months. In mid-1983 it appears that the Fed is once again trying to restrain money supply growth to intermediate if not long-term goals. Our judgment is that monetary policy will essentially offset any further widening of the full-employment budget deficit, if in fact that does occur, and hence that the growth rate of the United States economy will remain below 4% average for the next several years even though the economy is clearly so far away from full employment and full capacity. Those who would make the opposite judgment -- that the full-employment deficit will remain near its current level of 3% of GNP and that monetary policy will not interfere with this long-term stimulative process -- would undoubtedly predict a significantly higher rate of growth for the remainder of the decade. Once again we would submit that it is judgment rather than econometrics which is the critical question here.

Conclusion

The results presented in this paper have suggested that the basic underlying econometric structure of the U.S. economy has shifted radically over the postwar period, and that forecasts based strictly on econometric models -- even though they accurately incorporate all present knowledge at the time of estimation -- will give inaccurate forecasts unless tempered with a large degree of judgment. In particular, the behavior of individuals, corporations, and financial markets to inflation, and the degree to which the monetary authorities will seek to offset what would otherwise be fiscal stimulative policies, will in large part decide the future course of both real growth and inflation.

To the extent that most econometricians have erred in their forecasts over the past 20 years, their tendency has been to overstate the contributions of changes in fiscal policy and understate the changes in monetary policy; the latter appear to have been somewhat more stable. Interest rates are presumably still an important determinant of aggregate demand -- as both Keynesians and monetarists would agree -- yet the determinants of interest rates have changed so radically over the past 30 years, and the coefficients of interest rates in both the consumption and investment functions are so unstable that they do not permit a stable underlying econometric structure. The hope of econometricians 20 and 30 years ago that this structure could be found with greater applications of research and high-powered computers appears to have been in vain.

Econometric and Empirical Evidence on the Relationship between Survey Data and Official Data and its Relevance for Monitoring the Business Cycle

P.J. Yaun
Confederation of British Industry
London

INTRODUCTION

The Confederation of British Industry's quarterly Industrial Trends Survey, established in 1958, consists of postal questionnaires sent to senior executives in UK manufacturing firms. Nearly 2000 completed questionnaires are returned to CBI in each Survey*.

Some questions in the Survey ask about movements in variables which are measured by official statistics. For these variables (for example output and employment in manufacturing) one might expect to see a close relation between the qualitative results from the Survey and the quantitative official estimates.

If this is indeed so the Survey results for these questions will provide a good indication of the direction and size of changes in official figures when they become available some months later. It also implies that Survey data about variables not measured by official statistics may also be very worthwhile inputs into analysis of the current economic situation and outlook. Thus the data not only gives the user a "head-start" in the preparation of accurate short-term forecasts but also gives additional up-to-date economic information.

---

* For an excellent description of the Survey see Klein and Moore (1981).

INTERPRETATION OF THE SURVEY RESULTS

But how exactly should the Survey results be interpreted? The results are available in terms of the weighted percentage of firms replying "Up", "Same" and "Down" to a particular question. Usually the results are presented for convenience in "balance" form - simply the difference between the figures for "Up" and "Down".

One might expect that these balances would be related to the percentage change in the official variable but it has also been suggested that balances might also reflect the level of the official variable. In the case of the business optimism question in the Survey ("are you more, or less, optimistic than you were four months ago about the general business situation in your industry?") around half the respondents currently answer in terms of the level of optimism rather than the change. The evidence from the 1982 Survey of Answering Practices* suggests that the optimism question is the only Survey question that is interpreted in this way by a significant number of respondents nevertheless it is obviously crucial in analysing the Survey results that the way in which firms respond is correctly understood.

CAUSATION

Consider the survey balances to a question asking about the trend over the past four months (eg. for numbers employed). Respondents answer the question after they have observed the movement in numbers employed hence we can argue that the movement in the official series causes the balance to be recorded.

---

* see C P H Burton (1983)

In the question on future trends in numbers employed the causation between balances and official variables is more awkward to establish. Expectations concerning the movement in employment are likely to "cause" both the recorded Survey balance and the actual movement. There is therefore little direct causal link, prima facie, between the balance itself and the outturn.

Nevertheless we can establish a direct relationship on a number of assumptions concerning expectations.* Alternatively if we assume that manufacturers cannot readily alter numbers employed within a few months expectations are likely to be fulfilled with the outturn identically equal to the expectation.

GENERAL SPECIFICATION

We turn next to the general specification of the relationship between balances and official variables. Most questions ask for directions of trends over past and future four month periods and it is known that the majority of respondents answer in terms of the whole of the four month period in comparison with the whole of the previous four month period. Assuming a linear specification and including a constant for generality** the relationship between the official variable and the backward-looking balance might be:-

$$B_t = \alpha + \beta\left(\frac{\Delta X}{X}\right)_{t-1} \qquad (1)$$

---

* For example, assuming rational expectations we also need to assume that the outturn is uncorrelated with both the expectation error and the error in the relationship between the balance and the outturn otherwise the estimated coefficients in this relationship will be biased.

** A priori we might expect the constant to have value zero.

where we are considering, for example, a balance recorded in the January Survey being explained by the percentage change in the official variable between the third and fourth quarters of the previous year.*

Contrast this with the relationship implied by the theory suggesting that balances reflect the level of the official variable:-

$$\Delta B_t = \gamma + \delta\left(\frac{\Delta X}{X}\right)_{t-1} \tag{2}$$

Differencing (1) and adding to (2) gives:

$$\Delta B_t = \rho_o + \rho_1\left(\frac{\Delta X}{X}\right)_{t-1} + \rho_2\left(\frac{\Delta X}{X}\right)_{t-2} \tag{3}$$

where $\rho_o = \gamma/2,\ \rho_1 = \dfrac{\beta+\delta}{2},\ \rho_2 = \beta/2$

If the theory implicit in (1) is correct then in (3)

$$\rho_o = 0 \quad \text{and} \quad \rho_1 + \rho_2 = 0$$

and if (2) is correct then

$$\rho_2 = 0 \text{ and } \rho_o \text{ is not necessarily zero}$$

---

* In considering the forward-looking results the time-script on the outturn variable would be "t" and the January balance would be explained by the movement between the fourth and first quarters.

These hypotheses are equivalent if $\rho_0 = \rho_1 = \rho_2 = 0$ implying $\Delta B = 0$ Therefore, as expected, it will be difficult to distinguish between the two rival theories when the balances are changing only slowly.

ESTIMATION

Past Employment

Equation (3) was estimated using OLS with an assumed white noise error term for the period 1960Q1 to 1982Q4. B_t is the quarterly balance for the trend in numbers employed over the past four months, E_t is the official series for UK manufacturing employment. The following result was obtained (standard errors in brackets):-

$$\Delta B_t = \underset{(\cdot 77)}{-\cdot 31} \; + \underset{(1\cdot 91)}{15\cdot 58} \left(\frac{\Delta E}{E}\right)_{t-1} - \underset{(1\cdot 90)}{15\cdot 48} \left(\frac{\Delta E}{E}\right)_{t-2} \qquad (4)$$

$$\bar{R}^2 = \cdot 43 \qquad DW = 1\cdot 85 \qquad SE = 6\cdot 41$$

On this data, therefore, one cannot reject the joint hypothesis that $\rho_0 = 0$ and $\rho_1 + \rho_2 = 0$ at usual significance levels. On the other hand one can reasonably reject the hypothesis that $\rho_2 = 0$.

In addition setting $\rho_0 = 0$ and $\rho_1 + \rho_2 = 0$ and estimating by OLS with a white noise error term gives:-

$$\Delta B_t = \underset{(1\cdot 84)}{15\cdot 60} \left(\left(\frac{\Delta E}{E}\right)_{t-1} - \left(\frac{\Delta E}{E}\right)_{t-2}\right) \qquad (5)$$

$$\bar{R}^2 = \cdot 45 \qquad DW = 1\cdot 85 \qquad SE = 6\cdot 34$$

whereas setting $\rho_2 = 0$ and estimating by OLS gives:-

$$\Delta B_t = -\cdot 17 + 1\cdot 52 \left(\frac{\Delta E}{E}\right)_{t-1} \qquad (6)$$
$$\quad (\cdot 99) \quad (1\cdot 08)$$

$\bar{R}^2 = \cdot 01 \qquad DW = \cdot 99 \qquad SE = 8\cdot 43$

Clearly there is little statistical doubt on the above data that as far as the 'past employment' question is concerned the interpretation of the balances is that they represent the change in the official variable.

Future Employment

Using the general form (3) to investigate whether balances relate to changes or levels in the official variable the following results for the 'future employment' question (over a similar estimation period to that for past employment) were obtained:-

$$\Delta B_t = -\cdot 25 + 16\cdot 84 \left(\frac{\Delta E}{E}\right)_t - 16\cdot 69 \left(\frac{\Delta E}{E}\right)_{t-1} \qquad (7)$$
$$\quad (\cdot 96) \quad (2\cdot 38) \qquad\qquad (2\cdot 37)$$

$\bar{R}^2 = \cdot 36 \qquad DW = 2\cdot 86 \qquad SE = 7\cdot 97$

$$\Delta B_t = 16\cdot 83 \left\{\left(\frac{\Delta E}{E}\right)_t - \left(\frac{\Delta E}{E}\right)_{t-1}\right\} \qquad (8)$$
$$\quad (2\cdot 28)$$

$\bar{R}^2 = \cdot 38 \qquad DW = 2\cdot 86 \qquad SE = 7\cdot 88$

$$\Delta B_t = -\cdot 05 + 1\cdot 68 \left(\frac{\Delta E}{E}\right)_t \qquad (9)$$
$$\quad (1\cdot 17) \quad (1\cdot 25)$$

$\bar{R}^2 = \cdot 01 \qquad DW = 2\cdot 05 \qquad SE = 9\cdot 88$

Here again the statistical evidence points to the conclusion that the balance relates to <u>changes</u> in the official variable rather than its <u>level</u>. However the high values of the Durbin-Watson coefficient in equations (7) and (8) are slightly disconcerting as they suggest the likelihood of serially correlated errors. Consequently equations (7) - (9) were re-estimated with a first-order autoregressive error term. The justification for the inclusion of a lagged error term is that the trends questions are phrased in terms of a four-month change and not over a quarter year* thus one might expect a priori a significant coefficient on the lagged error term. The following results were obtained:-

$$\Delta B_t = -{\cdot}16 + 19{\cdot}33 \left(\frac{\Delta E}{E}\right)_t - 19{\cdot}10 \left(\frac{\Delta E}{E}\right)_{t-1} \qquad (10)$$
$$\quad ({\cdot}60) \quad (1{\cdot}80) \qquad\qquad (1{\cdot}80)$$
$$\bar{R}^2 = {\cdot}49 \quad DW = 2{\cdot}20 \quad SE = 7{\cdot}11 \quad \rho = -{\cdot}43\ ({\cdot}15)$$

$$\Delta B_t = 19{\cdot}21 \left\{\left(\frac{\Delta E}{E}\right)_t - \left(\frac{\Delta E}{E}\right)_{t-1}\right\} \qquad (11)$$
$$\quad (1{\cdot}76)$$
$$\bar{R}^2 = {\cdot}50 \quad DW = 2{\cdot}20 \quad SE = 7{\cdot}07 \quad \rho = -{\cdot}43\ ({\cdot}15)$$

$$\Delta B_t = -{\cdot}06 + 1{\cdot}65 \left(\frac{\Delta E}{E}\right)_t \qquad (12)$$
$$\quad (1{\cdot}14) \quad (1{\cdot}22)$$
$$\bar{R}^2 = {\cdot}01 \quad DW = 1{\cdot}99 \quad SE = 9{\cdot}87 \quad \rho = -{\cdot}02\ ({\cdot}68)$$

These results give further evidence in favour of the "changes" interpretation. The negative signs on the autocorrelation coefficients imply that businessmen tend to compensate for inaccurate forecasts made in the previous period.**

---

* In its early years the Survey was conducted three times a year and the wording of the questions were not altered when the Survey became quarterly in 1972. Trends data prior to 1972 has been linearly interpolated to give a quarterly series.

** Re-estimating equations (4) - (6), the past employment specifications, with an AR error term gave "insignificant" coefficients on the lagged error term in equations (4) and (5). In equation (6), where the coefficient on the explanatory variable is "insignificant" the coefficient on the lagged error term is +0.5 and significant.

Past Output

Questions about past and future movements in output have only been asked in volume terms since 1975 thus there are much shorter time-series with which to test the rival propositions.* Equations in similar specifications to those for employment data were estimated both with and without a first-order autoregressive error term.

The results were not quite as conclusive as those for employment. Looking at those including lagged error terms for 'past output' (even though none of these were 'significant') we have:-

$$\underset{}{\Delta B_t} = \underset{(2{\cdot}10)}{{\cdot}46} + \underset{({\cdot}80)}{3{\cdot}01}\left(\frac{\Delta X}{X}\right)_{t-1} - \underset{({\cdot}79)}{2{\cdot}04}\left(\frac{\Delta X}{X}\right)_{t-2} \qquad (13)$$

$$\bar{R}^2 = {\cdot}45 \quad DW = 1{\cdot}89 \quad SE = 8{\cdot}84 \quad \rho = {\cdot}20\ ({\cdot}44)$$

$$\Delta B_t = \underset{({\cdot}52)}{2{\cdot}47}\left\{\left(\frac{\Delta X}{X}\right)_{t-1} - \left(\frac{\Delta X}{X}\right)_{t-2}\right\} \qquad (14)$$

$$\bar{R}^2 = {\cdot}48 \quad DW = 1{\cdot}89 \quad SE = 8{\cdot}58 \quad \rho = {\cdot}25\ ({\cdot}38)$$

$$\Delta B_t = \underset{(2{\cdot}50)}{1{\cdot}65} + \underset{({\cdot}85)}{3{\cdot}10}\left(\frac{\Delta X}{X}\right)_{t-1} \qquad (15)$$

$$\bar{R}^2 = {\cdot}33 \quad DW = 1{\cdot}88 \quad SE = 9{\cdot}60 \quad \rho = {\cdot}29\ ({\cdot}35)$$

(B_t is the absolute change in the backward looking output balance and X_t is the implied index of UK manufacturing output; standard errors in brackets, data 75Q2 to 82Q4.)

---

* Questions regarding output expectations are asked in CBI monthly surveys which are conducted as part of the Harmonised EEC Business Survey. For the purposes of this section no account is taken of data outside the main quarterly surveys.

The coefficient on the explanatory variable in (15) is significantly different from zero, unlike in equations (6) and (12) for employment and although one cannot reasonably reject the hypothesis that the coefficients on $\left(\frac{\Delta X}{X}\right)_{t-1}$ and $\left(\frac{\Delta X}{X}\right)_{t-2}$ sum to zero in (13) it seems far less clear cut than in equations (4) and (10).

Future Output

With the forward-looking output question this also appears to be true viz:

$$\Delta B_t = \underset{(1{\cdot}68)}{\cdot 75} + \underset{(\cdot 78)}{2{\cdot}73}\left(\frac{\Delta X}{X}\right)_t - \underset{(\cdot 78)}{1{\cdot}40}\left(\frac{\Delta X}{X}\right)_{t-1} \tag{16}$$

$$\bar{R}^2 = \cdot 29 \qquad DW = 2{\cdot}02 \qquad SE = 8{\cdot}76 \qquad \rho = \cdot 00\ (3{\cdot}4)$$

$$\Delta B_t = \underset{(\cdot 59)}{2{\cdot}02}\left(\left(\frac{\Delta X}{X}\right)_t - \left(\frac{\Delta X}{X}\right)_{t-1}\right) \tag{17}$$

$$\bar{R}^2 = \cdot 28 \qquad DW = 2{\cdot}02 \qquad SE = 8{\cdot}86 \qquad \rho = \cdot 06\ (\cdot 77)$$

$$\Delta B_t = \underset{(1{\cdot}77)}{1{\cdot}45} + \underset{(\cdot 79)}{2{\cdot}44}\left(\frac{\Delta X}{X}\right)_t \tag{18}$$

$$\bar{R}^2 = \cdot 24 \qquad DW = 2{\cdot}04 \qquad SE = 8{\cdot}96 \qquad \rho = \cdot 06\ (\cdot 77)$$

Thus even though the results of the survey of answering pratices (op.cit) suggest that respondents answer in terms of the change in the variable concerned for both output and employment the results of this econometric exercise per se indicate that there may be more doubt about this in the case of output. Although it must be remembered that the output time-series used has rather less observations* than that of employment the suggestion that some respondents might be answering in terms of levels rather than changes is obviously very important in accurately interpreting the survey results. In particular it has clear implications for the specification of forecasting equations if the change in the balance (as well as the balance itself) were to be included in forecasting changes in the official series for output. It could completely alter ones view, based on business survey results, of where the economy was in the business cycle. With these thoughts in mind let us now turn to the specification and estimation of forecasting equations.

FORECASTING EQUATIONS

Specification

We now consider whether we can derive a forecast of the official variable from the recorded Survey data. This of course represents a reversal of the implied causation that we have been considering up until now. Taking employment first we might consider a linear specification of the following form:-

$$\left(\frac{\Delta E}{E}\right)_t = \alpha + \beta B_t \qquad (19)$$

---

* However analysis of the employment data over a similar reduced period did not suggest that the shorter time-series was the reason for the inconclusive results for output.

where B_t is the future employment balance in quarter t and E is the number of employees in manufacturing. Alternatively we might include the change in the balance as an additional explanatory variable ie.

$$\left(\frac{\Delta E}{E}\right)_t = \alpha + \beta B_t + \gamma \Delta B_t \tag{20}$$

Estimation

(i) Employment

The two above specifications were estimated by OLS over the 60Q1 to 80Q4 period with a first-order autoregressive error term and the following results were obtained:-

$$\left(\frac{\Delta E}{E}\right)_t = -\cdot 27 + \cdot 033\, B_t \tag{21}$$
$$\quad (\cdot 05) \quad (\cdot 002)$$
$$\bar{R}^2 = \cdot 87 \qquad DW = 1\cdot 98 \qquad SE = \cdot 27 \qquad \rho = \cdot 43$$
$$(\cdot 15)$$

$$\left(\frac{\Delta E}{E}\right)_t = -\cdot 28 + \cdot 038\, B_t - \cdot 013\, \Delta B_t \tag{22}$$
$$\quad (\cdot 06) \quad (\cdot 003) \quad (\cdot 003)$$
$$\bar{R}^2 = \cdot 90 \qquad DW = 1\cdot 87 \qquad SE = \cdot 24 \qquad \rho = \cdot 55$$
$$(\cdot 12)$$

The results suggest, on conventional grounds, that the addition of an extra term is justified as it is both "significant" and improves the fit. Nevertheless on forecasting performance over the next eight quarters (1981 and 1982) equation (21) does rather better than (22). Equation (21) has lower mean absolute prediction error and root mean square error and, using Hendry's Q-statistic one cannot reject the null hypothesis of parameter stability between the estimation and forecast periods at the 5 per cent level of significance whereas one can in equation (22). In (21) only five of the eight forecast errors are positive whereas in (22) the last seven are positive.

(ii) Output

For the future output question the following results were obtained:-

$$\left(\frac{\Delta X}{X}\right)_t = -1{\cdot}20 + {\cdot}086\, B_t \quad (23)$$
$$(\cdot34) \quad (\cdot017)$$
$$\bar{R}^2 = \cdot51 \qquad DW = 2{\cdot}10 \qquad SE = 1{\cdot}70 \qquad \rho = -\cdot21 \; (\cdot49)$$

$$\left(\frac{\Delta X}{X}\right)_t = -1{\cdot}03 + {\cdot}073\, B_t + {\cdot}064\, \Delta B_t \quad (24)$$
$$(\cdot33) \quad (\cdot017) \quad (\cdot035)$$
$$\bar{R}^2 = \cdot56 \qquad DW = 2{\cdot}16 \qquad SE = 1{\cdot}62 \qquad \rho = -\cdot24 \; (\cdot46)$$

In (24) the coefficient on B_t is not quite "significantly different from zero" but, despite this, equation (24) forecasts better (in terms of lower root mean square error) than (23) and in both equations parameter stability hypothesis cannot be rejected. Of course assigning to zero a coefficient that is insignificantly different from zero may be unjustified unless ones prior belief is that the coefficient's true value is indeed zero but nevertheless there again seems doubt between the rival specifications.

The clue to this problem is to be found in that none of these four estimated linear equations above forecast very well (ex post) over the 1981-82 period despite there being a reasonable fit, especially for employment, over the estimation period. What is peculiar about this particular forecast period is that the balances move considerably away from zero and thus the linear specification is called into question.

The point is that even though the survey data should simply be a mapping from one representation of an economic variable to another the linear relationship is merely an approximation because of the loss of information implicit in the qualitative data and particularly the survey balances. When the balances move further away from zero this approximation tends not to hold and the linear specification can mislead. Perhaps the change in the balance merely "picks up" the inaccuracy in the approximate relationship?

Further information can be gleaned by using the "Ups" and "Downs" separately rather than the balances, and with the aid of assumptions about firms' distribution of replies and sophisticated computer techniques functions that are non-linear in parameters can be estimated.* Nevertheless because much research work is, at the moment, focussed on the interpretation and analysis of balances it is important to know the strengths and limitations of this approach.

Improved Forecasting Equations

The aim of the remainder of this paper is to produce linear (in parameters) equations for manufacturing output and employment that would have forecast 1981-1982 better than equations (21) - (24) using balances and functions of balances only.

Evidence from scatter plots and previous work using simple

---

* see, for example, Keating (1983)

assumed distributions of firms' replies** suggests that functions using powers of balances might provide useful results. In the case of <u>employment</u> using cubic powers of rescaled balances produced very good forecasts over the 1981 - 1982 period.

$$\left(\frac{\Delta E}{E}\right)_t = -\cdot 23 + 2\cdot 48\ A_t + 5\cdot 04\ A_t^3 \qquad (25)$$
$$(\cdot 05) \quad (\cdot 29) \quad (1\cdot 31)$$
$$\bar{R}^2 = \cdot 89 \qquad DW = 2\cdot 13 \qquad SE = \cdot 25 \qquad \rho = \cdot 44\ (\cdot 15)$$
$$A_t = B_t/100$$

Estimation period: 60Q2 - 80Q4 by OLS AR(1) error

Forecasting performance (81Q1-82Q4):

$$MAPE = 11\cdot 2 \qquad RMSE = \cdot 24 \qquad Q = 7\cdot 67 \qquad \chi^2_8 = 15\cdot 51$$

...using fifth powers of the rescaled balances proved even better still...

$$\left(\frac{\Delta E}{E}\right)_t = -\cdot 24 + 2\cdot 81\ A_t + 10\cdot 23\ A_t^5 \qquad (26)$$
$$(\cdot 05) \quad (\cdot 24) \quad (2\cdot 75)$$
$$\bar{R}^2 = \cdot 89 \qquad DW = 2\cdot 11 \qquad SE = \cdot 25 \qquad \rho = \cdot 43\ (\cdot 15)$$

and mean absolute prediction error over the 81-82 period was 9.23 per cent with root mean square error .21 and Q-statistic 5.66, implying that the parameter stability hypothesis could not be rejected at the 5% significance level.

** see Yaun (1982), Appendix III

As can be seen from the chart below this equation (26) would have forecast manufacturing employment very well indeed during 1981 and 1982.

UK Manufacturing Employment

percentage change on previous quarter

Fitted & Forecast(+), Actuals(x)

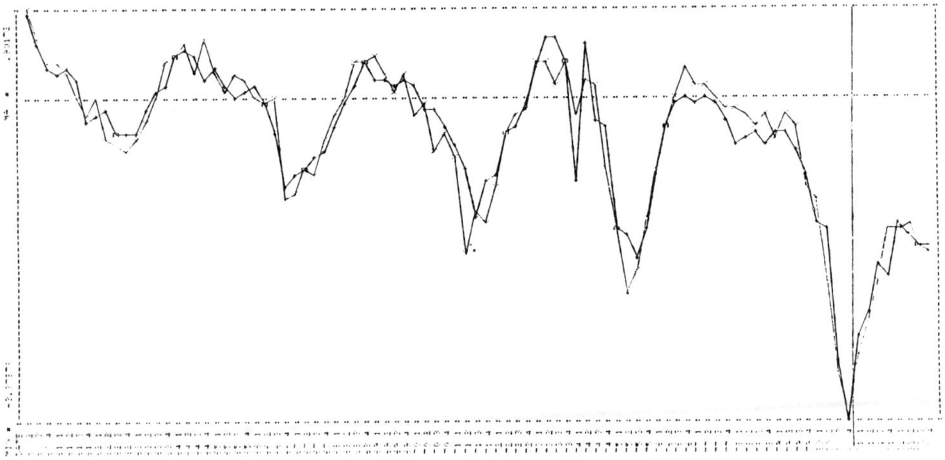

In the case of output however this method proved relatively unsuccessful with none of the powers of rescaled balances being "significant". The most favourable specification was found to be when the exponent of the rescaled balance was the only explanatory variable (apart from a constant) nevertheless this equation fitted no better than those using balances (and changes in balances) and its forecasts had unreasonably wide 95 per cent confidence limits.

A number of possible arguments can be advanced as to why these simple equations do not perform as well with output than with employment. First and foremost is that it is perhaps more difficult for businessmen to forecast output over the next four months as many unforeseen developments (eg. strikes, bad weather) can intervene. Secondly, because it is difficult to forecast output very accurately over the next four months some businessmen may actually only look one or two months ahead (despite the majority assertion in the 1982 survey of answering practices that they do not)*. Thirdly the official figures themselves may not perhaps measure accurately the extent and timing of changes in manufacturing output, although of course this charge might also be levelled at the UK manufacturing employment data.

---

* UK manufacturers are asked for four-month forecasts of output every month in the CBI Monthly Trends Enquirys which are carried out in the months between quarterly surveys. Averaging these monthly figures gave similar results to those reproduced in this paper. An alternative method of comparing Trends balances with official output data is to use these monthly forecasts against the changes in output compared with four months previously. This method, however, has two difficulties. Firstly that at the moment the implied index of output is not produced monthly, hence one has to use the official index which is not adjusted for stock changes and hence potentially liable to error. Secondly it appears that the majority of Survey respondents answer in terms of comparing four month periods as a whole in comparison with previous four month periods rather than through-the-period changes.

Instrumental Variables

Another approach for output was attempted. It could be argued (see for example Connolly (1975)) that the non-linearities in the relationship between Trends balances and official data manifest themselves in a correlation between the error term and the independent variable (the balance in forecasting equations) thus the Ordinary Least Squares technique is inappropriate as its use would result in biased coefficients. To circumvent this problem an instrumental variable (or indirect least squares) technique was used. Various "exogenous" variables were tried (world trade, world oil prices, US interest rates and UK government current spending) and the "best fit" seemed to be*:-

$$\underset{}{FQ_t = \underset{(10{\cdot}5)}{30{\cdot}0} - \underset{(\cdot 96)}{2{\cdot}80}\, USRS_{t-2} + \underset{(\cdot 62)}{1{\cdot}91}\, WT_{t-2}} \qquad (27)$$

$$\bar{R}^2 = \cdot 78 \qquad DW = 1{\cdot}56 \qquad SE = 8{\cdot}36 \qquad \underset{(\cdot 15)}{\rho = \cdot 74}$$

Nevertheless when the fitted values for FQ_t were plugged into an equation to explain the percentage change in the official output series the result was rather disappointing viz.

$$\left(\frac{\Delta X}{X}\right)_t = \underset{(\cdot 39)}{-\cdot 847} + \underset{(\cdot 023)}{\cdot 067}\, \widehat{FQ}_t \qquad (28)$$

$$\bar{R}^2 = \cdot 21 \qquad DW = 1{\cdot}90 \qquad SE = 1{\cdot}93$$

---

* USRS is the yield on three-month US Treasury bills and WT is the volume of OECD exports of manufactures (UK weighted).

CONCLUSION

This paper has addressed itself to two related issues. Firstly it investigated whether Survey balances refer to changes rather than the levels of comparable official statistics and thereby assisted in the interpretation of the results. Secondly it examined whether the balances alone could be used to produce accurate short-term forecasts.

In the case of questions referring to employment this econometric work supported by the 1982 CBI survey of answering practices suggest that the Survey balances are correctly interpreted as referring to the percentage change in the official series. For output however the econometric evidence is not quite so clear cut.

In forecasting equations the answers to the future employment questions provide good forecasts using balances only and these are further improved by addition of odd powers of the balances. With output however the forecasting performance of this methodology was less good.

It was suggested that there might be two reasons why these conventional methods produce relatively poor forecasts in the case of output. Firstly that because of the simplification necessary for collection and presentation of the data the balances themselves (and simple functions of them) do not adequately "pick up" the non-linearities implicit in so complex a relationship. Thus approaches based on non-linear techniques perhaps using data on "Ups" and "Downs" rather than the balances might produce better forecasts. Secondly that it reflects the difficulty of predicting output some months ahead in an uncertain world. This clearly points to the need for considered judgement in addition to careful econometrics.

Thus the CBI Industrial Trends Survey data can be used, provided it is done thoughtfully, as an excellent barometer of the business climate. In conjunctural analysis and in the preparation of short-term forecasts this survey and its correct interpretation is an invaluable asset.

References

Burton C P H (1983) — Answering Practices in the CBI Industrial Trends Survey - CIRET Workshop 1983

Connolly B L (1975) — Estimating Structural Relationships from CBI Industrial Trends Survey data - CIRET Conference 1975

Keating G B (1983) — The effect of answering practices on the relationship between CBI survey data and official data - Applied Economics 15, pp 213-224

Klein P A & G H Moore (1981) — Industrial Surveys in the UK, Applied Economics 13, pp 167-179 and 464-480

Yaun P J (1982) — A study of UK manufacturing investment using CBI Industrial Trends Survey - MSc project

Acknowledgements

The author would like to thank other members of the Economic Affairs Directorate (especially John Caff, Doug McWilliams, Charles Burton and Bahram Pesaran) for their comments in the preparation of this paper.

Recent Trends in Forecasting Methods

J.S. Armstrong
Wharton School
University of Pennsylvania
Philadelphia, Pa.

What have we learned about forecasting in the social sciences over the past quarter of a century? This paper reviews the research since 1960 to determine if it provides guidance for making better forecasts, better assessments of uncertainty, or gaining acceptance of our forecasts. As will be shown, the research has produced a number of valuable and surprising conclusions.

The first section of the paper presents forecasting principles that were believed to represent the best ideas on forecasting for an organization as of 1960. (Certainly, however, these principles did not represent current practice in 1960.) Following that, an examination is provided on the evidence produced since 1960.

Old-Fashioned Forecasting Principles, 1960 Style

To describe the context of the forecasting problem, consider the following situation. Suppose you were named the chief forecaster for a large corporation called Babo, Inc. Babo is the dominant firm in an oligopolistic market. You are responsible for the forecasting in the following areas:

a) the economy,

b) your industry,

c) effects of your company's actions and of competitors' actions,

d) your market share,

e) your company's costs,

f) your company's sales, and

g) your company's profits.

The previous forecaster, Nick Carter, assumed the position of chief forecaster at Babo in 1960, when he had instituted a set of forecasting procedures. The procedures were drawn from the academic literature and were regarded as amongst the most advanced for any organization in 1960.

Although Carter was ahead of his time, he proved to be amazingly rigid over the next quarter century. Babo's forecasting procedures today are exactly the same as they were in 1960.

Carter was forced into early retirement because of a report done by a consulting firm that specialized in forecasting. They suggested that Babo's forecasting procedures were outdated and that Carter was blocking change. Babo urges you to institute new procedures.

Although Babo's forecasting manual provided an extensive set of forecasting procedures, they can be summarized by the following eight guidelines. The first six guidelines refer to methods for making forecasts, the next one to estimating uncertainty, and the last one to gaining acceptance of the forecasts.

1. Decomposition should be used whenever feasible. This means that complex problems should be broken into a series of subproblems. Each subproblem would be solved and the results would then be synthesized. Of particular importance were decompositions to:

   a) separate the forecasting of company sales into industry sales and market share, and to

   b) estimate current status separately from forecasting change.

   It is also important to consider each consumer market as a separate problem.

2. Extrapolation should be used as one of the forecasting methods whenever data allow. The favored method is exponential smoothing of deaseasonalized data, using a trend estimate.

3. Obtain opinions from experts in the topic area and use it in highly structured ways, to:

a) estimate current status,

b) make forecasts of change,

c) forecast in situations where data on the variable of interest (e.g., on the sales variable) is absent or is of poor quality.

d) forecast the effect of actions by the firm when considering the reactions by other major competitors.

Expert opinion was <u>not</u> to be used to adjust the forecasts produced by objective methods.

4. Intentions surveys (e.g. consumers' intentions) should be used to forecast short-term behavior for relatively important events.

5. Causal-objective methods are preferred whenever sufficient data exist. They should be developed from <u>a priori</u> theory and estimates should be obtained from a variety of data sources. Substantial efforts should be made to obtain reliable data.

6. Combinations of forecasts taken from at least two different approaches are desired for all important forecasts. These forecasts should be weighted by the confidence one has in each forecast.

7. Uncertainty estimates should accompany the forecasts. The accuracy of this method in similar situations should be used as the primary means for assessing uncertainty. Judgmental assessments of accuracy should also be used.

8. Prior commitment should be sought among key decision makers on the potential use of the information <u>before</u> the forecasts are obtained.

Interestingly, when the above guidelines were developed by Carter, they were not based on much empirical evidence. They had been discussed in the literature, and they were not controversial from a theoretical viewpoint. However, these guidelines (except #4) were <u>not</u> commonly used by organizations.

You are interested in determining whether the empirical evidence obtained over the last 25 years has supported or refuted the above guidelines. To determine this, you conduct a literature review to try to cover all of the empirical research published over the past 25 years. Fortunately, research on forecasting methods has grown dramatically since 1960. Currently this area is experiencing faster growth than is typical for the social sciences. The publication rate for papers on forecasting is growing at about 8% per year, versus 6% in general for the social sciences (Armstrong, 1984b).

After completing the literature review, you circulated a summary among key people for comments. The comments were used to make revisions in your interpretations.

I used the above procedures to examine the evidence. The results are provided below in three sections: making forecasts, estimating uncertainty, and gaining acceptance by the users of the forecasts.

Making the Forecasts

The evidence on the eight guidelines for making forecasts is summarized in this section.

Decomposition

Although decomposition has been widely recommended for management science, little evidence exists on its value in forecasting (Armstrong, Denniston, and Gordon, 1975). Furthermore, evidence is lacking on how best to decompose problems and on the situations where decomposition is most useful. Still, no evidence exists to warrant change in Babo's guideline with respect to decomposition.

Extrapolation

In terms of effort, one of the most important areas for research on forecasting over the past quarter century has been on sophisticated extrapolation methods. However, the empirical research in the area, summarized in

Armstrong (1978a, p. 138-170) and Armstrong (1984a), supported especially by the simulation study by Gardner and Dannenbring (1980) and by the study of 1001 time series by Makridakis (Makridakis, et al., 1982), suggests there has been no gain in accuracy from sophisticated methods (see also McLaughlin, 1983). Thus, Babo's 1960 procedures still suffice. Babo's reluctance to change allowed them to avoid what might have been substantial expenditures on evaluating and implementing complex extrapolation methods.

Expert Opinion

The growth of research on judgmental forecasting has been dramatic. The number of publications in this area has been growing at about 14% per year over the past 30 years (Armstrong 1983b).

Expert opinion provides a useful way to estimate current status, although little direct evidence exists. Experts in the area often can make adjustments for recent events whose effects have not yet shown up in the data.

Surprising evidence has been obtained on forecasting change. For many years, it was suggested that expert opinion was especially relevant for long-range forecasts. The research shows it to be less accurate than objective methods in situations where large changes are expected (Armstrong, 1978a, p. 358-389). Also surprising is the finding that expertise, beyond a minimal level, is of little value in forecasting change (Armstrong, 1980). These findings challenge Babo's existing procedures. They should be modified to place more reliance on objective methods than on expert opinion (especially for longer-range forecasts) and to avoid the use of expensive experts when expert opinion is used to forecast change. These findings are counter-intuitive, and the reasons behind them are currently not well understood.

In situations where data are sparse (e.g. forecasting sales for a new product), the most important development in the past 25 years is "bootstrapping."

Bootstrapping involves translating judgmental forecasting into a set of procedures that can be carried out mechanically. This has been done by asking forecasters (either by "protocols" where forecasters describe each step in their thinking as they make judgmental forecasts, or by "retrospective process tracing models" where forecasters describe their procedures by memory), or, more commonly, by statistical inference (e.g., regressing a set of judgmental predictions against the information used by the judge). Research on bootstrapping has come from different fields, and this research indicates that bootstrapping forecasts are slightly better than the judgmental forecasts that were used to develop the model. Bootstrapping also reduces the cost of forecasting for situations requiring many forecasts. Finally, bootstrapping provides insight to the way in which judgmental forecasts are being made, thus offering the possibility of further improvement (e.g., it may turn out that the expert is using invalid relationships). Research on bootstrapping is summarized in Camerer (1981).

To forecast the effect of actions by the firm, it is sometimes important to forecast the reactions by other major participants in the system. Thus, in considering a major change in marketing strategy, Babo would like to forecast the reactions of its competitors, subsequent counter-actions by Babo, and so on. To make such forecasts, Babo tried to get the most knowledgeable experts and to provide them with all the relevant data. Research summarized in Armstrong and Walker (1983) suggests that substantially more accurate forecasts can be made by role-playing. The outcomes of these role-playing cases are then used as a basis for the prediction. Although the evidence is limited to only seven actual situations, the superiority of the role-playing predictions is dramatic. For these seven situations, "opinions" were correct for 20% of the predictions while "role playing" was correct for 70%. Furthermore, simple and relatively inexpensive designs have been sufficient to produce these gains. Further research on role playing would be of considerable value.

The most controversial of Babo's procedures was the recommendation that forecasts from objective methods should not be revised by expert opinion. This guideline was based on evidence from psychology (e.g., Kelly and Fiske, 1950). Some apparently contradictory evidence arose from studies in economic forecasting (e.g., Juster, 1972; McNees, 1975). Although the issue has not yet been resolved, the results might be explained as follows: the improvements from judgmental adjustments to economic forecasts may be due to gains in estimating current status, and these gains outweigh the loss in forecasting change. If so, the research suggests that no changes should be made in their procedures because Babo already makes separate estimates of current status and they incorporate judgmental evidence.

In general, the research on the use of expert opinion has led to dramatic and useful changes for forecasting.

Intentions

Research on the use of intentions has not produced dramatic changes. Nevertheless, the research in this area has been extensive and the results have been extremely pragmatic. For example, it is now known that valid intentions data can be obtained from mail and telephone surveys and at much lower costs than for personal interviews. Furthermore, the non-response problem is less serious, as we can achieve large response rates for mail and telephone surveys (often in excess of 70%), and the impact of the remaining non-response bias can be estimated (Armstrong and Overton, 1977). In addition, much has been learned about how to reduce response bias.

Causal-Objective Methods

The recommendation to use causal and objective methods whenever sufficient data exist has not held up well in light of the research. In particular, such methods have not been of significant value for short-term forecasting (e.g., Armstrong, 1978b). On the other hand, these forecasts have not been inferior. Thus, they might be used for important forecasts as one of several approaches that could be combined.

Years of experience with stepwise regression and other non-theoretical approaches to the development of causal models produced few successes and many absurd results (e.g. Armstrong, 1975). This supports Babo's guideline stressing that a priori theory should be used. Despite this evidence, models are often developed without the use of theory. This is partly due to technological advances such as the reduced costs of storing data with computers, and the low-cost procedures for exploratory analysis, such as stepwise regression. Also, academic researchers have often ignored causal approaches. Glaser's (1954) appeal for a priori analysis has gone unheeded in many areas (Inciardi, 1977).

Presumably, more data is better than less. So many sources of data would be expected to yield better estimates of causal relationships. This is valid, though not as important as originally thought. Multiple sources appear to be most important in cases where the existence or direction of the relationships is in doubt.

The quality of the data is also thought to be important. However, it has been difficult to find situations where highly reliable data are needed on causal factors. In fact, contradictory evidence exists. For example, unconditional forecasts (where the causal variables must be forecasted) were found to be superior to conditional forecasts in 8 of 10 published papers according to the review in Armstrong (1978a, p. 219). Furthermore, crude estimates of causal relationships, involving only proper specification of direction and a rough idea of magnitude, are often sufficient (Dawes and Corrigan, 1974; Dorans and Drasgow, 1978; Kerin and Newman, 1978). This finding might not be relevant, however, in situations where large changes are involved. This might produce significant cost savings for Babo, as they can reduce the amount spent for data on causal factors.

In general, the research has provided evidence in favor of simplicity. Among the vast literature on highly sophisticated methods, it is difficult to find any evidence that sophistication or complexity has improved forecasting accuracy. Methods of modest complexity have been found to be sufficient. Also, complexity generally increases costs and reduces understanding.

Combinations of Forecasts

One strategy that has long been advocated by academics and practitioners is to combine forecasts from different methods. This is thought to be especially useful if the methods are different, and if they draw upon different sources of data. Thus, it would be useful to combine forecasts from extrapolation, judgment, and econometric methods and to utilize data from independent sources such as data on consumers, production and trade, and causal factors.

Combinations of forecasts are intuitively appealing. They guard against mistakes or cheating and thus help to avoid large errors. They also utilize more information.

Surveys of forecasting methods used by organizations do not suggest that combined forecasts are widely used. Furthermore, combined forecasts have not been subject to much research. My survey and re-analysis of the published research produced ten studies with 18 comparisons (Armstrong, 1978a, pp. 263-268). These found modest benefits when combining different methods, as the error from the combination was better than the average forecast error on 10 of the 18 comparisons, the other 8 comparisons resulting in ties. On average, the forecast error was reduced by five percent when combining two methods. Recent evidence has suggested this strategy to be more powerful, especially when more than two forecasts are combined (Makridakis and Winkler, 1983). Combining is most appropriate when one is not sure, *a priori*, which method will yield the best forecast (and this is the typical situation).

Research to date suggests that equal weighting of the various forecasts is sufficient. A useful approach would be to start with the cheapest methods and average them.

Assessing Uncertainty

Previous accuracy still provides the best way to assess uncertainty. Therefore, to assess the uncertainty for a one-year forecast of automobiles, one should use the accuracy of previous one-year forecasts of automobiles where these forecasts were produced using the same method.

Judgmental assessments of uncertainty have been subject to numerous problems. For example, they typically underestimate uncertainty. Furthermore, as people gain expertise in an area, the tendency toward overconfidence increases (Fischhoff and MacGregor, 1982). One result is that claims by an expert about confidence in a forecast are virtually worthless. The implications for Babo are to put little emphasis on judgmental estimates of uncertainty and to ignore confidence claims by individuals, except in situations when feedback about outcomes is readily available and easy to summarize. Another useful technique, advocated by Benjamin Franklin, is to ask experts to summarize arguments *against* their prediction as well as those in favor; this leads to more realistic assessments of uncertainty (Koriat, Lichtenstein, and Fischhoff, 1980).

Prior Commitment

Evidence since 1960 supports the guideline that forecasters should gain specific prior commitment from decision-makers as to how they will use forecasts.

Without prior commitment, decision-makers are unlikely to be impressed by evidence that suggests changes in their existing beliefs (e.g. see Slovic and Fischhoff, 1977). Although little direct research has been done on this vital topic, we have learned something about methods for obtaining prior commitment. Research on the use of scenarios suggests that the evidence has a greater effect if decision-makers are presented with vivid accounts of the possible courses of action (Hamill, Wilson, and Nisbett, 1980). The likelihood of action can be modified if the decision-makers are asked to imagine themselves in the situation (Anderson, 1983), and also if they are asked to predict how they would react in that situation (Sherman, 1980). On the other hand, these vivid accounts may seriously distort the decision-makers' forecasts of the likelihood of various events (Gregory, Cialdini, and Carpenter, 1982).

Conclusions

In general, old-fashioned principles for forecasting have held up well over the past 25 years. Minor changes were found for six of the eight guidelines involving decomposition, extrapolation, intentions, combined forecasts, uncertainty, and prior commitment by decision makers. In these areas, the research provided support and also suggested more effective ways to implement the principles.

While the development of sophisticated approaches to the analysis of data has been the most popular research area, the payoff has been negligible. Nonetheless, this area still attracts most of the scientific research budget.

Research over the past 25 years has produced dramatic changes in the area of judgmental forecasting. The following guidelines are new:

a) judgment provides a poor approach to long-range forecasting,

b) high expertise on the topic is of little value in forecasting change, and

c) bootstrapping can provide more accurate forecasts than judgment, and it is typically less expensive.

A summary of some of this research on judgmental forecasting can be found in the collection of readings by Kahneman, Slovic and Tversky (1982).

Substantial change has also occurred with respect to causal models. It now appears that crude estimates of causal relationships are sufficient, with the possible exception of those situations involving very large changes.

The review of the literature also indicates that the research budget on forecasting is being misallocated. The exhibit provides a summary of those various research areas and suggests changes in the future research. The last column presents my opinions on the potential payoff for research in each area. Less should be spent on the areas of low payoff, such as the development of sophisticated approaches for extrapolation or the development of causal models. More should be spent where the payoff has been high, such as judgmental forecasting. Additional research on methods for gaining acceptance of forecasts also appears to be a promising area.

PROGRESS IN RESEARCH ON FORECASTING

Topic	Research Since 1960: Effort	Payoff	Examples	Future Research Prospects
Decomposition	Little	Low	• Helpful where uncertaintly is high	Good
Extrapolation	Very Much	Low	• Few differences in accuracy among methods	Poor
Expert Opinion	Much	Very High	• Bootstrapping more accurate • Limited value of expertise in forecasting large changes	Excellent
Intentions	Modest	Modest	• Ways to reduce response and non-response bias	Modest
Causal Methods	Very Much	Low	• Simplicity is a virtue	Modest
Combined Forecasts	Little	Modest	• Combinations yield substantial gains	Modest
Uncertainty	Little	Little	• Overconfidence in judgmental estimates • Argue against your forecast	Good
Implementation	Little	Modest	• Vivid examples lead to increased estimate of likelihood	Excellent

Anderson, Craig A., "Imagination and Expectation: The Effect of Imagining Behavioral Scripts on Personal Intentions," Journal of Personality and Social Psychology, 45 (1983), 293-305.

Armstrong, J.Scott, "Tom Swift and His Electric Regression Analysis Machine: 1973," Psychological Reports, 36 (1975), 806.

Armstrong, J. Scott, Long-Range Forecasting: From Crystal Ball to Computer. New York: John Wiley 1978a.

Armstrong, J. Scott, "Forecasting with Econometric Methods: Folklore vs. Fact," Journal of Business, 51 (1978b), 549-564.

Armstrong, J. Scott, "The Seer-Sucker Theory: The Value of Experts in Forecasting," Technology Review, 83 (June/July 1980), 18-24.

Armstrong, J. Scott, "Forecasting by Extrapolation: Conclusions from Twenty-Five Years of Research," Interfaces (forthcoming, 1984a).

Armstrong, J. Scott, "Do Judgmental Researchers Use Their Own Research? A Review of Judgment Under Uncertainty," Journal of Forecasting (forthcoming 1984b).

Armstrong, J. Scott; Denniston, W.B. and Gordon, M.M., "The Use of the Decomposition Principle in Making Judgments," Organizational Behavior and Human Performance, 14 (1975), 257-263.

Armstrong, J. Scott and Grohman, Michael, "A Comparative Study of Methods for Long-Range Market Forecasting," Management Science, 19 (1972), 211-221.

Armstrong, J. Scott and Overton, Terry S., "Estimating Nonresponse Bias in Mail Surveys," Journal of Marketing Research, 14 (1977), 396-402.

Armstrong, J. Scott and Walker, Harry S., "Validation of Role Playing as a Predictive Technique for Conflict Situations," World Future Society Bulletin, 17 (July-August 1983), 15-22.

Camerer, Colin, "General Conditions for the Success of Bootstrapping Models," Organizational Behavior and Human Performance, 27 (1981), 411-422.

Cocozza, Joseph J. and Steadman, Henry J., "Prediction in Psychiatry: An Example of Misplaced Confidence in Experts," Social Problems, 25 (1978), 265-276.

Dawes, Robyn M. and Corrigan, Bernard, "Linear Models in Decision Making," Psychological Bulletin, 81 (1974), 95-106.

Dorans, Neil and Drasgow, Fritz, "Alternative Weighting Schemes for Linear Prediction," Organizational Behavior and Human Performance, 21 (1978), 316-345.

Fischhoff, Baruch and MacGregor, Don, "Subjective Confidence in Forecasts," Journal of Forecasting, 1 (1982), 155-172.

Gardner, Everette S., Jr. and Dannenbring, David G., "Forecasting with Exponential Smoothing: Some Guidelines for Model Selection," Decision Sciences, 11 (1980), 370-383.

Glaser, Daniel, "A Reconsideration of Some Parole Prediction Factors," American Sociological Review, 19 (1954), 335-340.

Gregory, W. Larry; Cialdini, Robert B. and Carpenter, Kathleen M., "Self-Relevant Scenarios as Mediators of Likelihood Estimates and Compliance: Does Imagining Make it So?" Journal of Personality and Social Psychology, 43 (1982), 89-99.

Hamill, Ruth; Wilson, T.D. and Nisbett, R.E., "Insensitivity to Sample Bias: Generalizing from Atypical Cases," Journal of Personality and Social Psychology, 39 (1980), 578-589.

Inciardi, James A. and McBride, Duane C., "The Parole Prediction Myth," International Journal of Criminology and Penology, 5 (1977), 235-244.

Juster, F. Thomas, "An Evaluation of the Recent Record in Short-Term Forecasting," *Business Economics*, 7 (May 1972), 22-26.

Kahneman, Daniel; Slovic, Paul and Tversky, Amos, *Judgment Under Uncertainty: Heuristics and Biases*. London: Cambridge University Press, 1982.

Kelly, E. Lowell and Fiske, D.W., "The Prediction of Success in the VA Training Program in Clinical Psychology," *American Psychologist*, 5 (1950), 395-406.

Kerin, Giden and Newman, J. Robert, "Additional Considerations with Regard to Multiple Regression and Equal Weighting," *Organizational Behavior and Human Performance*, 22 (1978), 143-164.

Koriat, Asher; Lichtenstein, Sarah and Fischhoff, Baruch, "Reasons for Confidence," *Journal of Experimental Psychology: Human Learning and Memory*, 6 (1980), 107-118.

Makridakis, Spyros, et al.,"The Accuracy of Extrapolation (Time Series) Methods: Results of a Forecasting Competition," *Journal of Forecasting*, 1 (1982), 111-153.

Makridakis, Spyros and Winkler, Robert L., "Averages of Forecasts: Some Empirical Results," *Management Science*, 29 (1983), 987-996.

McLaughlin, Robert L., "Forecasting Models: Sophisticated or Naive?" *Journal of Forecasting*, 2 (1983), 274-276.

McNees, Stephen K., "An Evaluation of Economic Forecasts," *New England Economic Review* (November-December 1975), 3-39.

Sherman, Steven J., "On the Self-erasing Nature of Errors of Prediction," *Journal of Personality and Social Psychology*, 39 (1980), 211-221.

Slovic, Paul and Fischhoff, Baruch, "On the Psychology of Experimental Surprises," *Journal of Experimental Psychology: Human Perception and Performance*, 3 (1977), 544-551.

Summary of the Discussion

G. Poser
Technische Hochschule Darmstadt
Darmstadt

The discussion during the first session had to be kept in narrow time limits because the opening addresses used up more time than anticipated. Therefore the paper on forecasting methods presented by Scott ARMSTRONG could not be discussed in the audience.

What follows is a summary of the discussions of the papers of M. K. EVANS and P. J. YAUN.

G. GREEN as the main discussant of the paper presented by M. K. EVANS characterised it as stimulating and provocative, but in some parts as highly controversial. Although he agreed with EVANS' statement that judgement has to be considered to be part and parcel of any useful econometric forecast he was not convinced that the basic underlying econometric structure of the US economy has shifted radically over the postwar period as EVANS stated. GREEN argued that equations less simplistic in form, with variables that are less intercorrelated and dummy variables that allow for special events like Nixon's wage-price-controls would lead to more stable coefficients if the period is cut down into subperiods. As an example GREEN chose the wage-rate-function. Estimating the wage-rate-function of the BEA quarterly model for various subperiods - although different from those chosen by EVANS - he concluded, that the unemployment rate variable was significant for all subperiods except for 1979 to 1983 (a period with only 16 observations) and that the CPI variable did not reach more significance in the most recent subperiod as it did in EVANS' equation (the remaining variables having significant t-values in most cases). GREEN therefore did not want to accept EVANS' conclusion that econometric equations for most variables are highly unstable over time. Although he felt that judgement is an essential component of econometric forecasts he regards the equation structures as resonably stable and therefore assigns more weight to econometric equations and the statistical evidence in the model.

EVANS restricted his remarks to the wage-rate-function. He doubted that the inclusion of additional variables into this function - for instance a term for the composition of the unemployment rate or a dummy variable for the Nixon wage and price controls - would make the coefficient of the rate of unemployment variable more stable and significant. According to his experience with various different specifications - some sophisticated, some simple - dummy variables for wage and price controls during the Nixon administration would not make the equations more stable. He had also used a composition of unemployment terms. But he considered it a trick that backfired at the wrong time. Using this trick one could stabilize the coefficient of the unemployment term only at the risk and the expense of correcting all of the residual variables in another term which would then give wrong parameter estimates. EVANS therefore did not consider it a valid term. He emphasized that he has kept his functions simple on purpose because his 2o years' experience in forecasting had taught him that leaving out a couple of complicated terms did not diminish the efficacy of the equations in forecasting but - if anything - improved them.

Discussing P. J. YAUN's paper Ph. A. KLEIN pointed out that he agreed with the finding that net balances of answers to CBI survey questions on production and employment should be compared to changes in official statistics rather than to levels. But on other questions, for example the question on capacity which asks entrepreneurs whether their capacity is adequate in relation to expected demand the answers should be related to capacity levels in order to be comparable. KLEIN stated that it was not so much the character of the variable which determined the appropriate comparsion but how the survey question was worded. For the same reason this is also true for comparsions of net balances reporting future magnitudes. The decision whether to compare the surveys to changes or levels in quantitative magnitudes would not depend on either the variable or whether or not it refers to the past or the future but rather on how the question is worded. KLEIN was a little disturbed by YAUN's efforts to improve his correlation by using complex nonlinear variables because YAUN did not explain how to pick these complex interrelationships. Also he would not support YAUN's suggestion to include a lot of exogenous variables in order to improve the forecasts. Many exogenous variables - the oil shock or whatever - are factors which one could only know retrospectively.

W. H. STRIGEL called attention to the indifference interval. It is different for ex ante and ex post questions and its size and form might change over time. For the production variables for instance the indifference interval is shifted asymetrically in the direction of positive answers. For intended price reductions the indifference interval is shifted in the negative direction because often they are not reported. For ex ante questions the indifference interval as a rule exceeds that for ex post questions. It varies for different variables: it is relatively small for sales prices and relatively large for investment plans. It is difficult to conclude from changing indifference intervals that respondents have changed their intentions. It is a fact that reporting behaviour changes; this might have the same explanation as the change of relationships over time reported by EVANS.

G. NERB added that using third and higher powers is a scaling problem and would give better results in the quantification of qualitative data.

A. HART asked what was done about seasonal fluctuations and how various magnitudes were measured. What do respondents really count when they answer questions about production, for example? If they are working from sales data, then inventory figures have to be worked in. How is an upper bias introduced in inflationary situations? People who are attempting econometric work are tempted to be nominalists and to assume that variables which can be measured are a counterpart of a theoretical concept. That may not be the case. Regarding the paper by EVANS, the assumption that we know how to measure past changes in the stock of money is very rash. The institutional changes have been such that the content of the monetary variable is totally incomparable in recent quarters with what it was a few years back. As this is likely to happen to almost any series HART asked if it is feasible at all to find out what measurements were taken on.

YAUN answered that all questions he was dealing with in his paper were in seasonally adjusted terms. The vast majority of the participants claimed that they adjusted their answers themselves. But the respondents so far were not asked what they considered to be employment or output. Turning to the comments of STRIGEL he agreed that for forecasting purposes one really does have to look at as much information as one can possible get including any information about answering practices.

Second Session
Implication of Survey Data for Business Cycle Analysis

Chairman:

A. Piatier, Ecole des Hautes Etudes en Sciences Sociales

Paris

Business Cycle Analysis and Expectational Survey Data

V. Zarnowitz
NBER and
University of Chicago
Chicago, Ill.

Interest in business cycles is itself subject to a wave-like movement, waxing during and after periods of turbulence and depression, waning in periods of substantial stability and continuing growth. This can be well illustrated in the literature. At times, confidence in government institutions and actions persuaded many that cyclical instability had ceased to be a serious problem. Thus in the 1920s, monetary policies were expected to help maintain prosperity. In the 1960s fiscal fine tuning evoked similar hopes. The present is another time of disillusionment--now extending to either type of stabilization policy. The sequence of serious worldwide recessions in the last decade once more refuted the perennially attractive idea of business cycles having become obsolete. Beyond that, the credibility of both Keynesian and monetarist explanations of the recent developments has diminished. The profession is again paying more attention to the continued existence of business cycles.

This paper is part of a project in progress, which attempts to survey the recent work on business cycles in historical perspective. It concentrates on one set of phenomena in the complex story of this main form of economic instability and its interpretations. What is the role of foresight and the lack thereof under uncertainty in the theory of business cycles? What is the evidence from survey data on expectations and forecasts? The subject is broad and the work is far from finished, but some provisional results seem worth reporting.

The paper has four substantive parts. Section 1 discusses the expectational aspects of modern business cycle theories. Section 2 reviews the criticisms of the treatment of expectations. Section 3 summarizes the evidence. Section 4 provides some illustrations from my own empirical work.

1. Expectations in the Theory of Business Cycles

The "Konjunkturgebundenheit" of contemporary economic thinking, i.e., its dependence on whether prosperous or depressed business conditions prevail, is in itself an argument in favor of the importance of the "psychological factor."[1] Of the classics of business cycle literature, Pigou is most prominantly associated with the theory that, under uncertainty, interdependent expectations of businessmen generate widespread errors of optimism in expansions and of pessimism in contractions.[2] It is well known but still noteworthy that, for all their differences, Keynes shared with Pigou the emphasis on these processes of error diffusion, discovery, and reversal.[3] Later much further attention was given to the role of attitudes and expectations in business decisions (Hart, Shackle), consumer behavior (Katona, Juster), and the "contagious" cumulative processes of the business cycle (Jöhr).[4] Recently, Strigel examined the results of the Ifo business outlook surveys from a similar point of view.[5]

During business expansions, most series on output, employment, real income, and spending, etc., increase so that "good news" dominate and their cumulation fosters optimism; during business contractions, the opposite happens. This is simply a consequence of the persistence and pervasiveness of the fluctuations and not necessarily a source. To be possibly invalid and provoke disagreement, a theory of the "psychological" type must argue that errors of excessive optimism (pessimism) play a major independent part in generating booms (slumps). Thus, prospective profits are being overestimated for some reason in certain periods and such errors spread and grow until discovered in the markets for the "overproduced" goods and replaced for a time by similarly infectious and partly self-validating underpredictions. For the classics, access to more and better information on industry fortunes would help reduce individual forecast errors and their cumulation; for Keynes, this could not help much, since there is little knowledge on which expectations of the future yield from investment could draw.[6]

The first generation of formal theoretical models of cycles in aggregate output slighted the expectational factors. This is true of the stochastic, linear, and stable models (Frisch) and the deterministic, nonlinear, and unstable ones (Hicks).[7] But soon a reaction set in against the theories of the latter type. The dangers of volatile market psychology, investment collapse, etc., no longer loomed large in the midst of worldwide expansion and growing prosperity, even though "Keynesian" ideas were still ascendant. There was renewed recognition of the plurality of causes and diversity of elements in the individual business cycles (Duesenberry).[8] New influential theories cast expectations in prominent roles and at the same time imputed much more stability to the private sector than Keynes and his early followers did. The permanent income and life cycle hypotheses make consumption forward-looking rather than merely reactive, broadly wealth-dependent rather than income-constrained (Friedman, Ando and Modigliani).[9] The evolution of the investment function also pointed to the importance of longer-term expected ("permanent") output (Eisner), while relying as well on relative price variables such as the rental costs of capital (Jorgenson).[10] All these developments reduced the perceived significance of the accelerator-multiplier interaction and the associated cumulative movements making for instability.

The original monetarist theory which challenged Keynesian economics in the 1960s asserts that changes in the supply of money are the main determinant of changes in nominal income. The long-run version of this hypothesis reduces to the old quantity theory of how trends in money produce trends in prices, but there is much less clarity and agreement about the nature and direction of the money-income relation in the short run. Here one critical element is a relatively stable demand function for real money balances. The other is lags in wage and price adjustments, which arise because expectations are taken to be "adaptive," that is, backward-looking and involving gradual learning from, and correction of, past errors. Given both these conditions, autocorrelated disturbances in the form of alternating sequences of high and low monetary growth rates produce, via changes in expected relative prices and rates of return, fluctuations in aggregate demand and real economic activity, i.e., business cycles or growth cycles. The critical monetary impulses are treated as exogenous and mainly policy induced. The "feedback" influence from business activity to monetary growth is not analytically developed and integrated into a theory of how money, prices, and real factors interact in the short run. Instead, this is an essentially exogenous and monetary theory (Friedman and Schwartz).[11]

Under adaptive expectations (AE) short-term money changes are implicitly viewed as unanticipated and so are for some time the associated price changes. For example, people will tend to underestimate the rising prices caused by a sudden acceleration of monetary growth and hence overestimate their real money balances. This will induce portfolio adjustments in response to the altered relative prices or yields on a broad range of assets and then more transitory spending on goods and services to liquidate the extra amounts of "redundant" money. In the process, interest rates will first decline but then snap back as spending, income, and prices rise, overshooting the new equilibrium paths. This transmission process is seen as involving variable but on the average lengthy lags. As the adjustments in the price level are incomplete and those in wages may be particularly sluggish, employment and output react in a cyclical manner.

According to the "natural rate" hypothesis (Friedman, Phelps), the deviations of output, employment, and unemployment from their equilibrium levels can occur only if and as long as the expected rates of inflation differ from the actual ones.[12] However, such differences are eliminated only in an ill-defined "long run," which in this context is often treated as if it meant "on the average over the business cycle." The process of discovery and elimination of the price forecast errors is sluggish in a world of frequent monetary and real shocks, in which it is difficult to distinguish signals from noise, that is, absolute from relative price changes and persistent from temporary movements.

In the more recent equilibrium models, the hypothesis of AE is replaced by that of rational expectations (RE). Here expectations are basically like predictions of the relevant and valid economic theory: free of any bias and subject to random errors only (Muth, Lucas).[13] Economic behavior is guided by subjective probabilities which on the average agree with the observed frequencies of the events in question. These frequencies have predictive value, the processes to which they refer being assumed stable and known from past learning experience. Unlike in Knight or Keynes, there is no uncertainty here as to what the applicable objective probability disturbances are or whether they do in fact exist in any usable form.[14]

Under RE, all persistent monetary changes, inasmuch as they are predictable, will be correctly anticipated and met directly by proportional changes in prices and related nominal variables. Only random monetary impulses can lead to surprises and miscalculations which, in this view, are necessary to explain any cyclical movements in real variables. It is the resulting errors in price expectations, which must themselves be random and short-lived, that act as the proximate cyclical impulses in this class of models.

It is assumed that economic agents have timely and complete information about their own markets but only incomplete or lagged information about other "island" markets (Phelps) and about the economy-wide aggregates such as the money stock and the overall price level.[15] Supply and demand depend on perceived changes in a broad set of real variables, but that set is in practice limited to relative prices only. All agents are effectively treated as price takers, so quantity signals are disregarded. Suppliers compare their current price and wage opportunities with the expected (discounted future) opportunities and react positively to the excess of the former over the latter. These intertemporal substitution effects are typically elastic, reflecting strong competitive incentives to take advantage of temporarily higher real rates of return. Now a general price rise due to an unanticipated monetary stimulus is misperceived by agents as signaling increases in relative prices, which prompts simultaneous upward adjustments of output and employment throughout the economy. Only in time, after having made their decisions, will the agents discover that their relative price estimates were distorted as prices rose in other markets as well. A retrenchment will then follow. When prices unexpectedly fall or, which is more likely in our times, the actual inflation rates decline below the anticipated rates, misperceptions of the opposite sign are predicted to occur, which again will not be recognized and cleared up until they have caused a retardation or recession in real economic activity. Thus these theories originating mainly in the work of Lucas, Sargent, Wallace, and Barro rest on several strong, maintained hypotheses: intertemporal substitution on the supply side, rational expectations, and lags of information.[16]

The first generation of the RE models assumed flexibility of all prices and continuous clearing of all markets, including the labor market; they also implied the impotence of any monetary stabilization policy that is nonrandom and capable of being anticipated. These propositions are highly controversial and some critics regard them as entirely inconsistent with basic facts about the economy (Arrow, Solow, Tobin).[17] Empirical studies of intertemporal substitution show that it is difficult to test this hypothesis directly; the evidence is mixed but for the most part unfavorable (Lucas and Rapping, Hall, Altonji, and others).[18] The voluminous theoretical and empirical work on price determination and labor contracts identifies a number of reasons why prices and wages adjust gradually to changes in aggregate demand (Azariadis, Baily, Gordon, Okun).[19] Some of the more recent RE models reflect these developments by introducing contracts which predetermine the course of wages over some future time period (Phelps, Taylor, Fischer, McCallum).[20] Other models with RE retain continuous market clearing but rely largely or exclusively on real, not monetary, disturbances to explain business fluctuations (Kydland and Prescott, Black, King, Long, Nelson, Plosser).[21] The issues addressed in all these diverse studies are important for the analysis of business cycles but must be omitted from consideration in this paper which is limited to a single aspect of this work, namely the treatment of agents' expectations. The related problem of the accuracy of experts' forecasts will be noted later.

2. Critique

RE constitute the most common element in the recent theoretical work on business cycles at least in the U.S., and there is wide agreement that their use as a technical model-building principle has led to important developments and new insights (e.g., in the criticism of some aspects of macroeconometric models and the analysis of competitive markets with imperfect information).[22] Economics has always implicitly accepted the RE hypothesis in the analysis of steady states or stable market prototypes, where all active participants must be presumed to know the processes involved.

RE can be viewed as a condition of stochastic equilibrium, but general equilibrium theorists raise a number of sweeping objections against its application to macroeconomic dynamics (see note 17 for references). Contingent future markets are conspicuous by their absence. Information is limited and unevenly diffused. The subjective probability distributions underlying the forecasts of the individual decision-makers differ. No one can predict the evolution of other people's expectations. The counter-argument is that such criticisms, though they may be observationally correct, are not helpful. Some apply to more than the RE models and would preclude much innovative (and of necessity highly aggregative and abstract) theorizing (Lucas). Some neglect the many advances in the understanding and applications of the RE method, e.g., to the problem of diffuse or "asymmetrical" information (S. Grossman).[23]

The fundamental difficulty is not with the rationality of costly information uses, which it is only reasonable to assume, but with the availability of sufficient information, which certainly cannot be taken for granted. Two assumptions underlie what may be called the strong version of the REH: (1) that market incentives and penalties enforce continually and everywhere optimal, i.e., cost-efficient predictions, and (2) that economic agents generally possess adequate knowledge (data and models) so that their optimal predictions are at least unbiased (in practice, such knowledge should make most forecasts reasonably accurate). While (1) is presumably often well approximated, there seem to be no good a priori reasons why (2) should be always and everywhere true. It is the claim of <u>general</u> validity of the REH in its strong form (which is implicit in the macro-models built on this hypothesis) that many economists believe is greatly overstated.[24]

The equilibrium RE models contain no learning processes: they assume that agents have already learned all that they can know about the probability distributions they face. This fits best a stochastically stationary environment that has persisted long enough for people to have acquired the knowledge of its operation. Learning is impeded in a stochastic nonstationary environment, even without structural change, since nonstationary processes come in many varieties and may interact in complicated ways. Moreover, actions based on incorrect beliefs how the economy works cause outcomes that may themselves be misleading. Some authors have argued that the learning process, even if optimal in some (e.g., least squares) sense, may not converge to the rational-expectations equilibrium; however, convergence has been proven by others for some relatively simple situations. In any event, during the learning process, optimal predictions may be approximated by adaptive expectations (AE) with varying correction coefficients (Taylor, B. Friedman).[25]

In a nonstationary world with structural changes and a mixture of random and autocorrelated disturbances, uncertainty in the sense of Knight and Keynes is prevalent. Here AE based on "experience," i.e., the observed frequencies of past events modified in the light of recent changes, will often prove unreliable, but they are apt to include the bulk of the available information. (Of course, optimal predictions will also incorporate any genuine information about the future, e.g., credible news on prospective policy actions and domestic and foreign economic trends, but such inputs are in short supply.) The amount of valuable insight that can thus be obtained may be quite limited, but anyone who uses it the best way he can in actions concerning the inherently uncertain future would conform to a common sense definition of rational behavior.

A closely related argument is that uncertainty is associated with variations in nonstationary means resulting from "permanent" changes in levels or growth rates; in contrast, transitory, random deviations around stable trends are connected with calculable risk. Uncertainty is held to be essential to the persistence of cyclical contractions and the current RE models err in ignoring it. They should allow permanent changes to occur but not to be identified immediately. Stochastic shocks in the markets for commodities, money, and labor contain in each case a permanent and a transitory component. The two cannot be reliably separated: new information reduces but does not eliminate the confusion. The rational response to the shocks takes the form of gradual adjustments of beliefs about the permanent values of the endogenous variables, since the structure of information is such that adaptive or distributed-lag predictions are optimal (Brunner, Cukierman, Meltzer).[26]

3. Evidence

Consider testing for the "rationality" of any set of expectations or forecasts. Several related criteria have been formulated and used. Let X_t be the actual value and X^e_{jt} be the forecast of X_t made at the time $t - j$. Then the common test of unbiasedness is that the regression

$$X_t = a_j + b_j X^e_{jt} + u_{jt} \tag{1}$$

should yield estimates of the coefficents a_j and b_j that are not significantly different from zero and one, respectively. This test is weak, since RE are not merely free of systematic error but also efficient in the use of all relevant information, I_{t-j} ; the strict requirement is that

$$(X_t) = E(X^e_{jt} | I_{t-j}) , \tag{2}$$

where E is the expected value operator.

However, condition (2) is too general to be testable. The set I_{t-j} must be restricted and identified. For expectations or forecasts made regularly or by a replicable method, I_{-t-j} includes importantly the past errors knowable to the source of X^e_{jt} Here the requirement is that there be no significant autocorrelation among the errors u_{jt}, which could have been exploited to improve X^e_{jt} . Thus rationality can be rejected by the evidence of either bias or serially correlated residual errors or both. Of course, RE imply the equality of mean actual and predicted values; if $(a_j, b_j) = (0, 1)$ and $(u_{jt}) = 0$, $E(X_t) = E(X^e_{jt})$.

Another efficiency test is to check whether the survey data reflect the autoregressive properties of the variable in question. For example, let $j = 1$ and compare the regressions

$$(3) \qquad X_t = \sum_{i=1}^{n} \alpha_i X_{t-i} + \varepsilon_t \quad \text{and} \quad X^e_{1t} = \sum_{i=1}^{n} \beta_i X_{t=i} + \eta_t .$$

For the expectation errors to be orthogonal, i.e., uncorrelated with the information available from the past history of X, α_i must equal β_i for all i.

Forcasts are often made in each successive period for several periods ahead. In this case, a test of consistency of such forecasts (or expectations) is available. Consider, for example,

$$(4) \qquad X^e_{2t} = \beta_1' X^e_{1t} + \sum_{i=2}^{n} \beta_i' X_{t-i} + \eta_t' .$$

Here rationality requires that $\beta_i = \beta_i'$ for all i.

These tests have, of course, a common core and logic; they are simply different ways of checking on the properties of expectations conditional upon a certain set of information. If any exogenous variables generating X_t can be identified, further tests can be made to see whether their predictive power is fully reflected in X^e_{jt} .

Recent work using survey data has been preoccupied with tests for the rationality of inflation expectations. The most frequently used U.S. series are the one-step and two-steps ahead group average predictions from semiannual surveys of economic forecasters conducted since 1947 by Joseph A. Livingston, a syndicated financial columnist.

The balance of the evidence is that these data reject the REH according to at least some of the above tests. Thus failures to meet the criteria of efficiency and/or consistency are reported by Pesando and Carlson, failures to pass the unbiasedness tests by Wachtel and Gramlich. Pearce shows that univariate time-series (ARIMA) models would have predicted inflation better than the Livingston averages did, which also contradicts the rationality of the latter. Tests of individual forecasts predominantly fail the unbiasedness tests, confirming and amplifying the evidence for the aggregate forecasts, as shown by Figlewski and Wachtel. Moore notes the pronounced tendency of the Livingston averages to lag behind the actual inflation series. Most of the negative results relate to the 1970s, a decade of particularly large unpredictable inflationary shocks, but the earlier Livingston surveys do not fare much better. More favorable tests are reported by Mullineaux.[27]

Claims have been made that households predict inflation on the whole "more rationally" than economic and business forecasters, but the comparisons seem strained and inconclusive. The evidence comes from surveys of consumer attitudes which over time have dealt mainly with the direction, not the size, of the expected price changes. Some of the studies find that the hypothesis of unbiasedness cannot be rejected for these data, others merely that it is "not so decisively rejected" as the inflation forecasts by economists and business executives (Juster, Huizinga, Curtin, deLeeuw and McKelvey, Gramlich).[28] The conclusion that various surveys of price expectations produce as a rule mixed results, with a disturbingly large proportion of rejections, applies to European and Japanese as well as U.S. data (Aiginger, Papadia).[29]

Relatively few authors have tested expectations data for variables other than inflation. For many early forecasts of U.S. aggregative series (GNP, consumption expenditures, business outlays on plant and equipment, and industrial production in the 1950s and 1960s), there is evidence of significant bias (Mincer and Zarnowitz).[30] The most common pattern is underestimation of growth, i.e., of levels in upward-trending series, and somewhat less frequently of cyclical changes in general (Theil, Zarnowitz).[31] There are indications of adaptive learning behavior, with forecast revisions which are a fraction of the observed error (the smaller the longer the span of the forecast error). The AE models go back to the 1950s and have been used with some success in empirical research; whether they are "ad hoc" or, on the contrary, entirely "rational," depends on the structure and uncertainty of the available information (Cagan, Nerlove, Mincer, Frenkel, Mussa, Meltzer).[32]

Sales anticipations of U.S. manufacturing firms have been on the whole negatively assessed by Hirsch and Lovell, more positively by Pashigian and by Irvine. The latter study finds that the data pass most of the rationality tests before 1973 but not thereafter, and considers the possibility of a structural change associated with the first OPEC oil price shock. However, these Commerce data were discontinued in 1976.[33]

Underestimation of the mean actual change for 29 out of 39 variables covered is reported in a recent comprehensive compilation of tests on expectational survey data from several countries (Aiginger). These are surveys of businessmen covering a variety of operational variables (sales, orders, production, investment, inventories, selling prices); of consumers, concerning prices and financial situation; and of business analysts and economists, relating to GNP and its major components and the major price indexes. The prevalence of underprediction of average changes is attributed to asymmetries in the loss functions of economic agents: the loss from overoptimistic expectations tends to be larger than that for overpessimistic expectations. Given these asymmetries, the apparent biases in the survey data are themselves "rational" (on losses from forecasting errors, see Theil, Brainard, Waud, Johansen).[34]

The strongest evidence favorable to RE comes from the literature on "efficient markets" for financial assets and commodities. This is readily understandable since these are well-organized competitive auction markets with full price flexibility, where traders deal largely in standardized instruments, transaction costs are low, and prompt and general collection and dissemination of the information is vital and constitutes a central part of the functioning of the market itself.[35] Nevertheless, in this area, too, some test results unfavorable to the REH have been reported, namely for the interest rate forecasts surveyed in the Goldsmith-Nagan Bond and Money Letter. These are forecasts of representative interest rates one and two quarters ahead, made by active market participants. They were found to be in large part not unbiased or efficient and not always consistent (B. Friedman).[36]

However, survey data reflect *average* expectations whereas what matters in the marketplace are the expectations of *marginal* buyers and sellers. If the most resourceful participants succeed in eliminating unexpected profit opportunities, the market will behave in a way consistent with the REH, although many, perhaps even most, of the traders do not. Mishkin constructs forecasts of interest rate and inflation from bond market data and provides tests that fail to reject the rationality of the market interest rate forecasts. This is taken to suggest that "the Goldsmith-Nagan survey measures . . . are not an accurate description of the actual bond market forecasts" in the period 1959-69. But the concurrent bond-market predictions of inflation fail the rationality test, and Mishkin's argument that the 1960s were an unusual historical period because of rising inflation is not really persuasive. (The inflation forecasts in the 1970s seem generally worse yet, and this decade was in many respects even more "unusual." Long periods of tranquility are hard to find.)[37]

Clearly, the evidence from the surveys has certain important limitations and must be assessed with caution. But it is not good "positive economics" to dismiss it on the ground that only theories, not their assumptions, can be tested. Tests on the survey data focus on the issue of expectation formation. Where direct observations on expectations or forecasts are not used, the evidence generally consists of joint tests of an expectations hypothesis and the particular model incorporating that hypothesis. Diverse and rich expectational survey data are now available and in need of much careful exploration. Where independent tests based on such materials are in substantial agreement, they have lessons to impart that should be taken seriously.

4. Some Illustrations and Implications for Cyclical Analysis

Turning points in gross national product of the United States have been generally well predicted in the end-of-year forecasts for the next year, considerably worse in the earlier mid-year forecasts (Table 1, section 1). Few reversals occurred in this annual series. Directional changes over sequences of two semiannual periods or four quarters are much more difficult to anticipate and indeed these forecasts have not been much better than guesswork (sections 2 and 3 of the table). This and other evidence suggests that business analysts and economists are often able to recognize turns near the time they occur but not well ahead of the event (Zarnowitz, Fels and Hinshaw, Moore).[38]

Turning-point errors account for only 13 percent of all errors in a collection of annual forecasts of real GNP, 1959-76, but they are on the average 2 ½-3 times larger than other errors (Table 1, section 4). Real GNP is, of course, much more cyclical than nominal GNP and of central importance in business-cycle analysis and forecasting, but this analysis still understates the importance of turning points because it is limited to annual data. In the present-day practice of quarterly multiperiod forecasting, directional errors play a much larger and more adverse role yet; consider, for example, the widespread cumulative errors associated with missing a downturn and projecting continued growth instead (U.S., 1973-74, 1981) or with predicting an upturn prematurely (1982).

Realistically judged, annual GNP forecasts in the U.S. earn good marks; moreover, they have improved, compared with the earlier post-World War II years, in the 1960s and even in the turbulent 1970s. However, quarterly changes beyond the first two quarters ahead are much more difficult to predict than the year ahead, and here the record is actually much worse. A study of recent multiperiod predictions of real growth and inflation shows that their errors cumulated rapidly beyond the spans of 2-4 quarters. Underestimation of change is characteristic of most forecasts, but in periods of unanticipated retardations and recessions real growth tends to be overpredicted for some time as does the rate of price-level change in periods of unanticipated disinflation.[39]

I have applied tests of unbiasedness (based on regression equations of type (1) above) to a large set of forecasts by individual participants in quarterly business outlook surveys conducted since 1968 by the American Statistical Association and the National Bureau of Economic Research (ASA-NBER). Table 2, column 1, shows that only about 20 percent or fewer of the forecasters fail these F tests at the 10 percent significance level for five selected variables: percentage changes in nominal GNP, real GNP, and nominal consumer expenditures for durable goods, and levels of the unemployment rate and the changes in business inventories. In contrast, nearly 70 percent fail the tests for the forecasts of inflation (rate of change in the implicit price deflator). More detailed results would show that this contrast extends to each horizon but is particularly sharp for the longer ones (the targets include the current quarter and the four successive future quarters following each survey date).

Table 2, column 2, shows that about two thirds of the inflation forecasts and one-half of the inventory investment forecasts had autocorrelated errors; the corresponding proportions for the other variables range from 24 to 42 percent. These tests use series of errors based exclusively on data for past predictions and realizations that were available to participants in the successive surveys. The underlying argument is that the forecasters could and should have used this information so as to exploit and thereby eliminate all systematic elements in it. However, it must be noted that these computations required creation of a comprehensive computer file of successive vintages of the data covered. Keeping track of the many successive revisions in complex data, particularly the quarterly national income and product accounts, is not a small or low-cost operation in which forecasters can be expected to engage routinely.

In sum, tests of the REH produce results that are predominantly negative for the forecasts of inflation but much more favorable for those of real growth and some other important variables. These findings are generally consistent with others reported in the literature (Figlewski and Wachtel, McNees).[40]

Inflation has been underestimated most of the time during the 1970s in both the short and, particularly, longer forecasts. Mainly for this reason, the mean errors are generally negative for all nominal variables covered. They tend to be positive for the predictions of rates of change in real GNP (and accordingly negative for the unemployment rate), mainly because of the missed downturns in this period of surprisingly frequent recessions and stagflation (slow growth and high inflation) coming after a long period of prosperity in the 1960s. The first two lines in Table 3 provide a summary of the evidence for the above statements.

The most biased predictions are not necessarily the least accurate. For example, the inflation forecasts compare favorably with the real growth forecasts in terms of the average measures of relative accuracy and correlation between the predicted and the actual values (Table 3, lines 3 and 4). These comparisons show the ASA-NBER survey participants on the whole in a reasonably good light.

The group mean forecasts from a series of surveys have smaller variances of errors and hence are on the average more accurate than most of the corresponding forecast series of the individual participants. This is a strong conclusion, which applies to all variables and predictive horizons covered (Table 2, lines 5 and 6) and is consistent with evidence for different periods and from other studies.[41] However, a small number of the more regular survey members did perform better in most respects than the composite forecasts.

As noted earlier, failures to pass tests for rationality have been blamed in some writings on special features of this or that sample period (e.g., the Vietnam war inflation in the 1960s; OPEC and the supply shocks in the 1970s). Tests for the stability of coefficients (the F tests associated with Chow) have been applied to regressions of type (1) for the individual inflation forecasts to compare periods before and after 1974. For large majorities of the forecasters, the hypothesis that the coefficients remained the same could not be rejected.[42]

If the government has prompter access to information and better forecasts than the private sector, then its monetary stabilization policies can be effective even in the presence of rational expectations and full price flexibility (while otherwise, according to the same argument, agents and markets will anticipate and neutralize all such nonrandom discretionary policies). Comparisons of the annual January forecasts of the Council of Economic Advisors (published in the _Economic Report of the President_) with the more or less concurrent average forecasts from private surveys offer no evidence of any significant and consistent advantage on the side of the government. Thus the mean absolute error of GNP forecasts for 1962-68 was 1.3 percent for both the collected private predictions and those of the _Economic Report_ (Zarnowitz). The median forecasts from the November ASA-NBER surveys had slightly higher, those from the February surveys slightly lower, mean absolute errors than the corresponding _Economic Report_ forecasts for nominal GNP growth, real GNP growth, and inflation in 1969-76 (Moore).[43] It is usually not very difficult _in retrospect_ to find plausible reasons why some government policies proved reasonably effective, others ineffective or even counterproductive. The record of the policies is indeed mixed and the reasons vary, including prominently errors of judgment and foresight but not differences in such errors between the government and the private economy.

Expectations or forecasts for the same aggregate variables are likely to draw upon common, publicly available information and knowledge of certain established techniques and models. Informal exchanges, opinion polls, predictions publicized in the media and sold as expert advice--all these are ways in which forecast makers and users interact and influence each other directly and indirectly. In the process, the differences among the individual forecasts are likely to be reduced as many risk-averters may not wish to deviate much from the prevalent "consensus." Yet responsible forecasters will not simply imitate each other but use independent judgment so that their predictions will contain some independent information. Indeed, if simple or weighted averages of individual forecasts result in some net gains in accuracy, as is often the case, it is because these forecasts are to some extent diversified.

Table 4 compares the root mean square errors of the ASA-NBER group averages (M_s) with the corresponding measures for forecasts from a major corporation and two well-known econometric service bureaus (M_e). The ratios M_s/M_e vary between .84 to 1.59; when averaged across the target quarters, the range is narrowed to .95-1.11. There is considerable variation in the detail, but most of the ratios are close to one. IBM seems to be ahead of DRI, but gaps in reporting impair comparability here. The early Wharton forecasts often came out before the ASA-NBER surveys (and regularly precede the mid-quarter Wharton forecasts by approximately one month), so that they are at some informational disadvantage. The preponderance of $M_e/M_s > 1$ (except in the case of IBM) suggests that business economists' forecasts, which tend to be more judgmental, compare well with the forecasts constructed with the aid of large econometric models. However, it should be noted that the survey predictions benefit from the averaging of various inputs, including those from outside and inside econometric models (see below). To be sure, the model forecasts also include a large component of "judgmental adjustments," which have been shown to be on the average helpful. These findings are consistent with other evidence on the comparative accuracy of the leading corporate and econometric-model forecasters (McNees, Zarnowitz).[44]

The participants in the ASA-NBER surveys have been asked to rank the methods they use, and Chart 1 sums up the evidence on the relative importance of the different approaches on the average and over time. The most widely used set of procedures labeled the "informal GNP model" consists of predicting the major expenditure components of GNP, adding these figures to obtain the overall forecast, and checking and adjusting the results for plausibility and consistency. It is an eclectic approach in which judgment typically plays a large role, although various models of macroeconomic relationships are often employed as well. About three quarters of the forecasters have used it and some 50 to 60 percent ranked it first. Between 10 and 18 percent of the survey members (the proportion has been rising) relied mainly on their own ("inside") econometric models. About half of all participants reported subscribing to services of "outside" econometric models and nearly one-tenth ranked them first. Leading indicators were ranked second by a large majority of the forecasters, but this is a complementary approach seldom given the first rank, and so are the anticipations surveys. "Other methods" (write-in) is a rather negligible category.

Mean forecasts and their accuracy measures were computed and compared for three subsets of the group of the 79 "regular" participants in the ASA-NBER surveys, namely those who ranked first the informal GNP model (INF), the inside econometric model (INS), and the outside econometric model (OUT), respectively. Chart 2 superimposes the series of root mean square errors of the average forecasts of real growth made by the groups INS and OUT (broken lines) on the corresponding series for all participants (solid lines). The subscribers (OUT) perform better most of the time and on the average than the model proprietors (INS), particularly for Q0 (panel A), by smaller differentials for Q3 (panel B). This may be explained by the fact that OUT is dominated by large corporations using well-known econometric service bureaus and their own professional staff, whereas INS includes not only some of the leading models maintained by teams of experts but also a few models used exclusively by the reporting individuals.

Chart 3 shows for inflation forecasts what Chart 2 did for the real growth forecasts, using the same format. Here again OUT is visibly better than INS for Q0 (panel A). For the longer Q3 forecasts, however (panel B), the overall RMSE levels are virtually the same for the two groups. (These levels are shown on each of these graphs as the short horizontal lines labeled "means" in the right-hand margins.)

Although these differentials are apparently systematic, they are small, particularly for the longer forecasts, and of uncertain significance.[45] What is undoubtedly significant, even striking, are the high correlations among these forecasts and their errors, which are clearly demonstrated by these charts and others (not shown) for the different target variables covered. The averages for INF, the largest group, are not plotted in Charts 2 and 3 to avoid crowding, but their relative accuracy is high, close to that of OUT.

Finally, Table 5 provides detail on the relative accuracy and tests of unbiasedness for the real growth and inflation forecasts by the participants included in groups INS and OUT. It indicates that there is much differentiation among the individual forecasters. The group averages conceal this diversity. Sixteen of the 23 sources failed none of the F tests at the 5% significance level for their real GNP growth predictions, but only three (all in the OUT group) can boast of the same for their inflation predictions. The ratios of the individual to the overall group average RMS errors, M_i/M_{gi}, mostly exceed unity, reflecting the already noted gains from combining the forecasts, but 21 out of the total of 46 listed M_i/M_{gi} ranges include one or more ratios of less than one. The reader can locate a number of sources with excellent results for one or the other of the variables covered, and a few with very good results for both.

5. Concluding Observations

Recent theoretical work in macroeconomics has directed scholarly attention to the role of information and expectations in business cycles, which is certainly an important subject. What has been called the "rational expectations revolution" has stimulated much ingenious effort at model-building and -testing, which produced many interesting results. But the original claims on behalf of the new "classical" models with rational expectations and continuous market clearing have also encountered strong resistance by those who view them as greatly overstated or implausible. More importantly, there is considerable evidence that these models attribute to decision and policy makers more knowledge of how the economy works, better information and foresight, and prompter price adjustments in reaction to signals of change than people can have or make, given the complex dynamics of the modern world and the irreducible uncertainty about the future. Cyclical turning points in aggregate measures of economic activity more often than not surprise even expert forecasters, while lags in the public recognition of such events tend to be considerably longer yet. Early signals from leading indicators (which are generally sensitive and erratic series that are themselves difficult to predict) require confirmation and are sometimes ignored or disbelieved even after they get it. The speedups and slowdowns of inflation also usually arrive unanticipated. Indeed, the great majority of inflation predictions since the late 1960s fail the rationality tests and show a strong underestimation bias. This applies to both experts' forecasts and agents' expectations. Much less bias was found in the survey data for other variables of major importance for the analysis of business cycles.

It is probable that in many cases expectational data which fail to meet the strict rationality criteria in *ex post* tests would prove entirely consistent with optimizing *ex ante* behavior once the consequences of uncertainty, defective models (knowledge), and incomplete, tardy, or costly information are taken into account. But the concept of rational expectations in this general or weak sense does not have the striking, definite implications of the original strong version.

Where expectations are not strictly "rational," it does not follow that they must be merely extrapolative, regressive, or adaptive. In fact, past studies have found that such time-series models explain statistically at best little more than half of the variance of the expectations reported in surveys.[46] My own reading of survey data is that expectations are in general neither mere projections of the past nor flashes of intuition about the future. They are combinations of both extrapolative and autonomous components, which vary across individuals and change over time. The extrapolations are based on past data for both the variable to be predicted and other related factors: expectations are endogenous. But past developments and commitments, and current observations and news, also have implications for the future, which economic forecasters and agents try to extract and exploit.

Expectations matter a great deal but they are not all-important. Not all the past is bygones. The evidence that forecasts so often underestimate economic growth during recoveries and early expansions detracts from the hypothesis of excessive optimism (advanced in particular by Pigou and Jöhr). However, during the late expansion stages, when the high levels of activity suggest a "boom" but growth typically slows down, overoptimism does show up in that now the growth prospects tend to be overassessed. This continues _a fortiori_ in the earliest stage of contraction as a consequence of the widespread failure to recognize the downturn. Later, after the recession becomes evident, more of it is commonly anticipated and expectations may turn overpessimistic for some time. If the depressed conditions persist, these negative attitudes are likely to deepen and become in part self-validating (Keynes' case). But normally expectations of resumed growth soon assert themselves, sometimes prematurely as in 1981. As these observations suggest, predictions of the future almost inevitably contain strong elements of projections of the past: extrapolation of trends, regressivity toward the "normal," partial adjustments for recent errors. Expectations that affect the course of the economy can be presumed to be basically rational, that is, to use effectively the limited available knowledge and information, but they are diversified and need not always be self-validating and either stabilizing or destabilizing.

Footnotes

[1]Gottfried Haberler, Prosperity and Depression, 1937 (new ed., 1964), Harvard University Press, Cambridge, Mass., 1964, p. 471n.

[2]A. C. Pigou, Industrial Fluctuations, Macmillan, London, 1927, esp. chs. VI and VII.

[3]John Maynard Keynes, The General Theory of Employment, Interest, and Money, Macmillan, London, 1936, esp. chs. 11, 12, 15, 19, and 22.

[4]Albert G. Hart, Anticipations, Uncertainty, and Dynamic Planning, University of Chicago Press, Chicago, 1940; G.L.S. Shackle, Expectations in Economics, Cambridge University Press, 1949; George Katona, Psychological Analysis of Economic Behavior, McGraw-Hill, New York, 1951; F. Thomas Juster, Anticipations and Purchases, An Analysis of Consumer Behavior, NBER, New York, 1964; Walter Adolf Jöhr, Die Konjunkturschwankugen, J.C.B. Mohr, Tübingen, 1952, esp. pp. 588-618.

[5]Werner H. Strigel, Business Cycle Surveys, Campus Verlag, Frankfurt/New York, 1981, esp. chs. III and VII.

[6]Such knowledge is "usually very slight and often negligible" and so the expectations "being based on shifting and unreliable evidence . . . are subject to sudden and violent changes" (Keynes, 1936, pp. 149 and 315). Cf. Alfred Marshall, Money, Credit, and Commerce, Macmillan, London, 1923, pp. 260-261, and Pigou, op. cit., pp. 66-69.

[7]Ragnas Frisch, "Propagation Problems and Impulse Problems in Dynamic Economics," Economic Essays in Honor of Gustav Cassel, George Allen and Unwin, London, 1953; John R. Hicks, A Contribution to the Theory of the Trade Cycle, Oxford University Press, London, 1950.

[8]James S. Duesenberry, Business Cycles and Economic Growth, McGraw-Hill, New York, 1958.

[9]Milton Friedman, A Theory of the Consumption Function, Princeton University Press for the National Bureau of Economic Research (NBER), Princeton, 1957; Albert Ando and Franco Modigliani, "The 'Life Cycle' Hypothesis of Saving: Aggregate Implications and Tests," American Economic Review, March 1963, pp. 55-84.

[10]Robert Eisner, Factors in Business Investment, Ballinger Publishing Company for the NBER, Cambridge, Mass., 1978, esp. ch. 4; Dale W. Jorgenson, "Capital Theory and Investment Behavior," American Economic Review, May 1963, pp. 247-259.

[11]Milton Friedman and Anna J. Schwartz, "Money and Business Cycles," Review of Economics and Statistics, February 1963, supplement, pp. 32-64; A Monetary History of the United States: 1867-1960, Princeton University Press for the NBER, 1963.

[12]Milton Friedman, "The Role of Monetary Policy," American Economic Review, March 1968, pp. 1-17; Edmund S. Phelps, "Phillips Curves, Expectations

of Inflation and Optimal Unemployment Over Time," Economica, n.s., August 1967, pp. 254-281.

[13]John F. Muth, "Rational Expectations and the Theory of Price Movements," Econometrica, July 1981, pp. 315-335; Robert E. Lucas, Jr. "Expectations and the Neutrality of Money," Journal of Economic Theory, April 1972, pp. 103-124.

[14]J.M. Keynes, op. cit.; Frank M. Knight, Risk, Uncertainty and Profit, Houghton Mifflin, Boston, 1921.

[15]Edmund S. Phelps, "Introduction: The New Microeconomics in Employment and Inflation Theory" in Microeconomic Foundations of Employment and Inflation Theory, ed. by Phelps, Norton, New York, 1970, pp. 309-337.

[16]Robert E. Lucas, Jr. "An Equilibrium Model of the Business Cycle," Journal of Political Economy, December 1975, pp. 1113-1144; "Understanding Business Cycles," in Stabilization of the Domestic and International Economy, ed. by K. Brunner and A.H. Meltzer, North-Holland Publishing Company, Amsterdam, 1977, pp. 7-29; Thomas J. Sargent and Neal Wallace, "Rational Expectations and the Theory of Economic Policy," Journal of Monetary Economics, April 1976, pp. 169-183; T.J. Sargent, "A Classical Macroeconomic Model for the United States," Journal of Political Economy, April 1976, pp. 207-237; Robert J. Barro, "A Capital Market in an Equilibrium Business Cycle Model," Econometrica, 48, September 1980, pp. 1393-1417.

[17]Kenneth J. Arrow, "The Future and the Present in Economic Life," Economic Inquiry, 16, pp. 157-169; Robert M. Solow, "On Theories of Unemployment," American Economic Review, 72, pp. 1-11; James Tobin, "How Dead is Keynes?", Economic Inquiry, 15, October 1977, pp. 459-468.

[18]Robert E. Lucas, Jr., and Leonard A. Rapping, "Real Wages, Employment, and Inflation," Journal of Political Economy, 77, September/October 1969, pp. 721-754; Robert E. Hall, "Labor Supply and Aggregate Fluctuations," Carnegie-Rochester Series on Public Policy, 12, 1980, pp. 7-23; Joseph G. Altonji, "The Intertemporal Substitution Model of Labour Market Fluctuations: An Empirical Analysis," Review of Economic Studies, XLIX, 1982, pp. 783-824; J. G. Altonji and O. Ashenfelter, "Wage Movements and the Labor Market Equilibrium Hypothesis," Economica, 47, 1980, pp. 217-245; Kim B. Clark and Lawrence H. Summers, "Labor Market Dynamics and Unemployment: A Reconsideration," Brookings Papers on Economic Activity, 1, 1979, pp. 13-60; N.G. Mankiw, J. Rotemberg, and L.H. Summers, "Intertemporal Substitution in Macroeconomics," paper presented at the NBER Conference on Inflation and Business Fluctuations, April 30, 1982 (prel. draft).

[19]Costas Azariadis, "Implicit Contracts and Underemployment Equilibria," Journal of Political Economy, 83, December 1975, pp. 1,183-1,202; Martin N. Baily, "Wages and Employment under Uncertain Demand," Review of Economic Studies, 41, January 1974, pp. 37-50; Robert J. Gordon, "Output Fluctuations and Gradual Price Adjustment," Journal of Economic Literature XIX, June 1981, pp. 493-530; Arthur M. Okun, Prices and Quantities: A Macroeconomic Analysis, Brookings Institution, Washington, D.C.

[20]Edmund S. Phelps and John B. Taylor, "Stabilizing Powers of Monetary Policy under Rational Expectations," Journal of Political Economy, 85, February

1977, pp. 163-190; Stanley Fischer, "Long-Term Contracts, Rational Expectations, and the Optimal Money Supply Rule," ibid., pp. 191-205; John B. Taylor, "Aggregate Dynamics and Staggered Contracts," Journal of Political Economy, 88, February 1980, pp. 1-23; Bennett T. McCallum, "Macroeconomics After a Decade of Rational Expectations: Some Critical Issues," Working Paper No. 1050, National Bureau of Economic Research, December 1982.

[21]Finn E. Kydland and Edward C. Prescott, "Time to Build and Aggregate Fluctuations," Econometrica, 50, November 1982, pp. 1345-1370; Fischer Black, "General Equilbrium and Business Cycles," Working Paper, Massachusetts Institute of Techonology, rev. July 1982; Robert G. King and Charles I. Plosser, "The Behavior of Money, Credit, and Prices in a Real Business Cycle," Working Paper no. GPB 81-8, rev. November 1982, University of Rochester; Charles R. Nelson and Charles I. Plosser, "Trends and Random Walks in Macroeconomic Time Series: Some Evidence and Implications," Journal of Monetary Economics, 10, September 1982, pp. 139-162; John B. Long and Charles I. Plosser, "Real Business Cycles," Journal of Political Economy, 91, February 1983, pp. 39-69.

[22]Robert E. Lucas, Jr. "Econometric Policy Evaluation: A Critique" in Karl Brunner and Allan H. Meltzer, eds., The Phillips Curve and Labor Markets, North Holland, Amsterdam, 1976; William Poole, "Rational Expectations in the Macro Model," Brookings Papers on Economic Activity, 2, 1976, pp. 463-514.

[23]Sanford J. Grossman, "An Introduction to the Theory of Rational Expectations Under Asymmetric Information," Review of Economic Studies, XLVIII, 1981, pp. 541-559.

[24]See references in footnote 17 above.

[25]John B. Taylor, "Monetary Policy During a Transition to Rational Expectations," Journal of Political Economy, 83, October 1975, pp. 1,009-1,021; Benjamin M. Friedman, "Optimal Expectations and the Extreme Information Assumptions of 'Rational Expectations' Macromodels," Journal of Monetary Economics, 5, January 1979, pp. 23-41.

[26]Karl Brunner, Alex Cukierman, and Allan H. Meltzer, "Stagflation, Persistent Unemployment, and the Permanence of Economic Shocks," Journal of Monetary Economics, 6, October 1980, pp. 467-492; Allan H. Meltzer, "Rational Expectations, Risk, Uncertainty, and Market Responses," in Paul Wachtel, ed., Crises in the Economic and Financial Structure, Lexington Books, Lexington, Mass., 1982, pp. 3-22.

[27]James E. Pesando, "A Note on the Rationality of the Livingston Price Expectations," Journal of Political Economy 83, August 1975, pp. 849-858; John A. Carlson, "A Study of Price Forecasts," Annals of Economic and Social Measurement, 6 (1), Winter 1977, pp. 27-56; Paul Wachtel, "Survey Measures of Expected Inflation and Their Potential Usefulness" in Joel Popkin, ed., Analysis of Inflation: 1965-1974, Ballinger Publishing Company for NBER, Cambridge, Mass., 1974, pp. 361-395; Edward M. Gramlich, "Models of Inflation Expectation Formation: A Comparison of Household and Economist Forecasts," Journal of Money, Credit, and Banking, 11 (4), November 1979, pp. 447-456; Stephen Figlewski and Paul Wachtel, "The Formation of Inflationary Expectations," Review of Economics and Statistics, 63, February 1981, pp. 1-10;

Donald J. Mullineaux, "On Testing for Rationality: Another Look at the Livingston Price Expectations Data," Journal of Political Economy, 86 (2), April 1978, pp. 329-336.

[28]F. Thomas Juster, Statement presented in Hearings before the Task Force on Inflation of the Committee on the Budget, House of Representatives, 96th Congress, First Session (June), U.S. Government Printing Office, Washington, D.C., 1979, pp. 214-226; John Huizinga, "Real Wages, Employment, and Expectations,: Ph.D. Thesis, M.I.T. chapter 2; Richard T. Curtin, "Determinants of Price Expectations: Evidence from a Panel Study," in M. Laumer and M. Ziegler, eds., International Research on Business Cycle Surveys, Gower Publishing Company, Ltd., 1982; Frank deLeeuw and Michael McKelvey, "Price Expectations of Business Firms," Brookings Papers on Economic Activity, vol. I, pp. 299-313, 1981; E.M. Gramlich, op. cit., (quotation in text from p. 163).

[29]Karl Aiginger, "Empirical Surveyed Expectational Data and Decision Theory," paper presented at the 15th CIRET Conference, September 30-October 3, 1981, Athens; Francesco Papadia, "Rationality of Inflationary Expectations in the European Communities' Countries," EEC Working Paper, Brussels, March 1982.

[30]Jacob Mincer and Victor Zarnowitz, "The Evaluation of Economic Forecasts," in J. Mincer, ed., Economic Forecasts and Expectations, NBER, New York, 1969, pp. 3-46.

[31]Henri Theil, Economic Forecasts and Policy, North-Holland, Amsterdam, 1958; Victor Zarnowitz, An Appraisal of Short-Term Economic Forecasts, NBER, New York, 1967.

[32]Phillip Cagan, "The Monetary Dynamics of Hyperinflation," in Milton Friedman, ed., Studies in the Quantity Theory of Money, University of Chicago Press, 1956; Marc Nerlove, "Adaptive Expectations and Cobweb Phenomena," Quarterly Journal of Economics, 73, 1958, pp. 227-240; J. Mincer,ed., op. cit., pp. 83-111; Jacob A. Frenkel, "Inflation and the Formation of Expectations," Journal of Monetary Economics, 1, November 1975, pp. 403-421; Michael Mussa, "Adaptive and Regressive Expectations in a Rational Model of the Inflationary Process," ibid., pp. 423-442; A. H. Meltzer, op. cit.

[33]Albert A. Hirsch and Michael C. Lovell, Sales Anticipations and Inventory Behavior, Wiley, New York, 1969; B. Peter Pashigian, "The Accuracy of the Commerce-SEC Sales Anticipations," Review of Economics and Statistics, 46, November 1964, pp. 398-405; R. Owen Irvine, Jr. "Tests of the Rationality and Accuracy of Manufacturers' Sales Expectations," Working Paper Series, Board of Governors, Federal Reserve System, 1981.

[34]Aiginger, op. cit.; William Brainard, "Uncertainty and the Effectiveness of Policy," American Economic Review, 57, May 1967 (Papers and Proceedings, 1966), pp. 411-425; Roger N. Waud, "Asymmetric Policy Maker Utility Functions and Optimal Policy under Uncertainty," Econometrica, 44, January 1976, pp. 53-60; Leif Johansen, "Parametric Certainty Equivalence Procedures in Decision Making Under Uncertainty," Zeitschrift für Nationelökonomie, 40 (3/4) 1980.

[35]See Eugene F. Fama, "Efficient Capital Markets: A Review of Theory and Empirical Work," Journal of Finance, 25, May 1970, pp. 383-417; also Poole, op. cit.

[36]Benjamin M. Friedman, "Survey Evidence on the 'Rationality' of Interest Rate Expectations," Journal of Monetary Economics, 6, October 1980, pp. 453-465.

[37]Frederic S. Mishkin, "Are Market Forecasts Rational?" American Economic Review, 71 (3), June 1981, pp. 295-306.

[38]Victor Zarnowitz, op. cit., and "The Record of Turning Point Forecasts of GNP and Other Major Aggregates," paper presented at the Conference on Forecasting and Recognizing Turns in the Business Cycle, NBER, March 1968; Rendigs Fels and C. Elton Hinshaw, Forecasting and Recognizing Business Cycle Turning Points, NBER, New York, 1968; Geoffrey H. Moore, "Forecasting Short-Term Economic Change," Journal of the American Statistical Association, 64, March 1969, pp. 1-22.

[39]Victor Zarnowitz, "An Analysis of Annual and Multiperiod Quarterly Forecasts of Aggregate Income; Output, and the Price Level," Journal of Business, 52 (1), January 1979, pp. 1-33; "The Accuracy of Individual and Group Forecasts from Business Outlook Surveys," NBER Working Paper No. 1053, December 1982; "Rational Expectations and Macroeconomic Forecasts," NBER Working Paper No. 1070, January 1983.

[40]Figlewski and Wachtel, op. cit.; Stephen K. McNees, "The Rationality of Economic Forecasts," American Economic Review, 68 (2), May 1978, pp. 301-305.

[41]For references see the NBER W.P. No. 1053 by Zarnowitz.

[42]On the average across the different target quarters, the rejections accounted for 14 and 21 percent of the forecasters at the 5% and 10% significance levels, respectively.

[43]Geoffrey H. Moore, "The President's Economic Report: A Forecasting Record," NBER Reporter, April 1977; Victor Zarnowitz, "Forecasting Economic Conditions: The Record and the Prospect," in V. Zarnowitz, ed., The Business Cycle Today, NBER, New York, 1972, pp. 212-214.

[44]Stephen K. McNees, "An Evaluation of Economic Forecasts," New England Economic Review, November/December 1975, pp. 3-39; V. Zarnowitz, 1979, op. cit.

[45]Cf. V. Zarnowitz, "New Plans and Results of Research in Economic Forecasting," 51st Annual Report, National Bureau of Economic Research, September 1971, pp. 53-70 (esp. Table I-6, pp. 67-68).

[46]For a review of the evidence, see Karl Aiginger, "Empirische Informationen zur Bildung von Erwartungen," Ifo-Studien, 25, (1/2), 1979, pp. 83-135.

Table 1

Forecasts of Turning Points and Directions of Change in GNP and Real GNP, 1947-1976.

1. Annual Data, GNP, 1947-1965

Correct forecasts of Turning Points (TP) as percentage of	Forecasts Made Near the End of Preceding Year	Forecasts Made Near the Middle of Preceding Year
All predicted TP	93 (34)	60 (42)
All actual TP	74 (27)	50 (35)
All periods covered	89 (57)	64 (51)

2. Semiannual Data, GNP, 1947-1964

Correct forecasts of directional change as percentage of	Semiannual Change Forecasts, 1947-64: 0-6 months	Semiannual Change Forecasts, 1947-64: 6-12 months
All periods covered	73 (58)	62 (58)

3. Quarterly Data, GNP, 1959-1963

Correct forecasts of directional change as percentage of	Quarter-to Quarter Change Forecasts, 1959-63: 0-3 months	3-6 months	6-9 months	9-12 months
All periods covered	68 (65)	78 (77)	69 (72)	82 (82)

4. Annual Data, Real GNP, 1959-1976

	Number	Mean Absolute Error, % Points	Percentage of Total Absolute Error
Underestimation errors	33	1.12	46.8
Overestimation errors	21	.92	24.4
Turning point errors	8	2.85	28.8

NOTE: Forecasts or actual observations of no change are counted as half TP and half no TP. Figures in parentheses are the expected values on the assumption of independence and fixed marginal totals. The span 0-3 months refers to the change from the current quarter to the one ending three months hence; 3-6 months refers to the change from quarter ending three months hence to the one ending six months hence; etc.

SOURCE: V. Zarnowitz, "The Record of Turning Point Forecasts of GNP and Other Major Aggregates" (NBER draft manuscript) and G. H. Moore, "Forecasting Short-Term Economic Change," Journal of the American Statistical Association, March 1969, pp. 1-22. Section 4: V. Zarnowitz, "An Analysis of Annual and Multiperiod Quarterly Forecasts of Aggregate Income, Output, and the Price Level," Journal of Business, January 1979, p. 12.

Table 2

Percentages of Individual Forecasts That Failed the Tests for Unbiasedness and Serially Uncorrelated Errors, 1968-1979

Variable	Percent of Forecasts with Significant	
	tests	tests
Gross national product (GNP)	21.0	37.1
Implicit price deflator (IPD)	69.1	66.2
GNP in constant dollars (RGNP)	20.5	27.0
Unemployment rate (UR)	15.4	42.4
Consumer expenditures for durable goods (CEDG)	14.7	23.7
Change in business inventories (CBI)	17.2	50.0

NOTE: The level of significance is 10 percent. The F tests are for E_0: $(\alpha, \beta) = (0, 1)$, see eq. 1 and text above. These entries refer to all individuals who participated in at least 12 of the 42 quarterly surveys conducted in the period 1968:4-1979:1 (75 for CEDG, 79 each for each of the other variables). The Box-Pierce $Q = n(n + z) \sum_k^6 (n - k)^{-1} \rho_k^2$, where $\hat{\rho}_k = \text{cov}(u_t, u_{t-k})/\text{var}(u_t)$, tests for the presence of autocorrelation in the forecast errors. These entries refer to all individuals who participated in more than 12 consecutive surveys (18-20 depending on the target variable).

SOURCE: ASA-NBER Business Outlook Survey.

Table 3

Selected Statistics on the Properties and Accuracy of Individual Forecasts from Business Outlook Surveys, 1968-1979

		GNP	IPD	RGNP	UR	CEDG	CBI
1.	Mean of mean errors $(\bar{\bar{\varepsilon}}_i)$[a]	-0.1	-0.4	0.3	-0.1	-0.3	-1.7
2.	Underestimates, percent[b]	69	96	14	64	63	79
3.	Relative accuracy $(\bar{M}_i/M_a)$[c]	.3	.5	.9	.1	.9	.7
4.	Mean correlation $(\bar{\bar{r}}_i)$[d]	.5	.5.	.5	.8	.4	.5
	Percent better than group:[e]						
5.	Mean	20	26	22	29	24	33
6.	Range	13-35	11-37	18-27	8-42	19-31	29-38

NOTE: For symbols denoting the variables, see Table 2. All measures refer to the sample of 79 individual forecasters (75 for CEDG) who participated in at least 12 surveys. They are based on the corresponding statistics for the five target quarters Q0, . . . Q4 (where Q0 denotes the survey quarter, Q1-Q4 the four successive future quarters).

[a]Error ε is defined as predicted minus actual percentage change for GNP, IPD, RGNP, and CEDG, and as predicted minus actual level for UR and CBI. $\bar{\bar{\varepsilon}} = \frac{1}{n}\sum_i^n \bar{\varepsilon}_i$, where $\bar{\varepsilon}_i$ is the mean error of the ith individual's forecasts $(i = 1, \ldots, n)$.

[b]Percentage of individual forecasters with mean errors that are negative.

[c]Ratio of the average root mean square errors of forecasts to the root mean square value of the target series (the sum of its mean value squared and its variance).

[d] $\bar{r}_i$ = coefficient of correlation between predicted and actual values for the ith individual, corrected for the degrees of freedom. $\bar{\bar{r}}_i = \frac{1}{n}\sum_i^n \bar{r}_i$.

[e]Percentage of individual forecasts with root mean square errors (M_i) smaller than the corresponding root mean square errors for all forecasters who responded to the same surveys (M_{gi}). Mean and range refer to the percentage of cases where $M_i/M_{gi} < 1$ across the forecasts for Q0, . . ., Q4.

SOURCE: ASA-NBER Business Outlook Survey.

Table 4

Forecasts from Business Outlook Surveys and Econometric Models, 1968-1979

Model Compared with ASA-NBER and Period Covered[a]	Statistic[b]	Ratios of Root Mean Square Errors: Model/ASA-NBER[c]					
		GNP	IPD	RGNP	UR	CEDG	CBI
IBM, 1968-1979	Mean	.98	.95	.95	.98	.97	.96
	Range	.89-1.09	.90-.98	.86-1.03	.86-1.09	.91-1.01	.90-1.01
DRI, 1968-1979	Mean	1.06	1.05	1.08	1.07	1.01	.96
	Range	.97-1.09	.97-1.18	.91-1.26	.89-1.59	.87-1.10	.86-1.03
Early Wharton, 1975-1979	Mean	1.00	1.05	1.08	n.a.	1.06	1.11
	Range	.85-1.18	.84-1.120	.99.1.18	n.a.	1.01-1.12	.81-1.36
Mid-quarter Wharton, 1975-1979	Mean	.96	1.11	1.04	n.a.	1.02	1.10
	Range	.88-1.02	.96-1.29	.99-1.11	n.a.	.94-1.10	.86-1.28

[a] IBM (International Business Machines Corp.) and DRI (Data Resources, Inc.) forecasts are those reported to the ASA-NBER surveys. Wharton Econometric Forecasting Associates, Inc. forecasts are those reported by the source in the first month of each quarter ("early") and in the second month ("mid-quarter"). The ASA-NBER forecasts used here are the mean group forecasts.

[b] Mean and range of the ratios for Q0-Q4.

[c] The ratios are of the form M_e/M_s , where M_e is the RMSE for the given model and M_s is the RMSE for the business survey (ASA/NBER). For symbols denoting the variables, see Table 2.

n.a. not available.

Chart 1

Seventy-nine Regular Participants in the ASA-NBER Quarterly Business Outlook Surveys, Percentage Distributions by Reported Methods, 1968:4-1979:1 and Subperiods

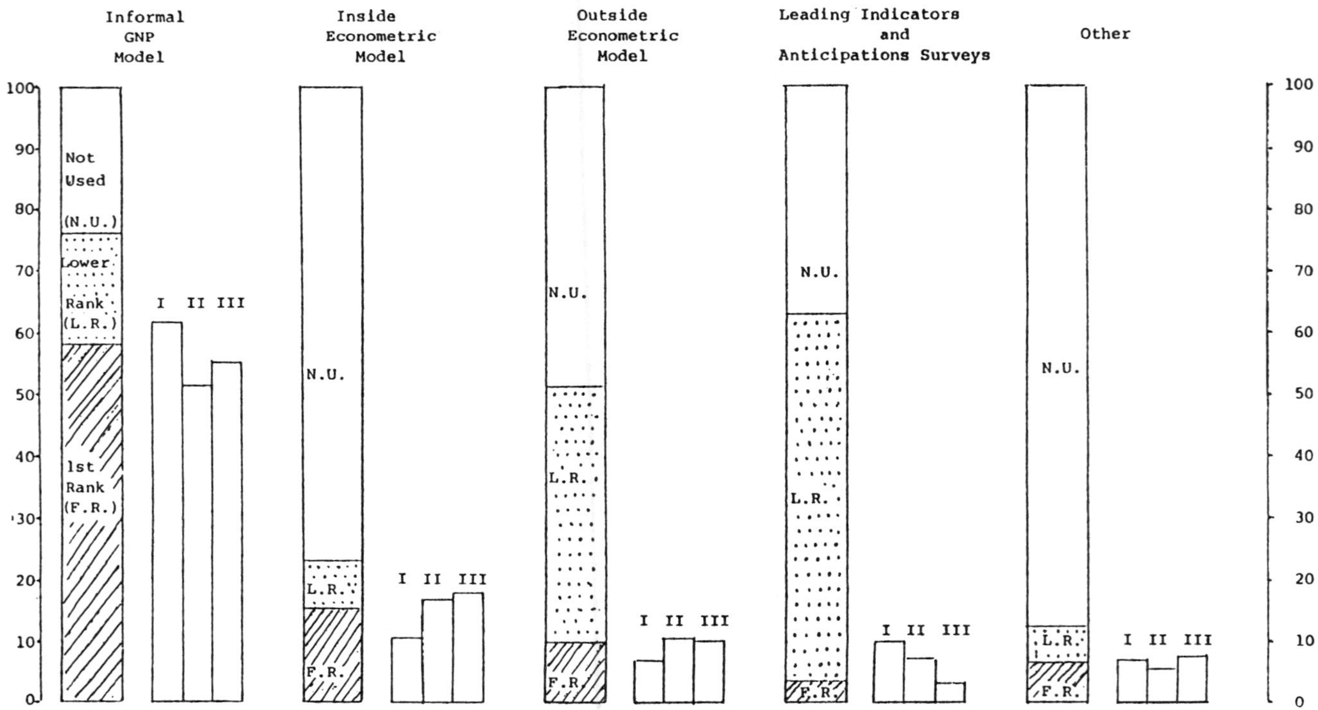

NOTE: The large bars (0-100%) refer to the total period 1968-1979. The small bars, marked I, II, and III, show the first-rank percentages only for the following subperiods, each containing 14 surveys: I, 1968:4-1972:1; II, 1972:2-1975:3; III, 1975:4-1979:1.

Chart 2

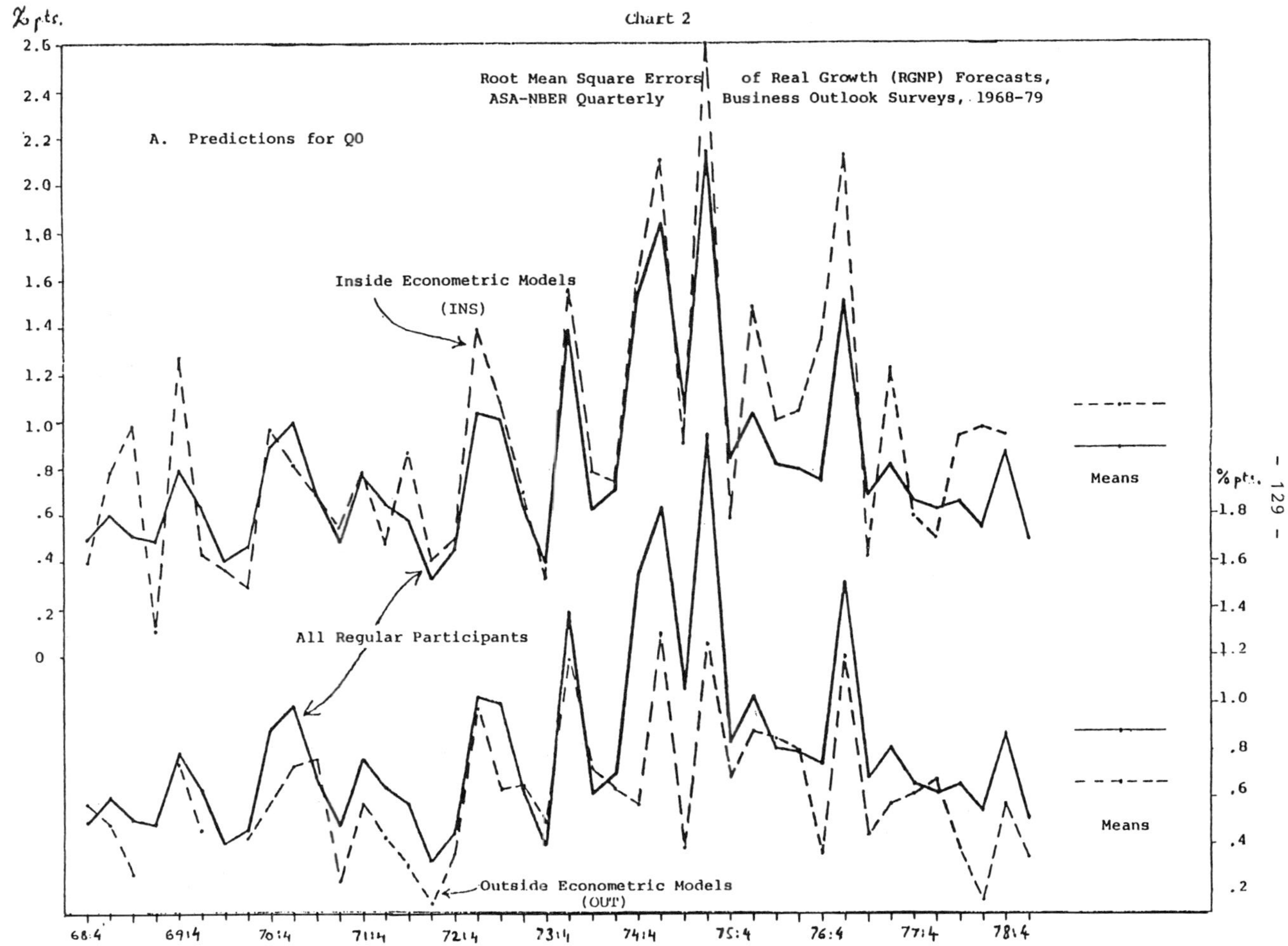
Root Mean Square Errors of Real Growth (RGNP) Forecasts,
ASA-NBER Quarterly Business Outlook Surveys, 1968-79
A. Predictions for Q0
% pts.
2.6
2.4
2.2
2.0
1.8
1.6
1.4
1.2
1.0
.8
.6
.4
.2
0
Inside Econometric Models
(INS)
All Regular Participants
Outside Econometric Models
(OUT)
Means
Means
% pts.
1.8
1.6
1.4
1.2
1.0
.8
.6
.4
.2
68:4
69:4
70:4
71:4
72:4
73:4
74:4
75:4
76:4
77:4
78:4

Chart 2
(concluded)

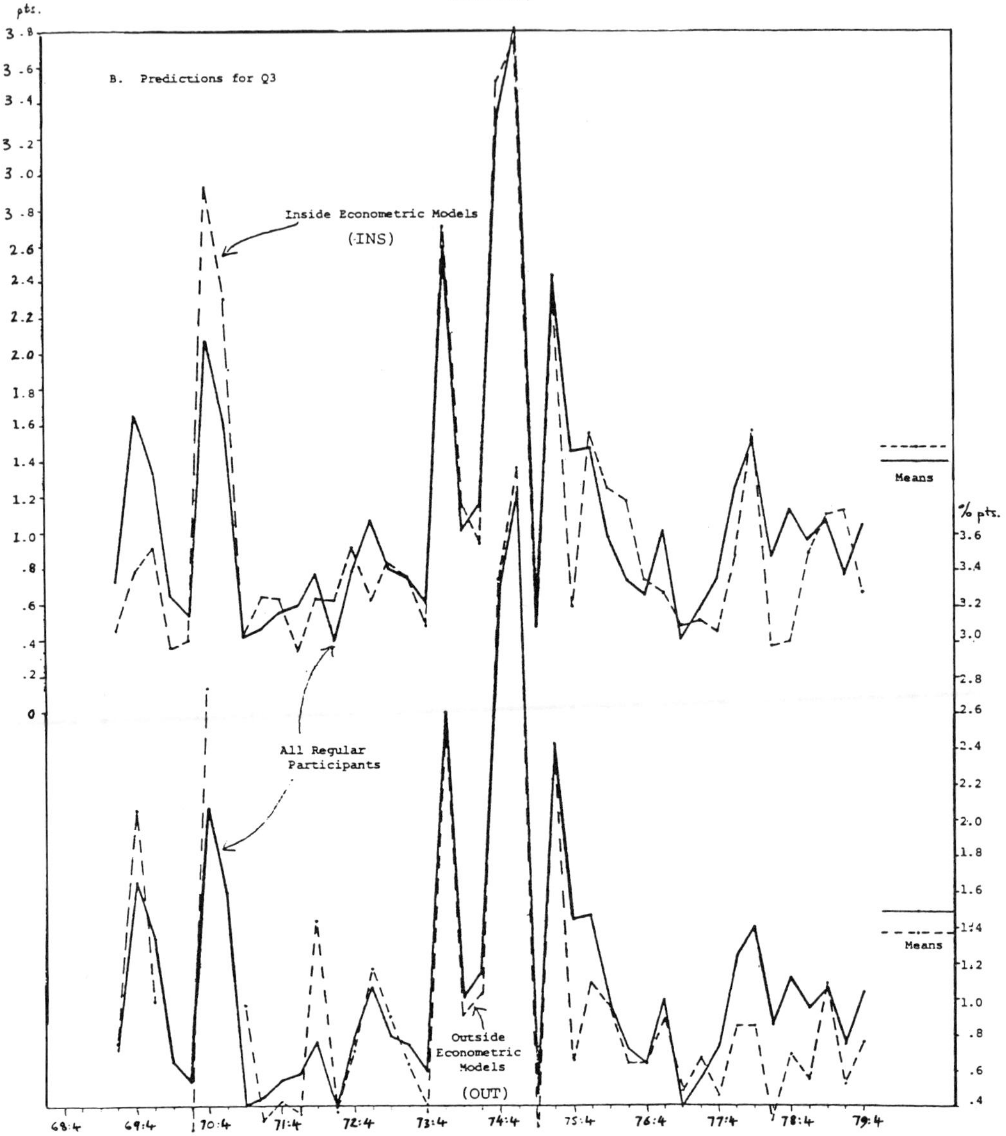

Chart 3

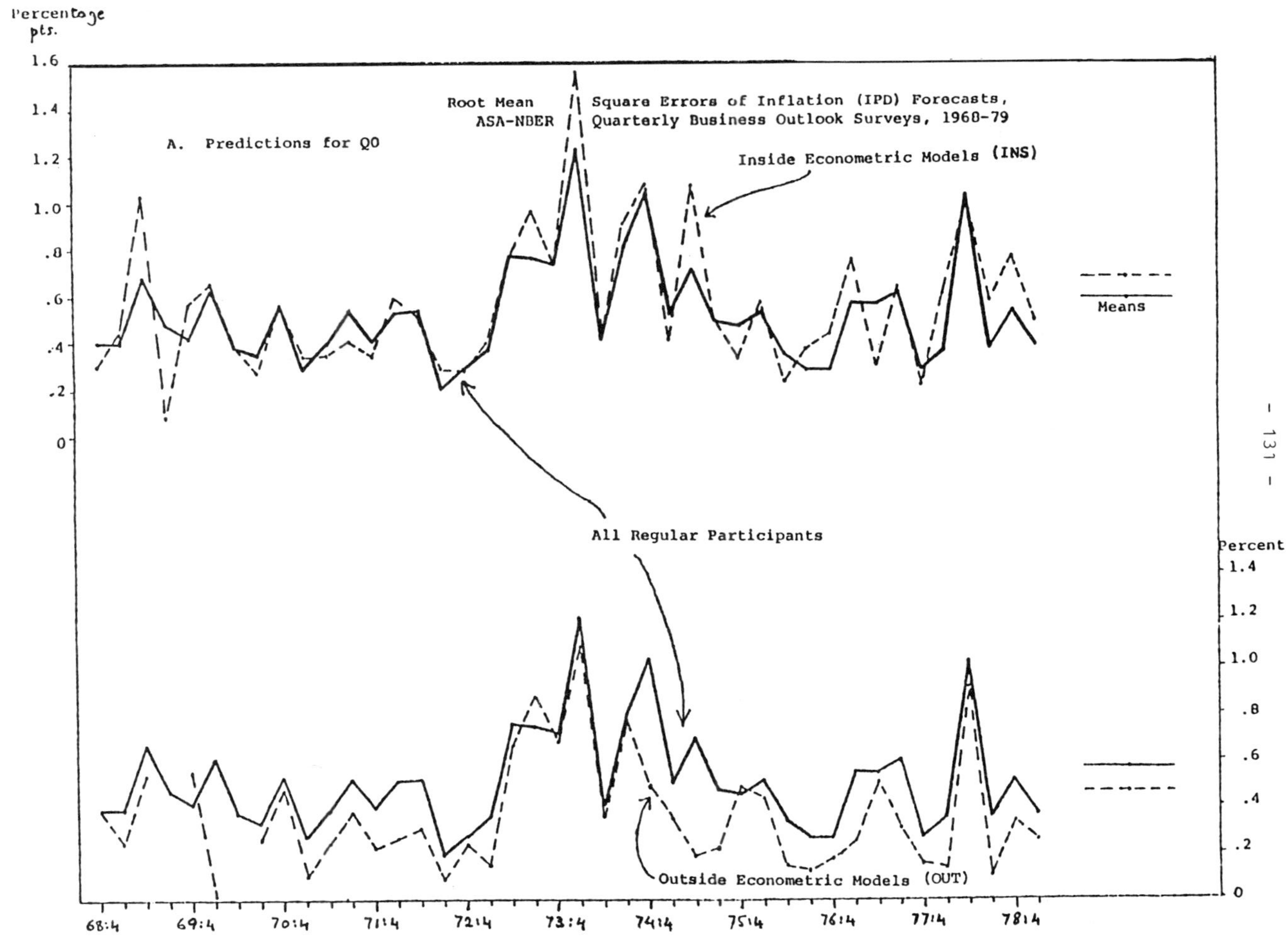
Percentage pts.
1.6
1.4
1.2
1.0
.8
.6
.4
.2
0
Root Mean Square Errors of Inflation (IPD) Forecasts,
ASA-NBER Quarterly Business Outlook Surveys, 1968-79
A. Predictions for Q0
Inside Econometric Models (INS)
Means
All Regular Participants
Outside Econometric Models (OUT)
Percent
1.4
1.2
1.0
.8
.6
.4
.2
0
68:4
69:4
70:4
71:4
72:4
73:4
74:4
75:4
76:4
77:4
78:4

Chart 3
(concluded)

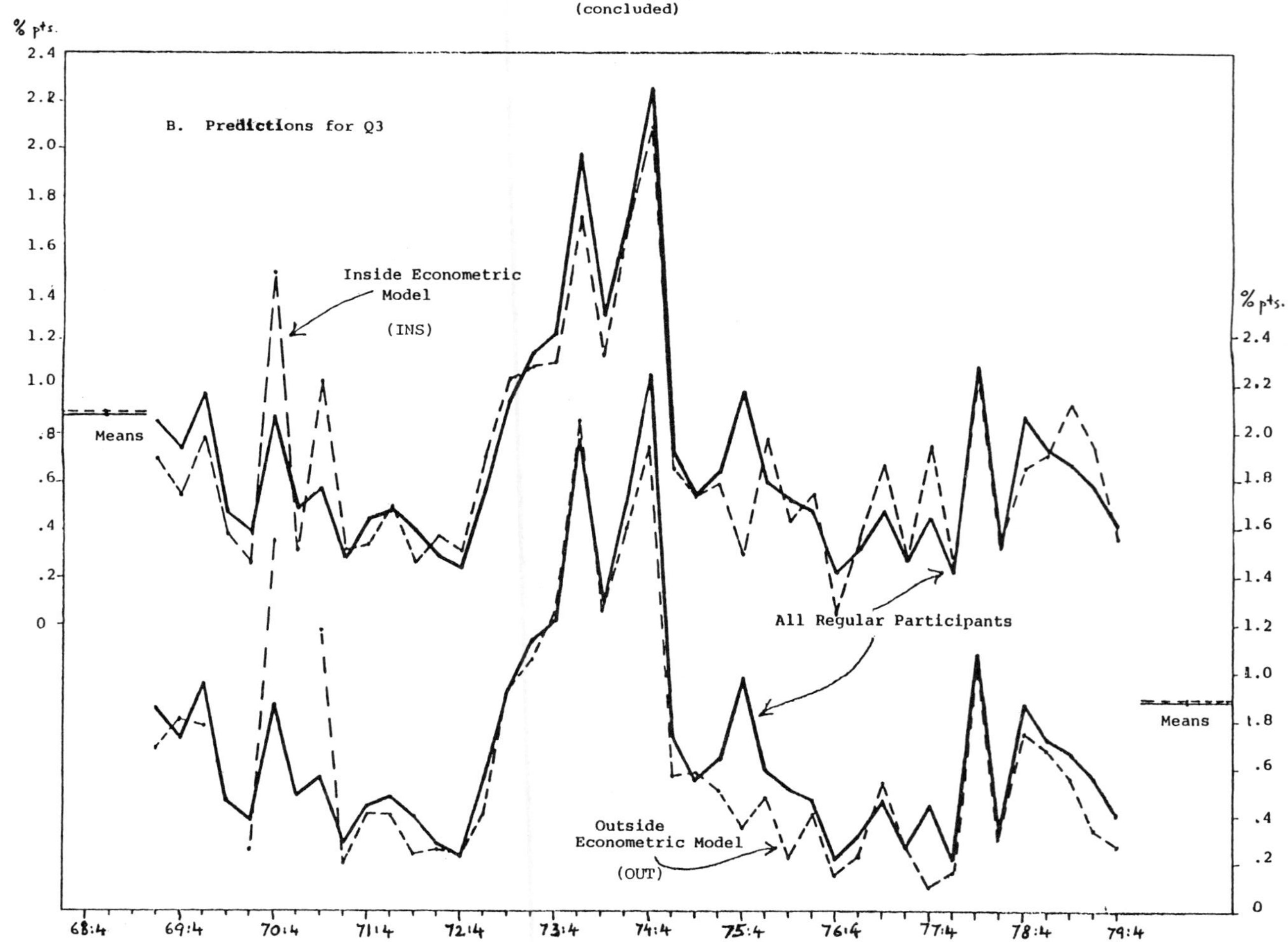

TABLE 5

TWENTY-THREE USERS OF ECONOMETRIC MODELS, SELECTED MEASURES OF RELATIVE ACCURACY AND TESTS OF BIAS, FORECASTS OF REAL GROWTH AND INFLATION, 1968-1979

Code #	Affiliation	Number of Surveys Covered	Forecasts of real growth (RGNP): Range of the M_i/M_{gi} ratios	Forecasts of real growth (RGNP): F-tests significant at the 5% level	Forecasts of inflation (IPD): Range of the M_i/M_{gi} ratios	Forecasts of inflation (IPD): F-tests significant at the 5% level
		(1)	(2)	(3)	(4)	(5)
			Inside Econometric Model (INS)			
31	Academic	35	1.15-1.59	4	1.33-1.49	5
40	Academic*§	24	1.06-1.60	0	1.13-1.30	2
42	Large mfg. company*	24	.98-1.28	0	.91-1.30	3
54	Large bank	34	.96-1.11	0	1.00-1.14	5
60	Government employee	17	.98-1.23	0	1.00-1.42	1
65	Large consulting firm*	30	1.00-1.13	1	.97-1.16	4
78	Large mfg. company	24	1.01-1.39	3	1.04-1.24	3
82	Business	34	1.01-1.31	1	.98-1.46	5
89	Large mfg. company*	28	.94-1.03	0	.89-1.01	3
93	Government employee	20	1.05-1.84	0	.93-1.46	4
108	Private consultant	27	1.16-2.30	4	1.14-1.84	5
124	Academic	18	1.10-1.59	0	1.17-1.52	3
133	Government employee	22	.78-1,50	0	.85-1.04	2
148	Academic	23	1.08-1.45	2	1.36-2.65	5
			Outside Econometric Model (OUT)			
1	Large mfg. company	22	.89-1.15	0	.92-1.22	4
8	Business	33	.99-1.22	0	1.03-1.32	5
16	Business	12	1.01-1.16	0	1.20-1.53	0
22	Business	29	1.01-1.41	1	1.01-1.87	4
44	Large bank	25	.67-1.10	0	.90-1.00	0
49	Large bank	40	.96-1.06	0	.99-1.06	5
81	Public utility	19	1.06-1.24	0	.94-1.16	3
86	Business	28	.91-1.18	0	.96-1.20	3
96	Consulting	16	1.01-1.65	0	1.09-2.44	0

*A well-known model.

§No adjustments to the model or other methods used.

The Use of Business Surveys in Short-term Forecasts. The French Experience

M. Devilliers
Institut National de la
Statistique et des
Etudes Economiques
Paris

INTRODUCTION

The remarkable usefulness of business surveys in forecasting is universally admitted,as testifies their world-wide development for the past thirty years.

In economic analysis and short-term forecasting, business surveys are in competition with other forecasting methods or tools : econometric models, cyclical analysis, ARIMA methods, quarterly accounts,.

INSEE's Economic Analysis and Short-Term Forecasting Department has these forecasting tools at its disposal. For ten years, it has tried to use them all together for the elaboration of its forecasts.
This paper intends to show what is, from INSEE's experience, the right place of business survey's results in the elaboration of short term forecasts.
It gets out a "balance sheet" of French business surveys strengths ans weaknesses ; it shows how business surveys can be complementary with other forecasting tools. It also tries to point out the main remaining difficulties in short-term forecasting and to propose new possible progresses.

I - INSEE'S EXPERIENCE

a) INSEE's business surveys :

For 30 years, gradually, INSEE has built up a wide set of business surveys.

The fifties were the experimentations period : the first survey was conducted in 1951 ; 3 000 entrepreneurs were asked, with a same questionnaire, in manufacturing, wholesaling and retailing, banking... There were two parts in the questionnaire : a part with questions relating to propects for the French economy, and a part with questions about the surveyed firm's situation. That first survey was a success ; so, it has been repeated every six months. The results obtained led to two changes : the part with questions related to firm's situation was developped, the other part reduced ; different questionnaires were perfected for the different sectors of the economy. Besides, the frequency of the surveys was increased progressively.
During the 60's, the set of surveys was stabilized (one of the most important step was in june 1962, the creation of the Commission of the European Communities monthly harmonized business survey). All the main series of business survey's results are now twenty years long ; so, their interest can be evaluated.

Table 1 shows the present set of business surveys carried out by INSEE.

TABLE 1	"monthly" survey	"quarterly survey"
Scheduled sectors	Manufacturing (foods, drink, and tobacco, excepted)	Manufacturing
Size of the sample	3 500	4 000
Frequency	Monthly (August excepted)	quarterly
main questions	- Production trend in recent months - Production expectations for the months ahead - Order books (above normal, normal, below normal ?) - Export order-books (above normal, normal, below normal ?) - Stocks of finished products (above normal, normal, below normal ?) - Selling price expectations for the months ahead - Expected development of economic situation in industry for the next four months - Expected development of inflation for the next four months	- Total demand trend in recent months - Foreign demand trend in recent months - Total demand expectations for the months ahead - Foreign demand expectations for the months ahead - Duration of assured production (*) (in weeks) - Stocks of finished products (in weeks of production) (*) - Stocks of raw materials (in weeks of utilizations) (*) - Capacity utilization (*) (%) - Selling price variation over the past three months (*) (%) - Selling price variation over the next three months (*) (%) - Variation of wages (*) (%) - Employment trend in recent months - Employment expectations for months ahead

(*) quantitative questions ; other questions are qualitative.

TABLE 1	Investment survey	Survey on financial situation	survey on foreign competition
Scheduled sectors	manufacturing	manufacturing	manufacturing
Size of the sample	5 000	4 000	4 000
Frequency	three time a year	twice a year	twice a year
main questions	- Investment trends and prospects : annual percentage change of investment expenditure at current prices* - Limits to investment - Investments'aims - Capacity trends and prospects (annual percentage change) (*)	- Corporate liquidity trend in recent months - Corporate liquidity expectations for the months ahead - Profit trend in recent months - Profit expectations for the months ahead - Reasons and consequences of profits variations - Difficulties about obtaining loans - Loans interest rate (*)	- Foreign competition trend in recent months - Difference between french producers'selling prices (%) and foreign producers' selling prices (*) - Profit margins'trend on export markets - Difference between profit margins in France and profit margins on export markets (%) (*) - Trend of deliveries time

(*) quantitative question ; other questions are qualitative.

TABLE 1	Trade survey	Building survey
Scheduled sectors	Wholesale and retail trade	Construction and public works
Size of the sample	7 000	3 000
Frequency	Six times a year	Quarterly
main questions	- Sales trend over the past two months - Orders expectations over the next two months - Stocks (above normal, normal, below normal) - Price trend in recent months - Price expectations for the months ahead - Liquidity situation - Investment expectations	- Order books (above normal, below normal) - Duration of assured production (*) (in months) - Production trend in recent months - Production expectations for the months ahead - Employment trend in recent months - Employment expectations for the months ahead - Price expectations for the months ahead - Liquidity situation - Investment expectations

(*) quantitative questions ; other questions are qualitative.

b) INSEE's other economic analysis tools

1) "METRIC"

METRIC, Modèle Econométrique Trimestriel pour la Conjoncture (Trimestrial Econometric Model for short term forecasting) was put in service at INSEE, in the autumn of 1977. This model was constructed to forecast the evolution of the economic situation and to facilitate the study of economic policy in the short term. It has two essential characteristics : a large number of exogenous variables that represent economic policy means, and its equations, which take into account, or at least as much as possible, economic behaviour in the short term (1) .

2) National quarterly accounts

INSEE prepares - and publishes - quarterly national accounts for French economy on the basis of usual quantitative time series. A provisional account is computed before the end of the quarter ; the missing quantitative data in component series are estimated by extrapolation or by econometric relations based on business surveys' results.

3) Cyclical analysis

INSEE doesn't publish any composite leading indicator for the French economy. Nevertheless, for many years, INSEE has done much work in cyclical analysis : leading, coincident and lagging indicators have been selected ; most of them are qualitative time series. Besides, the Organisation for Economic Cooperation and Development took the advice of INSEE when it developed a system of cyclical indicators.

---

(1) METRIC : Une modèlisation de l'économie française. INSEE publications 1980.

Four components of the OECD's composite leading indicator for France, published in the "Main Economic Indicators", are INSEE's business surveys'series : production expectations for the months ahead, consumer goods'stocks of finished products, consumer goods'order-books, expected development of economic situation in industry over the next four months.

c) <u>INSEE's short-term forecasts</u>

INSEE has published business outlooks and short-term forecasts since 1946. Now, INSEE's publication "Tendances de la Conjoncture" contains every three months an economic analysis of the three past quarters and a forecast for the three next quarters. Between quarterly forecasts, the prospects are made more precise in the comments of the monthly business survey.

Fig. 1
INDUSTRY SURVEY Climate indicators

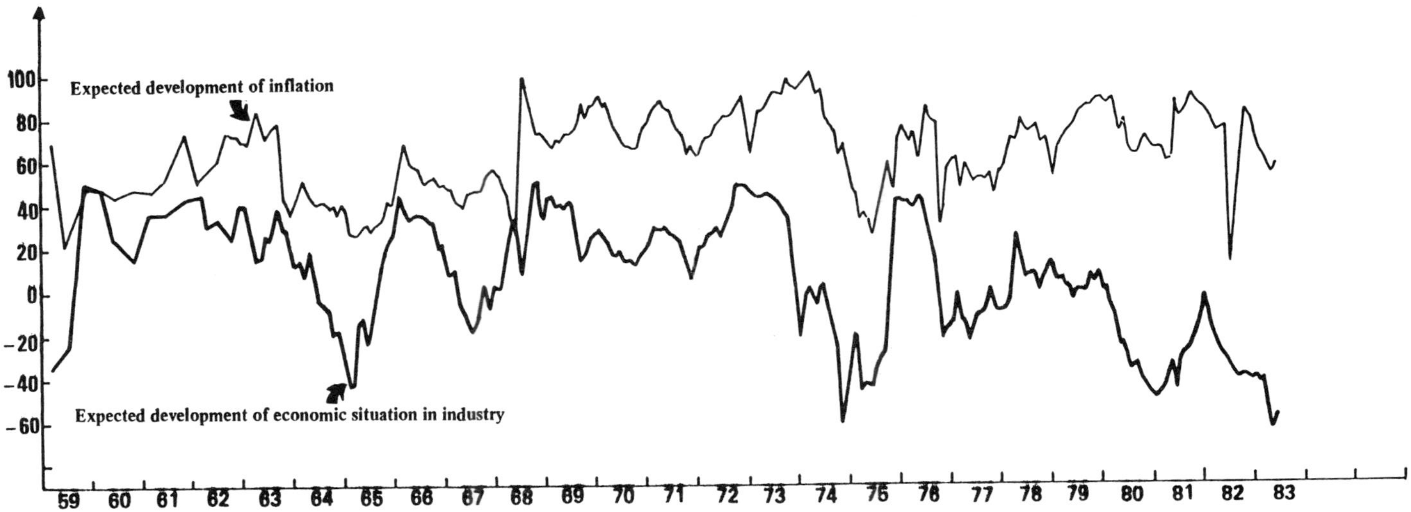

II) INSEE SURVEYS'STRENGTHS AND WEAKNESSES

This problem has been the theme of many CIRET conferences'papers or "CIRET STUDIEN" publications (2) (3) (4). But it is essential ; it is here dealt with succintly, on the basis of the French experience.

a) Informations on the past : ("The finger on the pulse of the economy" W.H. STRIGEL).

Informations given by business surveys on recent past are generally reliable. Besides, they are obtained very soon, before quantitative statistics. However qualitative data analysis is sometimes difficult : subjectivety in entrepreneurs'answers creates bias, quantifications are not always easy. So, the interest of business surveys'informations decreases as soon as quantitative data are available.

Business surveys'other advantage is to give a very full and coherent view of a sector.

From this, it can be concluded that business surveys are the best source of information on the recent past.

b) Informations on the future

Two types of informations on the future can be obtained from business surveys :

- Informations about the surveyed firms'anticipated situation ; generally, their aggregation lead to a reliable indicator. For instance, the results of the question

---

(2) M. ZIEGLER,30 years international exchange of experience on trade cycle surveys - CIRET STUDIEN n°29 1980.

(3) A. PIATIER, Business cycles surveys - Their utilization for forecasting - CIRET : 14th Conference - 1979.

(4) W.H. STRIGEL, Essays on trade cycle surveys - CIRET STUDIEN n°30 1981.

Fig. 2
INDUSTRY SURVEY

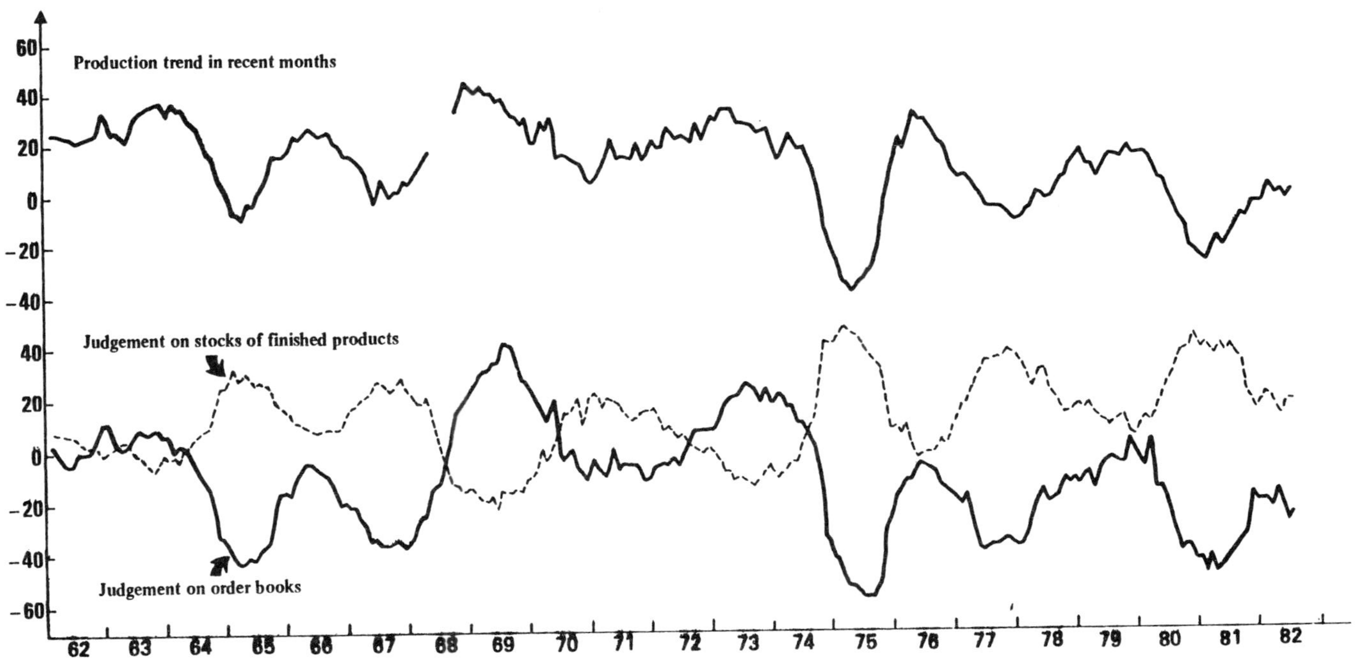

about "production trends for the months ahead" allow a good forecast of industrial production (see fig. 3). These informations can be called "real forecasting indicators". Their reliability, due to the entrepreneurs' perfect knowledge of their firms, is excellent for forecast for the next three or four months, fairly good for forecast for the 6 to 12 months, decreased beyond.

- Results of questions about the expected development of economic situation. They are "climate indicators" rather than forecasting indicators ; generally they are not closely correlated with quantitative variables like industrial production or GNP, (see fig. 1), but they are often leading indicators. The climate doesn't have much influence on entrepreneurs'decisions relative to production, but it may cause investment plans'revisions.

For the economist, the availability, at the same time, of "real forecasting indicators" and of "climate indicators" is very useful : he can base his forecast on the "real forecasting indicators" without being excessively influenced by the climate, since he can explain the differences between his analysis and the mass media's talk.

c) The cyclical behaviour

Business surveys'results are generally good cyclical indicators ; for instance, "the production trend in recent months" is an excellent coïncident one. The wide variations of business surveys'indicators clearly show the different phases of the cycle (see fig. 2 : judgement on order - books and judgement on stocks of finished products). Besides, most leading indicators are business surveys'time series (see § I b3).

Fig. 3
COMPARISON

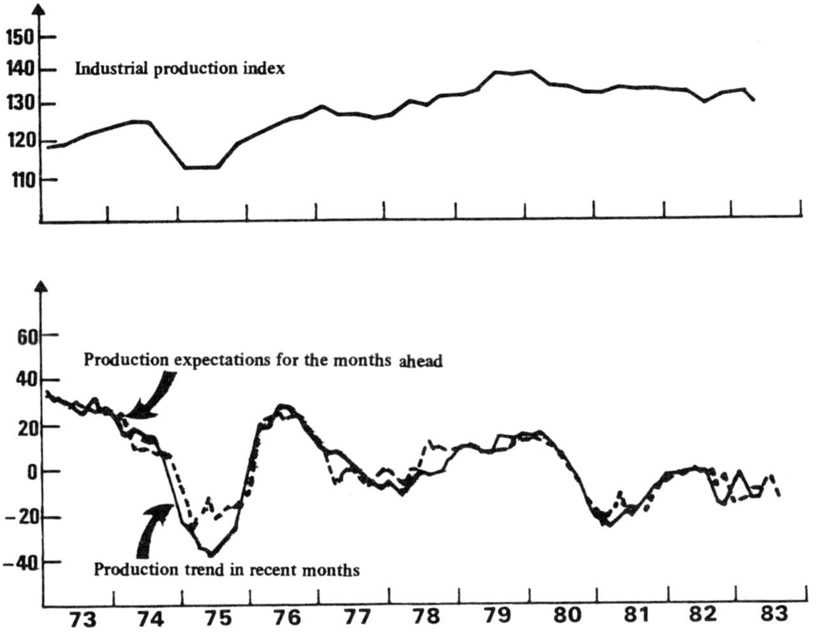

Fig. 4
INDUSTRY SURVEY

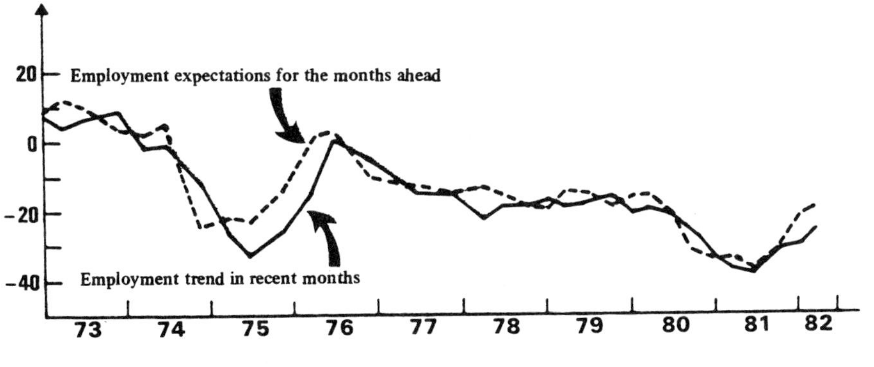

d) The reliability of business surveys'indicators

The reliability of business surveys'results depends on the questions. The reasons of these variations are not always easy to make clear ; they are connected with the problems of quality of entrepreneurs' informations. From INSEE's experience, the following classification can be obtained :

1) Matters for which business surveys'results are quite reliable

- production (manufacturing) : past trend and future trend (over the next three or four months) (see fig.3).
- order-books (manufacturing)
- past trend of employment (manufacturing, trade)
- past trend of investments
- selling prices (manufacturing) ; past trend and future trend (over the next three or four months)
- sales (trade)
- selling prices (trade) : past trend

2) Matters for which business surveys results are fairly reliable

- past trend of foreign demand (manufacturing)
- stocks ; present level (manufacturing, trade)
- capacity utilization (manufacturing)
- present financial situation (manufacturing, trade)
- future trend of raw materials purchases (manufacturing)
- investment trend over the next six months
- future trend of employment (industry ; trade ; over the next three or four months) (see fig. 4).
- future trend (over the next three or four months) of total demand.

Fig. 5
INDUSTRY SURVEY

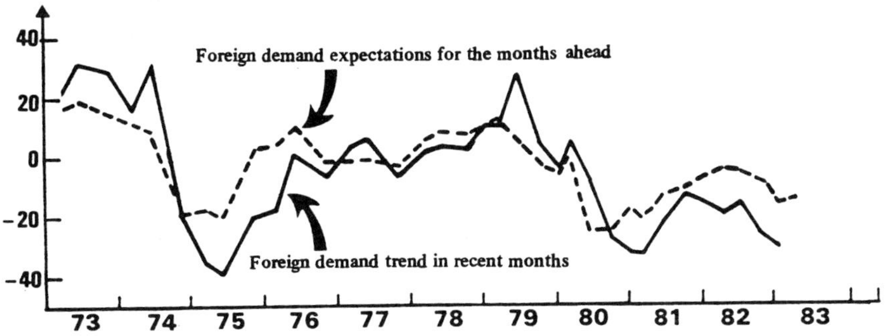

Fig. 6
SURVEY ON FINANCIAL SITUATION

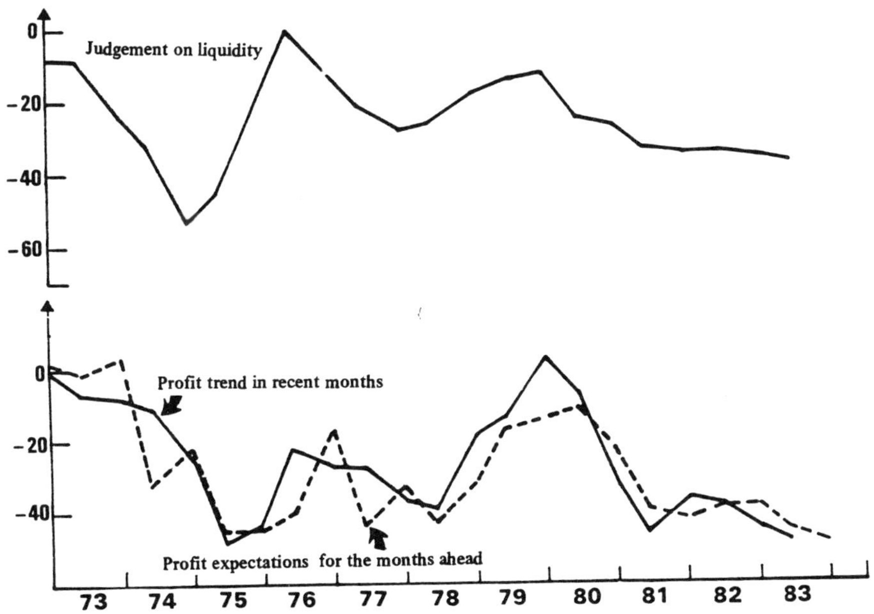

3) Matters for which business surveys'results are sometimes unreliable

- Future trend of foreign demand or exports

The comparison of "foreign demand expectations for the months ahead" and" foreign demand trend in recent months" (see fig. 5) clearly shows that managements have over-estimated the future trend of foreign demand since 1980 ; they have attributed too much importance to rumours of world recovery, maybe because they are unable to forecast precisely their exportations.

- Future trend of profit

Fig. 6 shows that entrepreneurs haven't forecast correctly the trend of profit in 1976, 1977, 1981... ; besides,turning points are not anticipated. It is shown in a CIRET 13th Conference paper (5) that, when they try to forecast profit, managements are excessively influenced by the climate ; this error can be corrected with the help of production expectations and selling price expectations, which are reliable.

- Investment expectations for the next 12 to 24 months

The magnitude of investment plans'revisions has increased for ten years. This problem is connected with the unreliability of profit expectations : at present time, in France, more than half of managements can't realize all the investments they wish (see fig. 7) ; the main reason of that difficulty is the decrease of profit.

---

(5) M. DEVILLIERS, An appraisal of the corporate liquidity and the profitability of firms by means of business surveys as well as the consequences on the firms'behaviour, CIRET 13th Conference. CIRET STUDIEN n°25.

Fig. 7
INVESTMENT SURVEY

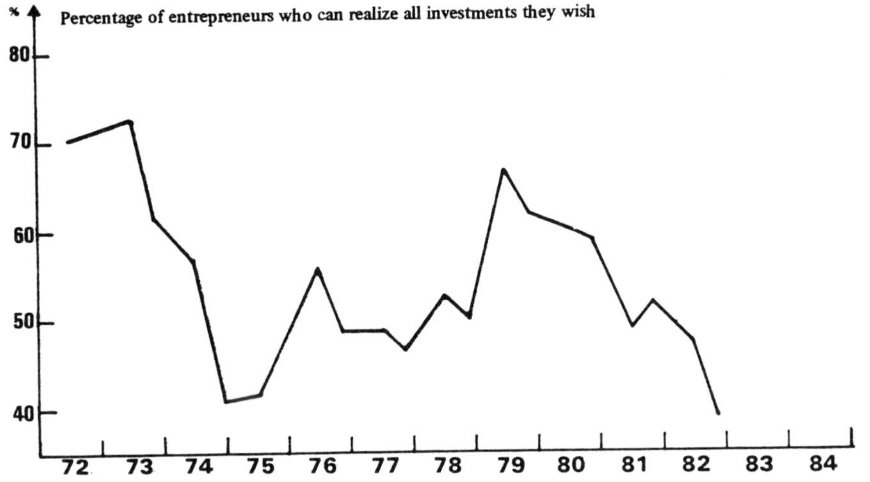

Fig. 9
JUDGEMENT ON STOCKS

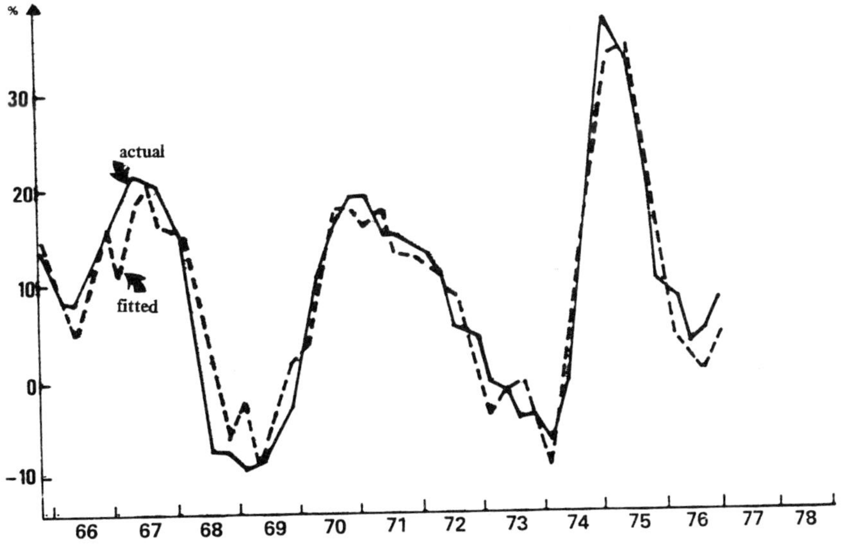

III) PLACES OF BUSINESS SURVEYS AND OF OTHER TOOLS, IN THE ELABORATION OF SHORT TERM FORECASTS

They are the consequences of surveys'strenghts and weaknesses. First, the place of business surveys in the period covered by economic outlook can be precised (see fig. 8). INSEE's economic outlooks cover six quarters,from $Q_0 - 2$ to $Q_0 + 3$ (Q_0 : present quater) ; business survey's place is from $Q_0 - 1$ to $Q_0 + 2$.

For quarters $Q_0 - 2$ and $Q_0 - 1$ (and partly for quarter Q_0 if a provisional account is available), quarterly accounts are the best tool for economic analysis : they are a synthesis of quantitative statistics, and they give estimations for variables that cause changes in economic agents'behaviour : entrepreneurial income, purchasing power, saving and increase in stocks.

For quarters Q_0 et $Q_0 + 1$, and partly for quarters $Q - 1$ and $Q_0 + 2$, business surveys are the best tool for information, economic analysis and forecasting.

For quarters $Q_0 + 2$, $Q_0 + 3$ and beyond, information available from business surveys is insufficient. So forecasts must be based on macroeconomic argument, or on econometric models.

Why must we prefer business surveys to econometric models for the forecasting of Q_0 and $Q_0 + 1$? The main reason is that an econometric model produces a forecast which is the mean path observed in the past from an economic situation clearly defined (the $Q_0 - 2$ quarterly account). In this forecast, trends at the begining of quarter Q_0 and economic agents'expectations, which can be known by business surveys, are not taken into account. Now, in the short run, economic agents'expectations are not always those than can be expected according to macro-economic analysis of past quarters, because economic agents are influenced by the climate. So, for the current quarter and the first next quarter, a better forecast than the model's one can be elaborated from business survey's results.

Fig. 8

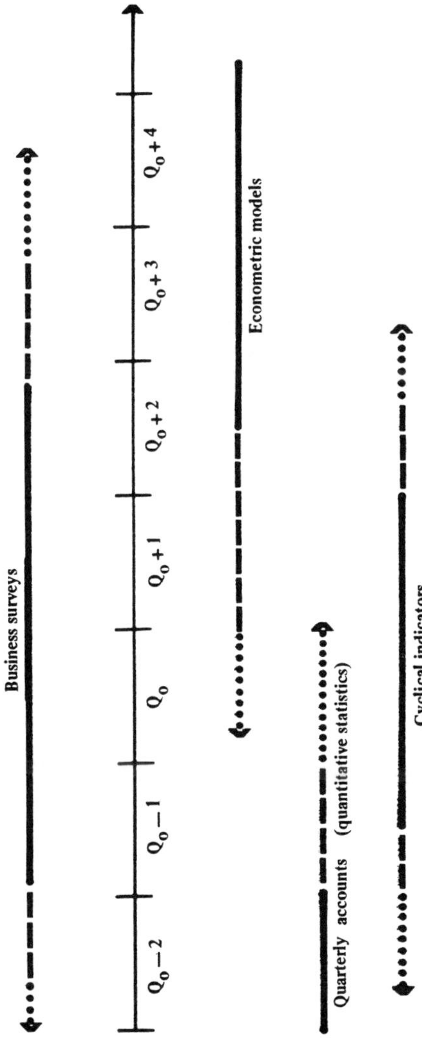
Business surveys
Q_0-2
Q_0-1
Q_0
Q_0+1
Q_0+2
Q_0+3
Q_0+4
Econometric models
Quarterly accounts (quantitative statistics)
Cyclical indicators

In all cases, the comparison of econometric model's forecast with business surveys'results is useful :

- If they agree, the forecast is very reliable.
- If they dont agree : economist must give preference business surveys'results over econometric models' forecast, because economic agents realize their expectations in major part in the short run. So, quarters Q_0 and $Q_0 + 1$ can be forecast correctly ; but it is difficult to forecast following quarters : in all likelihood, economic agents are going to revise their anticipations, since they are not adapted to the objective economic situation.

IV) POSSIBLE NEW PROGRESS IN SHORT-TERM FORECASTING

a) Improvements in business surveys'information

Business surveys information about future trends of foreign demand or exports is often unreliable (cf. § III d3). So, for many years, INSEE has tried to improve information on this matter.

- Entrepreneurs have been asked about deliveries time of export orders. Table 2 indicates the average percentage of orders delivered each quarter for all Q_0 quarters' export orders.

TABLE 2	Investment goods	Consumer goods	Intermediate goods
Q_0	26%	66%	58%
$Q_0 + 1$	13%	27%	32%
$Q_0 + 2$	8%	5%	6%
$Q_0 + 3$	5%	1%	2%
$Q_0 + 4$	6%	1%	1%
$Q_0 + 5 \rightarrow Q_0 + 8$	16%	0%	1%
$Q_0 + 9 \rightarrow Q_0 + 12$	16%	0%	0%
$Q_0 + 13 \rightarrow \ldots$	10%	0%	0%
	100%	100%	100%

This table shows that it is difficult to forecast exports with only the results of the questions about past trend of foreign demand, - which are reliable, cf. § III d2 - : for intermediate goods and consumer goods, deliveries times are short, and foreign demand past trends don't give any information about future exports ; only a share of investment goods'exports can be forecast.

- INSEE has carried out since 1973 a survey on foreign competition (6), which improve the knowledge of the french producers'behaviour. The perception of the competition by the producers can be precised. This survey shows also that the arbitrations about the prices and the quantities are an important component of the producers 'short term behaviour.

- An other way to forecast exports more precisely is to know sooner foreign countries'demand trends. The Commission of the European Communities'business survey is a good example. Can it be extended ?

b) Improvements in knowledge of entrepreneurs'behaviour

This theme is important : in France, it is obvious that entrepreneurs' behaviour has changed during the past 3 or 4 years ; maybe, because many entrepreneurs wish no more take large risks. The best way to improve knowledge of entrepreneurs'behaviour is probably to use micro data on individual firms (7) (8).

c) Taking account of business surveys'results in econometric models

As it is shown in § III, the synthesis of models'forecasts and of business surveys'results is essential ; it must be tried to take account of business surveys'results in econometric models.

---

(6) J. FAYOLLE, The INSEE survey on foreign competition ; CIRET 15th Conference - Athens -

(7) H. KÖNIG, M. NERLOVE, Micro-analysis of realizations, plans and expectations in the IFO business test by multivariate log-linear probability models CIRET 14th Conference - Lisbon.

(8) G. OUDIZ, Micro-analysis of realizations, plans and expectations in the INSEE business test by multivariate log-linear probability models. CIRET 14th Conference. Lisbon.

Qualitative data can be incorporated in econometric models. In METRIC (see §I.b) four surveys'variables are endogenous.

For example, the equation for the judgement on stocks is :

$$STK - \overline{STK} = 85{,}4 + 0{,}11 \times 10^{8} \frac{1}{NS} - 0{,}7\ AP - 140 \frac{DHS}{NS}$$

$$-70 \frac{DHS-1}{NS} + \sum_{i=o}^{3} C_i\ TRES_{-i} + \sum_{i=o}^{2} b_i\ RAPR_{-i}$$

$$C_o = 0{,}10 \ ; \ C_1 = 0{,}16 \ ; \ C_2 = 0{,}16 \ ; \ C_3 = 0{,}10$$

$$b_o = -9{,}5 \ ; \ b_1 = 3{,}4 \ ; \ b_2 = 16{,}4$$

AP = anticipated selling price
NS = level of stocks (volume)
DHS = final demand
TRES= judgement on liquidity situation
RAPR= ratio to trend of imported raw materials prices (see fig. 9)

An other way is to build a model based on qualitative data only. It is impossible to build a model of the whole economy, because qualitative data are not available on some matters : imports, government expenditures, exchange rates ..., but a partial model or sector's model is yet very useful.

For instance, at INSEE, J. FAYOLLE has constructed a model : "employment-prices - wages in manufacturing" based on business surveys'time series only (see fig. 10) (9).

---

(9) J. FAYOLLE, emploi-prix-salaires ; un modèle de court terme construit sur les variables d'opinion. Annales de l'INSEE 1983.

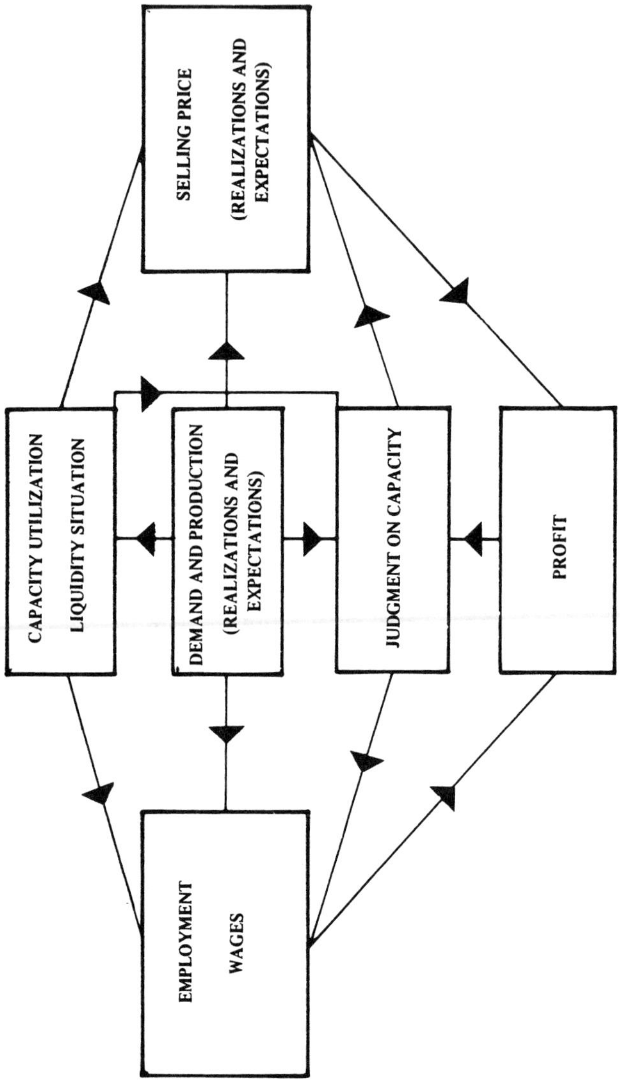
SELLING PRICE
(REALIZATIONS AND EXPECTATIONS)
CAPACITY UTILIZATION
LIQUIDITY SITUATION
DEMAND AND PRODUCTION
(REALIZATIONS AND EXPECTATIONS)
JUDGMENT ON CAPACITY
PROFIT
EMPLOYMENT
WAGES

Fig. 10

Fig. 11
RETAIL TRADE SURVEY

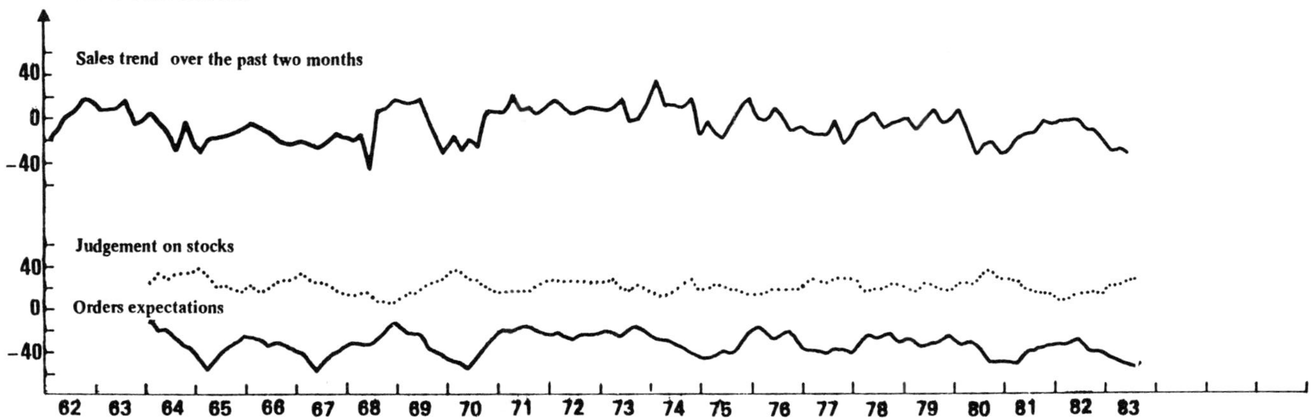

CONCLUSION

The development, for 30 years, of business surveys has led to a considerable progress in short term forecasting, for which expectations are essential. The association of business surveys with other forecasting tools, and particularly with econometric models lead to new improvements. The scientific nature of forecasting will increase. Short term forecasts will loose, to a large extend, the magical appearance inherited from ancient oracles, and will become more reliable.

The Anticipations Model: A Short-term Forecasting Model Based on Anticipations Data

W. Naggl
Universität München
Munich

Contents: Part I: Description of the model. 1. Concept of the model.- 2. The role of expectations in forecasting.- 3. Causality in the Anticipations Model.- 4. Data.- 5. Estimation methods.- 6. Selected regression estimates.- 7. Selected forecasts.- Part II: Forecasts for the West-German Economy with the Anticipations model. A. Forecasts up to the 4 th quarter of 1983.- B. Comparisons with other forecasts.- C. Plots of selected variables.- D. Summary of results and assumptions.

Empirical expectations variables have not played a prominent role in econometric modelling. The models of Tinbergen and Klein were followed by increasingly large models, such as the Wharton-model with several hundred equations, up to the Brookings-model with more than a thousand equations. St-Louis-type models, which explain aggregate income out of a single equation, mark the opposite trend in model building. Another major development was the incorporation of input-output matrices into econometric models, as in the Sysifo-model (Hansen, 1978) for West-Germany. Use of empirical expectations variables in these developments was either restricted to variants of existing models, such as the anticipations version of the Wharton-model (Adams, Duggal, 1974), or to parts of a model as in the METRIC-model (Artus et.al., 1977). Only the models of Friend and Taubman (1964), Fair (1971), Poser and Hecheltjen (1973), and Dramais (1983) are mainly based on anticipations variables.[1)] Also compare Uebe (1981) or Uebe, Huber, Fischer (1981).

Use of anticipations with regard to forecasts of specific variables progressed very rapidly. The realization function developed by Modigliani and Cohen (1957) was applied to econometric forecasts of investment, as by Modigliani and Weingartner (1958) or Eisner (1958). The predictive value of business test data was investigated by Theil (1961) and many others. Microeconomic expectations data is being investigated in order to study the expectations formation process (König, Nerlove, Oudiz, 1982).

The Anticipations model (A-Model) incorporates various forecasting uses of anticipations variables in a single, economy-wide, quarterly model of the real private economic activity in West-Germany. A special feature of the A-Model lies in the systematic use of variables with anticipatory character. 60 out the 400 variables in the A-Model are anticipations variables. The data on these empirical expectations is taken largely from business surveys. Due to the world-wide collection of business survey data, the approach of the A-Model can be applied to other economies as well.

The basic feature of this model, namely the exploitation of the time lead of empirical data on plans, expectations, and entrepreneurial judgment, is discussed in section 1 from the viewpoint of model building and in section 2 with regard to expectations variables. This is followed by a description of the causal mechanism of the model. Sections 4 to 6 deal with the data and estimation methods used and with some typical regression estimates. Ex-post and ex-ante forecasts are given in the last section.

1. Concept of the model

The A-Model, just like the Fair Model, has been constructed under the sole purpose of forecasting. The concept and approach of these two models are therefore similar. In practical forecasting, the A-Model is reestimated every quarter as new observations become available. Forecasts are not adjusted subjectively as is frequently the case. This is in correspondence with the Fair model. The main difference lies in the use of about 60 anticipations variables compared to three in the Fair Model. This quantitative difference also has a qualitative aspect, as will be shown below.

Estimation of a model under the sole purpose of forecasting implies the point-of-view that structural models (models designed to test hypotheses) do not automatically provide optimal forecasts. There is no mechanism that ensures that exogenous variables of a structural model are either controlled variables or easy-to-forecast. Moreover, structural models tend to be large, which makes them difficult to handle and to reestimate. Thus, if there exists a simpler way to arrive at satisfactory forecasts than by way of a structural model, then such an approach, being economical, would also be reasonable. Such a simplified approach consists in the attempt to estimate the model with regard to forecasting, such that the explanatory variables are no more difficult to forecast than the variables explained (Compare Fair, 1971, p. 3). I want to formulate this principle as the consequent search for ways of reducing the endogenous variables either directly or indirectly to variables which are easy to forecast. This is most frequently achieved by the use of leading variables, since such variables need not be forecast at all to the extent of their lead. As has been shown by Haitovsky, Treyz and Su (1974), model forecasts are improved considerably through a reduction in the error-of-forecast in the exogenous variables. The price for exploiting the lead of exogenous variables for forecasting purposes lies in the limitation of the forecast horizon to the time length of the lead. At the present stage, forecasts with the A-Model extend two quarters into the future.

The main difference between the Fair Model and the A-Model results from a higher degree of disaggregation and the use of a larger number of expectational variables in the latter. The logic of this approach can be found in the NBER-publications on leading indicators. (The A-Model obviously has similarities with a system of leading indicators.) Mitchell and Burns (1961, p. 166) wrote: "We can never be sure that unusual circumstances may mot make a series behave in an unprecedented fashion at the next revival or recession." and "...since the cyclical timing of single processes cannot implicitly be trusted, a measure of protection against surprises of the individual case may be won by combining indicators of numerous series (Burns, 1961, p. 36). The essence of these ideas can also be applied to econometric forecasting. Exogenous variables that are correctly specified in a model can nevertheless give a false signal occasionally, e.g. if lead-lag relationships are not entirely stable. A large number of exogenous variables can help to reduce the risk that such errors may have a decisive influence on the whole model.

2. The role of expectations in forecasting

Is it justified at all to use exogenous anticipations in forecasting? The Rational Expectations Hypothesis (REH) tends to answer this question negatively, due to the assumption, "that expectations of firms (or more generally, the subjective probability distribution of outcomes) tend to be distributed, for the same information set, about the prediction of the theory (or objective probability distributions of outcomes)" (Muth, 1961, p.316). The REH therefore favors endogenous use of anticipations.

The REH approach to expectations is in marked contrast to the widespread exogenous use of anticipations for forecasting. Leading indicators, like the Ifo-business-climate, expert forecasts, as collected by Zarnowitz, or realization functions as estimated by Eisner (1977), Nerb (1973), and others all exploit the lead of anticipations over realizations. An extensive investigation of expectations data conducted by Aiginger also showed that business surveys are not worthless with regard to forecasting: "...the variables examined exhibit an information lead" (1979, p.388). This is not to say that the diffusion of a certain method is the proof of its validity and it is certainly possible to find counter-examples to the result of Aiginger. However, arguments given by Shackle, Davidson, and others are very enlightening in this context, leading back to the reasons given by Katona (1951) for the collection and application of anticipations data. While the proponents of the REH assume that economic agents are forming subjective probability distributions for all events, Davidson argues that essential events need not necessarily have a probability distribution attached to them. The reason is that essential events, like investment decisions, are single events that are not usually repeated under the same circumstances. Very similarly, Katona (1951) has argued that essential decisions depend on structural changes in attitudes which can not be captured fully in a model. This is why business surveys on the results of essential decisions are conducted.

3. Causality in the A-Model

Production plans in industry and construction serve to forecast production in these sectors. In the short run, production is the main determinant of employment in industry and construction. (In construction, employment plans from business surveys also enter the employment function.) Due to adjustment costs, industrial employment adjusts to output with distributed lags.[2] Overall employment is determined by employment in industry and construction. This procedure is necessary since there exists very little data for the remaining sectors, especially for the services sector. It is justified by the fact that short-run cyclical movements are strongest in industry and construction and transmitted from there to other sectors rather than the other way around.

Industrial producer prices are forecast by lagged price expectations from business surveys. The product of output and prices relative to employment serves to forecast wages in industry and construction. Wages in other sectors are partly exogenous and partly determined by wages in industry. Given employment and wages (per employee), gross wage and salary income results by definition. Net wages and salaries are calculated by deduction of income taxes and social insurance payments. A large number of institutional regulations are included in the calculation of these deductions, since changes in the tax and insurance system are usually announced in advance, thus representing information on future determinants of the economy which is easily available. On the other hand, inclusion of too few institutional regulations could easily cause systematic forecast errors when these regulations are changed. Therefore the tax formula was replicated exactly, five tax categories and 17 income categories were considered, the yearly changing income basis for social insurance payments was calculated etc. Public transfer payments were calculated on the basis of regulations for old-age and pension payments, unemployment and family support etc.

Net wages and salaries, public transfers, and a short-term interest rate mainly determine private consumption. The imputed rent of private home owners contained in official consumption data

FLOW CHART FOR THE ANTICIPATION MODEL

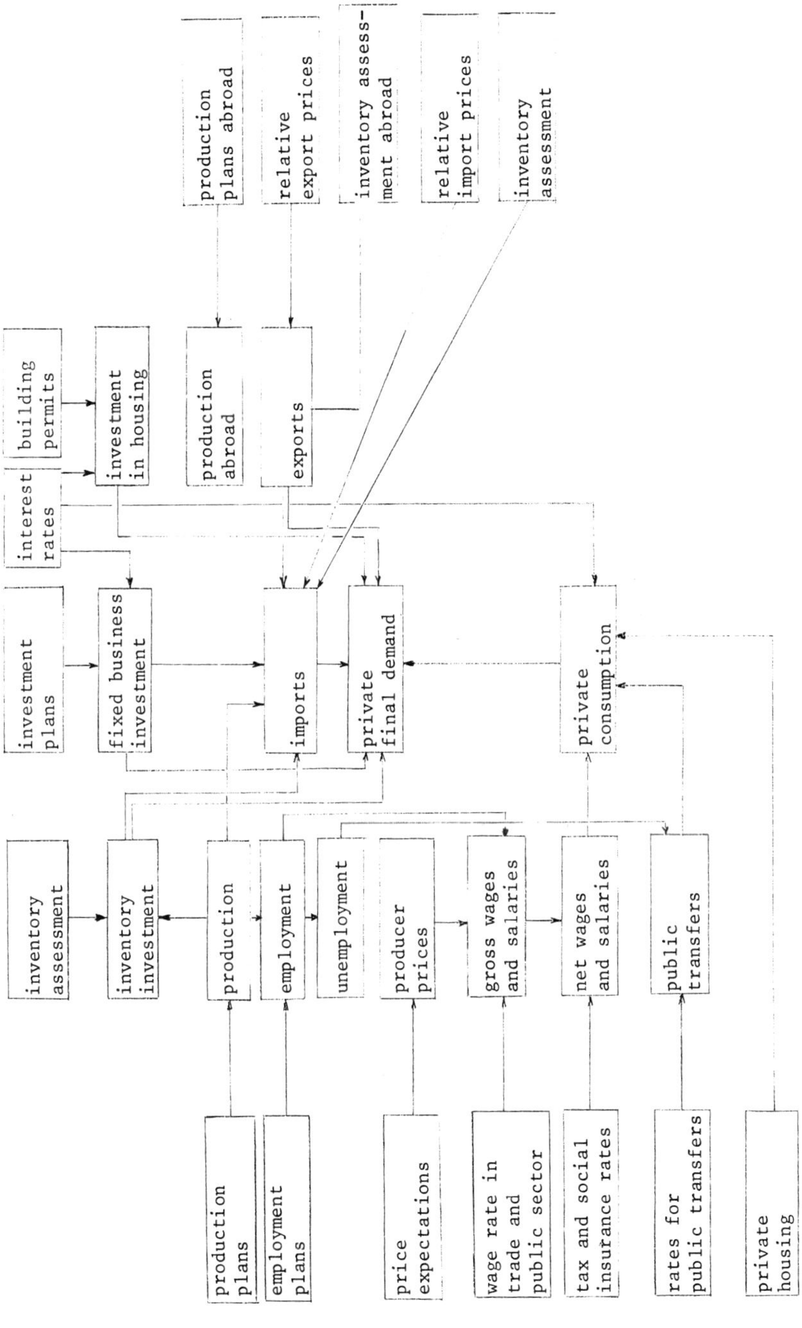

is forecast separately, since it is independent of current income.

Investment is explained by investment plans, accelerator relationships, and the lagged and unlagged spread between a short- and long-term interest rate. (In forecasting, the unlagged difference in interest rates has to be forecast exogenously, since the model contains no monetary sector so far.) Since investment plans are available for many sectors, fixed business investment is estimated by (eight) sectors. Investment plans refer to industry, construction, the railroad and postal service, and the energy sector. Investment in housing is forecast mainly by lagged construction permits. Inventory investment depends on a lagged inventory-assessment variable which serves as a proxy for planned changes in inventories.

Export forecasts are calculated by countries. To this end, industrial production in 14 of the most important OECD-countries is forecast by production plans from business surveys in those countries. Relative export prices together with production abroad (production level and accelerator) serve to forecast exports. Relative export prices were significant for nearly all of the countries investigated. At the present stage of the model, they have to be set exogenously in forecasting. Since the influence of export prices was frequently estimated with considerable lags, errors in these exogenous forecasts are only partially transmitted to export forecasts. Exports to OPEC-countries are made dependent upon the earnings of these countries which in turn are made a function of the exogenous price of crude oil and industrial production of OECD-countries.

Imports are explained by every component of private demand, including exports. Anticipations enter into import functions through lagged assessment of inventories. For example, the assessment of inventories in refineries is contained in the import function for crude oil (also compare ARTUS et.al, 1977).

Total private demand results by definition as consumption+investment+exports-imports, excluding trade in invisibles.

4. Data

Data on the variables explained in the model is taken from official statistics. Data is not deseasonalized prior to estimation. Seasonality in the data is accounted for by (0;1)-dummy variables. Due to lack of quarterly data, fixed business investment by sectors has to be estimated with yearly data. Total quarterly fixed business investment is explained by yearly investment for all sectors together and by the lagged business situation in industry, where the latter is introduced to approximate cyclical variations in investment over the year.

Investment plans for the railroad and postal service and for the energy sector, as well as building permits, are dimensioned in billions of DM. Other anticipations data used is collected by the method of business surveys and thus initially on a three-dimensional scale. Business test data was quantified as usual by taking balances of positive and negative replies in the survey. (Taking balances is certainly the most common and the best proven method of quantification. Business test data is therefore frequently published in the form of balances, as by the Ifo-Institute or by the OECD.) The author intends, though, to test other methods of quantification in later work. In the case of price expectations, allowance for differing weights between positive and negative replies might improve quantification (Praet, 1980). Another method of quantification consists in the approximation of individual changes[3)] surveyed in the business test by a normal distribution, as investigated by Theil (1952) and later by Carlson and Parkin (1975). It is not clear, though, whether this method is appropriate in cases where the share of either positive or negative replies is small (Foster and Gregory, 1977).

5. Estimation methods

At the present stage, the A-Model is recursive. It follows that OLS-estimates are consistent and consequently OLS was applied throughout. Lags were estimated with the Almon-method in cases where lags were distributed over more than four quarters. The Koyck-method was not applied. Autocorrelation in the residuals was estimated by the Hildreth-Lu-method (1960). Generally, however, a low value for the DW-Statistic was taken to indicate misspecification with regard to the functional form or the variables included. Inclusion of additional or different variables frequently led to an improvement of the DW in such cases. Only when the number of explanatory variables was limited from the beginning by data availability, as in the case of export functions, was a low DW simply followed by application of the Hildreth-Lu-method. From the above it is already clear that influencing variables were selected by exploratory methods. Due to limited data availability, alternative hypotheses had to be applied to the same set of data. However, regressions estimated in this way were tested for stability by out-of-sample ex-post forecasts over 12 to 20 quarters.

6. Selected regression estimates

Since a presentation of the entire model would take up too much space, the above description of causality of the model is supplemented instead by specific details on three typical regressions. The foreign trade sector, fixed business investment, and inventory investment have been described elsewhere (Naggl, 1981,82,83). A detailed publication of the entire model is intended by the author.

In the following, the forecasting equation for fixed investment in the energy sector is taken to demonstrate the approach to realization functions. Since investment in inventories is a special problem in forecasting, inventory investment is also discussed. Finally, the regression estimate for exports to the USA is taken in order to demonstrate the approach to export forecasts.

a) Fixed business investment in the energy sector

Electric power companies report on their investment plans in March of every year (t-1) for the following year (t). Since these investment plans are reported nine months prior to the beginning of the realization period, it is to be expected that original plans are modified considerably before execution. Sales, capacity utilization, and profits are typically introduced as variables affecting the execution of plans in the realization function (Eisner, 1977, p.1). Data on profits and sales of electric power companies are only published with a lag of a few years, however. Since this sector of the economy is highly regulated, profits can be left out as an explanatory variable. Data on sales is replaced by data on electricity generated. Capacity is specified instead of capacity utilization.

The influence of interest rates in the realization function has been denied by Evans with the argument that "modifications in investment will not be influenced by changes in the market rate of interest...because the funds have already been committed at the then existing rate of interest" (1969, p.105). This argument is not followed here, however, due to the long transition period from plans to realizations. Besides, decreases in interest rates, if unexpected, may very well lead to upward revisions of investment plans. An interest rate variable was therefore specified in the investment equation. This variable is calculated as the difference between the short-term interest rate on current accounts and the long-term interest rate on bonds.[4)]

Data on fixed investment in the energy sector is dimensioned in billions of DM at constant prices of 1976, as published in official statistics (Fachserie 18, Statistisches Bundesamt). The regression estimated with data from 1966 to 1981 is:

Coefficient (t-value) of					SEE	R^2	DW
C	IP	Z	Q_{-1}	K			
3.3 (3.1)	.33 (1.9)	-.32 (1.4)	1.33 (2.2)	-.37 (4.0)	.79	.936	1.85

C: Constant
IP: Investment plans in the energy sector, deflated by the price index for fixed investment, billions of DM, Ifo-Schnelldienst, Wirtschaft und Statistik.
Z: Difference between the interest rate on current accounts and the interest rate on bonds, per cent; Monatsberichte der Bundesbank.
Q: Electric power generation of regulated power stations, billions of kWH; Wirtschaft und Statistik.
K: Capacity of regulated power stations, billions of kW, Ifo-Schnelldienst.

Probably due to the early collection of plan data, investment plans can only explain one third of investment, whereas the variables representing plan revisions show a strong and significant influence in two out of three cases.

b) Investment in inventories

Investment in inventories is forecast by making use of the "assessment of inventories" (LU) variable from the business surveys[5] in industry and trade. This variable measures the deviation between actual and desired stocks, thus giving a measure for the inclination to change the level of stocks. It can also serve for forecasting, since assessment variables from business surveys contain information on future requirements (Anderson, Strigel, 1965). Estimation and prediction of inventory investment by assessment data alone is not possible, however, since the assessment of inventories in industry only covers finished products. Data on inventory investment on the other hand also contains changes in the stocks of raw materials and goods-in-process. In order to explain the latter, accelerator relationships have to be included in the investment function. This raises no additional problem for predictions, however, since production is forecast in the model. Inventory investment at constant prices of 1976 (Wirtschaft und Statistik) is estimated by the following regression for the sample period 1968.1 to 1982.4:

Coefficient (t-value) of								SEE	R^2	DW
C	S2	S3	S4	LU_{-2}	Q	$\dot{Q}$	K			
.8 (.2)	-15.3 (16)	5.9 (9.0)	-26.4 (18)	-2.0 (5.4)	.15 (2.0)	.13 (1.0)	-.11 (3.4)	1.66	.983	1.87

C: Constant
Sj: (0;1)-Seasonal dummy variables, j=2,3,4
LU: Assessment of finished goods inventories in industry and of total inventories in trade, with weights 0.67 and 0.33 respectively, balances from business surveys; Ifo-Institute and my own calculations (while Ifo weights with sales at the branch level, LU is weighted with inventories at the branch level here).
Q: Index of industrial production, 1976 = 100; Wirtschaft und Statistik.
$\dot{Q}$: change of Q over corresponding quarter of the previous year.

K: Inventories at the beginning of each period, calculated as cumulated investment; ibid and my own calculations.

The lagged assessment variable is significant with the expected negative sign. Further calculations showed that the influence of unlagged assessment on inventory investment was close to zero and insignificant, supporting the presumption that LU has a lead over investment. The accelerator influences inventory investment through first differences of production as well as the level of production together with the level of stocks.

c) Exports to the USA

Export functions in the A-Model typically contain a production variable of the importing country (in level and difference form) and relative export prices. In correspondence with the usual procedure, export functions were estimated in log-linear form.[6] The following regression was estimated for exports to the USA from 1972.1 to 1983.1, with exports deflated by average values (data is taken from Wirtschaft und Statistik):

Coefficient (t-value) of					SEE	R^2	DW
C	lnQ	$\ln\dot{Q}$	lnP	T			
-9.5 (5.2)	2.1 (5.0)	.4 (.4)	-1.7 (9.8)	.003 (1.2)	.070	.853	1.55

Lag weights

Lag	0	1	2	3	4	5	6	7	8	9	10	11	12	13	14	15
Q	.40	.30	.20	.10												
$\dot{Q}$	.30	.10	.05	.10	.20	.20	.05									
P	.10	.08	.06	.06	.05	.04	.04	.05	.05	.06	.07	.10	.07	.06	.06	.05

C: Constant
Q: Industrial production in the USA, 1975 = 100; Main Economic Indicators.
$\dot{Q}$: change of Q over corresponding quarter of previous year.
P: Export prices of investment goods relative to prices of producer goods in the USA, adjusted for exchange-rate changes; ibid and Wirtschaft und Statistik.
T: Trend
all Data, including data on exports, is in logarithms.

As for about one-half of the export functions of the model, considerable lags were estimated for output and relative export prices, with longer lags for the price variable than for production (also compare Magee, 1975, p.209). Since relative prices have to be forecast by simple extrapolation at the present stage of the model, long lags for prices are favorable to the calculation of export forecasts. Production is generally forecast by production plans with the exception of the USA, however, since production plans for this country are published with a lag of more than two quarters.[7)] Production forecasts for the USA are therefore taken from "Economic Outlook USA". Also, about one-half of the export regressions differ from the above regression by the inclusion of the lagged assessment of inventories in the importing country.[8)]

7. Selected forecasts

Every regression in the model has been tested for stability by out-of-sample ex-post and ex-ante forecasts. Ex-ante forecasts have already been published for sectoral fixed business investment and inventory investment (Naggl, 1982,83) which can now be compared with actual values. Since there exist no evaluations of comparable forecasts for West-Germany,[9)] it is not possible to compare the following measures of forecasting accuracy with results from other models. Comparison with naive forecasts is implicitly possible though, since Theil's inequality measure (TIM) takes the value 1 when "no change" is forecast. TIM < 1 is an improvement over "no change" forecasts. Furthermore, an investigation of annual GNP-forecasts by Zarnowitz (1979) showed that forecasts with naive models had practically no correlation with actual changes in GNP. This result is very likely to hold for investment forecasts as well. TIM and correlation coefficient between forecast and actual changes in fixed business investment and inventory investment in Tables 1 and 2 show better results in every case than would be expected for naive models.

TABLE 1: MEASURES OF EX-POST FORECASTING ACCURACY
REAL FIXED BUSINESS INVESTMENT 1977-1980

SECTOR	MAF	MF	%F	KK	TIM	BIAS
Energy	0,58	-0,50	5,2	0,44	0,63	0,43
Industry	0,75	-0,10	0,3	0,66	0,25	0,02
Construction	0,64	-0,64	18,0	0,70	0,51	0,66
Trade	0,31	-0,20	2,5	0,76	0,40	0,31
Housing	1,73	1,73	3,5	0,94	0,52	0,77

MAF = Mean absolute error, billions of DM.
MF = Mean error, billions of DM
%F = per cent error, MF relative to the level of Investment 1977-1980
KK = Correlation between forecast and actual changes in investment over the previous year
TIM = Theil's Inequality Measure
BIAS= contribution of unequal direction between forecasts and actual values to TIM

TABLE 2: MEASURES OF EX-POST FORECASTING ACCURACY
INVENTORY INVESTMENT AT CONSTANT PRICES, 1975.1-1980.4

Correlation Coefficient	0.91
Regression Coefficient of Actual on Predicted ...	0.97
Theil's Inequality Coefficient	0.22
Fraction of Error due to Bias................	0.06
Fraction of Error due to unequal Variation ...	0.02
Fraction of Error due to unequal Covariation	0.92
Root-Mean-Squared Error	1.09
Mean Error	-0.27
Mean Absolute Error	0.92
For Comparison: Mean Absolute Four Quarter Change in Inventory Investment	2.15

Ex-ante, total fixed business investment at constant prices was forecast in November of 1981 to increase by 1 per cent in 1982 over 1981, conditional on the assumption of a decrease in the spread in interest rates from 3.8 %-points to 2.3 %-points. However, interest rates increased in 1982 over the previous year and the spread in interest rates rose to 4.4 %-points. Insertion of this actual value of 4.4%-points into the investment functions gives a decrease of investment of 5%. This is fairly close to the actual decrease of 5.3% reported by the Statistisches Bundesamt[10)] for 1982.

Inventory investment for the four quarters of 1982 was forecast in June of 1982 (when no data on inventory investment for 1982 existed yet) at 6.6 billions of DM at constant prices of 1970.

Actual inventory investment for 1982 was only published at constant prices of 1976 at 4.1 billions of DM. The effect of the change in the base year of the deflator is not large, as can be seen from the following comparison:

Inventory Investment at constant prices of

	1970	1976
1980	12.1	14.2
1981	-0.5	-1.1

The change to the new base year of 1976 leads to somewhat larger absolute values of inventory investment during the last two years before the base year was changed. For purposes of comparison, the forecast value of of 6.6 billion DM is to be set at a slightly higher value. The error of forecast is still relatively small, though, considering the fact that published data on inventory investment is revised by as much as 1.5 billion DM from quarter to quarter.[11)]

Of course, not much can be inferred from just a few ex-ante forecasts. However, since ex-ante forecasts are now being made every quarter, beginning with the second quarter of 1983, a systematic evaluation of the forecasting properties of the model will be possible in the future.

SUMMARY

The A-Model is a quarterly econometric forecasting model for the real private product in West-Germany. Model forecasts include income generation by sectors and for the total economy, income redistribution, and all components of real private final demand. Fixed investment, exports, and imports are also forecast on a disaggregated level. A special feature of the model consists in the use of a large number of empirical plans and expectations as exogenous variables. 60 out of the 400 variables in the model are anticipations variables. The latter are taken largely from business surveys, whereas the variables explained in the model come from official statistics.

Use of anticipations data, as e.g. the assessment of inventories, results in very satisfactory forecasts of inventory investment which is difficult to forecast otherwise. The world-wide collection of business test data also enables forecasts of industrial production for nearly all of the OECD-countries within the model, which serve in turn for forecasts of exports by countries. Use of detailed information on economic activity in a large number of importing countries should contribute positively to the overall forecasting performance of the model, since the West-German economy is heavily dependent on exports. Ex-post and ex-ante forecasts conducted so far are very encouraging. Collection of business test data in many other countries makes it possible to apply the approach of the A-Model to those countries as well.

Forecasts with the A-Model are calculated regularly from now on at the end of every quarter for the following two quarters. Forecasts are calculated after reestimation of the model with the most recent data available and without any subjective adjustments of the forecasts.

PART II: FORECASTS FOR THE WEST-GERMAN ECONOMY WITH THE ANTICIPATIONS MODEL

A. FORECASTS UP TO THE 4TH QUARTER OF 1983, MADE IN JULY 1983

EX-ANTE FORECASTS ARE GIVEN IN HEAVY-FACED TYPE
PRIOR FORECASTS ARE GIVEN IN BRACKETS BENEATH ACTUAL VALUES

I. INCOME GENERATION

	ABSOLUTE VALUES					%-CHANGE OVER PRECEDING YEAR				
	82/4	83/1	83/2	83/3	83/4	82/4	83/1	83/2	83/3	83/4
INDUSTRIAL PRODUCTION INDUSTRY 1976=100	105.4	101.9	**105.6**	**101.2**	**110.5**	-5.9	-3.6	**-.8**	**2.4**	**4.8**
	(106.1)	(99.2)				(-5.3)	(-6.2)			
EMPLOYMENT IN INDUSTRY MIO	7.1	7.0	**6.9**	**6.9**	**6.9**	-4.1	-4.6	**-4.8**	**-4.6**	**-3.7**
	(7.2)	(7.0)				(-3.2)	(-4.7)			
OUTPUT IN CONSTRUCTION 1976 = 100	97.5	69.8	**102.8**	**108.9**	**103.9**	-4.6	.9	**-3.2**	**2.5**	**6.6**
	(98.4)	(71.2)				(-3.7)	(2.9)			
EMPLOYMENT IN CONSTRUCTION MIO	1.1	1.0	**1.1**	**1.1**	**1.1**	-4.5	-6.3	**-6.7**	**-6.7**	**-4.7**
	(1.1)	(1.0)				(-9.2)	(-7.6)			
EMPLOYEES, ALL SECTORS MIO	22.3	21.9	**21.9**	**22.0**	**22.0**	-2.0	-2.1	**-2.3**	**-2.3**	**-1.7**
	(22.4)	(21.9)				(-1.9)	(-2.1)			
UNEMPLOYED, TOTAL MIO	2.1	2.5	2.2	**2.3**	**2.5**	35.5	30.1	30.4	**30.6**	**22.2**
	(2.1)	(2.4)	(2.4)			(40.7)	(27.4)	(45.3)		
GROSS WAGES AND SALARIES, ALL SECTORS BIO DM	210.4	176.3	**184.8**	**188.4**	**213.0**	1.4	1.1	**.2**	**.2**	**1.3**
	(211.8)	(177.0)				(2.1)	(1.5)			

II. REDISTRIBUTION OF INCOME

	82/4	83/1	83/2	83/3	83/4	82/4	83/1	83/2	83/3	83/4
SOCIAL INSURANCE PAYMENTS, EMPLOYEES BIO DM	27.2 (27.2)	23.8 (24.0)	25.6	26.3	28.8	4.9 (4.8)	1.9 (2.9)	.4	3.5	6.0
INCOME TAX ON WAGES AND SALARIES BIO DM	37.0 ( )	24.0	29.7	31.0	37.8	4.5 ( )	-3.1	.4	2.8	2.0
NET WAGES AND SALARIES BIO DM	146.1 (146.6)	126.4 (126.8)	129.5	131.1	146.4	.1 (.4)	.1 (.5)	.1	-1.0	.2
PUBLIC TRANSFERS BIO DM	66.3 (67.5)	67.7 (67.1)	65.8	66.4	69.2	4.4 (6.3)	3.4 (2.3)	4.8	5.0	4.4
NON-PROFIT INCOME BIO DM	212.5 (214.1)	194.1 (193.9)	195.3	197.6	215.7	1.4 (2.2)	1.2 (1.1)	1.6	.9	1.5

III. PRIVATE CONSUMPTION

	82/4	83/1	83/2	83/3	83/4	82/4	83/1	83/2	83/3	83/4
NEWLY LICENSED PRIVATE CARS, MONTHLY AVERAGE 1000	92 (105)	147 (159)	175	117	123	-.7 (14.4)	5.5 (14.1)	20.7	27.6	33.7
PRIVATE CONSUMPTION AT PRICES OF 1976 BIO DM	182.5 (184.1)	165.5 (164.8)	173.6	174.5	189.5	-2.5 (-1.7)	-.5 (-.9)	2.0	3.2	3.8

IV. PRIVATE INVESTMENT AT PRICES OF 1976

	82/4	83/1	83/2	83/3	83/4	82/4	83/1	83/2	83/3	83/4 12)
INVENTORY INVESTMENT BIO DM	-16.5 ( )	8.8 ( )	-4.1	16.1	-11.9	.9 ( )	0.0 ( )	-1.3	1.5	4.6
INVESTMENT IN HOUSING BIO DM	19.0 (20.0)	12.7	17.2	18.8	19.8	2.7 (7.9)	-3.9	-5.5	3.6	4.1
FIXED BUSINESS INVESTMENT AT PRICES OF 1976 BIO DM	48.9 ( )	38.6	45.8	44.5	48.4	-4.4 ( )	-.0	.9	-3.0	-.9

FIXED BUSINESS INVESTMENT BY SECTORS AT PRICES OF 1976, YEARLY DATA

	1979	1980	1981	1982	1983	1979	1980	1981	1982	1983
ENERGY	13.2 (15.0)	14.3 (13.7)	14.0	14.0	14.8	-.4 (13.6)	8.7 (-8.7)	-2.2	.0	5.7
INDUSTRY BIO DM	47.5 (47.7)	51.3 (49.4)	47.8	40.8	38.4	8.3 (8.7)	8.0 (3.6)	-6.8	-14.7	-5.8
CONSTRUCTION BIO DM	5.8 (7.8)	5.4 (6.7)	4.2	2.6	2.7	19.6 (61.2)	-7.1 (-14.1)	-22.5	-37.2	4.1
TRADE BIO DM	14.0 ( )	13.8 ( )	12.2	9.9	9.9	3.6 ( )	-1.0 ( )	-11.9	-18.9	.1
TRANSPORTATION AND COMMUNICATION BIO DM	21.6 ( )	22.1 ( )	23.9	22.6	22.8	2.2 ( )	2.1 ( )	8.0	-5.2	.6
OTHER SERVICES BIO DM	40.5 ( )	41.3 ( )	39.9	39.1	41.0	21.0 ( )	1.9 ( )	-3.4	-1.8	4.8

V. EXPORTS OF GOODS AT PRICES OF 1976

	82/4	83/1	83/2	83/3	83/4	82/4	83/1	83/2	83/3	83/4
EXPORTS TO OPEC-COUNTRIES BIO DM	7.6	6.5	6.5	6.4	6.4	-13.9	-18.6	-12.6	-10.9	-15.8
	( )	( )				( )	( )			
EXPORTS TO NON-EUROPEAN DEVELOPING COUNTRIES BIO DM	7.0	6.8	6.5	6.5	7.1	-15.1	-5.7	-2.9	-.4	1.6
	( )	( )				( )	( )			
TOTAL EXPORTS BIO DM	86.2	82.8	81.8	78.7	86.7	-4.0	-4.9	-4.4	-1.0	.6
	( )	( )	( )			( )	( )	( )		
INDUSTRIAL PRODUCTION IN OECD-COUNTRIES[13] 1975=100	117.2	114.4	115.4	101.1	117.1	-3.7	-2.5	-1.8	-.9	-.1
	( )	( )				( )	( )			

VI. IMPORTS OF GOODS AT PRICES OF 1976

	82/4	83/1	83/2	83/3	83/4	82/4	83/1	83/2	83/3	83/4
IMPORTS OF MINING PRODUCTS	6.7	6.2	6.2	6.6	7.2	-8.1	-10.1	-10.0	4.1	8.0
BIO DM	(7.1)	(7.0)	(6.5)			(-3.0)	(2.4)	(-4.5)		
IMPORTS OF BASIC MATERIALS	17.6	18.5	19.7	17.8	20.7	-1.4	1.9	4.9	1.9	17.6
BIO DM	(17.8)	(18.7)	(20.2)			(-.2)	(2.5)	(7.4)		
IMPORTS OF INVESTMENT GOODS	19.8	18.7	19.9	18.4	20.7	2.7	-3.0	3.9	6.6	4.9
BIO DM	(19.4)	(17.6)	(19.9)			(.8)	(-8.8)	(3.7)		
IMPORTS OF CONSUMER GOODS	9.6	10.5	9.9	10.9	11.5	-2.5	3.2	6.9	11.8	19.7
BIO DM	(9.8)	(10.2)	(10.0)			(-.2)	(.0)	(7.8)		
IMPORTS OF FOOD AND	12.1	11.8	12.3	11.3	12.6	-1.0	2.5	2.5	3.9	4.0
FOOD PRODUCTS BIO DM	(11.9)	(11.3)	(11.6)			(-2.8)	(-1.4)	(-3.4)		
TOTAL IMPORTS	67.9	67.6	70.1	66.8	74.8	-.7	-.4	2.6	5.0	10.2
BIO DM	(67.5)	(66.6)	(70.2)			(-1.3)	(-1.7)	(2.7)		
BALANCE OF TRADE IN GOODS	15.2	11.9	9.3	9.5	9.2	6.5	6.5	-29.4	-18.9	-39.3
BIO DM	( )	( )	( )			( )	( )	( )		

VII. PRIVATE FINAL DEMAND AT PRICES OF 1976

	82/4	83/1	83/2	83/3	83/4	82/4	83/1	83/2	83/3	83/4
PRIVATE FINAL DEMAND AT	252.2	240.8	244.2	265.7	257.8	-3.3	-2.2	-1.7	.9	2.2
PRICES OF 1976[14)] BIO DM	( )	( )				( )	( )			

B. PLOTS OF SELECTED VARIABLES

I. INDUSTRIAL PRODUCTION 1976 =100

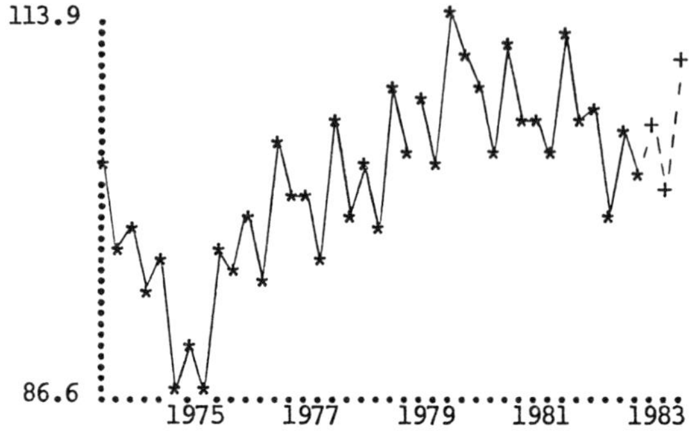

II. PRIVATE CONSUMPTION AT PRICES OF 1976

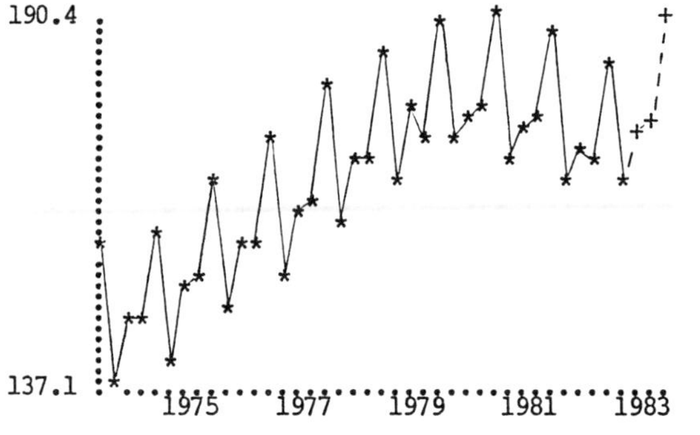

III. INDUSTRIAL PRODUCTION IN OECD-COUNTRIES

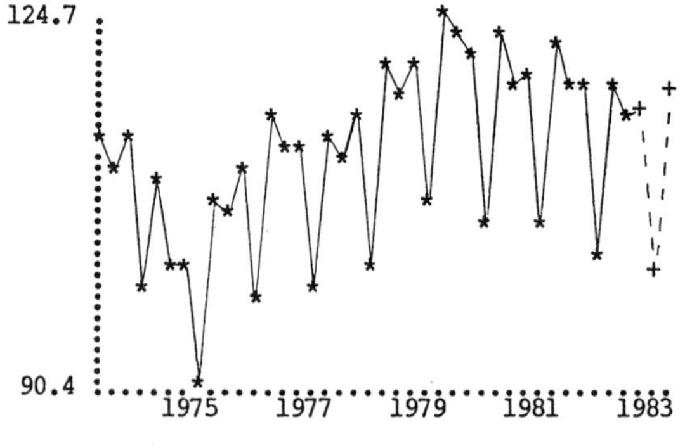

IV. EXPORTS OF GOODS AT PRICES OF 1976

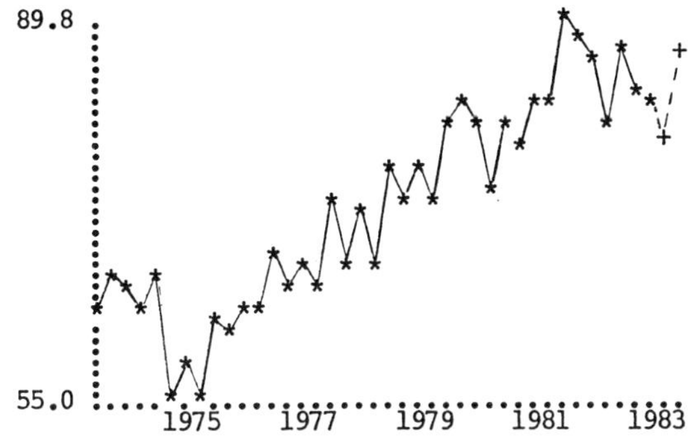

V. IMPORTS OF GOODS AT PRICES OF 1976

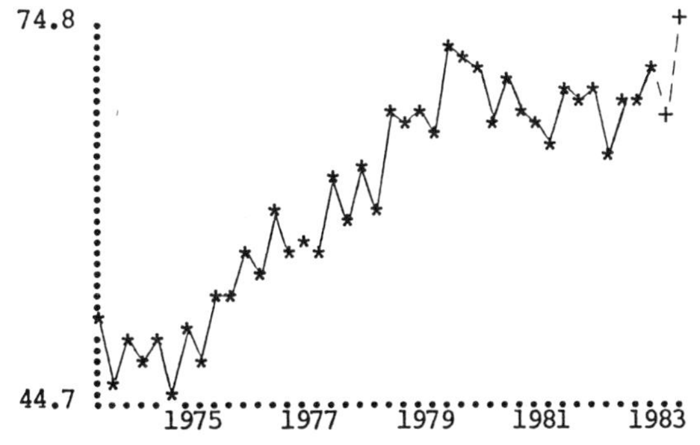

VI. PRIVATE FINAL DEMAND AT PRICES OF 1976

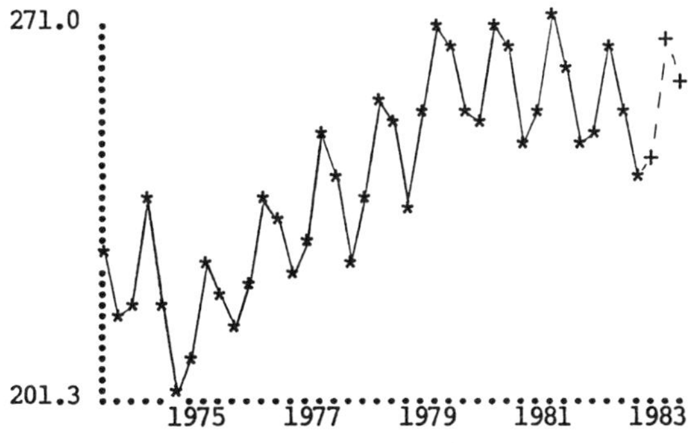

C. COMPARISON WITH OTHER FORECASTS

I. PRIVATE CONSUMPTION AT PRICES OF 1976

	%-CHANGE OVER PRECEDING YEAR 82/4	83/1	83/2	83/3	83/4
ANTICIPATIONS-MODEL	-2.5	-.5	2.0	3.2	3.8
RESEARCH INSTITUTES			-1.0	1.0	1.0
SYSIFO-MODEL			.7	1.0	1.7
COUNCIL OF ECONOMIC ADVISORS			-1.5	0.0	0.0

II. FIXED BUSINESS AND HOUSING INVESTMENT AT PRICES OF 1976

	82/4	83/1	83/2	83/3	83/4
ANTICIPATIONS-MODEL	-2.5	-1.0	-1.0	-1.2	.5
RESEARCH INSTITUTES			1.0	3.0	3.0
SYSIFO-MODEL			1.6	2.5	2.5
COUNCIL OF ECONOMIC ADVISORS			3.5	5.0	5.0

III. EXPORTS OF GOODS AT PRICES OF 1976

	82/4	83/1	83/2	83/3	83/4
ANTICIPATIONS-MODEL	-4.0	-4.9	-4.4	-1.0	.6
RESEARCH INSTITUTES				2.0	2.0
SYSIFO-MODEL				2.3	2.9
COUNCIL OF ECONOMIC ADVISORS				5.5	5.5

IV. IMPORTS OF GOODS AT PRICES OF 1976

	82/4	83/1	83/2	83/3	83/4
ANTICIPATIONS-MODEL	-.7	-.4	2.6	5.0	10.2
RESEARCH INSTITUTES				3.0	3.0
SYSIFO-MODEL				1.9	2.3
COUNCIL OF ECONOMIC ADVISORS				5.0	5.0

V. PRIVATE FINAL DEMAND OR GDP AT PRICES OF 1976

	82/4	83/1	83/2	83/3	83/4
ANTICIPATIONS-MODEL	-3.3	-2.2	-1.7	.9	2.2
RESEARCH INSTITUTES			-.5	1.5	1.5
SYSIFO-MODEL			0.0	1.8	2.7
COUNCIL OF ECONOMIC ADVISORS			-1.0	2.5	2.5

MONTH OF PUBLICATION OF THE RESEARCH INSTITUTES FORECASTS : 05/1983
MONTH OF PUBLICATION OF THE SYSIFO-MODEL FORECASTS : 03/1983
MONTH OF PUBLICATION OF THE COUNCIL OF ADVISORS FORECASTS : 11/1982

D. SUMMARY OF RESULTS AND ASSUMPTIONS

Output in industry and construction is forecast to increase in the third and fourth quarter of 1983 over the corresponding quarters of the preceding year. Employment in these sectors as well as total employment, however, is still going to decrease.

The decrease in employment causes low rates of increase in gross wages and salaries. Public transfers on the other hand are forecast to increase between four and five per cent during the third and fourth quarter of 1983, mainly due to high unemployment. Non-profit income (net) is largely determined by wages and salaries and will thus increase at low rates.

Real private consumption will grow at rates between two and four per cent, rates which are above the increase in income. Among others, private consumption benefits from high growth rates of expenditures on private cars.

Fixed business investment will not contribute to economic growth during the forecast period. This is due to high real rates of interest and the lag of fixed investment over the cycle. Exports will also continue to be low, mainly due to low economic activity in importing countries.

Inventory investment is forecast to exhibit a noteworthy increase in the fourth quarter of 1983 for the first time over a sustained period. Imports, unlike exports, are forecast to increase considerably, mainly due to increases in basic materials and consumer goods imports.

Altogether, real private demand is forecast to grow at moderate rates in the second half of 1983. Growth is due to consumption and inventory investment, whereas fixed business investment and exports will continue to be low during the forecast period.

Presently, prices and interest rates are not explained in the model. Forecasts are based on the assumption that various price increases range between 2 and 3.5 % per year and that interest rates do not change during the forecast period.

COMMENTS ON THE PRESENTATION OF FORECASTING RESULTS

The presentation of the predictions in section A is based on the availability of data on actual values. All data on time periods for which actual values do not exist when forecasts are calculated are called ex-ante forecasts. Ex-ante forecasts are distinguished from actual values by heavy-faced type. In addition to ex-ante forecasts, prior forecasts are given in brackets beneath actual values in order to allow comparisons between forecast and realized values.[15] (Where forecasts calculated formerly do not yet exist, the space between brackets remains empty.)

In section B, the development over time of selected variables is given graphically. This kind of presentation has the advantage to show up erratic movements in a simple way, whereas the change over the corresponding quarter of the previous year can give wrong impressions, if the base period is unusually high or low. Forecasts are distinguished in the graphical presentation by a change in symbols.

In section C, forecasts calculated with the A-Model are compared to forecasts from other models or institutions. In the first line of every group of forecasts, actual values are also given up to the first period of forecast in order to indicate the past development before the forecast period. Since forecasts by the council of economic advisors and by the research institutes are on a half-yearly basis, their forecasts take on the same value for the two quarters of a half-year. It goes without saying that only the most recent forecasts are used in the comparison. Since the comparison is made by the author of the A-Model at the time forecasts with that model are calculated, the other forecasts will usually have originated earlier. Forecasts referring to the same time period are in general - other things equal - the more precise, the later they have been calculated. Thus it is clear that the comparison of these forecasts originating from different periods is not made with the intention to compare the quality of the forecasts.[16] A range of possible future values may be helpful to those, however, who are interested in the results of forecasting.

FOOTNOTES

*) This work was supported by the Deutsche Forschungsgemeinschaft. The author would like to thank K. Hagn for helpful comments and suggestions. Any errors are the responsibility of the author.

1) Aiginger (1977) contains a summary table on the use of anticipations variables in econometric models.

2) In the case where errors of forecasts are not correlated positively, these errors can be offsetting over several periods. The values of longer lags need not be forecast anyway, since they are known at the time the forecast is made.

3) Since only the direction of changes is asked for in the business test (increase, no change, decrease) but not the amount of individual changes, quantification of business-test data has to be based on assumptions about the distribution of these individual changes. The usual method of taking balances e.g. implies the assumption that the frequency distribution of the individual changes is rectangular, as has been shown by Theil (1952).

4) Interest rate variables that are constructed similarly can be found in Evans (1969, p.191f) or Pindycke and Rubinfeld (1981, p.419f). Although this variable is not crucial for the estimates performed here, its logic is given, since it is rather uncommon. When interest rates are considered to be relatively high, the spread between short-run and long-run interest rates will also be high, since short-run loans are then preferred by debtors under expectations that interest rates will eventually go back to "normal" and vice versa. Also compare Evans (1969, p.192). In this way, the spread between interest rates incorporates expectations in a simple manner. The short-term rate used here is usually above the long-term rate. Generally, the spread between interest rates is high at the end of a boom and low at the end of a recession.

5) LU ist collected in the (Ifo) business survey with the following question: "We assess our stocks of unsold finished goods as being presently -too small -appropriate -too large."

6) The log-linear functional form is to be preferred where the variable investigated is linear in rates-of-changes which is probably frequently the case with exports. Further estimates conducted here showed a slight superiority of the log-linear functional form over the linear form, as measured by R^2.

7) Indicators of Industrial Activity, OECD, Paris.

8) Also compare the use of LU in import-functions of the METRIC-Model (Artus et.al, 1977).

9) There exists an evaluation of forecasts by industrial sectors performed by Gerstenberger (1983).

10) Fachserie 18, Reihe 1, 1982, preliminary report.

11) Compare Wirtschaft und Statistik, June and December of 1981.

12) In the case of inventory investment, changes over the preceding year are calculated as absolute changes rather than per cent changes.

13) Weights were derived from the shares of each country in German exports of 1980. The weights are for Australia 0.01, Canada 0.01, Austria 0.08, Belgium 0.11, Denmark 0.03, Finnland 0.01, France 0.18, Italy 0.12, Netherlands 0.13, Norway 0.02, Spain 0.02, Sweden 0.04, Switzerland 0.08, Great Britain 0.09 and USA 0.08.

14) Excluding invisible trade.

15) A systematic investigation of the quality of forecasts is reserved for later work.

16) The choice of forecasts compared was made according to the availability of forecasts and has nothing to do with the quality of these forecasts.

REFERENCES

ADAMS, F.G., DUGGAL, V.G., "Anticipations Variables in an Econometric Model: Performance of the Anticipations Version of Wharton Mark III", International Ecomomic Review, Vol. 15, No.2 (1974), 267-284.

AIGINGER, K., "The Use of Survey Data for the Analysis of Business Cycles", CIRET-Studien Nr. 24 (München, 1977).

AIGINGER, K., "Empirische Informationen zur Bildung von Erwartungen", Ifo-Studien, Vol. 25 (1979) 83-135.

ANDERSON O. jun., BAUER, R.K., GIEHL, R., "Zur Theorie des Konjunkturtests. Modelltheoretische Betrachtungen", Ifo Studien Jg. 1 (1955).

ANDERSON, O. jun., STRIGEL, W., "Aussagewert und Determinanten unternehmerischer Urteile und Erwartungen", Ciret-Studien Nr. 4 (Muenchen, Rotterdam, 1965).

ARTUS, P., et.al., "METRIC - Modele econometrique trimestriel de la conjoncture", Annales de l'INSEE, Vol. 26.27 (1977), 1-370.

BURNS, A.F., "New Facts on Business Cycles", in G.H. Moore (Ed.), Business Cycle Indicators. Volume I. (Princeton, 1961).

CARLSON, J.A., PARKIN, J.M., "Inflation Expectations", Economica, Vol. 42 (1975), 123-38.

DAVIDSON, P., "Rational Expectations: a fallacious foundation for studying crucial decision-making processes", Journal of Post Post Keynesian Economics, Vol. 5, No. 2 (1982.83).

DRAMAIS, A., "Use of Business Survey Data into a short-term Prediction Model", paper presented at the 16th CIRET-Conference, Washington, 1983.

EISNER, R., "Expectations, Plans, and Capital Expenditures: A Synthethis of Ex-post and Ex-ante Data", in M.J. Bowman (ed.), Expectations, Uncertainty, and Business Behavior, Social Science Research Council (New York, 1958).

EISNER, R., "More on Capital Expenditure Anticipations", Beitrag zur 13. CIRET-Konferenz (München, 1977).

EVANS, M.K., Macroeconomic Activity. Theory, Forecasting and Control (New York, Evanston, London, 1969), p.97.

FAIR, R.C., A Short-Run Forecasting Model of the United States Economy (Lexington, 1972).

FOSTER, J., GREGORY, M., "Inflation expectations: the use of qualitative survey data", Applied Economics, Vol. 9, (1977), 319-29.

FRIEND, J., TAUBMAN, P., "A Short-Term Forecasting Model", The Review of Economics and Statistics", Vol. 46 (1964), 229-36.

GERSTENBERGER, W., "Zur Treffsicherheit und analytischen Bedeutung von qualitativen und quantitativen Planangaben", in O. Anderson (Ed.), Qualitative und quantitative Konjunkturindikatoren (Göttingen, 1983), 39-68.

HANSEN, G., "Sysifo-Model Equation System, Version March 1978" (mimeographed paper).

HAITOVSKY, Y., TREYZ, G., SU, V., Forecasts with Quarterly Macroeconometric Models, NBER (New York, 1974).

HILDRETH, C., LU, J.Y., "Demand Relations with Autocorrelated Disturbances", Research Bulletin 276, Michigan State University Agricultural Experiment Station, 1960.

KATONA, G., Psychological Analysis of Economic Behavior (New York, Toronto, London, 1951).

KÖNIG, H., NERLOVE, M., OUDIZ, G., "Die Analyse mikroökonomischer Konjunkturtestdaten mit log-linearen Wahrscheinlichkeitsmodellen: Eine Einführung", Ifo-Studien, Jg. 28 (1982).

MAGEE, S.P., "Prices, Incomes, and Foreign Trade", In: P.B. Kenen (Ed.), International Trade and Finance: Frontiers for Research (Cambrigde, 1975), 175-272.

MITCHELL, W.C., BURNS, A.F., "Statistical Indicators of Cyclical Revivals", in G.H. Moore (Ed.), Business Cycle Indicators. Volume I. (Princeton, 1961).

MODIGLIANI, F., COHEN, K., The Role of Anticipations and Plans in Economic Analysis and Forecasting, Studies in Business Expectations and Planning No. 4 (Urbana, 1957).

MODIGLIANI F., WEINGARTNER, H.M., "Forecasting Uses of Anticipatory Data on Investment and Sales", Quarterly Journal of Economics, Vol. 72 (1958), p.38.

MUTH, J.F., "Rational Expectations and the Theory of Price Movements", Econometrica, Vol.(29), 315-35.

NAGGL, W., "Kurzfristige Schätzfunktionen für den Warenhandel der Bundesrepublik Deutschland", Weltwirtschaftliches Archiv, Vol. 117 (1981), 687-705.

NAGGL, W., "Erklärung und Prognose der realen Anlageinvestitionen nach Wirtschaftsbereichen", Ifo-Studien, Vol. 28 (1982), 193-212.

NAGGl, W., "Prediction of Inventory Investment with the Use of Business Survey Data", Konjunkturpolitik, Vol. 29 (1983), 89-99.

NERB, G., "Unternehmerische Antizipationen über den Bedarf an Arbeitskräften", Mitteilungen aus der Arbeitsmarkt- und Berufsforschung, Vol.6 (1973), 203-13.

PINDYCKE, R.S., RUBINFELD, D.L., Econometric Models and Economic Forecasting (Auckland, 1981).

POSER, G., HECHELTJEN, P., "The Use of Anticipation Data in a Quarterly Econometric Model of the Federal Republic of Germany's Economy, Vortrag auf der 11. CIRET-Konferenz, London, 1973.

PRAET, P., "A Comparative Approach to the Measurement of Price Expectations", Research Report (Brussels, 1980).

THEIL, H., Economic Forecasts and Policy, 2. Aufl. (Amsterdam, 1961), 31ff.

THEIL, H., "On the Time Shape of Economic Microvariables and the Munich Business Test", Review of the International Statistical Institute, Vol. 20 (1952).

UEBE, G., "Eine Übersicht zu den gesamtwirtschaftlichen ökonometrischen Modellen für die Bundesrepublik Deutschland, DIW-Vierteljahreshefte, Jg. 1981, 134-46.

UEBE, G., HUBER, G., FISCHER, J., The macroeconometric model a selected bibliography of macroeconometric models (Farnborough, 1981).

ZARNOWITZ, V., "An Analysis of Annual and Multiperiod Quarterly Forecasts of Aggregate Income, Output, and the Price Level", Journal of Business, Vol. 52, No. 1 (1979), 1-33.

Improving Forecasts with Survey Indicators. An Empirical Test

Ph. A. Klein
Pennsylvania State University
University Park, Pa.

Introduction

Government officials, economists, and businessmen in virtually all countries are increasingly interested in improving their ability to forecast the many significant variables which are reflected in both the business cycle and in growth rates. While forecasting has made progress in recent years there is much room for improvement. A technique which has gained favor in the period since the Second World War involves the use of the results of surveys of enterprises and consumers. While traditional work in the United States concentrated on quantitative indicators and paid somewhat less attention to qualitative indicators, in Europe the situation has been reversed, with quantitative indicators being extensively studied only in the past decade.

It is clear that both types of indicators can be useful. For some years Geoffrey H. Moore and I have experimented with combining qualitative and quantitative indicators.

In our previous work with qualitative indicators, we have tended to concentrate on determining turning points in indicators and relating these to

---

I wish to thank Mr. Thomas De Hora and his colleagues at the European Economic Community for much help in getting this study launched. In particular I thank Mr. Christopher Smyth who very kindly made all the initial calculations. At the Center for International Business Cycle Research at Columbia University, Chantal Dubrin made the final calculations with her customary efficiency. Finally, Geoffrey H. Moore made many very valuable contributions to the study as it developed.

growth cycle turns, with the hope of discovering reasonably reliable qualitative leading indicators for turns in quantitative series.

Some of the major results for the countries included in this paper are summarized in Table 1. We have found that production levels have a roughly coincident timing pattern at growth cycle turning points, while the survey net balances dealing with production, when put in comparable form, tend to lag. That is, the cumulated survey net balances lag the actual production levels. Because first differences in variables lead the series being first differenced, analyzing the same series as changes in levels moves the timing <u>vis a vis</u> turns to either shorter lags or from lags to leads. The table suggests that we have relatively few quantitative and qualitative series both available for the same country, but for the two we did have (West Germany and the U.K.), the survey net balances still lagged the actual production changes at growth cycle turning points. But as noted the work summarized in Table 1 concentrates exclusively on comparisons of series at turning points. While we have indeed discovered some useful indicators in this way as have many others, the leads are of variable length and hence of somewhat restricted use for forecasting. Moreover, if one wishes to forecast changes in variables rather than levels, the quantitative series being forecast--for example, production--is invariably far smoother in level form than in the change form. This suggests that there will be many false signals in forecasting changes in production. Unhappily, what the forecaster is most interested in is what is most difficult--namely, forecasting changes in, for example, the production index.

It is often asserted that prospective survey questions enhance the potential for forecasting. Thus, a survey question which asks what entrepreneurs think will happen "in the coming months" or "over the next four months"

TABLE 1

SURVEY NET BALANCES, PRODUCTION EXPECTED VS. PRODUCTION INDEX
(Timing--Lead (-) or Lag (+) in Months)

	Analyzed as Levels[a]			Analyzed as Change in Levels[b]		
	P	T	P+T	P	T	P+T
Survey Net Balances vs. Growth Cycle Chronology						
W. Germany	+8	+8	+8	-9	-4	-4
France	+5	+8	+6	---	---	---
Italy	+9	+9	+9	---	---	---
United Kingdom	---	---	---	---	---	-8
Production Index vs. Growth Cycle Chronology						
W. Germany	0	+2	+1	-16	-6	-11
France	+1	-1	0	---	---	---
Italy	+2	-3	-1	---	---	---
United Kingdom	---	---	---	---	---	-7
Survey Net Balances vs. Production Index						
W. Germany	+7	+7	+7	+6	+6	+6
France	+2	+8	+5	---	---	---
Italy	+6	+13	+10	---	---	---
United Kingdom	---	---	---	---	---	+3

Source: P. A. Klein and G. H. Moore, "Monitoring Business Cycles in Market-Oriented Economies," Forthcoming, National Bureau of Economic Research.

[a] The cumulated survey net balance is matched with the production index level for the same month.

[b] The survey net balance is matched with the change in the production index over the same span of months.

is believed to have greater leading qualities than a retrospective question such as "what has been the trend over the past months" or over the past four months. Geoffrey Moore and I have studied a number of questions asked in business surveys in both the retrospective and prospective form. The results with respect to production and production expectations in three major countries are summarized in Table 2.[1] For the United Kingdom we show a similar comparison utilizing new order data. Specifically we showed the timing of the results of the survey net balances for two questions in the EEC business survey: What are production expectations for the months ahead (up, unchanged, or down) and what are the production trends in the recent past (up, unchanged, or down). We noted that during the period under review, with the exception of a three month lead at troughs in France and a two month lead at troughs in Italy, the prospective survey questions do not produce results which lead those of the retrospective survey question. Our examination of new order data for the U.K. taken from the CBI survey showed the same pattern. We concluded in both studies that entrepreneurs are heavily influenced by what has happened to them in the recent past in saying what they think will happen to them in the near future.

In earlier work with forecasting foreign trade we have used simple correlation coefficients as a measure of the quality of the results.[2] The special contribution of correlation techniques is that they give one information not only about the length of the leads (if any) at the critical turning points, but enable one to gain insight into the overall likelihood that a particular indicator tracks cyclical changes with a useful degree of fidelity throughout a given time period.

In the case of production, for example, one is interested primarily in forecasting changes in production from one point in time. Because turning

TABLE 2

TIMING OF PROSPECTIVE vs. RETROSPECTIVE SURVEY DATA, AT GROWTH CYCLE TURNS, FOUR COUNTRIES 1958- 1979

Country	Timing, Average Lead (-) or Lag (+), in months		
	Peaks	Troughs	All Turns
France			
Recent Production Trends	-8	-2	-5
Production Expectations	-2	-5	-4
Italy			
Recent Production Trends	-8	-6	-7
Production Expectations	-4	-8	-6
West Germany			
Recent Production Trends	-12	-2	-7
Production Expectations	-2	+3	+1
United Kingdom			
Trend New Orders - Past	-12	-10	-11
Future Trend, New Orders	-9	-9	-9

Sources: Production data for France, Italy and West Germany from P. A. Klein and Geoffrey H. Moore, "Analysis of EEC Entrepreneurial Surveys and their Relationship to a System of Qualitative Indicators," unpublished report to the EEC, October, 1979. U.K. data on new orders: P. A. Klein and G. H. Moore, "The CBI Entrepreneurial Surveys: An Aid in Analyzing U.K. Business Cycles," revision of paper presented at 14th CIRET Conference.

points occur but rarely, more often than not what one is hoping to do is guess correctly, or reasonably correctly, by how much more production will have increased or decreased in three, six, or nine months into the future. This means that in addition to correctly forecasting changes in direction, one is interested in assessing amplitudinal changes as accurately as possible. Thus an ideal indicator of production (which had therefore a perfect correlation with actual production changes N months hence) would not only predict the turning points correctly, but would enable one correctly to predict the degree of change in both directions (i.e., during expansions and contractions) over periods for which analysts wish to forecast.

Accordingly, we have adapted these correlation techniques to the effort to forecast changes in a significant quantitative economic measure by means of qualitative indicators, specifically survey net balances summarizing entrepreneurial estimates of changes in production.

While the prospective survey net balance results cannot, therefore, be regarded as offering forecasting advantages over retrospective questions, there are still potential gains to be had from utilizing survey results as proxies for quantitative indicators. Specifically, there are two potential gains to be achieved by utilizing qualitative indicators. First, the survey net balances are invariably smoother than the quantitative series to which they are related. This suggests, of course, that in replying to survey questions the entrepreneurs engage in "mental smoothing." If there are exogenous factors which will affect actual magnitudes the entrepreneurs cannot anticipate them and so do not take them into account (in the case of prospective questions) and in the case of retrospective questions the entrepreneurs make allowances for them. They answer what has been the trend of production, orders, etc. in the recent past, allowing for the bad weather, strikes, or the myriad other factors which might in fact cause these variables to change from week to week. The "trend" in production therefore asks for a smoothed response. The actual series, however, rarely produces results as smooth as the qualitative series to which it can be related.

A second advantage which attaches to qualitative indicators is that they are almost invariably available earlier than the quantitative indicators to which they point. Hence, even were there no lead in the turning points of survey indicators in relation to the quantitative variable being surveyed, the fact that survey results can be processed and made available to both analysts and entrepreneurs more rapidly than governments can process quantitative statistics and make available means that there is an intrinsic forecasting advantage to be found in the qualitative indocators. We shall explore this explicitly here.

A Note on Methodology

We have noted that a major advantage in utilizing survey net balances for forecasting changes in quantitative variables is that the survey net balances are basically far smoother than the quantitative series. This paper will show the results of our efforts to apply correlations to data on production, new orders, and inventories. We shall illustrate the methodological problems as well as the forecasting potential of the method by referring to data on production.

The European Economic Community Business Survey asks about 20,000 enterprises in the manufacturing sector each month whether their production expectations for the months ahead are up, unchanged, or down. The replies are published each month in the form of the well-known net balances-- that is, the percentage giving positive less the percentage giving negative responses.

The initial problem is to relate the survey replies to changes in industrial production so as to consider the accuracy of the surveys. The term "the months ahead" is ambiguous, but we have adopted the convention of assuming it refers to the next four months. The Confederation of British Industry, which has conducted a survey of its own for many years, and which has conducted the survey for the EEC since Britain's entry into the Common Market, does in fact ask its own question in this form ("What are the expected trends in production for the next four months--up, same, down?").

The most obvious technique for relating survey results to actual production changes would be to take identical time spans--a January survey, asking for expected change in production over the next four months refers to production changes expected between February and May, a four month span. One could relate this to the expected change in the actual production index over the same four month span. On the face of it relating the percent change in the production index over four months to the results of the survey net balances asking for a change over a four month period ought to produce reasonable results. The difficulty is that the changes in the production index are so volatile--are, therefore, so full of irregular fluctuations as well as those which entrepreneurs can be expected to anticipate--that the correlation results can be expected to come out very badly.

It is essential, therefore, to attempt to smooth the actual changes in industrial production in order to find a production change series with which one may reasonably look for a relation to the survey net balances results. We have experimented with several ways to reduce the volatility in the production index changes for forecasting purposes. Because what we are looking for is evidence that the survey net balance results are useful in forecasting cyclical changes one technique we have tried is to compute the ratio of irregular (I) to cyclical (C) change for different spans, and to find the span which makes the I/C ratio closest to that which is found in the survey net balances, when the latter are analyzed in their original form.[3] This has the advantage of not smoothing the already quite smooth survey results. The I/C ratio can, of course, always be reduced for any time series by subjecting the series to some moving average. The well-known "months for cyclical dominance" (MCD) calculation smoothes a series by up to six months. MCD is the number of months that must elapse on average before cyclical changes are larger than irregular. In experiments with the production changes for Italy, Germany, the United Kingdom, and France, we found that in the case of the survey net balance for production changes the I/C ratio was below unity after two months in Italy, but even sooner in the case of the other three countries. In the case of the more volatile actual production index the I/C ratio does not get to unity for a number of months (Italy--5, France not even by 12, Germany after 4, and the U.K. after 5 months). Were we to utilize moving averages which varied according to the MCD for each series and each country one could be certain that the resulting forecasts would be based on series sufficiently smooth to reflect primarily cyclical changes. However, it would involve smoothing both the survey results and the actual quantitative series and this reduces the forecasting potential for the survey series.

Instead we have opted for calculating the I/C ratios for the production index changes, computed for spans of one to twelve months, and searching for the span which produces the I/C ratio nearest to that found in the unsmoothed survey net balances. The smoothing required in the quantitative production index, together with the relevant I/C ratios are as follows:

TABLE 3

I/C Ratios, Production, Four Countries[a]

Country	Survey Net Balances, Original Data	Production Index
Italy	2.23	2.10 (2)
France	1.09	1.10 (6)
Germany	1.49	1.36 (3)
United Kingdom	1.47	1.45 (4)

Note: The smoothing span in months, applied to the four month changes in the production index, is shown in parentheses.

[a] Source: Appendix Tables 1-4.

It will be seen that the I/C ratios are indeed quite close for the two series in the case of each country, but the fact that they are not below unity means that some irregular variation has not been suppressed. Nevertheless, because irregular variation in fact does occur, it is not inappropriate to ask, in effect, in the face of all that occurs in the real world, including irregular variation, how good a forecasting job is done by the business surveys?

Having smoothed the production index in this way, the primary question posed was how good a job the survey net balances do in tracking changes in industrial production, and how much lead time do the surveys give us? This goes beyond our previous work which was restricted to estimating leads at turning points. We conducted the test by utilizing ordinary least squares and searching for the highest correlation between the changes in the surveys and the changes in actual production. We searched by relating the survey results to the actual changes ten months before to ten months after the zero month. Additionally we examined the rate at which the correlations deteriorated. As is always the case there is a trade-off between the length of the lead and the accuracy of the forecast. The question we asked concerned the nature of the trade-off in each country and by how much one could increase the lead with only a moderate reduction in accuracy. In the process of conducting this experiment the usual significance tests were calculated and used in evaluating the results.

Finally, we factored in the difference in the publication lag between survey results and actual production changes. When this is added to the results of the correlation analysis the potential lead time over which the forecasts might anticipate the actual production changes, as well as the historical accuracy of the forecasts, could be assessed.

The forecasting usefulness of this procedure, though complicated, is illustrated for Italy in Figure 1. Let us assume we are dealing with a survey taken in month 6, for the four months ahead--thus the survey results are placed in month 10. It happens that the highest correlation in Italy is found by relating that survey result with the quantitative change ending in month 7. The quantitative series is the change in the production index calculated over four month spans, the resulting change having been smoothed by the two month period which showed the I/C ratio closest to that in the survey changes. Hence the two month moving average of the production changes ending in month 6 and month 7 is placed in month 7.

We know that the survey results for a survey taken in month 6 will be available in month 7. Even though this appears to vitiate the forecasting

FIGURE 1

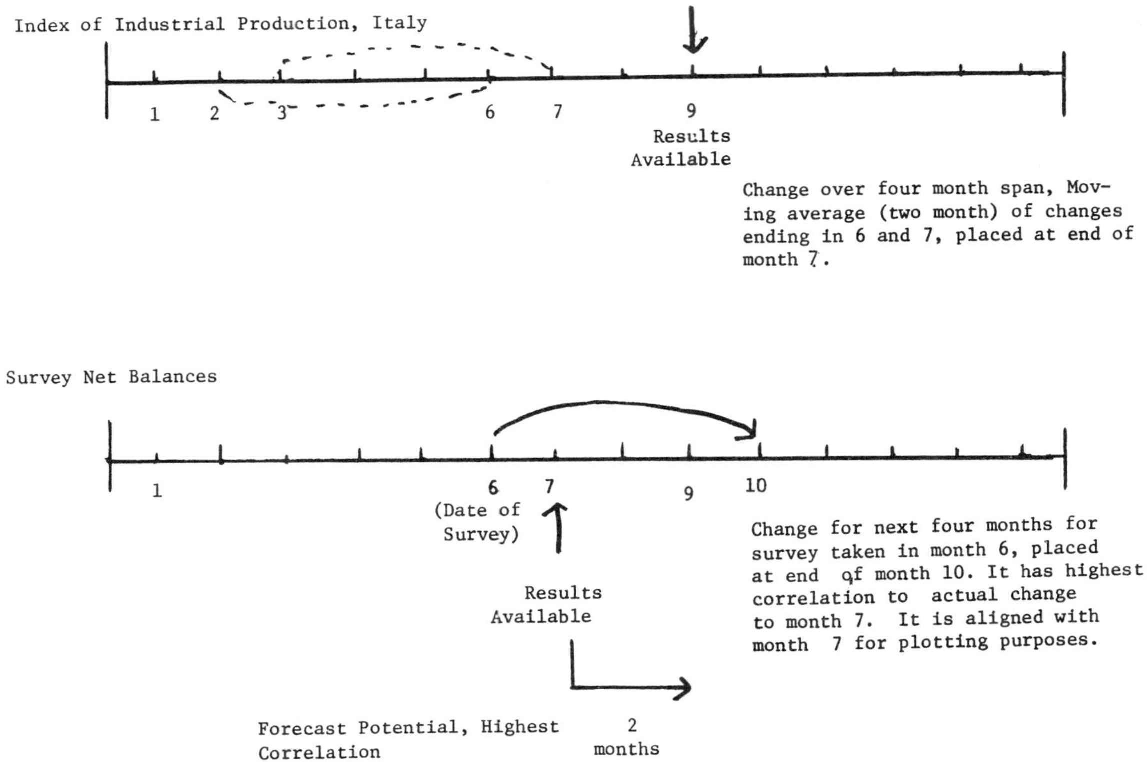
Index of Industrial Production, Italy
1
2
3
6
7
9
Results Available
Change over four month span, Moving average (two month) of changes ending in 6 and 7, placed at end of month 7.
Survey Net Balances
1
6
7
9
10
(Date of Survey)
Results Available
Change for next four months for survey taken in month 6, placed at end of month 10. It has highest correlation to actual change to month 7. It is aligned with month 7 for plotting purposes.
Forecast Potential, Highest Correlation
2 months

potential because the survey change ending in month 10 yields the highest correlation with the quantitative change ending in month 7, no conclusion can be reached without allowing for the time that elapses before the actual production data become available--in the case of Italian production this is six to eight weeks.[4] If we assume eight weeks this makes the actual change in the production index to month 7 available in month 9. Accordingly we may conclude that the survey results enable us to forecast production changes over four month periods by some two months before the actual production data will be available. If we settle for the longest lead with a correlation still reasonably near the highest, we can increase the forecast for Italian production changes by about two more months. How useful the forecast will be depends on the actual correlation coefficients, discussed for all four countries in the next section.

Before turning to the findings, one final comment is in order. Clearly forecasting changes in production constitutes one of the more difficult uses to which survey data can be put because the actual changes are so volatile. Were we to concentrate on forecasting levels of production, the actual series would be far smoother, and the correlation coefficients could be expected to be correspondingly higher for the behavior of the survey results. Entrepreneurs clearly are forecasting trends and not anticipating the myriad irregular events which they could not be expected to know about *ex ante*. A final way, therefore, to consider the forecasting potential of the surveys is to make the actual production changes approximate more closely the behavior which entrepreneurs can be expected to anticipate. We have attempted to do this by calculating the percentage changes in the index of industrial production by a method that reduces the irregularities more effectively than the method described above. We shall show the results of correlation of the survey results of production expectations over four months with the actual production changes, therefore, smoothed so as to approximate what entrepreneurs might be expected to anticipate.

Survey Results for Production Expectations

Utilizing the methodology outlined above we have examined the forecasting potential for the survey net balances dealing with production expectations for the four largest countries in the European Economic Community--France, Italy, the German Federal Republic, and the United Kingdom. Data utilized covered the period 1968-1982 for the first three countries and 1962-1982 for the United Kingdom.

We shall present first the results for each country based on efforts to correlate the production expectations over the next four months with changes in the production index over four months adjusted so as to smooth the production index to give the closest I/C ratios for the two production series in each country. The results for all four countries are summarized in Table 4 and are shown in Charts I-IV.[5] In the case of all the charts the changes are charted with the necessary alignment to reflect the best lead or lag found in conducting the search by means of ordinary least squares analysis. In each case, the charts show the surveys "lagging," but this needs to be interpreted with care. In relating production changes over the next four months to actual changes over a four month period we have found in each case that the survey change with the highest correlation with an actual change is for a period later than the quantitative change (Table 4, col. 4). However, finding that a survey of expected production changes four months hence is most closely correlated with an actual change three months before the end of the survey period means in effect that the highest correlation is for a period one month _after_ the survey month (Table 4, col. 4).

What may we conclude? With the exception of Germany, none of the "highest" correlations are above .50. Moreover, the entrepreneurs responding to the surveys appear to have a tendency to "forecast the present"-- that is, their attitude of what is apt to happen some months hence reflects strongly what in fact _is_ happening to their production changes at roughly the time of the survey (the highest correlations are usually with the change ending in the month after the survey month). These results echo the earlier timing analysis summarized in Table 2. This does not by any means mean that the survey results are not useful in forecasting. It is important to remember that the survey results have not been smoothed. In each case the survey results are smoother than the quantitative index even after it has been smoothed as described earlier. The moving averages used in smoothing the production indexes are three months for three countries, and four in the case of Germany. Inspection of the actual production changes so smoothed with the survey estimates shows how very volatile changes in the production index are.

If column 3 in Table 4 suggests that surveys of production expectations do not produce a significant lead over what in fact actually happens to production changes, the forecasting potential of the surveys cannot be assessed without factoring in the publication (or availability) lags in both the surveys (one month at most) and the quantitative series. (The latter lags are shown at the bottom of Table 4.) When these time periods are accounted for we find that using survey net balances as proxies for changes in production enables the forecaster to get an idea of what will happen to production changes from three weeks (Germany) to two months (Italy and the

TABLE 4

FORECASTING POTENTIAL, EEC SURVEY OF PRODUCTION EXPECTATIONS VS. ACTUAL CHANGES IN INDEX OF INDUSTRIAL PRODUCTION, FOUR COUTNRIES, 1968-1982.

Country (1)	Change Over 4 Months, Actual Index of Production, Moving Average of: (mos.) (2)	Timing, Survey Results Lead (-) or Lag (+) vs. Production-Actual Change As of Survey Month (3)	As of End Month Period (4)	R^2 (5)	Mean Absolute Errors (6)	Durbin-Watson Coeff. (7)	Surveys-Forecasting Potential, Including Publication Lags for Surveys,[a] Production Index[a] (mos.) (8)
Italy	2	-1	+3	.20	3.05	.51	2
France	6	-1	+3	.42	1.38	.32	1 1/2
Germany	3	0	+4	.59	1.20	.46	3/4
U.K.	4	-1	+3	.44	1.23	.45	2

[a]Survey results are available no later than the month following the surveys. Publication lags for the index of industrial production in these countries as reported by the OECD are:

Italy -- 6-8 weeks (assumed to be 8 in the table above)
France -- 6 weeks
Germany -- 6-7 weeks (assumed to be 7 in the table above)
U.K. -- 7-8 weeks (assumed to be 8 in the table above)

CHART I. Forecasting Potential of Business Surveys, Production Expectations vs. Actual Change in Industrial Production Index, Italy, 1968-1982, Highest Correlations

R^2--.20

Actual Production Changes--2 Month Moving Average

Survey Changes--3 Month Lag

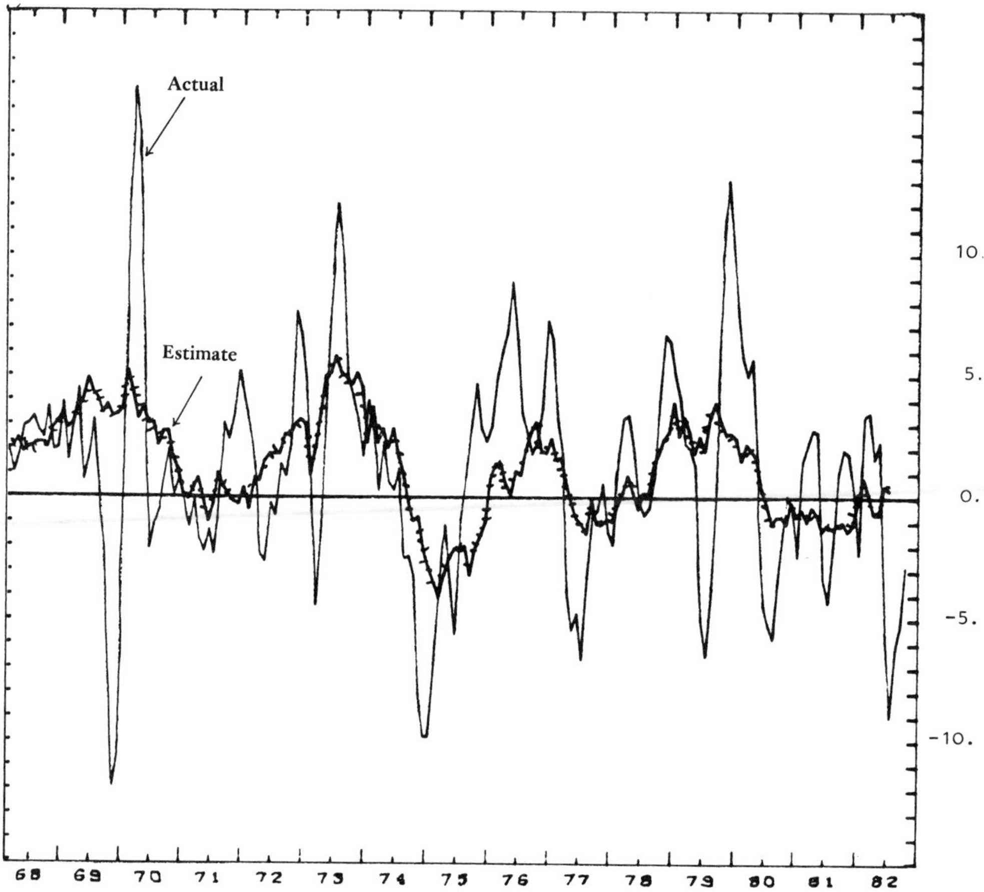

CHART II. Forecasting Potential, of Business Syrveys, Production Expectations vs. Actual Change in Industrial Production Index, France, 1968-1982, Highest Correlations

R^2--.42

Actual Production Changes--6 Month Moving Average

Survey Change--3 Month Lag

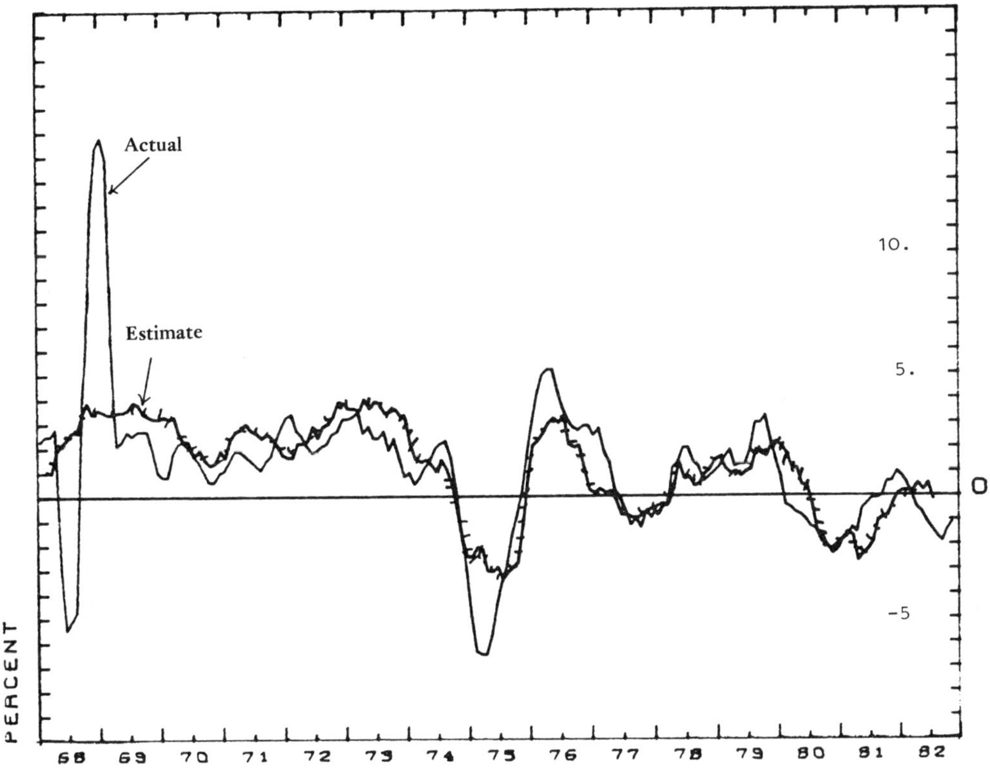

CHART III. Forecasting Potential of Business Survey, Production Expectations vs. Actual Change in Industrial Production Index, Germany, 1968-1982, Highest Correlations

R^2--.59

Actual Production Changes--3 Month Moving Average

Survey Changes--4 Month Lag

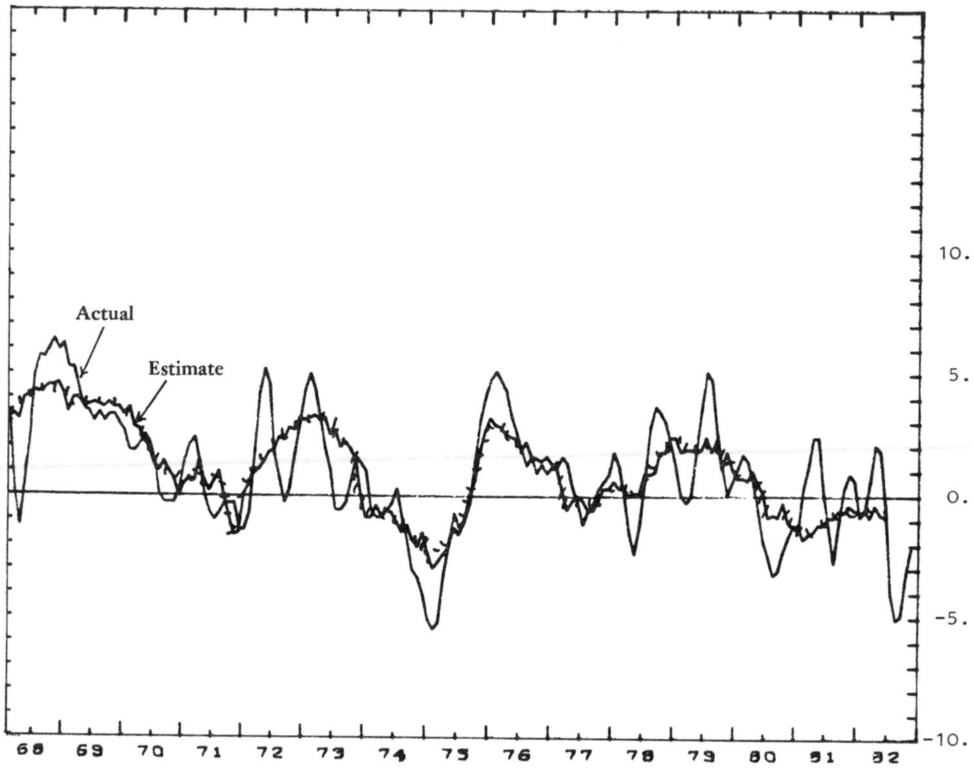

CHART IV. Forecasting Potential of Business Surveys, Production Expectations, vs. Actual Change in Industrial Production Index, United Kingdom, 1965-1982, Highest Correlations

R^2--.44

Actual Production Changes--4 Month Moving Average

Survey Change--3 Month Lag

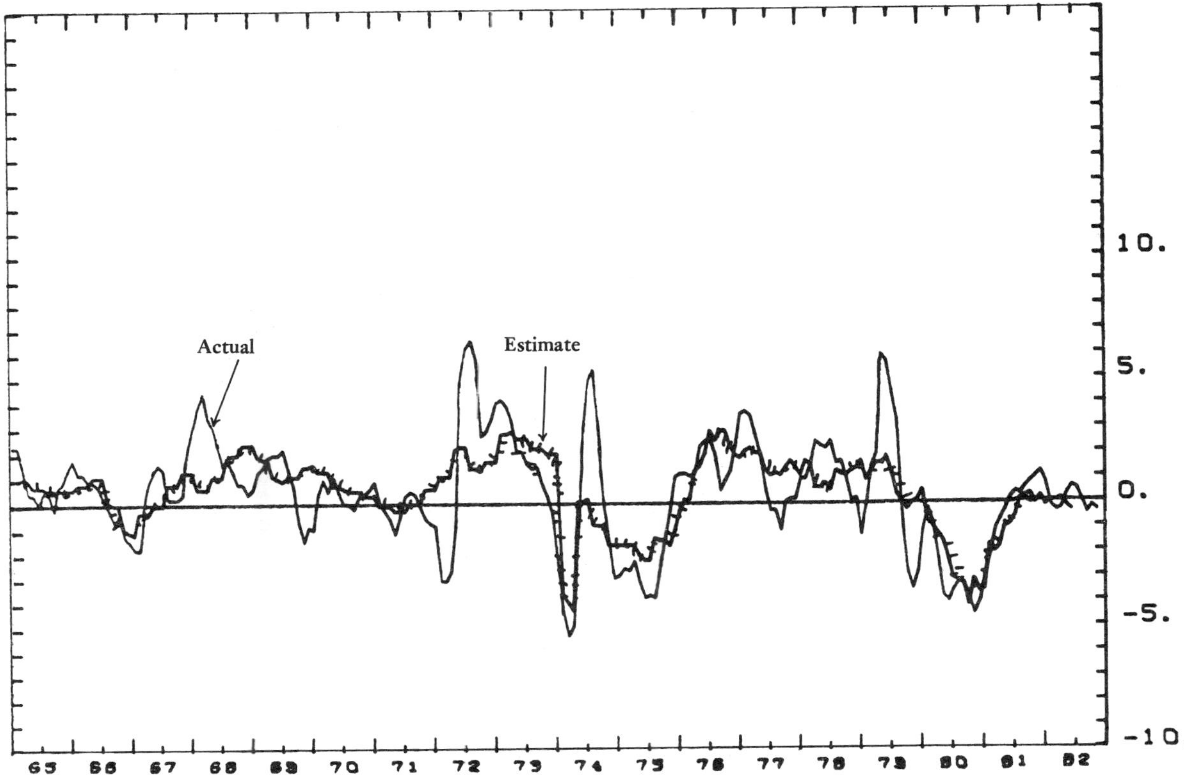

United Kingdom) earlier than the actual data on production changes will be available.

What entrepreneurs are likely to consider in responding to a survey involves their view of the trend of production in coming months. This as we have previously noted is anticipated production change which has been, therefore, "mentally smoothed" by the respondents. It is useful to see how much of the failure to forecast month-to-month changes in anticipated production over the next four months is due to the failure of entrepreneurs' expectations to include the myriad and often aberrant factors which produce high volatility in actual month-to-month changes in production over four month spans.

That this is a more accurate view of what the survey net balances reflect is suggested by findings shown in Table 5. This is based on the comparison of the survey results to the changes in the production index calculated by comparing the current month's index with the average index over a twelve month span ending six months ago. This is called a 12 month smoothed rate of change. It appears to approximate more closely the expected changes reported by entrepreneurs.

Here the real usefulness of the surveys comes into its own and can be shown graphically. The percent of actual production change captured by the surveys utilized as proxies for the not-yet-available quantitative data range from a high of 84% for Germany to a low of 50% for Italy, still high in comparison with our earlier findings (Table 5). The findings are shown in Charts V-VIII. The increased lead time given by using the surveys as opposed to waiting for the availability of actual production changes is more than two months for every country except the U.K., where it is still one month.

TABLE 5

FORECASTING POTENTIAL, EEC SURVEY OF PRODUCTION EXPECTATIONS VS. ACTUAL CHANGES IN INDEX OF INDUSTRIAL PRODUCT SMOOTHED OVER TWELVE MONTHS, FOUR COUNTRIES, 1968-1982

Country (1)	Timing, Survey Results Lead (-) or Lag (+) vs. Production-Actual Change: As of Survey Month (2)	As of End Month Period (3)	R^2 (4)	Mean Absolute Errors (5)	Durbin-Watson Coeff. (6)	Surveys-Forecasting Potential, Including Publication Lags for Surveys, Production Index[a] (mos.) (7)
Italy	-2	+2	.50	3.33	.54	-3
France	-2	+2	.59	2.38	1.03	-2 1/2
Germany	-2	+2	.84	1.69	.80	-2 3/4
U.K.	0	+4	.67	1.86	.63	-1

[a]Surveys are assumed available one month after the survey month. Actual production changes are available as shown in Table 4.

CHART V. Forecasting Potential, EEC Surveys of Production Expectations vs. Actual Changes in Index of Industrial Production, Twelve-Months Smoothed, Italy, 1968-1982

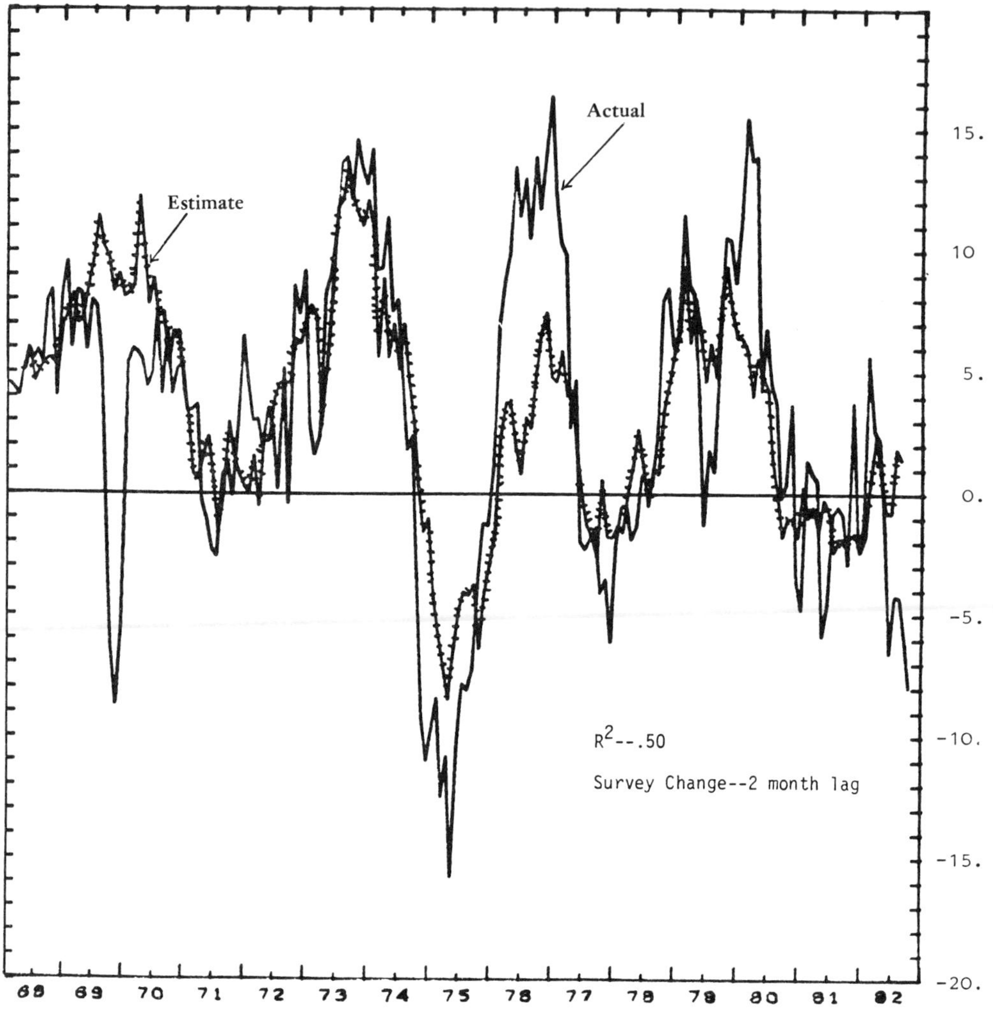

CHART VI. Forecasting Potential, EEC Surveys of Production Expectations vs. Actual Changes in Index of Industrial Production, Twelve-Months Smoothed, France, 1968-1982

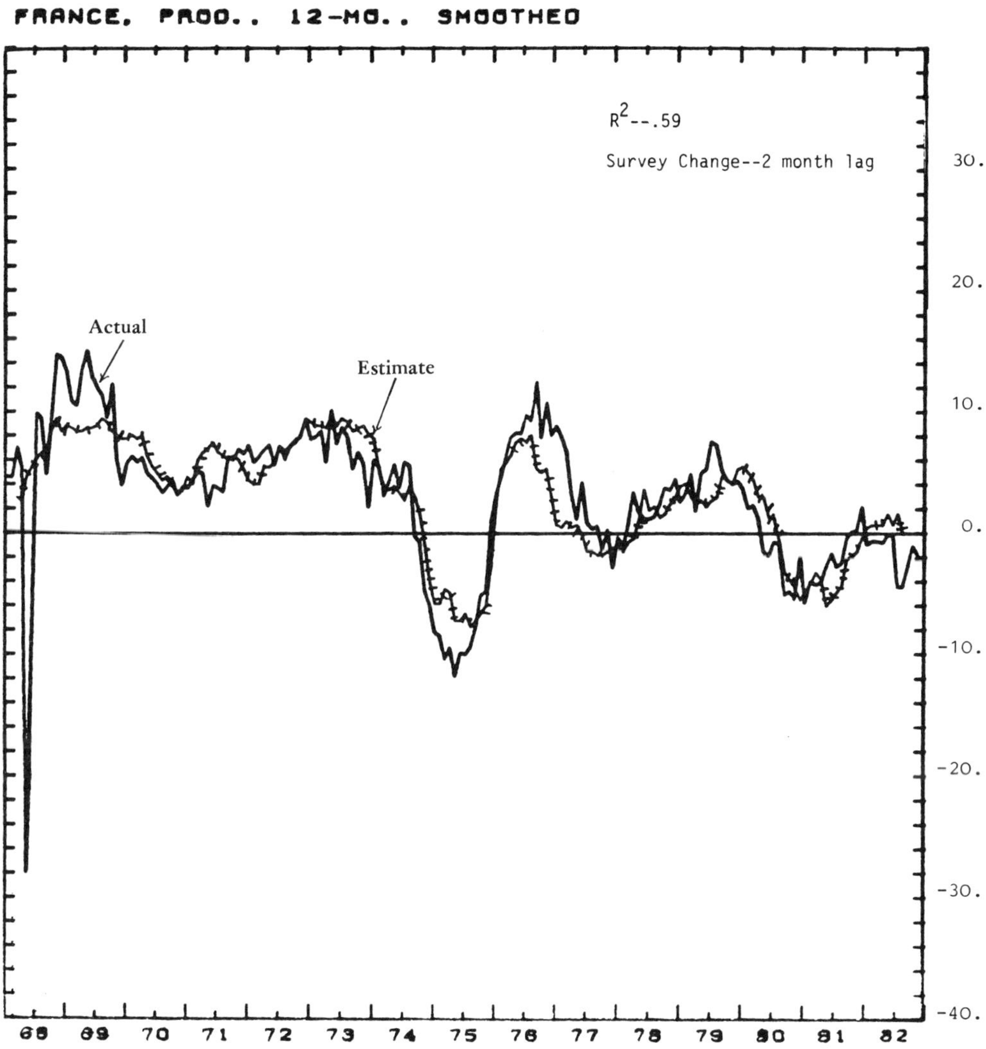

CHART VII. Forecasting Potential, EEC Surveys of Production Expectations vs. Actual Changes in Index of Industrial Production, Twelve-Months Smoothed, Germany, 1968-1982

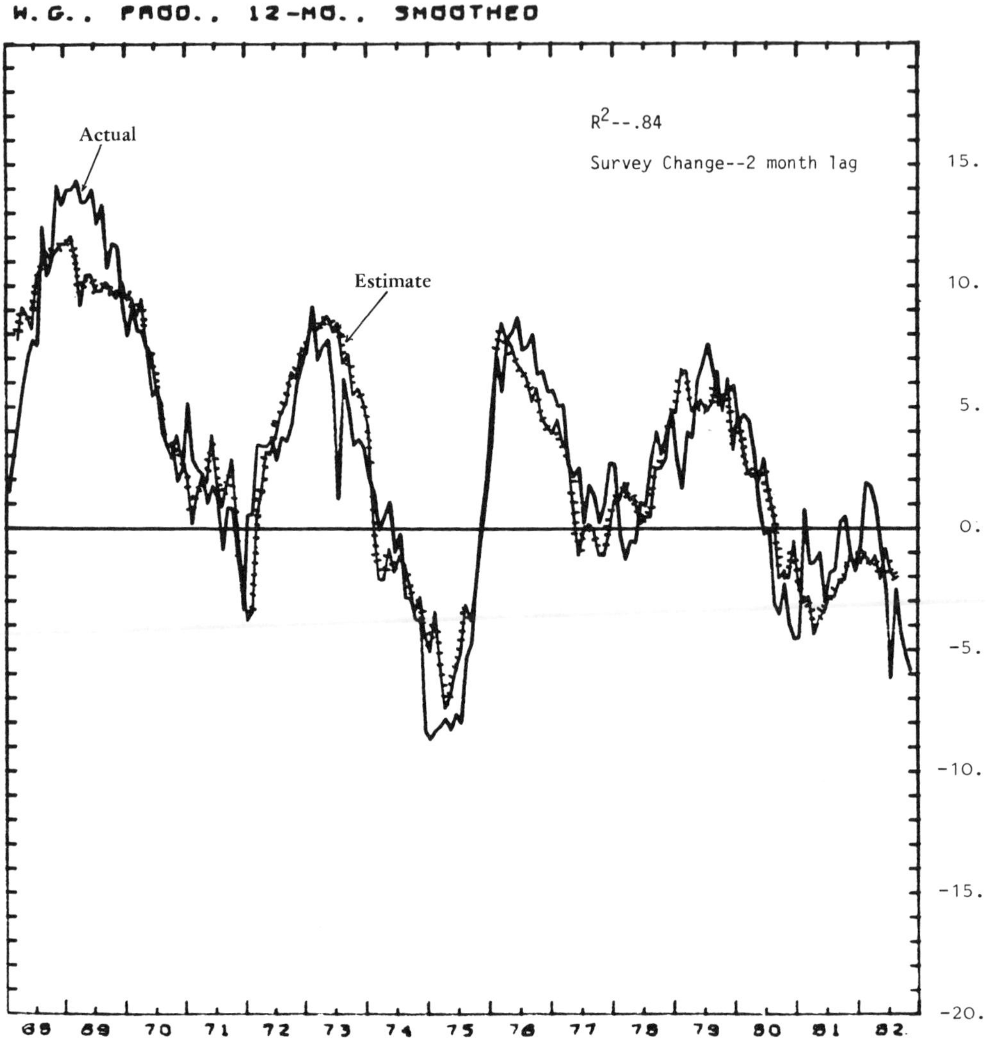

CHART VIII. Forecasting Potential, EEC Surveys of Production Expectations vs. Actual Changes in Index of Industrial Production, Twelve-Months Smoothed, United Kingdom, 1968-1982

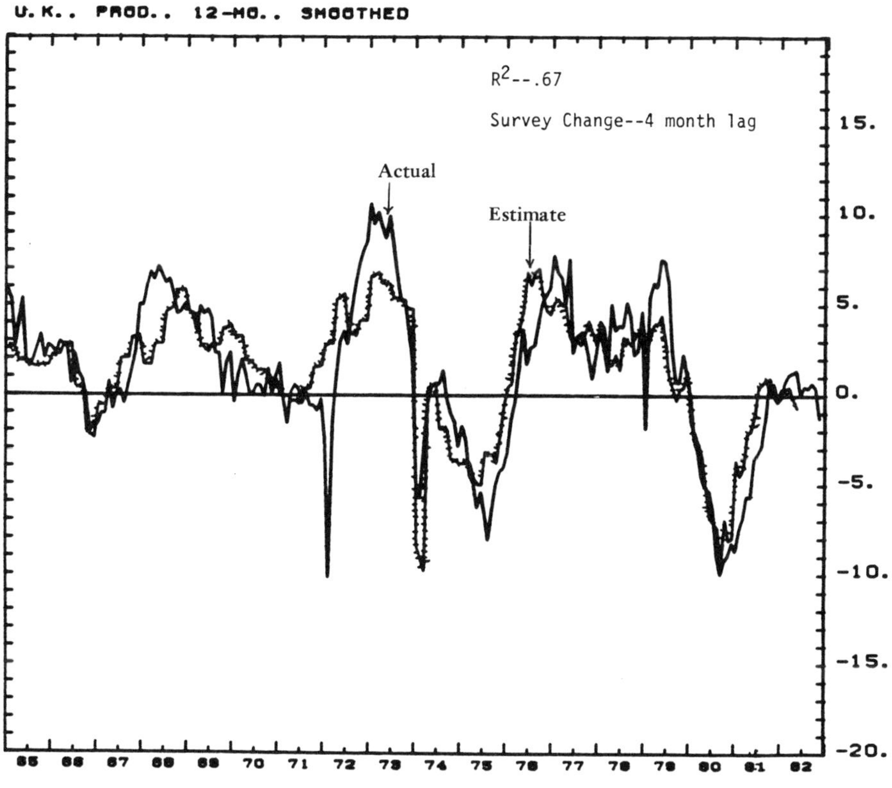

This comparison suggests that the entrepreneurs do a reasonably good job of anticipating what they can be expected to forecast--the overall trend of production changes over the months ahead.

Survey Results for New Orders

We do not have as complete a set of comparable quantitative and qualitative indicators for other variables but we can examine the behavior of new orders for the United Kingdom and for the Federal Republic of Germany.

In the case of the EEC survey of new orders we do not face the difficulty of having to cope with the spans of time covered as was the case with production expectations. The survey question asks whether order books are above or below normal. The survey net balances, therefore, are in effect a reflection of the entrepreneurs' view of their order book levels, mentally adjusted for trend (presumably "normal" would grow to larger amounts in a growing economy).

The problems in utilizing the survey results to monitor changes in new orders may be illustrated by reference to the German experience shown in Chart IX. The middle curve shows the monthly level of order books relative to normal as reflected in the survey net balances of entrepreneurs' replies. In order to relate this question appropriately to the quantitative series reporting the level of new orders during a month, it is necessary to take the first difference of the levels shown in the middle curve. That is, since the survey asks about "order books," which represent unfilled orders, the first differences of the survey net balances presumably represent the net flow of orders onto the books (new orders minus sales). This series is shown at the bottom of Chart IX. It is one of the few series on survey data which appears to be more volatile than its nearest quantitative equivalent (shown in the top curve of Chart IX).

CHART IX. New Orders, Investment Goods Industries, Volume Index, Survey Results of Level of Order Books, and Change in Survey Results, Germany, 1968-1982.

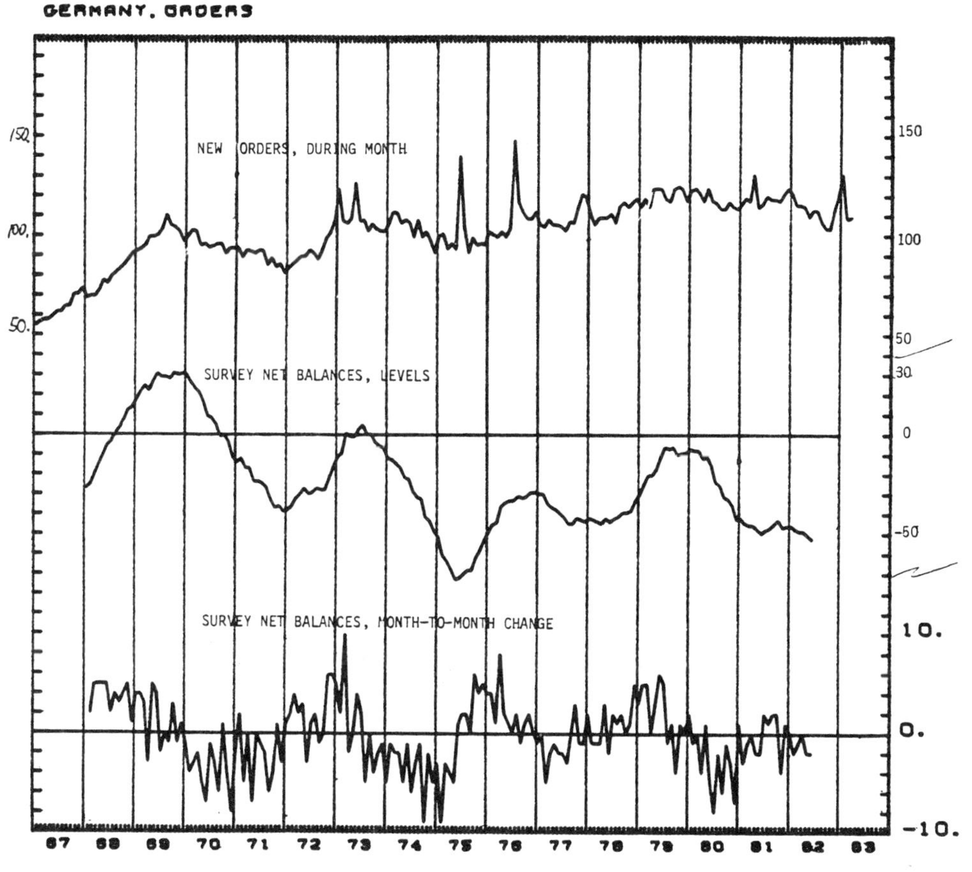

The difficulty in using the surveys to forecast actual changes in new orders is that the surveys (either in level form or in first difference form) reflect cycles more fully than does the quantitative series. Appendix Table 7 shows the results of searching for the highest correlation between the two. (Accordingly, we have not used the surveys to estimate orders as we did for production). Thus one must conclude that the chief virtue of the surveys must be that there is a publication lag of but one month for the surveys, compared to an eight week lag in data on German new orders as reported by the Bundesbank. This means that the surveys can be utilized as a proxy for new orders for a month before the latter become available. However, their ability to monitor actual month-to-month changes in new orders is very small.

The U.K. experience is summarized in the same manner in Chart X. The results of searching for a lag or lead with a useful correlation (Appendix Table 7) is similarly discouraging. The publication lag for U.K. data in new orders is a bit longer, however (ten to twelve weeks) with the result that there is a place for the survey data in forecasting changes in new orders. Again, however, the error in such forecasts is likely to be large indeed.

These results for the U.K. can be compared to our earlier results to underscore the importance of the working of these questions. The Confederation of British Industry did not, in its surveys prior to 1978, ask whether order books are above or below normal, but rather whether the trend in the past four months has been up, the same, or down. The change in the volume index of new orders was calculated as a change over a four month span in our earlier work, and it was both a volatile series and did not reflect cycles very much more sensitively than does the version of the series shown

CHART X. New Orders, Engineering Industries, Volume Index, Survey Results of Level of Order Books, and Change in Survey Results, United Kingdom, 1975-1982.

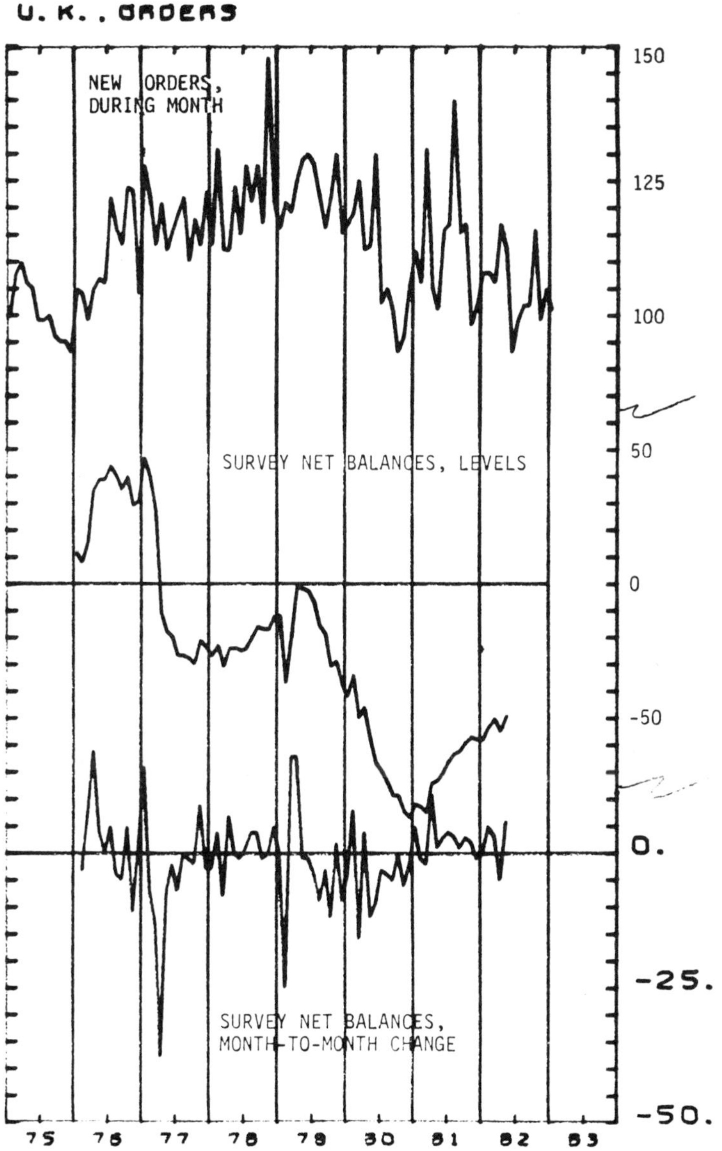

in Chart X. However, survey results were much more sensitive than those shown at the top of Chart X, as can be seen by examining Chart XI. According to Table 6 the CBI survey results lagged the new order volume index at turning points by an average of five months. (We did not compute the correlation coefficient.) The superior cyclical behavior of the previous survey results is partly the result of the way the question was worded, and partly that the question referred to a four month trend rather than to month-to-month changes. Again, however, the virtue of the surveys--their smoothness and prompt availability--is underscored.

Survey Results, Finished Goods Inventories

The final variable which we have attempted to examine to determine the forecasting potential of survey net balances has to do with inventories. In addition to the EEC survey results we have quantitative inventory data for Germany and for the United Kingdom. The EEC survey question asks entrepreneurs to state whether stocks of finished goods for the month were above normal, normal, or below normal. We can test the forecasting potential of this question in Germany, where there is a series available on inventory change, and for the United Kingdom, where there is a series available on the change in stocks and work in progress. As the latter suggests it covers more than finished goods and this is also the case for the German series. Finished goods inventories typically lag other measures of inventory at growth cycle turning points and the lack of correspondence in coverage between the qualitative and quantitative indicators needs to be kept in mind.

Our approach can be illustrated with the German experience (Chart XIII). We have assumed that when entrepreneurs judge the level of inventories they implicitly relate them to sales, so that what they are really telling the

TABLE 6

TIMING CBI SURVEY NET BALANCES, NEW ORDERS, TREND IN PAST FOUR MONTHS vs. CHANGE IN VOLUME INDEX, NEW ORDERS, FOUR MONTH SPAN

Turning Points Survey Net Balances New Orders, Trend in Past Four Months (1)		Change in Volume Index, New Orders, Four Month Span (2)		Lead (-) or Lag (+) in Month - Surveys vs. Volume Index (3) (1 vs. 2)	
P	T	P	T	P	T
12/59		9/59		+3	
	12/61		6/61		+6
		2/63		--	
			2/65		--
4/64		--			
	12/66		--		
4/68		2/68		+2	
	4/71		1/71		+3
8/73		7/73		+1	
	2/75		8/74		+6
11/76		5/76		+6	
	5/78		3/77		+14

Average Lead (-) or Lag (+):		P	T
	at P	+3	
	at T		+7
	at P + T	+5	

CHART XI

NET BALANCE OF NEW ORDERS, TREND IN PAST FOUR MONTHS,
CBI SURVEY, UNITED KINGDOM, 1959-79

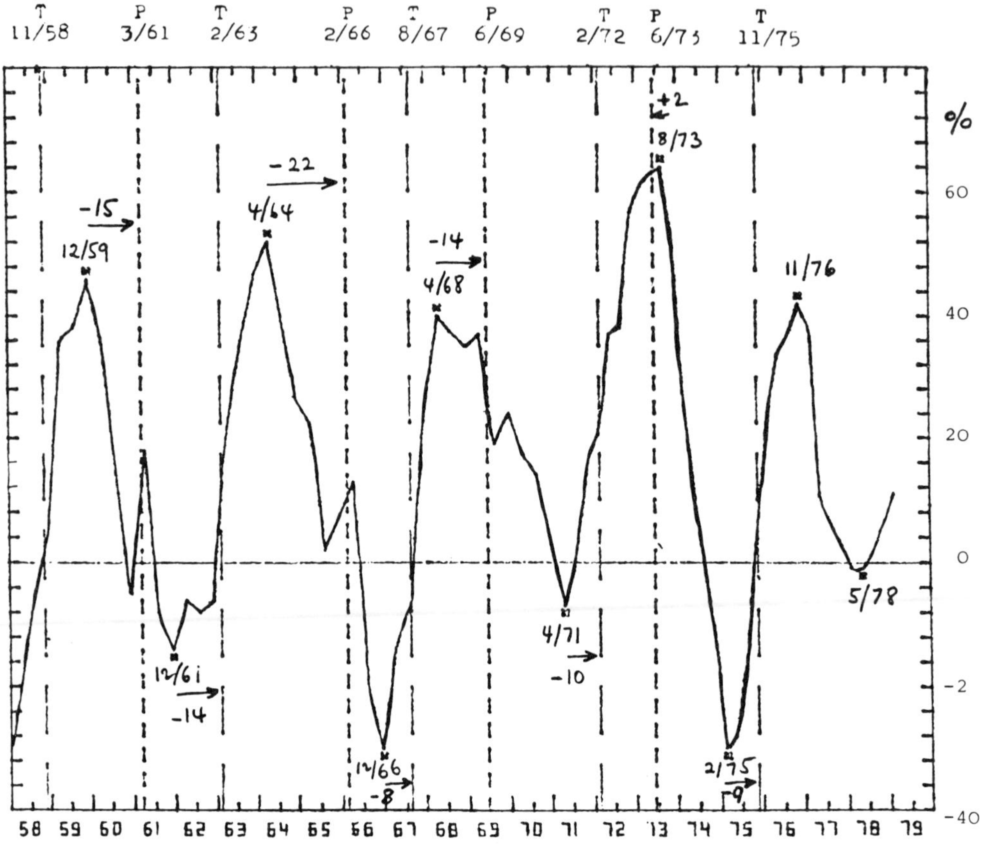

Data points are plotted in the mid-month of the four-month interval. Vertical lines are peaks and troughs in the United Kingdom growth cycle. Arrows indicate length of leads (-) or lags (+), in months.

Source: Industrial Trends Survey, Confederation of British Industry.

CHART XII

CHANGE IN VOLUME INDEX OF NEW ORDERS, FOUR MONTH SPAN, UNITED KINGDOM, 1958-79

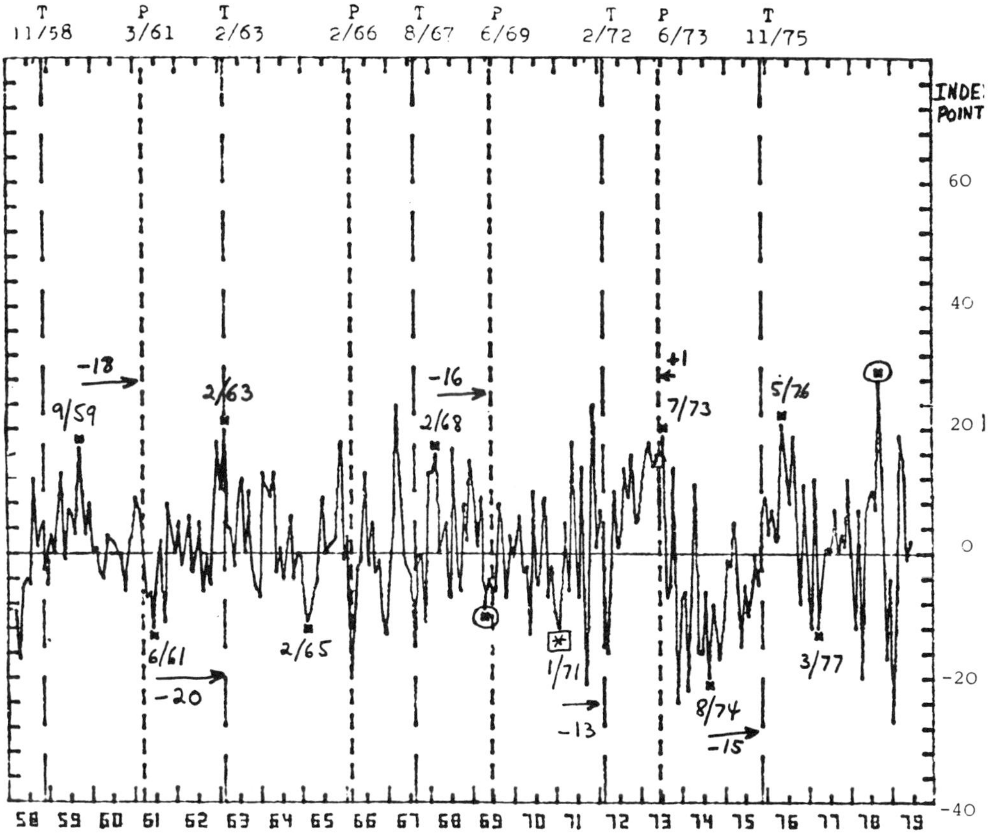

Data points are plotted in the mid-month of the four-month interval. Vertical lines are peaks and troughs in the United Kingdom growth cycle. Arrows indicate length of leads (-) or lags (+), in months.

Source: Central Statistical Office. Data are adjusted for seasonal variations.

CHART XIII. Inventory/Sales Ratio and Survey Results, Level of Finished Goods Inventories, Germany 1968-82.

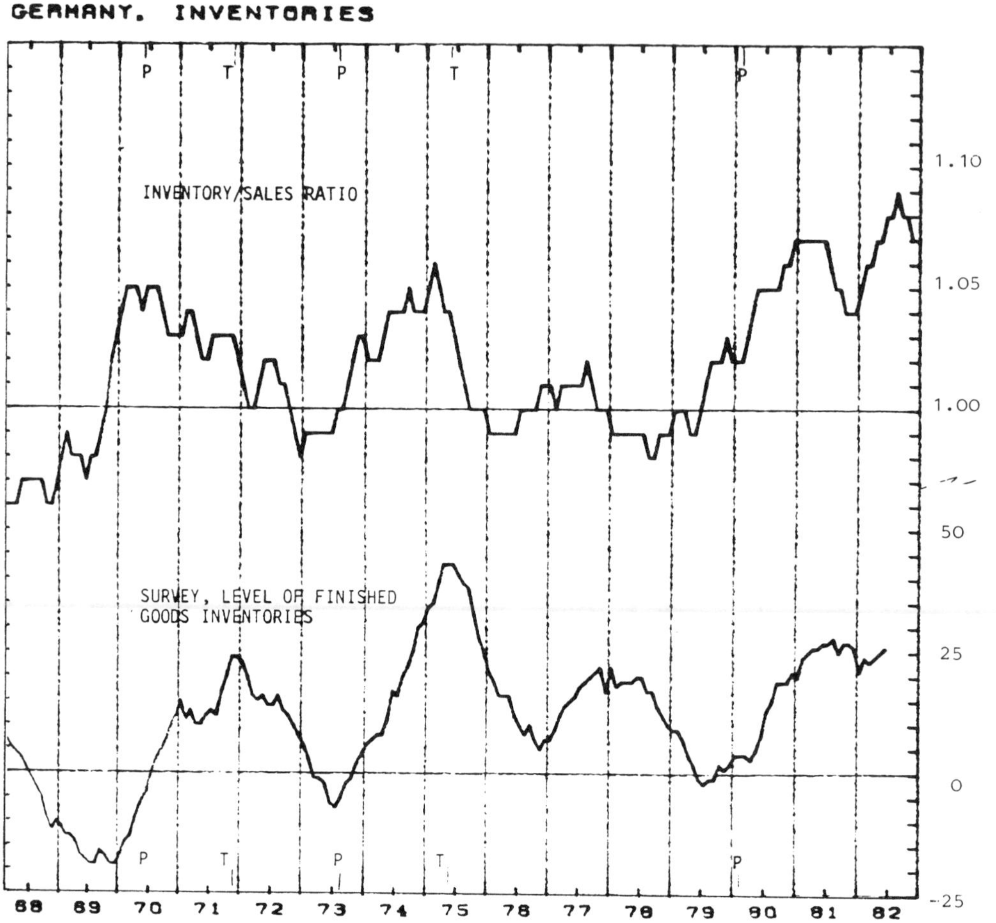

survey is whether their inventories relative to their sales are above or below normal. We have therefore calculated the inventory to sales ratio monthly and related it to the survey net balances reporting on the normality of inventories.[6]

Chart XIII suggests clearly that this method of interpreting the survey question dealing with inventories is appropriate and that the two are indeed closely related. However, the search for the highest correlation (see Appendix Table 8) suggests that the survey net balances will not be useful in forecasting the inventory/sales ratio. The highest correlation occurs at the month where the surveys are lagged ten months behind the inventory/sales ratio. Part of the lag is due to the concentration of the survey question exclusively on finished goods inventories, as noted above. Because data on German inventories are available about ten weeks after the period to which they refer, this means they lag the availability of the survey results by only a month or so. Therefore, the survey results will not help in forecasting the inventory/sales ratio. Were inventories broken into raw materials, work in progress, and finished goods, however, the survey results would no doubt not lag the quantitative ratio by this long.

Turning to the U.K. experience, Chart XIV suggests that the correspondence between the estimated inventory/sales ratio and the survey results is less close, and this is confirmed in Appendix Table 8, which suggests not only that the survey results lag the inventory/sales ratio by sixteen months for the highest correlation, but that this method captures only about half the monthly changes in the ratio. The publication lag for U.K. changes in industrial stocks is only seven to eight weeks, so that this lag will not offset very much of the lag in the survey results behind the actual

CHART XIV. Inventory/Sales Ratio and Survey Results, Level of Inventories, United Kingdom, 1975-1982.

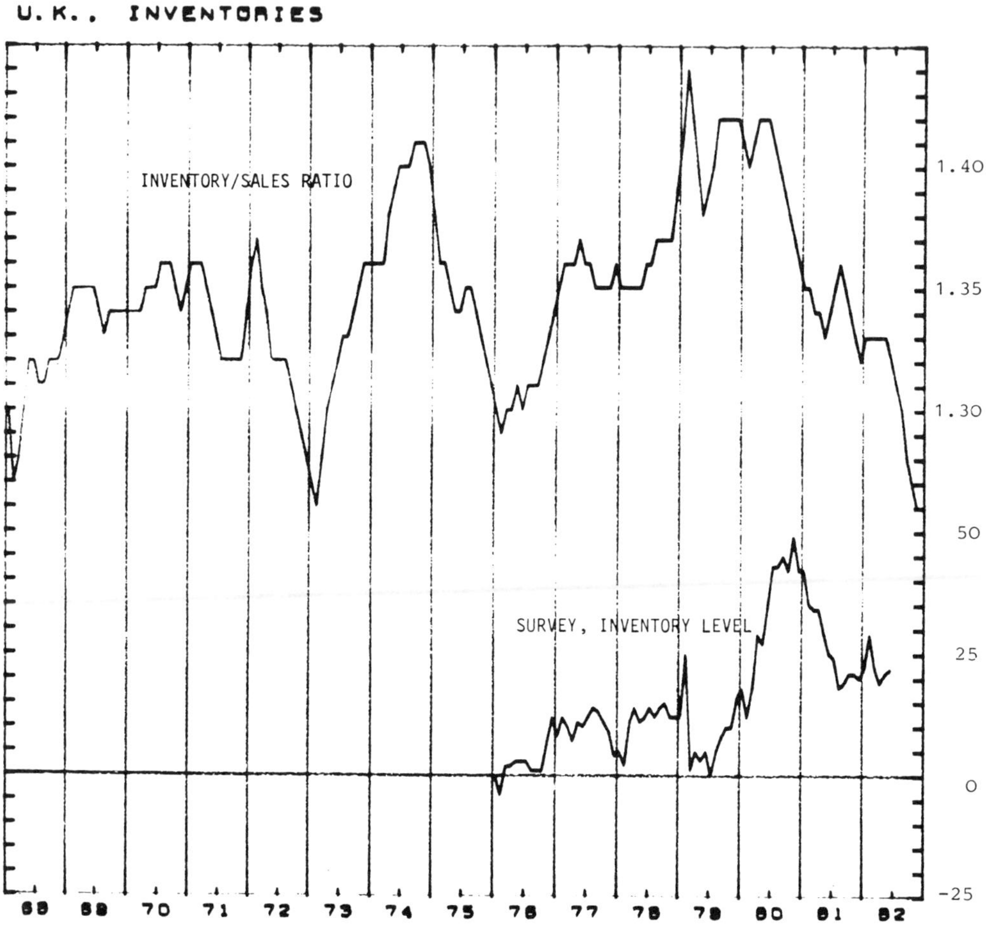

inventory/sales ratio. However, because we have based this exercise on the EEC survey results, the period of time covered is extremely short.

Conclusions

This exercise has concentrated on production, new orders, and inventories in four EEC countries. We have attempted to answer the question, "By how much can one increase the lead time for forecasting purposes by utilizing survey net balances as they become available as proxies for the actual production, new orders, or inventory data still to come?" Turning first to production, we have seen that the entrepreneurs tend to respond to questions asking for their anticipations of changes in production over the next four months by considering changes occurring at about the time of the survey and applying to them a "mental smoothing process." This means that the replies reflect what entrepreneurs think the trend of future production in likely to be. The results of comparing actual production changes with the survey net balances suggest that the greater promptness with which the survey net balances become available means that the survey results can add about two months to the lead time in forecasting actual production changes. Nevertheless, a lot of the actual change will be lost in this way because of the many factors which make actual month-to-month changes in production very volatile.

Both the explanatory power and the lead can be increased by utilizing the surveys in forecasting the trend of production. Entrepreneurs correctly anticipate well over half the change in actual future production trends. If the surveys are utilized to forecast these trends in production changes rather than short-run changes they can play their most useful role.

Our examination of the forecasting potential of survey results reporting on order book levels was restricted to Germany and the United Kingdom and was less successful than the test on production. The correlations were too low to justify estimating actual changes in order books from the survey results. However, there is a clear advantage in publication time attached to the survey results. Comparison with our earlier study of the CBI surveys, moreover, suggests that changing the form of the survey question might improve its ability to track actual order book changes.

Finally we examined the forecasting potential of survey questions dealing with inventories. Here the primary difficulty was that the fact that the survey concentrated on finished goods inventory, typically a lagging indicator, while the quantitative series available for the United Kingdom and Germany include other inventory as well. The correlation results for our estimate of the inventory/sales ratio and the survey estimate were quite high but there was a very long lag (approximately ten months for both Germany and the United Kingdom). This was partly to be explained by the finished goods concentration in the survey question, but not entirely. The publication lag gave the survey results a one month advantage over the inventory/sales ratios, not enough to offset their lag.

Overall, the study suggests that properly used, and carefully interpreted, the survey net balances can materially assist the forecaster. Care in dating the survey results and in relating them to quantitative series correctly adjusted is the key to utilizing the surveys for optimal forecasting results.

FOOTNOTES

1. In addition to the sources listed at the bottom of Table 2 the reader is referred to P. A. Klein and G. H. Moore, "The CBI Entrepreneurial Surveys: An Aid in Analyzing U.K. Business Cycles, Part I: New Orders," Applied Economics, April 1980, Part II: "Stocks, Profits, Business Confidence over the Business Cycle," Applied Economics, August 1980.

2. See for example the papers presented by P. A. Klein and G. H. Moore at the 13th CIRET Conference ("Forecasting Foreign Trade with Leading Indicators") and at the 14th CIRET Conference ("Further Applications of Leading Indicators to Forecasting Foreign Trade Flows and Balances").

3. A standard part of the computer analysis of time series includes the effort to ascertain the relative smoothness of each series. "C" is the average month-to-month change in the cyclical component of a seasonally adjusted time series. "I" is the average month-to-month change in the irregular component of a seasonally adjusted time series.

4. All publication lags are based on information provided to the OECD. In this particular case it is ISCO (Institute Nazionale per lo Studio della Congiuntura) which provides the data.

5. All the correlation results are shown in Appendix Table 5.

6. The technique was somewhat cumbersome and involves recognizing that real GNP less inventory change during the month represents final sales. Both inventories and final sales were expressed in constant prices. We cumulated the inventory changes from 1955, starting from an assumed level equal to sales (i.e., the inventory/sales ratio was assumed to be equal to one in 1st quarter 1955).

o o o

Editorial remark:

Due to limited space the appendix could not be included in this volume. Readers interested in these 8 pages are adviced to contact the author or the CIRET Office.

Summary of the Discussion

A. Piatier
Ecole des Hautes Etudes en Sciences Sociales
Paris

The discussant of the paper of V. Zarnowitz (G. Nerb, Ifo-Institute Munich) focussed his comments on the different kinds of surveys which can be used for forecasting purposes directly or indirectly. He stressed the advantages of surveys of business executives in forecasting turning points, and pointed out that numerous surveys in the United States are not nationally representative. He described the ASA-NBER survey and asked Prof. Zarnowitz to give the latest results.

An American participant mentioned industrial purchasers as the main agents of business fluctuations.

In his answer, Zarnowitz agreed to Nerb's remarks that there are no substitutes for suveys of executives, but he remained in favor of different kinds of surveys, giving examples of forecast results during the last ten years.

The second report was given by M. Devilliers (INSEE, Paris) on: the Use of Business Surveys in Short-term forecasts: The French Experience. The Comments of the discussant M. J. Courtois (Commission of the European Commission, Brussels) underlined that his personal experience in conducting the European Business Surveys was similar to the INSEE experience. He asked for some information on three points: usefulness and adequacy of general views of executives on production, climate, usefulness of forecasting exports by size of the firms, and reliability of yearly investment forecasts.

M. Devilliers in his answers explained why climate indicators are very useful. They are an important aid in forecasting influences of investment and employment. As to the second question, he regretted that we have no data for the prediction of export behaviour. In answer to the third question, he agreed that the quantitative outlook of entrepreneurs on investment had good forecasting records for only six months in the future.

A participant pointed out that the forecasting quality of the personal outlook on production, which is good in France, is unreliable in other countries.

The discussant of the paper presented by W. Naggl, University of Munich (H. König, University of Mannheim) admitted that for him, not being specialized in data analysis, it was difficult to judge the data used in the model. As he was interested in the theoretical structure of the model he regretted that the structure of the model was not given and he asked the author to give some information on this "black box".

He also claimed that survey answers are only individual judgements, being subjective in nature. Making a distinction between optimistic firms and pessimistic firms he pointed out that balances are sensitive to changes in attitudes. The problem of aggregation of micro data is also difficult: Results of business surveys are given in terms of positive and negative changes. "No change" answers also have to be taken into account. Although he agreed with the inclusion of anticipation variables in the model, he expressed some doubts concerning the structure of the model. Realizations are determined by previous periods' expectations; deviations of realizations from anticipations are captured by exogenous variables such as interest rates as an indication of the change in investment costs. It was also difficult for him to understand that investment plans of the last year were fulfilled totally in the following year. In many sectors plans were realized during a number of years. He gave the conditions for the use of Rational Expectations in modelling. To him it made more sense to assume that production is independent of variables such as expectations of inventories than to say that production is related to production plans. For inventory realization it is necessary to use explanatory variables such as economic policy measures, money holding, alternatives for capital investment, the relation between real wage determination, productivity changes, and the share of real profits.

The remarks on empirical results were focussed on the comparison with results of other econometric forecasts and on the fact that the rate of change is more important in short-term econometric models. For instance, the changes in investment activity in the energy sector for 1979/8o are overestimated. It is not clear that the figures in the anticipation models are consistent.

In his answer W. Naggl recognized the usefulness of such remarks. He admitted that balances of judgements contain noise and that it will be necessary to include other variables in the model, such as the availability of credits in long-term financing etc. Finally W. Naggl accepted G. Poser's conclusion that forecasts given today's state of the art are not good, but the way is open for important progress in methods.

The fourth paper by P. A. Klein (Pennsylvania State University) was devoted to an empirical test of improving forecasts with survey indicators. Observing that the traditional work in the United States is concentrated on quantitative indicators and in Europe on qualitative indicators, he has been experimenting with G. H. Moore with a combination of qualitative and quantitative data for the U.S., and evaluating the results of different European institutes in the use of business surveys. The results were better for the forecast of turning points than for the level of production.

The results of the analysis made by Klein for Italy, France, Germany and the United Kingdom were criticized first by the discussant, C.P.H. Burton (Confederation of British Industry, London) and secondly by other speakers.

For C.P.H. Burton, the calculation made by Klein for Great Britain did not give consistent results with his own results. Disagreeing with the broad conclusion of the paper he also paid attention to special problems. Survey data are more regular than the actual production figures.

For W. H. Strigel (Ifo-Institute, Munich) the lead between the business survey indicator and the production index is not three weeks but nearly two months. For the pre-month survey, the comparison with the official production index gives only a weak agreement. The "test of the test" made in Germany shows that firms often take the Ifo survey results as a guideline. Since so far no inconsistency has been reported, there is no reason for considering the business test results to be inadequate.

W.H. Strigel's assumption that the time series of the Ifo-survey with respect to changes mainly reflect pre-year changes was confirmed by means of graphical comparisons and regression analyses. Generally, the pre-year comparison gives considerably better results than the pre-month comparison (production plans/growth rates). For Strigel it seemed to be difficult to work with the relation between assessment of order-books and incoming orders because the first variable is affected not only by incoming orders but also by production or deliveries and by production capacities. Finally, he gave another example with the finished goods inventories and explained the behaviour of the firms. As a result of using inventory judgements as a cyclical component of inventories, he found a better coefficient of determination than Klein.

M. Devilliers explained why his results were different from Klein's results for France, more particularly for judgements on the production tendencies. The differences result from the statistical treatment of the data for May 1968 (a long strike during this month in all industrial sectors and also in the statistical offices).

Third Session
Consumer Surveys

Chairman:

R. Curtin, University of Michigan

Ann Arbor, Mich.

Plans and Attitudes from the Survey of Consumer Buying Expectations in Forecasting the Total Private Consumption

S. L. Öhlén
Statistiska Centralbyrån
Stockholm

1 INTRODUCTION

The empirical evidence of the significance of attitudes and anticipatory data in explaining the fluctuations in purchases of consumer goods is well documented during at least three decades. On the other hand it is harder to find papers where estimated models, using such data, are tested in actual forecasts and proved to give a higher prediction accuracy than models without attitude data. A common approach is to add attitude variables or indices to a model, estimate the coefficients, and usually some attitude variable is significant. A typical expression is "this study has shown that attitudes have a significant explanation of the dependent variable". From statistical point of view such a type of analysis is legitimate. There is however some danger in this approach because the probability to <u>find</u> a combination of variables and datasets which makes the attitude variable significant, is quite high. At the CIRET - Conference in Stockholm 1975 Mr Thomas Juster claimed in the discussion following his speach "Give me any data set of economic time series including attitudes and intentions and I could make almost every variable significant..." [1]. The discussion was quite lively and perhaps Mr Juster intended to be consciously provocative and that his true standpoint is more conservative. In my own experience with <u>time series data</u> during the last ten years, I have made the same conclusion as Mr Juster. This does not mean that I claim that significance analysis is irrelevant in the search for a new theory of consumer behaviour. What I mean is that efforts must be made to show the <u>prediction qualities</u> of estimated models. <u>The ultimate test of any time series model is its ability to predict future events</u>. Sometimes limited data sets restrict the analysis from going beyond the estimation period. Usually it is possible, and in my view an advantage, to partition the data set into two parts; one is used to estimate the model while the other part is used to predict the dependent variable using the estimated model.

---

1) I have not checked with Mr Juster about his exact words. However, the message was clear.

In this paper I have made a compromise in the discussion of significance aspects and prediction qualities with a greater weight to prediction performance.

Suppose that predictions $P_{j1},\ldots, P_{jn}$ of future or unknown outcomes $\theta_1,\ldots, \theta_n$ are to be made with the use of model "j" selected from a set of models. Aggregated costs C_j are induced by the predictions through associated decisions $d_{j1}, d_{j2},\ldots, d_{jn}$. We assume that the cost function C_j associated with n predictions has the following form:

$$C_j = w_1 \ddot{m}_j + w_2 \ddot{s}_j; \qquad (2.1)$$

where

$$\ddot{m}_j = \sum_{i=1}^{n} \frac{|P_{ji}-\theta_i|}{n}; \qquad (2.2)$$

$$\ddot{s}_j^2 = \sum_{i=1}^{n} \frac{(|P_{ji}-\theta_i| - \ddot{m}_j)^2}{n} \quad ; \qquad (2.3)$$

w_1 and w_2 are positive constants. If every prediction is correct, model j raises no cost at all. If the cost C_j associated with model j is less than the corresponding cost C_k associated with model k, we shall use the expression "model j <u>dominates</u> model k". Sometimes we use the expression "is better than".

The selection of the cost function (2.1) is a matter of convenience. The average error (2.2) is easy to handle for a user of forecasts. We call $\ddot{m}_j$ the <u>average error</u>. "Mean error" or "<u>mean prediction error</u>" is used in the sense of "mathematical expectation". $\ddot{s}_j$ is called "<u>average deviation</u>" of the errors.

In this paper we evaluate models or variables by comparing $(\ddot{m}_j, \ddot{s}_j)$ associated with model j with $(\ddot{m}_k, \ddot{s}_k)$ associated with model k. When speaking of "model j is better than model k" one of the following conditions is fulfilled.

1. $\ddot{m}_j < \ddot{m}_k$, $\ddot{s}_j < \ddot{s}_k$

2. $\ddot{m}_j < \ddot{m}_k$, $\ddot{s}_j = \ddot{s}_k$

3. $\ddot{m}_j = \ddot{m}_k$, $\ddot{s}_j < \ddot{s}_k$

For those readers who prefer other measures of prediction accuracy, we show the following measures in the tables introduced by Theil in his book "Applied Economic Forecasting", Ch.2. Under the assumption that the observed error structure will continue, the knowledge of these measures can be used for optimal linear correction of the forecasts. However, we are not considering this subject in the paper.

$$U_j^{\,2} = \frac{\Sigma(P_{ji} - \theta_i)^2}{\Sigma\,\theta_i^2}; \qquad U_j^M = \frac{n(\bar{P}_j - \bar{\theta})^2}{\Sigma(P_{ji} - \theta_i)^2};$$

$$U_j^S = \frac{n(s_j - s_\theta)^2}{\Sigma(P_{ji} - \theta_i)^2}; \qquad U_j^C = \frac{2n(1-r_j)s_j s_\theta}{\Sigma\,(P_{ji}-\theta_i)^2};$$

$$U_j^R = \frac{n(s_j - r_j s_\theta)^2}{\Sigma(P_{ji}-\theta_i)^2}; \qquad U_j^D = \frac{n(1 - r_j^2)s_\theta^2}{\Sigma(P_{ji}-\theta_i)^2};$$

Notations:

P_{ji} = The ith prediction with model j

θ_i = True outcome of the ith prediction

$\bar{P}_j$ = Mean of the predictions with model j

$\bar{\theta}$ = Mean of the true values

s_j = Standard deviation of the predictions with model j

s_θ = Standard deviation of the true values

r_j = Correlation coefficient between the predictions with model j and the true values.

2 THE SWEDISH SURVEYS OF CONSUMER BUYING EXPECTATIONS

Since October 1973 Statistics Sweden (SCB) has carried out current quarterly surveys of consumer buying expectations (HIP). The HIP-surveys contain questions on attitudes to economic development and buying plans. Buying plans are measured on an eleven-degree scale and the planning horizon is 3, 6, 12 and 24 months. One of the main purposes of the surveys is to obtain data, which could be used in forecasting the demand for consumer durables.

The household investigated is defined as follows:

i) two adult persons (man and woman) living together, married or cohabitating, and their children

ii) one adult person and his/her children,

A child is defined as a person under 18 years old without children of his/her own. The population contains all households in Sweden according to the definition above with the exception of:

a) households where the head is 75 years old or more

b) households consisting of persons in public care for a long period

c) households living abroad for at least one year after the date of the investigation

From October 1973 to April 1979 the sample size has been 10 000 HIP-households. From July 1979 till now the sample consists of about 6 600 households every quarter. It is stratified by income with a higher probability being given to households in higher income classes. There are five rotational groups each one containing about 1 300 households. Each group is interviewed in five consecutive quarters. It is then replaced by a new group. Two consecutive quarters have 4/5 of their respective samples in common. The interviews are mainly carried out by telephone. If the household does not have a telephone or if there are other special reasons, the interviewer makes a personal call. In October 1982 the unweighted non-response was 11,5 per cent. The object non-response[1] is distributed over the different response categories according to the respondent distribution. Before the non-response is distributed, the sample is divided into six income classes. The distribution of non-response in every income class is based upon the assumption that the non-respondents and the respondents should give the same answers to the questions.

Sources of non-response in October 1982 in per cent:

Refusal	7,3
Not available	3,7
Sickness	0,1
In hospital, nursing home etc	0,3

The mean non-response of the surveys in January, April and October is approximately 13 per cent. The mean non-response of the July surveys is about three per cent higher. The increased non-response in July is mainly due to "not available" (holidays). The rate of non-response is decreasing and is at present quite low.

---

1) The object non-response corresponds to the number of households with which no contact has been made. The non-response has been due to one of the following reasons:

a) the representative of the household refuses to participate in the survey
b) no representative of the household has been found
c) the representative of the household is unable to participate in the survey on account of illness
d) the representative of the household is in hospital, in a nursing home, in prison etc

Since 1977 the usefulness of the HIP-information in forecasts, has been investigated in collaboration between SCB and the Department of Statistics at the University of Gothenburg . The empirical evidence from these studies of cross sections- and time series data supports the conclusion that buying plans are very useful in explaining purchases of cars. However, we have not been able to show that attitudes have any predictive value in quarterly purchases of cars. The experiences from cross sections data are that buying plans are outstanding in explaining purchases of cars.

In the autumn of 1979 the National Research Institute raised the question whether the HIP-surveys could be used to improve forecasts of private final consumption expenditures. The evidence from the following investigations supported the conclusion that attitudes were not useful in very short term forecasting of private final domestic consumption expenditures . On the other hand, buying plans could be used in quarterly consumption functions with good prediction properties. When the forecasting horizon is increased to six months or perhaps more, the indication is that the importance of attitudes is increasing. However, buying plans are still important determinants of future consumption expenditures.

---

2) Öhlén S.: "The Use of Buying Plans and Attitudes in Forecasting Purchases of Goods and Services". Preliminary Report 1977:1. SCB.

Öhlén S.: "The Use of Buying Plans in Forecasting the Demand for Cars". Oct. 1979. SCB.

3) Öhlén S.: "Plans and Attitudes from the Surveys of Consumer Buying Expectations in Forecasting the Private Final Domestic Consumption Expenditures in Sweden". 1979-12-17. SCB.

The papers are all written in Swedish.

3 CONSUMPTION FUNCTIONS

We are studying consumption functions (cf) of the following type:

$$C_t = C1(Y_{t-k}, C_{t-k}; k=0,1,) + C2(P_t, A_t) + e_t \qquad (4.1)$$

where C1 and C2 are linear functions with unknown parameters and:

Y_{t-k} = Lagged disposable income

C_{t-k} = Lagged private final consumption

P_t = Variables regarding planned purchases of cars measured at the beginning of t

A_t = Attitude variables measured at the beginning of t

e_t = Random variable

The private final consumption in period t is determined by two functions C1 and C2, where C1 includes variables from national accounts (NA - variables) and C2 is a function of variables from the Swedish surveys of consumer buying expectations.

<u>Special cases of (4.1)</u>

We are studying the following special cases of model (4.1):

Special case	Notation
a) C2 = 0 for every value of P_t and A_t I.e. plans and attitudes are supposed to have no effect on consumption.	NA - MODEL
b) $C2(P_t, A_t) = C2(A_t)$ Attitudes but not plans have an effect on consumption.	ATTITUDE-MODEL I

Special case	Notation
c) $C2(P_t,A_t) = C2(D(A_{jt}))$ Plans do not have any effect on consumption. Attitudes are related to consumption through a discriminant function D of attitude variables A_{jt}	ATTITUDE-MODEL II
d) $C2(P_t,A_t) = C2(P_t)$ Plans but not attitudes have an impact on consumption	PLAN - MODEL

Specification (4.1) including plans and attitudes is called MODEL I.

The analyses have been carried through according to the following scheme.

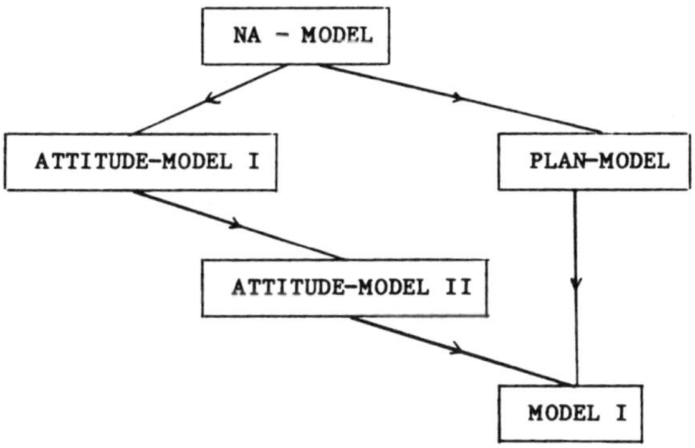

We tried to find the "best" NA-MODEL from a limited set of national accounts variables with different lags. The performance of the NA-MODEL was tested and the distribution of the prediction errors studied. To this model we added attitude variables. Plan variables were included in the same way. The ATTITUDE-MODEL I could be improved by adding indices of the separate attitude variables by means of discriminant analysis. The results from the ATTITUDE-MODEL II and the PLAN-MODEL were combined in MODEL I.

4 DATA AND VARIABLES

In the following t is indicating a six months period while k is indicating a three months period. C(t) and C_t will be used synonymously, indicating the private final consumption expenditures in the six months period t. C_k indicates the consumption during quarter k. The position of the variables on the time axis is shown in chart 1. Y indicates disposable income. The time series regarding six months consumption consists of 16 observations from the first six months of 1974 to the last six months of 1981. Data on national accounts are in fixed prices and are not seasonally adjusted.

National accounts variables

The following national accounts variables have been investigated:

NATIONAL ACCOUNTS VARIABLE	VAR NO
$C_{k-4} + C_{k-3} = C_{t-2}$	1
$C_{k-3} + C_{k-2}$	2
$C_{k-2} + C_{k-1} = C_{t-1}$	3
$C_k + C_{k+1} = C_t$ = Dependent var.	4
$Y_{k-4} + Y_{k-3} = Y_{t-2}$	5
$Y_{k-3} + Y_{k-2}$	6
$Y_{k-2} + Y_{k-1} = Y_{t-1}$	7
$Y_{k-1} + Y_k$	8
$Y_k + Y_{k+1} = Y_t$	9

Chart 1. NATIONAL ACCOUNTS VARIABLES

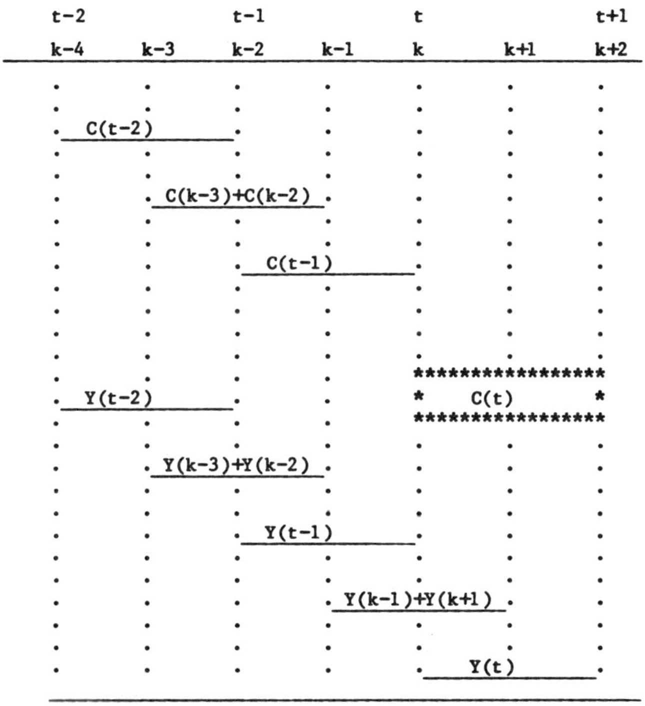

<u>Buying plan variables</u>

Notations:

N^n_{jT} = The number of households in the population with plan "j" according to the plan scale for purchase of a new car in the next T months.

j = 0%, 10%,..., 100%

T = 3,6,12,24

j = 0% is equivalent to "no chance of purchase" while j = 100% is equivalent to "absolutely sure". N^s_{jT} is the corresponding notation for second-hand cars while N_{jT} refers to new <u>or</u> second-hand cars.

The surveys of consumer buying expectations provide estimates $\hat{N}^n_{jT}$, $\hat{N}^s_{jT}$ and $\hat{N}_{jT}$ of the corresponding population totals. The estimates are uncertain for T = 3 and some j because of few observations. For that reason, we have transformed the 11-degree scale to a 5-degree scale according to the table below.

j %	k	Chance of purchase
0	0	Not a chance
10	1	
20	1	10 % - 30 %
30	1	
40	2	
50	2	40 % - 60 %
60	2	
70	3	
80	3	70 % - 90 %
90	3	
100	4	Absolutely sure

According to the 5-degree scale N_{1T} indicates the number of households in the population with 10 % - 30 % chance to buy a new or second-hand car in T months. Because of a strong negative correlation between the number of households with no plan and the number of households <u>with</u> a buying plan, we have restricted ourselves to households with buying plans. Beside the separate variables, we have tried the following aggregations:

$N^n_{.T}$ = Total number of households in the population with plans to buy a new car within T months

$N^s_{.T}$ = Total number of households in the population with plans to buy a second-hand car within T months

$N_{.T} = N^n_{.T} + N^s_{.T}$ = Total number of households in the population with plans to buy a car within T months.

Attitude variables

At present the Swedish surveys measure attitudes regarding:

1. Unemployment

2. The change of the personal financial situation since the last 12 months

3. The expected development of the financial situation of the family in the next 12 months

4. The change of the total family income since the last 12 months

5. The expected change of the total family income in the next 12 months

6. The perceived change of the general price level since the last 12 months

7. The expected change of the general price level in the next 12 months

8. The expected change of the general economic situation in Sweden in the next 12 months

Among the attitudes above, we shall restrict ourselves to show results regarding the variables below:

A1= The percentage of the families who think that their personal financial situation has improved since the last 12 months

A2= The percentage of the families who think that their personal financial situation has deteriorated since the last 12 months

A3= The percentage of the families who think that their personal financial situation is going to improve in the next 12 months

A4= The percentage of the families who think that their personal financial situation is going to deteriorate in the next 12 months

A5= The percentage of the families who think that the general economic situation in Sweden is going to improve in the next 12 months

A6= The percentage of the families who think that the general economic situation in Sweden is going to deteriorate in the next 12 months

A7= The percentage of the families who think that the rate of unemployment is going to decrease in the next 12 months.

The variables A1,...A7 have all been multiplied by ten. When we talk about an attitude variable $\hat{Aj}_t$, where t indicates a six months period, we mean the estimate of the population value Aj_t from the survey at the beginning of t. I. e. in predicting the consumption of the first six months of 1978, we have used the January survey. When predicting the last six months of 1978, the July survey is used.

When the predictions P_t and P_k of C_t and C_k are to be made using HIP-survey data, we have a delay of approximately two months before the predictions can be calculated. However, we have a delay regarding national accounts of about one quarter (when the first preliminary statistics of C_t and C_k are availiable) and they are uncertain. Therefore, the forecasts reduce the information gap about four months in the case of quarterly predictions and about seven months in the case of six months predictions.

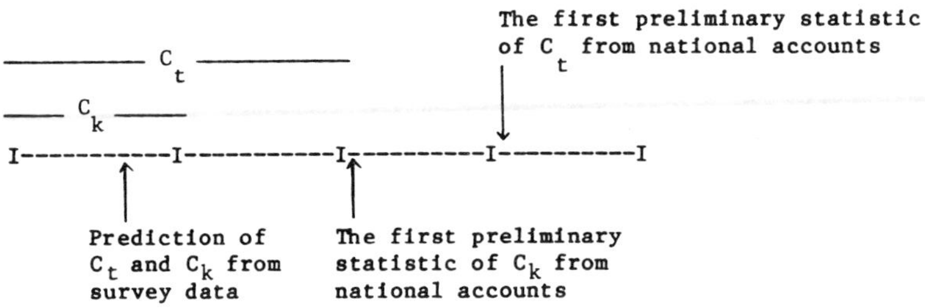

Restriction: Because of the limited number of observations regarding six months models, we must restrict the number of included variables. We have chosen to investigate significance properties with the use of all 16 observations. The prediction properties are tested through predictions of seven outcomes of the consumption variable C_t. In chapter ten regarding quarterly forecasts, we have used a varying number of outcomes of the dependent variable in studying the prediction properties and the distribution of the predicting errors.

5 NATIONAL ACCOUNTS MODEL

In the case of the national accounts model, we have restricted the maximum number of independent variables to three, because the NAMODEL will later be enlarged by attitude- and plan variables. The analysis for finding a best lag structure among the NA-variables in chapter 5 has been carried out as follows:

Criterion for specifying the NA-MODEL

Find the NA-variables, not more than three with significant regression estimates giving the smallest prediction errors during 1978:2 - 1981:2

According to that criterion, the optimal NA-MODEL has the following simple form:

$$\hat{C}_t = \underset{(2.10)}{14\,283} + \underset{(6.92)}{0.527}\, C_{t-1} + \underset{(10.44)}{0.285}\, Y_t + e_t; \qquad (6.1)$$

$$R^2 = 0.91 \qquad SE = 881.7 \quad DW = 1.53 \quad N = 16$$

where e_t is the residual, R^2 the multiple correlation coefficient, SE the standard error and DW is Durbin Watson's test for positive autocorrelation of the residuals. The numbers given within parentheses are t-values of the estimates. By developing C_{t-1} in terms of Y_{t-1} and C_{t-2} with the use of the recursive structure, the model could be brought into the form below:

$$\hat{C}_t = 25\,777 + 0.147\, C_{t-3} + 0.285\, Y_t + 0.150\, Y_{t-1} + 0.078\, Y_{t-2} + u_t; \qquad (6.2)$$

where u_t is a random variable.

Predictions with the NA-MODEL

In the estimation of (6.1), we have used all 16 observations. In table 1, we show ex - post forecasts with this model. The forecasts are assumed to be made for the first time 1978:2, the last six months of 1978. Nine observations are known to us when the forecast of $C_{1978:2}$ is to be made. The disposable income $Y_{1978:2}$ is not known but we assume that $Y_{1978:2}$ is known[4]. We estimate the model on the basis of the known observations 1974:1 - 1978:1. The estimated model is shown in the column with the head of "1978:2". The coefficient for lagged consumption is 0.516, while the coefficient for disposable income is 0.316. Below every estimate the t-test of the estimate is shown in brackets. R^2 is the multiple correlation coefficient. For the definition of the other measures of the table, we refer to chapter 2. If we use this estimated model, the prediction error of the consumption 1978:2 would be 0.5 per cent less than the actual value. The next forecast, 1979:1 is made accordingly with the use of <u>ten</u> observations for estimating the model. All predictions are made with the reestimated models shown in the table. This approach is quite interesting when attitude variables are included in the NA-MODEL because we get a picture of the stability of the regression coefficients. The NA-MODEL produces two "high" errors; 1979:1 and 1980:2, where the errors are -1.6 and 1.5 per cent. The average error $\ddot{m}$ is 0.697 per cent of actual consumption while average deviation is 0.682.

---

4) Because Y_t is an explaining variable in the attitude- and plan models in the next chapters, the dominance properties of the models will not change because of this assumption, unless the estimated coefficient for Y_t is different in the models. The "ex ante" prediction errors will of course increase when Y_t must be estimated.

The average error 0.697 is to be considered as quite normal in comparison with alternative consumption functions with a more elaborate structure using NA-variables of Swedish data. In spite of its quite simple structure the NA-MODEL is not so bad in the sense of prediction accuracy.

The question now, is whether attitudes and/or buying plans from the HIP-surveys could improve the NA-MODEL in the sense of:

1) better explaining the variations of private final consumption expenditures.

2) reducing the prediction errors.

In the next chapter, we investigate the "added prediction value" of the attitude variables defined in chapter 2. Then we try to find a discriminant function of attitudes, which could be used instead of separate attitudes.

6 ATTITUDE - MODELS

6.1 Single attitude variables

In table 2 we show the results of including the attitude variables $\hat{A}1_t,\ldots,\hat{A}7_t$ in the consumption function (6.1) one by one. In the table, we show the estimated models when all 16 observations are used for estimating the models. When attitude variable $\hat{A}1_t$ is added to (6.1), the coefficient of $\hat{A}1_t$ is 13.92 with a t-value of 2.86. The coefficient of multiple correlation R^2 has increased from 0.91 to 0.948. On the last row, we show the average error, when the model is used for predicting the consumption during 1978:2 to 1981:2 in the same way as is described in chapter 6. The average error associated with the inclusion of $\hat{A}1_t$ is 0.94 per cent. Below $\ddot{m}_j$ we show the average deviation $\ddot{s}_j$, where j indicates the jth attitude variable. $\hat{A}1_t$ gives an average deviation of 0.86 per cent. The inclusion of A1 in the NA-MODEL increases the fit but increases also the prediction errors.

All attitude variables have the sign we would expect; a positive attitude has a positive effect on consumption and a negative attitude has a downward impact. All variables except $\hat{A}2_t$ are significant. Traditional significance analysis indicates that attitudes do in fact have an impact on private final consumption expenditures. The table shows however, that we must be cautious if we believe that this circumstance (significance of the variables) would guarantee the success of looking into the shadows of the future. The unemployment variable $\hat{A}7_t$ and the expected future economic situation in Sweden $\hat{A}6_t$ give a minor improvement of the average error. The major effect from including these variables into the model is that the risk of getting large errors has decreased. $\hat{A}7_t$ reduces the average deviation from 0.67 to 0.33 per cent. We would say that these attitudes specify models which dominate the NA-MODEL. For this reason we show the predictions in detail in table 3 and 4. The reestimation of the models has been done accordingly to table 1.

6.2 Discriminant analysis of attitude variables

The attitude variables $A1_t, \ldots, A7_t$ are strongly correlated to each other. Therefore, we have tried to find an index of the separate variables depending on the multivariate distribution of the variables. We have used discriminant analysis to extract a suitable index. In the estimation of the latent roots and latent vectors, the correlation matrix of the attitude variables $A1_t, \ldots, A7_t$ below has been used.

CORRELATION MATRIX OF ATTITUDE VARIABLES $A1_t, \ldots, A7_t$

	$A1_t$	$A2_t$	$A3_t$	$A4_t$	$A5_t$	$A6_t$	$A7_t$
$A1_t$	1.00	-0.896	0.911	-0.855	0.233	-0.590	0.540
$A2_t$		1.00	-0.937	0.932	-0.259	0.532	-0.519
$A3_t$			1.00	-0.950	0.385	-0.680	0.551
$A4_t$				1.00	-0.527	0.765	-0.663
$A5_t$					1.00	-0.879	0.747
$A6_t$						1.00	-0.818
$A7_t$							1.00

The latent roots and vectors to the matrix above are shown in table 5. The largest root is 5.10, which gives a normalised vector (0.382, -0.387,..., 0.352). The first principal component

$$\hat{Y}_{1t} = 0.382\ A1_t - 0.387\ A2_t + 0.410\ A3_t - 0.428\ A4_t + 0.286\ A5_t - 0.384\ A6_t + 0.352\ A7_t; \qquad (7.1)$$

explains 72.9 per cent of the variance of the individual attitudes. From table 5, we can see that the first three components explain 96.7 per cent of the variance. $\hat{Y}_{1t}$ could in a certain sense be treated as an index of "general optimism", in which every single attitude is given the same weight. $A5_t$ is the most important factor in the second principal component, while the unemployment attitude $A7_t$ is dominant in the third component.

We have included every principal component $\hat{Y}_{1t},\ldots,\hat{Y}_{2t}$ in the NA-MODEL. Both single components and several components have been tried in combination. The best index in prediction sense is the second component $\hat{Y}_{2t}$ below:

$$\hat{Y}_{2t} = -0.349\ A1_t + 0.372\ A2_t - 0.270\ A3_t + 0.136\ A4_t + 0.616\ A5_t - \\ - 0.371\ A6_t + 0.362\ A7_t; \qquad (7.2)$$

We show the model with this index of attitudes in table 6. The index has the notation $ATTIND_t$ in the model and it is significant when the sample size is 15 or more. The index has a positive influence on consumption expenditures. The estimated coefficient of the index is stable if $N > 10$. In prediction sense this model, named ATTITUDE-MODEL II, dominates the NA-MODEL and also the model in table 4 with the unemployment attitude variable $A7_t$. The average error is reduced to 0.54 and the average deviation to 0.26 per cent.

Some conclusions may be drawn from the impact of the attitude index on consumption expenditures. For instance, suppose that the variables $A1_t,\ldots, A6_t$ have the same value A_t. I.e. the number of families with optimistic attitudes is the same as the number of families with pessimistic attitudes. The $ATTIND_t$-variable then takes the value

$$\begin{aligned} ATTIND_t &= A_t(-0.349 + 0.372 - 0.270 + 0.136 + 0.616 -0.371) + \\ &\quad + 0.362\ A7_t\ ; \\ &= 0.134\ A_t + 0.362\ A7_t > 0 \end{aligned}$$

This means that the index has a positive impact on consumption expenditures independent of the attitudes regarding unemployment $A7_t$. The reason for this is that the positive impact stemming from positive attitudes is greater than the impact stemming from negative attitudes.

7 PLAN-MODEL

We have investigated the buying plans within three and six months (T=3, 6) by adding the variables to the NA-MODEL. Besides the variables mentioned in chapter 2, we have investigated the discriminant functions of the variables for T=3 and T=6 in order to find a plan index for a general propensity to consume. For reason of space, we shall not show these analyses in this paper. We restrict the presentation to one variable, which in a satisfactory way relates buying-plans to consumption expenditures. We shall yet make some general remarks:

1. Buying plans in T=3 months are better predictors than buying plans in $T \geq 6$ months
2. In general buying plans improve the NA-MODEL
3. Buying plans are usually significant

The best buying plan variable is $N^n_{.3}$, the number of households with plans to buy a new car in the next three months. This variable gives the model an interesting structure discussed in chapter 9. We give the variable a simpler notation.

P_t = The number of households in hundreds who at the beginning of t have plans to buy a new car within three months

This variable puts the NA-MODEL into the following form:

$$\hat{C}_t = 8\,447 + \underset{(1.55)}{0.570}\, \underset{(9.66)}{C_{t-1}} + \underset{(13.70)}{0.282\, Y_t} + \underset{(3.28)}{7.87\, \hat{P}_t} + u_t; \qquad (8.1)$$

$$R^2 = 0.954 \qquad DW = 1.08 \qquad N = 16$$

One of the effects of adding this variable to the NA-MODEL is the reduction of the constant from 14 283 to 8 447. The weight of the lagged consumption has increased from 0.527 to 0.570, while the coefficient of disposable income is almost the same. From a prediction point of view, this model is an improvement in comparison with ATTITUDE-MODEL II with the attitude index. In table 7 we show the prediction errors produced by the PLAN-MODEL. The average error is reduced to 0.42 and the average deviation is 0.47 per cent.

The plan variable has a positive impact on consumption and the regression coefficient is quite stable. One large prediction error (1979:2) causes the average deviation to be relatively high in comparison with the ATTITUDE-MODEL II.

In the last chapter regarding six months forecasts, we combine the influence of attitudes and plans in a consumption function with extraordinary prediction performance and some interesting properties.

8 COMBINATION OF ATTITUDES AND BUYING PLANS

Through including two attitude variables regarding the future, the NA-MODEL was improved; the average prediction error was reduced from 0.70 per cent to 0.62. The attitude index reduced the errors to 0.54. The buying plan variable reduced the errors further to 0.42 per cent. The buying plan model is however not better than the attitude index-model according to the cost function in ch. 2 because the "index-model" has a lower average deviation than the buying plan model. By including the simultanous impact of the attitude index and the buying plans in the NA-MODEL, it is possible to reduce the prediction errors even further.

MODEL I

$$\hat{C}_t = \underset{(2.22)}{11\ 527} + \underset{(10.29)}{0.527}\ C_{t-1} + \underset{(13.45)}{0.269}\ Y_t + \underset{(2.48)}{5.94}\ \hat{P}_t + \underset{(1.90)}{3.05}\ ATTIND_t;$$

$$R^2 = 0.965 \qquad SE = 603.3 \qquad DW = 0.915 \qquad N = 16 \qquad (9.1)$$

The t-value of $ATTIND_t$ should be higher. In table 8, we show the prediction errors with MODEL I and the relevant estimates of the parameters. The t-value of $ATTIND_t$ is quite low for the estimated model of 1978:2 and 1979:1 and N = 15 is not enough for making $ATTIND_t$ significant. With the exception of 1978:2 and 1979:1, the estimated coefficients of $ATTIND_t$ are quite stable. The coefficients of $\hat{P}_t$ varies between 5.70 - 6.02.

From prediction point of view MODEL I is a major improvement, compared to the earlier models. The average error of the predictions is 0.15 per cent with an average deviation of 0.10. Beside this extraordinary prediction performance. MODEL I has an interesting and surprising property described in the next section.

Planned private consumption expenditures on cars

It is interesting to note that the term $\hat{\gamma}\hat{P}_t$ where γ is the regression coefficient could be identified as "planned private consumption expenditures on cars". Could the estimated $\hat{\gamma}\hat{P}_t$ by chance bee used as a proxy for realised car consumption, and if so, what is the difference between "planned" and "realised" car consumption? We could not expect that "planned consumption" would be a perfect predictor of "realised consumption" because:

1. People change their buying plans
2. We do not know the true values of P_t and γ.

Even if we knew the true values γ and P_t, we must expect a difference between "planned" and "realised" car consumption because of 1. above.

The estimate of γ from table 9, 1978:2, is 6.02. The estimate $\hat{P}_{1978:2}$ = 371 and $\hat{\gamma}\hat{P}_t$ = 6.02 * 371 = 2 233 million Swedish crowns. The actual consumption expenditures on cars 1978:2 was 2 183, which makes a difference of 2.3 per cent of actual consumption. Although this prediction was unusually successful, it is not a coincidence. In table 9, we show "planned consumption" in the sense above and the actual outcomes during the prediction period. The average difference between "planned" and "realised" consumption is 10.2 per cent. As can be seen, "planned consumption" is usually less than actual consumption. The main explanation for this is that some of the households with no plans to buy, actually buy a car. This is a well known experience of using buying plans in predicting future purchases.

I shall end the discussion regarding six months predictions by making some comments on a possible implication from the results above. The estimates of the coefficients of MODEL I, supports a natural partition of the model into two separate models; one explaining car consumption $C2_t$ and the other explaining $C1_t = C_t - C2_t$. The traditional consumption function is split into disaggregated models of consumer behaviour. In the present case, the disaggregation is quite simple.

TABLE 9. Planned and actual car consumption expenditures in fixed prices 1978:2 to 1981:2.

t	Planned consumption	Actual consumption	Difference in per cent
1978:2	2 233	2 183	2.3
1979:1	2 059	2 408	-14.5
1979:2	2 046	2 171	- 5.8
1980:1	1 898	2 101	- 9.7
1980:2	1 609	1 974	-18.5
1981:1	1 978	2 033	- 2.7
1981:2	1 610	1 964	-18.0

A simple disaggregated consumption structure

$$C2_t = \gamma P_t + \varepsilon_t \tag{9.2}$$

$$C1_t = \alpha + \beta_1 C_{t-1} + \beta_2 Y_t + \beta_3 ATTIND_t + u_t \tag{9.3}$$

$$C_t = C1_t + C2_t \tag{9.4}$$

Suppose that this disaggregation could be expanded to the following consumption structure:

$$C_{1t} = C_1(P1_t, Z1)$$
$$C_{2t} = C_2(P2_t, Z2)$$
$$\cdot$$
$$\cdot$$
$$C_{kt} = C_k(Y_t, C_{t-m}, ATTIND_t)$$
$$C_t = C_{1t} + C_{2t} + \ldots + C_{kt}$$

where $P1_t$ and $P2_t$ indicate buying plans for the goods or services defining C_{1t} respectively C_{2t}, $ATTIND_t$ is an attitude index (not necessarily of the type we have used). Other information Z may be needed. Suppose that the primary purpose is to predict the aggregate consumption C_t and that the models have been estimated. Let the disaggregated predictions be $\hat{C}_{1t}, \hat{C}_{2t},\ldots, \hat{C}_{kt}$ and

$$\hat{C}_t = \hat{C}_{1t} + \hat{C}_{2t} + \ldots, + \hat{C}_{kt}$$

Competing to this disaggregated prediction of C_t is of course to specify C_t directly and use this estimated consumption function to predict C_t. However, it seems easier to give the disaggregated models a behavioural or causal structure than the aggregated consumption function. If this is true it seems to me that the disaggregated prediction of C_t would dominate the direct prediction of C_t.

9 QUARTERLY FORECASTS OF PRIVATE FINAL CONSUMPTION EXPENDITURES 1977:3 - 1982:4

Most of our experience of the prediction value of attitudes and buying plans concern quarterly forecasts of the private final consumption expenditures. In this last chapter, we shall briefly deal with quarterly forecasts using buying plans in the consumption function.

MODEL

$$C_k^N = \alpha + \beta Y_{k-4} + \lambda_1 D1 + \lambda_2 D2 + \lambda_3 D4 + \varepsilon_t; \qquad (10.1)$$

$$C_k^T = \gamma_1 P_k^n + \gamma_2 P_k^s + u_t;$$

$$C_k = C_k^N + C_k^T;$$

where α, λ_1, λ_2, λ_3, β, γ_1 and γ_2 are parameters, ε_k and u_k are random variables and:

Y_{k-4} = Lagged disposable income

P_k^n = The number of households who at the beginning of k have plans to buy a new car within three months

P_k^s = The number of households who at the beginning of k are absolutely sure that they are going to buy a second-hand car within three months

D1 = Dummy for quarter 1

D2 = Dummy for quarter 2

D4 = Dummy for quarter 4

C_k^T = Transitory consumption

C_k^N = Normal consumption

C_k = Private final consumption expenditures.

Final consumption C_k is assumed to be decomposed into normal consumption C_k^N and transitory consumption C_k^T. Normal consumption is explained by lagged disposable income and seasonal components, while transitory consumption is explained by planned purchases of new and second-hand cars. Dummies are used because we have used data on consumption expenditures not seasonally adjusted.

We show the estimated model in table 10. The coefficient of D1 was insignificant. Below the estimated model we show 22 forecasts with the estimated model. We have used the first 15 observations for estimating the model. We must point out that the forecasts are in fact ex ante predictions in the sense that we do not need to make separate predictions of the independent variables. When the forecast is made, we do know the values to be put into the model. The model has not been reestimated when the forecasts are made; all forecasts are made with the use of the estimated model shown in the table.

Some remarks: The forecasting period is divided into two parts; 1977:3 - 1979:2 and 1979:3 - 1982:4. During the first part of the prediction period, the sample size of the HIP-surveys was 10 000 households. From 1979:3 the sample size has been 6 600 households. When survey estimates are used in consumption functions or predicting a population characteristic, we must be aware of the dependency between prediction accuracy and sample size. If the sample size is reduced, we must expect that the prediction errors would increase. Table 10 is a very good example of this. The average mean of the prediction errors for the first 8 quarters is 0.84 per cent of actual consumption. If the model is estimated with N = 23 (1973:4 - 1979:2) and the consumption during 1979:3 - 1982:4 predicted with that model, the average error increases to 1.83 per cent.

TABLE 1. NA-MODEL Prediction Errors in Per Cent of Actual Private Final Consumption Expenditures 1978:2-1981:2.

	1978:2	1979:1	1979:2	1980:1	1980:2	1981:1	1981:2	Prediction accuracy measures %
Constant	12 544 (1.10)	12 031 (1.14)	9 535 (0.91)	9 795 (1.07)	9 731 (1.18)	12 832 (1.68)	12 869 (1.81)	$U = 0.944$ $U^M = 23.78$
C_{t-1}	0.516 (4.10)	0.517 (4.39)	0.556 (5.42)	0.554 (6.33)	0.556 (6.20)	0.536 (6.25)	0.535 (6.89)	$U^S = 43.08$ $U^C = 33.15$
Y_t	0.316 (6.04)	0.322 (7.08)	0.316 (6.92)	0.315 (7.99)	0.314 (8.50)	0.295 (9.20)	0.295 (9.84)	$U^R = 54.65$ $U^D = 21.58$
N	9	10	11	12	13	14	15	$r = 0.938$
R^2	0.88	0.89	0.88	0.90	0.90	0.91	0.91	$\ddot{m} = 0.697$ $\ddot{s} = 0.682$
Pred. error %	0.5	-1.6	-0.1	-0.1	1.5	0.0	1.0	$m = 0.030$ $s = 1.01$

C_{t-1} = Private final consumption expenditures

Y_t = Disposable income

N = Number of observations used for estimating the model

R^2 = Coefficient of multiple correlation

( ) below the regression coefficient = t-value of the estimate

TABLE 2. ATTITUDE - MODELS I. Average Errors in the Predictions of Private Final Consumption Expenditures in Per Cent of Actual Consumption Expenditures 1978:2 - 1981:2

Variable							
Constant	147 (0.02)	6 239 (0.77)	2 075 (0.24)	5 716 (0.85)	12 860 (2.42)	11 158 (2.31)	6 178 (1.09)
C_{t-1}	0.653 (8.67)	0.616 (6.76)	0.631 (7.40)	0.628 (8.20)	0.543 (9.14)	0.596 (10.59)	0.619 (9.95)
Y_t	0.302 (13.30)	0.307 (10.46)	0.305 (11.54)	0.307 (12.34)	0.276 (13.02)	0.276 (14.35)	0.282 (13.75)
$\hat{A}1_t$	13.92 (2.86)						
$\hat{A}2_t$		-4.81 (-1.60)					
$\hat{A}3_t$			13.63 (2.04)				
$\hat{A}4_t$				-6.86 (-2.46)			
$\hat{A}5_t$					7.17 (3.08)		
$\hat{A}6_t$						-3.75 (-3.81)	
$\hat{A}7_t$							7.14 (3.32)
R^2	0.948	0.928	0.935	0.942	0.951	0.960	0.955
$\ddot{m}_j$ $\ddot{s}_j$	0.94 (0.86)	1.21 (1.16)	0.94 (0.47)	1.07 (0.75)	0.80 (0.84)	0.62 (0.50)	0.65 (0.33)

TABLE 3. ATTITUDE - MODELS I Prediction Errors in Per Cent of Actual Private Final Consumption Expenditures 1978:2 - 1981:2.

	1978:2	1979:1	1979:2	1980:1	1980:2	1981:1	1981:2	Prediction accuracy measures %
Constant	14 360	14 561	14 991	15 025	12 602	12 919	11 589	$U = 0.761$
	(1.66)	(1.84)	(2.00)	(2.32)	(2.05)	(2.51)	(2.27)	$U^M = 7.97$
C_{t-1}	0.577	0.575	0.552	0.552	0.580	0.579	0.597	$U^S = 22.80$
	(5.87)	(6.39)	(6.99)	(7.85)	(8.76)	(9.77)	(10.22)	$U^C = 69.23$
Y_t	0.265	0.263	0.275	0.274	0.275	0.273	0.271	$U^R = 36.97$
	(5.91)	(6.50)	(7.92)	(9.22)	(9.16)	(12.24)	(12.02)	$U^D = 55.06$
$\hat{A6}_t$	-6.14	-5.99	-5.01	-5.02	-4.45	-4.54	-4.02	$r = 0.940$
	(-2.36)	(-2.60)	(-3.06)	(-3.31)	(-3.07)	(-3.78)	(-3.51)	$\ddot{m} = 0.62$
N	9	10	11	12	13	14	15	$\ddot{s} = 0.50$
R^2	0.945	0.950	0.949	0.958	0.953	0.963	0.958	$m = -0.22$
Predic. error %	0.26	0.94	0.04	-1.22	0.16	-1.21	-0.51	$s = 0.80$

C_{t-1} = Lagged private final consumption expenditures

Y_t = Disposable income

$A6_t$ = 10* The percentage of the families who think that the general economic situation in Sweden is going to deteriorate in the next 12 months

N = Number of observations used for estimating the model

R^2 = Coefficient of multiple correlation

TABLE 4. ATTITUDE - MODELS I Prediction Errors in Per Cent of Actual Private Final Consumption Expenditures 1978:2 - 1981:2.

	1978:2	1979:1	1979:2	1980:1	1980:2	1981:1	1981:2	Prediction accuracy measures %
Constant	710	549	2724	6065	5760	6694	6228	$U = 0.724$
	(0.06)	(0.05)	(0.31)	(0.79)	(0.83)	(1.07)	(1.05)	$U^M = 0.704$
C_{t-1}	0.678	0.668	0.638	0.608	0.614	0.610	0.619	$U^S = 38.63$
	(5.08)	(5.25)	(6.70)	(6.96)	(7.97)	(8.58)	(9.29)	$U^C = 60.65$
Y_t	0.286	0.299	0.303	0.293	0.292	0.282	0.280	$U^R = 52.69$
	(6.22)	(7.39)	(8.35)	(8.66)	(9.20)	(11.31)	(11.79)	$U^D = 46.59$
$\hat{A7}_t$	10.27	9.62	8.28	7.25	7.18	7.67	7.29	$r = 0.954$
	(1.94)	(1.92)	(2.43)	(2.30)	(2.43)	(2.93)	(2.97)	$\ddot{m} = 0.65$
N	9	10	11	12	13	14	15	$\ddot{s} = 0.33$
R^2	0.93	0.93	0.935	0.94	0.94	0.95	0.95	$m = 0.055$
Predic. error %	-0.95	0.67	1.14	-0.30	0.66	-0.66	-0.19	$s = 0.777$

C_{t-1} = Lagged private final consumption expenditures

Y_t = Disposable income

$A7_t$ = 10* The percentage of the families who think that the rate of unemployment is going down in the next 12 months.

TABLE 5. Latent Roots and Vectors to the Attitude Variables $\hat{A1}_t, \ldots, \hat{A7}_t$

Latent root	Coefficients of the latent vector							Explained variance by the vector	Total explained variance
	A1	A2	A3	A4	A5	A6	A7		
5.10	0.382	-0.387	0.410	-0.428	0.286	-0.384	0.352	72.9	72.9
1.39	-0.349	0.372	-0.270	0.136	0.616	-0.371	0.362	19.9	92.8
0.27	0.231	-0.010	-0.247	0.208	-0.362	0.222	0.813	3.8	96.7
0.15	0.630	0.486	0.048	0.323	-0.150	-0.452	-0.185	2.1	98.8
0.043	0.490	-0.302	-0.444	0.186	0.536	0.341	-0.180	0.6	99.4
0.031	-0.023	0.096	0.704	0.514	0.281	0.373	0.114	0.4	99.8
0.01	0.201	0.614	0.050	-0.592	0.138	0.455	0.053	0.2	100.0

TABLE 6. ATTITUDE-MODEL II. Prediction Errors in Per Cent of Actual Private Final Consumption Expenditures 1978:2-1981:2.

	1978:2	1979:1	1979:2	1980:1	1980:2	1981:1	1981:2	Prediction accuracy measures %
Constant	15 159.7 (1.33)	14950.2 (1.40)	14842.2 (1.50)	15548.1 (1.77)	14764.4 (1.88)	16589.0 (2.49)	16132.8 (2.63)	$U = 0.594$ $U^M = 30.58$
C_{t-1}	0.537 (4.31)	0.530 (4.57)	0.523 (5.04)	0.518 (5.52)	0.529 (6.51)	0.518 (7.03)	0.525 (7.99)	$U^S = 31.74$ $U^C = 37.68$
Y_t	0.271 (4.19)	0.278 (4.66)	0.285 (6.30)	0.281 (7.04)	0.281 (7.46)	0.269 (9.18)	0.268 (9.71)	$U^R = 38.39$ $U^D = 31.03$
$ATTIND_t$	7.34 (1.12)	5.13 (1.12)	4.37 (1.69)	4.31 (1.79)	4.22 (1.88)	4.62 (2.32)	4.54 (2.43)	$r = 0.980$ $\ddot{m} = 0.54$
N	9	10	11	12	13	14	15	$\ddot{s} = 0.26$
R^2	0.907	0.913	0.915	0.929	0.930	0.941	0.942	$m = 0.32$
Pred. error %	1.05	0.50	0.34	-0.41	0.73	-0.35	0.41	$s = 0.54$

C_{t-1} = Lagged private final consumption expenditures

Y_t = Disposable income

$ATTIND_t$ = Discriminant function $\hat{Y}_{2t} = -0.349\ \hat{A1}_t + 0.372\ \hat{A2}_t - 0.270\ \hat{A3}_t + 0.136\ \hat{A4}_t + 0.616\ \hat{A5}_t - 0.371\ \hat{A6}_t + 0.362\ \hat{A7}_t$;

N = Number of observations used for estimating the model

R^2 = Coefficient of multiple correlation.

TABLE 7. PLAN - MODEL. Prediction Errors during 1978:2 to 1981:2 in Per Cent of Actual Private Final Consumption Expenditures.

	1978:2	1979:1	1979:2	1980:1	1980:2	1981:1	1981:2	Prediction Accuracy Measures %
Constant	10 048 (1.00)	9 444 (1.02)	7 245 (0.80	7 092 (0.90)	7 206 (1.02)	1 922 (1.26)	8 259 (1.43)	U = 0.599 U^M = 6.57
C_{t-1}	0.545 (4.93)	0.545 (5.28)	0.579 (5.90)	0.580 (6.60)	0.579 (7.61)	0.576 (8.29)	0.570 (9.21)	U^S = 29.11 U^C = 64.32
Y_t	0.289 (6.04)	0.297 (7.13)	0.291 (7.02)	0.291 (8.25)	0.291 (8.85)	0.284 (11.13)	0.285 (12.03)	U^R = 40.56 U^D = 52.87
$\hat{P}_t$	6.93 (1.72)	6.83 (1.82)	7.27 (1.94)	7.28 (2.11)	7.27 (2.24)	7.76 (2.78)	7.70 (2.93)	r = 0.965 $\ddot{m}$ = 0.42
								$\ddot{s}$ = 0.47
N	9	10	11	12	13	14	15	m = -0.157
R^2	0.927	0.932	0.922	0.936	0.938	0.949	0.950	s = 0.630
Predic. error %	-0.64	-1.34	-0.04	-0.01	0.51	0.20	0.22	

$\hat{P}_t$ = An estimate of the number of households who have a positive plan in the beginning of t to purchase a new car in the next three months.

Other notations are explained in table 6.

TABLE 8. MODEL I. Prediction Errors during 1978:2 to 1981:2 in Per Cent of Actual Private Final Consumption Expenditures.

	1978:2	1979:1	1979:2	1980:1	1980:2	1981:1	1981:2	Prediction accuracy measures %
Constant	1 185	11 308	11516	11 747	11 302	11 561	11 498	$U = 0.177$
	(0.95)	(1.09)	(1.22)	(1.42)	(1.55)	(1.86)		$U^M = 13.21$
C_{t-1}	0.547	0.548	0.551	0.549	0.555	0.554	0.555	$U^S = 61.88$
	(4.47)	(5.00)	(5.65)	(6.30)	(7.48)	(8.43)	(9.68)	$U^C = 24.75$
Y_t	0.279	0.278	0.274	0.273	0.272	0.269	0.269	$U^R = 63.82$
	(4.36)	(4.98)	(6.48)	(7.43)	(7.97)	(10.67)	(11.48)	$U^D = 22.74$
$\hat{P}_t$	6.02	5.85	5.70	5.77	5.81	5.94	5.94	$r = 0.999$
	(1.10)	(1.35)	(1.49)	(1.65)	(1.79)	(2.11)	(2.28)	$\ddot{m} = 0.15$
$ATTIND_t$	2.26	2.63	3.11	3.06	3.01	3.06	3.04	$\ddot{s} = 0.10$
	(0.29)	(0.56)	(1.22)	(1.33)	(1.41)	(1.63)	(1.77)	$m = -0.066$
N	9	10	11	12	13	14	15	$s = 0.178$
R^2	0.93	0.94	0.94	0.95	0.95	0.96	0.96	
Predic. error %	-0.14	-0.29	0.15	-0.25	0.16	-0.08	-0.01	

$\hat{P}_t$ = An estimate of the number of households in the beginning of t who have a positive plan to purchase a new car in the next three months.

C_{t-1}, Y_t, $ATTIND_t$ and the other notations are explained in table 6.

TABLE 10. Quarterly Forecasts of Private Final Consumption Expenditures 1977:3–1982:4

VARIABLE	$\hat{B}$	$s(\hat{B})$	t-value
Constant	11 482.5	4 006.43	2.866
Y_{k-4}	0.583	0.115	5.075
D2	-2 548.31	484.297	-5.262
D4	-3 770.01	1 352.87	-2.787
P_k^n	5.728	1.859	3.081
P_k^s	6.686	2.325	2.876

R^2 = 0.949   N=15   DW=1.848
SE = 624.837   F(5,9)=33.39

F O R E C A S T S

Time k	FORECAST	ACTUAL CONSUMPT.	ERROR %		PREDICTION ACCURACY MEASURES %
1977:3	36 948.1	36 854	0.255	Sample size of the HIP-surveys= 10 000 households	
:4	42 040.8	42 211	-0.403		U = 1.82
1978:1	38 673.2	37 466	3.222		U^M = 11.28
:2	38 798.6	38 624	0.452		U^S = 0.11
:3	36 784.9	37 204	-1.127		U^C = 88.57
:4	43 128.3	42 828	0.701		
1979:1	38 921.6	38 812	0.282		U^R = 0.91
:2	39 936.2	40 049	-0.282		
:3	37 614.8	37 664	-0.131	Sample size of the HIP-surveys = 6 600 households	U^D = 87.79
:4	43 105.4	43 731	-1.431		r = 0.963
1980:1	38 687.7	39 380	-1.758		$\ddot{m}$ = 1.33
:2	39 174.9	39 451	-0.700		$\ddot{s}$ = 1.28
:3	36 889.5	38 297	-3.675		m = -0.60
:4	42 037.7	43 448	-3.246		s = 1.83
1981:1	38 780.5	38 525	0.663		
:2	39 071.8	39 667	-1.501		
:3	37 586.5	37 229	0.960		
:4	44 049	44 025	0.055		
1982:1	37 721.6	39 439	-4.355		
:2	40 674.5	40 185	1.218		
:3	36 796.3	37 804	-2.666		
:4	45 463.3	45 339	0.274		

$\hat{B}$ = Regressions estimate
$s(\hat{B})$ = Standard deviation of the estimate

The Role of Attitudes in Consumer Spending

O.D.J. Stuart
Bureau for Economic Research
University of Stellenbosch
Stellenbosch

Introductory remarks

As a result of the work done by Katona - and others who base their research on similar lines - many researchers in the field of consumer behaviour accept the thesis that certain types of consumer spending are functions of consumers' ability to buy and their willingness to buy. The former is usually taken to refer to income, credit etc. whilst willingness to buy is determined by the interrelation of many attitudes and expectations.

It should be mentioned, though, that many economists are sceptical about the measuring of attitudes and the use of quantified attitudes in demand or consumption functions. They argue that consumer sentiment - as attitudes and expectations are usually referred to - can be explained by hard data and this makes the costly consumer surveys, attempting to directly measure sentiment, redundant. A valid counter argument is that survey data yield information which have unique features and thus may be extremely useful for purposes of forecasting. The survey data are also available well in advance of official data and are not subject to revision. These matters, by themselves, probably justify the continuation of consumer surveys aimed at the measuring of attitudes.

It is usually argued that changes in sentiment lead changes in spending which is of a discretionary nature. This has led to the practice of isolating spending on durable goods in order to test the explanatory value of attitudinal data. In this regard one should keep the level of affluence of the community in mind. It is surely plausible to argue that in rich societies neither changes in income nor changes in sentiment are likely to have any impact on even sizeable outlays because all purchases by the very affluent could be done impulsively. At the other end of the scale the very poor possess virtually no discretion when making purchases and the latter are thus mostly essential in nature. It would thus appear as if the importance of sentiment as an explanatory factor in consumer spending may well be a function of the income distribution within a country or community.

The points raised in the above paragraph put a question mark over the practice of selecting spending on durables and motor-cars as proxies for discretionary spending. Although one never or very seldomly encounters the extremes sketched in the previous paragraphs communities do tend to be either rich or poor. If the income distribution is fairly skewed towards higher incomes then sentiment will affect the spending on durables. However, it is also possible that in cases where the distribution is skewed towards low incomes, discretion may be exercised in the buying of even non-durables.

It follows, from the above, that the impact of sentiment on discretionary spending may be negligible in extremely affluent societies as well as in very poor societies. The role of attitudinal data is thus not independent of the income distribution and hence it does not follow that attitudes are bound to perform well in the demand functions of country A simply because they did so in country B.

The aim of this paper flows directly from the issues raised in the previous paragraphs; the aim is to investigate the use of sentiment data in explaining private consumption expenditure in South Africa. In order to get an idea of how well these data perform in extreme vs not-so-extreme discretionary purchases their roles are investigated with regard to spending on durable goods as well as to non-durable goods.

Measuring of consumer sentiment

In previous paragraphs reference to consumer attitudes has been made in a rather matter-of-fact manner implying that attitudes can be measured and quantified in a manner which enables one to investigate their role in consumer spending. It should be pointed out, however, that many of the issues raised by Katona have not been resolved and a great deal of uncertainty still prevails with regard to the methodology of measuring attitudes as well as with the selection of the attitudes to be measured. With regard to the latter the difference in opinion on "buying intentions" and "consumer attitudes" may be cited as an example of an issue which has not really been resolved.

The sentiment measures used in this paper are those of the Stellenbosch based Bureau for Economic Research (BER) and they differ little from those of the Survey Research Center (Michigan) and the European

Economic Community. The rationale for the type of questions asked had been advocated by Katona over decades and is well expounded by Pickering (9) in a recent article. The argument runs that a consumer is more likely to buy durable goods when he has confidence in the future and has a reasonably high degree of satisfaction with the present situation. When one makes the reasonable assumption that changes in confidence are not necessarily highly correlated with changes in income one has to conclude that a close relationship between changes in income and changes in purchases of durable goods is unlikely to exist.

An argument of Katona, elaborated upon by Pickering (9), essentially says that purchases of durables are more likely to occur when people feel confident. The latter could relate to general economic conditions or to the personal circumstances of the individual. In fact, the definition of consumer confidence can be quite problematical and one suspects that many co-called confidence measures are in fact measuring something else. Broadly speaking, though, it is plausible to argue that, to be confident, an individual must have a favourable expectation about as well as a favourable perception of recent developments within a certain sphere. Let us for the sake of argument restrict our reasoning to economic development. The following are possible attitudes which consumers may have regarding economic conditions.

		Expectations		
		Better	Same	Worse
Perceptions	Better	BB	BS	BW
	Same	SB	SS	SW
	Worse	WB	WS	WW

The letters shown in the box refer to different degrees of confidence; for instance, BB refers to an individual who has perceived better economic conditions and expect them to improve further. Such an individual's level of confidence surely must be higher than one with a WW-response (poor conditions perceived and expecting a further deterioration). Because of a belief that perceived as well as expected conditions help to shape confidence the BER questions respondents on both. The average value should provide one with the intensity of the implied confidence - in the diagram BB relates to high confidence as against WW which relates to a lack of confidence.

The areas on which data are collected are shown below, together with the response categories provided for. The numbers in brackets are weights which are used to quantify the responses and comment on this procedure follows in paragraphs to come.

A. Opinion on economic development over the past twelve months.

(a)	Considerable improvement	1
(b)	Slight improvement	$\frac{1}{2}$
(c)	Slight deterioration	$-\frac{1}{2}$
(d)	Considerable deterioration	-1

B. Opinion on economic development over the next twelve months.

(a))
(b)) As for A
(c))
(d))

C. Opinion on economic development over the next five years.

(a))
(b)) As for A
(c))
(d))

D. Description of the household's <u>current</u> financial situation.

(a)	Debts are increasing	-1
(b)	Forced to dissave	$-\frac{1}{2}$
(c)	Income just sufficient	0
(d)	Can save a little	$\frac{1}{2}$
(e)	Can save a lot	1

E. Opinion on current financial situation compared with that of a year ago.

(a)	Considerably better	1
(b)	Slightly better	½
(c)	Same	0
(d)	Slightly worse	-½
(e)	Considerably worse	-1

F. Expected financial situation over the next twelve months.

(a))
(b))
(c)) As in E.
(d))
(e))

G. Development in <u>rates</u> of price increases during the past twelve months.

(a)	Increased faster	1
(b)	Remain unchanged	0
(c)	Increased more slowly	-1

H. Expected development in <u>rates</u> of price increases during the next twelve months.

(a))
(b)) As in G.
(c))

I. Opinion on the suitability of the present time for saving.

(a)	Definitely favourable	1
(b)	Probably favourable	½
(c)	Probably unfavourable	-½
(d)	Definitely unfavourable	-1

J. Will be able to save money in the next 3 months.

(a)	Yes	1
(b)	Probably	$\frac{1}{2}$
(c)	Probably not	$-\frac{1}{2}$
(d)	No	-1

K. Suitability of the time for undertaking purchases such as furniture, washing-machines, refrigerators etc.

(a)	Right time	1
(b)	Neither right nor wrong	0
(c)	Wrong time	-1

The questions are posed quarterly to a representative sample of heads of households and provide the BER with a mass of information. The responses should help the researchers at least to form a subjective opinion of the frames of mind consumers are in. However, the raw data must somehow be ordened to enable the analyst to make meaningful interpretations. The method followed is outlined in the section below.

The quantification of consumer sentiment

It is obvious that the responses to a question can be summarized in various different manners. For instance, some analysts (21) prefer to restrict their interpretation of survey results to the analysis of inter-survey changes in optimistic answers, whilst the most popular method appears to be the use of net balances or methods based on them. The BER has, up to now, calculated weighted averages for each separate question by using the response categories and the weights shown in the previous section. In order to avoid negative values one hundred is added to the weighted mean of each question. This method produces an "index" which fluctuates around 100 and varies between the extremes 200 and zero.

When assessing the consumer market the researcher then has got indices at hand which summarize the views of consumers on the following matters:

(a) Economic matters in general.
(b) Financial situation of households.
(c) Rates at which prices are changing.
(d) Conditions for saving.
(e) Conditions for buying.

Each of the sentiment measures may be used as an indicator on its own, but researchers frequently prefer to combine questions in order to calculate a composite index of consumer confidence (sentiment). Two methods are popular in this regard - after appropriate questions have been selected, and their responses have been quantified as shown above. In the one approach the index values are simply summed and averaged. An alternative method is to apply weights to selected questions and then obtain a weighted mean in order to compute an index of consumer confidence.

One can argue against the method of assigning equal weights to the different questions and even the particular set of questions selected may be frowned upon. It can hardly be denied that some questions are more relevant at certain stages of the business cycle and that certain questions are on the average more important than others. Although it is extremely difficult to decide which questions are more important at certain times there are techniques available which can be used for ascertaining the weights for questions.

It is stated above that one can argue with the method of assigning equal weights. However, one can also argue with the method of differential weighting. Once weights have been ascertained, they have to be retained if one does not wish to change the index values with every survey. This implies that a rigidness, similar to equal weighting, is built into the indices. It could also be stated that equal weighting probably introduces systematic errors (as does differential weighting) and in this respect there is no conclusive evidence that one method is superior to the other. In a later section of this paper, however, the explanatory power of both types of indices are researched by means of regression analysis.

An analysis of the sentiment data

Apart from the problematical area of weighting of questions and responses one is also confronted (as was hinted at above) with the problem as to which questions should be used to establish a composite index. Different attitudes are usually highly correlated and it could thus be argued that little new information is obtained by measuring all of them and then averaging the scores. The intercorrelations of attitudinal indices are shown below.[1)]

Correlation matrix of BER attitude measures

	ECOA	ECOB	ECOC	PRB	PRF	FINC	FINB	FINF	BUY	SAVE	SAVEY
ECOA	1,0										
ECOB	0,84	1,0									
ECOC	0,32	0,76	1,0								
PRB	0,08	-0,08	0,29	1,0							
PRF	0,46	0,02	0,50	0,42	1,0						
FINC	0,50	0,57	0,37	0,42	0,21	1,0					
FINB	0,73	0,51	0,02	0,49	0,50	0,76	1,0				
FINF	0,78	0,86	0,59	0,10	0,07	0,74	0,76	1,0			
BUY	0,87	0,58	0,01	0,21	0,58	0,38	0,81	0,66	1,0		
SAVE	0,53	0,59	0,36	0,28	0,10	0,84	0,79	0,82	0,49	1,0	
SAVEY	0,58	0,60	0,32	0,40	0,29	0,93	0,81	0,82	0,50	0,90	1,0

It is clear that many of the variables are highly correlated and as such the measurement of certain attitudes may in fact be duplicated. Note for instance the very high correlation between ECOA and ECOB as well as between FINB and FINF. These correlations imply that consumers could be basing their expectations of changes in the economy and their finances on perceived changes in these magnitudes. One notices, however, that BUY is also highly correlated with FINB, FINF, ECOA and ECOB. Assuming a certain line of causality it could be argued that perceived good economic performances are projected into the future and so is a perceived sound financial situation. Given these favourable

1) A description of the notations used in this paper may be found in an addendum.

attitudes consumers then consider the time as being opportune for making sizeable money outlays. The opposite reasoning is followed when the signs of the correlation coefficients are all negative. Note also that ECOB and ECOC are highly correlated thus substantiating the suggestion that consumers simply project perceptions into the future - in this instance short-term expectations into the longer term, but both originating in perceptions.

These high intercorrelations could imply that other aspects of consumer sentiment are ignored or underweighted. If this is true it implies that research should be done to find questions to fill these gaps whilst at the same time minimising the overlap in sentiment measures calculated on the basis of the existing questions. However, it should be borne in mind that although the questions were designed to permit an insight into the way the consumer assesses <u>different</u> aspects of his environment(s) it is almost self evident that events within this environment(s) are bound to affect either all consumers or certain groups of consumers in a similar manner and the result will obviously be an informational overlap in what the questions convey about the respondents' frame of mind. Although there are overlaps, and sizeable ones at that, each question will nevertheless probably also contributes something unique. In order to eliminate overlaps and highlight the uniqueness mentioned, the technique of principal components could be put to good use.

The discussion above leads to the conclusion that the totality of consumers' experience over the years covered by the surveys as measured by the responses to the questions mentioned may be represented by an <u>overlapping</u> group of eleven areas which together make up a particular lump of variability. The principal component technique effectively summarizes the major <u>separate</u> sources of variability in the data by transforming a given set of variables into a new set of composite variables or factors which are <u>orthogonal to each other</u> (4, 16).

The results of a principal component analysis of the BER data are shown below. Surveys are taken as replications and the period 1975:4 to 1981:3 is covered.

Principal component analysis of responses to eleven attitudinal questions

	No rotation			Varimax rotated		
	COMA	COMB	COMC	VCOMA	VCOMB	VCOMC
ECOA	843	011	-501	304	918	167
ECOB	802	-467	-279	396	641	609
ECOC	399	-863	037	281	077	906
PRB	321	627	482	589	-044	-616
PRF	346	795	-307	097	591	-698
FINC	846	-012	440	925	212	097
FINB	901	348	037	719	612	-208
FINF	931	-285	-036	661	575	425
BUY	764	307	-500	260	918	-134
SAVE	867	-085	334	867	292	182
SAVEY	905	038	336	903	337	067

Variance explained by each factor before rotation:

COMA = 57,2% COMB = 20,9% COMC = 12,1%

(Please note that the figures appearing in the body of the table are factor loadings and thus also fractions. Decimal points are not shown, however).

The first three factors explain 90,1 per cent of the total variance in the data. The number of common factors was decided upon by applying Kaiser's criterion.

COMA loads significantly on all variables except PRB and PRF. It would appear to represent consumers who have perceived good economic conditions and think that these are likely to persist over the short-term future. The favourable economic conditions caused personal financial situations to become more relaxed, this was perceived by consumers and they expect that the financial situation of households is likely to improve further. As a result of these circumstances consumer liquidity and confidence is high hence they consider it a good time to buy and still have money to save. It would appear as if this component links confidence with liquidity and COMA may possibly be regarded as a liquidity indicator. It also shows that consumers base their expectations on their perceptions and it would probably not be incorrect to follow Van Raaij (3, p 103) and to call this component an optimism - pessimism indicator.

COMB loads significantly on ECOC, PRB and PRF. It appears that consumers who have perceived price increases project these into the future and conclude that such a development would harm the economy in the long run. The other loadings of this component are insignificant but their signs appear to underscore the reasoning that price changes are likely to harm the economy and financial situations and this could cause a buy-before-things-get-worse outlook.

COMC loads significantly on ECOA and BUY and the signs of the loadings are negative, suggesting that poor economic situations are likely to damp consumer spending and boost savings.

The varimax-rotated solution is easier to interpret as is clearly shown in the above table.

VCOMA loads significantly on past prices, personal finances and on matters related to saving. It seems to say that the current financial situation of households is easy, has improved over the year before surveying and is expected to continue improving during the post-survey year. This has led to a building-up of monetary liquidity but in view of experiences during a year of price changes consumers prefer to save their money.

VCOMB essentially says that consumers have enjoyed good economic times which they think will continue for a further year. This has led to an improvement in their personal finances which in their opinion is likely to improve further and because of a fear of price increases they consider it as a good time to buy durable goods.

VCOMC has to do with price changes, the general economy and consumers' anticipated financial situation. Apparently perceptions of declines in the <u>rate</u> at which prices have increased are projected into the future. At the same time these developments are expected to lead to a more sound economic environment - a spin-off of which will be an improved personal financial situation.

The factor analysis has thus confirmed that at least three orthogonal factors can be extracted from the intercorrelated BER survey data. Not all of them, however, lend themselves as obvious candidates to be considered in a demand function. Of the six described COMA and VCOMB appear to be the most logical choices. COMA because it does load on BUY, makes economic sense and could be interpreted as a liquidity index or, if one so desires, even as an index of consumer confidence. COMB is best left alone because of its heavy loadings on price variables. COMC is also a good candidate suggesting that ECOA and BUY could be combined to form a sentiment variable explaining consumer spending.

Of the factors obtained by varimax rotation VCOMA and VCOMB appear to measure contrasting streams of thought and it would be interesting to see how they perform in regression runs. VCOMC certainly makes sense, economically speaking, that is, but one wonders whether it is not best to steer clear of indicators which build a rigidness into the possible impact of inflation on consumer behaviour.

<u>Regression and correlation analyses</u>

As was pointed out earlier the dependent variables used are CD and CN; the former because it is the most logical proxy for discretionary spending and the latter to ascertain whether sentiment data could not be used with good effect to explain changes in a spending category which is made up of items which are for the most part essential in nature. The time span chosen is 1975:4 to 1981:3 which covers roughly one business cycle measured from peak to peak. The coefficients of variation for CD and CN are 17,5% and 5,3%, respectively, and this to a certain extent illustrates the difference in discretion that consumers had with regard to the buying of CD type goods vs CN type goods during the period mentioned.

Before turning to regression as such, the correlations between CD and the variables which are considered to be potential determinants of changes therein are discussed as is CN's correlation with its determinants. It should be stressed that in this paper it is assumed that causality is running uni-directional - from sentiment measure to expenditure. Also, the object of the correlation analysis is simply to obtain a clearer insight into the data and to offer tentative suggestions about the use of the measures. Hopefully, the exercise will not be viewed as a Galtonian overrating of the value of correlation coefficients.

It is clear that consumers' assessment of short-term past and future economic development correlates highly with both CD and CN. Their expectations of developments in the economy over the longer term (five years) show a low correlation with both CN and CD. As the time lags are made longer, however, the correlation improves suggesting that the influence of ECOC on CD, in particular, takes time to materialise. It is also possible that this particular measure will show higher correlations with costlier items such as houses and, perhaps, cars.

Perceptions of changes in the rate at which prices have changed, correlate fairly highly with CD but show low correlation coefficients with CN. Lagged values of PRB, apparently, have little influence on CD but it would appear that the impact of PRB on CD is almost an immediate one. Anticipations of changes in the rate at which prices change do, apparently, have an influence on both CD and CN suggesting that during the time span under review consumers have been inclined to buy in advance of anticipated changes.

Consumers' assessment of their current financial situation correlates fairly highly with CD but insignificantly with CN. In both categories the correlation coefficients become smaller as lags become longer. FINB correlates very highly with both CD and CN but in both categories (CN in particular) the introduction of lags causes declines in the correlation coefficients. This could imply that consumers base their purchases - in particular those of durable goods - on perceived changes in their personal finances and to a lesser extent on expected changes. One should take note, however, of the fact that FINF and CD correlate highest with a two period lag which means that an expectation of a change in personal finances eventually leads to a change in CD. The impact of FINF on CN is much more immediate and falls away as lags become longer.

Correlation coefficients showing correlations between CD and CN, respectively, with various sentiment measures

		ECOA	ECOB	ECOC	PRB	PRF
CD:	No lags[1)]	0,581	0,322	-0,161	0,665	0,600
	1 Period lags	0,726	0,573	0,078	0,622	0,557
	2 Period lags	0,839	0,765	0,354	0,440	0,477
CN:	No lags	0,781	0,463	-0,168	0,287	0,654
	1 Period lags	0,836	0,599	-0,077	0,210	0,621
	2 Period lags	0,187	0,628	0,147	0,039	0,517

		FINC	FINB	FINF	BUY	SAVE	SAVEY
CD:	No lags	0,690	0,890	0,512	0,782	0,631	0,710
	1 Period lags	0,680	0,891	0,663	0,843	0,648	0,752
	2 Period lags	0,586	0,837	0,730	0,897	0,616	0,627
CN:	No lags	0,401	0,752	0,534	0,878	0,502	0,568
	1 Period lags	0,233	0,634	0,515	0,865	0,290	0,392
	2 Period lags	0,080	0,483	0,410	0,875	0,077	0,129

		CONFA	CONFB	CONFC	COMA	VCOMA	VCOMB
CD:	No lags	0,604	0,369	0,814	0,641	0,848	0,645
	1 Period lags	0,756	0,603	0,878	0,783	0,848	0,782
	2 Period lags	0,865	0,769	0,909	0,864	0,744	0,877
CN:	No lags	0,736	0,487	0,826	0,721	0,631	0,787
	1 Period lags	0,777	0,590	0,778	0,721	0,453	0,824
	2 Period lags	0,750	0,587	0,741	0,645	0,225	0,792

1) Lags refer to sentiment measures.

What consumers think and have to say about the propitiousness of a certain time period for the buying of high priced goods correlate very highly with their actual spending. The latter is not restricted to CD only, as one would have expected, but CN and BUY also correlate highly. In the case of CD the lagging of BUY pushes up the correlations but not in the case of CN.

It is interesting to find that SAVE correlates positively with both CD and CN. In the case of the latter the correlations decrease as the lags increase but this does not hold for CD. It would thus appear as if this particular question measures something more than is asked for. The correlations imply that when consumers report a good time to save the very factors inducing them to say so are also inducing them to buy. The correlation coefficient between BUY and SAVE is 0,49 which do imply that the two variables have something in common. It appears as if people who respond by saying conditions favour saving resort to a great deal of discretionary spending. The SAVEY measure seems to underscore this deduction and apparently tells the researcher that although the consumer has the ability to save he will not necessarily do so. As was shown earlier, BUY and SAVEY are also highly correlated which could imply that some of the money that consumers ostensibly have put aside for saving find their way into the pockets of traders in durable goods.

To sum up the findings with regard to the correlations between single question based attitude measures and CD or CN, it could be stated that almost all of them are highly correlated with the dependent variable and should thus be valuable instruments in explaining consumer spending. The fact that so many of them correlate highly when lagged with either CD or CN implies that they possess leading indicator characteristics. It is also clear that the influence of sentiment on consumer spending is not restricted to spending on durable goods - as is so often advocated - but spending on non-durables is apparently also effected by consumer sentiment.

It was previously argued that composite indicators should be formed to get rid of multicollinearity in regression functions. The correlation coefficients of five such measures with CD and CN also appear in the table under discussion. Attention is first paid to the correlations between these measures and CD. All the sentiment measures with the exception of VCOMA - the first component of a varimax rotated factor analysis - correlate higher when lagged by two periods. Given two period lags, and the correlation coefficients as shown in the table, there is little difference between the measures - one appears to be as good as the other. Judged on correlation coefficients alone, one cannot but feel that the principal component based measures do not perform as well as was expected. In fact, CONFC, which is merely the mean of BUY and FINF, performs best. Note the similarity between CONFA and VCOMB; keeping in mind that VCOMB is made up of virtually the same variables as CONFA but with differential weights used in VCOMB compared to equal weights in CONFA.

In contrast to CD not all the composite measures correlate highly with CN - a noticeable example is VCOMA, while the correlation coefficients depicting the correlation of CONFB and lags thereof with CN are also rather low. All the measures lose some of their influence on CN when the time lags are longer than one quarter. This could be a further indication that the influence of sentiment on CN is rather short-lived and also that consumers react differently to identical exogenous stimuli. It is important, however, to take note of the fact that lagged composite measures do correlate highly with CN and as such they could prove to be important inputs in a forecast exercise.

It can be stated with a great deal of confidence that the multi-question based sentiment variables correlate highly (in lagged and unlagged form) with both CD and CN and are thus potential explanatory variables in regression runs. The fact that they also correlate satisfactorily in lagged form makes them candidates for inclusion in forecast functions. Or, failing that, they could be used as leading indicators to assist forecasters when making quantitative projections.

The models chosen for testing the sentiment variables in conjunction with hard data are:

$CD = a + bY + cCD1 + d\ X$

$CD = a + bY + cCD1 + d\ W$

$CN = a + bY + cCN1 + d\ X$

$CN = a + bY + cCN1 + d\ W$

where different lags are experimented with in the X and W vectors. A key to the symbols appears in the addendum.

In more popular form and using the conventional notation, the basic model can be written as

(1) $C_t = a + bY_t + cC_{t-1} + d\,Z$
where Z is a vector of sentiment variables which can for a moment be ignored.

This model was derived from two different theoretical approaches, namely the habit persistence hypopthesis of Brown (22) and the permanent income hypothesis of Friedman (23). The model can be derived by introducing a partial adjustment mechanism as follows:

Assume (i) $C^*_t = a + bY_t$
where C^*_t is desired consumption expenditure. The adjustment function is:

(ii) $C_t - C^*_{t-1} = k_1\ (C^*_t - C_{t-1}),\ 0 < k_1 < 1$

This implies that consumers do not immediately adjust to their desired level of consumption, but a coefficient of adjustment k_1, comes into play. Combine (i) and (ii) to obtain:

(iii) $C_t = k_1\ a + k_1\ b\ Y_t + (1 - k_1)\ C_{t-1}$ which is a simplified version of equation 1.

The model can also be derived by basing the arguments on the concepts of permanent income, expected income or normal income as the flow equivalents of wealth variables. These concepts are, however, immeasurable and approximations have to be made for empirical work. If a permanent income variable is generated by a Koyck type system of exponentially declining weights on current and past incomes then the underlying model of consumption expenditure yields an estimating equation which is statistically indistinguisable from equation 1.

Write: (iv) $C_t = a + bY^e_t$ where Y^e_t = permanent income

(v) $Y_t^e = k_2(Y_t + (1 - k_2)\ Y_{t-1} + (1 - k_2)^2\ Y_{t-2} + \dots)$

or by applying Koyck's transformation, equation (v) may be written:

(vi) $Y_t^e = k_2\ Y_t - (1 - k_2)\ Y_{t-1}^e$

By combining (vi) and (iv) and applying a bit of mathematical juggling it follows that:

(v) $C_t = k_2\ a + k_2\ bY_t + (1 - k_2)\ C_{t-1}$

which brings one back to a simplified form of equation 1:

$$C_t = a + b\ Y_t + c\ C_{t-1}$$

The results obtained in regressions where consumption expenditure on durable goods featured as the dependent variables are discussed in the next few paragraphs. A table in which the main results are summarised is given below.

The selection of the variables to be included in the X vector was done on the basis of their correlation with CD as well as on their performance in functions not quoted or discussed in this paper. As is shown in the above table, the lagged dependent tends to dominate the functions, especially in functions where the single-question based sentiment measures appear in unlagged form. The adjusted R^2 values are quite satisfactory and so are the Durbin Watson d statistics. It should be mentioned that the latter are biased because of the presence of a lagged dependent. Tests were made along lines as suggested by Malinvaud (24, p. 562) and on basis of that the functions were judged as satisfactory.

It is clear that the single-question sentiment measures do contribute to the explanation of CD in both unlagged and lagged form. Equation 12, for instance, shows that BUY2 is significant, CD1 is highly significant and Y also has a t-value close to 2. The structure of this latter function makes it a good candidate for purposes of forecasting.

Measures of confidence which are based on multi-question responses appear not to perform much better than single-question sentiment measures. The multi-question based measures which performed best are CONFA2 and VCOMB2. The former is the consumer confidence index of the Bureau for Economic Research and is computed from the responses of five

REGRESSION ANALYSIS: SELECTED RESULTS

(Dependent variable : CD. Figures in brackets are t-values.
Refer to first paragraph after table for comments on the use of D.W. with CD1).

CONSTANT	Y	CD1	FINB	BUY	ECOA	SAVEY	$\bar{R}^2$	D.W.
1. -1136,6	0,037	0,657	12,60				0,898	2,1828
	(1,35)	(5,18)	(2,8)					
2. -776,3	0,028	0,774		7,25			0,905	2,0645
	(1,1)	(8,63)		(3,2)				
3. -681,3	0,044	0,892			1,211		0,873	2,2183
	(1,39)	(9,90)			(1,6)			
4. -1415,0	0,047	0,834				10,29	0,883	2,1582
	(1,63)	(8,70)				(2,11)		
			FINB1	BUY1	ECOA1	SAVEY1		
5. -591,7	0,043	0,832			1,651		0,881	2,3358
	(1,45)	(8,39)			(1,99)			
6. -1419,1	0,060	0,648	11,33				0,883	2,1847
	(2,21)	(3,91)	(2,07)					
7. -899,7	0,043	0,750		6,38			0,882	2,4887
	(1,46)	(6,00)		(2,06)				
8. -1393,8	0,061	0,828				7,30	0,872	2,0537
	(2,13)	(7,16)				(1,50)		
			FINF2	BUY2	ECOA2	ECOB2		
9. -397,4	0,039	0,723			2,626		0,904	2,0821
	(1,48)	(7,06)			(3,10)			
10. -798,6	0,047	0,788				3,35	0,896	2,1316
	(1,79)	(8,26)				(2,71)		
11. -1464,9	0,059	0,839	7,17				0,872	2,0340
	(2,07)	(7,61)	(1,52)					
12. -1017,7	0,045	0,627		9,72			0,905	1,8967
	(1,77)	(5,09)		(3,19)				

CONSTANT	Y	CD1	CONFA	CONFX	CONFE	CONFA1	CONFC1	$\bar{R}^2$	D.W.
13. -761,7	0,039	0,885	2,991					0,8743	2,2044
	(1,20)	(9,78)	(1,64)						
14. -1248,6	0,025	0,745		13,224				0,9095	2,03715
	(0,937)	(8,1)		(3,40)					
15.-1732,6	0,083	0,735			16,00			0,8873	2,1587
	(1,1)	(6,09)			(2,30)				
16. -811,3	0,044	0,817				3,819			
	(1,51)	(7,85)				(1,97)		0,8806	2,3870
17. -1418,3	0,045	0,698					12,30	0,8849	2,4223
	(1,57)	(5,01)					(2,18)		
			COMA1	VCOMA1	VCOMB1	CONFA2			
18. -982,9	0,047	0,798	5,662					0,8821	2,3795
	(1,62)	(7,37)	(2,04)						
19. -1871,1	0,062	0,733		12,41				0,8785	1,9954
	(2,25)	(5,20)		(1,87)					
20. -786,9	0,042	0,800			4,22			0,8824	2,3279
	(1,41)	(7,46)			(2,06)				
21. -777,3	0,043	0,688				6,21		0,9039	2,0344
	(1,68)	(6,24)				(3,11)			
			CONFB2	CONFC2	COMA2	VCOMB2			
22. -1004,9	0,050	0,790	5,028					0,8913	2,1123
	(1,84)	(7,94)	(2,50)						
23.-1737,2	0,053	0,595		16,07				0,8917	1,9006
	(2,00)	(3,71)		(2,51)					
24.-1075,6	0,050	0,697			7,918			0,8943	1,9767
	(1,90)	(5,71)			(2,64)				
25.- 745,9	0,039	0,674				6,59		0,9023	2,0104
	(1,49)	(5,80)				(3,15)			

questions where the questions receive equal weights. VCOMB2 is a variant of this index. It is the second component of a varimax rotated factor analysis of survey data and consists of virtually the same questions as CONFA2. The main difference is that factor loadings are used to weigh the different questions incorporated in VCOMB2. It is clear that equation 21 and 25 hardly differ and it could thus be concluded that indices obtained by equal weighting of questions are not necessarily inferior to those obtained by the unequal weighting of questions.

Unfortunately multicollinearity makes if difficult to include more than one sentiment variable in a demand function. Many attempts were made, all of which yielded unsatisfactory results.

Estimation of private consumption expenditure on non-durable goods on similar lines proved to be very difficult. As it turned out the functions

$CN = a + bY + cCN1 + d\ X$

and $CN = a + bY + cCN1 + d\ W$

were of little practical value, mainly because of multicollinearity problems. In a full specification CN1 dominated to the extent that Y and whatever sentiment measures were included were rendered insignificant. In addition very high values of D.W. pointed to significant negative autocorrelation. The best function found with this specification is:

$$CN = 481,\ 20 + \underset{(1,67)}{5,27\ BUY2} + \underset{(7,42)}{0,888\ CN1} + \underset{(0,32)}{0,008Y}$$

with adjusted $R^2 = 0,929$
D.W. = 2,4972

In an attempt to improve the situation the following specifications were put to the test:

$CN = a + bY + c\ X$
$CN = a + bY + c\ W$

In these specifications <u>the sentiment measures were significant in all regressions</u> but disposable income remained an insignificant explanatory variable. In addition, the D.W. values dropped dramatically; most of them were in the range 0,5 to 0,7 suggesting the presence of positive autocorrelation and the misspecification of functions – probably on account of the ommission of a variable or variables.

Next, it was argued that disposable income, which is made up of wages and salaries plus income from property, is possibly not the best income variable to use in this regard. As a result of data problems, and also because it is sometimes argued that income measures merely explain the trend present in the dependent variable, it was decided to use the specification below: (Interestingly enough, Y had virtually no trend over the time span under consideration whilst CN had – hence, perhaps, the poor performance of Y.)

$$CN = a + bT + c\ X$$
$$CN = a + bT + c\ W$$

where T = 1, 2, 3 24

Overall, it can be stated that multicollinearity seriously affected the regression results – the latter were not very different from those found in functions which contained CN1. The trend variable T tended to force sentiment variables into insignificance. One favourable result was the fact that all the D.W. values were pushed higher, but they still hinted at significant positive autocorrelation.

The following CN functions are worthy of mention:

(i)	6131,7 + 5,41 FINB1 + 48,32 T		$\bar{R}^2$ =	0,9332
	(2,07)	(6,95)	D.W. =	1,1689
(ii)	6056,9 + 6,62 BUY2 + 42,08 T		$\bar{R}^2$ =	0,9363
	(2,35)	(7,98)	D.W. =	1,1644
(iii)	5879,9 + 6,93 VCOMA + 50,08 T		$\bar{R}^2$ =	0,9335
	(2,1)	(15,93)	D.W. =	1,1344
(iv)	5955,4 + 6,9 CONFC2 + 46,96 T		$\bar{R}^2$ =	0,9318
	(1,95)	(11,45)	D.W. =	1,1899
(v)	5985,6 + 5,7 VCOMA2 + 51,7 T		$\bar{R}^2$ =	0,9322
	(2,0)	(17,3)	D.W. =	1,2945

In sum: it can be stated that consumer spending on non-durables during the time span considered is difficult to explain by means of regression functions. Many structural changes took place, such as a gradual redistribution of income which must have had an impact on non-durable spending. In addition to this the introduction of colour television at the beginning of the investigation period changed consumption patterns of durables which tended to spill over into the non-durable goods area. Not surprisingly, thus, meaningful regression functions are difficult to come by but it can be stated with a great degree of confidence that the results suggest very strongly that consumer sentiment does have an influence on private expenditure on non-durable goods.

Forecasting

No empirical work with regard to forecasting is presented in this paper. It must, however, be stressed that the work reported on suggests that consumer sentiment measures are likely to be powerful instruments for purposes of short-term forecasting. Most of them perform best in regression functions when they are introduced with a two quarter lag. Evans (25) and Angevine (11), amongst others, argue that consumer sentiment measures can be endogenised by using hard data. Whilst not arguing the validity of their arguments one should perhaps always first take note of the quality of the hard data as well as the time lags involved - usually the data are released with long time lags and then in preliminary form only. In this regard the survey data clearly outperform them.

Concluding remarks

The use of sentiment data in explaining private consumption expenditure was the central theme of this paper. Brief mention was made of the work of Katona in particular whilst the measuring of consumer sentiment in South Africa was researched in more depth. Methodological aspects were discussed and put to tests which eventually lead to the isolation of a variety of sentiment measures. These were used, alone and in conjunction with other data, in regression analyses and it is concluded that sentiment plays an important role in the buying of durable goods. The role of sentiment is also significant in non-durable spending and all the results suggest that sentiment can be put to good use when forecasts of consumer spending are made.

NOTATION

(Values "1" and "2" denote lags)

ECOA= Economic development over past twelve months.

ECOB= Economic development over next twelve months.

ECOC= Economic development over next five years.

PRB = Rate of price changes last twelve months.

PRF = Rate of price changes next twelve months.

FINC= Current financial situation of households.

FINB= Development in financial situation over the past twelve months.

FINF= Development in financial situation over the next twelve months.

BUY = Good time to buy?

SAVE= Good time to save?

SAVEY = Ability to save next three months.

COMA= Principal component analysis, first component.

COMC= Principal component analysis, third component.

VCOMA)
VCOMB) As above but after varimax rotation of the axes.
VCOMC)

CD = Private consumption expenditure on durable goods, seasonally adjusted quarterly data at an annual rate, constant 1975 prices.

CN = Private consumption expenditure on non-durable goods, seasonally adjusted quarterly data at an annual rate, constant 1975 prices.

Y = Personal disposable income, seasonally adjusted quarterly data, deflated with implied consumption deflator with 1975 = 1.

X = Set of single-question sentiment variables.

W = set of multi-question sentiment variables.

CONFA= (ECOA + ECOB + FINB + FINF + BUY)/5.

CONFB= (ECOB + FINF)/2.

CONFC = (BUY + FINF)/2.

$\bar{R}^2$ = Coefficient of determination adjusted for degrees of freedom.

D.W. = Durbin Watson d statistic.

REFERENCES

1. De Jonge, W.
Changing economic conditions in turbulent times in: Fitting Research to Turbulent Times, ESOMAR, Vienna. 1982.

2. Van Raaij, W.F.
Consumenten vertrouwen en verwachtingen in een periode van recessie, Erasmus Universiteit, Rotterdam, 1980.

3. Van Raaij, W.F. and H.J. Gianotten.
Consumer confidence, expenditure and curtailment in: Fitting Research to Turbulent Times, ESOMAR, Vienna, 1982.

4. Adams, F.G.
Consumer attitudes, buying plans and purchase of durable goods: A principal components time series approach in: Review of Economics and Statistics, Vol. 46, 1964.

5. Katona G.
Psychological Economics, New York, Elsevier, 1975.

6. Williams, R.A. and L.V. Defris.
The roles of inflation and consumer sentiment in explaining Australian consumption and savings patterns, in: Journal of Economic Psychology, Vol.1, No.2, 1981.

7. Juster, F.T.
An expectational view of consumer spending prospects in: Journal of Economic Psychology, Vol. 1, No. 2, 1981.

8. Pickering, J.F.
A behavioural model of the demand for consumer durables in: Journal of Economic Psychology, Vol. 1, No. 1, 1981.

9. Contogiannis, E.
Private consumption functions in South Africa: A disaggragation in: Finance and Trade Review, Vol. XIII, No. 1, 1978.

10. Rayfuse, B.
The leading indicator properties of surveyed consumer attitudes and buying intentions, Bank of Canada Technical Report, 1982.

11. Angevine, G.E.
Forecasting consumption with a Canadian consumer sentiment measure in: Canadian Journal of Economics, Vol. VII, No. 2, 1974.

12. Juster, F.T. and P. Wachtel.
Anticipatory and objective models of durable goods demand in: American Economic Review, Vol. LX11, No. 4, 1972.

13. Linden, F.
The measure of consumer confidence in: Across the Board, Conference Board, New York, April 1979.

14. Thomas, R.W.
The effect of averaging components on the predictability of the index of consumer sentiment in: Review of Economic and Statistics, Vol. LVII, No. 1, 1975.

15. Ward, A.V. and J.F. Pickering.
Preliminary testing of the explanatory power of the EEC consumer Attitudes Survey in the United Kingdom in: Applied Economics, Vol. 13, No. 1, 1981.

16. Child, D.
The essentials of factor analysis, Holt, Rinehardt and Winston, London: New York 1973.

17. McDonnel, J.S.
The application of consumer survey data in: The Austrialian Economic Review, 3rd Quarter 1979.

18. Juster, F.T. and P Wachtel.
Anticipatory and objective models of durable goods demand in: American Economic Review, Vol. 72.

19. Angevine, G.E.
Forecasting consumption with a Canadian consumer sentiment measure in: Canadian Journal of Economics, Vol. VII, No. 2, 1974.

20. Nerb, G.
Informational content of consumer surveys, 12th Ciret conference, Stockholm, 1975.

21. Heald, G.
British experience of consumer anticipation surveys 1961-1971. 11th Ciret conference.

22. Brown, T.M.
Habit resistance and lays in consumer behaviour in: Econometrica, July, 1952.

23. Friedman, M.
A theory of the consumption function, Princeton Univ. Press for NBER, 1957.

24. Malinvaud, E.
Statistical methods of econometrics, North-Holland, 1970.

25. Evans, M.R.
Macroeconomic activity : theory, forecasting and control, Harper & Row, New York, 1969.

Experience in Belgium with Business Surveys in Trade. Element of Forecasting the Evolution of Private Consumption

B. Meganck/G. Maes
Banque Nationale de Belgique
Brussels

Preliminary remarks

It is known by experience that the evolution of private consumption, being an important accelerating or decelerating factor in business cycles, is not always easy to accurately determine or forecast. We have, it is true, a certain number of quantitative indicators at our disposal, which, however, have a considerable disadvantage in that the more complete and precise they are, the longer it takes before they are published. As such, their use for the analysis of business cycles is rather limited. In order to remedy this, as it is the case for other sectors of the economy, one has to fall back upon the instrument of business surveys.

In order to be able to quickly obtain an approximate idea of the private consumption evolution, most countries, as a general rule, make use of consumer surveys. Another possible quick approach to this evolution, resides in organizing business surveys in trade. As a consequence, this paper will aim at evaluating to what degree the results of these business surveys are useful in determining the evolution of private consumption.

The first part of this paper will illustrate how a composite indicator of the business cycle evolution in trade may be distilled from the diversity of information gathered by the surveys. In the second part, the usefulness of this indicator will be tested and, as concerns Belgium, it will be discussed whether this indicator yields better results than the usual consumer surveys. Finally, in the last part, the chronology of this indicator in trade will be checked against identical indicators in the manufacturing industry.

Part 1 : Calculation of a composite indicator of the main results of the monthly business surveys in trade

1.1 General considerations

As mentioned in the introduction, the diagnosis of business cycles in trade, just as in the other sectors of the economy, is hampered because the availability of quantitative indicators is very often delayed. This situation can of course partly been remedied by conducting monthly business tests ; the business surveys institute of the National Bank of Belgium started these kinds of tests some 25 years ago. At the beginning, only a limited number of sectors in the branches wholesale trade, retail trade and imports were examined, but as time passed, a number of new sectors were added to this list.

However, notwithstanding the surveys, it is not always possible to immediately synthetize the evolution of the aggregated short-term economic activity from the numerous modifications contained in the answers to the different questions. From the search for one objective measure the idea developed to create a composite business cycle indicator in trade , synthetizing a number of data from the surveys.

For about two years, the Research Department of the National Bank of Belgium has been making use of, by way of experiment, those data of the monthly business surveys in trade in order to calculate a composite indicator. Time series elaborated on the basis of those monthly tests seemed sufficiently homogeneous and spread over a long enough period of time thus enabling their statistical distinctive numbers to lend themselves for that purpose.

1.2 Calculation of a composite indicator in trade

1.2.1 Choice of the branches of trade

Although the National Bank conducts surveys in different branches of trade, particularly in the wholesale trade sector, the major distributive trades, the retail trade and imports, only the results of the surveys in the wholesale trade and the major distributive trades were used for the calculation of the synthetic indicator. Only in both of those branches were the questions harmonious enough so that a homogeneous series could be formed.

The following sectors in the wholesale trade and/or the major distribution trades were taken into consideration : textile articles, footwear, cars, electric household appliances (incl. radio, T.V., Hi-fi), food articles and cleaning and maintenance products.

1.2.2 Choice and treatment of the time series embodied in the composite indicator

1.2.2.1 Choice of the time series in composing the composite indicator

In principle, it could be assured that all the time series figuring in the survey are incorporated in the composite indicator. However, there is a chance, as shown by the composition of other composite indicators, that not all time series could be used for that purpose ; these would not reflect the business cycle trend as accurately.

In order to check this, use was made of the so-called "component analysis". It was thereby supposed that, to be taken into account as a time series for the composite indicator in trade, a certain degree of correlation was needed between the time series considered and the main component, regarded as the business cycle component. This led to the following result :

	R (1)
- turnover trend	0.88
- evaluation of the sales level	0.91
- selling-price trend	0.54
- evaluation of stocks of goods	0.60
- demand expectations for the following three month period	0.61
- expectations concerning orders to be placed with national furnishers for the following three month period	0.85
- expectations concerning orders to be placed with furnishers abroad for the following three month period	0.87

Consequently, to be taken into account as a series for calculating the composite indicator, it was pragmatically assumed that the correlation coefficient had to amount to 0.85 or more ; if not, the series considered were turned down. This rigid marginal condition finally caused the elimination of three questions, notably those concerning prices, stocks of goods and demand expectations. As regards the first two series, the result is not surprising as in recent years, prices and stocks of goods have been increasingly influenced by extra-business cycle factors (adjustment of exchange rates, price stop, highly fluctuating exchange rates). Moreover, the series concerning demand expectations seems to deviate considerably from the main component, even if its "leading"-character is taken into account.

---

(1) Correlation coefficient between the time series considered and the first component.

1.2.2.2 Treatment of the series composing the composite indicator

From the inquiry into the different time series of the business survey, it has appeared that, besides the business cycle pattern, some of them also contain movements of a more seasonal or accidental nature. In order to prevent these movements from complicating the interpretation of the cyclical evolution, it is advisable to eliminate them as much as possible and to consider only the cyclical component.

On the basis of the criteria used by the Census X-11 seasonal adjustment program, it may be stated that all the series appearing in the indicator, with the exception of the evaluation of the sales level, show a clear and stable seasonal pattern ; consequently, their seasonal component must be removed.

Furthermore, even after seasonal adjustment, all series still seemed to be somewhat too volatile so that the business cycle evolution remained slightly concealed. In order to remedy this situation, a weighted moving average of the last three months, centered on the last month, was made of the series ; a period of a maximum of three months was used in order not to overretard the business cycle turning points (1).

---

(1) The result of this is that the turning point of the business cycle is delayed by approximately one month.

1.2.3 Determination of the reference period

In order to turn the time series considered into a common basis, a reference period had indeed to be determined. For that purpose, the period July 1974 - June 1981 was chosen, particularly for the following two reasons :

- the economic context in which the business surveys took place, was radically modified after the first oil crisis. An economic climate which would have simply been thought normal at the time, would now be considered very satisfactory, whereas an economic climate apparently above average today would have been found to be poor previously. A change in the structural nature has thus taken place and this should lead to a significant lowering of the average. In order to take into account the break of structure in the participants' answers, it seemed necessary not to involve any more data from before that period for the calculation of the new curve ;

  the period considered likewise gives sufficient guarantee as to the neutrality in the business cycle field : the number of months the business cycle is oriented downwards, is almost as great as the number of months it is oriented upwards.

1.2.4 Calculation of the composite indicator

A first step into the calculation of the curve consists in amalgamating time series with different meanings. These time series themselves are made up of the balances of the positive and negative answers of the participants in the monthly business surveys. The working method is as follows : for each time series, an arithmetical mean of the monthly balances of the corresponding questions, during the reference period, is calculated (1). This mean (average) is given a value figure of 100 points ; a value figure of 0 point is given when their balance amounts to - 100, in other words when all the answers are negative. This means that each monthly balance may be given a value figure by means of a simple division (2).

Afterwards, the calculation of the composite indicator can be kept very simple by making an ordinary arithmetical mean of the different series. By doing so, however, the statistical features of each series are not taken into account. Firstly, the data of a certain series have a wider range of variation than those of another series, or in other words, the same changes in points within the scale in the series considered do not always have the same meaning, so that those points as such must not be added up immediately. Secondly, in response to the above-described method of conversions in the new scale, the changes in the balance of the answers will gain importance as the mean (average) is closer to the absolute minimum. In these conditions, it is advisable to grant to each series a certain weight which takes into account the spreading of the individual data and the position of their average. In other words,

---

(1) The state of the economy during one month will be appraised in relation to the standard (mean) shown by a particular series : more favourable or less favourable depending on whether the replies for the month are higher or lower than the standard.

(2) The following formula was used :

$$S_i = (x_i - m_i) \cdot \frac{100}{100 + m_i} + 100$$

whereby i = 1 ... 4 series ;
x_i = balance of that series in a certain month ;
m_i = arithmetical mean of the monthly balances of that series in the period July 1974-June 1981 (standard or mean) ;
s_i = value of x_i expressed on a base July 1974-June 1981 = 100.

a series the data of which have a wider range of variation and the average of which is closer to the absolute minimum, will be attributed a smaller weight (1).

Finally, the combination of the two above-mentioned criteria leads to the following weights :

- turnover trend	23.03 p.c.
- evaluation of the sales level	20.94 p.c.
- expectations concerning orders to be placed with national furnishers	30.41 p.c.
- expectations concerning orders to be placed with foreign furnishers	25.62 p.c.
Total	100.00 p.c.

The combination of the distinctive series, weighted as indicated above, yields as a final result a composite indicator which should reflect the business climate in trade.

---

(1) In order to determine the weight of each series, the following formula was used :

$$w_i = \frac{\dfrac{100 + m_i}{\sigma_i}}{\displaystyle\sum_{i=1}^{4} \dfrac{100 + m_i}{\sigma_i}}$$

whereby $i = 1 \ldots 4$ series ;
σ_i = standard deviation of that series ;
m_i = arithmetical mean of that series ;
w_i = weight of that series.

Part II : Evaluation of the composite indicator in trade as an instrument for determining and forecasting the private consumption

2.1 Situation of the trade sectors : being the object of the survey in the total private consumption

As it has been mentioned before, the composite indicator in trade described in part I comprises the following major sectors : textile articles, footwear, electric household appliances, cars, food articles and cleaning and maintenance products. From the table below, it appears that in the period 1974-1981 (1), according to the National Statistical Institute (Ministry of Economic Affairs), the sectors mentioned represented a part of the total private consumption fluctuating between 28.6 and 27.4 p.c.

---

(1) The most recent information at present (March 1983) available in the National Statistical Institute, relates to the year 1981.

Evolution of the private consumption at constant prices

	Total private consumption (a)	Consumer expenditure for food, textile, footwear, electric household appliances, cars and cleaning and maintenance products (b)	Other consumer expenditure (a) - (b)	Part of the consumer expenditure for food, textile, footwear, electric household appliances, cars and cleaning and maintenance products in the total private consumption $\frac{(b)}{(a)}$
	Percentage changes			Per cent
1974	3.8	4.2	3.7	28.2
1975	1.2	0.9	1.3	28.1
1976	5.4	7.3	4.7	28.6
1977	1.6	- 0.5	2.4	28.1
1978	3.0	1.4	3.6	27.6
1979	3.8	3.7	3.8	27.6
1980	2.6	3.2	2.4	27.8
1981	- 0.9	- 2.1	0.0	27.4
	average percentage change (c)			
74-81	2.6	2.3	2.7	
	standard deviation (d)			
74-81	1.8	2.8	1.4	
	$\frac{\text{standard deviation}}{\text{average percentage change}} = \frac{(d)}{(c)}$			
74-81	0.69	1.22	0.52	

Source : National Statistical Institute. Calculations of the National Bank of Belgium.

As it appears from the table, the standard deviation of the percentage changes of the total private consumption, in per cent of the average percentage change, seems to be considerably smaller than the standard deviation of the collective sectors which are included in the composite indicator in trade (namely 69 against 122 p.c.). Consequently, these sectors are subject to larger fluctuations than the private consumption components, in particular services, which are not incorporated in the composite indicator (namely 122 against 52 p.c.). In other words, the consumer expenditure concerning food articles, cleaning and maintenance products, textile articles, footwear, electric household appliances and cars, together constitute the driving force behind the fluctuations in the total private consumption. In the context of a business cycle analysis - where it is of particular importance to note or forecast short-term fluctuations - this is an important observation.

However, the importance of those short-term fluctuations also means that the National Statistical Institute's data (only available on a yearly basis) are neither suited for making a business cycle analysis, nor for discovering links with the composite indicator. As a consequence, other statistical sources will be needed for the purpose at hand.

2.2 Available statistical material

There exists a certain number of quantitative series, each of them illustrating a partial aspect of the private consumption in Belgium, for instance : sales index in the food sector, number of registered travellers/km at the railways, number of registered radio and television sets .... It's difficult, of course, to form, on the basis of these separate series, a global idea of the evolution of private consumption, if only because the periodicity of their publication is often irregular. As a consequence, it must be made possible to gather all this divergent information into one series, the frequency of which is high enough to enable a business cycle analysis. Such a synthesis is made by the "Département d'économie appliquée de l' Université Libre de Bruxelles" (Dulbea) on a monthly and quarterly basis (1). Moreover, this synthesis is published with a much smaller delay than the yearly data of the National Statistical Institute (2). Unfortunately, the Dulbea data, which are published twice a year, have, as far as the recent period is concerned, a very provisional character. As such, it is not excluded that, after the first publication, they still undergo important modifications (3). The data concerning the private consumption are adjusted for their accidental and seasonal influences by Dulbea itself (4) ; it is in this form that the evolution of the private consumption will be confronted with the composite indicator in trade.

---

(1) H. Glesjer, - Présentation de l'économie belge en 200 séries. Cahiers Economiques de Bruxelles, n° 20, 4th quarter 1963.

(2) This does not prevent the Dulbea-data from being marred by such a delay, compared with the composite indicator in trade. Rignt now (March 1983), the most recent Dulbea-information available concerning the private consumption dates back to June 1982. The composite indicator, to the contrary, relates already to February 1983.

(3) In a study of J. Vuchelen en E. Ghysels, the Dulbea-data are compared with the official and final indices. Characteristic of this is that Theil's disparity coefficient (the "U-coefficient") declines considerably as the moment of the Dulbea-publication comes closer to the official publication. This comparison, however, relates to GNP-data. E. Ghysels and J. Vuchelen, - The use of Dulbea-GNP-figures in business cycle analyses. Cahiers économiques de Bruxelles, n° 89, 1st quarter 1981.

(4) This happens on the basis of the Census X-11 program. The adjustment for the accidental influences causes a delay of the smoothed series of about 1 month, compared with the non-smoothed series.

As already shown in the table above, the inquiry will be limited to the evolution of private consumption at constant prices. It should be evident that the composite indicator does not comprise any series inquiring directly (from the participants in the business surveys) about the evaluation of any price evolution . Furthermore, it is not very probable that even in an indirect way, the composite indicator could be influenced by price evolution. In two of the series which are incorporated in the indicator, nl. the turnover trend and the evaluation of the sales level, the participants in the business survey are asked to compare the present situation with that of the previous month. Thus, the possible difference in impact price evolution may have on the evaluation of turnover and sales level in two different but subsequent months must be considered as marginal. As concerns the two other series taken up in the indicator, nl. the expectations concerning orders to be placed with national and foreign furnishers, it is not requested to make a comparison with the situation during the previous month, but experience has shown that those series too are not influenced by price evolution. This could be deducted, among other things, from the absence of a trend movement in the series mentioned.

2.3 Relation between the composite indicator in trade and the evolution of the private consumption

In the search for a relation between the composite indicator in trade on the one hand, and private consumption on the other hand, the following analysis emphasizes two factors.

It could substantially be the concern of the business cycle analysts, to verify inhowfar the composite indicator supplies rather quickly reliable information which makes it possible to discover and/or forecast the turning points and the tendencies in the evolution of the private consumption. Such an inquiry can be shown and demonstrated using a graphic model.

Besides, it seemed interesting to try to quantify the possible relation between both quantitative and qualitative indicators, although the quantifying of qualitative data, on the basis of which the composite indicator is composed, has to be approached with the necesarry circumspection (1).

The test of the composite indicator in trade as an instrument to forecast the evolution of the private consumption had to limit itself to the observations in the period July 1974 - June 1982. Indeed, on the one hand, the composite indicator only starts in July 1974 for the reasons mentioned in part I ; on the other hand, the most recent Dulbea-datum available right now (March 1983) concerning the private consumption relates to the month of June 1982.

2.3.1 Graphic inquiry of the cyclical evolution and specifically, the turning points of the private consumption

If one considers the period mentioned as a whole, it appears from chart 1 that the trend movement of the Belgian private consumption at constant prices shows a break for the first semester of 1980.

This break may be attributed to - as concerns Belgium - the delayed reaction of the private consumer expenditure after the second oil-shock. From that moment the private consumption has been showing a slightly downward trend.

---

(1) G. Gugerell, - The use of consumer surveys in Austria ; 14th Ciret Conference, Lisboa 1979, p.46.

National Bank of Belgium *Chart 1.*

EVOLUTION OF PRIVATE CONSUMPTION AT CONSTANT PRICES :
BELGIUM, 1973 - 1982
Quarterly data, indices 1975 = 100 1

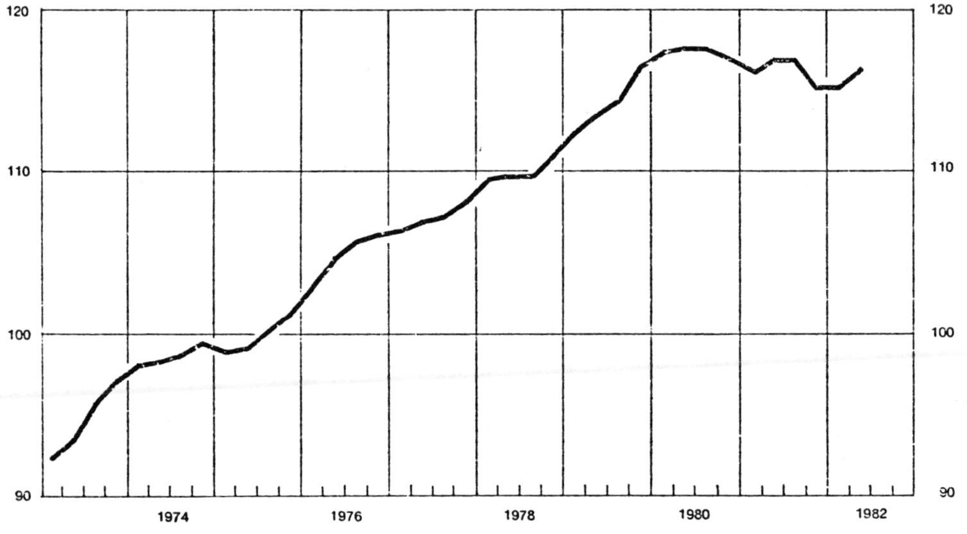

1 Seasonally adjusted and smoothed series.
Source : Dulbea.
St 83/4/216-1

In the graphic inquiry of the relation between the evolution of the composite indicator in trade and private consumption, we shall remove from the latter the trend-component, in order to be able to show very clearly the cyclical movements (1). Although in that way, the trend influences are eliminated, just like the modifications resulting from them, it nevertheless seemed indicated to have the test of the composite indicator relate to two separate sub periods. As it will be stated further on, in recent years, a number of government measures have indeed been taken which, much more than in previous years, have influenced the short-term movements in the private consumer expenditure and which have highly affected the homogeneity of the total period July 1974 - June 1982. Consequently, the period July 1974 - June 1982 has been split up into two periods, the separation of which was situated in the second quarter of 1980, thus more or less coinciding with the break in the trend-picture of private consumption. Likewise by doing so, one prevents the trend adjusted values of the private consumption, which are necessarily the result of two different trend equations (2), from being coupled in one way or another (in the charts), particularly in the period round about the break in the trend picture.

2.3.1.1 Third quarter 1974 - second quarter 1980

From chart 2, it clearly appears that the large movements in the evolution of the composite indicator on the one hand and in the evolution of the percentage ratios to trend of the private consumption (volume data) on the other hand, evolve in a rather parallel direction.

---

(1) The composite indicator itself doesn't show a trend movement.
(2) The first equation covers the period up to the break in the trend picture, nl. third quarter 1974-second quarter 1980. The second equation covers the period thereafter, nl. June 1980 - June 1982.

Chart 2.

National Bank of Belgium

COMPOSITE BUSINESS CYCLE INDICATOR IN TRADE AND CYCLICAL EVOLUTION OF PRIVATE CONSUMPTION :
3rd quarter 1974 - 2nd quarter 1980
Quarterly averages

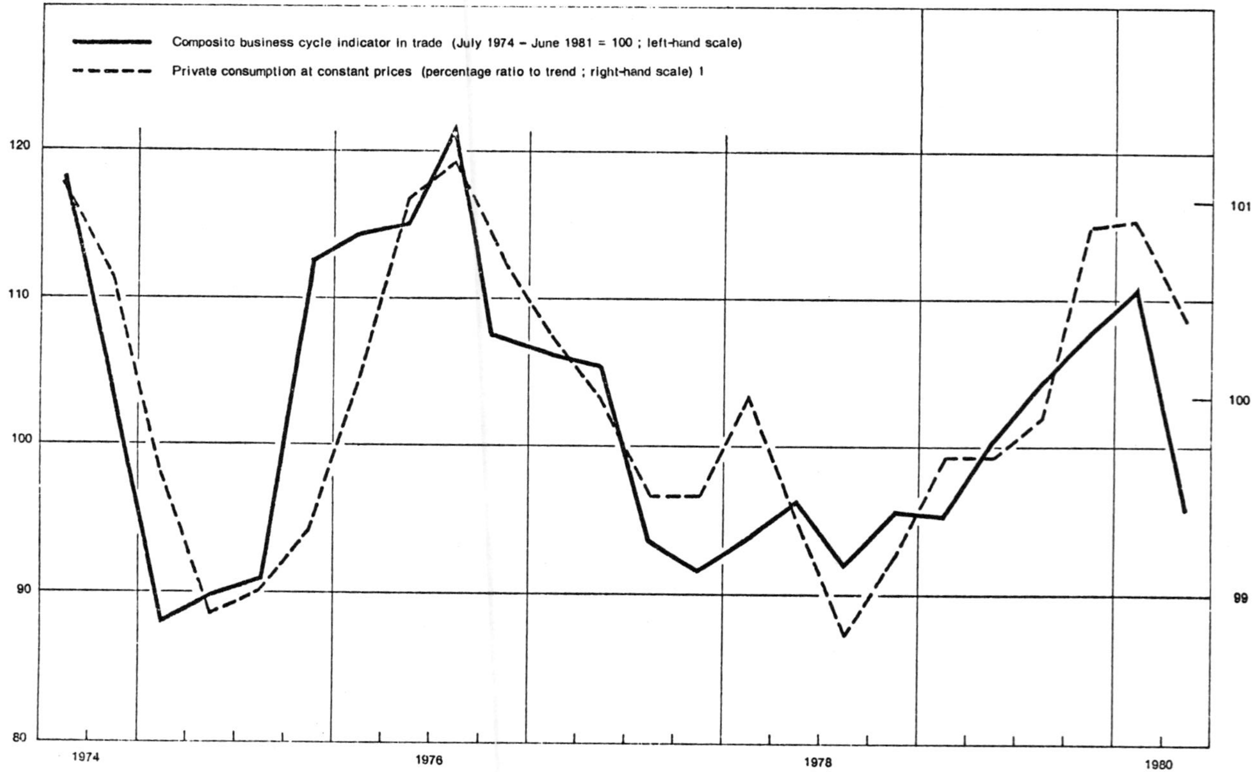

1 Calculations of the National Bank of Belgium
Source : Dulbea and National Bank of Belgium

St 83/4/216-2

Moreover, the composite indicator seems to be very apt to determine the turning points - which particularly interests us in the context of this inquiry - and even to anticipate them. It can generally be noticed that the turning points in the evolution of the composite indicator are either one quarter ahead, or coincide with the turning points of the cyclical evolution of private consumption. One will remember that the smoothing of the composite indicator and of the Dulbea-data in both cases caused the same lag, nl. of about one month, compared with the non-smoothed data ; as a consequence, the smoothing itself does not lend itself to making mistakes in interpreting the mutual position of the turning points.

Despite how parallel the movements in the composite indicator and the ratios to trend in the private consumption may be, it doesn't prevent the fluctuations in the former from being much larger than those in the latter. We can hereby refer to the observations already made in the table on p. 11. This difference in amplitude of the fluctuations does not appear from chart 2, in which the composite indicator in trade and the ratios to trend of private consumption are drafted according to a different scale.

Starting from the experience of the period third quarter 1974 -second quarter 1980, one could conclude that, notwithstanding the big delay in the publication of the quantitative data relating to the private consumption, it is possible to get an idea of the recent evolution of this private consumption on the basis of the composite indicator and even of the expected evolution for the near future. However, one must take into account the difference in amplitude of the fluctuations.

2.3.1.2 June 1980 - June 1982

In order to have a number of reliable observations at one's disposal, the analysis here takes place on the basis of monthly data.

In chart 3, we can again make mention of a parallelism between the evolution of the composite indicator and the cyclical evolution of private consumption. However, this parallel evolution is clearly less pronounced than in chart 2 ; this fact, just like the underlying government measures will be illustrated in item 2.3.2.2.

Notwithstanding this smaller parallelism, the inflexion points in both series perfectly correspond with each other : the minima of the ratios to trend in the private consumption (February 1981, December 1981) follow with a one-month delay the minima in the composite indicator ; also the record of July 1981 comes one month after the turning point in the composite indicator. Thus, the chronological relation appearing from chart 2 for the period 1974-1980, nl. that the composite indicator in trade is 0 to 1 quarter ahead, seems to be confirmed.

As concerns the amplitude of the fluctuations, it must be pointed out once again that the composite indicator and the ratios to trend in the private consumption were drafted in chart 3 according to a different scale.

If one starts from the experience in the period June 1980-June 1982, a period which was more than ever disturbed by a number of important government interventions, one could again conclude that, notwithstanding the big delay in the publishing of quantitative data concerning the private consumption, it was nevertheless possible to gauge the recent evolution and even

Chart 3.

COMPOSITE BUSINESS CYCLE INDICATOR IN TRADE AND CYCLICAL EVOLUTION OF PRIVATE CONSUMPTION :
June 1980 – June 1982
Monthly data

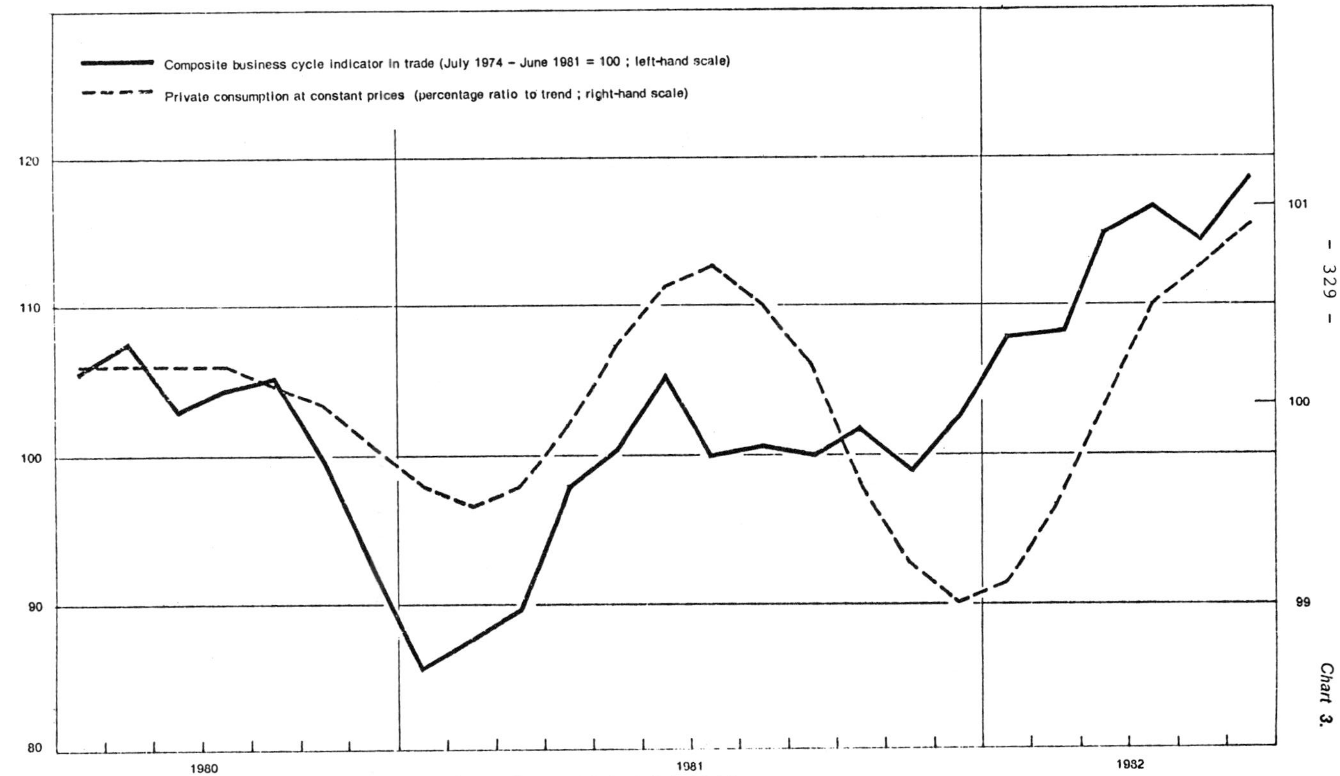

St 83/4/216-3 · 1 Calculations of the National Bank of Belgium. – Source : Dulbea and National Bank of Belgium.

the near future of that private consumption and more specifically on the basis of the composite indicator. For, a clear relation was established between the turning points in the indicator and in the private consumption during that period.

2.3.2. Attempt to quantify the relation between the composite indicator in trade and private consumption

2.3.2.1 Third quarter 1974 - second quarter 1980

If time (1) and the composite indicator in trade in the previous quarter are considered as explanatory variables for the private consumption, one obtains the following equation :

$$PC_t = 90.88 + 0.06\ SC_{t-1} + 0.87\ Trend$$
$$(87.7) \quad (6.5) \quad (61.0)$$

$R^2 = 0.99$

D.W. = 1.84

whereby PC_t = private consumption in quarter t (at constant prices ; index 1975 = 100)

SC_{t-1} = composite indicator in trade in the previous quarter (average July 1974 - June 1981 = 100)

Trend = trend variable (1, 2 ... 23)

The low regression coefficient of SC_{t-1}, nl. 0.06, points once again to the fact that the fluctuations in PC_t take much smaller proportions than those of SC_{t-1} (2).

---

(1) In order to take into account the important trend determined rise of the private consumption in the period mentioned.

(2) The equation with the composite indicator in the same quarter as the explanatory variable takes the following form :

$$PC_t = 90.49 + 0.06\ SC_t + 0.86\ Trend$$
$$(73.5) \quad (5.2) \quad (53.7)$$

$R^2 = 0.99$

D.W. = 1.15

2.3.2.2 June 1980 - June 1982

As has already been mentioned in the comments to chart 3, the parallelism between the variables examined for this period is more or less disturbed : if one attempts to quantify the relation between private consumption and the composite indicator in trade, one obtains a not very convincing equation, notably :

$$PC_t = \underset{(83.7)}{113.36} + \underset{(3.1)}{0.05\ SC_{t-1}} - \underset{(-5.9)}{0.10\ Trend}$$

$R^2 = 0.58$

D.W. = 0.31

whereby PC_t = private consumption in the month t (at constant prices ; index 1975 = 100)

SC_{t-1} = composite indicator in trade in the previous month (average July 1974 - June 1981 = 100)

Trend = trend variable (1, 2 ... 25)

The results of this regression are drafted in chart 4, and notably the real evolution of the private consumption is compared with the evolution as it is estimated on the basis of the two variables of time and composite indicator in the previous month.

From this, it appears that the relation seems to have been particularly disturbed during the period May-August 1981 and November 1981-February 1982 (1).

---

(1) The deviation between the real and the estimated value in June 1982 is perhaps attributable to the provisional character of the Dulbea-data.

Chart 4.

National Bank of Belgium

REAL AND ESTIMATED EVOLUTION OF PRIVATE CONSUMPTION :
Indices 1975 = 100 ; monthly data

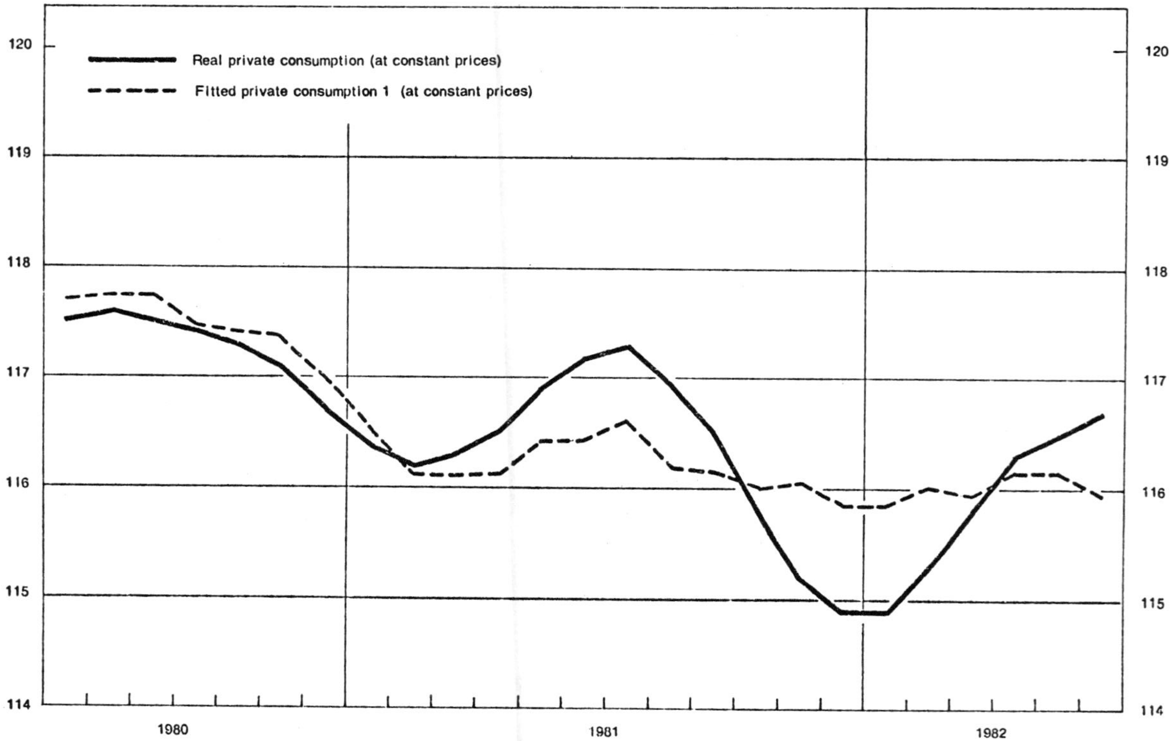

1 Estimation by means of the variables «time» and «composite indicator in trade of the previous month». Calculations of the National Bank of Belgium.
Source : Dulbea.

In fact, the Belgian government proceeded to a "Maribel" operation, reducing on the one hand the employers' social security payments from the 1st of July 1981 onwards, and increasing on the other hand, between the 18th of June and the 1st of September 1981, the rate of indirect taxes for a whole series of products. This Maribel operation - long beforehand announced in the media - led to an anticipated purchasing wave by consumers during the period May-August 1981 and to the compensating reaction afterwards, nl. a shrinking of the consumer expenditure in the winter 1981-1982. On the contrary, the government measures and the fluctuations in private consumption resulting from it, seem to have influenced the composite indicator much less. Participants of the survey rigthly considered the thus induced fluctuations in consumer expenditure as being reversable and they were not prepared to modify for that reason their appraisal of the economic situation in the monthly surveys and more specifically "the expectations concerning orders to be placed with national and foreign furnishers".

If one tries to trace the influence of the Maribel operation on private consumption on the basis of a dummy variable, the value of which amounts to 1 in the period May-August 1981, -1 in the period November 1981-February 1982 and 0 for the rest of the period (1), the following equation is obtained :

$$PC_t = \underset{(222.7)}{113.66} + \underset{(7.4)}{0.05}\ SC_{t-1} - \underset{(-13.7)}{0.09}\ \text{Trend} + \underset{(11.3)}{0.80}\ \text{dummy}$$

R^2 = 0.95

D.W. = 1.87

whereby PC_t = private consumption in the month t (at constant prices ; index 1975 = 100)

SC_{t-1} = composite indicator in trade in the previous month (average July 1974 - June 1981 = 100)

Trend = trend variable (1, 2 ...24).

---

(1) In view of the very provisional nature of the data for the month of June 1982, it has been omitted.

From the regression coefficient of SC_{t-1} it emerges that, as has already been noticed, the fluctuations in SC_{t-1} take on much larger proportions than in PC_t.

To conclude Part II it could be stated that the composite indicator in trade is a valuable instrument to determine and forecast private consumption. However, sometimes one has to take into account important incidental factors, such as for instance a sharp increase in the consumer tax, influencing the composite indicator and the private consumer in a divergent way. For the business cycle-analyst, it is of importance to evaluate this factor too, along with the evolution of the composite indicator in trade, and to take it into account in the estimate of the short-term evolution of private consumer expenditure.

2.4 Relation between the "sentiment indicator" of the Consumer surveys and the evolution of private consumption

The Survey Institute of the National Bank does not organize consumer surveys itself. Since 1974, however, and as far as Belgium is concerned, one has had at his disposal the results of the inquiries made by the National Statistical Institute under the auspices of the consumer survey of the Commission of the European Community. Three times a year, notably in the months January, May and October, the consumers are surveyed in order to know their assessment of the economic and financial situation. A "consumer confidence index" (CCI-index) is likewise formulated. This index is the arithmetical mean of the replies to the following five questions :

- the financial situation of households now compared to 12 months ago ;
- the financial prospects of households over the next 12 months ;
- general economic situation now compared to 12 months ago ;
- the prospects for the general economic situation over the next 12 months ;
- the advisability of making major purchases (of consumer durables) now.

As it likewise happened to the composite indicator in trade in the previous paragraphs, the relation between the CCI-index and the evolution of the private consumption will again be examined in two subperiods.

From chart 5, covering the period second half 1974 - first half 1980, it immediately appears that the parallelism between the evolution of the CCI-index on the one hand, and the percentage ratios to trend of private consumption on the other hand, is not very significant (1). Also the chronological

---

(1) If one attempts to quantify the relation between the private consumption and the CCI-index, the data relating to the private consumption must be converted beforehand into a frequency which corresponds more or less to that of the CCI-index (observations in January, May and October). This happened by making each year the arithmetical mean of the months December, January, February and March ; of the months April, May, June and July ; and finally of the months August, September, October and November. Notwithstanding tests with different lags between the variables, one obtained as the best result only an equation with a very low value for the "Student-test" of the variable CCI-index, nl. 1.1 :

$$PC_t = \underset{(15.3)}{90.78} + \underset{(1.1)}{0.06\, CCI_{t-2}} + \underset{(24.0)}{1.11\, Trend}$$

R^2 = 0.97

D.W.= 1.55

whereby PC_t = private consumption in the four-monthly period t (at constant prices ; index 1975 = 100)

CCI_{t-2} = index of the consumer confidence with lag of 2 four-monthly periods (index 1975 = 100)

Trend = trend variable (1, 2 ... 18)

Chart 5.

National Bank of Belgium

CONSUMER CONFIDENCE INDICATOR AND CYCLICAL EVOLUTION OF PRIVATE CONSUMPTION:
2nd half 1974 - 1st half 1980

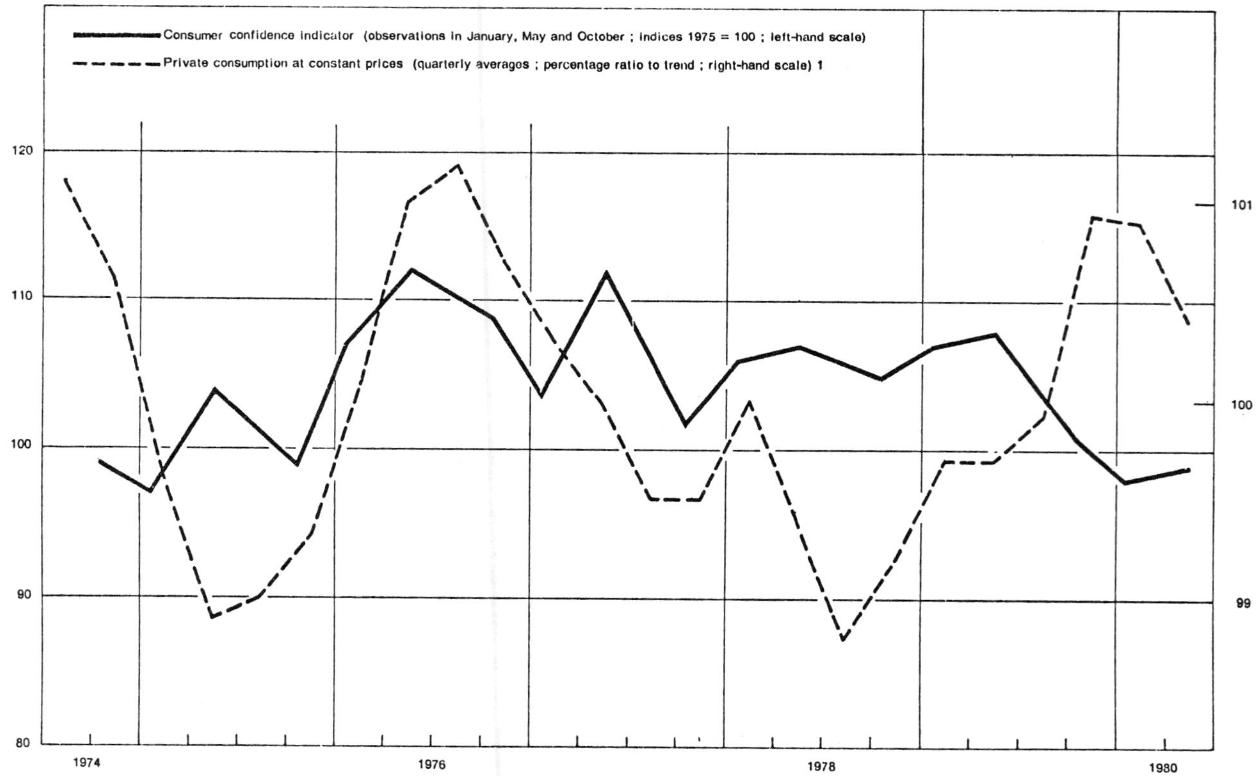

1 Calculations of the National Bank of Belgium. - Source : Dulbea, European Economic Community, Consumer survey.

St 83/4/216-5

relation between the turning points of both series can not easily be determined.

Chart 6 which covers the most recent subperiod, only confirms what has already been noticed in chart 5 (1).

In other words, the CCI-indicator seems to be a considerably less efficient indicator for determining the cyclical evolution in private consumption. This is partly attributable to the structure of the indicator, where only 3 observations per year are available, which moreover are separated from each other by a different timelag. Another reason for this disparate evolution could at first sight be found in the fact that the series, on the basis of which the CCI-index is formulated, cover a wider field than only the private consumption. Let us note that if only the results of the question "the advisability of making major purchases (of consumer durables) now" are taken into account, that question being a part of the CCI-index and - contrary to this index - exclusively being related to the private consumption or a part of it, it appears from chart 7 that this series is closely related to the CCI-index itself. Consequently the relation between the series "advisability of making major purchases now" and private consumption must likewise be weak.

---

(1) In view of the small number of observations for the CCI-index in that period, nl. 8, there was no attempt to quantify the relation.

CONSUMER CONFIDENCE INDICATOR AND CYCLICAL EVOLUTION OF PRIVATE CONSUMPTION:

1980 - 1982

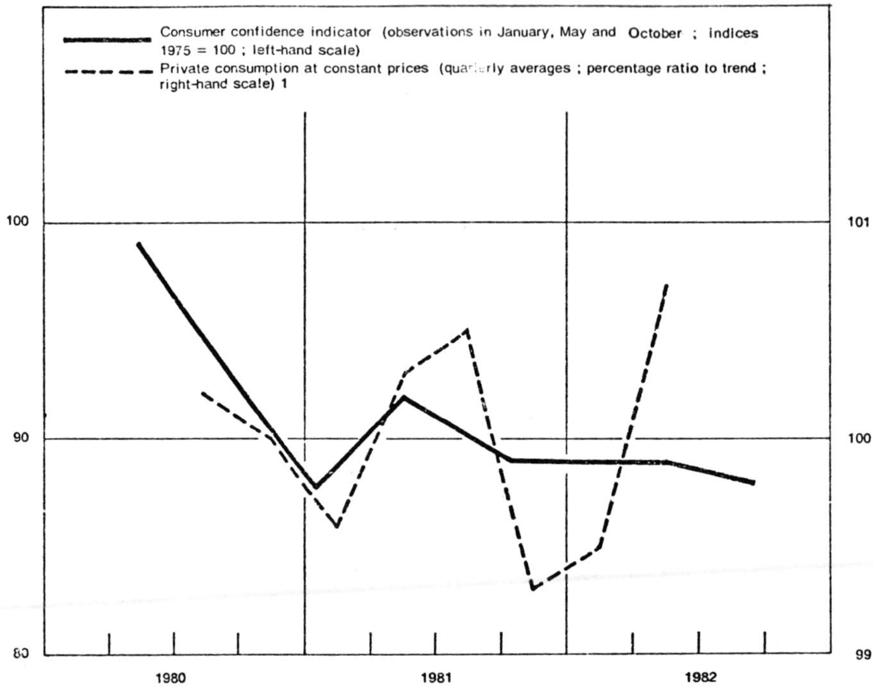

1 Calculations of the National Bank of Belgium.

Source : Dulbea; European Economic Community, Consumer survey.

St 83/4/216-6

Chart 7.

National Bank of Belgium

CONSUMER CONFIDENCE INDICATOR AND INDICATOR OF THE ADVISABILITY OF MAKING MAJOR PURCHASES

Observations in January, May and October

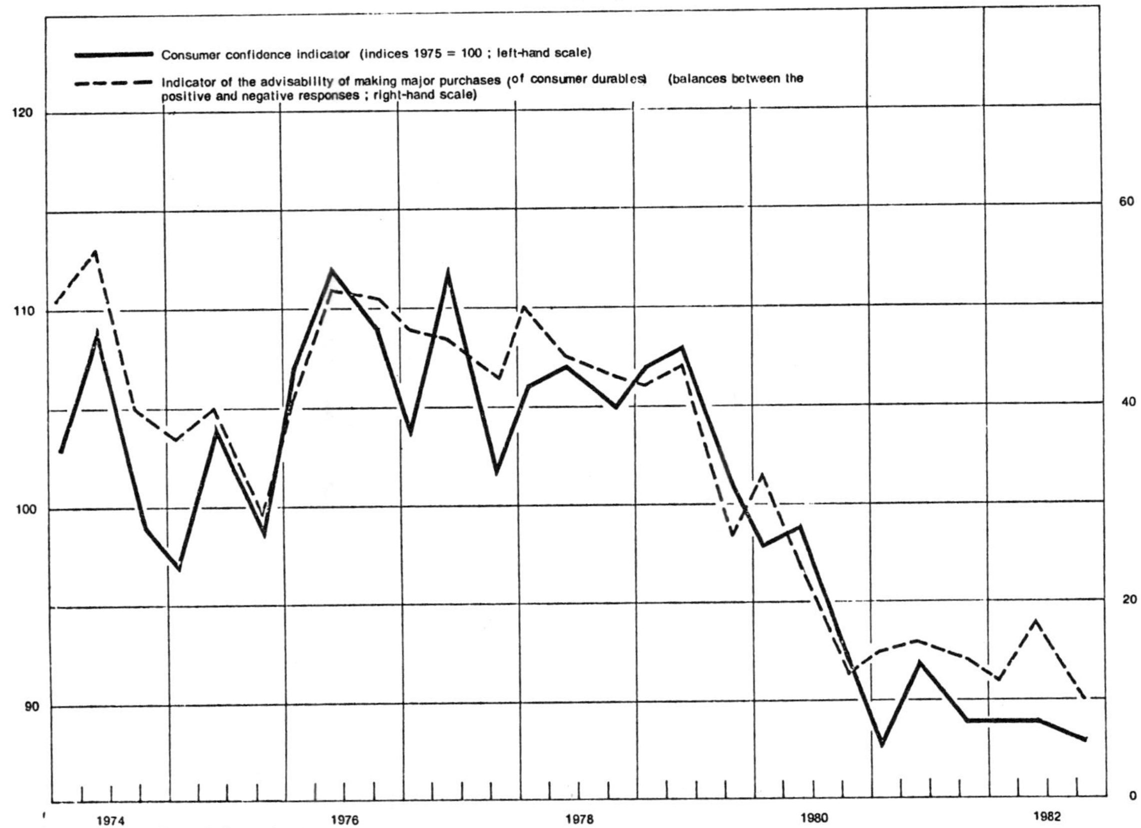

Source : European Economic Community; Consumer survey.

St 83/ 4/ 21..-7

Part III : Business climate in the manufacturing industry, in trade and consumer confidence

In order to get an idea of the chronological relation between the business cycles of several major sectors of the Belgian economy, it is necessary to verify how the business indicators related to trade and consumer confidence are situated in relation to the qualitative indicator reflecting the business climate in the industry. Therefore, a comparison was made between, on the one hand, the composite indicator in the manufacturing industry, calculated by the National Bank in almost the same way as the one for trade, and, on the other hand, the composite indicator in trade and the index of consumer confidence.

The comparison between the indicators (chart 8) leads to the following observations :

- for the whole of the period considered, the composite indicator for industry and the one for trade seem to show a rather similar cyclical pattern ; even though the amplitudes of the fluctuations are sometimes different. Thus, in the period 1974-1975, the deterioration was more considerable in industry, while in the period 1980-1981 it was more substantial in trade. This seems to be largely connected with structural breaks having occurred in those periods in the sectors considered ;

- the index of consumer confidence, on the contrary, seems to relate considerably less well to the cyclical evolution in industry ; it appears to be much less sensitive to business fluctuations than the composite indicator in trade ;

Chart 8.

National Bank of Belgium

BUSINESS CLIMATE IN MANUFACTURING INDUSTRY, IN TRADE AND CONSUMER CONFIDENCE: 1974 - 1982

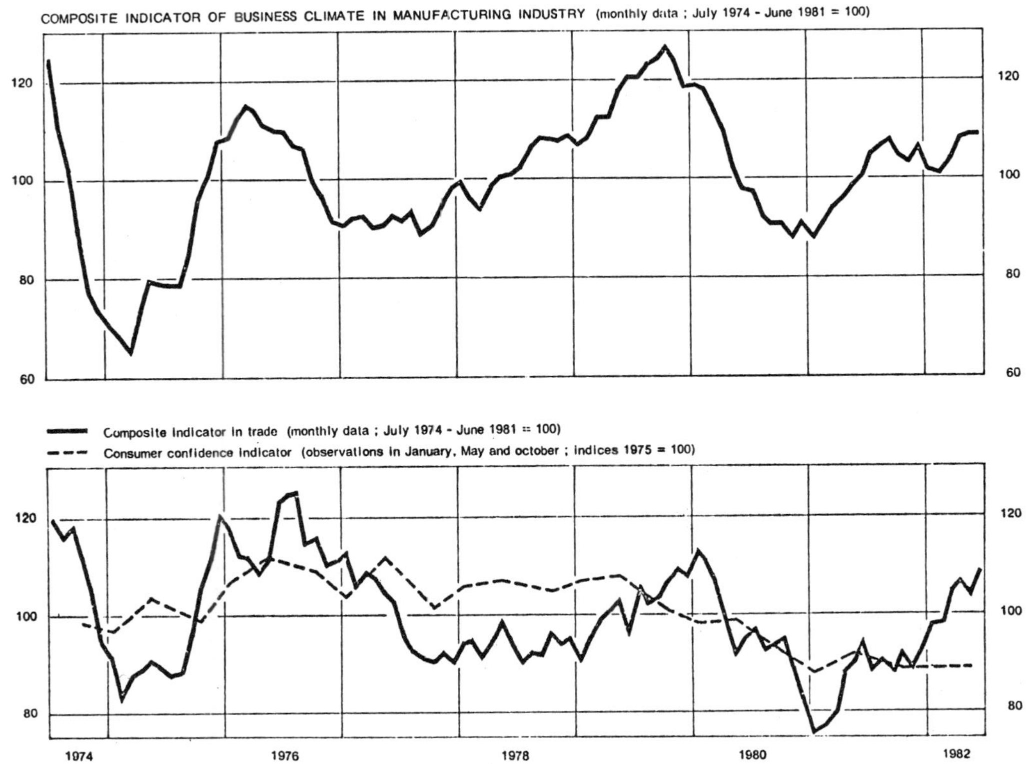

Source : National Bank of Belgium; European Economic Community, Consumer survey.

St 83/4/216-8

- the composite indicator in the manufacturing industry generally anticipates the trade indicator by a few months. From this perspective, it can thus be stated that the indicator in trade less quickly defines the cyclical turning points in the business cycle. At certain moments, the consumers confidence index gives the impression of having a leading character. But, as we have already mentioned before, one can hardly define the turning points so their significance must be highly relativized.

Conclusion

The purpose of this analysis has been to show that the composite indicator in trade is an efficient instrument for business diagnosis concerning private consumption. As such, it gives an exact idea of the cyclical evolution of the private consumption of which it defines rather accurately the turning points. It is true it cannot be considered as a real strong "leading" indicator ; this does not prevent it, however, from being of real significance for the study of the recent past and the near future due to its quick availibility.

Moreover it has been shown through the analysis that, without intending to detract from the specific features of consumer surveys in general, the composite indicator in trade is a more useful and precise instrument to define and forecast private consumption as far as Belgium is concerned. Its more general application to other economies and cultures remains an interesting point for study especially where Institutions are looking for more accurate and precise tools for measuring consumer behaviour.

Summary of the Discussion

R. Curtin
University of Michigan
Ann Arbor, Mich.

Most of the discussion of Schmiedeskamp's presentation involved his view that consumer attitudes trends cannot be adequately summarized by an Index based on a fixed combination of questions over time, and that consequently the use of an overall summary index should be avoided. Several participants pointed toward the need to use sentiment indices in the econometric models, even if the indices do not capture all the available information, so as to facilitate macroeconomic hypothesis testing. Schmiedeskamp responded that the integration of macroeconomic models and consumer sentiment data may be best approached in a two-step procedure. First, the usual econometric model would be used to generate forecasts under the assumption that the underlying behavioral parameters would not change over the forecast horizon. Second, the forecasts are then judgmentally adjusted based on the consumer sentiment information. Several participants agreed that the goal of the development of a single indicator of consumer sentiment is unrealistic, as no single measure will be infallible at all times, but nonetheless thought that a composite index of indicators is needed--a small list of indicators that is both manageable and reliable. Several participants noted the need for a profile of different aspects of consumer sentiment, which allows some aspects to become relatively more important at certain times. Not only could the type and number of aspects vary over time, but how the individual components are combined into an overall index could also change over time. Such added complexity in the structure of an index of consumer sentiment would not prevent its use in econometric models, but it would require special attention and model specification. A contrasting view was also offered: further increases in forecast accuracy are likely to stem more from new and improved survey measures of sentiment, rather than from raised analytic techniques for index construction.

As the contribution by J.Schmiedeskamp was not presented in writing it could not be included in this volume. An abridged version may be published in "CIRET Study" no. 34.

Ohlen was questioned on whether the model he outlined was used to estimate the change in consumption, as well as the level of consumer expenditures. Ohlen responded that this model had only been estimated based on consumption levels. Ohlen also reiterated his belief that sample size, rather than the different lengths of the forecast horizons, was one of the most important sources of increased forecasting errors.

The discussion of Stuart's paper affirmed his view that the classification of certain expenditures as discretionary depends on the overall economic characteristics of the population studied. For some countries, or population subgroups, certain nondurable as well as durable goods can be viewed as discretionary expenditures.

The discussion of the paper by Meganck and Maes centered around several points: the use of moving averages which may mask turning points, the limited number of business sectors included in the data base, and the construction of a consumer confidence index. Meganck responded that raw data series had too much noise to distinguish true signals, and thus smoothing was necessary to identify turning points. Meganck agreed that the business survey should cover more sectors, and consequently the estimates would exhibit greater stability. In response to a question on why their consumer confidence index did not exhibit cyclical sensitivity, Meganck laid most of the blame to small sample sizes (approximately 1,000 households out of a population of 10 million). Several questions involved the use of single indicators, rather than multiple indicators as is more usual for business sector analysis.

As part of an extended discussion, several audience members recommended the use of Box-Jenkins techniques, which base forecasts only on information from the series' own past. Other participants, of course, disagreed with this strategy, and stated that expectational measures are needed in addition to data on past events.

Another issue involved the use of anticipatory data versus commitment data, the latter indicating that plans have been put in place, start dates set, and so forth. Some defended the use of commitment data when there does not exist adequate theory to assess anticipatory measures, and consequently a relevance criteria must be used--the commitment criteria.

Another suggestion involved the estimation of a system of demand equations, not just equations which forecast demand for durables. Such a systematic approach would, it was argued, add greater validity and reliability to the results. It was pointed out that such techniques as principal components analysis can be imbedded in a simultaneous equations approach to forecasts of consumer demand.

Fourth Session
Investment Surveys

Chairman:
A.G. Hart, Columbia University
New York, N.Y.

Response of Prices and Production to Unanticipated Demand Shocks: Some Microeconomic Evidence

H. König
Universität Mannheim

M. Nerlove
University of Pennsylvania
Philadelphia, Pa.

1. Introduction

Two paradigms, in principle based upon different assumptions about the response of economic agents to disturbances in markets, characterize the debate in macroeconomics of the last decade. On the one hand, beginning with the work by Patinkin [1965], Clower [1965] and Leijonhufvud [1968], the main conceptional framework of Keynesian theory has been substantially reconsidered. In view of sluggish price movements in most Western economies, a number of short-run macroeconomic models have been developed assuming that prices adjust only after quantities have fully adjusted. Malinvaud [1977] argues that such sluggish adjustment is more than a purely institutional fact and that, due to uncertainty and information and transactions costs, the first reaction of firms to changes in the environment is more often a revision of quantities than a revision of prices. The new "Disequilibrium Macroeconomics," therefore, posits fixed prices (and price expectations) for the short-run, movement in prices between two periods is treated as "autonomous," and "...it is not significantly influenced...by the formation of demands and supplies... ."[1]

The polar case has been stressed by protagonists of the "New Classical Equilibrium Economics," especially in the context of rational expectations. Here it is assumed that universal auction markets allow economic agents to adjust instantly to perceived nominal demand changes and only imperfect information prevents economic agents from selecting the quantity that would maintain an aggregate equilibrium.[2]

The question whether real world adjustment processes are better described by the paradigm of neo-Keynesian disequilibrium or new classical equilibrium theory cannot be settled on a priori grounds. The answer, however, is most important for the question of the effectiveness of macroeconomic policy.[3]

1) Malinvaud [1977], p.12.

2) For a discussion see Gordon [1981].

3) See, e.g., Barro [1979], Gordon [1981], Laidler [1981].

This paper attempts to shed some light on the empirical relevance of these paradigms. It analyzes, at the microlevel, firms' reactions in terms of production plans and price anticipations to expected demand changes and to surprises in demand, i.e. deviations of expected from actual demand during the previous period and the effects of such demand shocks on deviations of _ex post_ prices and production from their _ex ante_ values.

Firms choose production, order backlogs and inventory levels to meet changes in demand and may choose prices as well. Even if they operate in reasonably competitive markets, they have some power to determine prices for their outputs. However, imperfect information about their demand functions and about competitors' reactions to changes in their own actions, as well as costs of communication and the heterogeneity of goods, may result in incomplete responses of prices to demand shocks. Although the macroeconomic literature for both types of models does not refer much to the role of inventories and unfilled orders, their importance as buffers are well known. Especially in models of firm behavior, inventories and backlogs have been discussed as instruments for production smoothing and for damping of price adjustment processes.[4)]

As will be seen, changes in order backlogs and inventories are strongly related to appraisals of their variables, the latter being significant determinants of the adjustment processes. Appraisals may also be considered as indicators of previous period excess demand or excess supply, i.e., for the constraints firms face, but they contain also implicit information about firms optimization process. Given perceived demand conditions and the firm's cost function, a firm will determine its optimal stock of inventories and order backlogs. If actual inventories (backlogs), for instance, are too low compared to the optimal level, the firm will alter its price and output plans.

Although this study is primarily directed to revisions of production plans and price anticipations due to changes in demand, our results show how these are connected with actual price movements and changes in production levels. Surprises in production and in prices are related

---

4) See, for example, Maccini [1981], Reagan [1979], Blinder [1981].

which reports on one survey that it plans to increase its production over the coming months in fact does so as reported in a subsequent survey. Methodological problems related to the analysis of cross-classified data, particularly of the kind one encounters in the German and French business tests, are dealt with elsewhere at some length. (See Nerlove (1981) for references.)

A log-linear probability model represents a particular parametrization of a set of discrete probabilities (*a priori* positive) characterizing counts in a multidimensional contingency table. The logarithms of the probabilities are represented as the linear sum of terms analogous to the main and interaction effects of standard analysis of variance models. The importance of the parametrization to the analysis of ordinal categorical data of the sort found in many economic surveys lies in the following characteristics: (1) Because the relation between two or more variables is characterized by interactions of successively higher order, it is possible to eliminate some parameters in a way which still allows two or more variables to be related to one another. (2) The bivariate interaction effects may be used to construct a measure of partial bivariate association between pairs of ordinal variables, for example, as a suitable generalization of the Goodman-Kruskal gamma coefficient (see Kawasaki 1979 and Goodman and Kruskal 1979), and to formulate a chi-square test for the significance of association between pairs of variables. (γ ranges between +1 for perfect positive association and -1 for perfect negative association). (3) The model also lends itself to a convenient parametrization of conditional probabilities in terms of a subset of the main and interaction effect parameters which characterize the joint probabilities.

Systems of probability statements relating a number of categorical variables have been considered by Maddala and Lee [1976], Lee [1981], Ottenwaelter and Vuong [1981], and Vuong [1981]. Vuong [1981]considers the most general case and derives conditions for the identification of systems of conditional probability statements, in which conditional variables in some probability statements are conditioning in others. His work is summarized and extended in Ottenwaelter and Vuong [1981]. The conditions are similar to those for the identification of a to unanticipated demand shocks and to changes in inventories and backlogs. Given production plans and price anticipations, therefore, it is possible to infer actual changes in production and prices from a system of relationships which relate these variables to unancticipated changes in demand over time.

Finally, there is a second question which is treated here. Since the publication of the General Theory, it has commonly been believed that price responses are asymmetric during the business cycle. Stickiness of prices (and nominal wages) during the downswing has been considered the main case for Keynesian demand management. In this paper we also examine the evidence of any changes in reaction patterns over time.

2. A Recursive Log-Linear Probability Model for Prices and Production

In this section we formulate a series of conditional probability statements relating realized changes in prices and production for French and German firms to a number of other variables such as previously anticipated price changes and production plans, demand anticipations, unexpected changes in demand, changes in inventories and appraisals of finished products and order backlogs and a measure of supply constraint. Data on changes in costs, in addition to information reflecting capacity or other supply constraints, are not available in the Ifo and INSEE business-test surveys on which we base our analysis. Thus it is only possible to infer somewhat indirectly the relative importance of changes in production and changes in prices in response to demand shocks.

Conditional, Recursive Log-Linear Probability Models

The data with which we deal in this paper are almost all categorical consisting of trichotomous responses of individual firms to survey questions. The data may be cross-classified for each respondent by question so that, for example, it is possible to see whether a firm recursive system of simultaneous equations in econometric theory but somewhat less restrictive. For simplicity consider the case of three categorical variables, A_1, A_2, A_3, the distribution of which is characterized by some joint probability law:

$$(1) \quad \Pr\{A_1, A_2, A_3\} .$$

Suppose that for theoretical reasons we believe that underlying the joint probability is a "structural" system of conditional probability laws:

$$(2) \begin{cases} \Pr\ \{A_1 \mid A_2, A_3\} \\ \Pr\ \{A_2 \mid A_3\} \\ \Pr\ \{A_3\} \end{cases}$$

Provided

$$(3) \begin{cases} \Pr\ \{A_2 \mid A_1, A_3\} = \Pr\ \{A_2 \mid A_3\} \\ \Pr\ \{A_3 \mid A_1, A_2\} = \Pr\ \{A_3\}, \end{cases}$$

it is possible to estimate each of the "structural probabilities separately. Moreover, the system of conditional probabilities uniquely determines the joint probability law (1).[5)]

In what follows we formulate such a system of conditional log-linear probability models which has the objective of describing the probability law governing changes in prices and in production as reported in the Ifo and INSEE business test surveys. This model represents a step in an ongoing effort to study the formation and revision of firms' plans and anticipations at a highly disaggregated level. In most macro-economic models and other studies involving time-series data, one can

5) This is a consequence of the fact that a complete set of univariate conditional probabilities derived from an underlying joint probability law uniquely determines the joint probability law and is determined by it. See Nerlove and Press [1976]. As a consequence of (3), no restrictions need be imposed on the "structural" probabilities in (2) in order to ensure that they are derivable from the same underlying joint distribution.

infer how expectations are formed and how they influence plans and behavior only indirectly by observing the outcomes of decisions made by the firms and the values of variables representing external forces affecting these firms. Such inferences can be tested only indirectly within the context of the behavioral model assumed. This means that errors in the formulation of a behavioral model affect conclusions regarding expectation formation and plans. Therefore, it is essential to obtain independent evidence on the actual micro-data themselves - on expectations and plans at the firm level. In our work, we devise models which attempt to explain variations in expectations, plans and realizations of economic variables as reported in survey of firms. In the present paper we are especially concerned with how expectations and plans once formed are or are not translated into realized changes in prices and production. Empirical evidence on this process bears on the issues in current macroeconomic theory discussed in the first section of this paper.

The French and German Business-Test Data

For France data are available for twenty-nine surveys conducted by the Institut Nationale de la Statistique et des Etudes Economiques (INSEE) between June 1974 and June 1982. The surveys were conducted three times per year until June 1978 (March, June, and November) and four times a year thereafter (January, March, June and October) and cover approximately 3000 firms. For Germany, data are available for the period January 1975 - December 1979 and June 1980 - September 1982 collected by the Ifo Institut für Wirtschaftsforschung. The data are collected monthly, for about 8000 products in the early period and about 10,000 in the later period, with respect to eleven basic questions and quarterly, on a rotating basis, for the so-called Sonderfragen. Unfortunately, we have the responses for the Sonderfragen only for a few of the months in 1977 (January, March, April, May, and June), although the data are complete in 1980-82.

Although the French and German economies are similar in many ways (level of industrialization, concentration, product mix, openness), it is believed by knowledgable observers that there are important structural and institutional differences particularly with respect to the way in which prices and production respond to various shocks to the respective systems (de Ménil and Westphal, 1982). For this reason we believe that a comparative study of the French and German surveys may be especially illuminating with respect to the relative effects of demand shocks and supply bottlenecks on changes in prices and in production. We show, indeed, that there are significant differences between the two groups of respondents.

The variables are taken from responses to the German (Ifo) and French (INSEE) surveys and are summarized in Table 1. Variables for

Table 1: French (INSEE) and German (Ifo) Business Test Variables

Variable	Plans or Expectations	Realizations	Appraisals
Business Conditions (Ifo)	G*	G	--
Demand (INSEE)	D*	D	D^a
Production	Q*	Q	--
Inventories of Finished Products	--	L (INSEE)	L^a
Backlog of Orders	--	S (Ifo)	S^a
Domestic Selling Prices	P*	P	--
Incoming New Orders (Ifo)	--	A	--
Supply Constraints	--	--	BOT

changes in the backlog of orders for French firms and for changes in inventories of finished products for the German firms have been constructed from continuous data (the latter from the so-called Sonderfragen). Nearly all the data are in categorical form: Increase (+), no change (=), or decrease (-); or greater than normal (+), normal (=), or less than normal (-); or too large (+), about right (=), or too small (-). For France, which has experienced a relatively higher rate of inflation during the period, continuous data on price anticipations and realizations are available, and these have been used to recategorize the responses so as to correct the almost complete absence of reported decreases.[2)]

We have also constructed a variable BOT for both French and German firms designed to reflect actual or anticipated constraints to expanding production. For German firms if expansion is hindered by lack of orders we say there is excess capacity, if it is not hindered, we classify the firm in a neutral category, whereas if the firm is hindered for any reason other than lack of orders, we classify the firm as constrained. For French firms, the questions are phrased somewhat differently: Firms are asked if they would receive additional orders could they advantageously expand production with present means; if a firm answers yes, it is asked whether nevertheless it is constrained by insufficient equipment, personnel, difficulties of obtaining parts or supplies, or for some other reason. If a firm answers yes but does not indicate any constraint, we classify the firm as unconstrained; if it answers yes and that is nonetheless constrained, we classify it as moderately constrained. If it answers no, that it could not advantgageously expand if it had additional orders, we classify it as severely constrained.

In the analyses reported in this paper, we use data on German establishments only at three-month intervals, corresponding to the dates of the Sonderfragen concerning inventories, necessitating the

2) The categories used for both anticipated and realized price changes for French firms are

"++" = > 5%

"+" = > 0% and $\leq$ 5%

"0" = $\leq$ 0% .

aggregation of some responses for each establishment over time.[3)]

The French responses refer to anticipated changes until the date of the next survey or to realized changes since the data of the last survey; our analyses use data at intervals corresponding to the intervals between surveys. Many of our analysis, require the definition of the discrepancy between a prior plan or anticipation and a subsequent realization. This is defined by the contingency table in Figure 1for the *ex ante* variable X^*_{-1} and a subsequent realization, X, as ΦX.

Figure 1:

$\Phi X \equiv X$

X \ X^*_{-1}	+	=	-
+	=	+	+
=	-	=	+
-	-	-	=

In earlier work, we found incoming orders, A, to be a better measure of demand than G, but G* to be a plausible measure of expected future demand. Consequently, ΦD is constructed using A and G^*_{-1} for the German respondents.

---

3) The method of aggregating the German data is as follows: Let X_t be a realization reported on the survey taken at date t; it refers to the change over the preceeding month. Let $\bar{X}_t$ be the aggregate referring to the preceeding three months. The method is as follows:
   If the sign of X_{t-i}, i=0,1,2 is identical, set $\bar{X}_t$ equal to that sign.
   If the responses differ in sign for each survey, the establishment is deleted.
   If the sign of X_{t-i}, i=0,1,2 is equal for two periods and the sign for the third period is not opposite in sign, set $\bar{X}_t$ equal to the sign of the categories reporting changes; otherwise the establishment is deleted.
   We have also looked at relationships using only the middle month (i=1) value. This method has the advantage of retaining more firms in the sample, particularly those firms which exhibit a great deal of variability over short periods of time. The results, however, are not much different from those reported here.

The Model

In our description of the model and results, we use the notation appropriate to the French data, it being understood that appropriate modifications should be made in connection with the German survey. For example, in the case of Germany D* represents expected future business conditions (G*), whereas demand realizations, D, are incoming new orders (A). Also the interpretation of L^a, inventory appraisals is reversed in sign: For the French data the first category is "greater than normal", the second "normal", etc., while for the German data the first category is "too small", the second "sufficient", etc.

The *ex ante* variables of our model are:

- D* : Expected future demand;
- P* : Anticipated price changes;
- Q* : Planned changes in production.

The *ex post* or realized variables are:

- D : Demand or incoming new orders;
- L : Changes in inventories of finished production;
- S : Changes in order backlogs;
- P : Realized price changes;
- Q : Realized changes in production.

The *appraisal* variables are:

- L^a : Aprraisal of inventory levels;
- S^a : Appraisal of order backlogs;
- BOT: Perception of constraints to expansion of production.

Both BOT and D are taken to be purely exogenous, although our findings suggest that BOT reflects much the same set of underlying latent variables which are reflected in S^a and L^a. The observed variable which "drives" our system is not D itself but rather ΦD, unexpected changes in demand. Unfortunately, the surveys contain very little information on changes in costs or input prices.

The model focuses on the determination of price anticipations and production plans and the reasons why the *ex post* values differ from the *ex ante* values of prices and production, i.e.. ΦP and ΦQ. There are, however, two implicit "identities" in the model relating previous anticipations or plans to their *ex post* values reported on a subsequent survey:

$$(1)\begin{cases} P \equiv P^*_{-1} \text{ "+" } \Phi P \\ Q \equiv Q^*_{-1} \text{ "+" } \Phi Q. \end{cases}$$

Because of the categorical nature of the variables, these are not true identities, nor do the plus signs represent actual addition.

The model we formulate is recursive in the sense defined above. Expectations of future demand are determined by past unexpected changes in demand in an "adaptive" manner. These unexpected changes in turn affect changes in inventory levels and order backlogs, which, together with expectations of future demand and BOT, are reflected in appraisals of these variables. Appraisals, expectations of future demand, and perceptions of capacity constraints determine price anticipations and production plans, which, by the implicit identities (1), determine realized changes in prices and production.

Determination of expectations of future demand:

$$(2)\quad \Pr\{D^* \mid D^*_{-1}, D\}$$

In previous analyses reported in Nerlove [1981], we found that a simple error-learning or "adaptive" expectations model explained changes in all three *ex ante* variables better than a number of other simple mechanical models which we estimated. The results were highly stable over time and showed a large and very significant positive association between changes in an *ex ante* variable and previously unexpected changes. We adopt a similar but somewhat more flexible formulation here for D^*, but formulate an explanation of P^* and Q^* below with greater economic content.

Unanticipated changes in production and prices

(3) $\Pr\{\Phi P, \Phi Q \mid \Phi D, L, S\}$

It is common sense that a firm's plans and expectations will be revised when unexpected events occur. The theory of the imperfectly competitive firm does not, of course, predict what will happen to prices and output given an upward shift in the demand function that a firm faces. If demand is highly elastic or if firms are reluctant to raise prices once announced, one can be reasonably confident that the quantity supplied will increase. The response of prices remains conjectural, but the more competitive are firms, the greater the likelihood of some increase in prices when demand increases. Thus, even over the short time horizon implied by the period between survey dates, we would expect unanticipated changes in demand to be positively associated with discrepancies between actual and planned production changes and more weakly, but still positively, associated with discrepancies between actual and anticipated price changes. The relation should differ depending on the levels of order backlogs and inventories of finished products capable of absorbing some of the unanticipated changes in demand. Changes in inventories and backlogs reflect the extent to which firms actually do buffer unexpected changes in demand in this way.[4)]

4) It is interesting to note that when the unconditional relationship between unanticipated changes in prices and in production is estimated, a strong positive association between ΦP and ΦQ is found, but that when this relationship is conditioned on ΦD, the association all but disappears, i.e., the two variables are nearly conditionally independent given unanticipated changes in demand.

Changes in inventories and order backlogs

(4) $Pr\{L, S \mid \Phi D, BOT\}$

If we had quantitative data on sales, production, and inventories or order backlogs, we would expect these variables to be related by identities:

Change in inventories ≡ production - sales.
Change in order backlogs ≡ orders - production.

Because the data are categorical, no such formulation is possible. However, it is possible to make a probability statement regarding the conditional probability of changes in inventory levels and order backlogs given the direction of unexpected changes in demand. We expect the association between L and ΦD to be negative and between S and ΦD to be positive (a fall in inventory levels or an increase in order backlogs is associated with an unexpected increase in demand). To the extent that it is costly to change levels of prices or production and in the presence of capacity constraints, we would expect firms largely to satisfy unexpected demand changes out of inventories or by drawing down order backlogs. But if capacity is unconstrained and prices do not adjust in the short run, a large part of the increase may be met by changing production.

Inventory and order backlogs appraisals

(5) $Pr\{L^a, S^a \mid D^*, L, S, BOT\}$

How a firm regards its current inventory level presumably depends mostly on its expectations of future demand in relation to how costly it may be to change current levels of production. One measure of the latter is how rapidly actual inventory or order backlog levels have recently been run up or down. Of course, we do not have, or do not use, quantitative information on these changes. Moreover, the sign and magnitude of the effect may be related to the cause of the fluctuation, whether purposefully or because of unexpected changes in demand or capacity constraints. Moreover, the firm's current perception of how easy or difficult it might be to expand production should affect its appraisal of inventories or order backlogs. As suggested above, however, it is moot whether these perceptions can be treated as exogenously determined in this context.

We expect to find a strong positive association between L^a or S^a and D*. If actual inventory levels or order backlogs have recently risen, we would expect firms to regard current levels as too high, and vice versa. If demand is expected to increase, any current level of inventories will, *ceteris paribus*, be regarded as too low and any current level of order backlogs too high. The presence of capacity constraints should be associated, *ceteris paribus*, with an appraisal of inventory levels as too low and order backlogs as too high.

Production plans and price anticipations

(6) $Pr\{P^*, Q^* \mid D^*, L^a, S^a, BOT\}$.

We have a strong *a priori* belief that planned changes in production and anticipated price changes ought to be related to expected future changes in demand and to one another.[5] *Ceteris paribus*, current appraisals of inventory levels and order backlogs ought also to be associated with these plans and anticipations: too low a level of inventories or too high order backlogs should be associated with

---

5) It is noteworthy that the relations

$Pr\{\Delta P^* \mid \Phi P\}$ and $Pr\{\Delta Q^* \mid \Phi Q\}$

provide strong and stable explanations of changes in price anticipations and production plans, but these probability statements contain little economic content. The notation ΔX is based on a definition similar to that for ΦX above.

planned increase in production and, perhaps with some anticipated upward adjustment in prices. The effect of perceived constraints to the expansion of production depends on whether such constraints are expected to persist in the future: If they are not, current constraints should be associated with planned increases in production but no anticipated changes in prices; if they are expected to persist, no planned increases in production should be anticipated but prices should be expected to increase.

The foregoing system of five conditional probability statements plus the two implicit identities, relating price anticipations and production plans to subsequent realizations, forms a recursive system which relates realized price and production changes to unexpected changes in demand and the presence or absence of impediments to the expansion of production. The latter may indirectly reflect changes in cost conditions.

3. Empirical Results

The results of estimating the five conditional probabilities using a conditional log-linear probability model for each are presented in summary from the Tables 2-6. The estimates are restricted to main effects and bivariate interaction configurations (except for the estimates on which the tests of time stability are based. Although we have estimates for 28 pairs of surveys for the French firms and potentially for 9 or 10 such pairs for the German firms, we have chosen two dates for each group for presentation here. For the German firms the dates are June 1977 and August 1982; for the French firms the dates are June 1975 and March 1980. These dates were chosen, in part, to obtain contrasting results for surveys widely separated in time and, in part, because in the first period both economies were entering a boom phase of the business cycle and in the second both were in recession.

Table 2: Model Pr $\{D^* | D^*_{-1}, D\}$

configuration	German firms: June 1977 γ (t-value)	June 1977 χ^2 (Prob.)	August 1982 γ (t-value)	August 1982 χ^2 (Prob.)	Time-stability χ^2 (Prob.)	French firms: June 1975 γ (t-value)	June 1975 χ^2 (Prob.)	March 1980 γ (t-value)	March 1980 χ^2 (Prob.)	Time-stabiltiy χ^2 (Prob.)
(D^*, D^*_{-1})	0.555 (6.2)	62.2 (0.000)	0.487 (7.9)	162.0 (0.000)	8.0 (0.093)	0.461 (9.1)	136.0 (0.000)	0.742 (16.9)	183.0 (0.000)	6.8 (0.149)
(D^*, D)	0.642 (10.3)	105.0 (0.000)	0.577 (11.0)	187.0 (0.000)	13.7 (0.006)	0.407 (7.5)	151.0 (0.000)	0.124 (2.0)	73.4 (0.000)	15.7 (0.004)
number of observations	1527		2546		4073	1737		1469		3206

a) partially estimated

Table 3 : Model Pr {ØP, ØQ ⋮ ØD, L, S}

configuration	German firms June 1977 γ (t-value)	June 1977 χ^2 (Prob.)	August 1982 γ (t-value)	August 1982 χ^2 (Prob.)	Time-stability χ^2 (Prob.)	French firms June 1975 γ (t-value)	June 1975 χ^2 (Prob.)	March 1980 γ (t-value)	March 1980 χ^2 (Prob.)	Time-stability χ^2 (Prob.)
(ØP, ØQ)	0.150 (1.7)	19.3 (0.001)	0.077 (0.8)	9.59 (0.048)	4.7 (0.321)	0.055 (0.3)	2.50 (0.64)	-0.059 (0.4)	0.27 (0.99)	5.4 (0.251)
(ØP, ØD)	0.178 (2.1)	11.9 (0.018)	0.123 (1.44)	6.58 (0.160)	4.6 (0.329)	-0.227 (1.4)	4.43 (0.35)	0.168 (1.4)	4.04 (0.40)	1.7 (0.787)
(ØP, L)	-0.094 (1.1)	1.93 (0.748)	0.002 (0.0)	13.5 (0.009)	6.7 (0.152)	-0.146 (1.1)	9.37 (0.05)	-0.152 (1.4)	4.05 (0.40)	6,4 (0.170)
(ØP, S)	0.177 (1.5)	19.9 (0.001)	0.155 (1.3)	26.8 (0.000)	3.2 (5.3)	0.017 (0.2)	2.77 (0.60)	0.009 (0.1)	2.38 (0.58)	3.9 (0.417)
(ØQ, ØD)	0.537 (10.0)	131.0 (0.000)	0.648 (18.1)	338.0 (0.000)	4.8 (0.307)	0.808 (17.1)	164.0 (0.000)	0.649 (21.5)	150.0 (0.000)	2.3 (0.675)
(ØQ, L)	-0.179 (2.6)	14.2 (0.007)	-0.048 (1.1)	20.9 (0.000)	9.0 (0.062)	0.235 (2.0)	6.48 (0.17)	0.149 (1.28)	2.31 (0.68)	8.0 (0.093)
(ØQ, S)	0.213 (2.2)	10.1 (0.040)	0.240 (3.2)	65.1 (0.000)	19.0 (0.001)	0.031 (0.4)	4.53 (0.34)	-0.105 (1.1)	3.49 (0.41)	2.0 (0.730)
number of observations	1527		2546		4073	574		565		1139

a) partially estimated

Table 4: Model Pr {L, S | ØD, BOT}

configuration	German firms					French firms				
	June 1977		August 1982		Time-stability	June 1975		March 1980		Time-stability
	γ (t-value)	χ^2 (Prob.)	γ (t-value)	χ^2 (Prob.)	χ^2 (Prob.)	γ (t-value)	χ^2 (Prob.)	γ (t-value)	χ^2 (Prob.)	χ^2 (Prob.)
(L, S)	-0.209 (2.5)	66.5 (0.000)	-0.251 (4.6)	47.6 (0.000)	12.6 (0.014)	-0.147 (2.0)	6.65 (0.156)	-0.020 (0.3)	0.29 (0.97)	8.4 (0.079)
(L, ØD)	-0.171 (2.7)	15.9 (0.003)	-0.135 (3.5)	18.4 (0.001)	9.6 (0.048)	-0.205 (2.3)	13.1 (0.01)	-0.296 (3.6)	17.6 (0.0)	1.4 (0.847)
(L, BOT)	0.380 (5.7)	31.2 (0.000)	0.095 (1.2)	28.0 (0.000)	11.2 (0.025)	0.211 (2.5)	12.4 (0.01)	0.236 (3.7)	14.3 (0.01)	1.6 (0.816)
(S, ØD)	0.863 (30.8)	202.0 (0.000)	0.691 (19.8)	271.0 (0.000)	20.8 (0.000)	0.108 (1.6)	9.85 (0.04)	0.030 (0.4)	4.19 (0.38)	12.8 (0.012)
(S, BOT)	-0.404 (4.7)	27.8 (0.000)	-0.227 (1.8)	32.5 (0.000)	2.8 (0.601)	0.017 (0.3)	3.75 (0.44)	0.070 (1.4)	5.96 (0.20)	2.1 (0.723)
number of observations	1527		2546		4073	706		645		1351

a) partially estimated

Table 5: Model $\{L^a, S^a \mid L, S, G^*, BOT\}$

configuration	German firms: June 1977 γ (t-value)	June 1977 χ^2 (Prob.)	August 1982 γ (t-value)	August 1982 χ^2 (Prob.)	Time-stability χ^2 (Prob.)	French firms: June 1975 γ (t-value)	June 1975 χ^2 (Prob.)	March 1980 γ (t-value)	March 1980 χ^2 (Prob.)	Time-stability χ^2 (Prob.)
(L^a, S^a)	0.765 (11.6)	133.0 (0.000)	0.782 (11.8)	262.0 (0.000)	5.2 (0.263)	0.618 (0.8)	23.7 (0.000)	0.488 (3.9)	35.4 (0.000)	2.98 (0.561)
(L^a, L)	-0.755 (13.5)	233.0 (0.000)	-0.346 (3.7)	42.6 (0.000)	75.2 (0.000)	-0.885 (17.0)	169.0 (0.000)	-0.897 (19.0)	159.0 (0.000)	1.27 (0.867)
(L^a, S)	-0.081 (0.6)	4.51 (0.342)	-0.357 (2.6)	38.7 (0.000)	15.2 (0.004)	-0.015 (0.1)	1.77 (0.87)	0.050 (0.4)	2.08 (0.72)	4.19 (0.381)
(L^a, D^*)	0.533 (3.3)	11.0 (0.026)	0.555 (4.2)	58.7 (0.000)	2.6 (0.625)	0.165 (0.8)	4.39 (0.36)	-0.204 (1.3)	5.17 (0.28)	1.84 (0.765)
(L^a, BOT)	-0.709 (9.2)	78.6 (0.000)	-0.421 (2.8)	43.2 (0.000)	12.4 (0.015)	-0.384 (2.5)	7.97 (0.09)	-0.276 (2.5)	10.2 (0.000)	6.98 (0.137)
(S^a, L)	-0.137 (1.2)	4.85 (0.303)	0.173 (1.6)	18.8 (0.000)	10.2 (0.037)	0.216 (1.2)	11.0 (0.03)	-0.277 (1.8)	8.56 (0.07)	9.49 (0.050)
(S^a, S)	0.720 (11.9)	141.0 (0.000)	0.839 (19.0)	272.0 (0.000)	6.1 (0.193)	0.306 (2.7)	8.35 (0.08)	0.262 (3.3)	10.9 (0.03)	4.21 (0.378)
(S^a, D^*)	0.317[a] (2.1)	7.3[a] (0.026)	0.169 (0.9)	13.7 (0.000)	1.8[a] (0.398)	0.605 5.2)	27.3 (0.0)	0.596 (7.2)	50.8 (0.000)	7.72 (0.103)
(S^a, BOT)	-0.722 (8.9)	151.0 (0.000)	-0.787[a] (13.8)	196,0[a] (0.000)	4.0[a] (0.132)	-0.410 (3.9)	26.1 (0.000)	-0.440 (6.5)	39.3 (0.000)	5.17 (0.271)
Number of observations	1527		2546		4073	466		473		939

a) partially estimated

Table 6: Model {P*, Q* | D*, L^a, S^a, BOT}

configuration	German firms: June 1977 γ (t-value)	German firms: June 1977 χ^2 (Prob.)	German firms: August 1982 γ (t-value)	German firms: August 1982 χ^2 (Prob.)	German firms: Time-stability χ^2 (Prob.)	French firms: June 1975 γ (t-value)	French firms: June 1975 χ^2 (Prob.)	French firms: March 1980 γ (t-value)	French firms: March 1980 χ^2 (Prob.)	French firms: Time-stability χ^2 (Prob.)
(P*, Q*)	0.233 (1.6)	21.5 (0.000)	0.449 a) (5.7)	27.4 a) (0.000)	3.9 a) (0.139)	0.056 (0.5)	4.66 (0.32)	-0.040 (0.4)	0.92 (0.920)	0.7 (0.952)
(P*, D*)	0.273 (1.4)	10.7 (0.030)	0.311 (1.6)	4.0 (0.406)	3.0 (0.556)	0.197 (1.8)	5.92 (0.20)	0.045 (0.5)	1.46 (0.831)	1.0 (0.909)
(P*, L^a)	0.110 a) (0.3)	6.8 a) (0.033)	0.356 (1.6)	22.9 (0.000)	1.1 a) (0.572)	-0.036 (0.3)	3.04 (0.55)	-0.023 (0.3)	4.19 (0.38)	1.1 (0.895)
(P*, S^a)	0.276 (1.3)	1.7 (0.799)	0.081 (0.3)	10.2 (0.037)	3.0 (0.563)	0.125 (1.1)	1.40 (0.84)	0.040 (0.5)	6.38 (0.17)	0.4 (0.984)
(P*, BOT)	-0.064 (0.5)	1.9 (0.763)	-0.122 a) (1.7)	4.08 a) (0.253)	0.03 a) (0.983)	-0.063 (0.7)	1.74 (0.77)	-0.054 (1.0)	1.65 (0.80)	6.9 (0.137)
(Q*, D*)	0.954 a) (47.9)	233.0 a) (0.000)	0.904 (42.1)	603.0 (0.000)	2.8 a) (0.251)	0.914 (27.7)	226.0 (0.000)	0.946 a) (48.1)	141.0 a) (0.000)	0.8 a) (0.674)
(Q*, L^a)	-0.013 (0.1)	4.3 (0.367)	-0.116 (0.8)	18.3 (0.001)	4.2 (0.378)	0.281 (1.6)	10.8 (0.03)	0.098 (0.5)	4.43 (0.35)	3.5 (0.482)
(Q*, S^a)	0.153 (1.1)	17.7 (0.001)	0.286 (2.0)	22.5 (0.000)	9.7 (0.047)	0.686 (4.6)	26.6 (0.000)	0.540 (4.6)	25.7 (0.000)	1.3 (0.857)
(Q*, BOT	0.010 (0.1)	7.1 (0.129)	0.033 (0.2)	4.67 (0.322)	2.1 (0.727)	-0.231 (1.6)	5.21 (0.27)	-0.122 (1.1)	1.82 (0.77)	4.1 (0.390)
Number of observations:	1527		2546		4073	554		593		1147

a) partially estimated

For each bivariate configuration of the conditional probability, we report a component γ-coefficient, an asymptotic t-statistic, the χ^2 for the entire configuration, and its associated upper-tail probability. Except for cases in which a configuration has been estimated only partially, due to an empty cell in the marginal table corresponding to the configuration, there are 4 degrees of freedom associated with the χ^2-value. For partially estimated configurations, there are 2 associated degrees of freedom.

The tests of time stability are based on estimating a model in which bivariate and trivariate configurations including a variable T (=0 for the first survey, =1 for the second survey of the pair). A significant χ^2-value (4 degrees of freedom) for a trivariate configuration (X,Y,T) indicates significant lack of stability of the bivariate configuration (X,Y) over time.

Often component γ-coefficients are not significantly different from zero (judged by the associated t-statistics), while the χ^2-statistic for the configuration is significant. Such a result is an indication of a non-monotonic relation between the two variables, since the γ-coefficient measures the strength of monotonic association only.

Instead of discussing all estimates in detail, we focus our attention on the main results:

- As in previous studies[6)] production plans for both French and Germans are significantly related to demand expectations and appraisals of order backlogs. Firms which evaluate their backlog of orders as higher than normal exhibit a higher probability of reporting planned increases in production. Appraisals of inventories, however, are of minor importance with respect to production plans, the association being low and unstable over time.

- For German firms there exists a positive association between price anticipations and production plans, a similar relationships is not displayed by the French data. Also, for German firms, in terms of t and χ^2, price anticipations are positively related to the appraisals

6) See Nerlove [1981] for references.

of inventories implying that firms which evaluate their inventories as too low (compared to normal) exhibit a higher probability of anticipated increases. For French firms, however, such a relationship cannot be observed.

- Given unexpected changes in demand, discrepancies in price anticipations and production plans appear to be conditionally independent for French but not for German firms. For both French and German firms, however, unplanned changes in production are always positively and significantly associated with unexpected changes in demand. In general, unanticipated changes in prices are not related to unexpected changes in demand. For German firms, changes in order backlogs and inventories display the relation to unexpected changes of production we expected a priori. Firms which report increases in backorders exhibit a higher probability of reporting increases in actual production above that which had been planned; firms which experience a decrease in inventory levels show a similar response . For French firms, these reaction patterns are not observed.

- Appraisals of backlog of orders and inventory levels are conditionally dependent. Appraisals of, and corresponding changes in, levels are significantly associated for both French and German firms, and associated with bottlenecks, indicating that firms with capacity constraints have a higher probability of reporting backlogs (inventories) higher (lower) than normal. Demand expectations and appraisals also display a significant positive association, the exception being French appraisals of inventory levels.

- Given unexpected changes in demand and bottlenecks, changes in inventory levels and backlogs or orders are conditionally independent for French but not for German firms. Changes in inventories are negatively associated with unexpected changes in demand for both German and French firms implying that firms draw on inventories in case actual production is higher than planned production. German firms also exhibit a strong positive association of changes in backlogs of orders and unexpected changes in demand, this

Table 7: χ^2-statistics and probabilities for time-stability of main effects.

configuration	German firms	French firms
(P*)	2.6 (0.274)	8.5 (0.015)
(Q*)	6.5 (0.039)	5.5 (0.063)
(ØP)	10.0 (0.007)	5.1 (0.077)
(ØQ)	8.2 (0.016)	17.7 (0.000)
(L^a)	13.0 (0.002)	9.4 (0.009)
(S^a)	2.2 (0.336)	1.4 (0.508)
(L)	40.7 (0.000)	44.1 (0.000)
(S)	18.3 (0.000)	44.4 (0.000)
(D*)	20.7 (0.000)	14.6 (0.001)

relationship being weaker for French firms. A similar pattern can be observed for bottlenecks. For German firms reporting bottlenecks the probability of reporting increases (decreases) in order backlogs (inventories) is larger, while, however, French firms display only a significant positive association between changes in inventories and the bottleneck variable.

- For both French and German firms there exists a strong and stable association between demand expectations in consecutive periods as well as between past actual demand changes and expected future demand changes.

- Tests of time stability for the bivariate interactions are presented in columns 6 and 11 for each table. With the exception of the configuration (Q^*, S^a) in $Pr\{P^*, Q^* \mid D^*, L^a, S^a, BOT\}$ for the German firms the null hypothesis of stability is accepted. The same is not the case for many of the other probability statements of the model: The configurations $(\Phi Q, L)$ and $(\Phi Q, S)$ in $Pr\{\Phi P, \Phi Q \mid \Phi D, L, S\}$ are unstable for German firms and $(\Phi Q, L)$ is unstable for French firms. Four of eight interactions in $Pr\{L^a, S^a \mid L, S, D^*, BOT\}$ are unstable, although only one, (S^a, L), is for the French firms; most interactions in $Pr\{L, S \mid \Phi D, BOT\}$ and $Pr\{D^* \mid D^*_{-1}, D\}$ are unstable for the German firms; many fewer are for the French firms. Since the two survey dates at which the probabilities have been estimated differ with respect to phase of the business cycles, we conclude that we have found considerable evidence for asymmetric behavior for German firms over the course of the cycle, but that French firms appear to be much less affected. In particular, there is no evidence for asymmetric price behavior for French firms; only for German firms is there some evidence that the relation between P^* and Q^* changes over the course of the cycle.

- Further light on the question of how the business cycle - changes in the macroeconomic environment in which firms operate - affects their behavior, may be gleaned from Table 7. In this Table we report the χ^2-tests for stability of the main effects for the endogenous variables in the different equations. Nearly all are significant, some highly so, suggesting that macroeconomic variables affect most firms simmultaneously, in the same direction, with respect to production plans, surprises in prices and production, inventory appraisals expectations of future demand, and so forth. Notably, such macroeconomic effects do seem to play a role in French firms' price anticipations but not in those for German firms. This is especially interesting in view of the fact that nothing internal to the firm seems to have anything to do with French firms' price anticipations.

Conclusion

This paper has examined the determinants of firms' price anticipations and production plans and their responses to unexpected demand shocks. Two important conclusions emerge: First, there exists a remarkable difference between French and German firms with respect to pricing policy. For French firms, price anticipations as well as actual price changes are independent of expected demand changes and demand shocks. In general, the results suggest that prices are determined largely by costs and that firms react to demand shocks primarily by changes in production. Even if firms face supply constraints, revisions of production plans are more likely to occur than revisions of price anticipations. These results support the position taken by Malinvaud [1977].[7] For German firms, however, our results indicate that firms may react by changing both production and prices when demand changes; however, firms are more likely to react with changes in production than with changes in prices. Thus the empirical evidence provides strong support for the hypothesis central to disequilibrium economic for French firms, to a somewhat lesser extent for German firms. Second, with respect to asymmetric behavior during the course of the business cycle, our results give considerable support to the hypothesis for German firms with respect

7) See also Kawasaki et. al. [1982].

to the formation of demand expectations, demand disturbances, supply constraints, and in relation to changes inventories and backorders, and with respect to the relationship between price anticipations and production plans. For French firms, our results provide almost no evidence for instability for those bivariate interaction effects which are significant in both sample periods.

Some caveats are in order: First, the evidence presented is restricted to the comparison of two sample periods for French and German firms. We stress that a more elaborate analysis over the whole course of the business cycle is necessary. Second, firms are considered to be homogenous in forming anticipations and plans as well as in their reactions to demand shocks. As is well known, market structure may be of considerable importance for pricing behavior. Differences in the market structure may not only affect the price policy of the firm but also result in different reaction pattern in production, investment plans, and so forth.[8)] Preliminary studies taking into account the degree of concentration of specific industry groups, however, did not yield significant results with respect to the estimated interaction effects. Finally, we emphasize againg that the surveys contain almost no information on changes in costs.

The absence of information on changes in costs may be expected to affect primarily our ability to explain changes in price anticipations and realizations to the extent these are related to cost conditions and not to demand shocks. However, neglect of changes cost conditions need not bias the result that production plans and realizations are strongly and significantly affected by demand shocks since tha latter are likely to be nearly independent of changes in cost conditions <u>at the level of the individual firm.</u>

---

8) See Monopolkommission [1976].

References

Barro, R. J. [1976], "Rational Expectations and the Role of Monetary Policy." Journal of Monetary Economics, 2: 1-32.

Blinder, A. S. [1982], "Inventories and Sticky Prices: More on the Microfoundations of Macroeconomics." American Economic Review, 72: 334-348.

Clower, R. W. [1965], "The Keynesian Counterrevolution: A Theoretical Appraisal." in: F. H. Hahn and F. P.Brechling (eds.), The Theory of Interest. London.

Gordon, R. J. [1981], "Output Fluctuations and Gradual Price Adjustment". Journal of Economic Literature, 19: 493-530.

Kawasaki, S. [1979], Application of Log-Linear Probability Models in Econometrics. Ph. D. dissertation, Department of Economics, Northwestern University.

Kawasaki, S. and J. McMillan, K. F. Zimmermann, [1982], "Disequilibrium Dynamics: An Empirical Study." American Economic Review, 72: 992-1004

Laidler, D. [1981], "On Says Law, Money and the Business Cycle". Research Report No. 8106, University of Western Ontario.

Lee, Lung-Fei, [1981], "Fully recursive probability models and multivariate log-linear probability models for the analysis of qualitative data." Jour. Econometrics,16: 15-69.

Maccini, L. J. [1981], "On the Theory of the Firm underlying Empirical Models of Aggregate Price Behavior." International Economic Review, 22: 609-624

Maddala, G. S. and Lee, Lung-Fei, [1976], "Recursive models with qualitative variables." Annals of Economic and Social Measurement, 5/4: 524-545.

deMenil, Georges and Westphal, Uwe, [1982], "The transmission of international disturbances: A French-German cliometric analysis, 1972-80." European Economic Review, 18: 41-73.

Malinvaud, E. [1977], The Theory of Unemployment Reconsidered- Basic Blackwell. Oxford.

Monopolkommission [1976], Mehr Wettbewerb ist möglich. Hauptgutachten 1973/1975. Baden-Baden. Nomos Verlagsgesellschaft.

Nerlove, M. [1981], "Expectations, Plans, and Realizations in Theory and Practice." Presidential address to the Econometric Society. Forthcoming in Econometrica, September 1983.

Nerlove, M. and Press, S. J. [1976], "Multivariate log-linear probability models for the analysis of qualitative data." Discussion paper No. 1, Center for Statistics and Probability, Northwestern University.

Ottenwaelter, B. and Vuong, A. 1981 , "Modèles conditionnele log-linéaires de probabilité et systèmes récursifs." Annales de l'INSEE, 44: 81-120.

Patinkin, D. 1965 , Money, Interest, and Prices; An Integration of Monetary and Value Theory. New York. 2nd ed. Harper and Row.

Reagan, P. B. 1979 , "Inventories and Asymmetrics in Price Adjustment." Working Paper, Nov.

Vuong, Q. H. 1981 , Conditional Log-Linear Probability Models: A Theoretical Development and an Empirical Application. Ph. D. dissertation, Department of Economics, Northwestern University.

* The research on which this paper is based has been supported by the U.S. National Science Foundation and the Deutsche Forschungsgemeinschaft. We are indebted for able research assistance to G. Flaig and K. Zimmermann, University of Mannheim, and to D. Ross, Northwestern University. Our colleague G. Oudiz, Centre d'Etudes Prospectives et d'Informations Internationales generously provided access to the French data. Ross also made numerous helpful expository suggestions.

HANDOUT for "Response of Prices and Production to Unanticipated Demand Shocks," by H. Koenig and M. Nerlove

Table 1: French (INSEE) and German (Ifo) Business Test Variables

Variable	Plans or Expectations	Realizations	Appraisals
Business Conditions (Ifo)	G*	G	—
Demand (INSEE)	D*	D	D^a
Production	Q*	Q	--
Inventories of Finished Products	—	L (INSEE)	L^a
Backlog of Orders	—	S (Ifo)	S^a
Domestic Selling Prices	P*	P	--
Incoming New Orders (Ifo)	—	A	—
Supply Constraints	—	—	BOT

Figure 1: Definition of a "Surprise"

$\phi X \equiv X$ \ X^*_{-1}	+	=	-
+	=	+	+
=	-	=	+
-	-	-	=

(1) $P \equiv P^*_{-1}$ "+" ϕP

$Q \equiv Q^*_{-1}$ "+" ϕQ

(2) $Pr \{D^* | D^*_{-1}, D\}$

(3) $Pr \{\phi P, \phi Q | \phi D, L, S\}$

(4) $Pr \{L, S | \phi D, BOT\}$

(5) $Pr \{L^a, S^a | D^*, L, S, BOT\}$

(6) $Pr \{P^*, Q^* | D^*, L^a, S^a, BOT\}$

The Results: Tables 2-7

Table 2: Model Pr $\{D^* | D^*_{-1}, D\}$

configuration	German firms					French firms				
	June 1977		August 1982		Time stability	June 1975		March 1980		Time stability
	γ (t-value)	χ^2 (Prob.)	γ (t-value)	χ^2 (Prob.)	χ^2 (Prob.)	γ (t-value)	χ^2 (Prob.)	γ (t-value)	χ^2 (Prob.)	χ^2 (Prob.)
(D^*, D^*_{-1})	0.555 (6.2)	62.2 (0.000)	0.487 (7.9)	162.0 (0.000)	8.0 (0.093)	0.461 (9.1)	136.0 (0.000)	0.742 (16.9)	183.0 (0.000)	6.8 (0.149)
(D^*, D)	0.642 (10.3)	105.0 (0.000)	0.577 (11.0)	187.0 (0.000)	13.7 (0.008)	0.407 (7.5)	151.0 (0.000)	0.124 (2.0)	73.4 (0.000)	15.7 (0.004)
number of observations	1527		2546		4073	1737		1469		3026

Table 3: Model Pr (ØP, ØQ | ØD, L, S)

configuration	German firms					French firms				
	June 1977		August 1982		Time Stability	June 1975		March 1980		Time Stability
	γ (t-value)	χ^2 (Prob.)	γ (t-value)	χ^2 (Prob.)	χ^2 (Prob.)	γ (t-value)	χ^2 (Prob.)	γ (t-value)	χ^2 (Prob.)	χ^2 (Prob.)
(ØP, ØQ)	0.150 (1.7)	19.3 (0.001)	0.077 (0.8)	9.59 (0.048)	4.7 (0.321)	0.055 (0.3)	2.50 (0.64)	-0.059 (0.4)	0.27 (0.99)	5.4 (0.251)
(ØP, ØD)	0.178 (2.1)	11.9 (0.018)	0.123 (1.44)	6.58 (0.160)	4.6 (0.329)	-0.227 (1.4)	4.43 (0.35)	0.168 (1.4)	4.04 (0.40)	1.7 (0.787)
(ØP, L)	-0.094 (1.1)	1.93 (0.748)	0.002 (0.0)	13.5 (0.009)	6.7 (0.152)	-0.146 (1.1)	9.37 (0.05)	-0.152 (1.4)	4.05 (0.40)	6,4 (0.170)
(ØP, S)	0.177 (1.5)	19.9 (0.001)	0.155 (1.3)	26.8 (0.000)	3.2 (5.3)	0.017 (0.2)	2.77 (0.60)	0.009 (0.1)	2.88 (0.58)	3.9 (0.417)
(ØQ, ØD)	0.537 (10.0)	131.0 (0.000)	0.648 (18.1)	338.0 (0.000)	4.8 (0.307)	0.808 (17.1)	164.0 (0.000)	0.649 (21.5)	150.0 (0.000)	2.3 (0.675)
(ØQ, L)	-0.179 (2.6)	14.2 (0.007)	-0.048 (1.1)	20.9 (0.000)	9.0 (0.062)	0.235 (2.0)	6.48 (0.17)	0.149 (1.28)	2.31 (0.68)	8.0 (0.093)
(ØQ, S)	0.213 (7.2)	10.1 (0.040)	0.240 (3.2)	65.1 (0.000)	19.0 (0.001)	0.031 (0.4)	4.53 (0.34)	-0.105 (1.1)	3.49 (0.41)	2.0 (0.730)
number of observations	1527		2546		4073	574		565		1139

Table 4: Model Pr {L. S | ϕD. BOT}

configuration	German firms: June 1977 γ (t-value)	June 1977 χ^2 (Prob.)	August 1982 γ (t-value)	August 1982 χ^2 (Prob.)	Time stability χ^2 (Prob.)	French firms: June 1975 γ (t-value)	June 1975 χ^2 (Prob.)	March 1980 γ (t-value)	March 1980 χ^2 (Prob.)	Time stability χ^2 (Prob.)
(L, S)	-0.209 (2.5)	66.5 (0.000)	-0.251 (4.6)	47.6 (0.000)	12.6 (0.014)	-0.147 (2.0)	6.65 (0.156)	-0.020 (0.3)	0.29 (0.97)	8.4 (0.079)
(L, ϕD)	-0.171 (2.7)	15.9 (0.003)	-0.135 (3.5)	18.4 (0.001)	9.6 (0.048)	-0.205 (2.3)	13.1 (0.01)	-0.296 (3.6)	17.6 (0.0)	1.4 (0.847)
(L, BOT)	0.380 (5.7)	31.2 (0.000)	0.095 (1.2)	28.0 (0.000)	11.2 (0.025)	0.211 (2.5)	12.4 (0.01)	0.236 (3.7)	14.3 (0.01)	1.6 (0.816)
(S, ϕD)	0.863 (30.8)	202.0 (0.000)	0.691 (19.8)	271.0 (0.000)	20.8 (0.000)	0.108 (1.6)	9.85 (0.04)	0.030 (0.4)	4.19 (0.38)	12.8 (0.012)
(S, BOT)	-0.404 (4.7)	27.8 (0.000)	-0.227 (1.8)	32.5 (0.000)	2.8 (0.601)	0.017 (0.3)	3.75 (0.44)	0.070 (1.4)	5.96 (0.20)	2.1 (0.723)
number of observations	1527		2546		4073	706		645		1351

Table 5: Model Pr $(L^a, S^a \mid L, S, D^*, BOT)$

configuration	German firms: June 1977 γ (t-value)	German firms: June 1977 χ^2 (Prob.)	German firms: August 1982 γ (t-value)	German firms: August 1982 χ^2 (Prob.)	German firms: Time Stability χ^2 (Prob.)	French firms: June 1975 γ (t-value)	French firms: June 1975 χ^2 (Prob.)	French firms: March 1980 γ (t-value)	French firms: March 1980 χ^2 (Prob.)	French firms: Time Stability χ^2 (Prob.)
(L^a, S^a)	0.765 (11.6)	133.0 (0.000)	0.782 (11.8)	262.0 (0.000)	5.2 (0.263)	0.618 (0.8)	23.7 (0.000)	0.488 (3.9)	35.4 (0.000)	2.98 (0.561)
(L^a, L)	-0.755 (13.5)	233.0 (0.000)	-0.346 (3.7)	42.6 (0.000)	75.2 (0.000)	-0.885 (17.0)	169.0 (0.000)	-0.897 (19.0)	159.0 (0.000)	1.27 (0.867)
(L^a, S)	-0.081 (0.6)	4.51 (0.342)	-0.357 (2.6)	38.7 (0.000)	15.2 (0.004)	-0.015 (0.1)	1.77 (0.87)	0.050 (0.4)	2.08 (0.72)	4.19 (0.381)
(L^a, D^*)	0.533 (3.3)	11.0 (0.026)	0.555 (4.2)	58.7 (0.000)	2.6 (0.625)	0.165 (0.8)	4.39 (0.36)	-0.204 (1.3)	5.17 (0.28)	1.84 (0.765)
(L^a, BOT)	-0.709 (9.2)	78.6 (0.000)	-0.421 (2.8)	43.2 (0.000)	12.4 (0.015)	-0.384 (2.5)	7.97 (0.09)	-0.276 (2.5)	10.2 (0.000)	6.98 (0.137)
(S^a, L)	-0.137 (1.2)	4.85 (0.303)	0.173 (1.5)	18.8 (0.000)	10.2 (0.037)	0.216 (1.2)	11.0 (0.03)	-0.277 (1.8)	8.56 (0.07)	9.49 (0.050)
(S^a, S)	0.720 (11.9)	141.0 (0.000)	0.839 (19.0)	272.0 (0.000)	6.1 (0.193)	0.306 (2.7)	8.35 (0.08)	0.262 (3.3)	10.9 (0.03)	4.21 (0.378)
(S^a, D^*)	0.317[a)] (2.1)	7.3[a)] (0.025)	0.169 (0.9)	18.7 (0.000)	1.8[a)] (0.398)	0.605 5.2)	27.3 (0.0)	0.596 (7.2)	50.8 (0.000)	7.72 (0.103)
(S^a, BOT)	-0.722 (8.9)	151.0 (0.000)	-0.787[a)] (13.8)	196.0[a)] (0.000)	4.0[a)] (0.132)	-0.410 (3.9)	26.1 (0.000)	-0.440 (6.5)	39.3 (0.000)	5.17 (0.271)
Number of observations	1527		2546		4073	466		473		939

a) partly estimated

Table 6+ : Model Pr (P*, Q* | D*, L^a, S^a, BOT)

configuration	German firms					French firms				
	June 1977		August 1982		Time Stability	June 1975		March 1980		Time Stability
	γ (t-value)	χ^2 (Prob.)	γ (t-value)	χ^2 (Prob.)	χ^2 (Prob.)	γ (t-value)	χ^2 (Prob.)	γ (t-value)	χ^2 (Prob.)	χ^2 (Prob.)
(P*, Q*)	0.233 (1.6)	21,5 (0.000)	0.449[a)] (5.7)	27.4[a)] (0.000)	3.9[a)] (0.139)	0.056 (0.5)	4.66 (0.32)	-0.040 (0.4)	0.92 (0.920)	0.7 (0.952)
(P*, D*)	0.273 (1.4)	10.7 (0.030)	0.311 (1.6)	4.0 (0.406)	3.0 (0.556)	0.197 (1.8)	5.92 (0.20)	0.045 (0.5)	1.46 (1.831)	1.0 (0.909)
(P*, L^a)	0.110[a)] (0.3)	6.8[a)] (0.033)	0.356 (1.6)	22.9 (0.000)	1.1[a)] (0.572)	-0.036 (0.3)	3.04 (0.55)	-0.023 (0.3)	4.19 (0.38)	1.1 (0.895)
(P*, S^a)	0.276 (1.3)	1.7 (0.799)	0.081 (0.3)	10.2 (0.037)	3.0 (0.563)	0.125 (1.1)	1.40 (0.84)	0.040 (0.5)	6.38 (0.17)	0.4 (0.984)
(P*, BOT)	-0.064 (0.5)	1.9 (0.763)	-0.122[a)] (1.7)	4.08[a)] (0.253)	0.03[a)] (0.983)	-0.063 (0.7)	1.74 (0.77)	-0.054 (1.0)	1.65 (0.80)	6.9 (0.137)
(Q*, D*)	0.954[a)] (47.9)	233.0[a)] (0.000)	0.904 (42.1)	603.0 (0.000)	2.8[a)] (0.251)	0.914 (27.7)	226.0 (0.000)	0.946[a)] (48.1)	141.0[a)] (0.000)	0.8[a)] (0.674)
(Q*, L^a)	-0.013 (0.1)	4.3 (0.367)	-0.116 (0.8)	18.3 (0.001)	4.2 (0.378)	0.281 (1.6)	10.8 (0.03)	0.098 (0.5)	4.43 (0.351)	3.5 (0.482)
(Q*, S^a)	0.153 (1.1)	17.7 (0.001)	0.286 (2.0)	22.5 (0.000)	9.7 (0.047)	0.686 (4.6)	26.6 (0.000)	0.540 (4.6)	25.7 (0.000)	1.3 (0.857)
(Q*, BOT)	0.010 (0.1)	7.1 (0.129)	0.033 (0.2)	4.67 (0.322)	2.1 (0.727)	-0.231 (1.6)	5.21 (0.27)	-0.122 (1.1)	1.82 (0.77)	4.1 (0.390)
Number of observations	1527		2546		4073	554		593		1147

a) partly estimated

Table 7: χ^2 **- Statistics and Probabilities for Tests of Time Stability of Main Effects.**

Configuration	German firms	French firms
(P^*)	2.6	8.5
	(0.274)	(0.015)
(Q^*)	6.5	5.5
	(0.039)	(0.063)
(ϕP)	10.0	5.1
	(0.007)	(0.077)
(ϕQ)	8.2	17.7
	(0.016)	(0.000)
(L^a)	13.0	9.4
	(0.002)	(0.0009)
(S^a)	2.2	1.4
	(0.336)	(0.508)
(L)	40.7	44.1
	(0.000)	(0.000)
(S)	18.3	44.4
	(0.000)	(0.000)
(D^*)	20.7	14.6
	(0.000)	(0.001)

Tax Incentives and R&D Expenditures

R. Eisner/S.H. Albert/
M.A. Sullivan
Northwestern University
Evanston, Ill.

Company-funded research and development expenditures in the United States showed rapid real growth in the 1960's, slipped in the first half of the next decade and rebounded thereafter. Finally increasing at almost nine percent in 1980, despite a mild recession, they reached a level of $30.5 billion, or 1.16 percent of GNP. In 1981 the tax laws were amended to offer various incentives to further that growth.

The major new provision was a 25 percent tax credit for increases in certain types of R&D expenditures. The credit began with expenditures in the latter half of 1981 and was scheduled to expire at the end of 1985.

In the spring of 1982, with the support of the National Science Foundation, we undertook an ongoing analysis of this experiment in process. Our objectives have been to estimate tax incidence and effect on R&D expenditures. Initial reports are to be found in Eisner (1982) and Collins (1983). Now, after the credit has been in effect some two years, we offer further but still preliminary analysis.

We have thus far been able to develop and use three main bodies of data. These came first from the regular McGraw-Hill spring capital expenditure surveys of 1981, 1982 and 1983, which include a section on R&D expenditures and expenditure anticipations. In 1982, on our behest, McGraw-Hill added several special questions dealing with the new tax credit. In 1983 they undertook a special "supplementary research and development survey," for which we drafted the questionnaire.

Our second primary source of data has been Compustat series for some 800 firms from 1973 to 1982, first taken for recent years from Business Week reports of July 5, 1982 and June 20, 1983. Finally, we have secured from the Office of Tax Analysis of the U.S. Department of the Treasury a special run by three-digit and four-digit industry of information from tax form 6765, used by firms in reporting their R&D tax credit for 1981. Both the Business Week-Compustat and McGraw-Hill data were for individual companies, in the latter case by code number to preserve anonymity of survey responses.

Our analysis will combine an analytic examination of the incremental R&D tax credit and empirical exploration of the survey and relevant financial and tax data.

I. ANALYTICAL FRAMEWORK

1. Statutory and Effective Credits

Under the Economic Recovery Tax Act of 1981, businesses are offered a credit for increasing qualified research activities. These generally relate to company-financed current expenses, including wages, supplies, rental or lease costs (but not depreciation) and 65 percent of contract research. R&D conducted outside of the United States, financed by government or in the social sciences is excluded.

The credit is incremental in character, amounting to 25 percent of the excess of current R&D expenditures over a base which is company-specific and shifts in time. For 1981 qualified expenditures are limited to those after June 30 and the base consists of half of qualified expenditures of all of the year 1980. For 1982, the base consists of the arithmetic mean of qualified expenditures of all of 1980 and 1981. For 1983, 1984 and 1985, the base for each year is the mean of qualified expenditures for the three preceding years. The credit is currently scheduled to expire at the end of 1985, although the Treasury has now joined supporters of its extension beyond that year.

The definition of the base is modified, however, by the requirement that it may never be less than 50 percent of current qualified expenditures. Thus, as R&D exceeds 200 percent of its normally defined base, the redefined base is increased 50 cents for each additional dollar of R&D expenditures, reducing the marginal incremental tax credit from 25 percent to 12.5 percent for such expenditures.

Since the credit is against business income tax liabilities, it is not applicable to current taxes in the very considerable number of cases where firms do not have current tax obligations. Unused credits can be carried back three years and carried forward 15 years.

As of this date, final regulations for implementing the credit have not been promulgated. More than usual latitude has perhaps hence been available to taxpayers in calculation of the credit, particularly in the categorization of "qualified" R&D expenditures.

Systematic analysis of the terms for this credit for increasing research activities suggests a number of significant effects, not all perhaps anticipated by framers of the legislation. First, rather obviously, since qualified expenditures are all defined in nominal terms, in periods of inflation firms may enjoy substantial tax reductions with no real increase in R&D expenditures, and even with some substantial decline. Second, since the credit applies to increments in "qualified" expenditures, the amount of the credit depends both on the proportion of R&D expenditures qualified in the current year and the proportions qualified in base years. Shifts from the base year to the current year in proportions of R&D expenditures deemed qualified can have major effects upon the magnitude of tax credit, with no change in total R&D expenditures.

But most important, the fact that increases in current R&D expenditures over what they would have been without the credit may or may not increase the current credit and may or may not decrease future credits offers a varied menu of consequences, some fairly bizarre. For among the possibilities are the following: 1a) qualified current R&D expenditures will not be increased to an amount in excess of the base and therefore the current credit will be identically equal to zero; 1b) qualified current expenditures will be more than twice base-period expenditures so that each additional dollar of current qualified expenditures will raise the redefined base by 50 cents and limit the marginal credit to 12.5 percent of each additional dollar of expenditures; 1c) qualified expenditures will be within the range of 100 percent and 200 percent of the base, so that the full 25 percent current credit will be enjoyed; 2a) qualified expenditures in each of the succeeding three years will be between 100 and 200 percent of their base; 2b) qualified expenditures in one or more of the succeeding three years will be less than 100 percent of their base; 2c) qualifying expenditures in one or more of the succeeding three years will be more than 200 percent of their base; 3a) a lack of tax liabilities in the current and three preceding years will prevent current use of the credit and induce a carry-forward; 3b) lack of tax liabilities in future years will cause deferral of the effects of current R&D expenditures on future credits.

The various combinations of possibilities 1a to 1c, 2a to 2c and 3a or 3b are further complicated by uncertainties for each firm as to the state of the world in which it will fit. A firm contemplating an increase in qualified R&D expenditures may find it difficult to evaluate the likely impact on future bases and credits.

Take, for example, an informed firm anticipating qualified expenditures above base but less than twice as much as base in each of the years 1981 to 1984. In considering whether to increase its R&D budget in 1981 it would have had to reckon that each additional dollar of R&D spending in the latter half of that year would generate not only a 25 cent reduction in tax liabilities for that year but also a 12.5 cent consequent increase in tax liabilities in 1982 and 8.33 cent increases in tax liabilities in each of the years 1982 and 1983. (The 1982 base, equal to the mean of 1980 and 1981 qualified expenditures, would be raised by 50 cents, and the 1982 and 1983 bases, each of which is the mean of qualified expenditures over the three previous years, would each be raised by 33.33 cents.) The 25 cent tax saving on each additional dollar of qualified R&D expenditures in 1981 would hence generate increased taxes of 29.2 cents over the years 1982, 1983 and 1984.

Taking account of the consequent increase in future tax liabilities, the effective rate of tax credit for 1981 expenditures,[1] at a discount rate of 10 percent, is then actually 0.5 percent, a small fraction of the 25 percent statutory rate. Indeed, at a rate of discount of 8.8 percent, the effective rate of the tax credit becomes zero and, at rates of discount below 8.8 percent, the effective rate of tax credit is in fact negative. In this latter instance the incremental tax credit offers short-term, current gain but penalizes firms over a longer-run three-year period for R&D expenditures in 1981. A firm with a rate of discount less than 8.8 percent would be better advised to reduce its current qualified R&D expenditures, accepting the resultant reduction in current R&D tax credit, in order to reduce its base and hence raise its tax credits for future years.

Consequences for years after 1981 for firms with current and anticipated tax liabilities whose growth in qualified research over base falls in the zero to 100 percent range are not quite as extreme. Again, however, the effective rate of tax credit with a ten percent rate of discount is relatively low, 4.3 percent rather than the current credit of 25 percent.

There are other combinations, however, in which the effective rate of tax credit may be negative, and sharply so. Again assuming a 10 percent rate of discount and tax liabilities in all relevant years, a firm with current qualified expenditures more than 100 percent above its base period amount, but with expected future increases over base in the zero to 100 percent range in each of the three following years, will find its effective rate of tax credit is -8.2 percent. For each additional dollar of current qualified expenditures will reduce the firm's current taxes by 12.5 cents while future taxes are raised by 8.33 cents in each of the three following years, for a total increase of 25 cents. The present value of this future tax increase is 20.7 cents, as against a 12.5 cents current tax saving for each increase of one dollar in qualified current R&D expenditures.

An even more extreme situation arises when an increase in current R&D expenditures will still leave them below their base period amount. Such an increase in qualifying current expenditures generates no current tax saving but may reduce future credits by increasing bases for future years. In the event that future years' qualifying expenditures would be above their bases by more than zero but less than 100 percent, losses in future credit would total 25 cents for each dollar increase in current expenditures. At a rate of discount of 10 percent, the effective credit is -20.7 percent. Far from decreasing taxes by 25 cents, each addititional dollar in qualifying current R&D expenditures would thus <u>raise</u> the present value of tax liabilities by 20.7 cents. In these instances of negative effective tax credits, the response to the incremental R&D tax credit by rational, informed firms, cost of adjustment and intertemporal complementarity considerations aside, would be not to increase but rather to reduce current qualified R&D expenditures.

The necessity of carry-forward in years where there are no tax liabilities or insufficient tax liabilities in both the current and three preceding years also operates to reduce the effective rate of tax credit. For the "normal" case where there are and will be taxes to be offset and where qualified expenditures are growing by between zero and 100 percent of their base, the effective rate of tax credit on marginal qualified R&D expenditures is positive. This is so, even though, other things being equal, future tax credits are reduced dollar for dollar for current increases. Because of the discount factor, current reductions in taxes have a greater present value than future increases.

To the extent that realization of a current tax credit must be deferred because of the lack of current tax liabilities, however, this discount advantage is lost. Increases in qualified current R&D expenditures lower future credits and postpone additional current credits until the future. For example, a firm contemplating \$12 million of additional expenditures in 1982, foreseeing no tax liabilities for 1982, 1983 and 1984 but anticipating tax liabilities in 1985, would derive no tax advantage from the incremental credit. The increased expenditures of \$12 million in 1982 would generate a \$3 million tax credit which would be carried forward to 1985. It would also reduce by \$1 million the tax credits for 1983 and 1984, to be carried forward to 1985, and also reduce by \$1 million the tax credit for 1985 itself. The net effect would thus be zero, a carry-forward of \$3 million of tax credits from 1982 to 1985 minus a reduction of \$3 million in tax credits for 1985 directly and carried forward from 1983 and 1984.

The one situation in which the credit would be most effective is that in which a firm is spending more than base in the current year but anticipates being below base in the three subsequent years. The effective marginal rates of tax credit, if there are current taxes to be offset, is then equal to the statutory rates, 25 percent, or 12.5 percent for expenditures more than 100 percent above base.

All of the analysis thus far has been based on the assumption that the incremental tax credit will be extended indefinitely beyond its current legal date of termination. If in fact the credit is expected to die at the end of 1985, increases in qualified R&D expenditures in 1983 can reduce anticipated future credits only in 1984 and 1985. Increases in expenditures in 1984 can reduce anticipated future credits only in 1985. And increases in expenditures in 1985 will have no impact on future credits.

Thus, again assuming a 10 percent rate of discount, the effective rate of tax credit in 1983 for firms which are and expect to be in the "normal" range of growth over base (positive but less than 100 percent) will equal $.25 - .0833\ (1.1^{-1} + 1.1^{-2})$, or 10.54 percent. For 1984 the effective rate of tax credit will equal $.25 - .083\ (1.1)^{-1}$, or 17.42 percent. And for 1985 the effective rate of credit will finally take on its full statutory rate of 25 percent.

Analogous calculations would be in order for firms in other categories. Thus in 1983 a firm with qualified expenditures more than 100 percent above mean qualified expenditures of the three previous years, but expecting to be in the normal range in 1984 and 1985, would find its effective rate of credit, with a 10 percent rate of discount, equals $.125 - .0833(1.1^{-1} + 1.1^{-2})$, or -1.196 percent. This compares with the even more negative rate of -8.22 percent, noted above, on the assumption that the credit will not terminate at the end of 1985.

In 1984 a firm in the 12.5 percent current rate category but expected to be in the normal range in 1985, would find its effective rate of credit positive, amounting to $.125 - .0833(1.1)^{-1}$, or 4.92 percent. And in 1985 the effective rate would be 12.5 percent. We may note, finally, that if the credit is in fact expected to terminate at the end of 1985, the incentive to reduce expenditures for firms that would in any event be below base would become progressively less in the final years. It would be completely gone in 1985.

2. Magnitudes of Company Tax Savings and Treasury Revenue Losses

Treasury revenue losses from the R&D credit are difficult to predict, however, because of its incremental character. (Treasury losses due to the investment tax credit, dependent on the flow of investment in eligible equipment, are relatively easier to forecast since changes in spending are relatively more volatile than their levels.) Further, since the R&D credit is tied to expenditures in nominal terms, the rate of inflation has a major impact. With changes in rates of inflation generally more difficult to predict than changes in real growth, the problem of anticipating revenue losses from the R&D tax credit is further compounded. And most importantly, changes in the ratio of qualified or eligible expenditures to total R&D spending, what we shall refer to as eligibility ratios, will have what may appear to be an overwhelming impact on the amounts of credit claimed.

Certain things can be predicted, however, in terms of the definition of the R&D credit. First, since for 1981 it applies only to qualified expenditures after June 30, while for the years 1982 through 1985 it applies to all qualified expenditures, we might expect an approximate doubling of the credit from 1981 to 1982. This effect is immediately modified, however, by the shifting nature of the base. For 1981 the base, aside from the 100 percent growth limitation, is equal to half of qualified 1980 expenditures. Hence, the base is lagged 1.25 years, from the second half of 1981 to all of 1980. For 1982, though, the base, calculated as a mean of 1980 and 1981 qualified expenditures, is lagged on average 1.5 years, while for 1983, 1984 and 1985 the average lag of the base is two years. For generally increasing rates of qualified expenditures, the increasing average lag of the base tends to increase the increment in expenditures subject to the credit.

Thus, if qualified R&D expenditures were growing at a constant annual rate of 10 percent and the credit for 1981 were calculated on the difference between half of 1981 expenditures and half of 1980 expenditures the credit as a fraction of 1980 qualifying expenditures would be

$$.25\ (1.1 - 1)/2 = 0.0125,$$

Recognizing the 1.25 year lag in the base for 1981, however, it is more appropriate to assume that R&D expenditures were growing throughout 1980 and 1981. Thus a 10 percent per annum growth would imply a half-year growth in expenditures of $(1.1)^{.5} - 1$, or 4.88 percent. Again normalizing so that total expenditures in 1980 are 1.0 and in 1981 are 1.1, we have a sequence for the four successive half-years of 0.488, 0.512, 0.537, 0.563. For each dollar of 1980 expenditures, the credit for 1981 is then

$$.25(0.5631026 - 0.5) = 0.0157757.$$

Thus, for firms whose R&D is growing at 10 percent per year, the effect of calculating the credit on the difference between R&D expenditures in the latter half of 1981 and half of all of 1980 expenditures rather than on half the difference between the totals for both years is to raise our estimate of the credit, from 0.0125 to 0.0158 per dollar of 1980 R&D, or some 26.2 percent.

For 1982, the credit would be

$$.25\ [1.21 - .5\ (1 + 1.1)] = .04.$$

Had there been no increase in the average lag of the base, with a 10 percent growth in R&D expenditures, the credit would have increased from 0.0158 to 0.0338, or 115 percent. With the increase in the lag of the base, however, the increase in the credit, from 0.0158 to 0.04, is 154 percent.

A similar increase in the amount of the credit due to the increasing lag of the base then takes place in 1983. For this year the credit will equal $.25\ [1.1^3 - {}^1/_3(1 + 1.1 + 1.1^2)] = .0569167$, a 42.3 percent increase in the credit over that of the previous year where, without lengthening of the base, the credit would have increased by only 10 percent. For the years 1983, 1984 and 1985 the average lag of the base will have reached its equilibrium value of two years and there will be no further increases in the credit from this factor.

It is important to recognize that the increasing length of the base will tend to increase the credit more, for any given rates of real growth, the greater is the inflation factor in R&D spending. Even with no real growth and a constant rate of inflation, the R&D tax credit would grow from 1981 to 1982 and from 1982 to 1983 along the lines that we have indicated.

Two further factors affecting the trend of revenue loss or company tax saving may be cited. First, there is a transitional factor. The first year tax credit, in 1981, may tend to be unduly high where firms, perhaps oblivious of future losses of the credit, may be inclined to classify large portions of 1981 R&D expenditures as qualified and as occurring after June 30. There is no incentive to set 1980 qualifying expenditures high as they contribute only to raising the base and therefore lowering the tax credit for future years. There may hence be a substantial, one-time increase in the eligibility ratio from 1980 to 1981. If the eligibility ratio has been unduly inflated for all of 1981, there may then even be a regression or declinein 1982.

Second, small swings in the eligibility ratio can have a major impact on the amount of the tax credit. A relatively modest shift in the eligibility ratio, from 65 percent to 70 percent from 1980 to 1981, for example, would increase by some 59 percent the R&D credit resulting from a 15 percent growth over base.

Finally, to the extent that R&D spending follows the business cycle, the credit will tend to be pro-cyclical, reducing taxes in time of boom and inflation and increasing them in time of recession. Downturns in the rate of growth of R&D expenditures and, a fortiori, actual declines, not only reduce the tax credit and hence increase taxes in time of recession. By lowering the base they tend, as a corollary, to increase tax credits and thus lower taxes in future years of boom. Further, since the credit is not refundable but is merely an offset to tax liabilities, its effect in increasing firm net income will be all the less in recessions when, because of low profits, there may be no tax liabilities. The consequent carry-forward of the credits will increase net income all the more at the peak of a business cycle when there are tax liabilities to be offset.[2]

3. Summary

The incremental tax credit for qualified R&D expenditures has a number of perverse and possibly unanticipated effects. For some firms, particularly in 1981, but to a considerable extent in other years as well, the marginal impact of the credit on qualified expenditures is negative. They find themselves better off by lowering 1981 expenditures in the interest of claiming a credit or larger credit in future years. In any event, the effective value of the credit, that is, the reduction in cost of additional current R&D expenditures resulting from the current credit net of the present value of consequent losses of future credits, is likely to be very low. Common values are in the order of zero to 3 or 4 percent, depending upon rates of discount, rather than the 25 percent statutory rate.

If the credit is expected to expire at the end of 1985, however, the effective rate of credit rises in 1983, 1984 and 1985, reaching its statutory level in that last year. As a corollary, as the credit termination date is approached, firms below base will lose their incentive to cut expenditures in order to claim credits in the future.

The definition of the company-specific base with an increasing lag over the first two years contributes to sharply rising values of the credit from 1981 to 1983. If rates of inflation, rates of growth of real R&D expenditures and eligibility ratios were stable, the growth of the credit itself would be stable over the last years of the credit under current law.

Both inflation and cyclical effects are substantial. Higher rates of inflation swell the tax credit with no changes or even declines in the real rate of growth of R&D. The Treasury may lose substantial amounts of tax revenues because of increases in nominal R&D expenditures while real expenditures are declining. The amount of the credit will not only tend to be considerably less in periods of recession but the low base set in recessions will raise future credits, in time of subsequent booms, all the more.

II. OFFICE OF TAX ANALYSIS DATA

The preliminary tabulation of R&D tax credit data made available to us by the Office of Tax Analysis is based on a sample of 2,678 1981 returns representing 11,029 business taxpayers. These were blown up and aggregated in 97 industries. A number of returns, including those of some large firms, had not been received. The OTA estimates that the data thus far available account for some 80 percent of 1981 R&D expenditures.

Since the data were from form 6765 used to file reports of eligibility for the tax credit, they are essentially limited to firms who claimed qualified R&D expenditures after June 30, 1981 exceeding half of their qualified expenditures in all of the year 1980. Thus, in effect, the OTA data are truncated at zero with regard to rates of growth of qualified R&D.

The tabulations indicate qualified R&D expenditures of $6,448 million for the population represented by this sample, as shown in Table 2.1. This entailed an increase of no less than 42.7 percent over the $4,519 million base from 1980. The tentative credit was then $408.4 million but lack of tax liability against which to offset it reduced this total by $176.6 million — some 43.2 percent — so that the total credit claimed currently in the population represented by the sample comes to $231.8 million. The Office of Tax Analysis, apparently relying upon additional information for firms not included in the sample, estimates from these data that the total credit "claimed" in 1981 — presumably the "tentative credit" in view of the sample data — was some $600 million[3].

Extensive cross section analysis of the data for these 97 industries indicated little relation between growth in qualified expenditures and the ratio to assets of the credit actually claimed, as indicated in equations (2.1) and (2.3). There was some evidence of a negative relation between the growth in R&D and the ratio to assets of credit earned but not claimed because of lack of tax liability, as shown in equations (2.2) and (2.3).

(2.1)

$$QR\&DG = \underset{(0.116)}{0.972} - \underset{(0.000182)}{0.000035}\ CRARAT$$

$$\hat{R}^2 = -0.010 \qquad n = 97$$

(2.2)

$$QR\&DG = \underset{(0.119)}{1.070} - \underset{(0.000384)}{0.000585}\ TLARAT$$

$$\hat{R}^2 = 0.014 \qquad n = 97$$

(2.3)

$$QR\&DG = \underset{(0.117)}{1.020} - \underset{(0.000175)}{0.000304}\ CRARAT + \underset{(0.000465)}{0.002345}\ LLARAT - \underset{(0.000378}{0.001318}\ TLARAT$$

$$\hat{R}^2 = 0.209 \qquad n = 97$$

QR&DG = Qualified R&D growth

CRARAT = CRDCCL ÷ ASSETS

TLARAT = (TNTCRD - CRDCCL) ÷ ASSETS

LLARAT = (CROLIM - TNTCRD) ÷ ASSETS

where CRDCCL = Credit currently claimed

TNTCRD = Tentative credit (without regard to existence of taxes to be offset)

CROLIM = .25 (QUAL R&D - BASE), thus the credit calculated from industry aggregates as if no firms had qualified R&D expenditures either below or more than twice their base

ASSETS = "total assets," financial and non-financial.

This last result is subject to several possible interpretations. It may, of course, represent a quite spurious correlation between industries if, for one reason or another, more firms without tax liabilities are in industries with relatively greater R&D intensity.

The negative relation may, however, stem from a greater reluctance to raise R&D expenditures on the part of firms with lower profits. Or it may reflect the fact that firms unable currently to enjoy the tax credit increase their R&D expenditures less than firms that are able to realize it.

The significantly positive coefficient of LLARAT in (2.3) would seem to reflect the considerable number of firms in the OTA sample reporting qualified R&D more than twice their base and hence running into the 50 percent base limitation.

III. COMPUSTAT DATA

We took initially the Compustat R&D data as reported in Business Week in 1982 and 1983. Putting together data in the two reports, we had the R&D expenditures of 690 companies for 1980, 1981 and 1982. The 1980 sum of $27,355 million in R&D expenditues for these firms was nearly 90 percent of the NSF estimate of nationwide company-financed R&D in that year.

The rate of growth of R&D in this sample, which in view of its coverage leaves little room for bias, was 14.9 percent from 1980 to 1981, far less than the 43 percent growth of qualified expenditures over base in the OTA tabulation. It slackened sharply to 11.3 percent from 1981 to 1982. This reduction in growth would suggest that, if the eligibility ratios were constant over these years, the increase in tentative credit from 1981 to 1982 would be considerably less than what would have been predicted on the assumption of constant growth rates. Had the 1980-81 R&D growth rate of 14.9 percent been maintained, the tentative credit, on the assumption of a constant eligibility ratio, would have grown some 160 percent. But as shown in Tables 3.1 and 3.2, under that assumption of constant eligibility ratio, the actual increase in tentative credit which is indicated is in the order of 122 percent.

Estimation of tax credits from annual R&D data is complicated for 1981 by the restriction of qualified expenditures to those after June 30. We have imputed second-half-of-year figures by assuming steady growth over the year 1981 equal to the annual growth of 1981 over 1980. Thus, 1981 R&D expenditures after June 30 are calculated as:

$$\text{(3.1)} \qquad RD81\text{-}II = RD81/[(RD80/RD81)^{.5} + 1],$$

where RD81 and RD80 are the annual R&D expenditures for 1981 and 1980, respectively.

The eligibility ratio of .6329144 used in calculating tentative credits in Tables 3.1 and 3.2, and elsewhere in this section, was derived, as explained in Eisner (1982), p. 13, by assuming that the proportions of R&D cost not eligible in computation of the credit correspond to "Other R&D costs" for 1979 as listed in NSF (1981, Table B-51, p. 43), "Distribution of R&D Costs by Industry." We have maintained the same eligibility ratio in a number of our calculations in this paper, in the interest of comparability with the earlier analysis and on the basis of data from our McGraw-Hill special supplemenatry R&D survey, discussed below.

Tables 3.1 and 3.2 make clear that with constant eligibility ratios the variation among industries in growth of tentative credit for 1981 to 1982 is substantial. In computers (listed under "Info. Proc."), where the year-over-year rate of growth of R&D expenditures actually increased from 15.3 percent to 22.7 percent, the indicated tentative credit grew by 244.9 percent. At the other end of the scale were containers, where with a decline in the rate of growth of R&D for the entire industry from 5.8 percent to -16.9 percent, the percent change in the tentative credit was -17.1 percent. In fuel, where the year-over-year rate of growth in R&D expenditures declined from 31.7 percent to 6.2 percent, the growth in the tentative credit was only 19.7 percent and in automotive parts and equipment, where the rate of growth in R&D declined from 18.7 percent to 4.6 percent, the rate of growth in the credit was only 25.2 percent.

The Business Week reports of company R&D expenditures were not accompanied by information on taxes currently payable. This information is of course available on the original Compustat tape. Utilizing a set of 592 companies for which information on R&D expenditures for the years 1980, 1981 and 1982, and on taxes for the years 1981 and 1982 was to be found on the tape, we still had a very large, if somewhat smaller coverage of R&D, as indicated in Table 3.3. Rates of growth were just about the same as in the Business Week reports, now 14.8 percent from 1980 to 1981 and 11.4 percent for 1981 to 1982. We may also note that R&D expenditures are highly concentrated. The great bulk, over 76 percent in the sample and perhaps almost as large a percentage in the population as a whole, were financed by firms whose 1982 R&D expenditures were $100 million or more. This relates to only 66 out of the total of 592 firms in our Compustat sample.

Coming as close as the data permitted to the definition in the law and in our mathematical appendix, we calculated the credit currently claimed as equal to the tentative credit where the federal income tax payable was positive and zero where the federal income tax was zero or negative. On this basis, as shown in Table 3.4, the nationwide tentative credit of $465 million in 1981 is reduced to a currently claimed credit of $402 million. This reduction of 14 percent, we must note, is far less than the 43 percent reduction found in the OTA data. That difference offers a considerable puzzle. It is not clear how much it may relate to errors in reporting on the forms or in the preliminary and incompletely checked OTA file given to us or how much the discrepancy may be due to our inability to take account in the Compustat data of other tax credits or adjustments which may have precluded current claims of a new incremental R&D credit. The difference may also relate to inclusion in the OTA sample of smaller firms or others without information on the Compustat tape.

What is all the more startling, however, is the much greater falloff in credit currently claimed indicated in our Compustat data for 1982. The combination of business recession and increasing tax deductions from the accelerated cost recovery system apparently brought a considerably larger number of firms into the no-tax category. With the ratio of the credit currently claimed to the tentative credit falling to 65.2 percent in 1982, the credit currently claimed rose only from $402 million to $682 million.

The percent increases in the tentative credit were clearly positively associated with the amount of 1982 R&D spending, as shown In Table 3.5, but this may well reflect in part the consequence of our categorization on the basis of 1982 R&D. To the extent that individual firm R&D spending has random variation from year to year, those firms with more spending in any one year would on average have higher rates of growth than those firms having low spending in that year.

Two classes of firms would not receive R&D tax credits: those where R&D does not exceed base and those where R&D exceeds base but where no federal income taxes are payable. Undertaking that division for 1981, we note in Table 3.6 that 112 of the 592 firms have R&D below base. This proportion was largest, however, among firms doing the least R&D (15 out of 32 for firms of 1982 R&D less than $1 million and only 4 out of 66 for firms spending $100 million or more). Hence firms with R&D below base accounted for only 6.1 percent of R&D expenditures by the 592 firms in the sample. Another 83 firms, accounting for 13.1 percent of R&D expenditures, did have R&D greater than base but had no federal income taxes which the credit might offset.

Thus, in 1981, 80.7 percent of R&D expenditures in this 592-firm set were undertaken by companies which presumably were receiving the R&D tax credit. The proportions descended progressively for the different amount-of-R&D categories, from 83.3 percent for those spending $100 million or more in 1982 down to 43.7 percent for those in the under $1 million category.

Similar data for 1982, presented in Table 3.7, indicate that only 52.7 percent of qualified R&D expenditures were undertaken by firms receiving the credit. For 15.3 percent of R&D expenditures were made by firms whose qualified R&D did not exceed their base. And no less than 32.1 percent, or $6,480 out of $20,215 million, occurred in firms where R&D exceeded the base but there was no federal income tax payable. The proportion of total R&D taking place in firms which received a credit was somewhat smaller still, 45.9 percent, in the set of 92 firms with R&D expenditures under $1 million.

Differences among industries were sharp. We note that 98.7 percent of R&D expenditures of $959 million in the drug industry were made by firms that should have been able to claim the credit. But for motor vehicles and parts, in which total R&D expenditures came to $3,147 million, only 9.6 percent (or $301 million) were made by the 7 out of 17 firms claiming a current credit.

In Tables 3.8 and 3.9, both again calculated on the assumption of the constant elibibility ratio (of 0.6329144) for all firms in 1980, 1981 and 1982, we may note readily the substantial variation across industries in both the tentative credit and the credit currently claimed. For the compilation of

592 firms the tentative credit in 1981 was 4.05 percent while the credit currently claimed was 3.50 percent of qualified R&D. For 1982, as shown in Table 3.11, calculated from Table 3.10, those ratios were respectively 4.24 percent and 2.76 percent. The ratio of credit currently claimed to qualified R&D in 1982 varied among industries from 5.04 percent for other manufacturing, 4.83 percent for paper, 4.82 percent for drugs, 4.65 percent for food, and 4.46 percent for computers, to 0.06 percent for nonferrous metals, 0.24 percent for ferrous metals, 0.43 percent for lumber, wood and furniture, and 0.62 percent for motor vehicles and parts.

Table 3.12 makes clear the heavy concentration of R&D expenditures among the largest companies as measured by net sales. In our set of 592 firms, $20 billion of the $31.9 billion total R&D expenditures in 1982 were made by the 52 firms with net sales of $5 billion and over. As may be noted in Table 3.13 these firms, which accounted for 66.8 percent of 1982 sales of all of those in the compilation, accounted for only 58.4 percent of the total credit currently claimed. Thus, as seen in Table 3.14, since the percent increases in R&D were least among the firms with sales of $5 billion and over, their shares of the total tentative credit of the firms in the compilation were considerably less than their shares of total R&D: 56.5 percent and 57.3 percent for 1981 and 1982, respectively, for the tentative credit, as against 63.3 percent and 62.6 percent for 1981 and 1982 for R&D.

A concentration of R&D expenditures among the largest firms is also indicated in Table 3.15 where companies are categorized in terms of number of employees. Here we note that 120 companies with 25,000 or more employees, or 20.3 percent of a total of 592 companies in the compilation, accounted for 1982 employment of 8,645,000 or 76.8 percent of total employment, and 1982 R&D expenditures of $25,869 million or 81.0 percent of total R&D. We can see further, in Table 3.16, that the companies with employment of 25,000 or over accounted for 82.0 percent of the total credit currently claimed by firms in our compilation. This last represents a higher proportion than for the tentative credit, which was some 77 and 78 percent in 1981 and 1982, respectively, as shown in Table 3.17. There, we also note that the rates of growth of R&D, both from 1980 to 1981 and from 1981 to 1982 seemed generally lower in the largest firms.

The tax credit estimates presented thus far from Compustat data have all been constructed on the assumption of a constant eligibility ratio. In the special supplementary R&D survey run for us by McGraw-Hill, however, we have received responses regarding qualified expenditures and total company funds for research and development which enable us to estimate eligibility ratios industry-by-industry and year-by-year. We have utilized annual aggregate eligibility ratios derived from these McGraw-Hill responses to estimate qualified expenditures and consequent tax credits with the Compustat data.

Since the McGraw-Hill responses suggest a relatively low eligibility ratio in 1980 and a relatively high one in 1981, estimates of tax credits which are based upon them are generally higher for 1981 than those utilizing a constant eligibility ratio. In Table 3.18, we note that the tentative credit claimed for 1981, making use of these variable eligibility ratios is $586 million, rather than the $465 million estimated on the assumption of a constant eligibility ratio. The credit currently claimed for 1981 rises to $507 million from the $402 million calculated with the constant eligibility ratio. The estimates of $1,028 million and $670 million for tentative credit and credit currently claimed in 1982, respectively, differ little, however, from the estimates prepared on the assumption of a constant eligibility ratio. Table 3.19 presents a distribution of eligible R&D and the tentative credit and percent increases in each by category of 1982 R&D, applying these variable aggregate eligibility ratios. It is thus analogous to Table 3.5, calculated with a constant eligibility ratio. Similarly, Table 3.20, cross-classifying firms by their amount-of-1982-R&D category and their 1981 tax credit situation, it is analogous to Table 3.6, but uses the variable eligibility ratios.

We have also prepared estimates of the tax credit from aggregates of Compustat R&D expenditures for the years 1980, 1981 and 1982, based to the 1980 NSF total of Company Funds for R&D. Working with the aggregates implies ignoring the limitations: that credits are not negative for companies for which qualifying expenditures are less than their base and that the base can never be less than 50 percent of current qualifying expenditures. The first limitation implies that our aggregate estimates will be less than estimates from individual company expenditures because in the aggregate firms with expenditures below base will offset some of those with expenditures above base. Failure to take account of the 50 percent base limitation, however, will tend to make the aggregate estimates higher.

In fact, the estimates from aggregates, ignoring limitations, tend to be somewhat less than those calculated by summing estimated credits for individual firms. This is particularly true in 1982, where a larger proportion of firms showed qualifying expenditures below base.

Assuming the usual constant eligibility ratio, the estimate of the tentative tax credit from the aggregates, ignoring limitations, was $451 million for 1981, as against $465 million from the individual firm data, as shown in Table 5.1. For 1982, the estimate from the aggregates is $989 million, as against $1,046 million in the data from individual firms.

Working with the variable eligibility ratios taken from the McGraw-Hill supplementary R&D survey, our estimate from the aggregates of the credit without limitations is $579 million in 1981, almost identical with the $586 million estimate from the individual firm data. For 1982, our estimate from the aggregates is $960 million, as against $1,028 million from the individual firm data.

We have undertaken some preliminary exploration of cross-sectional relations among R&D, sales and net income. Regressions of R&D on lagged R&D, changes in R&D, sales, sales changes and net income are shown in Table 3.21 for 1980, 1981 and 1982.

The cross-sectional differences in R&D are overwhelmingly explained by previous R&D and the previous change in R&D. To the extent that the tax credit is encouraging firms with increasing R&D to increase their R&D still more, we might expect higher coefficients of the lagged change-in-R&D variable in 1981 and 1982 than in 1980. It is apparent that this is not so, although the change-in-R&D variable does have a higher coefficient in 1982, when the credit was in effect for the entire year and increased expenditures did less to lower the future base and hence reduce future credits than they did in 1981.

One might have expected that if the tax credit were effective in increasing R&D expenditures the coefficients of the current net income variable, which would include tax credits, would be higher in 1981 and 1982 than in 1980. This too was not the case.

We observe also that both the sales change and net income variables are positively related to R&D expenditures, suggesting accelerator and profitability determinants of R&D spending. To the extent that these determinants were dominant, the possible role of marginal tax credits might be reduced.

As we have noted in section I, while the tax credit may have some effect of increasing R&D expenditures for firms over base, it may also induce firms under base to lower qualified R&D spending in the interest of securing credits in the future. To test this hypothesis, we have compared R&D spending below and above "base" for the years 1976 to 1980, before the incremental tax credit was in effect and the years 1981 and 1982 when the credit was operative. We define the "base" for all years alternatively as that applicable for 1981, that is, half of the (qualified) R&D expenditures of the previous year, and as that in effect for 1982, half of the (qualified) R&D expenditures of the two previous years. In the comparisons in terms of the 1981-type base, we take as R&D expenditures qualified for the credit the imputation of second-half-of-year expenditures defined in (3.1).

As may be seen in Table 3.22, we can find no evidence of effect of the incremental tax credit in this test. The differences between the mean excess of R&D over "base" and the mean shortfall of R&D below "base" are expressed as percents of previous R&D. They turn out to be no greater, and indeed somewhat smaller, by either measure of base, in the years 1981 and 1982 than in the five years before 1981 when there was no incremental tax credit.

A substantial amount of further statistical analysis of the Compustat data, utilizing both time series and cross sections, will be undertaken in an effort to detect possible effects of the tax credit on R&D.

IV. McGRAW-HILL DATA

The special supplementary R&D survey undertaken on our behalf by McGraw-Hill brought responses from 81 firms who indicated the R&D tax credit that they claimed in 1981 along with the R&D expenditures. Blowing up these responses in accordance with (the reciprocal of) the ratio of the sum of R&D expenditures reported and the NSF estimate of company funds for R&D in each industry for 1980 (NSF, 1983b, Table B-5), yields an estimate of the tax credit of $684 million, as shown in Table 4.1.

It is unfortunately not clear whether the tax credits reported were restricted to those currently claimed or included as well credits carried back or forward because of lack of current federal taxes payable. Interpreting these answers as relating to the "tentative credit," whether or not there were tax liabilities, the resultant estimate is still high in comparison with the estimate of $465 million from Compustat data and even with the estimates from OTA data. There the tentative credit, it may be recalled, came to $408 million from a sample thought to be 80 percent complete although, as noted above, Treasury Assistant Secretary Chapoton presented an estimate of $600 million.

The blowup of 77 McGraw-Hill firms reporting tax credits for 1982 came to only $884 million, however, which is less than the $1,046 million tentative credit estimated from the Compustat tape, although more than the $682 million currently claimed. In terms of internal consistency, the rate of growth of the reported credit from 1981 to 1982, only 29 percent, is extremely low in relation to both analytical predictions and calculations from the Compustat data on assumptions of constant eligibility ratios.

Results substantially similar to those in direct reports of the credit are derived when we calculate it on the basis of qualified expenditures, reported by a slightly smaller number of respondents. These expenditures when blown up to national aggregates, as shown in Table 4.2, would appear to have grown only by 7.89 percent in 1981 and 7.56 percent in 1982. The survey questionnaire asked, however, for "qualified research expenses used in base period calculations" and further stipulated, "Please enter annual or annualized amounts; for the 1981 credit only half-year base percents were used." Thus, as in our estimates with the Compustat annual data, we imputed second-half-of-year figures from year-over-year growth. In this instance we compute 1981 qualified R&D expenditures after June 30 as

$$(4.1) \qquad RDQ81\text{-}II = RDQ81/[(RDQ80/RDQ81)^{.5} + 1] ,$$

where RDQ81 and RDQ80 are qualified R&D expenditures in 1981 and 1980, respectively.

As indicated in Table 4.3, with these imputations for 1981 expenditures after June 30, the tentative credit in 1981 comes to $634 million. It then rises only to $907 million in 1982, falls to $809 million in 1983 and rises again to $952 million in 1984.

In Table 4.4 we present total R&D projections derived from responses in the R&D section of the main McGraw-Hill capital expenditure survey. In Table 4.5, assuming again a constant eligibility raio of 0.6329144 for all years, we show tentative credits from a sample of 205 firms blown up to NSF nationwide totals. For 1981, the tentative credit estimate of $442 million is close to the Compustat figure of $465 million but well below the $634 million from the reported qualifying expenditures of the smaller number of 78 firms in the McGraw-Hill supplementary R&D survey. For 1982, however, our projected tentative credit from the 205 firms in the capital expenditure survey is $974 million, consistent on the one hand with the greater lag in the 1982 base and, on the other, the decline in the year-over-year rate of growth of R&D expenditures, from 16.51 percent from 1980 to 1981 to 11.68 percent from 1981 to 1982. The forecast expenditures in the McGraw-Hill surveys would then indicate additional growth in the tentative credit to $1,477 million in 1983, essentially because of a further lengthening in the lag of the base, but a moderate decline to $1,308 million in 1984 and a further decline to $1,238 million in 1985, reflecting the cumulative consequences of a slackened projected growth of R&D.

We next assume that eligibility ratios for all firms were identical in each year but changed from year-to-year as did the ratios of the aggregates of qualifying expenditures and total company-funded expenditures from intersecting supplementary-R&D-survey subsets of 74 firms reporting this information for the years 1980 to 1982 and 52 firms reporting for the year 1982 to 1984. Results of the consequent calculations, shown in Table 4.6, suggest a tentative tax credit of $586 million in 1981, $954 million in 1982, $1,388 million in 1983, $1,307 million in 1984 and $1,281 million in 1985 (this last on the assumption of the same eligibility ratio in 1985 as in 1984).

We have utilized NSF estimates of industrial R&D for the years 1980 through 1984 to supplement the estimates of future tax credits from the McGraw-Hill data. The results are estimates of the credit without limitations calculated from these aggregative NSF data as shown in Table 4.7. We may note first that the estimates from these aggregates for the years 1981 and 1982 are quite close to the Compustat estimates for these years. Estimates for future years of course depend critically on forecast growth in nominal R&D. Estimates from the NSF projections, assuming our constant eligibility ratio, were $491 million of tax credit without limitations in 1981, $1,019 million in 1982, $1,354 million in 1983 and $1,513 million in 1984. Estimates prepared on the basis of the variable eligibility ratios from the McGraw-Hill supplementary R&D survey prove sensitive to the high eligibility ratio in 1981. The estimated credit without limitations would rise from $620 million in 1981 to $995 million in 1982, more slowly to $1,197 million in 1983 and then more rapidly again to $1,529 million in 1984.

Responses to the McGraw-Hill supplementary R&D survey permit certain suggestive tests of the effect of the incremental tax credit on R&D expenditures. As shown in Table 4.8, among 71 reporting firms, the mean growth in total R&D in 1981 was 15.8 percent. For 64 firms reporting, the ratio of the change in qualifying R&D to total previous R&D was 21.3 percent. The similar ratio for nonqualifying expenditures was -4.4 percent. If we were to treat these as a sample, the differences in rates of change in qualifying and nonqualifying expenditures would clearly be statistically significant as the standard error of that difference of 25.7 percent is only 5.0 percent.

The regression coefficients indicate an analogous story for 1981. The cross-section coefficient of 5.051 of the change in qualified expenditures on the tax credit is clearly significant. The regression coefficient of the tax credit for nonqualified R&D expenditures is in fact negative although the difference from zero is not statistically significant.

The differences for 1982 are not nearly as striking. The mean rate of growth of R&D was only 10.2 percent. The change in qualified R&D divided by lagged total R&D was 8.6 percent while a corresponding ratio for nonqualified

R&D was 2.1 percent. Where there had been a difference of 25.7 percent in 1981 there was thus a difference of only 6.5 percent in 1982. The cross-section regression coefficient of qualified R&D on the tax credit was a smaller but still highly significant 3.467 while that for nonqualified R&D was virtually zero.

What these relationships suggest is that there was a substantial surge in R&D reported to be qualified in 1981. The tax credit was of course, as its definition requires, greater the greater was the growth in qualified R&D. That growth in qualified R&D, however, was considerably offset by a reduction in non-qualified R&D. One might infer that the tax credit was effective in inducing an increase in qualified R&D and a substitution of qualified R&D for non-qualified R&D. One might also infer, alternatively, that there is little evidence of any real impact on R&D, but rather a reclassification of R&D so that a considerably larger portion of the total was classified as qualified in 1981 than in 1980.

With the big increase in the eligibility ratio in 1981, however, there was little room for further growth in qualified R&D relative to total R&D. Hence the difference in rates of increase between qualified and nonqualified R&D very greatly narrowed in 1982.

V. CONCLUSIONS

Our analytical section has indicated a number of the prime characteristics of the incremental tax credit for R&D.

For one thing, it can be expected to grow rapidly in amount over its first three years, 1981, 1982 and 1983. Much of the growth from 1981 to 1982 is obviously fore-ordained by the fact that the 1981 credit applies only to expenditures after June 30. The progressive lengthening of the lag of the base over all of the first three years, however, offers predictable consequences of increases in the credit, magnified in the context of generally growing expenditures.

Second, the amount of the credit is sensitive to nominal rates of growth of R&D, whether due to real growth or inflation. A credit may be earned by firms which are merely paying more for the same or even less R&D than previously.

Third, the amount of credit is sensitive to changes in the eligibility ratio, that is the proportion of total R&D deemed or accepted as qualified. Proportionally small reclassifications of expenditures as qualified for credit will cause proportionately large changes in the credit.

Fourth, the shifting, company-specific nature of the base reduces drastically the incentive effect of the credit. Since increasing current expenditures reduces future credits, the effective rate of credit, taking into account the present value of future losses of credit, is far lower than the nominal 25 percent rate of current credit. With 1981 expenditures counting as half of the base for 1982 as well as one-third of the bases for 1983 and 1984, the effective rate of credit in 1981 is indeed generally close to zero. For later years the effective rate of credit for firms with tax liabilities and increasing R&D is in the order of only a few percent.

Fifth, for a number of firms the effective rate of credit is negative. This occurs in particular where R&D is already below base and the credit is not sufficient to induce an increase of expenditures to a level above base. Firms in such a situation may be induced by the existence of the credit to lower current expenditures, on which no credit is earned in any event, in order to lower the base for future years and thus earn a credit or greater credit then.

A second category of firms for which the effective rate of credit may be negative includes companies where qualifying expenditures are more than 100 percent over base. Since these firms in effect raise their current base by 50 cents with each dollar of additional expenditures their current tax credit is actually at a rate of only 12.5 percent instead of 25 percent. With future bases being fully raised by current expenditures, their loss in future credits with any reasonable rate of discount is more than the current gain.

In addition, firms with no federal income taxes currently payable and also unable to take advantage of the three-year carry-back provision may lose the advantage of the credit. If a carry-forward of one or two years is necessary, the present value of tax savings is reduced. If the carry forward is three years, the effective rate of credit is brought to zero.

We have analyzed vast amounts of data from the Office of Tax Analysis of the U.S. Treasury Department, Standard and Poor's Compustat tape and tabulations, and individual company responses from both the regular McGraw-Hill spring surveys and a special supplementary R&D survey undertaken for us. Results of the analysis serve generally to flesh out our analytical predictions.

The "tentative tax credit," ignoring the issue of current tax liabilities against which it would have to be offset, appeared to run in the broad neighborhood of $500 million in 1981 and roughly double that in 1982, despite the slackening rate of growth in R&D in that year. Forecasts of the future tax credit suggest some further increase in 1983, but the forecasts for 1984 are mixed.

A considerable number of firms, accounting for substantial proportions of R&D expenditures, fall into categories for which the effective credit is negative or zero. In 1982, for example, 128 firms out of 592 in our Compustat sample, accounting for 15.3 percent of R&D expenditures in that group, appeared to have R&D equal to or below base. These firms could benefit by reducing current expenditures. An additional 154 firms, accounting for no less than 32.1 percent of total R&D expenditures, had no federal income taxes payable in 1982. What they will gain from the credit will depend upon in which direction and how far it will have to be carried.

The OTA data indicated a huge falloff for 1981, of some 43 percent, from tentative credit to credit currently claimed. The corresponding figure for 1981 estimated from the Compustat data was only about 14 percent. If the OTA data are in fact correct for 1981, the trend in the Compustat data for 1981 to 1982 suggests that perhaps well over half of 1982 R&D would have been undertaken by firms unable to claim the credit in 1982 because of lack of tax liabilities in that year.

The sensitivity of the credit to eligibility ratios is supported in several bits of evidence. First, the direct estimates of the 1981 credit from both OTA and McGraw-Hill data are significantly larger than is indicated in either Compustat or McGraw-Hill R&D tabulations. This suggests that firms did indeed increase their eligibility ratios in 1981 as against 1980. That may have been accomplished by counting as qualified R&D in 1981 expenditures that had not been so classified in 1980. It may also have been accomplished by crediting to the second half of 1981 expenditures for goods and services which in 1980 were spread relatively evenly over the year. Firms in a position to do this could enjoy a greater 1981 tax credit without increasing the base and thus reducing credits in future years. The answers to explicit questions in the McGraw-Hill supplementary R&D survey dealing with qualified and total company-financed R&D expenditures do in fact suggest a sharply higher eligibility ratio in 1981.

The R&D tax credit, like R&D expenditures themselves, is concentrated heavily among firms which are large, whether measured in terms of R&D expenditures, sales or number of employees. The concentration of the credit is somewhat less among large firms than is R&D itself, however, because R&D is apparently growing proportionately somewhat less among large firms.

Efforts to find in the data measures of the effectiveness of the tax credit are still very preliminary. Analytical considerations suggest that the effectiveness may indeed be hard to detect, partly because the credit is by its definition tied to increases in R&D, whether it causes them or not, and partly because the effective rate of credit is generally small, and in many instances zero or negative. Our data appear consistent with the view that levels of current R&D expenditures are largely accounted for by previous R&D levels and broadly determining economic conditions such as sales and profitability.

By one hypothesis the credit, if it were affecting firms' decisions, might have been expected to result in greater increases in R&D by firms with R&D above base and lesser increases, or greater decreases, for firms with R&D below base. A comparison of such increases and decreases in R&D for the years 1976 to 1980, before the adoption of the tax credit, and the years 1981 and 1982, did not indicate that the credit was having this impact.

A comparison of changes in qualified and nonqualified R&D and their relations with the tax credit indicates a substantial upsurge in R&D reported as qualified in 1981, significantly offset by a decline in nonqualified R&D. Qualified R&D apparently increased somewhat more rapidly than nonqualified R&D in 1982 but the growth in total R&D decreased sharply.

We have thus as yet been unable to detect reliable evidence that the credit is having a positive impact on total R&D expenditures. Our analysis is still too incomplete, however, to sustain any definite conclusion on this issue.

While companies interested in tax benefits would understandably wish to see the credit extended, analytical considerations indicate that the credit will become increasingly effective in 1983, 1984 and 1985 if it is not expected to be extended. For if firms do not anticipate that the credit will be extended, the loss of future credits as a result of increasing current expenditures will be reduced by one-third for expenditures undertaken in 1983, by two-thirds for expenditures undertaken in 1984 and entirely for expenditures undertaken in 1985. By that last year, for firms with tax liability and with qualified R&D above base but less than 100 percent above base, the effective rate of credit would be raised to the full 25 percent.

Without judging the issue as to whether any R&D tax credit is socially desirable, certain revisions would seem likely to improve the one currently in effect.

First, while the 50 percent limitation does not apparently relate to a large proportion of R&D, its negative incentive effects can be considerable where it does come into play. To the extent that our major concern is for increasing R&D expenditures and not for distributing the benefits of reduced taxes in some more egalitarian fashion, it would appear that the 50 percent base limitation might well be removed. If it is not entirely removed, at the least, future bases should take into account the limitation on the current base. Where the 50 percent limitation is currently in force, each dollar of current qualified expenditure in excess of base might better generate only 50 cents toward increasing future bases. This would eliminate the anomaly by which, for firms in this category, each dollar increase in R&D expenditures would generate only 12.5 cents in current credit while losing 25 cents in future credits.

A second significant revision, in the interest of increasing incentives, would entail eliminating or reducing the asymmetry as between firms with R&D above base and firms with R&D below base. This might of course be accomplished directly by levying a negative credit, or an additional tax, equal to 25 percent of reductions in qualified R&D spending. Since this would certainly be viewed with extreme distaste by firms affected, a more practical solution would be to combine such a tax for declining R&D with a general credit on all R&D over, say, 80 percent of base. Thus firms with decreasing R&D would lose some of the general credit and would hence be discouraged from such reductions, but might never have to pay a net tax relating to R&D.

The most important and fundamental revision, however, would relate to altering the moving, company-specific nature of the base. It is this feature which results in firms generally losing dollar for dollar in future credits the amounts that they gain in current credits from increasing their R&D expenditures. Under the current law, firms whose R&D is increasing and expected to increase over base within the zero to 100 percent range, and who have and expect to have tax liabilities to be offset, in effect gain only the interest savings of postponing taxes over a three year period, rather than eliminating them.[4]

Several methods are available which would alter this provision in the interest of increasing the effective incentive. First, the company-specific base could be retained but left fixed at, say, the average of 1980, 1981 and 1982 qualified R&D expenditures (with possibly some exceptions or adjustments for new firms). This would imply rapidly growing amounts of R&D credits over the years but would mean that the effective rate of credit would be equal to the statuatory rate for firms which have current tax liabilities and are not subject to the 50 percent base limitation. It would also generally offer an incentive to firms to minimize their reductions in R&D.

Somewhat more complicated to administer, but less costly in terms of tax revenues, would be a provision to start with a company-specific base, say of R&D expenditures of 1980, 1981 and 1982, but to adjust that base in accordance with national or industry movements in R&D. Thus if a firm were in an industry where R&D in 1983 grew by 10 percent, its base in calculating its R&D tax credit for 1984 would be raised by 10 percent. The credit for each firm would hence relate to increases in R&D spending over a base which is both company-specific but adjusting to movements of R&D among companies in similar situations. Unless the industry were unduly small in relation to the size of the firm — and this could be avoided by appropriate grouping of industries — each firm would have a full 25 percent effective credit as an incentive to increase its expenditures. Its increased expenditures would contribute to raising the base and reducing future credits for everybody but would have a trivial effect in raising its own base and reducing its own future credits. By having the base increase on the basis of industry experience rather than company-specific experience, we would achieve the maximum incentive impact along with the minimal Treasury tax loss associated with an incremental credit.

Finally, the impact of the R&D tax credit would be increased by making it refundable or a direct subsidy rather than a credit. This would mean that the considerable number of firms in the economy not paying federal income taxes would also have an incentive to increase R&D spending. With the vastly increased depreciation deductions implicit in the accelerated cost recovery system, the investment tax credit and credits for foreign taxes, we have reached the point where many existing credits, let alone new ones, can be realized only by selling or merging firms. Unless we are to restore the corporate income tax by eliminating most or all of the existing incentives, deductions or loopholes, depending on one's view, new credits such as those for R&D would have to be refundable, regardless of taxes, to avoid significant losses of whatever incentive effects they have.

Alternatively, and this may well be a better path to take, the corporate income tax as such might be eliminated, presumably with shares in real corporate earnings attributed to the individual stockholders. Then business tax incentives or "tax expenditures" might be eliminated and we could readily move to direct subsidies of those private expenditures and activities which we find it in the social interest to encourage.

References

Chapoton, John E. Statement before the Subcommittee on Taxation and Debt Management of the Senate Committee on Finance, *Treasury News*, R-2159, May 27, 1983. Quoted in part in *Tax Notes*, June 6, 1983.

Collins, Eileen L. *An Early Assessment of Three R&D Tax Incentives Provided by the Economic Recovery Act of 1981*, National Science Foundation, PRA Report 83-7, April 1983.

Eisner, Robert. *An Early Assessment of the Effects of the Incremental Tax Credit on Industrial R&D*, National Science Foundation, Division of Policy Research and Analysis, August 31, 1982.

National Science Foundation. *Research and Development in Industry, Funds, 1979, Scientists and Engineers, January 1980, detailed statistical tables* NSF 81-234 [NSF(1981)]

______________. *Science Resources Studies Highlights*, NSF 83-316, July 22, 1983 [NSF(1983a)].

______________. *Research and Development in Industry, Funds, 1981, Scientists and Engineers, January 1982, detailed statistical tables* [NSF(1983b)].

FOOTNOTES

1 In all instances, it should be recalled, effective rates relate to marginal and not total R&D expenditures. The distinction is illustrated in "Appendix A. Short-term and Long-term Effects of R&D Changes on Incremental Tax Credit."

2 A number of the relationships discussed above are presented more rigorously in "Appendix B. Mathematical Exposition."

3 Statement of John E. Chapoton, May 27, 1983, page 8.

4 These interest savings would, however, prove a perpetual stream if the indicated conditions remain in effect.

A P P E N D I X

LIST OF TABLES

o o o

Editorial remark:

Due to limited space tables and appendices could not be included in this volume. Readers interested in these 57 pages are adviced to contact the authors or the CIRET Office.

The Realization of Investment Plans of Finnish Manufacturing Firms

I. Pyyhtiä
Bank of Finland
Helsinki

INTRODUCTION

Since 1963 the Bank of Finland has conducted a survey of the short-term investment plans of Finnish industrial firms for use in economic forecasting. The maximum time horizon covered in the survey is one and a half years. Respondents are requested to provide information on investment outlays in current prices. In addition, the survey includes questions on capacity utilization and the share of external financing in total investment. The survey is carried out twice a year, in spring and autumn. Firms are selected by stratified random sampling according to industrial sector and size of enterprise.

This paper examines the usefulness of the survey results for business cycle forecasting. The statistical properties of the sample have been dealt with elsewhere and are not therefore touched upon here. Rather, the aim is to explain *ex post* discrepancies between survey data and the official statistics on investment solely by means of economic factors. In assessing the reliability of the survey results for forecasting purposes, data on both actual and planned investment outlays are analyzed. The predictive ability of the survey data is measured by applying the method of ordinary least squares and the inequality coefficients developed by Theil.

To meet forecasting needs, an attempt is made to explain deviations between planned and realized investments *ex post*. The choice of explanatory variables is based on the assumptions of general investment theory and, in particular, Modigliani's realization function. Consideration is also given to evaluating the effects of financial variables. The analysis is carried out by industrial sector and according to the length of the forcasting horizon. The approach applied in this study is essentially an exploratory investigation of the data, with frequent recourse to *ad hoc* hypotheses. The intention in the future is to utilize the survey data in reserach work of a more theoretical nature.

2 EVALUATION OF SURVEY DATA

2.1 The Survey as a Predictor of Actual Investments

In the first stage of the analysis, survey figures on actual investments are compared with corresponding data in the official statistics. This comparison is believed to give some indication of the overall forecasting accuracy of the survey. In the regression performed for total industry, the coefficient of multiple determination received a value of .914 when the time series were expressed in the form of annual percentage changes (Table 1). The results obtained in the sectoral analysis were slightly poorer, partly because of deficiencies in the sampling at the industry level.

Bearing in mind the pronounced cyclical variation which has characterized industrial investment in Finland, the survey has described past developments in actual investment comparatively well.

TABLE 1 ESTIMATES OF REGRESSION EQUATIONS RELATING FINAL FIGURES FOR INVESMENT IN THE INDUSTRIAL STATISTICS TO INFORMATION ON ACTUAL INVESTMENT IN THE INVESTMENT SURVEY, 1964 - 1977

Equation	Volume of investment, annual percentage change	Constant	Bank of Finland survey: volume of investment, annual percentage change	R^2
1.1	Total industry	1.730 (1.33)	0.850 (10.80)	.914
1.2	Manufacturing	1.022 (0.48)	0.753 06.52)	.780
1.3	Wood-processing industry	0.222 (0.06)	0.717 (5.37)	.724
1.4	Metal industry	3.429 (0.64)	0.999 (5.44)	.729
1.5	Other manufacturing	-0.490 (0.16)	0.888 (5.70)	.747
1.6	Non-residential construction in manufacturing	0.555 (0.29)	0.971 (13.28)	.941
1.7	Machinery and equipment in manufacturing	-0.310 (0.10)	0.986 (5.64)	.743

Numbers in brackets are t-statistics of estimates

2.2 Measuring the Predictive Power of the Survey

In the following, anticipatory data obtained from the survey are compared with *ex post* figures in the official statistics. This could give a somewhat biased picture of the modification of investment plans, since the survey data and the published figures are known to differ from each other to some extent. Such an analysis is nonetheless essential from the point of view of forecasting.

A distinctive feature of the Bank of Finland Survey, as, too, of other surveys, has been the tendency for underestimation to increase with the lengthening of the planning horizon (Figure 1). No convincing explanation for this has been put forward, but it could be associated with the high inflation of the 1970s and also with the fact that not all the costs of an investment can be taken into account at the planning stage. When changes in investment plans and realized investment are compared over different planning horizons, it is seen that the prediction of the timing of turning points becomes more difficult as the time horizon increases (Figure 2 and Figures I.1 - I.5 in the Appendix).

The regression results show that the investment plans for the longest time horizon of the survey, one and a half years, explain more than half of the variation in actual capital outlays (Table 2). Moreover, the regression coefficients indicate that the investment survey tends to overestimate the variation of realized investment; i.e., it is unable to forecast the turning points with complete accurary. As the time horizon shortens, so the predictive power of investment plans

FIGURE 1

ACTUAL INVESTMENT IN MANUFACTURING AND INVESTMENT PLANS FOR DIFFERENT TIME HORIZONS IN THE SURVEY 1964 - 1978

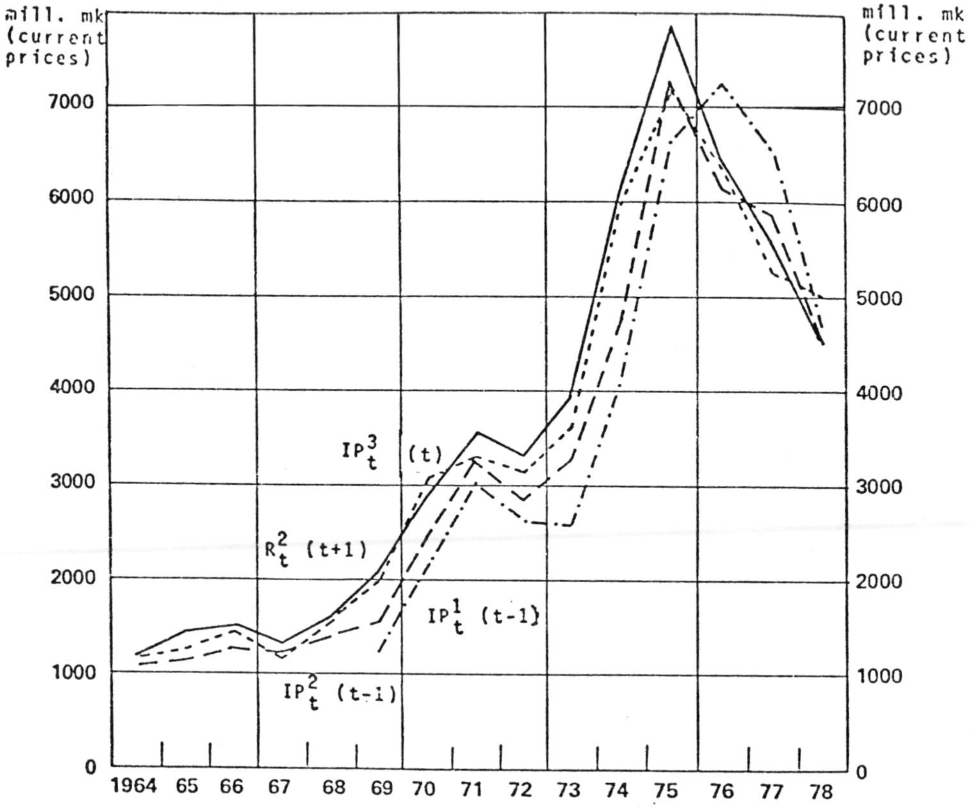

———	R^2_t (t+1)	actual investment in year t as reported in autumn survey of year t+1
—·—·	IP^1_t (t-1)	investment plans for year t in spring survey of year t-1
—— ——	IP^2_t (t-1)	investment plans for year t in autumn survey of year t-1
— — —	IP^3_t (t)	investment plans for year t in spring survey of year t

FIGURE 2

ACTUAL INVESTMENT IN MANUFACTURING AND INVESTMENT PLANS FOR DIFFERENT TIME HORIZONS IN THE SURVEY 1964 - 1978

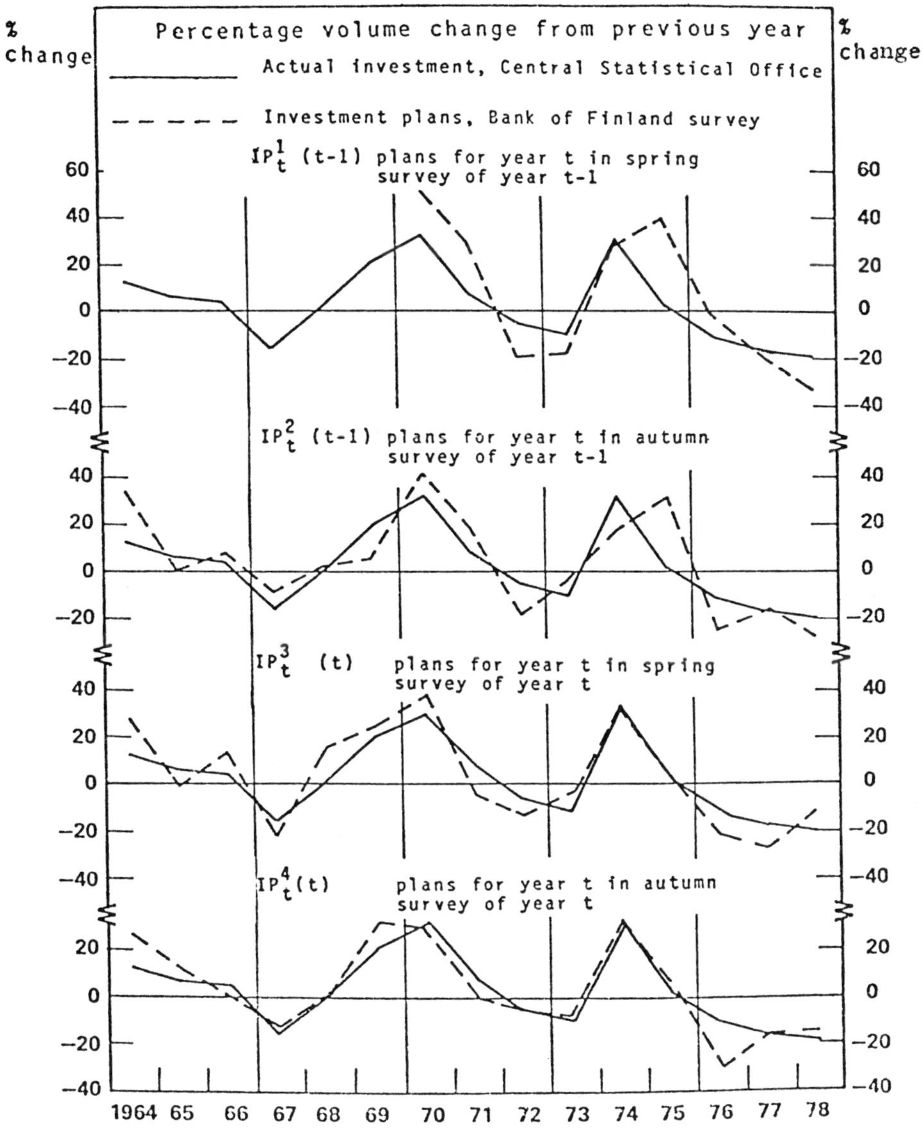

improves. Thus, the spring survey explains 83 per cent of the variation of actual investment outlays in the same year when the data are expressed in the form of percentage changes.

TABLE 2 ESTIMATES OF REGRESSION EQUATIONS RELATING ACTUAL INVESMENT IN MANUFACTURING TO PLANNED INVESTMENT OVER DIFFERENT HORIZONS IN THE SURVEY, 1964 - 1978

Equation	Volume of manufacturing investment, annual percentage cange	Constant	Regression coefficient	Volume of planned investment, annual percentage change	R^2
3.1	I_t	-0.259 (0.06)	0.451 (3.17)	IP^1_t (t-1)	.589
3.2	I_t	1.190 (0.43)	0.557 (4.30)	IP^2_t (t-1)	.587
3.3	I_t	0.960 (0.55)	0.683 (8.01)	IP^3_t (t)	.832
3.4	I_t	0.858 (0.51)	0.733 (8.48)	IP^4_t (t)	.847

Numbers in brackets are t-statistics of estimates

IP^1_t (t-1) = investment plans for year t in spring survey of year t-1

IP^2_t (t-1) = investment plans for year t in autumn survey of year t-1

IP^3_t (t) = investment plans for year t in spring survey of year t

IP^4_t (t) = investment plans for year t in autumn survey of year t

The overall forecasting accuracy of investment plans and their relative performance for individual indsustries can also be measured by applying the inequality coefficient criterion - the standardized root-mean-square prediction error - formulated by Theil (H. Theil, Applied Economic Forecasting, Amsterdam 1971).

$$U = \sqrt{\frac{\frac{1}{N}\sum_{1}^{N}(x_i^e - x_i)^2}{\frac{1}{N}\sum_{1}^{N}x_i^2}} , \qquad (1)$$

where

X_i = actual value

X_i^e = predicted value

N = number of observations

U can take values ranging from zero to infinity. It is equal to zero when the forecast is perfect, i.e., when every $X_i^e = X_i$. It takes the value 1 in the case of a so-called naive forecast , where the prediction procedure involves extrapolating on a no-change basis. Hence, in order for the sign of the predicted change to be estimated correctly, on average, the inequality coefficients calculated for the forecasts should have values of less than one.

The calculated inequality coefficients indicate that the forecasting accurary of investment plans in the survey improves as the time horizon diminishes (Table 3). Only in a few cases do investment plans with

TABLE 3. Root-mean-square prediction errors of invetment plans, 1965 - 1976 (calculated on the basis of percentage volume changes in planned and actual outlays)

Time horizon of survey, % volume change	Bias component BC	Inefficiency component IC	Stochastic component SC	Root-mean-prediction RMS²	Square error % distribution BC	IC	SC	RMS²	Standardized RMS²
IP_t^1 (t-1)	52.13	101.58	200.67	354.38	14.7	28.7	56.6	1.63	1.28
IP_t^2 (t-1)	3.88	45.35	104.10	153.33	2.5	29.6	67.9	0.71	0.84
IP_t^3 (t)	0.04	2.37	41.05	43.46	0.0	5.5	94.5	0.20	0.45
IP_t^4 (t)	0.21	0.22	24.10	24.53	0.9	0.9	98.2	0.11	0.33
R_t^5 (t+1)	0.00	1.70	53.96	55.66	0.0	3.1	96.9	0.26	0.51
R_t^6 (t+1)	0.04	0.16	24.50	24.70	0.2	0.7	99.1	0.11	0.33

IP_t^1 (t-1) = investment plans for year t in spring survey of year t-1

IP_t^2 (t-1) = investment plans for year t in autumn survey of year t-1

IP_t^3 (t) = investment plans for year t in spring survey of year t

IP_t^4 (t) = investment plans for year t in autumn survey of year t

R_t^5 (t+1) = estimates of actual investment in year t in spring survey of year t+1

R_t^6 (t+1) = estimates of actual investment in year t in autumn survey of year t+1 a time horizon of one and a half years predict better than the no-change forecast. By contrast, the predictive power of the plans is already better, on average, than the no-change extrapolation when the time horizon has shortened to slightly more than a year. However, differences in the forecasting accuracy of plans are observable at the indudstry level. The investment plans of the metal indsutry perform better than other sectors in this respect.

The RMS prediction error can be decomposed into a systematic and a stochastic component. Moreover, the systematic element can be further broken down into bias and inefficiency components, i.e.

$$\frac{1}{N}\sum_{1}^{N}(x_i^e - x_i)^2 = (\bar{x}_i^e - \bar{x}_i)^2 + (s_{x_i}^e - s_{x_i})^2 + 2(1 - R)s_{x_i}^e s_{x_i}, \qquad (2)$$

where

$\bar{x}_i^e$ ja $\bar{x}_i$ = means of predicted and realized changes

S = standard deviations of predicted and realized changes, and
R = correlation coefficient of predicted and realized changes

The first term on the right-hand side of the equation, the bias component, refers to errors in central tendency, i.e., differences between the means of actual and predicted values. It takes a positive value if systematic over - or underestimation is present in the plans, otherwise it is zero. The second term, the inefficiency component, is zero if and only if the standard deviations of predicted and actual changes are equal. Finally, the third term, the stochastic component, is zero if the correlation coefficient of predicted and realized changes is one, i.e., if the time series are completely identical in form.

In general, it is possible to reduce the proportion of the total forecast error due to bias and inefficiency by the refinement of forecasting tehniques. The stochastic proportion, on the other hand, tends to increase as the total error of the forecast declines. This can be seen in Table 3, which shows that the share of the stochastic component grows appreciably as the time horizon of the survey shortens.

The foregoing analysis shows the desirability as regards the use of the survey in forecasting of discovering what factors are reponsible for the poor predictive ability of the survey when the length of the planning horizon is extended beyond six months. Also supporting the inclusion of additional explanatory variables in the regression equations relating realized investments to planned investments is the presence of autocorrelation in the residual terms.

3 EXPLAINING CHANGES IN INVESTMENT PLANS

3.1 General

Attempts to explain changes in investment plans have been made using both surveys and econometric models. The information obtained varies somewhat from country to country, presumably because of the type of survey and survey methods applied as well as differences in the structure of production and investment and in institutional characteristics.

In Finland, changes in investment intentions have typically been rather pronounced over the longest time horizons covered in the survey. This seems to be connected with the openness of the economy, the concentration of exports in the cyclically-sensitive sectors and hence the tendency to display greater-than-average cyclical variations. As a consequence, movements in corporate and industrial profitability have also fluctuated sharply, and differently, it would seem, from expectations. Given this background, the realization function approach employed by Modigliani represents a worthwhile point of departure in the development of a model for forecasting investment.

Financial variables have also been identified as an a important factor influencing investment behaviour in the short-run. At least during the 1960s and 1970s, conditions in Finnish financial markets were characterized by credit-rationing, under which market forces were unable to equate the demand for and supply of funds because of, it is claimed, the underdeveloped state of the markets. In view of the preliminary nature of the present study, a partial recourse to ad hoc hypotheses was necessary when constructing the investment function. The aim in the future is to carry out a closer investigation of expectations formation hypotheses.

3.2 The Realization Function

The central idea underlying realization functions is that firms' original investment plans are "rational" in relation to the information available at the time the plans are formulated. Subsequently, plans are modified in response to changes in the economic environment in which firms operate. Likewise, Modigliani's realization function (F. Modigliani - H. Weingartner, "Forecasting Uses of Anticipatory Data on Investment and Sales", Quarterly Journal of Economics, 1958:1) is based on the assumption that desirable and realized investment are determined in the light of conditions prevailing at different times. By constructing separate equations for the initially planned investment and the _ex post_ desirable investment and then combining them to form a single investment function, he derived a realization function in which modifications of investment plans are explained by changes in sales expectations, i.e.,

(3) $$I_t = IP_t\,(t-1) + \beta\gamma\alpha[S_{t+1}(t) - S_t\,(t-1)]$$

where

I_t = realized investment in period t

IP_t (t-1) = investment planned in period t-1 for period t

β = coefficient measuring the speed of adjustment of initial plans

γ = coefficient measuring the speed of adjustment of the capital stock

α = capital-output ratio

$S_{t+1}(t)$ = sales expectations in period t for period t+1

$S_t(t-1)$ = sales expectations in previous period

Eliasson (G. Eliasson, "Kreditmarknaden och industrins investeringar", Uppsala, 1967), like Modigliani, uses the acceleration theory as a stating point for his realization function, but he also gives explicit consideration to the influence of financial variables on the basis of the "Accelerator Residual Funds" theory (J.R. Meyer - R.R. Glayber, "Investment Decisions", Economic Forecasting and Public Policy, Boston, 1964). In so doing, he thus incorporated the external financing of industry in the realization function. In addition, efforts have been made to integrate investment and financial behaviour within the framework of financial planning models. Eliasson used production as the expectations variable in his specification of the realization function, whereas Modigliani had information on sales expectations at his disposal. Modigliani did not include financial variables in his model but he pointed out that any change in a firm's environment would lead to a revision of investment plans.

3.3 Formulation of the Realization Function

Because of the availability of survey data on sales in many countries, sales anticipations have frequently been employed in investment realization functions as the variable describing firms' profit expectations. Sales, moreover, provide the quickest indicator of developments in the demand for products and, ultimately, in a firm's profitability. In Finland, however, reliable and uniform data on sales and sales anticipations is lacking and hence in this study gross profits are used directly as the expectations variable. Koskenkylä used value added in production as the expectations variable in his formulation of the realization function. (H. KOSKENKYLÄ, The Investment Realization Function in Finnish Manufacturing Based on Partial Adjustment and Adaptive Expectations Hypotheses, The Finnish Economic Journal, 1971:4.) A fairly close relationship exists between profits and investment in Finland, due in part to the country's corporate tax legislation. Substituting gross profits (P) for sales in equation (3) yields

$$I = IP(t-1) + \beta\gamma\alpha\,[P_{t+1}(t) - P_t(t-1)]. \qquad (4)$$

In its present form, however, the model does not lend itself to empirical testing because of the lack of empirical observations on expectations.

Profit expectations in industry are assumed to be

dependent on the course of profits in the current and preceding periods. The expectations function can be expressed by the following equation:

$$P_{t+1}(t) = bP_t + (1-b)P_{t-1}, \qquad (5)$$

where the adjustment coefficients b and 1-b are determined by empirical experimentation. The lag distribution is limited to two periods since annual data is being used to study short-term variations in investment plans. One could perhaps interpret the expectations distribution presented here as a variant of the adaptive expectations model. (M. NERLOVE, Adaptive Expectations and Cobweb Phenomena, The Quarterly Journal of Economics, 1958, pp. 230 - 236.) According to the adaptive model, the revision of expectations in each period is in some fixed proportion to the forecast error in the previous period, the relevant equation taking the form

$$P_{t+1}(t) - P_t(t-1) = b\,[P_t - P_t(t-1)]. \qquad (6)$$

The coefficient b measures the speed with which expectations are adjusted in response to the observed expectations error. As a special case, the adaptive model can also be presented with a geometrically distributed lag structure, i.e.,

$$P_{t+1}(t) = b \sum_{j=0}^{\infty} (1-b)^j P_{t-j}. \tag{7}$$

By inserting expression (5) into equation (4) we obtain an equation (8), which is amenable to estimation

$$I_t = \alpha IP_t(t-1) + \beta[b\Delta P_t + (1-b)\Delta P_{t-1}], \tag{8}$$

where β equals $\beta\gamma\alpha$. The coefficient of investment plans, α, allows for the possibility of systematic bias over the planning horizon.

Financial markets in Finland and other Nordic countries are commonly asserted to operate by way of credit rationing. In other words, the interest rate does not equate the demand for and supply of credit; rather, demand tends to exceed supply for most of the time. (E. KOSKELA, A Study of Bank Behaviour and Credit Rationing, Helsinki 1976. See also, A Quarterly Model of the Finnish Economy, Bank of Finland, Series D:29, 1972.) In such conditions, the availability of domestic credit is largely dependent on the tightness of conditions in the financial markets, which, in turn, can be regulated to a fairly large degree by the central bank. Hence, investment equations formulated for a credit rationing enonomy often include an indicator of the tightness of financial markets as a measure of external financing. By contrast, Eliasson's realization function is based on some kind of investment budget thinking. Realized investment can diverge from planned investment either if the investmet budget differs from the planned budget or if income is different than anticipated, in which case the originally planned investment is no longer optimal in relation to actual income.

In addition to a variable measuring the firm's internal financing, it is also desirable to introduce into the realization function a variable, M, describing the availability of external finance. A more precise specification of the financial variable is left, together with the adaption coefficient c, to empirical testing, since earlier studies on a comparable realization functions using Finnish data do not exist. (P. KUKKONEN, The Transmission of Monetary Policy through Credit Rationing: The Case of Finland, Conference on Monetary Policy in Open Economies, Helsinki, August 1975; Cf. H. KOSKENKYLÄ, op. cit. p. 299.) Hence we obtain the following expression for the realization function:

$$I_t = \alpha \, IP_t(t-1) + \beta[b\Delta P_t + (1-b)\Delta P_{t-1}] \qquad (9)$$

$$+ \gamma[c\Delta M_t - (1-c)\Delta M_{t-1}].$$

It is also the aim in the empirical tests to examine whether variables describing price expectations and capacity utilization should be added to the model. It seems likely, however, that movements in profits will be fairly closely correlated with capacity utilization, and thus a separate capacity utilization variable may not be needed. The model will be tested in current price form, which means that changes in the price level will be partly reflected in the profits variable.

4 EMPIRICAL TESTING OF THE REALIZATION FUNCTION

The realization function was tested in difference form so that the trend common to both investment and plans would not interfere with the explanation of changes in investment plans. The most appropriate weighting structure for the variable describing income expectations was found by experimentation. The model to be estimated took the following form:

$$\Delta I_t = \alpha \Delta IP_t(t-1) + \beta[b\Delta\Delta P_t + (1-b)\Delta\Delta P_{t-1}]. \qquad (10)$$

The tests showed that the explanatory power of the equation was highest when b had the value 0.9. Omitting the lagged term $\Delta\Delta P_{t-1}$ raised the overall explanation of the model somewhat. The difference was not very great, but the term 0.1 $\Delta\Delta P_{t-1}$ is in any case of little significance in the model. Without the lagged profits variable, the model simplifies to

$$\Delta I_t = \alpha IP_t\ (t-1) + \beta\Delta\Delta P_t \qquad (11)$$

according to which the revision of investment plans depends on changes in profits. The expectation function corresponds to a static model where expectations of the future values of a variable are the same as the actual value of the variable at the moment plans are formulated. Expectations can also be static with respect to the variable's rate of change, i.e., the present rate of growth is expected to be maintained in the near future as well.

An attempt was made to analyze the effect of the financial variable, i.e. of a firm's external financing, on changes in investment plans by trying out different credit availability indicators. Neither the monetary tightness indicators describing the general conditions prevailing in credit markets nor the marginal rate of interest on central bank debt, used as a measure of banks' profitability, received significant coefficients in the estimations. In part, this may be explained by the fact that lags between indicators of monetary tightness and fixed investment have been found in econometric studies to be 1 1/2 - 2 years in length on average. (A Quarterly Model of the Finnish Economy, op. cit. and H. HALTTUNEN - S. KORKMAN, Central Bank Policy and Domestic Stability in a Small Open Economy, Bank of Finland , 1981, Series D:47.) The realization functions, however, are concerned with adjustment over considerably shorter intervals. An additional factor could be that industry is normally in a more favourable position than the other sectors of the economy as regards access to credit. Furthermore, the monetary tightness indicators generally measure credit availability with respect to the banking sector, whereas industry met less than one-fifth of its credit requirements through borrowing from banks over the estimation period. The credit expansion variable, which to some extent corresponds to the bank credit variable tried by Eliasson in his study, unexpectedly received a negative sign.

Since the variables describing money market conditions did not generate significant coefficients, it was decided to try central bank credit and foreign capital imports directly as a variable in the realization function. Significant coefficients were obtained as a result. The lagged financial variable did not receive significant coefficients in the estimation and was therefore dropped from the final equation.

Reflected quite strongly in the financial variable is some kind of credit budget thinking since it deals with the principal marginal components of the banks' credit expansion. The question is only to which sector this finance is directed in each cyclical phase. On the other hand, the financial variable can also be interpreted as an indicator of businessmen's expectations of future credit availability.

The causal relationships as regards the financial variable are not clear, and the notion of a budget or identity is more relevant here. On occasions, however, credit policy may have also curbed investment activity in industry. In 1976 and 1977, the original invesment plans were scaled down for the first time during the history of the survey (Figure 1). This period coincided with the pursuit of tight monetary policies by the Bank of Finland in response to inflation and a high level of external indebtedness.

Initially, realization, functions were estimated only for manufacturing. The same form of the function was then applied mechanically to different industrial sectors and categories of capital goods. A more detailed analysis using disaggregated functions could give quite different empirical findings. The final estimation results are presented in Table 4a, 4b, 4c and in Figures I.6 - I.8 of the Appendix. The estimated model was in the form.

TAULUKKO 4a REGRESSION RESULTS: REALIZATION FUNCTIONS FOR INVESTMENT PLANS IN INDUSTRY

$$\Delta I_t = \alpha \Delta IP^1_t (t-1) + \beta \Delta \Delta P_t + \gamma \Delta \Delta M_t$$

Investment plans for the following year in the spring survey of the current year, 1969 - 1978. Numbers in brackets are the t-statistics of the coefficients

Change in value of investment		α Value of investment	β Value of gross profits	γ Value of external financing	R^2	DW
(5.1)	Total industry	0.770 (4.86)	0.164 (1.36)	0.355 (2.52)	.783	1.491
(5.2)	Manufacturing	0.629 (5.65)	0.199 (2.76)	0.310 (3.81)	.914	1.165
(5.3)	Wood-processing industry	0.684 (14.44)	0.020 (0.69)	0.109 (3.98)	.963	1.014
(5.4)	Metal industry	0.870 (6.21)	0.338 (2.47)	0.019 (0.43)	.853	2.210
(5.5)	Other manufacturing	-0.162 (0.82)	0.153 (1.27)	0.135 (2.12)	.547	1.567
(5.6)	Non-residential construction in manufacturing	0.445 (1.53)	-0.001 (0.01)	0.208 (2.86)	.569	2.142
(5.7)	Machinery and equipment in manufacturing	0.516 (1.78)	-0.146 (1.12)	0.283 (1.87)	.546	1.450

TAULUKKO 4b REGRESSION RESULTS: REALIZATION FUNCTIONS FOR INVESTMENT PLANS IN INDUSTRY

$$\Delta I_t = \alpha \Delta IP^2_t\,(t-1) + \beta \Delta\Delta P_t + \gamma \Delta\Delta M_t$$

Investment plans for the following year in the autumn survey of the current year, 1964 - 1978.

Change in value of investment		α Value of investment	β Value of gross profits	γ Value of external financing	R^2	DW
(5.8)	Total industry	0.775 (5.16)	0.208 (1.85)	0.143 (1.11)	.714	2.078
(5.9)	Manufacturing	0.744 (5.75)	0.272 (3.61)	0.142 (1.75)	.792	1.774
(5.10)	Wood-processing industry	0.802 (9.76)	0.046 (1.08)	-0.014 (0.40)	.886	2.802
(5.11)	Metal industry	0.927 (6.49)	0.225 (1.81)	-0.028 (0.65)	.814	2.709
(5.12)	Other manufacturing	0.489 (2.19)	0.253 (2.66)	0.093 (1.94)	.595	1.315
(5.13)	Non-residential construction in manufacturing	0.869 (6.18)	0.048 (1.66)	0.112 (3.25)	.878	2.767
(5.14)	Machinery and equipment in manufacturing	0.890 (4.09)	-0.020 (0.23)	0.177 (1.91)	.742	1.709

TAULUKKO 4c REGRESSION RESULTS: REALIZATION FUNCTIONS FOR INVESTMENT PLANS IN INDUSTRY

$$\Delta I_t = \alpha \Delta IP^3_t(t-1) + \beta \Delta \Delta P_t + \gamma \Delta \Delta M_t$$

Investment plans for the current year, 1964 - 1978.

Change in value of investment		α Value of investment	β Value of gross profits	γ Value of external financing	R^2	DW
(5.15)	Total industry	0.942 (10.46)	0.022 (0.41)	-0.020 (0.25)	.935	.619
(5.16)	Manufacturing	0.800 (7.35)	0.059 (1.21)	-0.016 (0.21)	.872	1.047
(5.17)	Wood-processing industry	1.045 (5.41)	0.105 (1.44)	-0.126 (2.05)	.693	1.932
(5.18)	Metal industry	0.810 (3.78)	0.062 (0.33)	0.035 (0.59)	.604	2.423
(5.19)	Other manufacturing	0.779 (5.27)	0.133 (2.45)	0.010 (0.26)	.831	1.197
(5.20)	Non-residential construction in manufacturing	0.875 (11.70)	-0.034 (2.46)	0.034 (1.46)	.960	2.709
(5.21)	Machinery and equipment in manufacturing	0.877 (3.18)	-0.195 (2.41)	0.096 (0.82)	.658	2.080

$$\Delta I_t = \alpha \Delta IP_t(t-1) + \beta \Delta\Delta P_t + \gamma \Delta\Delta M_t.$$

The results show that, almost without exception, investment plans occupy the most important position in the equations. When weighted for the variance of the investment plans, the proportion of total explanation was about a half for the first plans (Table 4a). - i.e. those with a time horizon of one and a half years in the survey - about 2/3 for the second plans (Table 4b) and roughly 4/5 for the third set of plans (Table 4c).

Similarly, the financial variable was an important additional regressor for the first plans and the profits variable for the second plans. However, the importance of profits in explaining changes in investment plans was distinctly greater than credit when all plans over different time horizons were compared with the final figures for actual investment. The third plans - i.e. those reported in the spring of the year of realization - were so close to the final figures that neither profits nor the financial variable received significant coefficients in the equations. Here the difference between planned and realized investment would seem to be due mainly to random factors and technical matters relating to the compilation of statistics.

The profits variable did not receive significant coefficients in the regressions for the wood-processing industry, non-residential construction or investment in machinery and equipment. In the wood-processing industry this was evidently because the explanatory power of investment plans was markedly higher than in other sectors. Investments in the forest - based industries have typically involved comparatively large-scale acquisitions, which once under way are rather difficult to interrupt, and short-term changes in plans have apparently been fairly small. The separation of the realization functions into non-residential investment and machinery and equipment is perhaps rather arbitrary, since both categories of capital good are generally associated with investments. This may explain the poor fit of the relevant equations in the regression analysis.

By contrast, the financial variable received a low t-value in the regression equations for the metal industry. The reason for this may be that, owing to the smaller size of projects in this sector, the metal industry has tended to rely more on equity for financing its investment than has been the case in the forest-based industries.

5 CONCLUSIONS

The Bank of Finland survey data and the official statistics on investment in industry have corresponded fairly well with each other. This is despite the fact that the investment survey data are obtained through sampling, whereas the official figures are based on a survey with almost complete coverage. However, some distortion may also be present in the official statistics because of the lack of information on totally new projects.

By contrast, the data on individual sectors and investment goods have not conformed as well with the official figures as have the total industry and manufacturing data. In the case of the sectoral data, the deviations are probably mainly due to the fact that the official industrial statistics are collected by establishment whereas the investment survey is conducted more on an enterprise basis.

The predictive power of the investment survey is greatly dependent on the length of the time interval covered in the survey. As the horizon increases firms have systematically underestimated their investments, with the exception of the years 1976 and 1977.

Even when uncorrected, the spring survey investment plans for the current year predict the actual course of investment in that year fairly well. The forecasting power of investment plans has been noticeably weaker in other manufacturing than in other sectors, which is perhaps attributable to the heterogeneity of this branch and thus also to shortcomings in the survey.

When utilizing the spring and autumn investment plans for forecasting investment in the following year, the plans should be corrected by means of realization functions. Investment plans are closely correlated with firms' perceptions of the economic outlook at the time the plans are made. If they revise their assessment of the likely couse of economic events, the investment plans respond fairly sensitively to these changes. The correction of investment plans for forecasting purposes requires that the forecaster's judgement of future economic developments is better than that of firms. Here one can perhaps justifiably claim that public institutions involved in economic policy decision-making do frequently possess this information advantage.

There is also a correlation between investment plans and the credit policy pursued by the central bank, although the causal relationships are not so obvious. Credit policy may, at times, have induced changes in the investment plans of industry. But, while credit policy has probably rarely acted as a direct constraint on investment by industrial enterprises, it may have influenced firms' expectations and hence also investment plans at the time they were being formulated.

FIGURE I.1

ACTUAL INVESTMENT IN MACHINERY AND EQUIPMENT BY MANUFCTURING INDUSTRY AND INVESTMENT PLANS FOR DIFFERENT TIME HORIZONS IN THE SURVEY

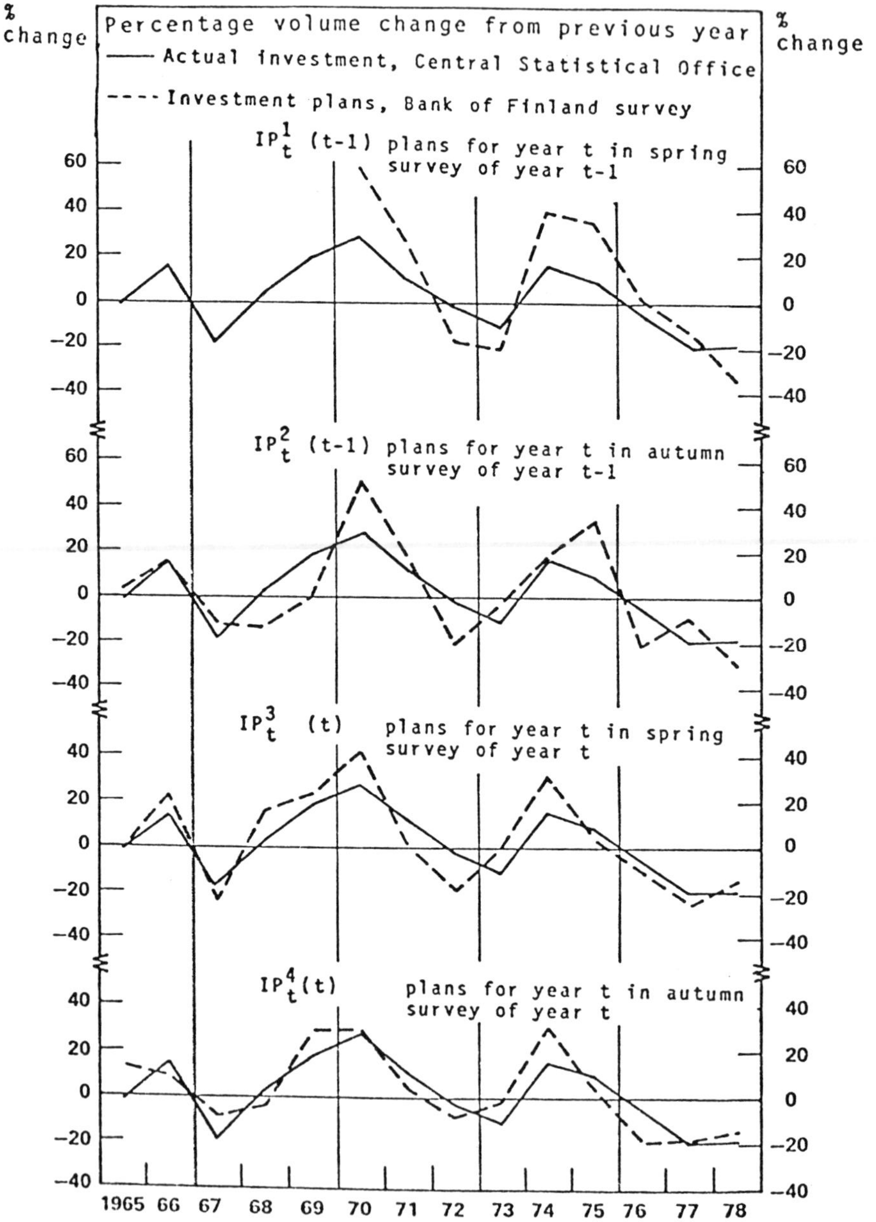

FIGURE I.2

ACTUAL INVESTMENT IN NON-RESIDENTIAL CONSTRUCTION BY MANUFCTURING INDUSTRY AND INVESTMENT PLANS FOR DIFFERENT TIME HORIZONS IN THE SURVEY

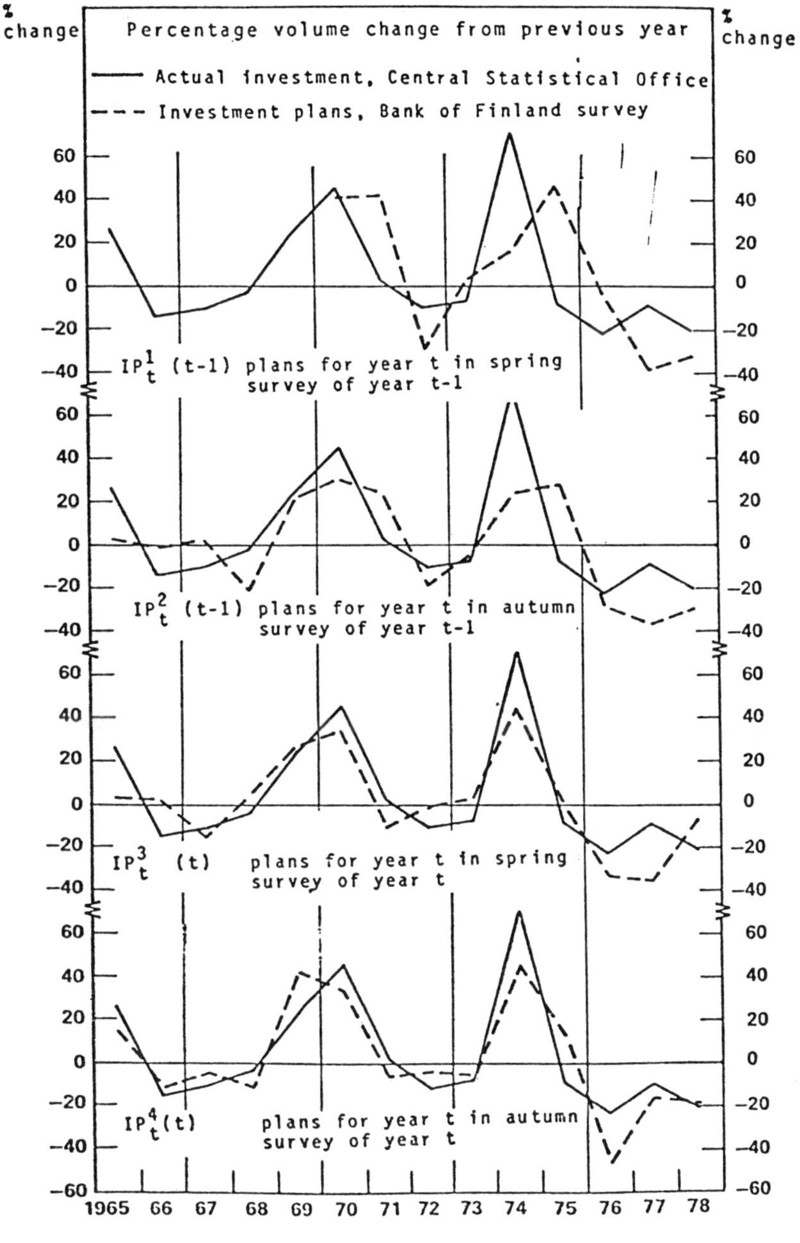

FIGURE I.3

ACTUAL INVESTMENT IN WOOD-PROCESSING INDUSTRY
AND INVESTMENT PLANS FOR
DIFFERENT TIME HORIZONS IN THE SURVEY

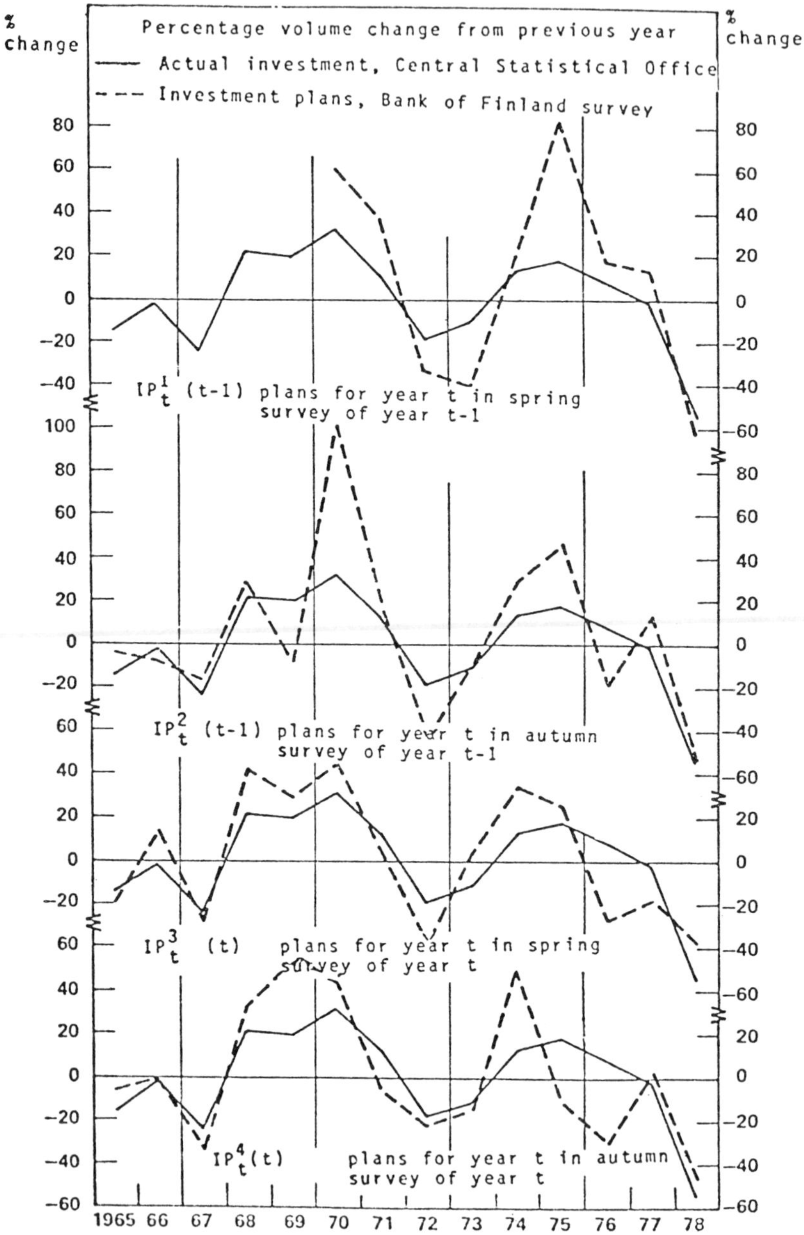

FIGURE I.4

ACTUAL INVESTMENT IN THE METAL INDUSTRY
AND INVESTMENT PLANS FOR
DIFFERENT TIME HORIZONS IN THE SURVEY

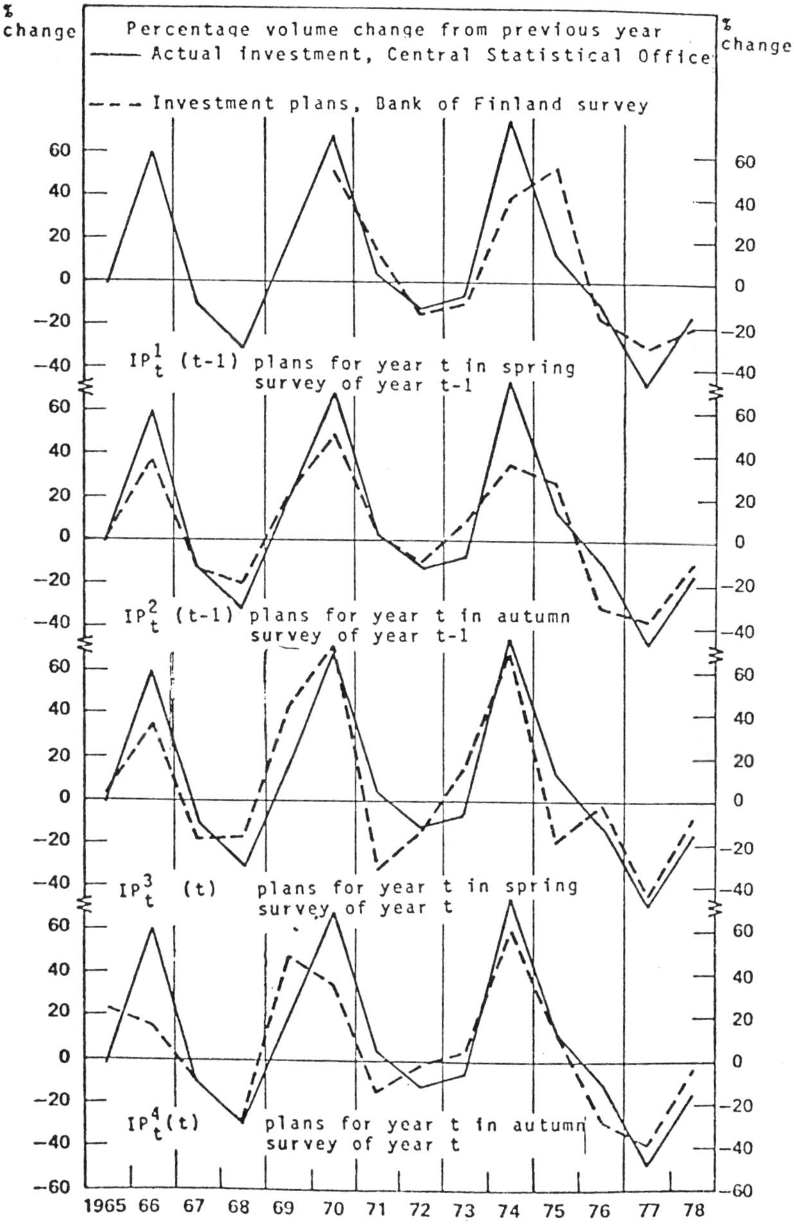

FIGURE I.5

ACTUAL INVESTMENT IN OTHER MANUFACTURING
AND INVESTMENT PLANS FOR
DIFFERENT TIME HORIZONS IN THE SURVEY

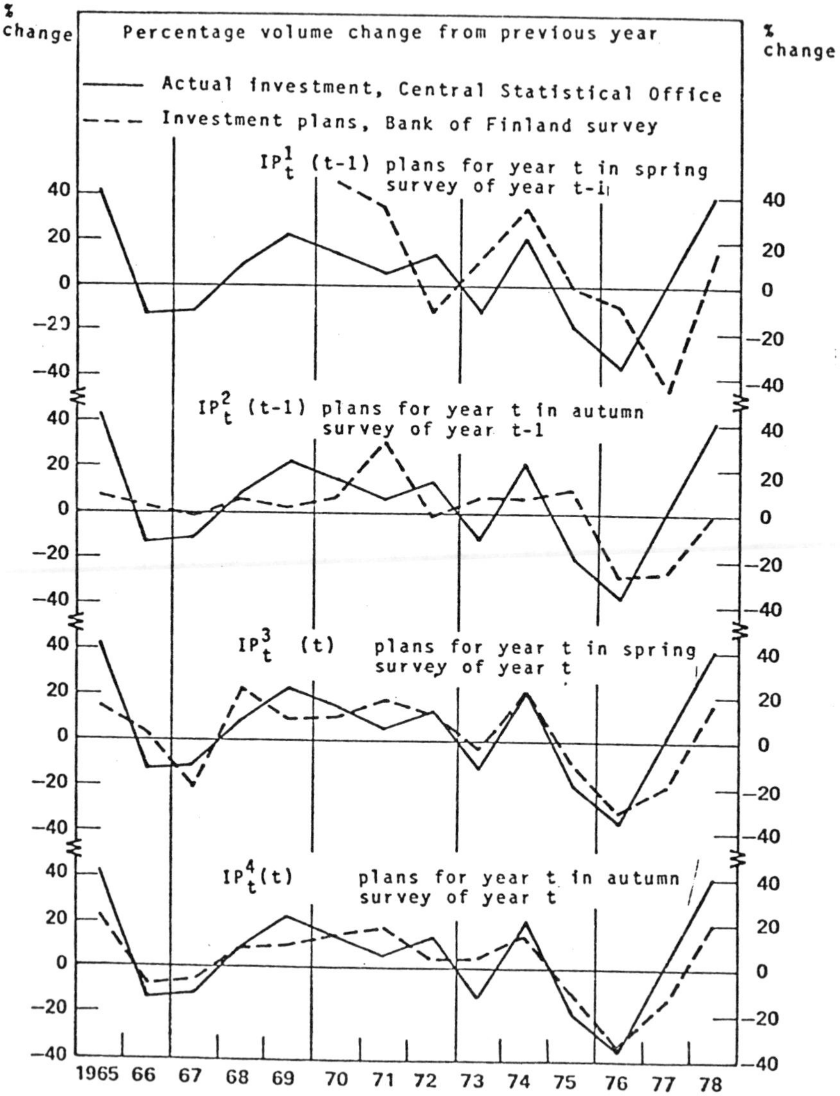

FIGURE I.6

MANUFACTURING INVESTMENT

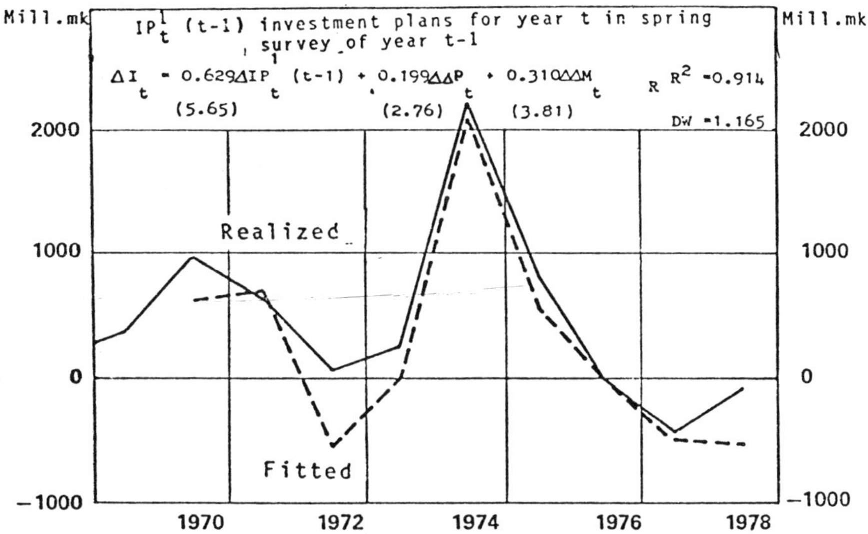

FIGURE I.7

MANUFACTURING INVESTMENT

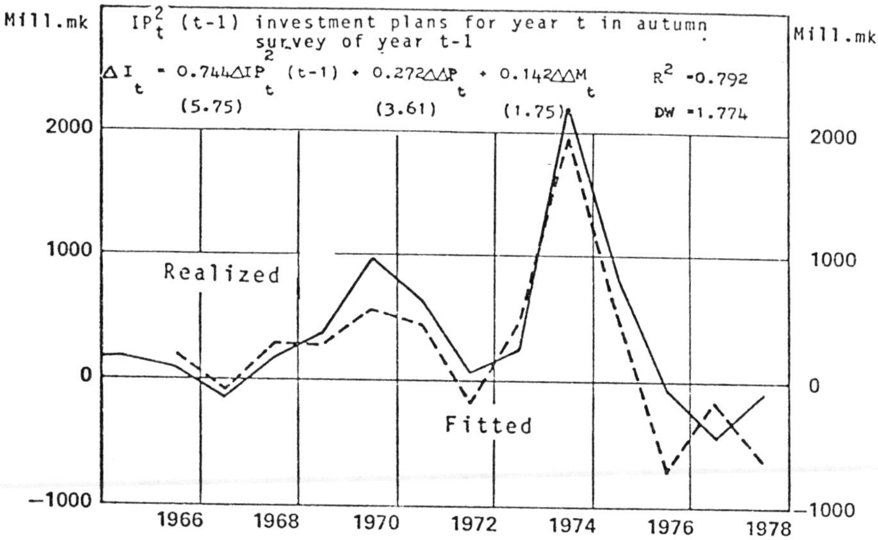

FIGURE I.8

MANUFACTURING INVESTMENT

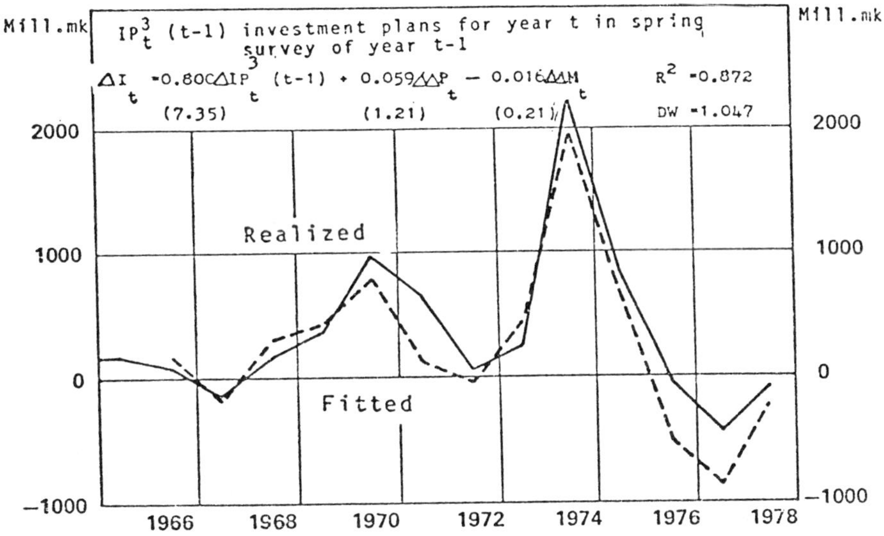

REFERENCES

ELIASSON, G. Kreditmarknaden och industrins investeringar, Uppsala, 1967

HALTTUNEN, H. KORKMAN, S., Central Bank Policy and Domestic Stability in a Small Open Economy, Bank of Finland, 1981, Series D:47

KOSKELA, E., A Study of Bank Behaviour and Credit Rationing, Helsinki 1976.

KOSKENKYLÄ, H., "The Investment Realization Function in Finnish Manufacturing based on Partial Adjustment and Adaptive Expectations Hypotheses, The Finnish Economic Journal, 1971:4.

KOSTIAINEN, S., "Assets and Liabilities of Finnish Industry, 1961 - 1978, Bank of Finland Monthly Bulletin, December 1980.

KUKKONEN, P., The Transmission of Monetary Policy through Credit Rationing: The Case of Finland, Conference on Monetary Policy in Open Economies, Helsinki, August 1975,

MEYER, J.R., - GLAUBER, R.R., Investment Decisions, Economic Forecasting and Public Policy, Boston 1964.

MODIGLIANI, F. - WEINGARTNER, H., "Forecasting Uses of Anticipatory Data on Investment and Sales", Quarterly Journal of Economics 1958:1.

NERLOVE, M., "Adaptive Expectations and Cobweb Phenomena", Quarterly Journal of Economics 1958.

A Quarterly Model of the Finnish Economy, Bank of Finland 1972, Series D:29.

THEIL, H., Applied Economic Forecasting, Amsterdam 1971.

Summary of the Discussion

A.G. Hart
Columbia University
New York, N.Y.

Discussion of Paper No 12, by H. König and M. Nerlove, entitled

RESPONSE OF PRICES AND PRODUCTION TO UNANTICIPATED DEMAND SHOCKS: SOME MICROECONOMIC EVIDENCE

Professor Nerlove's opening remarks started, as it were, in the midst of discussion, since he presented a "handout" in which the authors clarified a number of points in response to some written queries from the chairman a few weeks previous to the meeting. The Nerlove remarks were in good part an amplification of the handout. Since these clarifications will doubtless be incorporated in the draft for publication, while all discussants were responsive to the handout, the discussion comes closer to comment on the final draft than is usual at such sessions.

All the discussants accepted with enthusiasm the two-country approach of the paper, and the applicability of the evidence on the question whether unexpected changes in demand lead primarily to price adjustments (tempered by changes in inventory and in unfilled orders) or primarily to production adjustments (with inventory and unfilled orders as buffers). There seemed to be unanimous admiration of the procedures adopted, avoiding the weaknesses and exploiting the advantages of "categorical" data, and treating conditional probability propositions as "quasi-equations".

Professor G. Ronning, as assigned discussant, while enthusiastic about the paper's approach, expressed misgivings (shared by some other discussants) as to the findings of differences between French and German response patterns. The effort to match cyclical situations between the two authors (explained by the authors as derived from cyclical macro indicators rather than from a consensus in tendency surveys) did not seem fully successful. Some arbitrariness seemed to be introduced by the technique of deriving *ex post* data for Germany from a chaining of three monthly reports (which the authors agreed would reduce apparent variability) while all French data and *ex ante* data for Germany came from quarterly surveys. There was concern also as to whether the more inflationary pattern of the French economy handicapped establishment of comparable forecasts and experience on the side of price.

Minds did not fully meet as to the importance and feasibility of decomposing the sample by industries. The authors, taking it for granted that such a decomposition would be into a number of distinct industrial groups, were doubtful that added computer costs would be warranted, considering that the industry tables corresponding to the tables of the text and handout would contain many empty cells. Discussants felt that if a large number of industries could not be sorted out, it would still be rewarding to make a single split. It was pointed out that the role of order backlogs is quite different as between industries producing to order (as do most durables) and industries selling off the shelf (as do most nondurables). For the first group, a rise of unfilled orders generally is good news, signalling that a rise of "sales" in the sense of orders placed, has initiated a rise in output. For the second group, a rise of unfilled orders indicates, on the contrary, that "sales" (synonymous with shipments of goods which are largely standardized) have turned to be blocked by bottlenecks.

Discussion of Paper No 13, by R. Eisner, S.H. Albert and M.A. Sullivan, entitled

TAX INCENTIVES AND R&D EXPENDITURES

Professor Eisner's opening remarks offered primarily a less technical version of the paper proper, followed up by some comments from his co-authors. This presentation offered a welcome opportunity to bring to life the tabular materials.

Discussion was opened by W. Gerstenberger, who welcomed the widening of the CIRET "spectrum" through demonstration of the use of survey materials to test policy measures. He also gave voice to several concerns which turned out to be shared by other discussants and by the authors:

(a) Whether such "incentive" programs are made known correctly and effectively to the enterprises the program aims to influence.

(b) Whether such programs will not effect primarily the way enterprises describe activities in their accounting, rather than the activities themselves.

(c) Whether respectable design of such programs is attainable unless they incorporate "theoretical" analysis of the quality found in this paper, rather than fragmentary and tendentious analysis in the service of lobbyists and of political sponsors of the programs.

(d) Whether *ex post* analysis of effects should not be on some other basis than a "ceteris paribus model".

(e) Whether an "incentive program" for R&D can be warranted (expecially in the form of subsidy rather than "tax expenditure as recommended by the authors) in face of the presumption that pushing any activity beyond what enterprise would spontaneously choose may waste resources.

The authors' responses were sharply focused. As to (a), they pointed out that R&D expenditures are highly concentrated in a rather small number of enterprises, which had to be well informed if only because of their involvement in organizations lobbying for the program. However (linking b to a), the financial and accounting groups in the enterprise may well have arrived at a clear picture of the preferred incentives some time ahead of the actual directors of R&D; a sharp rise in the proportion of R&D falling into the subsidized categories from year to year suggests manipulation of data. As to (d), the authors argued that "effects" can only be measured against some image of "what would have happened otherwise", so that some sort of "ceteris paribus" is unavoidable. And as to (e), they pointed out that since results of R&D become known rather rapidly to users they have something of the character of "public goods", and must be presumed to have favorable externalities that deserve public support if an effective and economical program can be installed.

It came out in discussion that those who read and heard the paper had not fully registered a major remediable effect explained in the "theoretical" analysis: namely, that the _company-specific_ nature of the moving base against which creditable increments of R&D are measured in the hope of avoiding benefits paid on R&D which would have been undertaken without the benefits, was a flaw of design. Because the base is company specific, early creditable expenditures lead to decreases in the amount that can be credited in later years. This defect, Professor Eisner points out, can be cured by using a moving base which reflects industry aggregates of R&D.

Discussion of Paper No 14, by I. Pyyhtiä, entitled

THE REALIZATION OF INVESTMENT PLANS
OF FINNISH MANUFACTURING FIRMS

The author's opening remarks consisted chiefly of a reading of key passages from the advance text, supplemented by helpful comments on how to interpret the tables and equations.

Discussion was limited by the pressure of time. M. Devilliers, as assigned discussant, offered helpful comparisons of Finnish with French experience. These comparisons led to queries as to whether use of extrapolation for profit expectations might not run into the same difficulties as in France, and as to whether the systematic underestimation of expenditures in the surveys might be due (as in France) to the contributions of small companies. The author's comments indicated that responses had been classified by size of company (as well as in several other dimensions), and small companies did not show exceptional underestimates. The use of profits as proxy for sales (which the author tells us are not covered in Finnish surveys) is also worrisome. The predictions in NORDIC ECONOMIC OUTLOOK (well known to Finnish business men, and taking account of evidence available to the Finnish Central Bank) might offer a more useful proxy.

Paper No 15, by J.A. de Souza, entitled

INFLUENCE OF LONG-TERM EXPECTATIONS UPON THE
INVESTMENT PLANS OF ENTERPRISES

unfortunately arrived only on the day of this session, so that no discussion was possible. An abstract of this paper will be published in CIRET Study No 34.

Fifth Session
Uses of Business Survey Indicators on a Company Level

Chairman:

Å. Lönnqvist, Statistiska Centralbyrån
Stockholm

Sectoral Indicators by Use of Survey Data

H.-J. Dormayer/J.D. Lindlbauer
Ifo-Institut für Wirtschafts-
forschung
Munich

1. Basic observations

Our work regarding industry indicators is based on the observation that economic time series which are affected by the business cycle tend to reach their cyclical turning points at different times. This phenomenon was already enlisted for diagnosing and forecasting business cycles as far back as the last century[1]; extensive use of it is primarily made by the NBER which started publishing indicator lists in the 1930s[2].

This study is also based on earlier work we did on macro-indicators[3] and on branch indicators[4]. The idea is to demonstrate the economic relationships between the individual time series and the various industries in order to utilize in an optimal way the time lags among them in economic forecasting.

---

1) See: Wagemann E., (1928), p. 105 et seq.

2) See: Mitchell W.C. and Burns A.F. (1938).
Moore G.H. (1950).
Moore G.H. and Shiskin J. (1967).

3) See: Gerstenberger W., Lindlbauer J.D., Nerb G., Strigel W.H. (1969).
Lindlbauer J.D., Nerb G., Roberts Ch.C. (1973).

4) See: Nerb G., Ruppert W., Stock K. (1979).
Dormayer H.-J., Lindlbauer J.D. (1982).

It goes without saying that the qualitative indicators constructed by the Ifo Institute have a special role in this. But quite objectively, the good experiences we had had with these data, justify their use as well.

Two cyclical diffusion processes form the logical foundation of the studies on branch indicators which shall be illustrated by means of two graphs. The first building block consists in the horizontal diffusion of a business cycle impulse through the different variables of a sector. The example presented in Fig. 1 shows that in the past a cyclical change in the printing industry was first indicated by business expectations, then by the assessment of the current business situation and, after another lag, by the behavior of the cyclical component of net production. Measured by the maximum correlation coefficient between the individual series, expectations lead assessments by an average of two quarters and net production by another two quarters (see Appendix, pp. 32 - 34). The second example shows by means of the change in the cyclical component of net production that the different sectors react to cyclical impulses with systematic time lags. In this case cyclical turning points of the average of all sectors of the manufacturing industry occurred one quarter after those of drawing and cold-rolling mills (see Appendix pp. 35 - 37). Electrical engineering also lagged drawing and cold-rolling mills by one quarter.

Fig. 1

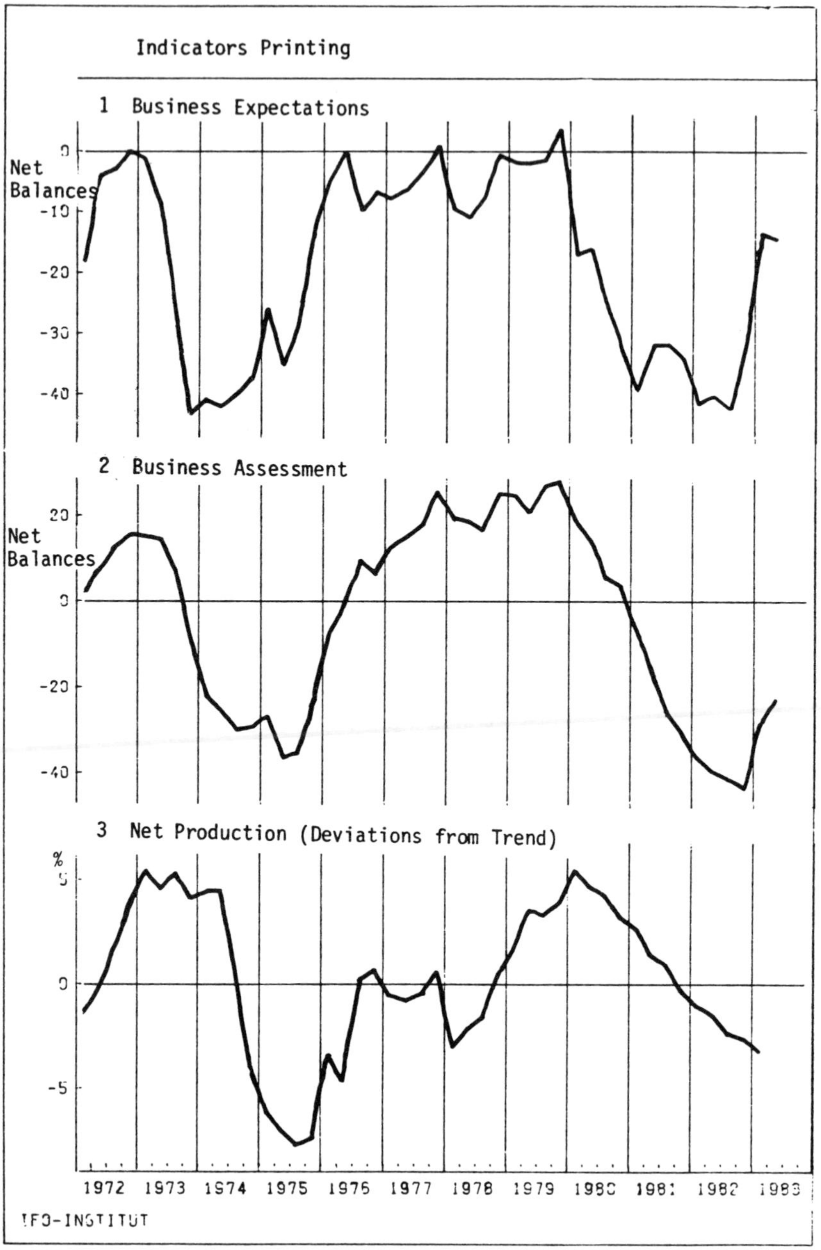
Indicators Printing
1 Business Expectations
Net Balances
0
-10
-20
-30
-40
2 Business Assessment
Net Balances
20
0
-20
-40
3 Net Production (Deviations from Trend)
%
5
0
-5
1972 1973 1974 1975 1976 1977 1978 1979 1980 1981 1982 1983
IFO-INSTITUT

Fig. 2

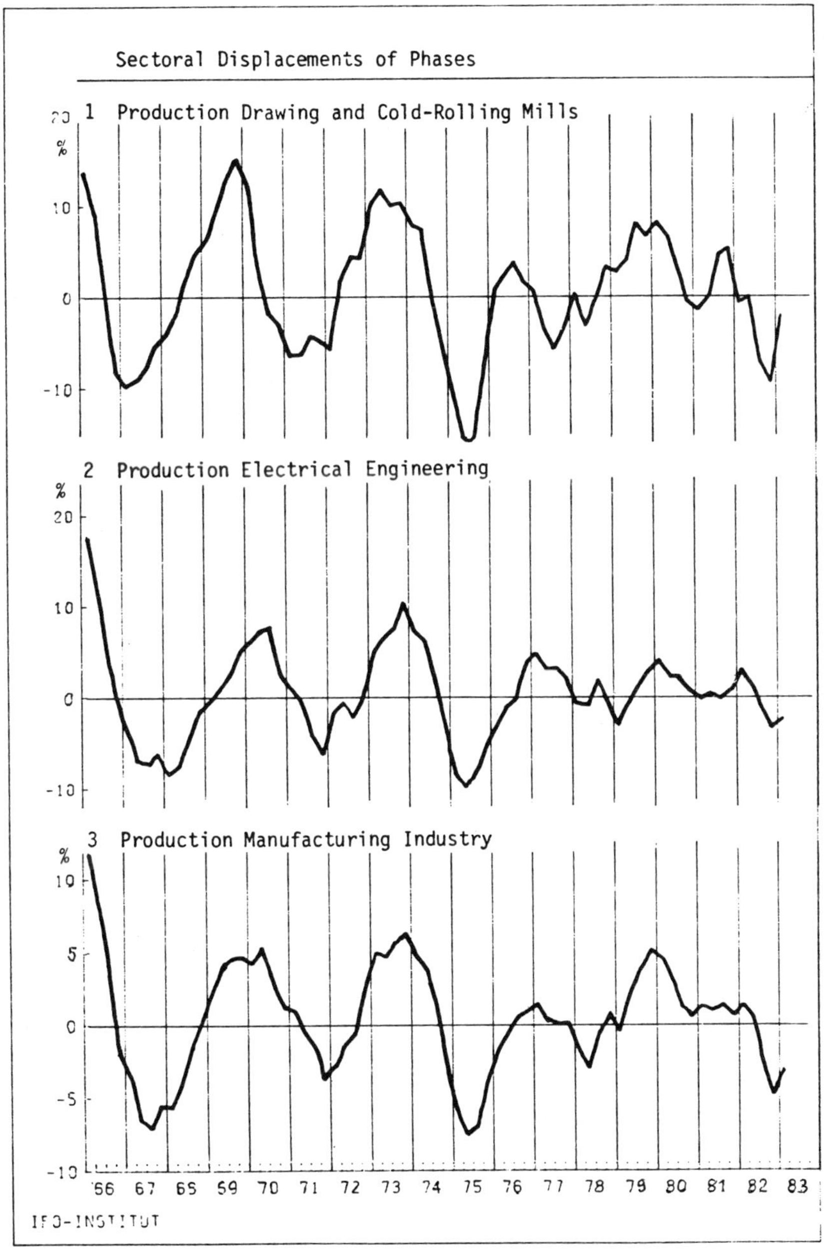
Sectoral Displacements of Phases
1 Production Drawing and Cold-Rolling Mills
%
10
0
-10
2 Production Electrical Engineering
%
20
10
0
-10
3 Production Manufacturing Industry
%
10
5
0
-5
-10
66 67 68 69 70 71 72 73 74 75 76 77 78 79 80 81 82 83
IFO-INSTITUT

The usefulness of observing individual industry business cycles is thus obvious: if industries can be found which cyclically lead either the total average or individual other industries, then the early indicator function of these industries can support the forecast of total economic activity or of that of the lagging industries. The advantage becomes even more evident if the industry lead and the lead of the variables can be combined in a favorable way.

2. Theoretical principles and methodology of the study

Given the large number of economic time series supplied by modern statistics, it is not difficult to present many such examples of lead-lag behavior. Reliable indicators for forecasting can only be obtained, however, if the existence of an economic relationship between the indicator series and the reference series can be determined. In searching for the economic relationship of sequential business cycle movements one primarily looks to business cycle theory and its most prominent explanations, i.e. the multiplier-accelerator mechanism[1], the inventory cycle[2], and the psychological approach[3]. Unless one desires to be led by these explanatory attempts to the sources of cyclical impulses, indicator research quickly reveals that these theories can or must primarily be utilized in explaining disturbances in the desired cyclical sequence.

The indicator approach is based on the idea that a business cycle impulse enters the economic system via auto-

---

1) See: Samuelson P.A. (1939), Hicks J.R. (1950).

2) See: Metzler L.A. (1941), Tichy G.J. (1976), p.155 et seq.

3) See: Jöhr W.A. (1952).

nomous demand or from abroad and is then diffused as derived demand through all economic sectors until it arrives at the raw materials. This concept would imply, however, that final demand first initiates a long ordering process all the way to the raw materials which is followed by the production-delivery process in the opposite direction. The waiting time to the very last delivery of the final product would be too long - but ideal for the construction of indicators. The normal existence of inventories of industrial raw materials, intermediate products, and final products makes the task much more difficult for the indicator researcher. To generate a business cycle impulse it suffices to have a large number of firms at any production or distribution stage change their expectations and increase their inventories by stepping up output or purchases. In addition, the adjustment of inventories to supposed or actual demand changes ensures, via the well-known mechanisms of the inventory cycle, not only that the amplitudes of the cyclical movements are widened, but also that cyclical turning points are possibly advanced[1]. This may then lead to the absurd case, at least for the designer of indicator systems, that the cyclical turning points of the industrial raw materials sectors precede those of the true causes, i.e. the final demand sectors. A good theoretical explanation of indicators is further impeded by the fact that producers of industrial raw materials and intermediate goods gear their expenditures for labor or machinery to their own business cycles. This way the derived, advanced business cycle again affects part of final demand. This effect is certainly all but negligible as the industrial raw materials and intermediate goods sectors have a 47 % share of total manufacturing output.

---

1) Cf. Lösch, H.P. (1969).

Besides inventory investment, plant and equipment purchases are also held responsible for generating business cycles with a forward displacement of the phases.

These theoretical considerations already promise a lot of difficulties for the use of delivery interrelationships between economic sectors in the construction of indicators.

What about the formation of horizontal indicators? It is based on the company decisionmaking process which causes lagged adjustment responses to exogenous changes (such as cyclical impulses). It makes sense to distinguish between production to order and production for inventory. In production to order, orders determine production. Hence, chronologically production activity follows orders received. The trend of the latter may frequently be predicted by the intensity of inquiries. In production for inventory a change in demand initially affects the supplier's finished goods inventories. Production is rather independent of these: it may have been adjusted in advance, if the entrepreneur has correctly foreseen the change, it may ignore the change as insignificant or it may follow later when the new trend has turned out to be a lasting one after all. Correspondingly, in the latter case judgements and expectations should be of significantly greater importance for actual production activity. This does not exclude, however, that these variables may also be good early indicators for production to order.

The time-series on judgments and expectations, necessary for these comparisons, are supplied by the Ifo Business Test[1]. Since this kind of business survey has meanwhile become quite well-known internationally we shall limit our explanation to the variables used in this paper. There are

---

1) Cf. Marquardt W. and Strigel W.H. (1959), Strigel W.H. (1981).

four of them: assessment of current business, assessment of inventories, expectations regarding business over the next six months, and the business climate consisting of the average of the last two variables mentioned.

The questions selected here from the Ifo Business Test, which are put monthly to about 12,000 firms in the manufacturing industry, retail and wholesale trade and the construction industry, are:

- We judge our business situation regarding product X to be good/satisfactory/bad.
- We judge our inventories (retail trade) to be too low/adequate/too high.
- Over the next 6 months our business situation regarding good X will, in cyclical terms, i.e. excluding purely seasonal variations, be rather more favorable/about the same/ rather more unfavorable.

The overall result is derived by aggregating the individual firms' judgment and tendency reports. For any given aggregate (product, product group, industry) the individual responses are weighted according to their relative importance. Then the weighted results are summed up over the various answer choices and, finally, these sums are expressed as percentages of the total number of responses. For each question three results are derived, to wit the shares of positively, indifferently and negatively responding survey participants. Netting the positive and the negative percentages yields a single number per question and month, which becomes one element of a time series (net balance). The early reply deadline, the 5th day of the following month, and the high standardisation of the company responses permit an up-to-date processing of the results which may be available as early as three weeks after the end of the reporting month.

Past work on the indicator characteristics of the Business Test variables revealed that the expectations time series have a greater lead, but also much more random movement than the judgments. As a compromise an average of the two - the business climate - is therefore frequently used as indicator[1].

Advantageous for the employment of Business Test results as indicators are, above all, three special features of the survey: In the Ifo Business Survey the product group is primarily chosen as survey unit. Therefore tha data are available in disaggregated form. This is particularly important for tracing cyclical impulses over several successive production and trade stages and forms the basis of the construction of branch indicators. The only disadvantage is that corresponding data from the official statistics are usually not available at this level of disaggregation. In addition, in the Ifo Business Test there is constant adjustment to the structural changes in the economy. This yields continuous time series over an unlimited - at least in terms of the method - period of time. Finally, the survey results are especially suitable for business cycle observation because, unlike most quantitative series, they don't contain a long-term trend and the short-term disturbance factors (season, irregular component) also have a markedly smaller effect in relation to the cyclical component than they do in the series of the quantitative statistics.

3. Selection of industry indicators

The first step towards an industry indicator is - as with any indicator design - the determination of the reference variable. In the case of overall indicators such variables are usually used which constitute a measure of the current

---

1) Cf. Strigel W.H. (1977), p. 67 et seq.

state of the economy, such as capacity utilization or the cyclical component of production, sales, etc. In this case, the early indicators are generally taken from the same sector - i.e. the total aggregate - and comprise such variables as orders received, assessment of the business situation etc. The concept of industry indicators wants to go beyond this approach of horizontal early indicators and would like to include in the analysis data from the supplier and customer sectors as vertical components. In order to get the maximum possible lead of the indicator, the selection of a "good" horizontal early indicator from the sector under observation suggests itself as reference series.

The next step is the search for the main customer sectors and for series which may serve as early indicators on that stage. Before the selection process can be continued, a filter stage must be inserted, on which the series in the selection, including the reference variable, are reduced to the cyclical component.

In this process those components are eliminated which are irrelevant to the business cycle analysis, but can distort the comparison of the time series, e.g. irregular or seasonal influences or long-term trends. Elimination of possible trends is of special importance, since the Business Survey data don't have such a long-term growth component. The cyclical component is isolated by means of one of the popular seasonal adjustment methods[1]. Using the cyclical component the comparison of the time series can now determine the "best" or a "good" indicator. The criteria for assessing an early indicator are primarily the length and the constancy of the lead as well as the accuracy of the forecast. The lead length and the forecasting accuracy will often compete in such a way that the forecast will become the more accurate the shorter the forecasting period. Optimal compromises must then be found from this.

---

1) Cf. for example: Goldrian G. (1973).

The closeness of the relationship between two variables or their respective time series is measured by the Bravais-Pearson correlation coefficient (R). The direction of the relationship is given by the sign of the coefficient. A positive sign implies a direct, a negative sign an inverse relationship. The square of the correlation coefficient (R^2) is called the coefficient of determination. It indicates the share of the variance of one variable which is explained by the other variable.

Of major interest for the problem of early indication is the lag between different time series rather than the analysis of parallel time series or indicators. Correlation analysis is a simple method for determining such lags. One of the two series to be analyzed is successively shifted by one time unit. A correlation coefficient is calculated for each shift interval. The absolutely highest correlation coefficient is assigned, together with the respective lead/lag, to the analyzed series. The only criterion for the determination of the time lag is, therefore, the maximum correlation coefficient.

The absolute height of each maximum is considered the measure of the accuracy of the lead/lag structure found and thus of the suitability of the leading series as early indicator. At this time, conclusions in the sense of statistical significance or a confidence interval cannot be derived, however. One proceeds according to the principle "the higher the maximum correlation coefficient the more accurate is the determined time lag". In practice subjective lower limits for the correlation maxima are generally used in the selection of relevant indicator series. I.e. those time series are considered early indicators whose correlation maximum occurs with a lead of at least one period and whose value exceeds a previously fixed limit. As a rule this value lies between 0,6 and 0,8 in the analysis of Business Survey series on the industry level.

The relationship between indicator series and reference series may also be classified in the following way:

$\|R\| \geq 0{,}8$	very strong relationship/ very good indicator
$0{,}8 > \|R\| \geq 0{,}6$	strong relationship/good indicator
$0{,}6 > \|R\| \geq 0{,}4$	medium relationship/ medium indicator
$0{,}4 > \|R\| \geq 0{,}0$	no relationship to speak of/ bad indicator

It should be emphasized, however, that these are subjective values based on experience and not "objective statistical data" permitting more extensive interpretation.

Another criterion for the assessment of the accuracy of a determined lead/lag may be obtained from the graphical presentation of the correlation coefficients over the displacement period in a so-called correlogram (see Appendix). In general, the more distinctly the maximum value differs from its neighboring values, the more accurate is the found lead/lag structure. In interpreting the results it should be kept in mind that correlation analysis is an examination of averages over the whole period under consideration. An average lead or lag is determined. Changes in the time structure occurring over time are not explicitly shown. In all cases the graphical analysis is, therefore, consulted in the selection of the "best" indicator, at least in a supplementary way. A comparative graph of the reference variable and the indicator shows very quickly whether the calculated average lead remains constant over time, and in addition, whether there are extensive distortions of the relationship as the result of special behavior exhibited by one or the other series and in which period they occur. From this the cause of the disturbance can often be deduced which possibly permits improving the forecast if the same disturbance should reappear in the future.

By means of this analysis it is possible to systematize the indicators according to the most important criteria, i.e. length of the lead, constancy of the lead, and accuracy of the forecast.

4. Application of the indicators

The characteristics of the indicator revealed in this way will determine its area of application.

The more accurately an indicator hits the reference variable, the greater will be one's inclination to quantify this relationship and to use the indicator either alone or together with other supplementary variables in model forecasts. To determine the relationship between the indicators (X) and the reference variable (Y), the regression method is frequently used:

1. Simple linear regression
   i.e. only one indicator variable is included
   $Y_T = b + a \cdot X_{T-s}$

2. Multiple linear regression
   i.e. several indicator variables are included
   $Y_T = b + a_1 X_{1,T-S1} + a_2 X_{2,T-S2} + \ldots + a_n X_{n,T-Sn}$

where T = period for which the forecast is to be made
S, S1-Sn = lead (in periods) determined by the correlation analysis.

Since the relationship between X and Y must here necessarily be of a stochastic nature, the regression equations may not be interpreted as functional equations. An exact forecast of Y is dependent on the closeness of the relationship between X and Y. Under certain conditions (known distribution, etc.) it is possible to state a confidence interval for the forecast value. This interval can be expected to become larger with increasing indicator lead. A statistical derivation as well as a presentation of the different tests of the coefficients shall not be given here.
Besides the quantitative estimate of the future values of the reference series (forecasting the course), there is the "simpler" possibility of forecasting the turning points. Here the cyclical behavior of the reference series in T periods is deduced from a change in the direction of the indicator series, where T corresponds to the average lead of the early indicator.

An extension of the information which an indicator may supply to a customer stage is imaginable in several ways:

For one, several indicators may be selected from the customer sector and ordered according to decreasing forecasting horizon and/or increasing accuracy. Moreover, the reference sector is likely to have more than one customer sector. In this case indicators are chosen for several or all customer sectors. These may again be used individually or they may be combined into one or several total indicators. For determining the weights several possibilities suggest themselves in this case: shares of the various customer sectors in total sales, regression coefficients or arbitrary weights found by trial and error - since the regression will usually be of little use because of multicollinearity.

The success of the indicators described so far was based on the fact that they permit the observer to use information which also serve as a basis for the decisions of the customer sector. This way decisions of the customer sector may be anticipated. It seems reasonable to take another step in this direction and to develop indicators for the customers of one`s own customer sectors. This can only be successfully done in exceptional cases, as sales relationships usually branch very quickly and can scarcely be measured even on the second stage.
One may assume, however, that each customer stage will try in turn to gather significant information from its own customer sectors so that this information will already be concentrated in their judgments and expectations.

5. Real- world examples

5.1 Product flow lags in the textile sector

Tracing a cyclical impulse over several customer stages should theoretically be easiest in a sector which comprises many stages and whose sales to the outside or whose purchases from the outside are relatively insignificant.

A sector which sufficiently meets these requirements is the textile sector. It consists of the textile industry, the clothing industry as well as trade in textiles and clothing and comprises all the stages from the initial processing of the textile raw material to the sale of the final product to the consumer.

It is relatively well isolated from other economic sectors. A close relationship exists only to the chemical industry as the major supplier of intermediate products (synthetic fibers, dyes). Most of the natural fibers (wool, cotton) are imported. The other stages and the proportion of the output of one stage which is supplied to another are presented in Fig. 3.

For this paper the intermediate production stages of wool wash, yarn production and fabric production were combined. Three stages remained for the comparison: Textile intermediate products, textile consumer goods as well as trade in textiles and clothing. Concerning the manufacturing industry there are no official statistics for this subdivision. Therefore only time series from the Business Survey were used for the comparison.

The working hypothesis for this case is: the cyclical impulse enters the system via retail trade, is transmitted to the consumer goods producers after completion of a decision process and there initiates another decision process, which causes the transmission of the impulse to the producers of intermediate products. This entire process requires a time measurable in months or quarters, so that, corresponding to the diffusion of orders a clear lag shift between respective time series can be determined.

The early indicator chosen for the retail trade was "inventory assessment", as inventory are to be considered the trigger for orders from the consumer goods industry. "Assessment of the business situation" was used to represent the cyclical state on the two industry stages.

Fig. 3

Product-Flow Textile Industry

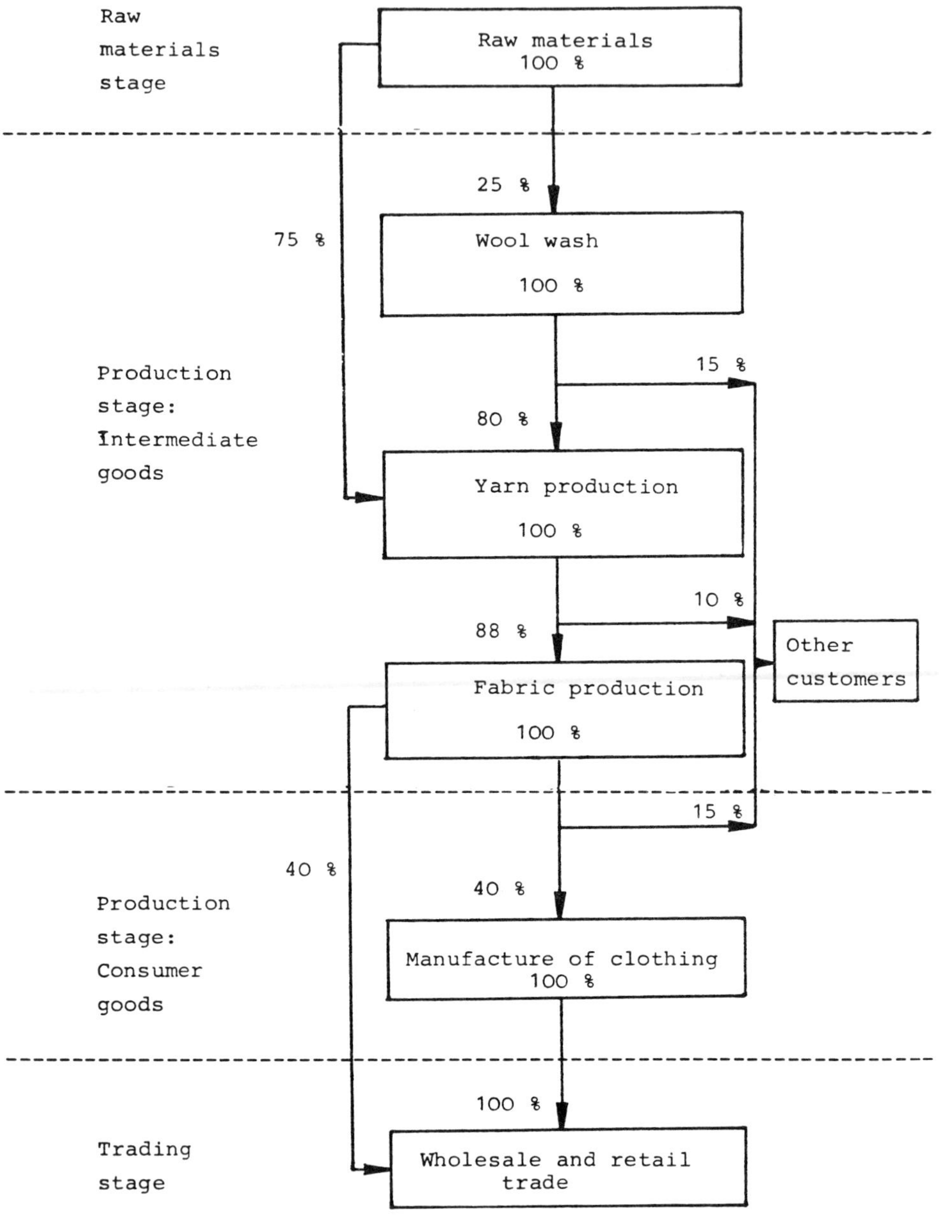

The result of this comparison is shown in Fig. 4. It should be pointed out that the inventory assessment of retail trade is presented inversely, i.e. the case of inventories being too high which, from a cyclical point of view, is a negative judgment, was graphed with negative values. The first thing noted is that the, at times rather diffuse, variations in judgment on the retail stage become rather marked cyclical movements on the stage of the producers of intermediate products. In addition at the marked turning points the retail trade judgments always had a clear lead over the assessments of the business situation of the industry sectors. The lead relationships between the industry sectors are not unambiguous: At some turning points the consumer goods lead (1972/73, 1973/75), at others the intermediate goods lead (1979/80, 1981/82).

The correlograms of these comparisons confirm the optical impression (cf. Appendix, pp. 38-40):

Relationship	Lag	Correlation Coefficient (R)
Retail trade vs.	- 2	0.690
Consumer goods producers	- 1	0.675
Retail trade vs.	- 2	0.527
Producers of intermediate products	- 1	0.531
Consumer goods producers vs. producers of intermediate products	± 0	0.620

The inventory assessments of the retailers in textiles and clothing thus had a lead of 1 to 2 quarters over the business assessments of the producers of textile consumer goods as well as the producers of textile intermediate products. The correlation coefficients for the one-quarter leads did not differ significantly from those for the two-quarter leads. Furthermore, the relationship between retail business and consumer goods business is evidently somewhat closer than that between retail business and intermediate products business. No average lead of one or the other sector was established for the relationship consumer goods-intermediate goods.

Fig. 4

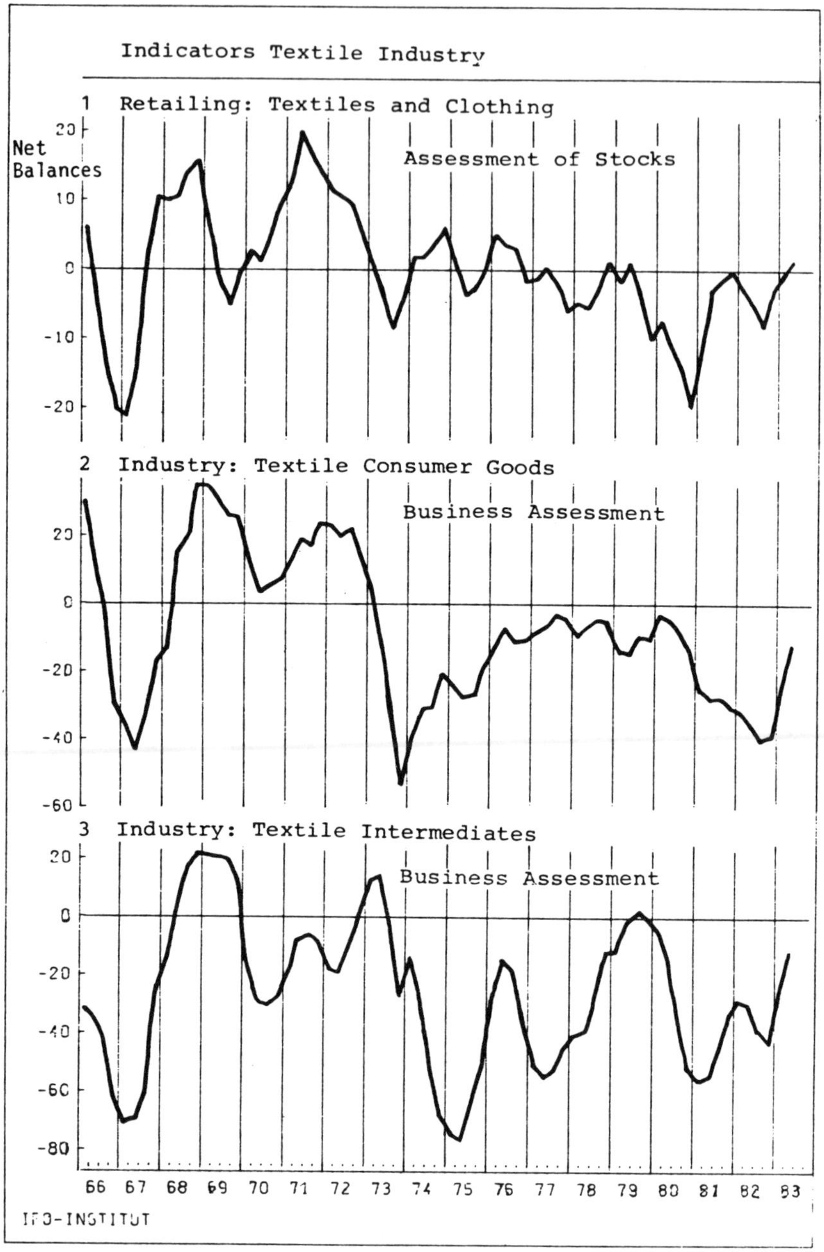

Indicators Textile Industry
1 Retailing: Textiles and Clothing
Net Balances
Assessment of Stocks
20
10
0
-10
-20
2 Industry: Textile Consumer Goods
Business Assessment
20
0
-20
-40
-60
3 Industry: Textile Intermediates
Business Assessment
20
0
-20
-40
-60
-80
66 67 68 69 70 71 72 73 74 75 76 77 78 79 80 81 82 83
IFO-INSTITUT

The retailers' inventory assessment is thus a leading indicator for the business development in the production sectors. Another question is whether the producers don't already have information available which is at least as good. This question can be answered by a comparison of business assessments and business expectations, assuming that the expectations reported reflect the businessmens's state of information (cf. Appendix, pp.41-42):

Relationship	Lag	Correlation Coefficient (R)
Business expectation vs. business assesssment of producers of consumer goods	- 2	0.756
	- 1	0.789
Business expectation vs. business assessment of producers of intermediate goods	- 2	0.762

The results are quite unambiguous: Business expectations in the production sectors permit a more accurate forecast (R is higher) than the early indicator found, the lead being about the same.

A comparison of the retailers' inventory assessment and the business expectations on the production stages also leads to conclusion that many producers were already well aware of cyclical tensions on the retail level (cf. Appendix pp. 43-44).

5.2 Investment Lags

Cyclical impulses are, of course, not only transmitted to the suppliers of intermediate products, but also to the producers of investment goods. Although there are also accelerator effects in this relationship, relatively long leads should still be expected due to the more distinct and therefore more time-consuming decision processes regarding investment. Moreover, at the upper turning point of the cycle investments cannot be curbed as quickly as orders for materials. Lastly, the lower turning point occurs during periods of low capacity utilization, which means that investment decisions in these situations are likely to be delayed.

5.2.1 Production of Paper Machinery

These hypotheses shall first be tested for the case of paper production and the production of papermaking and preparing machines. Here again Bussiness Survey data will exclusively be used.

A certain difficulty in devising indicators derives from the fact that more than half of the paper machines produced are exported. Therefore it must be assumed that it is nevertheless the domestic economic situation which dominates the cyclical behavior of machinery production.

Fig. 5 shows the result of the comparison. Purely visually, business assessment in paper production seems to be a good early indicator of the paper-machinery producers` judgments with significant leads especially at the lower turning points. An exception is the most recent turnaround, in which interest-rate behavior, the change in government, and investment promoting policies led to a synchronization of turning points.

In contrast, the correlation turned out to be relatively low at R = 0.642, which may have been due to differences in the relative amplitudes of the two series as well as the large variations of the lead. On average, the judgments of the paper producers had a lead of 3 quarters over the judgments of the producers of paper machinery (cf. Appendix, p. 45).

The machinery producers would, however, not have done any better with their own business expectations. These did achieve an average lead of 6 quarters, but a lower level of accuracy at R = 0.577, which should be the decisive factor when leads are very long anyway (cf. Appendix, p. 46).

Fig. 5

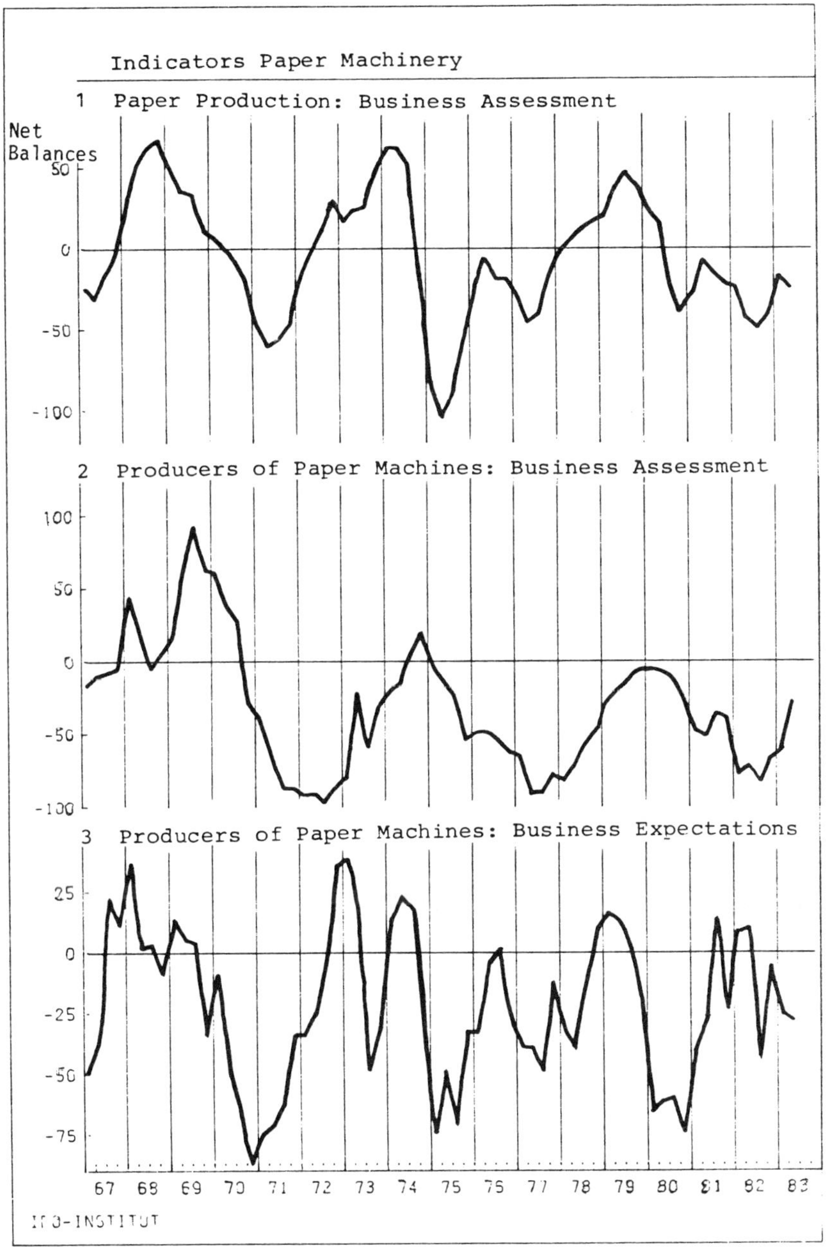
Indicators Paper Machinery
1 Paper Production: Business Assessment
Net Balances
50
0
-50
-100
2 Producers of Paper Machines: Business Assessment
100
50
0
-50
-100
3 Producers of Paper Machines: Business Expectations
25
0
-25
-50
-75
67 68 69 70 71 72 73 74 75 76 77 78 79 80 81 82 83
IFO-INSTITUT

5.2.2 Production of Construction Equipment

The second example of an investor relationship is taken from the construction sector. In contrast to the previously discussed sectors, here it is possible to use data from the official statistics as reference.

The analysis concerns the transmission of cyclical impulses from the construction industry to the producers of construction equipment. The major part of the output of construction equipment is exported, too; nevertheless, the cyclical behavior is determined by domestic demand.

In this case the reference variable is the index of real orders received for construction equipment, supplied by the Federal Statistical Office. As no disturbing trend could be proved to exist in these data, they were only seasonally adjusted. Chosen as early indicator were the business expectations of the construction industry. According to the visual impression of Fig. 6, the turning points with the most extreme upward or downward deviations, i.e. in 1969, 1975, 1979, and 1983, were indicated very early.

The maximum correlation coefficient, at R = 0.425, was calculated for a 3-quarter lead of the business expections of the construction industry versus the orders received by the producers of construction equipment (cf. App. p. 47). In this context it should be mentioned, however, that the comparison is impaired by the effects of investment-retarding (1973) or investment-stimulating (1975) economic policies which, while clearly reflected in the orders received, could not be predicted by early indicators.

Fig. 6

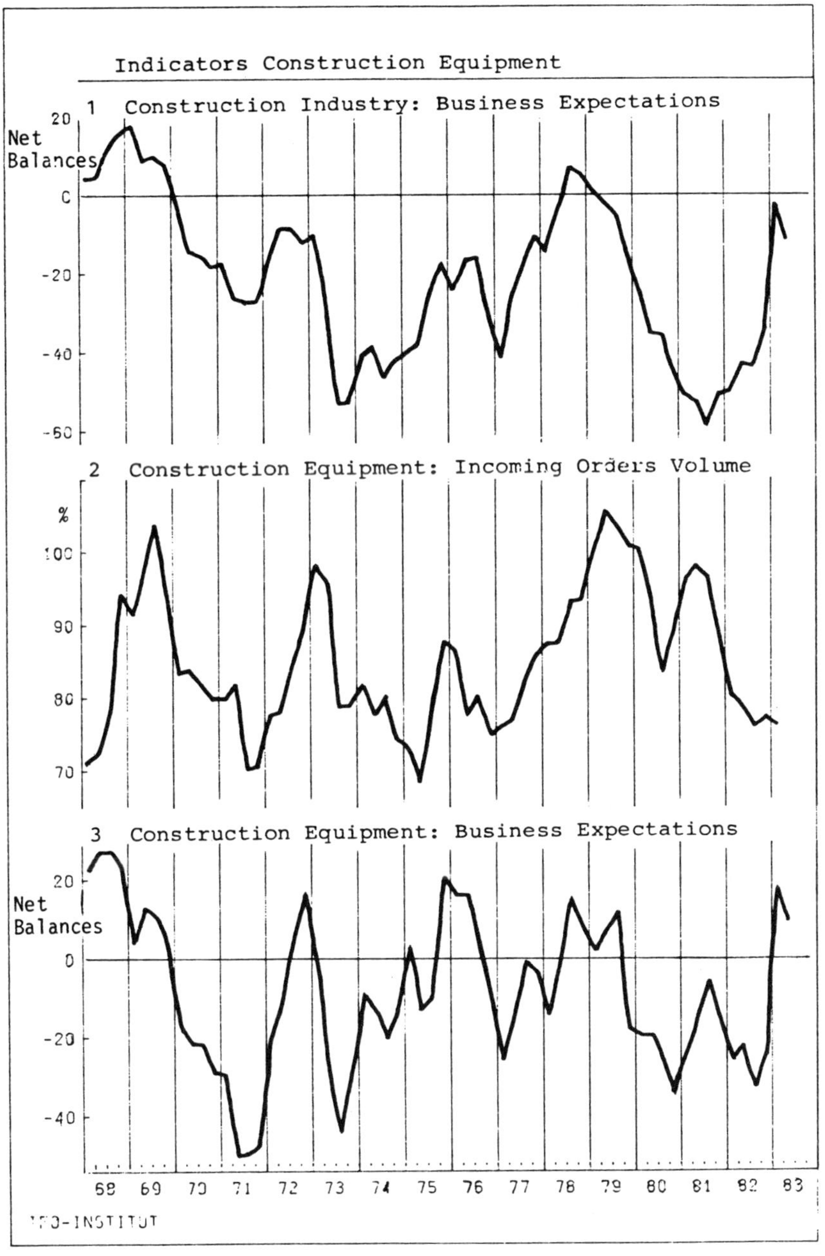
Indicators Construction Equipment
1 Construction Industry: Business Expectations
Net Balances
20
0
-20
-40
-60
2 Construction Equipment: Incoming Orders Volume
%
100
90
80
70
3 Construction Equipment: Business Expectations
Net Balances
20
0
-20
-40
68 69 70 71 72 73 74 75 76 77 78 79 80 81 82 83

The business expectations of the construction equipment producers did significantly worse as early indicators. They achieved an average lead of only one quarter over the orders received, with a maximum correlation coefficient of R = 0.314 (cf. Appendix, p. 48).

5.3 Multistage Indicator

The final example is taken from a company which devises indicators for its own sales by means of the Business Survey data. Among other things, the company produces electronic investment goods.

The reference variable is orders received by this company from the building materials industry. For company data, the original series exhibits especially strong short-term, mostly irregular variations. For this reason the data were not only adjusted for trend and seasonal influences, but were also especially smoothed. The result is the cyclical component. One could now look for an early indicator from the direct customer sectors of the building materials industry. This route was not chosen here. Rather an indicator was selected for the next customer stage, the construction industry (Fig. 7).

The indicator chosen was the "business climate" for the construction industry. The fact that the lead does not remain constant over time was accounted for by putting a tolerance band around the indicator.

This way an early indicator was found which has an average lead of 21 months.

Fig. 7

Business Climate in the Construction Industry
with Band (allowance for instability of the lead)

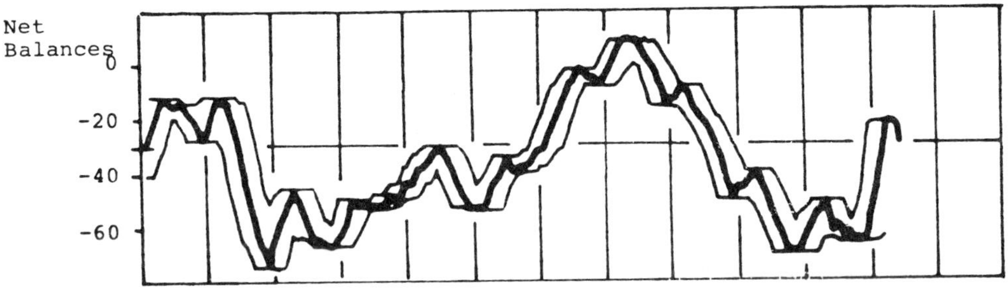

Domestic Orders Received
from the Building Materials Industry
Cyclical Component (deviation from trend in %)
Business Climate Band Construction (displaced by 21 months)

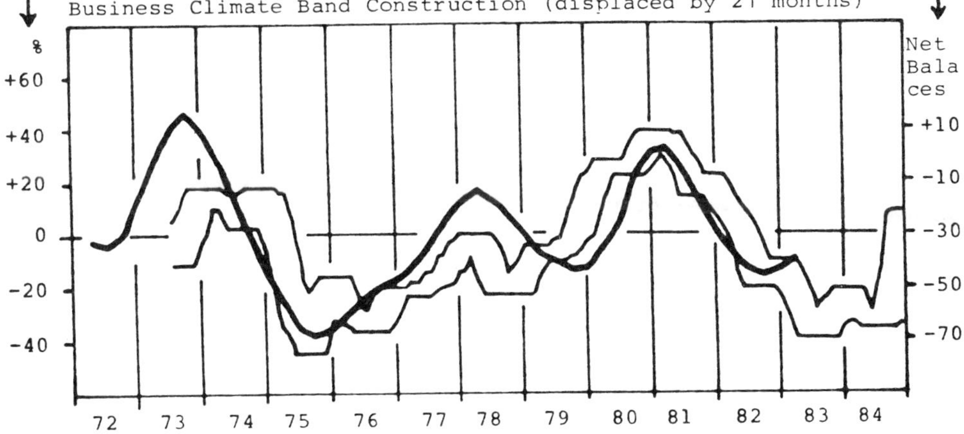

6. Summary

The fact that the cyclical movements of the subsectors of the economy are not synchronous, but temporally displaced with respect to each other, may be utilized for analyses of the economy as a whole as well as of individual industries - - if these displacements are systematic. In these cases, time series of those sectors which react first to cyclical impulses may be used as early indicators of the average total business development, but also of the business development of subsectors which react later.

In order to rule out mere coincidence, one must be able to find a logical explanation for the lead. The theoretical foundation for the development of industry or sectoral indicators is provided by the concept of cyclical impulses: A cyclical impulse enters into the system of the production or service sectors, either through private demand or public demand, economic policy, foreign demand, etc.. The change in demand in the sector which is affected first is then transmitted via demand to its suppliers of finished goods, intermediate products or investment goods. The transmission of the impulse requires decisions which are responsible for the lapse of time between recognizing a change and transmitting the impulse via changes in orders. If this period of time is long enough to become visible in the available monthly data, time series of the customer sectors become early indicators of the supplier sectors.

These ideal conditions for an indicator approach are primarily impaired by inventories. With the help of inventories the firms on most stages may to a limited extent become independent of demand. Instead of waiting for the impulse to arrive or to transmit it immediately, they may build up or deplete their inventories. In addition, accelerator effects on inventory investment or fixed investment may cause the cyclical turning points of the supplier sectors to occur before those of the customer sectors. While theoretical considerations do, therefore, provide logical support for systematic time lags between different sectors, the leads are not necessary and, at least, quite variable.

The possibility of using sectoral indicators in forecasting was empirically tested by means of quantitative data and also of the results of the Ifo Business Survey. The Business Survey provided information in the form of time series of businessmen's judgments and expectations. This appears to be of special importance, as these very variables have a significant influence on the transmission of cyclical impulses. In addition, the Business Survey results have the advantage over available quantitative statistics of being highly disaggregatable, which is a prerequisite for industry or sectoral analyses.

The study required the determination, in each case, of a reference variable for the sector for which early indicators are to be devised as well as the selection of those time series from customer sectors which are to serve as early indicators. Quantitative orders received or, as substitutes, assessments of the business situation were used as reference variables. Among the most useful early indicators were inventory assessments, judgments and expectations regarding the business climate (the average of business assessment and business expectations). We also investigated the question whether the early indicators found actually provided additional information to the companies in the respective reference sectors or whether their own business expectations already reflected the same state of information. The examples were chosen so as to permit the presentation of impulse chains via product flow as well as via investments.

It turned out that even in those cases, in which early indicators with significant leads can be developed, the information of the supplier sectors is frequently already up to date. Nevertheless, the search for leading indicators from the customer sectors is not only worthwhile for producers of investment goods. While here the success rate was high, i.e. greater accuracy and also a longer time horizon for the forecast could be achieved more often than for suppliers of consumer goods and their intermediate products, the proportion of firms which, in each case, reported the correct trend, revealed that in this sector as well only a minority of firms has this knowledge. Futhermore, not every company whose responses contribute to the overall accuracy of the expectations, is likely to have forecasted equally well in all cases.

It might be very interesting, indeed to find out how the good forecasters acquired their knowledge - possibly in the same way which was pursued here.

References

Dormayer H.-J., Lindlbauer J.D., (1982): Branchenspezifische Konjunkturindikatoren. Sonderhefte zum Allgemeinen Statistischen Archiv, Heft 20, edited by Andersen, O.

Gerstenberger W., Lindlbauer J.D., Nerb G., Strigel W.H.,(1969): Abschwung und Rezession im Spiegel quantitativer und qualitativer Statistik. CIRET-Studie Nr. 15. Ifo-Institut für Wirtschaftsforschung, München.

Goldrian G., (1973): Eine neue Version des ASA-II-Verfahrens zur Saisonbereinigung von wirtschaftlichen Zeitreihen. Wirtschaftskonjunktur. Ifo-Institut für Wirtschaftsforschung. 25 Jg. Heft 4. München.

Hicks J.R. (1950): A Contribution to the Theory of the Trade Cycle. Oxford.

Jöhr W.A., (1952): Die Konjunkturschwankungen. Tübingen.

Lindlbauer J.D., Nerb G., Roberts Ch.C., (1973): Ansätze zu einem Konjunkturindikatorensystem für die Bundesrepublik Deutschland. CIRET-Studie Nr. 20. Ifo-Institut für Wirtschaftsforschung, München.

Lösch H.P., (1969): Die Textilkonjunktur im Rahmen des allgemeinen Wirtschaftsablaufs. Ausmaß und Ursachen der erhöhten konjunkturellen Instabilität der Textilindustrie. Köln-Opladen.

Marquardt W. und Strigel W.H.,(1959): Der Konjunkturtest. Berlin-München.

Metzler L.A., (1941): The Nature and Stability of Inventory Cycles. Review of Economics and Statistics. Vol. XXIII, Nr. 3.

Mitchell W.C. and Burns A.F., (1938): Statistical Indicators of Cyclical Revivals. Bulletin 69, New York. NBER.

Moore G.H., (1950): Statistical Indicators of Cyclical Revivals and Recessions. Occasional Paper 31. New York. NBER.

Moore G.H. and Shiskin J., (1967): Indicators of Business Expansions and Contractions. Occasional Paper 103. New York. NBER.

Nerb G., Ruppert W., Stock K., (1979): Indikatoren für die betriebliche Marktbeobachtung. Ifo-Schnelldienst 35-36. Ifo-Institut für Wirtschaftsforschung, München.

Samuelson P.A., (1939): Interactions between the Multiplier Analysis and the Principle of Acceleration. Review of Economics and Statistics. Vol. XXI.

Strigel W.H., (1977): The "Business Climate" as Leading Indicator. In Search of Economic Indicators. Strigel W.H., editor. Berlin, Heidelberg, New York.

Strigel W.H., (1981): Business Cycle Surveys. Frankfurt.

Tichy G.J., (1976): Konjunkturschwankungen. Berlin, Heidelberg, New York. P 155 et seq.

Wagemann E., (1928): Konjunkturlehre. Berlin. 1: P 105 et seq.

o o o

Editorial remark:

Due to limited space the appendix (explanation of the correlograms) could not be included in this volume. Readers interested in these 18 pages are adviced to contact the authors or the CIRET Office.

+ Important parts of this work were extracted from: Dormayer H.-J., Hölter E., Lindlbauer J.D., Scheld M., Wenger E.: Branchenbezogene Konjunkturprognosen. Edited by Hahn D., University of Gießen. The research for this publication was supportet by the Deutsche Forschungsgemeinschaft.

The Variability of Relative Price Expectations, the Rate of Inflation and the Phillips Curve

S. Kawasaki
Internationales Institut
für Management und Verwaltung
Berlin

D. Gahlen
Universität Augsburg
Augsburg

A.J. Buck
Temple University
Philadelphia, Pa.

1. The Theory of Price Uncertainty

In view of the stagflation of the seventies, uncertainty about the inflation rate has become an important area of research. This uncertainty increases with increasing rates of inflation. It also has real effects and increases the cost of inflation. In this paper, using expectations data from the ifo Institute, we shall look into both propositions as they apply to Germany. Before going directly to the empirical tests, we provide an overview of the literature.

1.1 Inflation and the Certainty of Expectations

The monetarist view is that in their effects on the real sector of the economy, a stable price level and a fully anticipated inflation are identical; neither has a quantity effect. A fully anticipated inflation is "...the equivalent of a full indexing of all contracts" (Friedman (1977)). With this began a noteworthy, new orientation of economic research: Friedman took it up in his 1976 Nobel lecture. At the same time he proposed further research.

Friedman accepts a climbing Phillips curve. In his third stage inflation and unemployment are positively correlated. Connected with this are two interrelated empirical regularities:

a. With high rates of inflation its variability also increases.

b. The rate of inflation and the variance of relative price changes are positively correlated.

What follows is a review of both of these points. In the framework of a review of the literature we present in section 1.2 the results of studies of the relation between inflation and its own variability and in section 1.3 its relation to the variability of relative prices. Following that we go into the real effect of these variabilities. The literature review is brought to a close in section 1.5 with remarks on expectations and uncertainty.

1.2 Inflation and the Variability of Inflation

The previously mentioned notion that the concepts of price level stability and fully anticipated inflation ought to be compatible has been heavily criticized from the beginning. Okun (1971) pointed out that with higher rates of inflation these concepts should diverge. Gordon (1971) compared the fifties and sixties. Although the dependence between price stability and the rate of inflation was always positive, it was weaker in the sixties. This result is not surprising. In the fifties was the Korean conflict. The sixties were marked by moderate inflation and high growth. In the seventies we see supply side shocks. In view of these historical developments it is not astonishing that Logue and Willet (1976), in their study of 41 OECD and developing countries, found a positive relationship between the inflation rate and its variability for the period 1949-1970. For the highly industrialized countries this relationship exists only for the fifties. This is confirmed by the investigation of Katsimbris and Miller (1982), which ends in 1970.

It is not surprising that, for the Latin American countries with high inflation rates, we find the strongest relation between inflation and its variability. This has been found by Foster (1978) and Blejer (1979), among others. In any case, this positive correlation is well documented for western countries. Fischer (1981b) established the relation for the U.S. for the long term (1806-1979). Taylor (1981) investigated this dependence for the seven most important industria-
lized countries. The cross section result was that countries with a higher rate of inflation also experienced more variation therein. The time series analysis gave the same result: as the inflation rate in the same countries rose, so rose its variability.

Evaluation of the relevant empirical evidence permits the conclusion that there is a positive and significant dependence between the rate of inflation and its variability. But this relation is not linear. It begins at a definite threshold value of the inflation rate. With high rates of inflation its variability changes in an overproportionate manner.

1.3 Inflation and the Variability of Relative Prices

In a regime with a low rate of inflation, economic activity is coordinated by the system of relative prices. Taylor (1981) quite rightly proposes that "The true signals in relative price movements are benefits not costs." The problem relevant to us is formulated by Friedman (1977) as follows: "But the information in practice is transmitted in the form of absolute prices...If the price level is on the average stable or changing at a steady rate, it is relatively easy to extract the signal about relative prices from the observed prices. The more volatile the rate of general inflation, the harder it becomes to extract the signal about relative prices from the absolute prices."

Since the empirical research by Vining and Elwertowski (1976), it has been consistently found that there exists a positive relationship between the inflation rate and the variability of relative price changes (Jaffee and Kleiman (1977), Balk (1978), Parks (1978), Clements and Nguyen (1980), Hercowitz (1981), Fischer (1981a, b and 1982a) and Taylor (1981)). In view of the new interest in the relationship between the inflation rate and relative prices one must recall the earlier investigations of the same phenomenon e.g. Mills(1927), Graham (1930), and Glejser (1965). In Germany it has been ascertained that a positive relation between inflation and the variability of relative price changes exists. The relation is particularly strong in the seventies. Above all, an above average inflation rate is associated with greater variability in relative price changes (Buck and Gahlen (1983)).

1.4 Real Effects of Increased Variability

With increasing inflation we find increasing inflation variability and increased variability of relative price changes. Following Friedman (1977), these have negative real effects. These real effects are bound to the increasing uncertainty about the inflation rate: "...in such an environment, no one has single-valued anticipations. Everyone recognizes that there is great uncertainty about what actual inflation will turn out to be over any future interval" (Friedman, (1977)). But uncertainty and variability are not the same thing (see Section 1.5). In this section we give a short overview of the new empirical work on the Phillips curve.

Lucas has criticized the usual proposition of the Phillips curve. He argues that the Phillips curve is not based on a structural model. The empirical regularity is not independent of economic policy. Lucas (1973) comes to the conclusion: "The alternative explanation of the same observed tradeoff is that the positive association of prices and output arises because suppliers misinterpret general price movements for relative price changes. It follows from this view, first, that changes in average inflation rates will not increase average output, and secondly, that the higher the variance in average prices, the less favorable will be the observed tradeoff".

Lucas' interpretation provides a role for relative prices in the traditional Phillips curve. Nevertheless, the Friedman-Phelps hypothesis has unfortunately been reformulated; it is based on money illusion. Money illusion ought not be arbitrarily invoked. This is the message of the Lucas model: "...,the model asserts that the greater the variance of the general price level relative to the variance of market specific price changes, the less economic agents will be fooled into responding to nominal aggregate demand changes (Froyen and Waud (1980)). Moreover, "fooling" is meant to play the central role in the Friedman-Lucas message: Misunderstandings about relative prices have positive temporary quantity effects.

The Lucas model, which Friedman cites in his Nobel lecture, has called forth numerous empirical investigations of the Phillips curve and the Output-Inflation Tradeoff. We review the rudiments of the model in what follows.

In this case, the hypothesis to be tested is that nominal shocks have real effects only when they are misinterpreted as real shocks; then the elasticity of cyclical quantity changes will be determined by nominal demand changes (π). The reduced form is given by

$$Y_{c,t} = -\pi\delta + \pi DX_t + \lambda Y_{c,t-1} + U_t \qquad (1.1)$$

where $Y_{c,t}$ is the cyclical component of real social product, DX_t is changes in nominal social product with mean δ and variance σ_x^2 and $u \sim N(o, \sigma^2)$.

The test then is the question of establishing the relationship between π and σ_x^2. The two are negatively correlated. This holds true in the case of replacing σ_x^2 by the variability of inflation (σ_p^2). (Compare Lucas (1973), Alberro (1981), Froyen and Waud (1980)).

Going back to Friedman's Nobel lecture, there is a more direct test which avoids the two step procedure. Friedman also elucidates three Phillips curves or Output-Inflation tradeoffs:

a. In the long term there is no trade-off. The Phillips curve is vertical.

b. There are transitory shifts in the Phillips curve. Variability, uncertainty or noise lead to negative quantity effects.

c. The Output-Inflation tradeoff is valid only in the short term.

Friedman makes it quite clear that he regards the short and middle term Phillips curves as transition manifestations of the trade-off. The short term trade off disappears after the adjustment of expectations; the middle term trade-off after adjustment of institutions (Fischer (1982b)). For our period of investigation, we must start from the point that there are two effects at work: the "fooling" aspect and the "noise" aspect.

There are now numerous studies which capture the two effects simultaneously (Mullineaux (1980), Levi an Makin (1980), Blejer and Leiderman (1980, 1982), Buck and Gahlen (1983)). A general result is that the "fooling" aspect has positive quantity effects and the noise aspect has negative quantity effects.

This speaks directly for the inclusion of both effects in any analysis. Failure to include both will result in a specification error. Once more the literature demonstrates that "noise" and "fooling" apear at the same time in the seventies.

1.5 Variability and Uncertainty

For quite some time the empirical regularity between the variability of the inflation rate and the variability of relative price change on the one hand and aggregate prices and quantities on the other has been recognized. It is the usual form in such studies "... to establish as carefully as possible the structural form explanation underlying the reduced form correlation" (Taylor (1981)). There is no scarcity of such structural forms. Fischer (1981a) lists six different formulations which are all consistent with the empirical findings and between which one cannot discriminate. In the context of macroeconomics we will draw upon the contract-based and information based models.

The contract-based models argue that increased variability reduces the length of the optimal contract. Adhering to contracts only diminishes the efficiency of the market system. The information-based models argue that increased price variance reduces the efficiency of market prices by making factor allocation more difficult. It thus comes down to the divergence from Full-information-Output. As was mentioned, these theories are not conclusive. In any case, we propose the hypothesis - which is closely connected to both theories - that higher inflation rates raise uncertainty.

In the popular economics press this hypothesis has received

much attention in recent years. Pointed out are, for example, the shortening of planning horizons and the preference for financial investments. Microeconomic theories show that, for risk averse entrepreneurs, increased uncertainty yields reduced production and factor demand at the firm level (Sandmo (1971), Batra and Ullah (1974)).

How can one empirically measure uncertainty? In the literature it is quite commonplace to confuse uncertainty with variability (absolute and relative). Mullineaux(1980) correctly observes: "It appears that Friedman is treating the terms 'variability' and 'volatility' as roughly synonymous with 'uncertainty'. However, increases in variability are not necessarily accompanied by increased uncertainty. Recognizing this, we will nevertheless follow Friedman in using the terms 'uncertainty', and 'variability' interchangeably". Mullineaux can do this in good conscience. In related work Cukierman and Wachtel have found that the variance and uncertainty measures are positively correlated.

We will use expectations data for the reason that, the ARIMA-computed separation of expected and unexpected inflation is consistently criticized. Directly observed expectations data provide a better basis for this separation. The ifo data base is our replacement for the Livingston and Michigan data.

It is therefore lucrative to investigate the real effects of uncertainty about the inflation rate within the available price expectations data for Germany. The role of the distinction between expected and unexpected inflation is well known in this regard. With reference to these differences one can make a direct investigation.

Critical in this judgement is the noise variable. The Mullineaux and Makin-Levi studies use in this context the Livingston data. Livingston conducts a semiannual aggregate inflation survey of professional forecasters (for difficulties in the use of this data see Carlson (1977)). The variance of responses can be used as an indicator of uncertainty.

Cukierman and Wachtel (1979) suggest that "...suppliers in different markets will have different views about the general level of prices". With this in mind, it is hard to understand why survey results about the overall inflation rate (be they from experts or the public) should be the basis for the noise variable. It may be that the subjective calculation of the inflation rate is different with higher rates of inflation. Nevertheless, the Livingston responses are seldom identical with those of different market participants. This is noted by Cukierman and Wachtel (1979).[1]

It is adviseable to consider the confusion between variability, uncertainty and expectations formation. In this connection Cukierman and Wachtel observe "in the concluding section to our earlier paper, we came close to identifying inflation variance with uncertainty". They then define the degree of inflation uncertainty as the variance of forecast error. These errors are the difference between the Livingston expected inflation series and the actual inflation rate.[2] This appears to correspond to Klein's definition. He asks: "How much uncertainty now exists regarding future price changes, i.e. what is the variance of the expected price change distribution?" Under the label of uncertainty he is interested in the probability of differences in subjective price expectations.[3] Fischer apparently returns to this view (1981b). He carries this out in reference to the Livingston and Michigan surveys: "Each person could in principle hold his views with no uncertainty, in which case the dispersion of expectations would say nothing of subjective inflation uncertainty. But then, high dispersion would certainly imply that most people's plans were made on the basis of inaccurate beliefs about inflation. It is more plausible that the relationship between the variance of inflationary expectations within the surveys and the mean expected rate does reflect subjective uncertainty about inflation that has grown with expected inflation".[4]

In this paper we take the following positions: First, when expectations and surprises are dealt with, the use of subjective data is to be given preference to autoregressive equations. This is valid in view of the many studies which use survey and econometric computations for the same purpose. The AR processes are based on doubtful theoretical representations. The survey process is a direct measure.

Second, the subjective data provide a direct response to the "fooling" question of Lucas and others. Usually only the aggregate unexpected inflation rate is considered. The empirical works about the output inflation tradeoff are macroeconomic country studies. Therewith one cannot reveal market differences. Here the basis of the Lucas (1975) and Barro (1976) models will be widened in order to capture different market conditions. Parks (1978) considered different supply and demand conditions. Going further, Cukierman and Wachtel (1979, 1982a, b) have proposed that inflationary expectations are not uniform across markets. Cukierman (1982) has proposed that market participants can distinguish between permanent and transitory market changes only with some difficulty. Bordo (1980), in the context of contract theory,[5] finds support for differing price flexibility. Other models include the role of inventories, export etc. All of these rigorous theories of market differences are consistent with the empirical evidence.[6]

With the ifo data set we can directly test the same hypothesis on a market or industry level.

Third, the equation ought to be

$$X_t = \alpha_0 + \alpha_1 t + \alpha_2 X_{t-1} + \alpha_3 (DP_t - DPE_{t-1}) + \alpha_4 DPE_{t-1} + \alpha_5 VP_{t-1} + \alpha_6 VPE_{t-1} + \alpha_7 D1 + \alpha_8 D2 + \alpha_9 D3 + U_t \tag{1.2}$$

where X_t is either net production, number of workers or hours worked. DP_t is the actual price change from t-1 to t. DPE_t is the expected price change from t to t+1. VP_t and VPE_t are the variances corresponding to DP_t and VPE_t. And D1, D2, D3 are seasonal dummies for the 1st, 2nd and 3rd quarters. All of the price variables are computed from the ifo data set.

Recall from the previous section that the ifo respondents report, in a qualitative fashion, on previous price changes. Because of the discrepancy between DPE and the actual series from the Statistiches Bundesamt we have constructed DP from the ifo using the same method applied to DPE.

Also the disaggregation in the ifo data allows us to fit (1.2) to fifteen industries as well as the aggregate of all industries.

The considerations of our second proposition make such a branch specific investigation more purposeful.

Fourth, on the branch level regard should be given to absolute prices. After consideration of the Friedman citations, the industry level decision makers must filter signals about relative prices and the inflation rate from the absolute price level. On that basis, an unexpected price increase can be misinterpreted as a real price effect and have a positive quantity effect (fooling). On the other hand, an increased variance in inflationary expectations leads to many decisions being based on false price signals (noise).

Fifth, looking closely at VPE_{it} one is struck by the fact that the distribution of expectations is conditioned by different understandings of the aggregate inflation rate and market specific relative prices. This measure was the intention of Cukierman and Wachtel (1979, 1982a, b). But it was not measured. Rather, they used $VP_t = EVPE_{it}$.

Sixth, one can correctly claim that VPE_{it} is a better measure of uncertainty than the measure used by among others Mullineaux, Levi-Makin and Cukierman-Wachtel. The measure should reflect the confusion about relative prices and the inflation rate. In their theoretical section Cukierman and Wachtel are quite clear: "The realized (market) price...reflects both movements in the general level of prices (due to aggregate supply and demand shocks) as well as movements which are market specific. Producers in the market use this price, ..., to improve their forecast of the current general price level. Since equilibrium prices on different marekts differ in general (owing to different realizations of the market specific shocks), predictions concerning the current general level of prices also differ across markets. As a consequence there is some distribution of inflationary expectations across markets at a given time". These abundant theoretical ideas cannot be captured by the Livingston data. The data of the Michigan SRC give better results. Nevertheless, the measure VPE_{it} is necessary for a direct test. This measure can be constructed directly from the ifo data.

Seventh, the foregoing studies show that "fooling" and "noise" are positively correlated. It then follows that both must be calculated. We surmise therefrom, that expected inflation must also be included.

2. Data Bases and Variable Construction

2.1 The Federal Statistical Office Data[7]

From a number of the special series we were able to construct quarterly data for our fifteen industry study. See Table 2.1 for the included industries for the following variables: net production (defined as gross production minus materials consumption), paid hours of work per man per week[8] (this is the sum of contractual and overtime hours) and number of workers. The time period for all industries is 1960.1 through 1982.4.

As with all data sets there are a number of problems of which the user should be aware. Probably the most crucial problem is the changing base year for the computation of net production and producer prices. As always, such changes involve revised weighting schemes. In converting to a single base year we have not tried to correct for changing weights. With rare exception, the changing weights have not radically altered the way in which the industry time series evolve (see the citations in footnote 7). As we are dealing in rates of change, a cost-benefit analysis led us to decide against re-weighting the data.

Our seventeen industries are drawn from a larger set (forty) of industries categorized on the basis of a system similar, but not identical, to the NACE scheme. The current system was adopted in 1977 and is a revision of the SYPRO system used since 1961. Since our industries are highly aggregated (corresponding roughly to the 3 digit level in the American SIC code) we felt that the altered economic classification scheme was not of great concern.

Of more interest is the manner in which a firm is classified. In its response to the statistical office the firm must indicate its point of economic emphasis with regard to output. At the end of each year the approximately 2100 firms in the survey may change their category. The important, or disturbing, point is that all of a firms output, workers, etc. are categorized according to its point of emphasis rather than being distributed to its perhaps quite different economic activities.

Lest this method cause too much concern, the Statistical Office has done a thorough study to demonstrate that it is very difficult to put a single firm in more than one category. Further, a study has been made of firm homogeneity. A firm is said to be homogeneous if its employees are engaged principally in the point of emphasis of that firm. The results show that 77.2% of all firms are homogeneous. The least homogeneous of our industries are shown in Table 2.2.

2.2 ifo Data

The second source of our data is the ifo-Kunjunkturtest survey. The survey covers industrial enterprises, construction, wholesale and retail trades. In the present paper we have used only the survey of industrial enterprises. The questionnaire, used since 1960, is shown in Table 2.3. There are several unique features in the ifo data base.

The most unusual aspect of the ifo survey is the class of

respondents. In the most popular surveys (from a use-intensity point of view) the respondents are either professional forecasters (Livingston) or households (Michigan SRL). The ifo survey relies on managers in industrial firms. Thus, our survey respondents are active participants in the price setting mechanism and may be presumed to have more complete information. Also, the industry grouping allows us to investigate certain micro-based macro-hypotheses on an industry-by-industry basis.

The ifo surveys are conducted monthly, although we do not avail ourselves of this degree of disaggregation. Because the Statistical Office data is quarterly we had to take three month averages of the survey results.

The survey questions permit only three directional responses; increase, the same and decrease. In order to be useful for the tests of hypotheses outlined in the previous section the qualitative data had to be converted to quantitative data. The procedure is outlined in the next section.

The more immediate concern is compatibility between the ifo data and the data from the Statistical Office. The original basis for classifying the ifo data was SYPRO. As far as possible, the data have been reorgnized to fit the Systematik des Investititionstests in Handel. This is fairly close to the method now used by the Statistical Office. Given the catalog, the firms are assigned on the basis of institutional affiliation, EEC grouping or functional characteristics of output. We have used the final classification scheme as it most closely resembles the results of the Statistical Office catalog.

Table 2.1

Industries in the Study

	Begin	End
Stone and Earth	60.1	82.4
Non-ferrous metal forging	66.1	82.4
Mineral oil manufacture	66.1	82.4
Chemicals	66.1	82.4
Machine tools,	60.1	82.4
Automotive	60.1	82.4
Steel and light metal construction	61.1	82.4
Electronics	60.1	82.4
Fine machinery, optics and watches	60.1	82.4
Ceramics	60.1	82.4
Textiles	60.1	82.4
Clothing	60.1	82.4
Paper Goods	60.1	82.4
Wood Working	60.1	82.4
Printing	63.1	82.4

Table 2.2

Industry Homogeneity

Industry	% Homogeneous Firms
Steel and light metal construction	70.6
Machine tools	73.9
Automotive	46.1
Electronics	81.6
Chemicals	85.3

Table 2.3

The ifo Questionnaire*

	Question	Type of Answer			
1.	Judgement of the business climate	+	=	-	
2.	Production compared to the previous month	+	=	-	
3.	Judgement of finished goods inventory	+	=	-	0
4.	Demand compared to last month (prior to 80.1 this question was: New orders over last month)	+	=	-	
5.	Unfilled orders compared to last month	+	=	-	
6.	Judgement of Unfilled orders	+	=	-	
7.	Domestic sales price compared to last month	+	=	-	
8.	Expectation for production output in the next 3 months	+	=	-	
9.	Expectation for domestic sale price in the next three months	+	=	-	
10.	Expectation of export business in the next three months (prior to 69.1 this question was: judgement of unfilled foreign business)	+	=	-	0
11.	Expectations for the business development in the next six months	+	=	-	
12.	Business climate (This is the geometric average of S from questions 1 and 11)			S	

*The responses from the firm participants are: +, up or good; =, the same or unchanged; -, down or worse; 0, not applicable. In addition to the proportion of responses coded in the + category the data base includes S(saldo), which is the difference between the + and - responses plus 100. From the proportion of + and S one can calculate the proportion in each category as follows: Note that in no case can the participants respond with an "I don't know".

Let A = the proportion of + responses

B = the proportion of - responses

C = the proportion of = responses

then

$$S = A - B + 100$$

$$B = A - S + 100$$

$$100 - A - B = C$$

2.3 Qualitative to Quantitative Data

Implementing qualitative response data in a study of the real effects of inflation uncertainty poses the very special problem of converting the categorical data to meaningful cardinal data. In the modern literature the first attempt at such a conversion for West Germany was Knöbll (1974). More recent pieces include works by Carlson and Parkin (1975). Batchelor (1981,1982) and Foster and Gregory (1977).

The conversion technique assumes that the individual respondent makes a judgement about the behavior of future prices P on the basis of a subjectively held probability distribution $f_i(P,\theta_i|\Omega_i)$. The judgement is based on the information set available to the individual, Ω_i and the set of parameters θ_i. The price is reported as an expected change only if the expectation differs from the current price P_0 by more than some threshold δ_i.

Aggregating across individuals, the survey results can be viewed as a sample from an aggregate probability density function $g(P, \theta \mid \Omega)$. We must assume for this purpose that the individual distributions are independent, belong to the same family and have finite mean and variance. If we further assume that the reporting-threshold is commonly held then the aggregate distribution is as shown in Figure 3.1.

The proportion of respondents expecting a fall in P, say A, and the proportion expecting a rise in P, say B, are estimates of the true proportions in g(.|.). Given the proportions and an assumed probability density, one can calculate the abscissae with some knowledge of the threshold δ.

In the present exercise we have assumed that log price changes follow a scaled t distribution with six degrees of freedom (Praetz (1972) and Carlson (1975)). That is,

$$Y_t = \ell n[P^e(t + \tau)/P(t)] \tag{3.1}$$

has a scaled t distribution; namely,

$$t_n = \sqrt{n/(n-2)}\,(Y_t - \mu_t)/\sigma_t \tag{3.2}$$

has student's t distribution with n degrees of freedom and where μ_t and σ_t are the mean and standard deviation.

To operationalize the choice mechanism described above, we suppose that the proportion of people expecting a price increase is given by

$$\begin{aligned} \text{Pr (the price will increase)} &= \text{Pr } (Y \geqslant \delta) \\ &= P_r(\sqrt{n/(n-2)}\,(Y_t-\mu_t)/\sigma_t \geqslant \sqrt{n/(n-2)}\,(\delta-\mu_t)/\sigma_t) \\ &= P_r\,(t_n \geqslant \sqrt{n/(n-2)}\,(\delta - \mu_t)/\sigma_t) \end{aligned} \tag{3.3}$$

Similarly, the proportion expecting a price decrease is given by

$$\text{Pr (the price will decrease)} = \text{Pr } (Y \leqslant -\delta)$$

$$= \Pr_n\left(t < \sqrt{n/(n-2)}\,(-\delta\ \mu_t)/\sigma_t\right) \qquad (3.4)$$

From the surveys we otain the proportions of expected price increases, A, and expected decreases, B. Combining these with 3.3 and 3.4 gives

$$a_t = \sqrt{n/(n-2)}\,(\delta - \mu_t)/\sigma_t \qquad (3.5)$$

$$b_t = \sqrt{n/(n-2)}\,(-\delta - \mu_t)/\sigma_t \qquad (3.6)$$

where a and b are the t values which cut off A and B in the upper and lower tails. Equations 3.5 and 3.6 may be solved for the mean and standard deviation at time t. Namely,

$$\mu_t = -\delta\,\frac{a_t + b_t}{a_t - b_t} \qquad (3.7)$$

$$\sigma_t = \delta\{2\sqrt{n/(n-2)}\}/(a_t - b_t) \qquad (3.8)$$

The remaining unknown is the threshold, δ. There are several methods for its determination (see Batchelor (1981) for this discussion). What we have done is to assume that over the long run, the respondents expectations coincide with the actual price changes reported by the Statistical Office. Thus

$$\hat{\delta} = \sum_{t=1}^{T} \ln\,(P_{t+1} / P_t) / \sum_{t=1}^{T} ((a_t + b_t)/(b_t - a_t)) \qquad (3.9)$$

This method has the advantage of always returning a positive value for the standard deviation if the two data sources are consistent.[9]

To recapilate what has been accomplished; without directly observing the responses of the j=1,...,k individual agents, DPE_{ijt}, we have been able to recover the mean forecast of the agents in the ith market, $DPE_{i.t}$, and the variance of those forecasts, $VPE_{i.t}$. Note that in the text the agent subscript j has been suppressed.

In operationalizing the procedure there are two additional problems. First is the problem of empty cells, which occurred in fewer than 5% of the observations. In order to revise the empty cells we adopted a pseudo-Bayesian technique which involved averaging the response for all industries at time t and replacing the empty cell by the average. The second problem is that of equal proportions in the plus and minus tails. Here again we used the all industry averages as replacements.

Having constructed the cardinal data one can check for its coherency with the Bundesamt data. In the latter the price change series are essentially monotone increasing for all industries. The pseudo-price-change series shows a great deal of variability with both price increases and reductions. Although there are other conference papers dealing more explicitly with this issue, we offer a number of explanations: the respondents to the two surveys may be different. Participation in the Bundesamt survey is mandatory, the ifo survey is voluntary. The nature of the question differs markedly between the two surveys. The incentives to answer honestly may differ between the surveys. And finally, the ifo data may be a reflection of changes in actual prices including discounts and premia while the Bundesamt data may be list prices.

The discrepancy between our cardinal series and the Bundesamt data may also b an artifact of our initial assumptions. In constructing the cardinal series it was assumed that the underlying expectations distribution was symmetric. The asymmetry in responses may be a more accurate reflection of prices reported in the official statistics.

3. Empirical Findings

To recapitulate and set the stage for presentation of results, the role of uncertainty in the Phillips tradeoff is widely recognized. We have in our review of the literature identified three sources of uncertainty: First is that associated with incorrectly forecasting the rate of inflation in the current period; denoted by S (for surprise) in the accompanying tables. Second is the uncertainty of an ex post nature, i.e. the distribution of actual relative price changes, denoted by VP. This reflects the extent to which there are forecast errors within the ith industry. Finally, there is uncertainty within the industry about the appropriate price increase; denoted by VPE.

From the literature we have inferred the following hypotheses about the uncertainty variables: The greater the surprise, $S = DP_t - DPE_{t-1}$, the greater should be output/employment/hours of work. This is essentially the Levi-Makin interpretation of the Phillips curve.

The effect of lagged VP on output etc. is expected to be negative. Due to past errors in setting relative prices, the price system is less efficient from an informational/allocation standpoint and thus firms do not optimize corrctly. (See Blejer and Leiderman on this point.)

Finally, the effect of VPE should also be negative. VPE is a reflection of the degree to which there is a consensus among respondents in the ith industry as to the rate of inflation expected to prevail. A larger VPE is consistent with greater uncertainty about the future. If managers are risk averse, then we expect increased VPE to adversely affect output etc.

Thus, we expand the Levi-Makin specification of the Phillips curve to appear as

$$X_t = \alpha_0 + \alpha_1 t + \alpha_2 X_{t-1} + \alpha_3 (DP_t - DPE_{t-1})$$

$$+ \alpha_4 DPE_{t-1} + \alpha_5 VP_{t-1} + \alpha_6 VPE_{t-1}$$

$$+ \alpha_7 DI + \alpha_8 D2 + \alpha_9 D3 + U_t \qquad (3.1)$$

Variable definitions follow equation 1.2. Since we are not using seasonally adjusted, detrended data we have included the lagged dependent variable, the time trend and the quarterly dummy variables.

Since equation (3.1) includes a lagged dependent variable, special care must be taken to eliminate the effects of possible correlation between the lagged dependent variable and the error term. Besides, a quarterly time-series model like (3.1) is most likely to have a serially correlated error structure. One of the most practical methods of dealing with this situation is the instrumental-variable method developed by N. Liviatan (1963). He proposed using a lagged independent variable as the instrument for the lagged dependent variable (we employed all the lagged dependent variables for this purpose). This method, given certain conditions, should give us a consistent, though inefficient, estimator.

Equation (3.1) was fitted to fifteen individual industries and their aggregate for three different dependent variables (production, working hours, and employment) with and without VP[10].

Since the models with VP suffered from high correlation between VP and VPE, we present only the results without VP in tables 3.1 through 3.3.

We also examined the significance of serial correlation by the Lagrange multiplier method developed by Breusch and Pagan (1980). Thus, we first estimate equation (3.1) without VP by OLS and then re-estimate it with the first four lagged OLS residuals as additional variables (namely, $\hat{u}_{t-1}$, $\hat{u}_{t-2}$, $\hat{u}_{t-3}$, and $\hat{u}_{t-4}$). Then F values for these û's are calculated in order to test the statistical significance of these serial correlations. The results are given in the last column of tables 3.1 through 3.3. They show that there are in all cases, except for two, statistically significant serial correlatons which may be either AR or MA or a mixture of both(Even in these two cases the second order term ($\hat{u}_{t-2}$) is statistically significant).

The coefficient on the "surprise" variable was on the whole positive although not always significant. The industries for which it is negative are worth noting. The stone and earth industry has undergone enormous reorganization since the war under the aegis of government intervention. The same is true for the steel industry, in addition to the excess capacity induced European recession in steel of the last 15 years. And, of course, the mineral oil industry has experienced drastic disturbances. The results for non-ferrous metals are not readily explained.

The coefficient on the variance of relative price changes VPE was expected to be negative. For two labor dependent variables the coefficient tends to be negative. In particular the working hour has negative coefficients for all but two cases. This seems to correspond to the fact that the response of working hours to business fluctuations is more flexible than the response of employment. However, the signs of coefficients in the production equation have no clear direction.

The variable DPE is anticipated inflation and is constructed from the Ifo surveys. The parameter estimates for this variable are sometimes significantly positive, sometimes significantly negative, and most often non-significant. This finding is weakly consistent with the Natural Rate Hypothesis and the preponderance of U.S. results. However, it is worth noting that in a similar study of West Germany using an AR process on actual price changes to construct DPE the Natural Rate Hypothesis was rejected (Buck and Gahlen, 1984, Economic Letters).

These results must be interpreted very carefully. For one thing, alternative estimation methods should be tried because the parameter estimates seem to be very sensitive to the choice of estimation method. Further, as we mentioned previously, there may be statistical inconsistencies between the Ifo data and the Statistisches Bundesamt data. Besides, the Statistisches Bundesamt data have undergone a few important statistical revisions, which may require more careful treatment of the data. Additional research will allow us to examine the time domain more carefully. That is, model statistical breaks at, for example, the oil price shock.

Other studies of inflation and uncertainty lead us to suspect a high degree of collinearity between DPE, S, VP and VPE. We could correct this problem with a Gram-Schmidt orthogonalization, thereby sorting out independent effects. More conventionally, a joint F-test would allow us to test for the joint significance of these variables.

In order to examine the real effects of price uncertainty more realistically, it is probably necessary to include materials' prices, wages, inventories, and capacity utilization as independent variables.

4. Conclusions

In this paper we have argued that there is an important role for uncertainty in structural models of the Phillips curve. Further, we assert that this relationship is valid at the industry level.

We have brought a new data source to bear on the question of uncertainty and the Phillips curve. This data consists of qualitative response survey conducted by the ifo Institute.

Following the work of Carlson and Parkin, among others, we have constructed cardinal series for actual and expected price changes. The actual relative price change variance and the variance of expectations were then constructed as measures of uncertainty.

Our results show that the "surprise" has positive real effects, as the theory predicts. However, the real effects of price uncertainty as measured by the variance of expected price changes (VPE) were weak and ambiguous except in the case of the working hour equation.

Footnotes

1. Mitchell and Taylor (1982) also criticize this point.
2. Fischer (1982a) uses the Michigan survey data for the same purpose.
3. It is quite another question if Klein's measure is one of uncertainty. On this point see Ibrahim and Williams (1978).
4. It would be useful to further document the confusion. Klein's paper is above all a font of issues. For example: How much unanticipated price change is expected.
5. Compare this with Taylor (1981) also.
6. Froyen and Waud (1980) make use of Cukierman's (1979) specification of the Lucas model. Theirs is, however, only a cross country study.
7. This section is based on a series of articles in Wirtschaft and Statistik. Complete references are given in the Bibliography.
8. Paid hours of work also includes vacation and sick time. In seasonally adjusted data this should not introduce undue bias in our results.
9. Of the fifteen industries, only Stone and Earth returned a negative value.
10. The total of industry variables are computed from the pooled raw data rather than as simple weighted averages of the observations for the individual industries.

Bibliography

Alberro, J. (1981)
"The Lucas Hypothesis on the Phillips Curve: Further International Evidence", Journal of Monetary Economics, Vol. 7, pp. 239-250.

Batchelor, R.A. (1981)
"Aggregate Expectations Under the Stable Laws", Journal of Econometrics, Vol. 16, pp. 199-210.

Batchelor, R.A. (1982)
"Expectations, Output and Inflation", European Economic Review, Vol. 17, pp. 1-25.

Batra, R. and Ullah, A. (1974)
"Competitive Firm and the Theory of Input Demand under Price Uncertainty", Journal of Political Economy, Vol. 82, pp. 537-549.

Balk, B.M. (1978)
"Inflation and its Variability: Some Comments and the Dutch Case", Economics Letters, Vol. 1, pp. 357-360.

Blejer, M.I. and Leiderman, L. (1980)
"On the Real Effects of Inflation and Relative Price Variability: Some Empirical Evidence", Review of Economics and Statistics, Vol. 62, pp. 539-544.

Blejer, M.I. and Leiderman, L. (1982)
"Relative Price Variability and Output-Inflation Tradeoffs in an Open Economy", Weltwirtschaftliches Archiv, Vol. 118, No. 4, pp. 640-649.

Bordo, M.D. (1980)
"The Effects of Monetary Change on Relative Commodity Prices and the Role of Long Term Contracts", Journal of Political Economy, Vol. 88, No. 6, pp. 1088-1109.

Buck, A., Gahlen, B. (1983)
"Relative Preise, Inflation und gesamtwirtschaftliche Aktivität", G. Bombach, B. Gahlen, A.E. Ott (editors), Makroökonomik heute - Gemeinsamkeiten und Gegensätze. Schriftenreihe des Wirtschaftswissenschaftlichen Seminars Ottobeuren. Tübingen.

Breusch, T.S. and A.R. Pagan (1980)
"The Lagrange Multiplier Test and Its Applications to Model Specifications in Econometrics", Review of Economic Studies, Vol. 47, pp. 239-253.

Carlson, J.A. (1977)
"A Study of Price Forecasts", Annals of Economic and Social Measurement. Vol. 6, No. 1, pp. 27-56.

Carlson, J. and M. Parkin (1975)
"Inflation Expectations", _Economica_, Vol. 42, No. 166, May, pp. 123-135.

Carlson, J.A. (1975)
"Are Price Expectations Normally Distributed", _Journal of the American Statistical Association_, Vol. 70, No. 352, December, pp. 749-754.

Clements, K.W. and Nguyen, P. (1980)
"Inflation and Relative Prices: The Australian Experience", Reserve Bank of Australia, Discussion Paper 8007.

Cukierman, A. (1979)
"The Relationship between Relative Prices and the General Price Level: A Suggested Interpretation", _American Economic Review_, Vol. 69, No. 3, pp. 444-447.

Cukierman, A. (1982)
"Relative Price Variability, Inflation and the Allocative Efficiency of the Price System", _Journal of Monetary Economics_, Vol. 9, No. 2, pp. 131-162.

Cukierman, A. and Wachtel, P. (1979)
"Differential Inflationary Expectations and the Variability of the Rate Inflation", _American Economic Review_, Vol. 69, No. 4, pp. 595-609.

Cukierman, A. and Wachtel, P. (1982a)
"Inflationary Expectations: Reply and Further Thoughts on Inflation Uncertainty", _American Economic Review_, Vol. 72, No. 3, pp. 508-513.

Cukierman, A. and Wachtel, P. (1982b)
"Relative Price Variability and Nonuniform Inflationary Expectations", _Journal of Political Economy_, Vol. 90, No. 1, pp. 146-155.

Fischer, St. (1981a)
"Relative Shocks, Relative Price Variability, and Inflation", _Brookings Papers on Economic Activity_, No. 2, pp. 381-431.

Fischer, St. (1981b)
"Towards an Understanding of the Costs of Inflation: II", _Carnegie Rochester Conference Series on Public Policy_, ed. K. Brunner, A. Meltzer, Amsterdam, Vol. 15, No. 1, pp.5-42.

Fischer, St. (1982a)
"Relative Price Variability and Inflation in the United States and Germany", _European Economic Review_, Vol. 18, pp. 171-196.

Fischer, St. (1982b)
"Adapting to Inflation in the United States Economy", R.E. Hall (editor), _Inflation, Causes and Effects_, National Bureau of Economic Research, New York.

Foster, J. and Gregory, M. (1977)
"Inflation Expectations: The Use of Qualitative Survey Data", Applied Economics, Vol. 9, pp. 319-329.

Friedman, M. (1977)
"Nobel Lecture: Inflation and Unemployment", Journal of Political Economy, Vol. 85, pp. 451-472.

Froyen, R.T. and Waud, R.N. (1980)
"International Evidence on Output Inflation Tradeoffs", American Economic Review, Vol. 70, No. 3, pp. 409-421.

Fuhr, M. (1980)
"Kartei im produzierenden Gewerbe als Aufbereitungsinstrument und Untersuchungsobjekt", Wirtschaft und Statistik, No. 11, pp. 760-770.

Fuerst, G. (1963)
"Der deutsche Beitrag zum Weltindustriezensus 1963", "Wirtschaft und Statistik", No. 5, pp. 255-259.

Glejser, H. (1965)
"Inflation, Productivity, and Relative Prices - A Statistical Study", Review of Economics and Statistics, Vol. 47, No. 1, pp. 76-80.

Gordon, R.J. (1971)
"Steady Anticipated Inflation: Mirage or Oasis?", Brookings Papers on Economic Activity, Vol. 2, pp. 499-510.

Graham, F.D. (1930)
"Exchange Prices and Production in Hyper-Inflation: Germany 1920-23", Princeton, N.J.: Princeton University Press.

Guckes, S. (1979)
"Zur Neuberechnung der Preisindizes auf Basis 1976", Wirtschaft und Statistik, No. 7, pp. 471-474.

Hercowitz, Z. (1981)
"Money and the Dispersion of Relative Prices", Journal of Political Economy, Vol. 89, No. 2, pp. 328-356.

Ibrahim, I.B. and Williams, R.B. (1978)
"Price Unpredictability and Monetary Standards: A Comment on Klein's Measure of Price Uncertainty", Economic Inquiry, Vol.16, No. 3, pp. 431-37.

Jaffee, D. and Kleiman, E. (1977)
"The Welfare Implications of Uneven Inflation", E. Lundberg (ed.), Inflation, Theory and Anti-Inflation Policy, pp. 285-307.

Katsimbris, G.M. and Miller, S.M. (1982)
"The Relation between the Rate and Variability of Inflation: Further Comments", Kyklos, Vol. 35, pp. 456-467.

Klein, B. (1975)
"Our New Monetary Standard: The Measurement and Effects of Price Uncertainty, 1800-1973", Economic Inquiry, Vol. 13, pp. 461-483.

Knöbl, A. (1974)
"Price Expectation and Actual Price Behavior in Germany", IMF Staff Papers, Vol. 21, No. 1, March, pp. 83-100.

Levi, M.D. and Makin, J.H. (1980)
"Inflation Uncertainty and the Phillips Curve: Some Empirical Evidence", American Economic Review, Vol. 70, pp. 1022-1027.

Liviatan, N. (1963)
"Consistent Estimation of Distributed Lags", International Economic Review, Vol. 4, pp. 44-52.

Logue, D.E. and Willett, T.D. (1976)
"A Note on the Relation Between the Rate and Variability of Inflation", Economica, Vol. 43, No. 170, pp. 151-158.

Mills, F.C. (1927)
"The Behavior of Prices", National Bureau of Ecnomic Research, pp. 251-286.

Mitchell, D.W. and Taylor, H.E. (1982)
"Inflationary Expectations: Comments", American Economic Review, Vol. 72, pp. 502-508.

Mullineaux, D.J. (1980)
"Unemployment, Industrial Production, and Inflation Uncertainty in the United States", The Review of Economics and Statistics, Vol. 62, pp. 163-169.

Okun, A.M. (1971)
"The Mirage of Steady (anticipated) Inflation", Brookings Papers on Economic Activity, No. 2, pp. 485-498.

Parks, R.W. (1978)
"Inflation and Relative Price Variability", Journal of Political Economy, Vol. 86, No. 1, pp. 79-95.

Potkowik, G. (1980)
"Revision der Systematik der Wirtschaftszweige", Wirtschaft und Statistik, No. 7, pp. 437-445.

Praetz, P.D. (1972)
"The Distribution of Share Price Changes", Journal of Business, Vol. 45, No. 1, January, pp. 49-55.

Sandmo, A. (1971)
"On the Theory of the Competitive Firm Under Price Uncertainty", American Economic Review, Vol. 61, pp. 65-74.

Sobotschinski, A. (1976)
"Die Neuordnung der Statistik des produzierenden Gewerbes", Wirtschaft und Statistik, No. 7, pp. 405-412.

Suesser, H.G. (1970)
"Untersuchung zur Homogenität und Heterogenität der Industrieunternehmen", Wirtschaft und Statistik, No. 10, pp. 497-504.

Taylor, J.B. (1981)
"On the Relation Between the Variability of Inflation and the Average Inflation Rate", (ed.) K. Brunner, A.H. Meltzer, Series on Public Policy, Vol. 15, pp. 57-86.

Vining, D.R. and Elwertowski, T.C. (1976)
"The Relationship between Relative Prices and the General Price Level", American Economic Review, Vol. 66, No. 4, pp. 699-708.

Figure 3.1

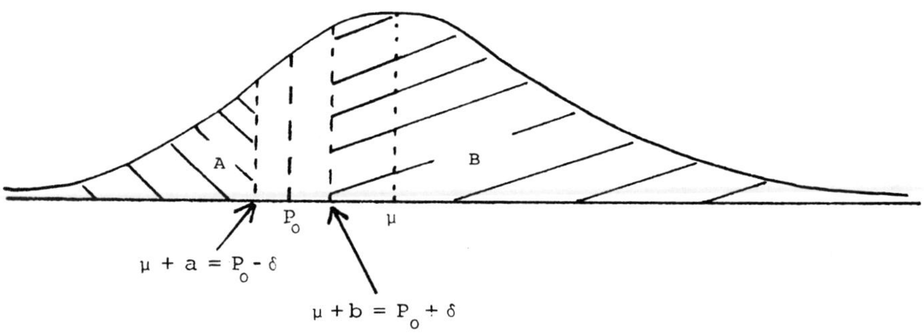

Table 3.1

Production Equation : Instrumental-Variable Method (t-ratios in parentheses)

	N. of obs.	CONSTANT	TIME	Q(t-1)	S	DPE	VPE	D1	D2	D3	F-value
1. Stone & Earth	73	.120 (.040)	.000 (.227)	.934 (1.857)	.561 (-2.843)	-4.643 (-2.443)	1.364 (.008)	.207 (1.290)	.589 (2.979)	.348 (8.969)	4.938
2. Non-Ferrous Metals	65	1.637 (3.107)	.003 (2.918)	.644 (5.474)	-.102 (-3.755)	.305 (.373)	-72.940 (-.598)	-.012 (-1.053)	-.035 (-3.352)	-.032 (-3.225)	5.299
3. Mineral Oil	65	-1.512 (-.417)	-.002 (-.663)	1.251 (2.164)	.008 (.009)	-2.225 (-.543)	1080.661 (.462)	-.024 (-.540)	-.016 (-.345)	-.025 (-.578)	100.398
4. Chemicals	65	2.491 (3.786)	.001 (3.304)	.634 (6.632)	5.567 (4.130)	6.614 (3.062)	3023.155 (1.585)	-.008 (-.518)	.028 (2.785)	.012 (1.207)	3.047
5. Machine Tools	73	2.570 (3.727)	.001 (3.620)	.622 (6.190)	5.357 (3.961)	6.092 (2.879)	2941.732 (1.611)	.000 (.026)	.035 (3.518)	.018 (1.860)	6.040
6. Automobiles	73	2.115 (1.219)	.003 (1.069)	.705 (2.748)	1.778 (.888)	3.939 (.974)	-2096.380 (-1.124)	-.056 (-1.985)	-.162 (-5.270)	-.116 (-6.715)	6.268
7. Steel and Light Metals	73	.696 (1.235)	.000 (.332)	.860 (7.815)	-.818 (-3.059)	-1.625 (-1.020)	50.574 (.110)	-.012 (-.822)	.061 (3.924)	.063 (5.386)	3.511
8. Electronics	73	1.938 (1.600)	.003 (1.522)	.727 (4.136)	1.827 (2.391)	-.023 (-.010)	136.979 (.127)	-.035 (-1.537)	-.036 (-2.391)	-.015 (-1.154)	8.384
9. Precision Machinery & Optics	73	3.748 (1.372)	.001 (.939)	.302 (.585)	6.302 (1.534)	5.579 (.840)	-522.328 (-.187)	-.059 (-1.771)	-.062 (-2.592)	-.018 (-.675)	13.296
10. Ceramics	73	2.229 (1.808)	.000 (1.353)	.424 (1.313)	3.615 (3.836)	2.589 (1.073)	97.440 (.106)	-.005 (-.349)	-.031 (-2.293)	-.026 (-2.122)	5.523
11. Textiles	73	.116 (.086)	-.000 (-.582)	.999 (4.106)	1.164 (2.948)	-1.492 (-.839)	308.082 (.394)	-.091 (-4.778)	-.188 (-8.175)	-.094 (-6.586)	8.573
12. Clothing	73	1.893 (1.171)	-.002 (-1.339)	.673 (2.255)	5.164 (2.122)	2.933 (.660)	-2651.099 (-1.773)	-.075 (-4.252)	-.117 (-6.671)	-.086 (-4.559)	3.340
13. Paper Products	73	-1.835 (-.847)	-.003 (-.977)	1.392 (3.078)	1.274 (.966)	-5.601 (-1.793)	3853.103 (1.726)	-.063 (-3.010)	-.067 (-3.943)	-.009 (-.481)	6.847
14. Wood Products	73	3.162 (1.800)	.004 (1.649)	.460 (1.525)	3.889 (1.676)	9.889 (1.428)	-3972.489 (-.814)	-.056 (-1.830)	-.029 (-1.136)	.005 (.234)	16.196
15. Printing	73	.946 (.648)	.001 (.697)	.831 (3.074)	.921 (1.234)	-1.041 (-.577)	-1582.524 (-1.915)	-.009 (-.993)	-.012 (-.867)	-.010 (-.963)	2.479
16. TOTAL	73	1.962 (1.102)	.002 (1.044)	.780 (3.826)	1.723 (2.654)	-.025 (-.011)	365.573 (.350)	-.010 (-.613)	-.021 (-2.054)	-.014 (-1.328)	7.312

The F-value for the Lagrange Multiplier test of serial correlation was calculated from OLS estimates with and without four lagged OLS residuals ($\hat{u}_{t-1}$, $\hat{u}_{t-2}$, $\hat{u}_{t-3}$, $\hat{u}_{t-4}$). Its distribution is asymptotically F(4,58) (F(4,50) for industry 2,3, and 4) under the null hypothesis that the coefficients for the residuals are all zero.

Table 3.2

Employment Equation : Instrumental-Variable Method (t-ratios in parentheses)

	N. of obs.	CONSTANT	TIME	E(t-1)	S	DPE	VPE	D1	D2	D3	F-value
1. Stone & Earth	73	-1.136 (-.633)	.001 (.536)	1.087 (7.537)	.001 (.017)	.577 (.864)	-166.559 (-1.684)	.041 (2.887)	.115 (6.689)	.072 (7.446)	3.853
2. Non-Ferrous Metals	66	.940 (2.275)	-.000 (-2.600)	.916 (24.832)	-.031 (-3.169)	.441 (1.806)	-62.503 (-1.440)	-.004 (-.971)	.005 (1.422)	.006 (1.620)	11.462
3. Mineral Oil	66	1.931 (3.284)	-.000 (-1.049)	.801 (13.309)	.134 (.726)	-.337 (-.563)	440.216 (1.381)	.000 (.037)	-.002 (-.232)	-.003 (-.345)	16.660
4. Chemicals	66	1.674 (2.626)	-.001 (-2.236)	.877 (18.789)	2.365 (4.026)	.259 (.384)	479.411 (.577)	-.012 (-2.235)	.002 (.557)	.008 (2.131)	13.032
5. Machine Tools	73	-.809 (-.555)	.000 (.554)	1.060 (9.914)	1.931 (3.019)	-.913 (-1.010)	-910.105 (-.923)	-.002 (-.250)	.005 (1.107)	.006 (1.456)	13.209
6. Automobiles	73	1.791 (1.284)	.000 (.802)	.863 (8.046)	.814 (1.050)	2.129 (1.989)	-127.766 (-.169)	-.010 (-1.196)	-.004 (-.475)	.001 (.196)	19.302
7. Steel and Light Metals	73	-1.981 (-.948)	.001 (1.012)	1.161 (6.813)	-.472 (-1.846)	-2.065 (-1.366)	-286.866 (-.563)	-.011 (-.767)	.017 (1.261)	.024 (2.074)	18.245
8. Electronics	73	1.122 (1.401)	-.000 (-1.489)	.918 (15.507)	1.137 (4.036)	-.295 (-.369)	-677.306 (-1.646)	-.004 (-.462)	.009 (1.404)	.007 (1.405)	19.403
9. Precision Machinery & Optics	73	-1.303 (-.494)	.001 (.419)	1.109 (5.034)	.640 (.402)	-.962 (-.544)	-522.025 (-.385)	-.006 (-.331)	.003 (.265)	.011 (1.082)	49.660
10. Ceramics	73	1.463 (1.257)	-.001 (-1.330)	.869 (8.382)	.790 (2.158)	.960 (1.493)	131.332 (.340)	-.008 (-1.313)	.003 (.516)	.010 (2.055)	9.691
11. Textiles	73	1.321 (1.640)	-.002 (-1.907)	.899 (14.624)	.213 (2.033)	.616 (1.828)	60.654 (.316)	-.007 (-1.539)	-.003 (-.945)	-.000 (-.041)	71.396
12. Clothing	73	3.356 (1.211)	-.003 (-1.345)	.740 (3.412)	2.772 (3.645)	2.308 (.998)	-400.680 (-.399)	-.021 (-3.166)	-.016 (-2.784)	-.017 (-2.479)	12.736
13. Paper Products	73	3.018 (2.053)	-.001 (-2.215)	.741 (5.867)	1.096 (2.823)	.579 (.841)	206.227 (.256)	-.003 (-.545)	.010 (1.736)	.008 (1.477)	15.534
14. Wood Products	73	-3.447 (-.808)	.001 (.741)	1.281 (3.685)	2.840 (1.905)	-4.572 (-.963)	-573.412 (-.295)	.013 (.660)	.018 (1.274)	.014 (1.434)	21.310
15. Printing	73	1.424 (1.497)	-.001 (-1.596)	.883 (11.270)	.155 (.538)	.810 (1.492)	-189.680 (-.342)	-.004 (-.865)	.003 (.373)	.007 (1.423)	11.433
16. TOTAL	73	.806 (.654)	-.000 (-.914)	.948 (11.742)	.677 (2.759)	.309 (.524)	-176.897 (-.404)	-.005 (-.853)	.006 (1.335)	.009 (2.171)	30.247

The F-value for the Lagrange Multiplier test of serial correlation was calculated from OLS estimates with and without four lagged OLS residuals ($\hat{u}_{t-q}$, $\hat{u}_{t-2}$, $\hat{u}_{t-3}$, $\hat{u}_{t-4}$). Its distribution is asymptotically F(4,58) (F(4,50) for industry 2,3, and 4) under the null hypothesis that the coefficients for the residuals are all zero.

Table 3.3

Working Hours Equation : Instrumental-Variable Method (t-ratios in parentheses)

	N. of obs.	CONSTANT	TIME	H(t-1)	S	DPE	VPE	D1	D2	D3	F-value*
1. Stone & Earth	73	.385 (.480)	-.000 (-.449)	.893 (4.355)	-.005 (-.127)	.049 (.213)	-64.430 (-1.679)	.029 (3.435)	.062 (7.065)	.034 (10.809)	216.645
2. Non-Ferrous Metals	66	1.012 (4.506)	-.000 (-2.628)	.733 (12.411)	-.028 (-3.673)	-.075 (-.403)	-70.692 (-2.110)	.003 (.841)	.009 (3.093)	.005 (1.693)	13.851
3. Mineral Oil	66	.433 (1.954)	-.000 (-.885)	.884 (15.085)	-.006 (-.140)	-.150 (-1.092)	-5.736 (-.080)	.003 (1.581)	.010 (4.721)	.006 (2.756)	5.911
4. Chemicals	66	.809 (3.212)	-.000 (-2.078)	.786 (11.838)	1.788 (3.679)	-.103 (-.213)	-429.283 (-.682)	.005 (1.300)	.018 (5.363)	.009 (3.031)	18.390
5. Machine Tools	73	.343 (.654)	-.000 (-.506)	.908 (6.558)	1.287 (2.331)	-.328 (-.576)	-366.072 (-.645)	.007 (1.542)	.017 (5.300)	.009 (2.953)	11.335
6. Automobiles	73	6.290 (.895)	-.002 (-.873)	-.672 (-.361)	.307 (.157)	5.268 (.797)	-1509.615 (-.491)	-.013 (-.441)	-.004 (-.118)	.007 (.350)	10.485
7. Steel and Light Metals	73	.885 (2.424)	-.000 (-2.139)	.767 (8.046)	-.169 (-3.395)	-.293 (-1.091)	-34.872 (-.477)	.004 (1.315)	.021 (7.126)	.015 (6.722)	5.444
8. Electronics	73	1.729 (2.475)	-.000 (-2.158)	.540 (2.917)	.369 (2.040)	.080 (.193)	-704.176 (-1.819)	.008 (1.740)	.013 (3.953)	.007 (2.440)	9.720
9. Precision Machinery & Optics	73	1.630 (1.511)	-.000 (-1.459)	.563 (1.955)	.758 (1.548)	.339 (.618)	-310.642 (-.763)	.002 (.352)	.009 (2.459)	.006 (2.098)	11.228
10. Ceramics	73	1.161 (1.934)	-.000 (-1.840)	.692 (4.369)	.673 (1.770)	.071 (.247)	-126.102 (-.427)	.005 (1.061)	.011 (2.478)	.005 (1.347)	8.552
11. Textiles	73	1.768 (2.436)	-.000 (-2.636)	.529 (2.736)	.053 (.617)	.611 (1.934)	-82.325 (-.940)	-.000 (-.131)	.002 (.793)	.001 (.521)	10.205
12. Clothing	73	-2.594 (-.803)	.001 (.737)	1.700 (1.952)	1.107 (1.852)	-2.183 (-1.161)	604.356 (.784)	.003 (.435)	.014 (1.929)	.002 (.391)	4.628
13. Paper Products	73	.866 (.889)	-.000 (-.684)	.770 (2.979)	.467 (3.282)	-.286 (-.584)	130.242 (.436)	.001 (.493)	.005 (2.544)	.002 (.884)	8.647
14. Wood Products	73	.098 (.127)	-.000 (-.032)	.973 (4.781)	1.100 (2.644)	-.973 (-2.033)	-22.130 (-.028)	.008 (2.681)	.016 (5.421)	.008 (3.276)	2.438
15. Printing	73	.065 (.099)	.000 (.251)	.982 (5.605)	.165 (1.265)	-.442 (-2.110)	-97.512 (-.599)	.004 (2.546)	.007 (3.612)	.000 (.108)	2.864
16. TOTAL	73	1.512 (.717)	-.000 (-.687)	.600 (1.080)	.340 (1.543)	.202 (.282)	-366.925 (-1.235)	.005 (.688)	.014 (1.962)	.008 (2.795)	10.988

* The F-value for the Lagrange Multiplier test of serial correlation was calculated from OLS estimates with and without four lagged OLS residuals ($\hat{u}_{t-1}$, $\hat{u}_{t-2}$, $\hat{u}_{t-3}$, $\hat{u}_{t-4}$). Its distribution is asymptotically F(4,58) (F(4,50) for industry 2,3, and 4) under the null hypothesis that the coefficients for the residuals are all zero.

Economic Rational Expectations and their Influence on Production and Inventory Decisions

K. Aiginger
Österreichisches Institut
für Wirtschaftsforschung
Vienna

1. Aim of the paper

This paper intends to bridge the gap between reported expectations (anticipations, forecasts) and the growing field of Microeconomic Theory of Uncertainty. Reported expectations are interpreted not as (conditional) expected values - as they are in mainstream economic literature and specifically in the Rational Expectations Hypothesis, but as optimal production or investment strategies resulting from maximizing an objective function.

Using such a concept it is easy to explain one of the most striking features of reported expectations, namely their persistent downward bias over a long period of time.

We survey the existing literature on the microeconomic theory of the firm, on inventory decisions and on investment decisions under uncertainty, focussing on the question whether the optimal production (investment, inventory) decision under uncertainty should be the same as under certainty and how it relates to the mathematically expected demand. Either deviation (optimal production plan smaller than under certainty or than expected demand) opens the possibility that "expected" and "realized" production will differ even in the long run.

In practice firms will not use the explizit maximization process derived in the models of chapter 3, but may use the rule of thumb (consistent with some of the models) that losses of the same size but different sign are judged differently (asymmetric losses, see chapter 4).

In chapter 5 empirical material is presented to determine which of the models are more likely to explain actual behavior, those which predict a downward bias of production and investment decision under uncertainty 1), those which predict neutrality or those which predict higher values for the decision variable 2).

2. The Interpretation of Reported Expectations as Optimal Decisions

2.1 Expected Values versus Loss Evaluating Decisions

In modern economics the concept of expectations is used nearly without exception in the sense of the mathematical expected value3). Consequences of these expectations or of errors in expectations should not be used in the formation of the expected value (the expected value is independent of tastes and beliefs). This concept reached its climax of popularity with the Rational Expectation Hypothesis by Muth (1961) and its extensive use in macroeconomic policy (for quite different papers in this field see Shiller 1978 or Batchelor and Sheriff 1980). Expectations there are considered as conditional expected value based on all available information (implying that expectations and realizations should differ only by a hopefully small, irreducable error term with zero expected mean).

We argue that in most cases where people form expectations, in most cases where expectations are relevant and, last not least, in most cases where people are asked to report their expectations there are consequences of expectations (of errors) which should be considered in the formation of the expectations. This incorporation of errors becomes most relevant if the consequences of errors are different for different signs of the error (asymmetric losses or gains).

These "loss evaluating" procedure is well known in decision theory, but its result is termed "action" or "decision" (in contrast to expectations). The literature on forecasting procedures (see HEY 1974) also posits that forecasts should in general consider the consequences of forecast errors and specificetly that unbiased forecasts (in the sense of zero mean error) are optimal only under symmetric and quadratic losses of forecast errors.

To my knowledge it has never been investigated whether and under what circumstances rationally formed sales anticipations, inflation forecasts and macroeconomic forecasts could (indeed should) be biased. The nearest related field to this problems seems to be uncertainty theory of the firm (and therefor we will try to exploit this field). This theory does not aim at explaining expectations and their deviation from realizations, but rather optimal values for a "decision variable" in a world of uncertainty about a "random variable".

Incorporating losses (or profits) into a concept for the formation of expectations is not an innocent concept. For the sake of keeping concepts apart we should perhaps reserve the term "expectation" for "pure" expectations in the sense of the mathematically expected value and refer to the loss (and profit) evaluating decisions as "actions". But it is very improbable that many agents use a two stage procedure forming a "pure" expectation first and then evaluate consequences to arrive at the optimal action, though this procedure may be argued to be optimal. Above all it is unlikely that people asked for their sales or inflation "expectations" do report their "pure" expectations. We want to label these reported expectations (plans, actions) as "economically rational expectations"4).

2.2 General Conditions for "Biased Expectations"

In this chapter we investigate under which general conditions the optimal value of a decision variable under uncertainty will be lower (larger) than under certainty.

We assume a utility function (1) in which utility U depends on the variable Z (which can be understood as profits): Z itself depends on two variables X and Y, (which usually are quantity produced and price). In the world of certainty X_0 is known and there exists an optimal solution Y* for the decision variable Y, under which profits are maximized (the second order condition is assumed to hold).

$$(1) \quad U\left[Z\,(X_0,\ Y)\right] \rightarrow \text{Max } Y^* \quad \text{(certainty maximum)}$$

Under uncertainty we assume maximization of expected utility (Neumann-Morgenstern Utility Maximization). Uncertainty exists about the variable X for which a probability density function f(x) is known, its expected value is assumed to be the same as the fixed value X under certainty (mean preserving introduction of risk).

$$(2) \quad E\,U\left[Z\,(X,Y)\right] \rightarrow \text{Max } \hat{Y} \quad \text{(uncertainty maximum)}$$

The optimal value of the decision variable labelled Y under uncertainty can be shown to be smaller (equal, larger) than the optimal value under certainty Y*, if U_{YXX} is smaller (equal or larger) than zero 5). (Rothschild, Stiglitz 1971, Diamand, Stiglitz 1974 etc.).

$$(3) \quad \hat{Y} \lesseqgtr Y^* \qquad \text{if} \quad U_{YXX} \lesseqgtr 0$$

Unfortunately this condition is not very useful, since U_{YXX} proves for most problems to be neither unambiguously positive nor negative. (see Hey 1981 or Kraus 1979). Either of following assumptions has to be made, the first of which is predominant in the literature, the second of which we will follow in this paper.

Assumption A: Linear Technology ... $Z_{XX} = 0$

$$d\,Y^* / dX > 0$$

$$(4) \quad U_{ZZ} \lesseqgtr 0 \rightarrow \hat{Y} \lesseqgtr Y^*$$

The first simplification refers to the relation between profits (the argument of the utility function) and the variable in which uncertainty exists. Z is assumed to be linear in X, that means that profit depends on X, but its expected value does not change with mean preserving variations of X. In this case it follows, that the relation between U and Z decides about the result. In case of risk aversion ($U_{ZZ}<0$) and a linear technology the optimal y. under uncertainty is unambigously smaller than that under certainty (Y*).

An alternative simplification is to assume risk neutrality. In this case the optimal $\hat{Y}$ is biassed downward if Z_{YXX} is negative 6).

Assumption 8: Linear Utility Function ... $U_{ZZ} = 0$

$$(5) \quad \text{If } Z_Y \text{ is } \begin{Bmatrix} \text{concave} \\ \text{linear} \\ \text{convex} \end{Bmatrix} \text{ in } X \Rightarrow \hat{Y} \lesseqgtr Y^*$$

Since the utility function is assumed to be linear, the bias comes from the relation between Z,X andY. Economically speaking the concavity of Z_Y in X stems from cost or demand conditions. Therefore we could label it as "economic" or "technological concavity".

In the economic literature the case of biased action in the case of risk aversion (or risk loving) is well known. But it seems that its impact on economic thinking is smaller, since people´s attitudes toward risk are unknown. Furthermore, there are arguments that firms should behave as if they were risk neutral 7), that repeating decisions can be based on the assumtion of risk neutrality and that entrepreneurs should be at least less risk averse (if not risk loving) than consumers.

Technological concavity 8) on the other hand can be measured objectively, prevails even under infinite repetitions and does not depend on the tastes of the entrepreneurs. We therefor want to focus on this point. Of course, technological concavity is not unknown in literature too, but it is characteristic that Lippman and McCall (1982, p212) in an article on the economics of uncertainty have to recall that "though in many circumstances, risk aversion is a fact ..., much economic behavior is a direct consequence of uncertainty and is independent of risk aversion".

In addition to technological concavity and risk aversion, there is another channel trough which the uncertainty obtains influence on the optimal decision. We want to give up the assumption, that the ex post control (e.g. the price) does change fast enough to guarantee equilibria. In disequilibria models there are ex post either unsold goods or unsatisfied demand, ex ante we have to calculate the costs for both of them (potentially unsold production plus potentially unsatisified demand). Uncertainty therefor unambigously increases expected cost and we have to equate expected marginal revenues and the sum of expected marginal cost of production and marginal cost of uncertainty. This reduces the optimal production under uncertainty (given convex costs under certainty). We want to label the extra costs of uncertainty as "marginal cost of uncertainty" (see chapter 3.2.1.2).

Finally decisions under uncertainty will differ from optimal decisions under certainty if "fine tuning" of the ex ante variable is feasible after the realization of the uncertainty variable has become known. This ex post flexibility will lead to a downward bias, if it is easier (less costly) to revise the preliminary decision in the upward direction (see chapter 3.5).

Technological concavity in equilibrium models, marginal cost of uncertainty in disequilibrium models and asymmetries in ex post flexibility are three channels through which uncertainty can alter decisions even in a world of risk neutrality.

3. Survey on Optimal Biases in Models of Expected Profit Maximization

3.1. Contents and Limitations

In this chapter we present several models each of which focus on one aspect of uncertainty. In most models there exists one decision and one random variable, together with very restrictive assumptions about the working of the economy. In the first group of models the crucial simplification is that the goods are perishable (one period models), in the largest part of the second group prices are assumed to be constant and the probability density function is assumed to remain the same for each period (i.i.d.-assumption), the third group deals with heterogeneous models about the influence of uncertainty on the factor input.

Here we do not present rigorous mathematical derivations of the results (most of the models are well known in literature), but want to explain which economic factor explains the bias (or the absence of the bias). In those models were the bias depends on the exact value of a parameter, we want to get a feeling about its critical magnitudes.

3.2. Microceconomic Theory of the Firm

3.2.1. Competition

3.2.1.1 Price Uncertainty

From the puristic point of view there exists only one model of the competitive firm. The firm must choose its optimal production (q takes the role of Y) in an environement of price uncertainy (p takes the role of X). The firm maximizes expected profit (equation 6) by equating marginal costs and expected price. Since uncertainty is assumed to be introduced in a mean-preserving way ($E\ p = p_o$, the known price under certainty), it does not change the optimal production ($q^*=\hat{q}$) The statistical explanation is the Z is linear in X, the economic background is that the actual prices change realized profits but not expected ones and the production decision can do nothing to reduce uncertainty.

$$(6) \qquad E\pi = \int_0^\infty \left\{ \left[p\, q - c(q) \right] \quad f(p)\, dp \right\}$$

$$(7) \qquad E\, p = c'(q)$$

$$(8) \qquad q^* = \hat{q}$$

3.2.1.2 Demand Uncertainty

In the second model the firm chooses again its optimal production (q=Y) but is uncertain about demand (x=X). This model contradicts that feature of the competitive model which assumes that any amount produced can be sold at the market price and is considered to be logically incompatible by some authors (z.B. Hey 1979). However, price or market share rigidities may lead to a situation where even in case of many producers and homogeneous goods there are unsold goods and backlogged orders. This can happen if the production decision fixes the market share of each producer and prices are fixed at least for one period so that markets do not clear. Then the competitive firm maximizes its

$$(9) \qquad E\pi = \int_0^q p.x\ f(x)\ dx + \int_q^\infty p.q\ f(x)\ dx - c(q)$$

$$(10) \qquad F(q) = \frac{p-c'(q)}{p}$$

$$(11) \qquad \hat{q} < q^* \qquad (\text{if } c''(q) > 0)$$

expected profit, bearing in mind that some output may not be sold. The result is that it produces less than under certainty, given that marginal cost are rising (the only case under which competitive output is well defined). This results stems statistically from the fact that the left hand side of the solution (as any distribution function) is increasing in q (starting with zero for q=0), while the right hand side is decreasing (starting from one for q = 0). They cross somewhere with p larger than marginal cost, which happens at an output less than that optimal for certainty. Economically the lower value stems from the fact that the lower production is necessary to allow for the extra cost due to the expected cost of unsold production.

Despite the conceptual problems with the pure competition model, this model is cited in the early literature (Hymanns 1966), and is very similar to the "newsboy model" (famous in inventory literature). The only difference to the latter is that inventory models usually assume constant marginal cost. In this case the comparison with certainty becomes elusive and expected demand may be the useful target for comparing the uncertainty results. This will be done in chapter 3.3.1. In the empirical part we will investigate whether competition under demand uncertainty is an empirically valid concept. Strong price fluctuations, lack of buffer stock inventories and small variations of backlogged orders for "relatively competitive industries" would contradict this model of demand uncertainty under competition.

3.2.2 Monopoly

The behavior of monopoly under uncertainty allows different assumptions, about the decision variable and it needs an assumption about the "nature of uncertainty".

3.2.2.1 Q-Mode

The easiest case is to assume that the monopolist decides on his optimal output (q = Y) and allows his uncertain demand curve, g(q,u), to decide about the selling price.

(12) $E\pi = \int \left[p\,(q)\,.q - c\,(q) \right] f\,(p)\,dp$

(13) $\hat{q} = q^*$ (see Leland 1972, Hey 1979)

His quantitiy decision is the same as under certainty, because his profits are linear in the prices. In economic terms this is explained by the fact that an eventually high price increases profits to the same extent as an eventually low price would reduce them 9).

3.2.2.2 P-mode

The monopolist who decides on his price (p = X) and allows the market to decide on his optimal output (q=g(p,u)) under reasonable conditions chooses a higher price than under certainty. The "reasonable conditions" consist of $c''>0, c'''\geq 0$, and a socalled "Principle of Increasing Risk" (defined by Leland 1972, assuming higher uncertainty of higher revenues). The economic reason for the higher prices is that they "insure" the monopolist against the possibility of eventually high marginal cost of production (in case of favorable demand). The difference to the Q-mode is that the second term of the objective function depends on the uncertainty variable (compare 14 versus 12).

$$(14) \quad E\pi = \int \left\{ p.q\ (p) - c\left[q\ (p) \right] \right\} \ f\ (q) \quad dq$$

$$(15) \quad \hat{p} > p^* \quad \text{if} \quad \begin{cases} c'' > 0,\ c''' \geq 0 & \text{Leland 1972} \\ \text{PIU} & \text{(Principle of increasing uncertainty)} \end{cases}$$

The higher price under uncertainty opens space for a lower conditional expected output under uncertainty $Eq|\hat{p} < Eq|p^*$ but this need not apply in all cases (for contradictory examples see Mills 1962, conditions for this tendency under assumptions of a normal distribution are given in Baron 1970).

3.2.2.3. P-Q-Model

If the monopolist is forced to fix price and quantity (p and q represent Y) the result of the joint optimization depends heavily on the fact whether uncertainty is additive or multiplicative. We follow Karlin and Carr (in Arrow 1962), who assume constant marginal costs and present their results.

If uncertainty is multiplicative, the optimal price is higher than under certainty, the optimal quantity is smaller under very probable conditions. This last-mentioned downward bias depends on two effects. The negatively sloped demand curve decreases optimal quantity because of the higher price (17), the second term constitutes the effect of sunk cost (due to high output). The effect is negative (lowering output) if p is is smaller than 2c.

(16) Multiplicative uncertainty: $x = g(p).u \qquad E(u) = 1$

(17) $\hat{p} > p^*$ (Karlin, Carr in Arrow et al. 1962)

(18) $\hat{q} = g\ (\hat{p})\ .\ F^{-1}\ (\frac{\hat{p}-c}{\hat{p}})$

If uncertainty is additive, the optimal price is lower than under certainty. The result on optimal output is ambiguous since the elasticity of demand tends to increase optimal output while the balance of foregone profits versus sunk cost still tends to decrease it as compared with certainty.

(19) Additive uncertainty: $x = g\ (p) + u \qquad E\ (u) = 0$

(20) $\hat{p} < p^*$ (Karlin, Carr in Arrow et al. 1962)

(21) $\hat{q} = g\ (\hat{p}) + F^{-1}\ (\frac{\hat{p}-c}{\hat{p}})$

At this stage of the literature the results become complicated. Nevin (1966) by means of numerical simulation shows that the result of a higher price under multiplicative uncertainty depends on Karlin's and Carr's assumption of linear cost. Zabel (1972) extends the results of

Karlin and Carr to dynamic models, showing that the tendency of the results remains valid, but conditions to guarantee unique solutions are more restrictive in case of multiplicative uncertainty. Zabel explains the difference in the price reaction (higher prices for multiplicative uncertainty) by the fact that multiplicative uncertainty allows higher prices to reduce uncertainty.

There is not much hope to obtain information about the "true" nature of uncertainty. It may be in between the concepts of multiplicative and additive uncertainty. Low values for the elasticity of demand and a profit share considerably below the cost share would make it more reasonable, that for any kind of the "nature of uncertainty" optimal quantity will be lower under uncertainty. Further empirical evidence can be gathered about the likelihood of the different modes 10).

3.3. Inventory Models

Looking into inventory theory constitutes a necessary complement of the microeconomic theory of the firm surveyed in the last chapter, since it starts where the latter ends, namely with the value of those goods which were not sold during the planning period. This extension is especially important for the cases of fixed prices (competition under demand uncertainty and monopoly under P-Q-mode) since only in these cases unsold products exist. For this reason we hope not to commit a serious omission if we concentrate on those aspects of inventory theory, which assume price rigidity.

Inventory theory aims not at determining the optimal production level, but usually at calculating the optimal stock on hand (inventory level coming from orders, production and past inventory decisions before the level of the uncertain demand is revealed). The possible result that planned inventories on hand should be lower than expected demand or lower than under certainty does not imply that production is lower than expected demand, but that expected inventories are negative.

Inventory theory covers an enormous research topic, work concentrates on two different lines. On the one side research efforts are engaged in mathematical aspects of the problem (existence and uniqueness of the solution for different classes of problems). On the other side, they are concerned with solving numerical inventory decisions of firms with a huge number of products in different plants and stages of fabrication. The question in which we are interested - whether uncertainty reduces or increases planned stocks on hand - lies in between. Very different answers are given to this question in the literature, or can at least be inferred from the formulas derived.

3.3.1. The Newsboy Model

This model is the starting point of neary every model on inventory decisions under uncertainty (see HILLIER and LIEBERMANN, 1980). In contrast to the competitive model under demand uncertainty usually constant marginal costs are assumed. Its relation to the market structure is neglected (it is not a monopolistic model since prices are given, it is not a competitive model since unsold goods are given). The results are the same as for the competitive model (3.2.1.2.). Production or inventories at hand are less than expected demand, if the profit share (p-c) is smaller than cost (c) or, what is identical, if p is not larger than two times c.

$$(22) \quad F(q) = \frac{p-c}{c} \Rightarrow (23)$$

$$(23) \quad \hat{q} < E(x) \qquad \text{if } p < 2c$$

Surprisingly, the evident conclusion, that under all reasonable empirical considerations producers should produce (or hold less stocks on hand) less than expected demand is not drawn.

3.3.2. One Stage Approximation of Holding and Goodwill Cost

Though constituting the starting point of inventory literature, the newsboy model is no real inventory model, since it places no value or cost on unsold products or missed opportunities. As a first approximation we could calculate a cost h on any unsold quantity and a goodwill loss g for any missed opportunity. It is important to note that this goodwill cost is additional to an implicit calculated revenue loss, so that the value of a missed opportunity is p+g. The resulting formula shows that a quantity less than expected demand is very likely, except if profits p-c and cost c are about equal and holding cost are much larger than goodwill cost

$$(24) \quad L(q) = \int_0^q (c+h)(q-x)\, f(x)dx + (p+g-c) \int_q^\infty (x-q)\, f(x)\, dx$$

$$(25) \quad F(q) = \frac{p+g-c}{p+g+h}$$

3.3.3. Dynamic Inventory Models

A truly dynamic inventory model places an expected value on an inventory which represents the discounted future revenues and costs of these inventories. The mathematical technique used is the solution of a recursion formula and treated in the mathematical programming literature. For references see HILLIER and LIEBERMANN 1980, VEINOTT 1966 or HAY 1981/pp.133-138).

The economically most important assumption concerns the question whether unsatisfied demand can be backlogged or not. If all demand can be backlogged any amount of unsatisfied demand of today leads to the same amount of "extra demand" tomorrow, revenues and cost of this unit have to be discounted. A parallel logic holds for inventories: if all goods are durable, any amount of inventories saves tomorrow´s production cost. Both considerations are included in equation (26).

Assuming α as the time discount factor, a as the durability parameter ($a = 1$ for durable goods, $a = 0$ for perishable goods), b as backlogging parameter ($b = 1$ if all demand can be backlogged) we reach the following formula (see appendix (1) for derivation)

$$(26) \qquad F(\bar{q}) = \frac{(p-c)(1-\alpha b) + g}{p+g+h-\alpha ac-\alpha b(p-c)} \qquad \bar{q} = q + I$$

This formula has the following properties:

- for infinite time discount ($\alpha=0$) or a and b equal to zero (complete loss of unsatisfied demand and stored products) it collapses into the newsboy formula (this is an eminently logical result).

- optimal stocks on hand (including production) decrease in b, since backlogging reduces the cost of low production.

- if b is zero (no backlogging), but goods are at least partly durable (a is not zero), optimal production is larger than in the static case even if goodwill and holding costs are equal ($g = h$), though it can be larger or smaller than expected demand.

- And finally - most surprising on first sight - in case of complete backlogging, complete durability ($b=a=1$), in absence of goodwill and storing cost ($g=h=0$) the decision is exactly the same as in the newsboy model. On second thought this is eminently reasonable since any unsatisfied demand increases future earnings, the only definite losses are goodwill and holding costs.

The question whether optimal stocks should be lower than expected demand now depends on several parameters. But the forces are very much the same as in the static case, specifically a small profit share will yield production (plus stocks) lower than expected demand under reasonable goodwill and holding costs For eample: p=1, c=0,9, g=h=0,2, a=b=1, α=0,9 yields F(q)=0,42, q<Ex.

3.3.4. A Digression on Prejudices of Mainstream Inventory Literature on the Impact of Uncertainty

We have demonstrated that it is quite plausible to assume that optimal inventory on hand should be lower than expected demand. If this is the case it follows that increasing uncertainty also decreases optimal inventory. A survey of the inventory literature reveals that just the opposite seems to be assumed there.

Dealing with the newsboy formula, some authors give numerical examples where profits are more than 50% of the price (Lange 1969) other give examples partly above and partly below this critical value (Petersen, Silver 1979). They never discuss how improbable it is to produce that much as expected demand. Arrow, Harris and Marshak (1951) assume cost of not satisfied demand 10 resp. 100 times higher than marginal production cost, similar asymmetries are implied in Karlin, Scarf and Beckman, Muth (both in Arrow et al. 1968) or Buchan, Koenigsberg 1963.

This assumption results from the fact that many inventory models implicitly or explicitly assume the non-backlogging case. Examples for disregaring backlogging without explicitly stating this assumption are the otherwise seminal books by De Groot (1970) and Hey (1981). De Groot arrives at the following dynamic formula (27), which implies for monthly production (where α is near 1), that any improbable production should be satisfied.

$$(27) \qquad F(\bar{q}) = \frac{p-c}{p-\alpha c} \qquad \text{for } \alpha \rightarrow 1, \quad \hat{q} \rightarrow \infty$$

The importance of the prejudice can be seen in the fact that several authors want to include backlogging, but disregard revenue from backlogged orders. Veinott (1966) in his seminal article on the status of mathematical inventory theory, obtains a formula where optimal production increases with the possibility of backlogging. This is due to the fact that he considers the cost of backloggs (the cost of production for those units backlogged, which would be saved if the sales were lost to a competitor) but not their revenues. The formula of Veinott furthermore differs from this paper (though the same derivation technique is used) by not differentiating between p (the opportunity cost of lost sales, which can be recoverd under backlogging) and g (the goodwill cost invariable lost due to shortage) Veinott comprises both components in $\mathring{p}$.

$$(28) \quad F(\bar{q}) = \frac{\mathring{p} + \alpha cb - c}{\mathring{p} + h + \alpha (cb - c\alpha)} \Rightarrow \frac{d\hat{\bar{q}}}{db} > 0 \quad \text{(Veinott 1966)}$$

What reasons are responsible for this prejudice of a whole stream of literature? Several hypotheses could be proposed:

- The first task of inventory literature was to explain (rationalize) inventory holding as an efficient behavior, uncertainty of demand was one possibility (precautionary motive).

- Changing from deterministic to stochastic models the assumption that demand must be met, is changed into a very high service level which has to be planned for (usually above 90%).

- Inventory theory often implicitly deals with input inventories, when they fall below a critical level, this could hamper the whole production process. In this case the cost of this one single input may well be below the cost of the missed opportunities (profit).

- Literature often refers implicitly to the retailer, where mark-up on inputs may be indeed 100%. But in this case the wages are paid out of this mark-up, maybe these are not considered as costs related with the inventories.

- Inventory theory was largely influenced by military thinking (see Journal of Naval Research etc). Here the implicit value of stockouts is nearly infinite. Look at a remark in Arrow et. al. 1951, P257: The penalty for depleted stocks may be very high". A horse, a horse, my kingdom for a horse" cried defeated Richard III.

- Balance sheets invariably show that there exist positive inventories. By disregarding orders as negative inventories, producing less than expected demand seems highly implausible.

In fact, the most realistic remarks stem from two authors who explicitly comprehend orders and inventories as two sides of the same phenomenon. Simon writes (1951, S250): "Depending on the commodity produced, the optimal inventory may also be positive or negative ... the former ships from stocks, the latter on orders" or Zarnowitz (1973 p.11) explicitly names unstable or sporadic demand as a reason to hold negative stocks (to produce on order) 8).

In the empirical part we will try to get some information on the relative size and variations of finished stocks versus orders, about their relative size, their variations and the behavior of net inventories in periods of uncertainty.

3.4. Investment Demand under Uncertainty

Results as to the effects of uncertainty are even less general as far as investment decisions are concerned. This is due to the fact that many models assume ex ante contol of one factor (usually investment) and ex post control of the other. The optimal strategy therefore depends on the subsitutability of the factors. The second reason is that some authors assume that the irreversibility of investment becomes important.

3.4.1 Both Factors as Ex-ante-control

If both factors (and therefore output too) have to be decided upon ex ante, the input demand corresponds to the chosen level of output. Is the output the same as under certainty (as demonstrated for price uncertainty under competition), input demand is the same, if it is lower (demand uncertainty) it is lower for both inputs (Batra and Ullah, 1974, Hartman, 1975).

3.4.2 Wages as Ex-post-control - Limitational Production Function, Fixed Prices

Nickell (1978) assumes that the capital input must be fixed before demand is known, thereby fixing also the upper limit of production. The sole ex-post variation is that wages can be saved if output is not demanded. Fixed prices and constant marginal costs renders a result (30) very similar to the newsboy model, but the possible saving of wages diminishes the tendency to produce less than expected demand (this tendency holds if investment is larger than half of gross profits, p-w).

$$(29) \quad F(q) = \frac{p-w-i}{p-w} \qquad \text{(Nickell 1978)}$$

$$(30) \quad \hat{q} < E(x) \qquad \text{if} \quad i > \frac{1}{2}(p-w)$$

3.4.3. Monopoly - Limitational Production Function: q=f(p).u

The firm facing a downward sloping demand curve, multiplicative uncertainty and a fixed technology chooses its capacity in a way to equate expected marginal revenue EM(q,u) and (constant) unit cost (w+i). Nickell shows, that it is very likely that the optimal capacity is lower than under certainty, since the necessary concavity of M (q,u) is given under either of the following conditions12): linear or quadratic demand curve or constant elasticity of demand (smaller than -1).

Table 1

Summary of the Theoretic Models

Mode	Literature	Main Result	Condition for Main Result	Economic Rational	Empirical Implikation (EI) Caveats (C) Critical Parameters (CP)
Competition - price uncertainty - q ex-ante mode					
Y : q X : p	Sandmo 1971	$\hat{q} = q^*$	-	$\underbrace{E(p)}_{p^*} = c'(q)$	EI: no involuntary inventories, no fluctations of involuntary inventories, expected production = actual production, actual price differs randomly from expected one
Competition - demand uncertainty - q ex-ante mode					
Y : q X : x	Hymans 1966	1) $\hat{q} < q^*$	$c''(q) > 0$	expected unsold quantity can be reduced	C: is this a competitive model ? CI: disequlibria inventories, forecast errors even in competitive markets, fixed prices CP: profit share versus costs
	"Newsboy-model"	2) $\hat{q} < Ex$	$p-c < c$ $(= p < 2c)$	opportunity cost of unsatisfied demand smaller than sunk cost	
Monopoly - demand uncertainty - q ex-ante mode					
Y : q X : p = f(q,u)	Leland 1972	$\hat{q} = q^*$	additive uncertainty, multiplicative uncertainty + PIU	production can do nothing to reduce price uncertainty	EI: no disequlibria, expected production = actual production, actual price differ from expected one randomly
	Nickell 1978	$\hat{q} < q^*$	multiplicative uncertainty $q=f(p).u \rightarrow p=f^{-1}(\frac{q}{u})$ and one of these conditions: $\varepsilon < -1$ q_p linear or quadratic	indirect influence via demand curve	C: depends on specific type of multiplicative uncertainty: is uncertainty additive or multiplicative (if the latter: is $p = g(q).u$ or $p = f^{-1}(\frac{q}{u})$?)

Table 1 continued

Mode	Literature	Main Result	Condition for Main Result	Economic Rational	Empirical Implikation (EI) Caveats (C) Critical Parameters (CP)
Monopoly - demand uncertainty - p ex-ante mode					
Y : p X : q = f(q,u)	Leland 1972	$\hat{p} \gtrless p^*$	if $c''' \gtrless 0$ PIU or additive demand	high price insures against eventually expensive production	EI: no disequilibria, expected price = actual price, actual production differs from expected one randomly
Monopoly - demand uncertainty - p and q ex-ante mode					
Y : p,q	additive uncertainty	$\hat{p} < p^*$	$c'(q) = c$	smaller price to reduce additive uncertainty, quantity smaller if p-c very small, but larger according to demand elasticity	EI: disequlibria inventories and backloggs, expected variables = realizations
	Karlin, Carr 1962	$\hat{q} \gtrless q^*$			
	multiplicative uncertainty	$\hat{p} > p^*$ q likely to be smaller than q^*	$c'(q) = c$	higher price (chosen to reduce multiplicative uncertainty) and small profits reinforce each other to lower production	EI: disequilibria inventories and backloggs, expected variables = realizations C: assumption of constant costs
Inventory models - demand uncertainty - fixed prices					
Y : q + I X : x	following the line of Veinott 1966	$\hat{q}$ + I likely to be smaller than E (x)	p fixed $c'(q) = c$	small p-c and symmetric holding and goodwill costs as well as symmetric backlogging and durability parameters	EI: disequlibria inventories and backloggs, net inventories negative, procyclical movement of planned net inventories, decreasing net inventories with increasing uncertainty CP: p - c : c; g : h; a : b

Table 1 continued

Mode	Literature	Main Result	Condition for Main Result	Economic Rational	Empirical Implikation (EI) Caveats (C) Critical Parameters (CP)
Factor demand models					
Y : K,L X : p	see e.g. Hey 1979 Hartman 1975	$\hat{K} = K^*$ $\hat{L} = L^*$	$\hat{q} = q^*$ "well behaved" production function	implication of the result for output	C: both factors under ex-ante controll, equilibrium model
Y : K,L X : x		$\hat{K} < K^*$ $\hat{L} < L^*$	$\hat{q} < q^*$ $c''(q) > 0$	implication of the result for output	C: the same as for the competitive model under demand uncertainty
Y : K,q^{max} X : x	Nickell 1978 p. 72 f	$\hat{K} \lesseqgtr K^*$	$i \gtrless \frac{1}{2}(p-w)$	i fixes upper limit of production, foregone profits have to be balanced only against i, since wages can be saved if demand is low	C: constant prices, constant unit wage, investment cost EI: strong fluctuations of wages (and employment) disequilibria inventories
Y : K X : p	Hartmann 1976	$\hat{K}$ likely to be larger than K^*	$\sigma < \frac{1}{1-\eta}$ competition ex-post controll	marginal product of labour rises with increasing rate	EI: uncertainty increase capital stock, fluctuations of wages (employment), investment anticipation = actual investment C: equilibrium model
Y : K X : p ex post decision: utilization rate	Kon 1983	$\hat{K}$ likely to be smaller than K^*	large utilization effect	possibility of unused capacity outweights advantages of large programs	C: disequilibrium in the sense of unused capacity
Y : K X : w	Nickell 1978 p. 80 f	$\hat{K}$ likely to be larger than K^*	$\sigma < \vert\epsilon\vert$ monopoly, L ex-post controll	low substitutability favours "reserve capacities"	EI: as in last case above
Asymmetric ex-post flexibilities					
Y : I^o or q^o X : x	e.g. Nickell 1978 p. 105 ff	$\hat{K} < K^*$ $\hat{q} < q^*$	upward revisions easier than downward revision	irreversibility of investment or production, cost differences in emergency reactions ($c_2 > c_1$)	C: easy results often dependent on constant price and cost assumptions EI: investment anticipation and production plans biased downward

(31) $E\,M\,(q,u) = w + i$

(32) $E\,M\,(q,u) = (1 + \frac{1}{\varepsilon})\ q^{1/\varepsilon}\ u^{-1/\varepsilon}$ (Nickel 1978)

this is concave in u if $\epsilon < -1$ or

q_p linear or quadratic

However we know from the discussion of monopoly output that this results depends on the assumption of a specific version of multiplicative demand, namely that q=f (p).u. If Leland's version was applied or if p=g(q).u, optimal production would be the same as under certainty (see footnote 9 in chapter 3.2.2.1).

3.4.4. Competition, Ex-post Variation of Labor under Price Uncertainty and CES-function

In this model (presented by Hartmann 1976 and Nickell 1978) labor can be chosen according to its marginal productivity after the true price is revealed. Optimal capital stock is lower or higher than under certainty, according to its substitutability (see equation 33), in relation to the scale parameter η. Except for a very high degree of substitutability, optimal capital stock will be larger than under certainty. This "convexity result" arises from the fact that the marginal product of capital increases with price even if labor were fixed, together with rising labor input it will increase at an increasing rate. We would like to mention another model, Kon 1983, in which lower capacity under uncertainty is much more likely, since Kon allows for the effect of potentially unused capacity (disequilibrium).

(33) $\hat{K} \lesseqgtr$ if $\sigma \gtrless \frac{1}{1-\eta}$ (Hartman 1976, Nickel 1978)

3.4.5. Monopoly, Ex-post Variation of Labor under Wage Uncertainty

In this model (Nickell 1978) wages are uncertain, but the amount of labor can be decided on after the wage rate becomes known. Again the elasticity of substitution becomes crucial, this time in relation to the elasticity of demand. Again it seems more likely that the elasticity will not reach the level necessary for lowering capital input in relation to certainty.

$$(34) \qquad \hat{K} \lessgtr K^* \qquad \text{if } \sigma \gtrless |\epsilon|$$

3.4.6 Investment Strategy for a Firm Facing an Upward Shift of its Demand of Unknown Extent.

Nickell shows that a firm choosing an optimal long-rund investment strategy and facing a demand shift, whose extent is not known (multiplicative uncertainty) will choose lower investment under very general conditions (the same as in equation 32, namely linear or quadratic demand curve or constant elasticity of demand of less than one). The result does not depend on some kind of adjustment cost or irreversibilities of investment, but on his assumption of the specific form of the multiplicativity of the demand shock.

3.4.7. Investment Strategy in Case of Irreversible Investments

A very realistic assumption concerning investment is that it can be increased if demand becomes known (probably after a specific lag), but cannot be reduced (or not more than given by its depreciation). This fact is (again shown by Nickell) another source sufficient to reduce investment in a uncertain environment.

3.5. Ex-post Flexibility

Up to now we have only shown that it is economically rational to have a production plan in which the quantity planned is lower than under certainty or lower than expected demand. This could be an explicit plan (for those firms for which q is the decision variable) or an implicit plan (resulting from the decision about the optimal p and given demand conditions). To get a deviation of plans from actual production (the phenomenon we want to explain) there must be some form of ex-post flexibility (fine tuning of the ex-ante-control variable).

There is special need for this in all the models where there is no ex-post control variable (and therefore on average unsatisfied demand for example in the P-Q-monopoly model or in competition under demand uncertainty or in the newsboy inventory model). In cases where there is an ex-post control (competition under price uncetainty) there is no evident need (since production equals demand), but if there are possibilities to change ex post (within limits or with higher costs) the variable first assumed to be an ex ante control variable, the optimal decision has to incorporate this ex-post flexibility.

The effect will be shown for a fix-price model, where c,c. and c. are the unit cost of normal production, of producing one additional unit during the planning period or respectively reducing it, a and b are the feasibility parameters of increasing respectively reducing production.

Assuming c. smaller than c. and/or a smaller than b introduces two sources of asymmetry: if it is cheaper and/or easier to increase production than to reduce it, then optimal production is smaller than in the newsboy model. Optimal production is very likely to be smaller than expected demand.

$$(35)\quad E\pi = p\int_0^q x\, f(x)dx + \int_q^\infty p.q\, f(x)dx - c.q + c_2 \int_0^q a\,(q-x)\, f(x)\, dy + (p-c_1)\int_q^\infty b\,(x-q)\, f(x)\, dx$$

$$(36)\quad F(q) = \frac{p-c-bp+bc_1}{p+bc_1-bp-ac_2}$$

c, c_1, c_2 unit cost for normal, emergency production resp. production cutback ($c_2 > c_1 > c$)

4. An Asymmetry Premium as a Rule of Thumb for Deriving Economically Rational Expectations

From the work of Simon 1978 or Cyert and March 1963 or others we know that we can expect people to behave with only limited (bounded) rationality. They will therefore not use the explicit form of the optimization process, but attempt to approximate the optimal decision by a rule of thumb. If people know that the economic consequences of high and low sales forcasts are different, we can say that they have a - maybe linear - loss function (37), where the parameter k tells how much worse it is to overestimate sales than to underestimate them by 1%. The second ingredient we need is to know the degree of uncertainty about the sales. Let us assume it to be a general symmetric density function with expected value E (x) and standard Deviation S.

(37) Linear loss function $f(x-y) = \begin{cases} k\,|x-y| & \text{if } x \leqslant y,\ k > 1 \\ x-y & x > y \end{cases}$

(38) General symmetric density: $f(x)$ ... symmetric, one sided monotonic for $x > 0$ and $x < 0$ (increasing for $-\infty < x < 0$)

(39) $\hat{y} = S\,F^{-1}\left(\frac{1}{k+1}\right)$ see Aiginger 1983

The optimal asymmetry premium is given by equation 39. It depends first on the degree of asymmetry (represented by k) and second on the degree of uncertainty (represented by S). This structure is exaxtly analogous to that for the risk premium which depends on the degree of risk aversion and the degree of risk (uncertainty).

In the newsboy example (3.3.1) the loss due to optimistic sales is the foregone costs, let us assume it to be 0,75. The loss due to a pessimistic forecast is the foregone profit p-c, let us assume it to be 0,25. K is therefore 3 (0,75/0,25). If demand is characterized by a normal distribution with standard deviation of 2, the value in the parenthesis is (1/4=0,25). Look into the standard table of normal distribution for F.(0,25) and you will find - 0,674, multiply this by 2 (the standard deviation) and you obtain an asymmetry premium of -1,35 for this problem. If your true mathematical expectation of sales is 7%, tell the surveying institute that the sales forecast used in your firm is 5,65%13).

Rules of thumb - like any approximation of a "structural" optimizing process by a "reduced form" as done by asymmetric loss functions - are not strictly optimal procedures in a changing environment (cost structures, demand conditions), but they reduce the information, search and planning costs and may therefor be optimal in a wider sense. As a matter of fact rules of thumb seem to dominate the optimization processes in real life. One of them is rooted in the beginnings of business economics and says that firms should be "cautious" in cases of uncertainty.

5. Empirical Evidence on the Validity of the Models and the Implied Bias

5.1. Evidence for Downward Biases in Expectations, Anticipations and Forecasts

The author reported in previous papers (among them in his CIRET-Conference paper in Athens 1981A, see also Aiginger 1983A, Aiginger 1981B, Aiginger 1977) that inflation forecasts, sales anticipations and investment plans were on average biased downward (result for 29 out of 39 variables).

The results were especially significant for business anticipations. Out of 14 series the average of anticipated changes was lower than that for actual changes in 13 series (statistically significant lower in 8 series, higher in one). The magnitude of this bias is different from country to country, depends on the questions asked in the survey and the time period covered. A typical result is that Japanese firms expected their production to increase by 2,92% (1953-1975), but actual production rose by 3,54%. This tendency prevailed after the recession in the mid seventies. Between 1976 and 1982 production rose actually by 1,97% on average, anticipated change was 1,63%.

5.2. Evidence on the Plausibility of Theoretical Models and Modes in Austrian Manufacturing

We have seen that there is a wide range of potential influences on the optimal decision under uncertainty. Some models forecast downward biases for the decision variable, some upward biases, some yield the same decision as under certainty. I would like to present a few empirical hints as to which of the models are more realistic descriptions of the manufacturing sector in a developed country. Indicators of the flexibility of prices and the development of inventories and backlogged orders should help us to judge the importance of equilibrium versus disequilibrium, the relative importance of finished good inventories versus backlogs and a questionaire should give us a hint on the relative importance of holding costs versus goodwill costs. Investment surveys can tell us a little bit about the flexibility of investment plans (which are usually assumed to be an ex ante control) and hopefully whether this ex post flexibility is symmetric or not. Two limitations of the material should be stressed: first we present only a few empirical results (more see in Aiginger 1983B) and the results can tell us only about the question how firms do behave, not how they should behave from the point of view of a normative theory.

5.2.1. Are Prices Flexible?

5.2.1.1. Price flexibility as measured by the standard deviation of industrial prices over time (quartely changes) is less than production flexibility as measured by the standard deviation of industrial production (period 1963-1982 3,65: 5,03 for the approximately the same mean see row 1 in table 2) 14).

5.2.1.2. Short term changes in prices as measured by the first order correlation coefficient of price changes with the previous period is even more stable, showing that prices move with long-run costs rather than as an ex post control, which closes unexpected disequilibria (R2=0,83:0,61, b=0,92:0,79 for prices resp. quantities, see row 2 in table 2).

5.2.1.3. Price expectations (as reported in the business test) exhibit a higher mean (M=18,9) and a higher standard deviation (17,2) than productions expectations (M=6,4, S=12,0), though the respective measures are the same or lower for realisations, indicating that price changes, if they occur, are planned, while an important part of production growth is unplanned (see table 2, 3rd row).

5.2.1.3. Price expectations are more succesful in explaining prices in 8 out of 10 German industries (1965-19834, 1 month lead) than production expectations (see table 2, 4th row). In Austria, expectations and ex-post development cannot be compared in a simple way, since realizations are available only from the quantitative statistics. It is no surprise that the net balances of the expectations and quantitative change in the realizations yields very low coefficients of determination on the branch level. At the aggregate level the correlation of price and quantities are approximately equal (with a slight superiority of production expectations, which evaporates in the seventies when industrial prices began to change).

5.2.1.4. Asked in a questionnaire what reactions within the planning period would happen in a case of a (positive or negative) demand shock only 20% said they would change prices (56% said they would change production Table 2, row 5, 1100 firms). Asked which influences prevailed on their prices the majority named supply factors (costs), demand was reported to be less important.

5.2.1.5 In an econometric investigation trying to estimate which part of a 1% change in demand was followed by change in production, inventories or price, the last one had nearly no weight. The method followed closely Hay's approach using Z-tranforms to obtain linear decision rules (Hay 1970). The results as to the relative importance of production versus price change correspond to that of Hay 1970 for lumber and paper industry (see table 2, row 6).

5.2.1.6. The tendency of short run inflexibility of prices (15%) remained true for smaller firms (less than 100 employees) and industries supposed to be competitive demonstrating that price inflexibility is given not only for monopolistic or oligopolistic firms. Therefore model 3.2.1.2 (competition with short run price inflexibility) cannot be ruled out a priori.

5.2.2. Are there Unwanted Inventories of Finished Goods?

5.2.2.1. The standard deviation of the inventory-sales ratio for finished goods is 0,7 (10% of its mean), its developement is not definitely procyclical (its relation to changes in production is insignificantly negative). Inventory fluctuations need not necessarily contradict the model of competition under price uncertainty, since they could be voluntary (varying anticipations for price increases). However fluctuations of inventories in the individual branches are less related to prices (R2 = 0.32) than to production (R2 = 0.58).

5.2.2.2. The evaluation of finished goods inventories in the business test shows that firms are not able to "fix" them at a desired level. There are periods (in booms) when the level of stocks is considered too low quarter after quarter and (much longer) periods when it is considered too high. This contradicts models of market clearing through rapid price response and models explaining inventories as profit maximizing speculative behaviour. This cyclically changing assessment is even stronger for branches considered as competitive (sector A in chart 1) than in those with considerable oligopolistic tendencies (sector B).

5.2.2.3. Asked for the importance of inventory changes within the planning period following positive or negative demand shocks, 48% answered that this was a prime reaction.

This tendency is somewhat less often reported by firms with less than 100 employees. 48% reports it to be the prime response to a demand

INVENTORY SALES RATIO FOR FINISHED GOODS AND THEIR ASSESSMENT (BUSINESS TEST) IN COMPETITVE (A) AND LESS COMPETITIVE (B) BRANCHES (AUSTRIA)

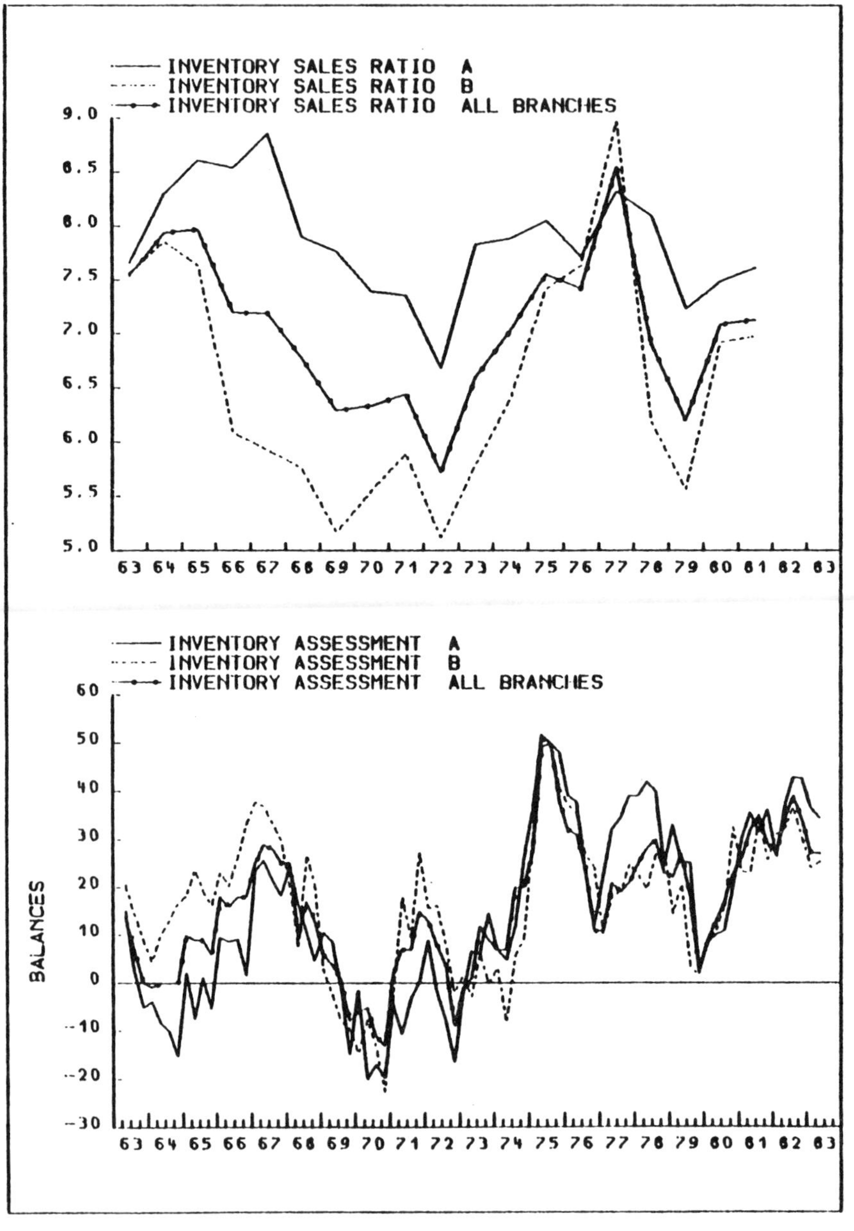

BUSINESS ANTICIPATIONS AND ACTUAL DEVELOPMENT
JAPAN 1963-1982

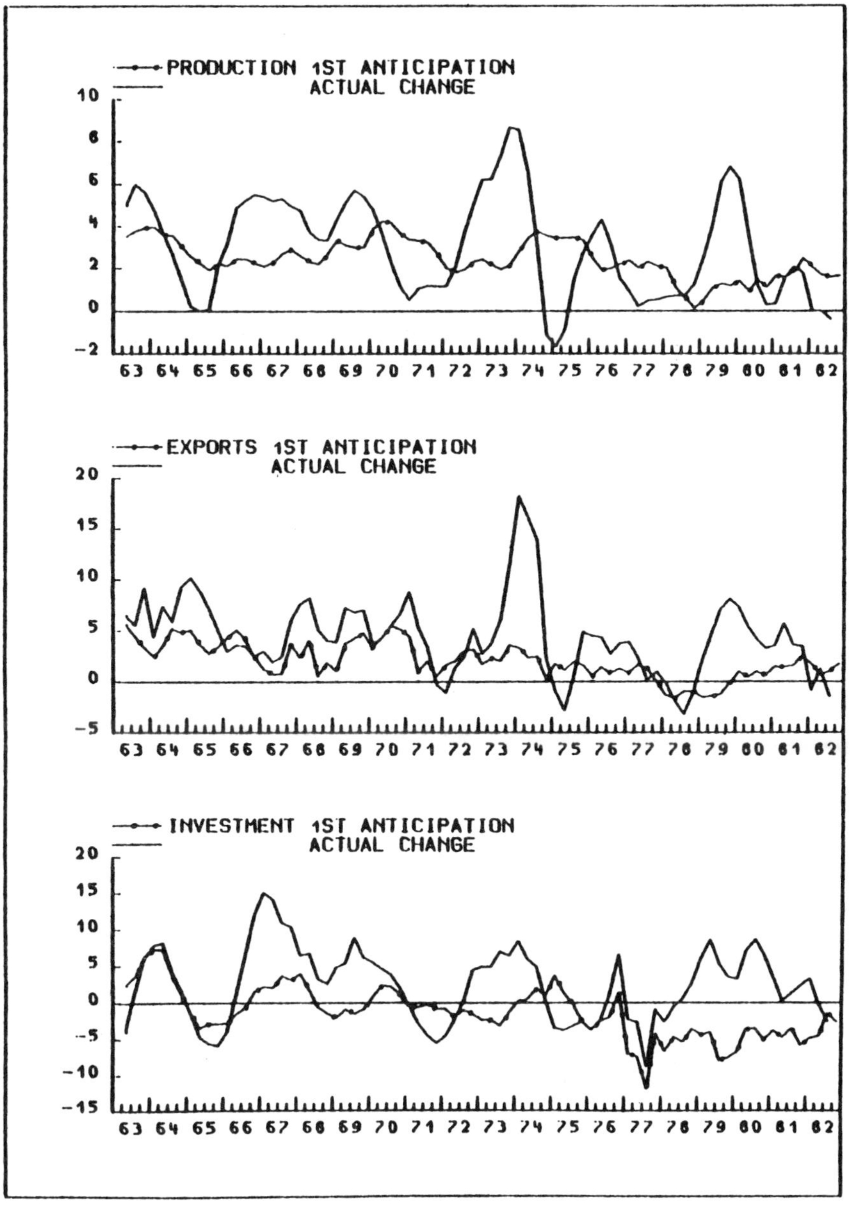

Table 2

Measures of Price-Flexibility versus Quantity-Flexibility

1) Mean (M), Standard Deviation (S), Coefficient of variation (V) of quarterly changes (R 4) 1963 - 82, Austria

	Prices			Quantities		
	M	S	V	M	S	V
1963-83	4,04	3,65	0,90	4,35	5,03	1,16

2) Coefficient (b) and R^2 of 1 st order autocorrelation (Austria)

b	t_b	R^2	b	t_b	R^2
0,92	19,11	0,83	0,79	11,10	0,61

3) Net balance and standard deviation of firms (Austria, 1963-82) for price resp. quantity changes in business test.

Balance	S	Balance	S
+ 18,92	17,23	+ 6,41	12,01

4) Predictive accurancy of business expectation in Germany (R^2)

Prices expectations outperform quantities in 8 branches
quantity expectations outperforms prices in 2 branches

5) Questionaire: how would you react within your planning period if demand is different from your sales forecast (Austria, 1.100 firms)

	All firms	Small firms
Price change	20 %	15 %
Quantity change	56 %	47 %
Inventories	48 %	34 %
Capacity change	16 %	21 %

6) Econometric test of changes in production, prices, orders as a result of an increase in demand of 1 %. (Austria, technique see Hay, 1970)

production	0,65	
prices	0,02	(not significant)
order build up	0,33	(residual)

R 4 .... relative change against same quarter in the last year

b, t_b .... regression coefficient, t-value

shock, 35% as a possible reaction in case of large surprises and only 32% report it as not feasible as it would be requested in the theoretic modell of the competitive firm.

5.2.3. Are Net Inventories Negative?

5.2.3.1. Using empirical data to compare the profit rate relative to costs shows that profits are approximately 6% of sales and 17% of value added (Austrian manufacturing, 1976/1979). Whichever measure we use the costs of foregone sales are much lower than that of sunk costs of overproduction. The difference is that large that we will get a production strategy which is less than expected demand, if inventory holding costs are not much higher than goodwill costs or backlogging is impossible for a large part of the industry. Testable implications of this asymmetry are that net inventories should be negative on average and decreasing (becoming even more negative) with increasing uncertainty.

5.2.3.3 Net inventories are defined as the difference between inventories of finished goods and backlogged order stocks. On average they are negative, though the data have some flaws (usually data on order backlog and on inventories do not have the same coverage, nor is the same sampling technique used).

In the US finished goods inventories (1954-1982) are reported to be on average 14% of annual sales (1,7 of one month), unfilled orders (in relation to annual shipments) 28%. The backlogs are reported only for branches which do have backloggs. If we devide reported backloggs by all sales the ratio still remains higher than the inventory-sales ratio.

In Germany (data by IFO Munich) finished goods amount to 7.5% of annual production (1980-1982), order backlogs to 24%.

Table 3

Inventories (Finished Goods) and
Order Backlog in %
of Annual Sales

U S A

	(1)	(2)	(3)	(4)	
	Inventory - Sales-Ratio	Order-Shippment-Ratio[1)]			Net-inventories
		All	Durables	Non Durables	(1)-(2) = (5)
1954-59	14,58	28,29	33,42	8,02	- 13,71
1960-69	14,17	27,09	32,40	6,09	- 12,86
1970-79	14,09	30,32	36,15	6,52	- 16,23
1980-82	14,08	31,39	38,08	5,03	- 17,31
Ø 54-82	14,22	28,90	34,49	6,53	- 14,68

Source: Economic Report of the President

1) For firms which do have backloggs
Unfilled orders in % of sales (including branches without backloggs): 16,30
Net inventories: -2,08 (14,22 - 16,30)

Germany

	(1)	(2)	(3)	(4)	(5)
	Inventory - Sales-Ratio	Evaluation as too high (+) or too low (-)	Order backlog	Evaluation as too high (+) or too low (-)	Net - inventorie (3)-(1)
1972	-	+ 13	23,5	- 25	
1980-82	7,5	+ 29	23,9	- 40	- 16,4
1970-79	-	+ 12	25,9	- 24	-

Source: IFO-Munich

Austria

	(1)	(2)	(3)	(4)	(5)	(6)
	Inventory - Sales-Ratio Total	Evaluation as too high (+) as too low (-)	Order backlog Total	excl. maschineries	Evaluation as too high (+) or too low (-)	Net - inventorie
Ø 73/74	6,8	+ 9,4	33,4	22,9	- 4,2	- 15,0
Ø 80/82	7,1	+26,5	39,0	25,8	-25,9	- 17,4

1) Excluding maschinery and those branches, not covered by order statistic

In Austria (1974-1981) finished goods inventories make up 8.2% of sales, if we substract those industries which are not covered by the order book statistics and the machinery industry (which possess as nearly on half of the order backlog) the inventory-sales ratio is 9,7%. The average order backlog is 37.5% for total industry, 24% if we exclude machineries.

The ratios are different for all countries, but net inventories are on average negative. It seems reasonable to conclude that order backlogs are approximately two times as important than finished goods inventories.

5.2.3.4. Backlogged orders are supposed to decline in bad times by business cycle economists, firms are suppossed to try to cut down planned inventories but are reported to accumulate involuntary inventories (see Tichy 1976). With a stronger tendency of the first component than of the second net inventories would increase in troughs (being less negative than usual).

Observed net inventories do not follow this presumtion, rather they follow the hypothesis that net inventories should decrease with greater uncertainty if F(y)<1/2 (see chapter 3.3.3).

In the USA the inventory-sales ratio reached 14.1% in the last three years (1980-1982) which was approximately the same as usually, unfilled orders increased to 31.4% of annual shippments which is definitely higher than usual. Net inventories therefor decreased to 17,3, to highest negative value of all periods reported in table 3.

In Germany inventory data are available only for 1980-1982 in business surveys. The order backlog decreased from 25.9% in 1970-1979 to 23.9%. The evaluation of these order books as being too low worsened even more. The same length or order books as in 1980-1982 (23.9%) had been reached

Table 4

Indicators of Asymmetry in the Ex-Post-Flexibility

1) Differences in the first reaction to a demand shock within the planning period (1.100 firms, Austria)

	positiv demand shock (all firms)	negative demand shock (all firms)	small firms positiv shock	small firms negativ shock	large firms positiv shock	large firms negativ shock
price	20	20	12	18	39	21
quantity	56	56	47	46	55	63
inventory	60	36	41	26	81	58
capacity	16	15	23	18	0	9

2) Differences in errors of same size and different size (1.100 firms, Austria)

	all firms	small firms	large firms
costs are about the same	21 %	18 %	30 %
larger for optimistic sales forecast	62 %	58 %	64 %
larger for pessimistic sales forecast	17 %	24 %	61 %

3) Estimates of holding cost versus goodwill costs (HOLT et al 1960)

	managers' estimation	simulation by the model
holding costs	139,8	152,6
penalty costs	166,8	126,0
hypothetical total costs	1 000,0	921,6

4) Order backloggs (mean, standard deviation) versus inventory holdings (mean, standard deviation), Austria

order backlogg Mean	order backlogg Standard deviation	finished goods inventory Mean	finished goods inventory Standard deviation
37,6	3,69	7,0	0,71

5) Changes in average of investment anticipations (1965-76, Aiginger 1977)

All firms	+ 14 %
Small firms	+ 31 %
Large firms	+ 9 %

6) Sign of average error for expectations, investment, expert's forecasts (Aiginger 1981):
expected changes on average larger (upward bias) that actual changes: 10 series
expected changes on average lower (downward bias) than actual changes: 29 series.

1972 (23.5). During that time the assessment as too low was -25%, now it is -40%. This means that desired order backlog increased, though actual backlog decreased.

Most remarkable is that within the aggregate of backlogs, those of durable goods increased, while those of nondurables decreased. This may be influenced by long term trends, but also conforms to the hypothesis that industries with on average negative net inventories, backlogs should be increased while in those with on average positive inventories, uncertainty should increase net inventories (decrease backlogs).

In Austria the finished goods/sales ratio remained approximately constant at 7,19%. The backlog of unfilled orders increased from 33.4% to 39.0 (after excluding machineries 22.9 resp. 25.8). Net inventories therefore decreased (becoming more negative). Desired net inventories will probable have turned even more into the negative since the order backlog is considered as insufficient (-26%) and finished goods evaluation have reached record marks in their evaluation as being too high (+27).

The Japanese inventory-sales level (total economy) is reported (Economic Survey, 1982) historically low at the beginning of the eighties 15).

5.2.4. Are there Ex-post Flexibilities?

5.2.4.1. Econometric techniques showed that 0.65% of a 1% demand change can be compensated by production within a quarter (see row 6 in table 2).

5.2.4.2. Firms reported in a questionaire (1100 firms in Austrian manufacturing) that reactions within the planning period were possible. Production is considered as the most flexible variable, it was named as prime response by 56%, as response in case of large disequlibrium by 29%, as not feasible by 15% (see row 1 in table 4).

Inventory response (which actually closes the gap between current supply and demand but leaves the stock level at a disequilibrium) was called as prime response by 48%, as not feasible by 18%.

Price response was called as prime response by 20%, as not feasible by 38%. Capacity change is a prime response by 16%, not feasible for 43%.

5.2.4.3. Deviations between sales anticipations and actual changes show that sales are not fixed ex ante, deviations between production plans and actual production show that production plans are not fixed and the especially large (on average positive) deviations of investment anticipations and investment plans show that not even the input of capital (considered as the ex ante control in the theory) is fixed without partial ex post flexibility.

5.2.4.4. Flexibility seems to be larger for smaller firms if we rely on differences in the forecasting performance for example of sales and investment anticipations). For large firms underestimation of actual investment during 1964-1976 (a boom period) amounted to 9 percent, for small firms (less than 100 employees) 31% (Aiginger 1977). In the questionnaire on possible reactions within the planning period, small firms in general were more reluctant to name strategies, probably because they regard their flexibility not as changes of plans because they do not have (nor need) well defined plans. That would mean that large firms have to fix prices and quantities before uncertainty is revealed (P-Q-mode) but then have some ex post flexibility, while small firms face P and Q as ex post control. This could imply an increasing market share for small firms in periods of uncertainty, which seems to be corroborated by empirical evidence (Aiginger - Tichy 1982).

The feasibility of price and inventory reaction increases, the feasibility of quantity and capacity change decreases with firm size.

5.2.5. Are these Flexibilities Symmetric (Up and Down)?

5.2.5.2. Entrepreneurs labelled more instruments as feasible in case of pessimistic forecasts, especially they are willing to let inventories become cut down, but will not build them up, indicating less goodwill costs than inventory holding cost and/or easy backlogging).

5.2.5.3. Investment plans are more often revised upward than downward

For small firms this tendency occupies up to one third of their annual investment programm (see row 5 in table 4).

5.2.5.4. Asked which errors are more costly, 21% of Austrian firms assessed upward and downward errors as equally costly, 63% reported optimistic forecasts as more costly, 16% overpessimistic forecasts. This asymmetry slightly increased with the size of the firms (see row 2 in table 4).

6. Conclusions

(1) This paper interprets reported expectations (e.g. sales or investment anticipations) as optimal plans of the entreprepeur in an uncertain environment and not as expected values in the mathematical sense. This latter concept is implizitly assumed if we evaluated the "reliability" of measured expectations according to a mean error criterium, or if we test some of the implications of the Rational Expectations Hypothesis.

(2) Optimal decisions under uncertainty coincide with optimal decisions under certainty - or with expected value of a random variable (e.g. expected demand) only under very restrictive conditions, which can be summarized under the label "symmetric losses due to same errors of different sign" (symmetric quadratic criterion function).

(3) Literature on uncertainty heavily concentrates on risk aversion (concave utility function) as the channel of impact of uncertainty. A concave utility function plus a linear technology (e.g. profit linear in the uncertainty variable X) is sufficient to bias the decision variable (Y, for example output) downward. In contrast we concentrate on concavity stemming from cost curves, production technology and demand elasticity, labelling this source of the bias as "concave technology". A linear utility function plus a certainty solution Z_Y concave in X are sufficient to bias the decision variable down. The same effect may stem from the expected costs from potentially unsold production and those from potentially unsatisfied demand (marginal costs of uncertainty) or from the fact that upward revisions of decision variables are easier (less costly) than downward revisions (asymmetric ex-post flexibilities). The three last mentioned tendencies yield downward biases for decision variables under uncertainty (as compared to certainty), which do not rely upon risk aversion.

(4) We show that there are many models which show the unambigous downward effect of uncertainty (e.g. 3.2.1.2), that there are some models in which solutions are the same as under certainty (e.g. 3.2.1.1) and there is a large class of models (3.3) in which the result depends on parameters taken by some cost components.

(5) The main source of a downward bias is the expected cost of unsold production which may not be sold if demand finally turns out to be unfavorable. This yields a downward bias (as compared to certainty) if production cost are convex and very likely a production plan lower than expected demand if costs are linear. The second bias is the more likely the smaller the profits are as compared to costs.

The main source of a neutrality of uncertainty is given if prices adjust ex post and there is no unsold quantity and no cost of late production. This yields for some models (examply in 3.2.1.1 or 3.2.2.1) a quantity decision independent of uncertainty.

A possible source for an input decision higher than under certainty is given in the case of low elasticity of substitution.

(6) We present empirical material demonstrating that prices are very unlikely to adjust quickly (using surveys, econometrics, comparing expectations and realizations, looking at involuntary inventory movements). Thus it becomes unlikely that models with prices as ex post controls are realistic, increasing importance of models incorporating unsold production and disequilibrium inventories.

(7) Ex post flexibility is not absent and may be even larger than presumed. But it concerns in the first place quantities, in the second place changes in inventories (and backlogs) and only to a minor extent prices. Changes in the net inventories represent of course only a partial flexibility, since they leave firms with a net inventory position higher or lower than planned.

Indeed formally the interpretation of reported expectations as decisions together with the fact that there are differences between expectations and realizations "needs" the element of ex post flexibility (otherwise expectations, however arrived at, have to be identical with realizations).

(8) There are indications that ex post flexibility is easier upward than downward. This fact is not popular in optimization literature since it is a new "Adhockery" (we usually have no knowledge whether and to what degree this flexibility is asymmetric). The only well known asymmetry in literature is the non negativity (irreversibility) of investment. This and any other asymmetric ex post flexibility constitutes another source (besides technological concavity) of a downward bias in optimal decision.

This asymmetry (that investment can be easily increased but not decreased) thwarts the impact of uncertainty to increase the optimal capacity suggested by the models of input uncertainty in case of low rates of substitution (3.4.5). If one input had to be fixed, it would be chosen to be high, but since a first decision can easily be revised upward it is actually chosen at relatively low levels (see upward bias in investment anticipations).

(9) Smaller firms seem to be more flexible in the sense, that they do not have to make decisions as early as large firms. Thus while large firms face price and output ex ante cotrols with partial ex post flexibility, small firms face a high degree of ex post flexibility of output and therefor can increase their market share in periods of uncertainty.

(10) Inititially intended only as a byproduct (introducing dynamic elements into a static model), we arrived at some surprising conclusions on the optimal level of inventories under uncertainty.

- we correct a well known formula in a seminal paper for the forgotten revenue from backlogged sales (Veinott 1966)

- we criticize literature with respect to unrealistic assumptions giving that uncertainty unambigously increases inventories

- we find empirical parameters to be in a region, where net inventories (planned) should be on average negative and

- predict that uncertainy will as a tendency lower planned net inventories

- we show that presently - if anything changed in the inventory position - we are in a period of declining net inventories (which may be due to increasing uncertainty or to declining demand), at least desired net inventories (which are negative) decreased.

These results are a byproduct of the main story of this paper but disputable on there own. If one does not believe this part, this should not prevent the reader from believing that reported expectations are optimal decisions and therefor should deviate from realizations in a persistent and predictable way.

(11) The decisions process of the firm consists of several stages in which it has to form a "pure" mathematical expectations and then consider the impacts of wrong decisions due to costs, production and demand conditions. The result of this process is an optimal decision or an economically rational expectation. I believe that a firm asked for its sales expectations will report this economically rational expectation and not the pure mathematical expectation. If the firm is (i) risk averse, or

(ii) faces a concave technology, or

(iii) there exists marginal cost of uncertainty (like potentially unsold production in disequilibrium models), or

(iv) asymmetric ex post flexibilities (with easier revisions upward), then the "economically rational" decision (optimal action) will differ from the expected value, being lower than the latter year after year.

Appendix 1: Derivation of a General Formula for the Optimal Inventory Starting Stock (after production, before demand is revealed)

In this appendix the formula (26) for the optimal inventory starting stock is derived using two different techniques (geometric row and dynamic programming). In both cases costs and prices are assumed linear (constant unit prices) and stable over time, the demand distribution is known and independently and identically distributed (i.i.d.), the solution is given for the infinite horizon.

Geometric Row Technique:

The first block (containing 4 terms) of Equation 1 shows the costs of producing, missing opportunity, inventory holding and goodwill costs (the first and third of these are relevant in the case of optimistic forecast, the second and forth in the case of overpessimistic forecast). The second block (containing 2 terms) tells us that for a proportion of a (indicating durability) of any disequilibrium future costs will be lower since the stored goods save towmorrow's production costs and that for a proportion b (indication backlogging possibility) there will be future profits out of backlogs (both factors properly discounted by α). The third and the fourth blocks are repetitions of this process with tomorrow's actual demand. Since the demand distribution is assumed to be i.i.d, the subscripts of x and y can be deleted, we can sum up terms (equation 2), diferentiate (3) and obtain the result (4).

Dynamic Recursion Technique:

The same result can be derived by a dynamic recursion. This method is far more flexible and usually applied in advanced inventory literature (see Veinott 1966, Hey 1981). In addition to the arguments in the first cited paper we include revenues from backlogs, in addition to those of the second paper costs and revenues from backlogs).

The equation 1 is the flow identity, defining the starting stock in t+1, depending on past demand, production and inventory position and of course durability and backlogging parameters.

$$(1)\quad C = \int_0^{y_1} c\ (y_1-x_1)\ f(x)dx + (p-c) \int_{y_1}^{\infty} (x_1-y_1)\ f(x)dx + h \int_0^{y_1} (y_1-x_1)\ f(x)dx$$

$$+ g \int_{y_1}^{\infty} (x_1-y_1)\ f(x)dx - \alpha \int_0^{y_1} a\ \ c\ (y_1-x_1)\ f(x)dx - \alpha \int_{y_1}^{\infty} b\ (p-c)\ (x_1-y_1)\ f(x)$$

$$+ \alpha \int_0^{y_2} c\ (y_2-x_2)\ \ f(x)dx + \alpha \int_{y_2}^{\infty} (p-c)\ (x_2-y_2)\ f(x)dx + \alpha h \int_0^{y_2} (y_2-x_2)\ f(x)dx$$

$$+ \alpha g \int_{y_2}^{\infty} (x_2-y_2)\ f(x)dx - \alpha 2 \int_0^{y_2} a\ \ c\ (y_2-x_2)\ f(x)dx$$

$$- \alpha^2 \int_{y_2}^{\infty} b\ (p-c)\ (x_2-y_2)\ f(x)dx + \ \ \ldots\ldots$$

$$(2)\quad C = \left[c\ (1-\alpha a)+h\right] \int_0^{y} (y-x)\ f(x)dx + \alpha \left[c\ (1-\alpha a)+h\right] \int_0^{y} (y-x)\ f(x)dx + \ldots\ldots.$$

$$+ \int_{y}^{\infty} (x-y)\ f(x)dx \left[(p-c)\ (1-\alpha b)+g\right] + \alpha\left[(p-x)\ (1-\alpha b)+g\right] \int_{y}^{\infty} (x-y)\ f(x)dx + \ldots. =$$

$$= \int_0^{y} (y-x) \left[\frac{c(1-\alpha a)+h}{1-\alpha}\right] f(x)dx + \int_{y}^{\infty} (x-y) \left[\frac{(p-c)\ (1-\alpha b)+g}{1-\alpha}\right] f(x)dx$$

$$(3)\quad \frac{\partial C}{\partial y} = \left[\frac{c(1-\alpha a)+h}{1-\alpha}\right] F(y) - \left[1-F(y)\right] \left[\frac{(p-c)\ (1-\alpha b)+g}{1-\alpha}\right] = 0$$

$$(4)\quad F(y)\ .\ \left[\frac{c(1-\alpha a)+h+g+(p-c)\ (1-\alpha b)}{1-\alpha}\right] = \frac{(p-c)\ (1-\alpha b)+g}{1-\alpha}$$

$$(5)\quad F(y) = \frac{(p-c)\ (1-\alpha b)+g}{p+g+h-\alpha a\ c\ -\alpha b\ (p-c)}$$

$$(1)\qquad I_{t+1} = \begin{cases} a\,(-x_t + q_t + I_t) & \text{wenn } x_t < q_t + I_t \\ b\,(-x_t + q_t + I_t) & \text{wenn } x_t > q_t + I_t \end{cases}$$

The recursion reads (2), V(I) is the maximum expected profit depending on I

$$(2)\qquad V(I) = \max_{q \geq 0} \int_0^{q+I} \left\{ [px - h\,(y-x)] + \alpha V\,[a\,(-x+y)] \right\} f(x)\,dx + \int_y^{\infty} \left\{ p\,y + \alpha bp\,(x-y) - g\,(x-y) + \alpha V\,[b\,(-x+y)] \right\} f(x)\,dx - c\,q$$

Differentiating for q (q = y-I) we get (3)

$$(3)\qquad 0 = \int_0^{\hat{q}+I} -h + \alpha V'\,[a(-x+\hat{y})]\,f(x)dx + \int_{\hat{q}+I}^{\infty} p - \alpha bp + g + \alpha V'\,[b(-x+\hat{y})]\,f(x)dx - c$$

Since $\hat{q}$ in equation (3) is given always in the form $\hat{q}$ + I there is a optimal post order stock $\hat{y}$. If I is smaller than $\hat{y}$ it is optimal to produce up to this quantity. If I<$\hat{y}$ we can write (2) in the form of

$$(4)\qquad V(I) = \int_0^{\hat{y}} [px + h\,(\hat{y}^*-x) + \alpha V\,[a\,(\hat{y}-x)]\,f(x)dx + \int_{\hat{y}}^{\infty} p\,\hat{y} + \alpha bp\,(x-\hat{y}) + g\,(x-\hat{y}) + \alpha V\,[b\,(-x+\hat{y})]\,f(x)dx - c\,(\hat{y}-I)$$

It follows that

$$(5)\qquad V'(I) = c \qquad \text{für} \quad I < \hat{y}^*$$

The other case ($\hat{y}$>I) need not be considered because it will not occur if we always start from an optimal inventory.

Putting (5) into (3), (6) and (7) follows, the last being identical to (36).

$$(6)\qquad (-h + \alpha a\,c)\,F\,(y^*) + [p - \alpha bp + g + \alpha bc]\,[1 - F\,(\hat{y}^*)] = c$$

$$(7)\qquad F\,(\hat{y}^*) = \frac{p - \alpha bp + g + \alpha bc - c}{p - \alpha bp + h + g + \alpha bc - \alpha ac} = \frac{(p-c)\,(1-\alpha b) + g}{p+g+h-\alpha b(p-c) - \alpha ac}$$

List of Abbreviations

1) All theoretical models will assume maximization of expected utility as the chosen decision technique. Uncertainty is not differentiated from risk (in the sense of Knight 1921), in contrast we assume a that the decision-maker has a probability distribution about the uncertainty variable (which Knight would have called risk). The rationale for this assumption is not that I believe that the concept of expected utility maximization is the only feasible one. The Keynesian view that "true" uncertainty changes the very behavior of agents (for example favoring the use of more flexible production techniques, reducing the willingness of people to undergo long term commitments etc, see Rothschild 1981) is probably the more realistic description for the impact of uncertainty albeit less operational. However proving the impact of uncertainty on the formation of economically rational expectations, is a harder task for Neumann-Morgenstern-maximizers than for Post Keynesians, who are inclined to believe it ex ante.

2) I want to thank the IFO Institute (Mr.Nerb, Mr.Lindlbauer) for providing me with data on their investment and business tests.

3) If we say the term expectation is used in the sense of the mathematical concept of the conditional expected value in mainstream economics, we do not deny that most authors on a theoretical level refer to expectations in the broader sense of the whole (subjective) probability function, instead of a point expectation (as represenbed by the conditional expected value). This follows the tradition of Muth, who starts describing expectations as subjective probability distribution (p.316, 1961). When appliing the concept into macroeconomic policy, however, nearly without exception the term rational expectations is restricted to the concept of the conditional expected value (see the recent surveys on the REH in the books by Mishkin 1983, Sheffrin 1983). This is specifically true in the New Classical Macroeconomics. As an exception we want to cite Lucas (1978), who presents a model in which

the agent's entire subjective probability distribution coincides with the true objective probability distribution. In most applications of the concept of the Rational Expectations Hypothesis, it is used in the sense of a conditional expected value (this operationalisation is necessary indeed to arrive at the policy impotency result), though it should be well known that this is only a good representation of the original idea in case of an objective criterion function).

4) The term "economically rational expectation" wants to express that people forming expectations do not only consider the mathematical concepts of probability densities or expected values, but also include the consequences of false expectations stemming from the economic system (cost functions, demand elasticities, disequilibria). This concept of economically rational expectations should not be confused with the concepts of either "bounded" rationality (Simon 1978), which stresses the cognitive limits of economic agents, or with the concept of "economically rational expectations" by Feige and Pearce 1976, which refers to the trade off between revenues and cost of information.

5) A suffix as usual denotes a partial derivative. All functions are assumed to be well-behaved in the usual sense (differentiable, integrals exist and are finite),

6) The proof makes use of the assumption that the second order condition for maximization under certainty holds ($Z_{YY}<0$) and of Jensen's Inequality for convex or concave functions. We prove the case of $\hat{Y}<Y^*$ defining Z_Y concave in X.

$$Z_Y(X_0, \hat{Y}) > EZ_Y(X, \hat{Y}) = 0$$

The inequality holds for any concave function (and so for Z_Y), the equality stems from the first order maximization under uncertainty.

It follows that $Z_Y(X_0, \hat{Y})$ is positive, and using $Z_{YY}<0$ this implies that $\hat{Y}$ is smaller than Y^* (where $Z_Y=0$).

7) See Nickell 1978, p.70f and p.84: If there exist n firms with identically but independently distributed random profits, then as $n \Rightarrow \infty$, any risk-averse investor will wish each and every firm to maximize its expected profit.

See also Nickell for objections to the empirical validity of this hypothesis (large firms, correllated movements of profits in business cycles).

9) There is one case in which the production decision is not indifferent from that under certainty. This is in case of multiplicative uncertainty, where the quantity is a function of the price times the random variable u. In this case the price follow the inverse relation $p=f^{-1}(\frac{q}{u})$ (while usually it is assumed that p=g(q).u). This is the case of Nickell (1978, see 3.4.3), here uncertainty gives under very likely conditions (see equation 32) a quantity lower than under certainty.

10) The decision about which mode is used may itself derive from profit maximization (see LIM 1980).

11) As far as empirical behavior is concerned, Tichy 1976 found evidence for procyclical changes in the inventory sales ratio for Austria; Streissler (1969) reported a increasing share of inventory investment within total investment in a period of rapid medium term growth in Germany.

8) We want to label consequences of uncertainty which do not stem from risk attitude as "technological". This use of the term "technological" concavity should be distinguished from the term "concave technique", which is sometimes used as a short cut description of a concave production function. Technological concavity in our sense may stem from cost curves as well as from demand curves.

12) These conditions are sufficient (see Nickell, 1978, p.91).

13A) Examples for non-linear loss functions see in Aiginger 1981, 1983. If the subjective probability function about possible states of nature do not follow a normal distribution, tables about the distribution function of the other family of distributions has to be used.

14) The larger standard deviation for quantities remains if we calculate prices by the means of actual sales, following the argument that price indices usually do not comprise discounts.

15) These results cannot constitute a proof of the hypothesis of net inventories declining with uncertainty, since the tendencies shown may be influenced by trends, structural changes or by decreasing expected demand. However, the data seem to be at greater variance with the presumption of business cycle experts, who maintain that backlogs are low and therefor net inventories should be large in troughs.

List of Abbreviations

U utility

Z argument of objective function (e.g. profit)

X "random variable"; X_o in world of certainty

Y "decision variable"

$\hat{Y}$, Y^* optimal decision in case of uncertainty resp. certainty

U_{XXY}, Z_{YXX} suffixes as usual denote partial derivatives

π profit

p price, ($\mathring{p} = p + g$)

$c(q)$ production costs (c' = marginal costs, c'' = second derivative), c = constant unit costs

c_1, c_2 cost of "emergency" production, production cutback

x, q quantity demanded, produced

$\bar{q} = q + I$ stock on hand (inventory after ordering, before demand); I starting stock before production.

E expectation operator

F (.) distribution function, f (.) density function (symmetric)

u additive or multiplicative error term in demand function

h, g cost of holding 1 unit of stocks respectively goodwill loss for 1 unit of unsatisfied demand

$\alpha = \frac{1}{1+r}$ discount factor (r = discount rate)

a, b durability parameter ($a = 1$ for durable goods, $a = 0$ for perishable goods) resp. backlogging parameter ($b = 1$ if no demand is lost, $b = 0$ if all demand unsatisfied today is lost)

w, i wages, investment (per unit of output)

M (q,u) marginal revenue (for a given q and u)

ϵ price-elasticity of demand

K ($\hat{K}$,K^*) capital stock (optimal under uncertainty resp. certainty)

$\tilde{\sigma}$ η elasticity of substitution, scale parameter

S standard deviation

k asymmetry parameter

REFERENCES

K. AIGINGER: The Use of Survey Data for the Analysis of Business Cycles, CIRET-Study, No. 14, Munich, 1977.

K. AIGINGER: Mean, Variance and Skewness of Reported Expectations and their Difference to the Respective Moments of Realizations. EMPIRICA 2/1979, pp. 217-165.

K. AIGINGER: Empirical Surveyed Expectational Data and Decision Theory. CIRET-Conference, Athens, 1981 (1981 A).

K. AIGINGER: Empirical Evidence on the Rational Expectations Hypothesis. EMPIRICA 1/1981, pp. 25-72, (1981 B).

K. AIGINGER: Die Wirkung von asymmetrischen Verlusten auf die Bildung von rationalen ökonomischen Erwartungen. Forthcoming in: Ifo-Studien, vol.29, 1983, (1983 A).

K. AIGINGER: Die Anwendung der Unsicherheitstheorie auf die unternehmerische Produktionsentscheidung in der österreichischen Industrie. (Mimeo 1983, 1983 B).

Y. AMIHUD, H. MENDELSON: Price Smoothing and Inventory. Review of Economic Studies, vol. 5o, 1983, pp. 87-98.

K.J. ARROW: The Future and the Present in Economic Life. Economic Inquiry, vol. 16, April 1978, pp. 157-169.

K.J. ARROW, T. HARRIS, J. MARSCHAK: Optimal Inventory Policy. Econometrica, vol.19, 1951, pp. 25o-272.

K.J. ARROW, M.D. INTRILLIGATOR: Handbook of Mathematical Economics. Amsterdam, New York, Oxford, 1982.

K. ARROW, S. KARLIN, H. SCARF: Studies in the Mathematical Theory of Inventory and Production. Stanford, 1958.

K. ARROW, S. KARLIN, H. SCARF: Studies in Applied Probability and Management Science. Stanford, 1962.

D.P. BARON: Price Uncertainty, Utility, and Industry Equilibrium in Pure Competition. International Economic Review, October 197o, 11, pp. 463-48o.

R.A. BATCHELOR, T.D. SHERIFF: Unemployment and Unanticipated Inflation in Post-war Britain. Economica, vol. 47, May 198o, pp. 179-192.

A.S. BLINDER: Inventories and Sticky Prices: More on the Microfoundation of Macroeconomics. Amerian Economic Review, vol. 72 (3) June 1982, pp. 334-348.

J. BUCHAN, E. KOENIGSBERG: Scientific Inventory Management. Prentice Hall, 1963.

D.W. CARLTON: Market Behavior with Demand Uncertainty and Price Inflexibility. American Economic Review, Sept. 1978, vol. 68, pp. 571-587.

R. CYERT, J. MARCH: Behavioural Theory of the Firm. Englewood Cliffs, 1963.

M. DE GROOT: Optimal Statistical Decisions, New York, 197o.

P.A. DIAMOND, J.E. STIGLITZ: Increases in Risk and in Risk Aversion. Journal of Economic Theory, vol. 8 (3), July 1974, pp. 337-36o.

Economic Report of the President, 1983, Washington, 1983.

E.L. FEIGE, D.K. PEARCE: Economically Rational Expectations: Are Innovations in the Rate of Inflation Independent of Innovations in the Measures of Monetary and Fiscal Policies? Journal of Political Economy, vol. 84 (3), June 1976, pp. 499-522.

P.C. FISHBURN: Mean - Risk Analysis with Risks Associated with Below - Target Returns. American Economic Review, vol. 67, March 1977, pp. 116-124.

R.J. GORDON: Output Fluctuations and Gradual Price Adjustment, Journal of Economic Literature, vol. 19 (2), June 1981, pp. 493-53o.

R. HARTMANN: Competitive Firm and the Theory of Input Demand under Price Uncertainty. Journal of Political Economy, vol. 83, December 1975.

G.A. Hay: Production, Price and Inventory Theory. American Economic Review, vol. 6o, 4/197o, pp. 531-545.

D.A. HAY, D.J. MORRIS: Industrial Economics. Oxford 1979.

J.D. HEY: Statistics in Economics. London 1974.

J.D. Hey: Uncertainty in Microeconomics. Oxford 1979.

J.D. HEY: Exonomics in Disequilibrium. Oxford 1981.

J.D. HEY: Goodwill-Investment in the Intangible University of York. Discussion Paper 46, 1982.

F.D. HILLIER, G.J. LIEBERMANN: Introduction into Operations Research, San Francisco, 198o.

A.A. HIRSCH, M.C. LOVELL: Sales Anticipations and Inventory Behavior. New York, London, Sydney, Toronto, 1969.

C.C. HOLT, F. MODIGLIANI, J. MUTH, H. SIMON: Planning Production, Inventories and Work Force, Englewood Cliffs, New York, 196o.

S.H. HYMANNS: The Price Taker: Uncertainty, Utility, and the Supply Functions. International Economic Review, September 1966, 7, pp. 346-356.

L.A. JOHNSON, D.C. MONTGOMERY: Operations Research and Production Planning, Scheduling and Inventory Control. New York, 1974.

T.F. JUSTER, R. COMMENT: A Note on the Measurement of Price Expectation. University of Michigan, Unpublished, 1978.

F.H. KNIGHT: Risk, Uncertainty and Profit. Boston 1921.

M. KRAUS: A Comparative Statics Theorem for Choice Under Risk. Journal of Economic Theory, vol. 21 (3), December 1979, pp. 51o-517.

Y. KON: Capital Input under Price Uncertainty: A Putty - Clay Technology Case. International Economic Review, vol. 24 (1), February 1983, pp. 1983-197.

H.E. LELAND: Theory of the Firm Facing Uncertain Demand. American Economic Review, June 1972, vol. 62, pp. 278-291.

C. LIM: The Ranking of Behavioral Modes of the Firm Facing Uncertain Demand. American Economic Review, vol. 7o, March 198o, pp. 217-224.

E.A. LÖWE, R.W. SHAW: An Analysis of Managerial Biassing. Evidence from a Company's Budgeting Process. Journal of Management Studies 5/1978.

R.E. LUCAS: Asset Prices in an Exchange Economy. Econometrica, vol. 46 (6), November 1978, pp. 1429-1446.

D.J. MULLINEAUX: Inflation Expectation and Money Growth in the United States. American Economic Review, vol. 7o, March 198o, pp. 149-161.

J.F. MUTH: Rational Expectations and the Theory of Price Movements. Econometrica, vol. 29, July 1961, pp. 315-335.

A.J. NEVIN: Some Effects of Uncertainty: Simulation of a Model of Price. Quarterly Journal of Economics, vol. 8o (1), 1966, pp. 73-87.

S.J. NICKELL: The Investment Decisions of Firms. Oxford 1978.

E. NOWOTNY, A. GUGER, H. SUPPANZ, H. WALTHER: Studien zur Wettbewerbsfähigkeit in der österreichischen Wirtschaft. Schriftenreihe des Ludwig Boltzmann Institutes für Wachstumsforschung, vol. 1, Wien 1981.

F. PAPADIA: EEC DG II Inflationary Expectations. European Community, Internal Paper 1981.

P.B. PASHIGAN: The Accuracy of the Commerce - SEC Sales Anticipations. Review of Economics and Statistics, November 1964, pp. 398-4o5.

D.K. PEARCE: Comparing Survey and Rational Measures of Expected Inflation. Journal of Money, Credit and Banking, vol. 11. November 1979, pp. 447-456.

J.E. PESANDO: A Note on the Rationality of the Livingston Price Expectations. Journal of Political Economy, vol. 83, August 1975, pp. 849-858.

R. PETERSEN, E.A. SILVER: Decision Systems for Inventory Management and Production Planning. New York 1979.

R.S. PINDYCK: Adjustment Costs, Uncertainty, and the Behavior of Firm. American Economic Review, June 1982, vol. 72, pp. 415-427.

K.W. ROTHSCHULD: Einführung in die Ungleichgewichtstheorie. Berlin, Heidelberg, New York, 1981.

M. ROTHSCHILD, J.E. STIGLITZ: Increasing Risk: 1. A Definition, 2. Its Economic Consequences. Journal of Economic Theory, vol. 2, 197o, pp. 225-243, resp. vol. 3, 1971, pp. 66-82.

J.C.R. ROWLEY, P.K. TRIVEDI: Econometrics of Investment. London, New York, Sydney, Toronto, 1975.

S.M. SHEFFRIN: Rational Expectations. Cambridge University Press, Cambridge, London, New York, 1983

R.J. SHILLER: Rational Expectations and the Dynamic Structure of Macro Economic Models, Journal of Monetary Economics, vol. 4 (1) 1978, pp. 1-44.

R.J. SHILLER: Do Stock Prices Move Too Much to be Justified by Subsequent Changes in Dividends? The American Economic Review, vol. 71, June 1981, pp. 421-436.

H.A. SIMON: Rationality as Process and as Product of Thought. American Economic Review, Papers and Proceedings, vol. 68, May 1978, pp. 1-16.

E. STREISSLER: Hayek on Growth: A Reconsideration of his Early Theoretical Work. In: Streissler, G. Haberler, F.A. Lutz, F. Machlup (Eds): Roads to Freedom, Essays in Honour of F.A. von Hayek, London 1969.

S.J. TURNOWSKY: Empirical Evidence of Price Expectations. Journal of American Statistical Association, vol. 65, December 197o, pp. 1441-1454.

P. WACHTEL: Survey Measures of Expected Inflation and Their Potential Usefulness. In: Joel Popkin (Ed.): Analysis of Inflation: 1965-1974. Studies in Income and Wealth, vol. 42, NBER, Cambridge MASS, 1977, pp. 361-395.

G. TICHY: Die Bedeutung der Lager für die Konjunktur. Empirica 1/1976, pp. 3-45 and 2/1976, pp. 153-196.

S.J. TURNOVSKY: The Theory of Production under Conditions of Stochastic Input Supply. Metroeconomica, vol. 23, 1971, pp. 51-68.

S.J. TURNOVSKY: Production Flexibility, Price Uncertainty and the Behavior of the Competitive Firm. International Economic Review, vol. 14 (2), June 1973, pp. 395-413.

A.F. VEINOTT: The Status of Mathematical Inventory Theory. Management Science, vol. 12, July 1966, pp. 745-777.

G. WINCKLER: Walrasianische und keynesianische Aspekte der Lagerhaltungstheorie. Österreichische Akademie der Wissenschaften, Wien 1977.

E. ZABEL: Multiperiod Monopoly under Uncertainty. Journal of Economic Theory, vol. 4, December 1972, vol. 5, pp. 524-536.

V. ZARNOWITZ: Orders, Production and Investment - A Cyclical and Structural Analysis. New York 1973.

V. ZARNOWITZ: Process and Performance in Economic Prediction. Paper presented to the 15th CIRET Conference, Athens 1981.

Summary of the Discussion

G. Poser
Technische Hochschule Darmstadt
Darmstadt

W. J. SCHEUTEN opened the discussion of J. D. LINDLBAUER's paper by stating that external data - like interest rates of illiquidities and bankruptcies - that could help to make better investment decisions were so rare that qualitative survey data were about the most important external data that entrepreneurs could rely on. One of the most important internal indicators is the order inflow - not just its level but its monthly changes and whether and to what extent orders had been withdrawn, postponed or advanced. At IBM this analysis was made for economic sectors because this company is differently affected by cyclical developments, by export and capital markets and other developments in the economy. For businessmen different developments of internal and external indicators seem to be especialy interesting because they need an explanation why the indicators go in different directions.

To use all the information contained in survey results, W. NAGGL suggested to break down the net differences and to look at the changes of increases and the changes of decreases separately. On the other hand he emphasized that disaggregation of the data would lead to problems with the irregular component.

Ph. A. KLEIN asked if new orders in each of the branches lead or lag business assessments.

H. KÖNIG mentioned that the application of the so-called latin structure approach, a method used in sociology, to Ifo-data has led to an indicator with a lead time of 2 to 3 months compared to the Ifo-business climate in the textile industry.

LINDLBAUER answered that he had tried combinations of indicators to minimize the effects of irregularities but that it was very difficult to analyse what happened from combined indicators. Turning to the problem of inventories he pointed out that although there should be clear lag relations between textile consumer goods and textile intermediates the data show that this is not the case. Sometimes consumer goods lead and sometimes intermediates do. According to LINDLBAUER this result might well be influenced by inventories but the data did not allow to investigate this question in more detail.

Jack CULLITY stated that the initial findings of the paper presented by KAWASAKI, GAHLEN and BUCK were encouraging but that there were a few open questions, one of them being how the variance of price expectations is related to disturbances.

W. GERSTENBERGER pointed out that the link between inflation on the one hand and variability of inflation and variability of relative prices on the other hand is connected with measurement. In addition he suggested that the costs of primary production factors be taken into account when the Philipps-curve is discussed.

R. A. BATCHELOR argued that the apriori assumption of the authors, namely that output and employment ought to be positively correlated with unexpected inflation and negatively correlated with the variance of expectations and the variability in the rate of inflation itself need not be correct. Furthermore, theory suggested that by relative price variability the slope of the Philipps-curve is determined rather then the underlying natural rate of output or employment.

G. POSER suggested that further work on this project take the market structure into account as a determinant.

Concerning the question about the connection between the variance of price expectations and the variance of relative price changes BUCK answered that this is still an open question that needs more work. As far as the development of the Philipps-curve is concerned, BUCK admitted that in disaggregation to the industry level they had omitted the costs of materials and the wage costs. Also the questions of the identification of the model and the underlying structure had to be left open. The suggestion that perhaps market structure plays some role in the models of uncertainty in the Philipps-curve was accepted as an issue that should be incorporated in future research.

In his discussion of K. AIGINGER's paper R. A. BATCHELOR pointed out that uncertainty was well able to increase rather than decrease employment, as he had already argued in the discussion of the previous paper. Consequently he underlined AIGINGER's conclusion that one could not conclude that uncertainty was bad for unemployment. But BATCHELOR had some reservations concerning AIGINGER's means of rationalizing his empirical observation that output expectations were chronically biased downward. AIGINGER assumed that firms are planning for a certain level of output which is less than what they really think is going to be required on an average. When continually a higher than expected demand comes in output kind of creeps upwards but the creeping output does not actually involve a rise in prices. BATCHELOR doubts that output is much more flexible than prices. The fact that the variance of prices is less than the variance of output does not explain exactly how the adjustment was going on. BATCHELOR concluded what was needed was some research into exactly how firms are answering questions to find out whether they make a distinction between the level of output they would produce under uncertainty, the level of output they planned, and the level of output they actually expect to wind up supplying.

Sixth Session
International Forecasting

Chairman:

C.F. Bergsten, Institute of International Economics
Washington, D.C.

Major Features of New Business Cycle Indicators in Japan

M. Baba
Kyoto University
Kyoto

N. Nomura
Economic Data Research Center
Tokyo

S. Tahara
Economic Planning Agency
Tokyo

I

It was in August, 1960, that the Economic Planning Agency (EPA) of Japanese Government began to prepare and make public the diffusion indexes (DI), which were in accordance with the method developed by National Bureau of Economic Research (NBER), as an official tool for analyzing and forecasting business cycles. Since then up to the present, these diffusion indexes have been made public at the end of each month. During this period, the DI were revised four times in 1965, 1966,1968 and 1979 with their components being replaced or the method of seasonal adjustment improved. The number of the components which was 20 at the outset, has been increased to 25 since the revision in 1966. In the seasonal adjustment of the components, a 12-month moving average method was used at the outset. Subsequently, however, an EPA Method which was an improved version of the preliminary stage of the Census Method, was adopted. Since 1981 the Bureau of the Census Method, x-11 program, has been in use.

In the 1979 revision, 10 components were replaced in an attempt to have the DI reflect as much as possible the structural change of the Japanese economy and the transformation of cyclical fluctuation which had occurred after the first oil crisis. This resulted in a more or less correction of the defect that though the leading indexes (the DI which had been computed on the basis of the leading components) signalled cyclical peaks before they were actually reached, they failed to signal troughs in advance or rather lagged behind them. In retrospect, however, we suspect that among all DI components, those related to production, inventory and finance occupied considerably too large weight as compared with those representing other fields.

Subsequently, the Japanese economy experienced the second oil crisis and an adjustment to it and the world economy also underwent a big change. As a consequence, there arose doubts and criticisms that the behaviors of the diffusion indexes which were revised in 1979 might not be reflecting the real picture of business cycles in Japan. As a result of more-than-one-year's cautious and close inquiries and analyses of economic statistics, the EPA prepared new diffusion indexes and made them public late in August this year.

For this fifth revision of diffusion indexes, the EPA proceeded with preparatory work paying attention to the following points among others. First, efforts should be made so that such fields as personal consumption expenditures, housing construction, corporate profits and profit margins might be covered as much as possible. These spheres ought to have been covered by DI components but had not hitherto necessarily been done so in full. Second, efforts should be exerted in finding indicators which would reflect changes in tertiary-industry activities in an appropriate form. Third, an examination should be made of a possibility of using anticipatory data. Fourth, efforts should be made in order that leading indexes might signal in advance not only the peaks of business cycles but also the troughs and that roughly coincident index components might cover important economic fields more extensively than ever. Fifth, the percentage changes from the same month of the preceding year of DI components should be examined positively so that the leading indexes might more clearly identify turning points in advance. Sixth, as much importance as possible should be attached and consideration be given to the Zarnowitz-Boschen's scoring system (economic significance, statistical adequacy, timing, conformity, smoothness, currency or timeliness) in selecting DI components.

II

Table 1 gives DI components which have been selected from among varieties and enormous quantities of economic statistics.

Table 1

Leading Indicators

1. Index of producer's inventory ratio to shipment (mining and manufacturing) (inverted)
2. Index of raw materials inventory ratio to consumption (manufacturing) (inverted)
3. New orders for machinery (private demands, excl. vessels and electric power)
4. Index of producer's shipment of construction materials *
5. Dwelling new construction started, number of units
6. Index of overtime worked (manufacturing) *
7. New passenger car registrations
8. Suspensions of business transaction with bank
9. Index of stock prices (total, Tokyo)
10. Money supply (M_2 + CD, money and quasi-money plus certificate of deposits) *
11. Nikkei index of commodity prices (total) *
12. Index of terms of trade

Roughly Coincident Indicators

1. Index of industrial production (mining and manufacturing)
2. Index of producer's shipment (mining and manufacturing)
3. Index of capacity utilization ratio (manufacturing)
4. Index of consumption of raw materials (manufacturing)
5. Electric power consumption of large users
6. Quantum index of imports
7. Construction started, floor space (mining and manufacturing)
8. Ratio of job offers to applicants (excl. new graduates)
9. Sales at department stores *
10. Net profits (all industries)
11. Sales of small and medium enterprises

Lagging Indicators

1. Index of producer's inventory of finished goods (mining and manufacturing)
2. Index of raw materials inventory (manufacturing)
3. Index of producer's shipment of capital goods (excl. transportation machinery)
4. Index of regular workers employment (manufacturing) *
5. Employment insurance beneficiaries (general insurance)
6. Living expenditure (workers household) *
7. Average contracted rate on loans and discounts (all banks)

* Percentage change from the same month of preceding year.

The new DI components are 30 in number, an increase of five from the old ones. Brief explanations are given below group by group about the components which have been removed from the list of DI components and the ones which have newly been added.

(1) Leading Index Components: New orders for construction works (private sector), excess of imports over exports (quantitative basis) and inventory investment of goods in process (mining and manufacturing) which were among old DI components, have recently become subject to irregular fluctuation so frequently that it has become very difficult to identify their cyclical peaks or troughs. Besides, the excess of imports over exports has ceased to show the behavior like a leading index. The components which have newly been chosen, include the five components of (a) index of producer's shipment of construction materials, (b) new dwelling construction started (number of units), (c) new passenger car registrations, (d) suspensions of business transaction with banks and (e) index of terms of trade. The index (a) manifests a turn in advance of the turns in both equipment investment and housing

investment, and its percentage change from the same month of the preceding year more clearly identities the turning points in advance. The component (c) indicates the trend of durable consumer goods most representatively and in Japan it has become able to observe their cyclical fluctuations considerably clearly since 1973 or thereabouts. With respect to the two components of the index of overtime worked (manufacturing) and the Nikkei index of commodity prices (total) which have been adopted as DI components continuedly from the old list of DI , it has been decided that their percentage changes from the corresponding month of the preceding year would be used beginning with the latest revision, in order to improve their cyclical timing (especially, their property of identifying turning points in advance).

(2) Roughly Coincident Index Components: While the eight components out of the 11 components of this kind remain unchanged from the old list of DI , there have been new additions of three components of (a) sales at department stores, (b) net profits (all industries) and (c) sales of small and medium enterprises. Since the component (b) is a quarterly statistical series which is suveyed by the Ministry of Finance, the behavior of the index of industrial production multiplied by the wholesale price index will be used as a substitute variable until the data becomes available.
The component (c) is what Small and Medium Enterprises Agency

estimates as the index of producer's shipment of small and medium enterprises (manufacturing) multiplied by the small and medium enterprises' wholesale price index (industrial goods).

(3) Lagging Index Components: Those which have been removed from the old list of DI components are the five components of (a) gross fixed capital formation (private sector), (b) yields of interest-bearing Telegraph and Telephone Bonds, (c) turnover of demand deposits, (d) ratio of loans to deposits (banking account) and (e) ratio of labor cost (manufacturing). Those which have been newly adopted in replacement of them are five components including (a') the index of producer's shipment of capital goods, (b') index of regular workers employment (manufacturing), (c') employment insurance beneficiaries, (d') living expenditure and (e') average contracted rate on loans and discounts (all banks). As regards the component (b), its conformity with the trend of demand and supply of private funds which would reflect domestic business conditions has become unclear due partly to the issuances of large amounts of national bonds in recent years. The component (c) which is calculated dividing bill clearance by deposit money balance, has come to show irregular fluctuations more frequently since 1979 due in part to the increases in receipts connected with foreign exchange transactions or in coupons of national bonds both of which are related only

sparsely with the trend of domestic economy. With respect to the component (d), its conformity with business cycles has recently become unclear as diversification progresses not only in corporate procurements of funds but also in households' investments of funds.

III

Now, let us examine the characteristics of new diffusion indexes, especially of leading index while comparing it with the old one.

Fig. 1 illustrates the behaviors of new leading index comparatively with the old one. The two curves in the lower part of the diagram depict the behaviors of these cumulative indexes. As will be seen, the new index displays its property of signalling in advance both peaks and troughs at reference cycle dates more satisfactorily than the old one. In order to see such a fact more precisely, we have prepared Table 2.

The table gives a comparison of the timing of coincident and lagging indexes of the new DI with that of the two indexes of the old DI for reference's sake. In this place, however, let us direct attention to the numerals (the number of months) in the leading index columns among others. (We have been unable in this table to compare the new and old DI in the period from the peak in 1951 to the trough in 1954, be-

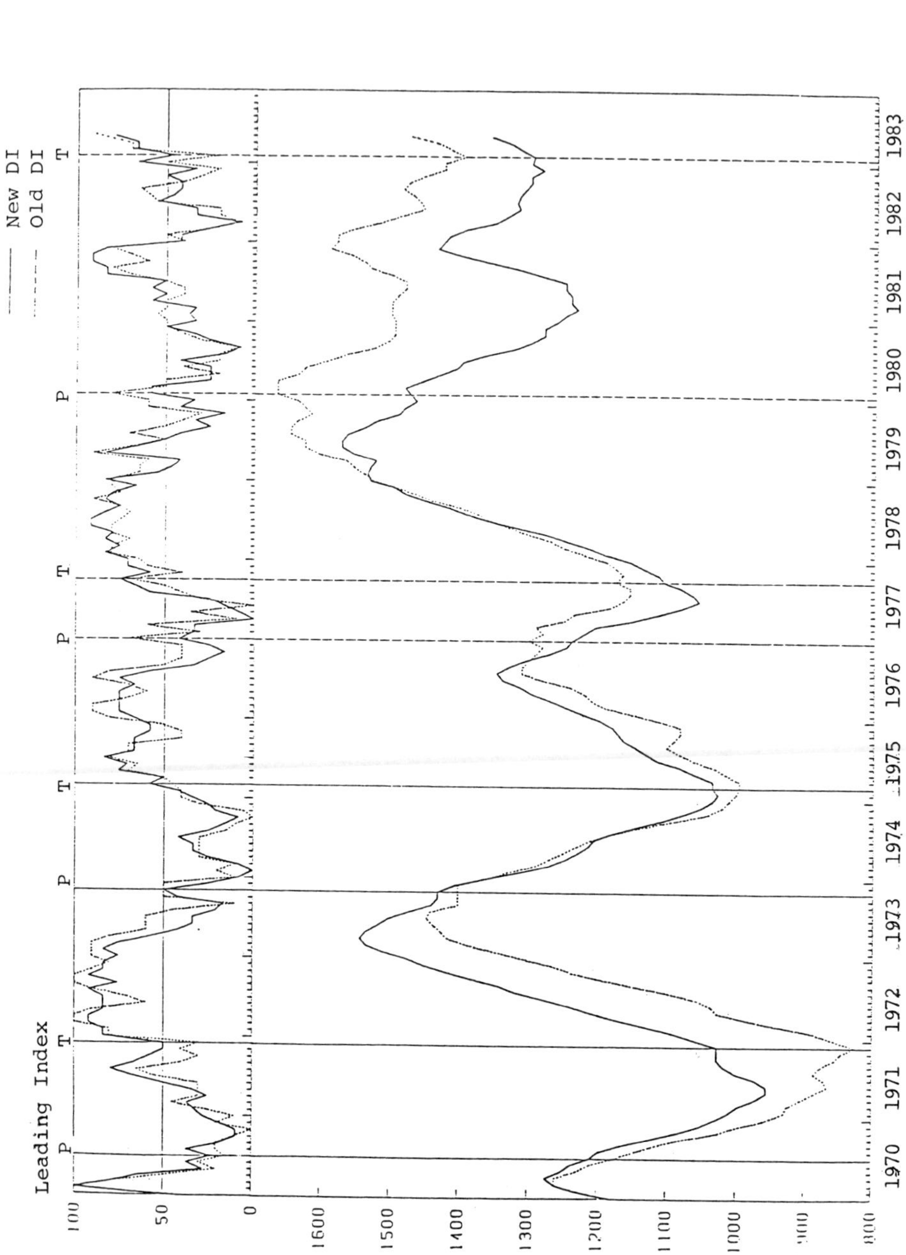

Leading Index
New DI
Old DI
P
T
P
T
P
T
P
T
100
50
0
1600
1500
1400
1300
1200
1100
1000
900
800
1970
1971
1972
1973
1974
1975
1976
1977
1978
1979
1980
1981
1982
1983

Fig. 1

T a b l e 2

(month)

Reference Dates			New DI			Old DI		
			Lead-ing	Coin-cident	Lag-ging	Lead-ing	Coin-cident	Lag-ging
June	1951	P	--	--	--	--	--	--
Oct.	1951	T	--	--	--	--	--	--
Jan.	1954	P	--	--	--	--	--	--
Nov.	1954	T	--	--	--	--	--	--
June	1957	P	-2	+1	+9	-2	+1	+9
June	1958	T	0	+1	+10	0	+1	+10
Dec.	1961	P	-4	+1	+7	-4	+1	+7
Oct.	1962	T	+1	+2	+8	+1	+2	+8
Oct.	1964	P	-7	+2	+2	-7	+2	+2
Oct.	1965	T	-2	0	+2	-2	0	+2
July	1970	P	-3	+1	+5	-3	+3	+9
Dec.	1971	T	-6	0	+8	0	0	+3
Nov.	1973	P	-7	+1	+9	-4	+1	+14
Mar.	1975	T	-1	+1	+5	+1	+1	+12
Jan.	1977	P	-5	0	+5	-4	0	+14
Oct.	1977	T	-3	-3	+12	-1	0	+11
Feb.	1980	P	-7	+2	+8	+2	+1	+16
Feb.	1983	T	-2	-2	--	0	0	--
Average Timing (1957-1983)		P&T	-3.4	+0.5	+6.9	-1.6	+0.9	+9.0
		P	-5.0	+1.1	+6.4	-3.1	+1.3	+10.1
		T	-1.9	-0.1	+7.5	-0.1	+0.6	+7.7
Average Timing (1970-1983)		P&T	-4.4	0.0	+7.4	-0.9	+0.8	+11.3
		P	-6.3	+1.0	+6.8	-2.0	+1.3	+13.3
		T	-3.0	-1.0	+8.3	0.0	+0.3	+8.7

cause we have failed to make the data retroactive to this period in a satisfactory form).

The timing of the new and old leading indexes had almost been same until the first oil crisis. In the subsequent period, however, the difference in timing between the two DIs has been quite conspicuous. While the old leading index completely failed to signal in advance the trough in March 1975, peak in February 1980 and trough in February 1983, the new leading index manifested the turning points one , seven and two months respectively in advance of these reference cycle dates. The fact that the new DI have a considerably better property of signalling business cycles in advance than the old DI , is quite clear from the number of months they manifested turning points before the actual peaks or troughs which are given in the average timing (in 1957-83 and 1970-83) in the lower column of the table.

In order that a leading index may become an indicator which is effective for analyzing and forecasting business cycles, it is, first of all, necessary that the timing of the index is good. It is, however, desirable in addition that the index will show as less irregular fluctuations as possible and also that it will have enough smoothness. Table 3 gives a comparison between the new and old DI in this respect on the basis of the figures for 1970 and subsequent years. The degree of fluctuating irregularly has been measured in this

Table 3

	Irregular Fluctuations (times)			Smoothness		
	Leading	Coincident	Lagging	Leading	Coincident	Lagging
New DI	4	5	8	1.77	2.52	2.10
Old DI	11	7	17	2.31	3.09	2.13

place by the frequency a DI broke for a time through the 50% line from downwards to upwards or vice versa (on the reference dates or on the dates not in their neighborhood); while $(\sqrt{\Sigma(\text{second order difference})^2 / \text{number of months}})$ has been used as the measure of smoothness. The less this value, the smoother is the index. As will be seen in Table 3, the new DI are more superior than the old one with respect of both frequency of irregular fluctuations and smoothness.

The EPA has not adopted the composit indexes (CI) as an offi-cial tool yet. However, when the CI are tentatively calcu-lated by the groups of leading, coincident and lagging index-es on the basis of new DI components and the timing to refer-ence dates of the calculated result is examined, the results will be as given in the left half of Table 4. The timing of Japanese leading and coincident indexes adopted at the Center for International Business Cycle Research (CIBCR) is given in the right half of the table for the sake of refer-ence. It must be noted, however, that it will be impossible to compare the EPA's CI directly with CIBCR's because Japa-nese reference dates set by CIBCR differ from those set by

Table 4

Reference Dates			CI Leading	CI Coincident	CI Lagging	CIBCR Leading	CIBCR Coincident
June	1951	P	-	-	-	-	-
Oct.	1951	T	-	-	-	-	-
Jan.	1954	P	-	-	-	-	-
Nov.	1954	T	-	-	-	-	-
June	1957	P	-4	-1	+7	-5	-1
June	1958	T	-3	0	+9	+3	+7
Dec.	1961	P	-8	+1	+5	-2*	-2
Oct.	1962	T	-3	+1	+8	0	+3
Oct.	1964	P	-8	+2	+1	-12	-1
Oct.	1965	T	-5	-2	+4	-2	+5
July	1970	P	-5	-1	+5	-5	-1
Dec.	1971	T	-7	-2	+8	+2	0
Nov.	1973	P	-9	0	+8	+3	-9
Mar.	1975	T	-2	0	+10	-1	-1
Jan.	1977	P	-7	0	0	-5	-
Oct.	1977	T	-3	-3	+10	+4	-
Feb.	1980	P	-9	0	+6	+2	0
Feb.	1983	T	-4	0	-	-	**
Average Timing (1957-1983)		P&T	-5.5	-0.4	+6.2	-1.4	0.0
		P	-7.1	+0.1	+4.6	-3.4	-2.3
		T	-3.9	-0.9	+8.2	+1.0	+2.8
Average Timing (1970-1983)		P&T	-5.9	-0.8	+6.7	+0.8	-2.2
		P	-8.3	-0.3	+4.8	0.0	-3.3
		T	-4.0	-1.3	+9.3	+1.7	-0.5

* Dec. 1959 .... peak
May 1960 ....trough

** Aug. 1980 ....trough
June 1981 .... peak

EPA.

IV

We have so far explained the contents and characteristics of Japan's new business-cycle indicators, diffusion indexes (DI). Some of the objectives which were set when the work of preparing new DI was started, have been achieved. However, there are on the other hand many issues which have not been solved in a satisfactory manner. These are problems left for the study or examination in future. Of importance among them is first of all the failure to discover indicators which would reflect directly and appropriately the cyclical fluctuations in the economic activities of government sector (for example, public investment) or in the activities of tertiary industries centering around service industry. There has been available in Japan since several years ago a statistical series in the name of "index of tertiary industry activities" which is compiled every quarter year by Ministry of International Trade and Industry. To our regret, however, it is not proper as an economic indicator in respect of currency or timeliness because it is considerably late in being made public.

Secondly, the data which are suveyed by such government agencies as EPA, Bank of Japan and Small and Medium Enterprises Credit Corporation have been examined in order to incorporate anticipatory or ex ante data into DI components, especially those which concern with entrepreneurs' judgment on business conditions: and a conclusion has consequently been reached that it is helpful for us to make effective use of them in order to improve the property of leading indexes to signal the turns of business cycles in advance. We have, however, shelved the adoption of anticipatory or ex ante data in the latest revision on the grounds that the use of ex post data should preferentially be considered.

Thirdly, the adoption of composite indexes (CI) has also been shelved in the latest revision because it was considered that there still remain problems which have to be examined further with respect to such issue as the trend adjustment of some components.

We believe that more studies have to be conducted on these points hereafter.

Use of Business Survey Data into a Short–term Prediction Model

A. Dramais
Commission of the
European Communities
Brussels

Foreword

The present paper describes the introduction of Business Survey Data into a short-term forecasting model named BUSY, proposed by the author to the services of the Commission of the European Communities. The full model is still being developed and all results quoted here should be considered as provisional. This is also the reason why only equations relative to the Business Survey Data themselves are presented.

In the model, Business Survey Data are used in the quality of expected variables, centering on expected output and expected inflation.

The paper will therefore start with the derivation of a new indicator for expected industrial production, using the Generalized Logit approach (Poirier, 1980). The methodology however is not applicable to all Business Expectation series since it requires the simultaneous availability of answers about forecast and realised evolution of the relevant series.

../..

The author is presently Head of Division, Commission of the European Communities. The paper, however, was written when the author was Associate Professor, Department of Applied Economics, University of Brussels. All views and opinions expressed in this study are those of the author and should in no way be attributed to the Commission Services.

Therefore, price expectations had to be derived in a more usual way, as the balance of answers between those expecting price increases (or acceleration of inflation) and those expecting a price decrease (or deceleration of inflation).

The second chapter will deal with the most critical issue, in the use of Business Survey Data into a model, i.e. the fact that they must themselves be generated endogenously by the model when more-than one-quarter ahead forecasts are envisaged.

The third chapter finally will introduce output and price expectations indicators into selected equations.

At present, the results cover four countries, i.e. France, Germany, Italy and the United Kingdom. Results for Belgium are also presented in the industrial production part. The Business Survey Data sample is based on monthly or quarterly data, all results being, however, converted ex-post into quarterly aggregates when introduced into the equations of the model in order to be compatible with quarterly national accounts and labour market data. Estimations were done on the 1969-1980 period, the data available for 1981-82 being used for testing the out-of-sample properties of the equations.

I. FORECASTING INDUSTRIAL PRODUCTION[1]

1. Introduction

The present economic situation makes economic predictions based on macroeconomic models a somewhat difficult art. This has entailed a revival in the analysis of expectations of economic agents, as shown by the increasing number of papers on rational expectations and related concepts.

The problem, however, is that expectations are generally unobservable and must be approached in an indirect way, through adaptive, autoregressive, ... processes.

Now, for some series at least, business survey data provide the explicit expectations of the participants about production indices, prices and sometimes employment in the next three to six months.

1 This chapter is a development of a former paper by A. Dramis and E. Waelbroeck-Rocha, "A probabilistic approach to the quantification of Business Survey Data", presented to the European Congress of the Econometric Society, Athens, Sept. 1979.

These surveys have however some drawbacks, the main one being that they recognize but three possible (subjective) answers to the future evolution of a time series : increase (+), decrease (-), or no change (=). This implies a loss of information compared with a complete numerical specification, and raises theoretical and empirical difficulties about the exact interpretation of a "no change" answer (Boas and Koerts, 1963). However, it also results in a considerable gain as to the speed with which data becomes available; since this availability factor is of major importance in short-term forecasting, the use of this kind of expectations is certainly worth considering.

This conclusion is of course far from being a new one, and has been considered by numerous authors since 1950 (2) with various degrees of success. In fact, it seems to us that the usual approach to business survey data quantification for predictive purposes suffers from too great a degree of "confidence" since, except for pure numerical transformations, business expectation data are taken as they are. In other words, expectations appear in predictive equations with fixed coefficients (obtained from the usual linear or non-linear estimation techniques) as if they were necessarily correct. Now, of course, these data are sometimes wrong, which may lead to worse predictions than those which could have been obtained without considering the business expectations.

The problem is therefore to correct the "increase" and "decrease" answer proportions. This was already recognized by H. Theil in 1966 using the information theory approach and proposing to correct the survey answers for their general (underestimation) bias as well as for seasonal factors and serial correlation, using time-series regressions. This approach however presumes a symmetrical behavior during the business cycle phases. Now,

---

(2) See e.g. O. Anderson (1951), Theil and Jochems (1960), Theil (1961), Kloek and Banning (1961), Adams (1964 and 1965), Lindlbauer (1968), Eisner (1971), Lonnqvist (1971), Nerb (1973 and 1975), Vanderlinden (1977) and the papers presented at the fifteen (to date) CIRET Conferences.

as has been shown notably by Anderson et al. (1956) this may not reflect the effective reaction patterns of businessmen.

In this study therefore we prefered to approach the correction of business survey data in a more probabilistic way, i.e. by weighting the expectations by their probability to be "true". These probabilities are computed from objective indicators coming from macro-economic indicators as proposed by Theil but also from informations contained in the business survey themselves, most notably in the "no change" answers (3). Besides they are allowed to follow a non symmetrical distribution.

The plan of this chapter is as follows : the next section will present the methodology and define the correction model used. Section 3 will describe the data and the estimation technique. Section 4 will be devoted to an empirical application on the harmonized business data published by the European Economic Commission.

2. Methodology

Let $\dot{y}$ represent the rate of growth of the quantitative variable to be predicted, and $\dot{y}_t^{t+n}$ the expected value of this rate of growth, made at time t for time t+n.
Let X be a vector of K exogenous variables, and $\dot{X}_t^{t+n}$ the vector of rates of growth of these variables as predicted at time t for time t+n.
Finally, let A_t^{t+n} represent the three dimensional vector of business expectations relative to $\dot{y}_t^{t+n}$, with $A_t^{t+n} = (A_t^{t+n}(+), A_t^{t+n}(-), A_t^{t+n}(=))$.

$A_t^{t+n}(+)$ represents the percentage of enterprises who, at time t expect their production to increase between time t and time t+n; $A_t^{t+n}(-)$ represents the percentage of enterprises who, at time t, expect their production to decrease between t and t+n, and $A_t^{t+n}(=)$ represents the percentage of enter-

(3) Since the development of our methodology, we learned about a similar (in spirit) approach by Nerlove et al. (1981) based on estimates of the conditional probability of realizations, given prior anticipation plans.

prises who expect their production to remain stable between period t and t+n.

In the absence of business survey data, a general predictive equation could be written :

$$\dot{y}_t^{t+n} = F\ (\dot{X}_t^{t+n},\ L\ (\dot{y}),\ L\ (\dot{X}),\ \alpha) + \varepsilon \qquad (1)$$

with L being a lag operator, and α a vector of coefficients.

Similarly, predictions based exclusively on business expectations could be written :

$$\dot{y}_t^{t+n} = G\ (A_t^{t+n}\ (+),\ A_t^{t+n}\ (-),\ A_t^{t+n}\ (=),\ \beta) + \eta \qquad (2)$$

with β being a vector of coefficients.

If expectations from business surveys were always accurate, predictions given by (2) should, on the average, be better than those given by (1) since they avoid the prediction error on $\dot{X}_t^{t+n}$.

Unfortunately, as we noted in the introduction, business expectations may be wrong so that for (2) to be correct the respective weights given to A_t^{t+n} (+), A_t^{t+n} (-) and A_t^{t+n} (=) in the equation should in some cases be reversed.

If we postulate that expectations are not pure random walk processes, it should be possible to define objective (or at least measurable) criteria according to which expectations are liable to be correct or erroneous, and link our problem to the standard Probit approach (Goldberger (1964), Cox (1970)).

Let Z_t^k be these k criteria, and $R\ (Z_t^k, \delta)$ be a function of these criteria, with coefficients δ. $R\ (Z_t^k, \delta)$ is called the realisation index.

At the individual level, we may suppose that there exists, for enterprise i, a critical value $\bar{R}_i$ such that if the realisation index for enterprise i is above the critical value the expectation will be correct, which we note $W_i = 1$. On the other hand, if the realisation index for enterprise i is below the critical value $\bar{R}_i$ the expectation will be false ($W_i = 0$) :

If $R_i (Z_k, \delta) \geq \bar{R}_i$ $\quad W_i = 1$

If $R_i (Z_k, \delta) \leq \bar{R}_i$ $\quad W_i = 0$

The critical value $\bar{R}_i$ is unknown, but varies between enterprises. If the size of the population is sufficiently large, we may suppose at first that these critical values $\bar{R}_i$ (i = 1, ..., n) are approximately normally distributed accross the population of enterprises.

We have thus (after suitable transformations of the raw data) :

$$\bar{R} = N (0, 1) \tag{3}$$

For a given value of the realisation index $R (Z_t^k, \delta)$, we will have W = 1 for all anticipators characterized by $\bar{R}_i \geq R (Z_k, \delta)$, and W = 0 for all anticipators characterized by $\bar{R}_i \leq R (Z_k, \delta)$.

The probability for W to be equal to one, given $R (Z_k, \delta)$, is thus straightforward :

$$P (W = 1 / R) = P (\bar{R}_i \geq R (Z_t^k, \delta)) = P (R)$$

$$= \frac{1}{(2 \pi)^{1/2}} \int_{-\infty}^{R} e^{-\frac{1}{2} u^2} du \tag{4}$$

And :

$$P (W = 0 / R) = P (\bar{R}_i \leq R (Z_t^k, \delta)) = 1 - P (R) = Q (R) \tag{5}$$

Since business survey data also include qualitative information about past realisations, we can compare the historical series of the realisations and the corresponding expectations, and determine at each point in time the proportion r_t of enterpreneurs for which W = 1, and the proportion $(1 - r_t)$ for which W = 0.

The likelihood function of the sample can then be written as :

$$L (\delta) = \prod_{t=1}^{T} (P (R (Z_t^k, \delta)))^{r_t} \cdot (Q (R (Z_t^k, \delta)))^{1 - r_t} \tag{6}$$

with :

$$P (R (Z_t^k, \delta)) = \frac{1}{(2 \pi)^{1/2}} \int_{-\infty}^{R (Z_t^k, \delta)} e^{-\frac{1}{2} u^2} du \tag{7}$$

$$Q\ (R\ (Z_t^{\ k},\ \delta)) = 1 - P\ (R\ (Z_t^{\ k},\ \delta)) \qquad (8)$$

The Probit model however is not the only one that may be used in this context and is certainly not the most tractable one from a numerical point of view.

Beside, a basic hypothesis of the Probit model is of course that the probability distribution of the critical values is symmetric. Now, as noted by Poirier (1980) if $P\ (W = 1\ /\ R)_t$ has a density function f (.) symmetric around zero, then $\frac{\partial\ P}{\partial\ R}$ must be the same when evaluated at values of R yielding values of P symmetric around ½.

In other words, the effect of an explanatory variable on $P\ (W = 1\ /\ R)_t$ is the same whether $P\ (W = 1\ /\ R)_t$ is equal to 0.10 or to 0.90 and there is no reason why it should necessarily be so.

Finally a case may be made for the use of logistic or "Logit" models in the frame of information theory (see Theil (1966)) as more appropriate than the normal or Probit ones. Furthermore, the Logit model, as shown by Prentice (1976) may quite easily be generalized so as to allow for non-symmetrical distribution.

More precisely we have then :

$$P\ (W = 1\ /\ R)_t = P\ [\bar{R}_i \geq R\ (Z_t^{\ k},\ \delta)]_t = [1 + \exp\ (- \underset{k=1}{\overset{K}{\pi}}\ Z_t^{\ k}\ \delta^k)]^{-\alpha} \qquad (9)$$

with $\alpha > 0$, all other variables and coefficients being as defined in the Probit model.

The log-likelihood function is the same as (6) i.e. :

$$\log L\ (\delta,\ \alpha) = \underset{t=1}{\overset{T}{\pi}}\ (1 - r_t)\ \log\ (1 - P_t) + r_t\ \log P_t$$

with P_t given by (9).

As shown by Prentice, if $0 < \alpha < 1$, the density function corresponding to equation (9) is negatively skewed; if $\alpha > 1$ it is positively skewed. Finally, when $\alpha = 1$ we obtain the usual symmetric Logit density.

We have therefore decided to use the following methodology :

(i) estimate the probability of success for the expectation from equation (9) using as approximation for the observed probabilities the success frequenties given from the comparison of expectations and later realisations (see below section 3 for a more complete description of the data);

(ii) test whether the symmetry parameter α is significantly different from one or not;

(iii) if it is not statistically different from one, compare the Logit and Probit models and select the best-fitting one;

(iv) compare the retained model with other approaches.

3. The data and the estimation technique

Our main concern is how to improve the quality of firms' forecasts of their own production, as shown by the firms' later-appreciation of what exactly happened, in order to insure what we should call the internal consistency of Business survey data. Then of course one should also check the external consistency of these data, i.e. are Business survey data really able to forecast and describe the real world, a problem that will not be tackled here since it would lead us too far. However we can at least say that if Business expectations are not even able to forecast their own realizations they can hardly be considered good forecasters of the real, quantitative world. Therefore, the internal consistency should be insured before any attempt to use these qualitative expectation data into a quantitative model framework.

The observations about the expectation/realization process may be described by a two-way contingency table with forecasts in columns and realisation in lines :

		expectation			
		(+)	(=)	(-)	
realisation	(+)	n_{11}	n_{12}	n_{13}	$n_{1.}$
	(=)	n_{21}	n_{22}	n_{23}	$n_{2.}$
	(-)	n_{31}	n_{32}	n_{33}	$n_{3.}$
		$n_{.1}$	$n_{.2}$	$n_{.3}$	

where n_{ij} represents the number of firms quoting an expectation of kind j followed by a realisation of kind i and $n_{.j}$ and $n_{j.}$ are the marginal totals.

When one wants to make a comparable study for several countries however the disaggregated micro data are not always available in a form suitable for the construction of the contingency table. All that we have for the EEC countries in fact are the marginal totals, given as the weighted proportion of firms in a given sector answering (+), (=) or (-). They involve therefore a risk of aggregation error since it is quite easy to build examples where an apparently perfect forecast in terms of the marginal totals is derived from very bad individual performances (see Nerlove et al., 1981, p. 6). However, they are what we must use.

There remains the problem of combination of (+), (=) and (-) into a synthetic forecasting indicator. Since in quantitative sectoral data, the occurence of an effective "no change" i.e. arithmetic zero growth is an uncommon phenomenon, most users of Business survey data prefer to build what is called a Balance indicator B, i.e. the difference between the proportions of (+) and (-). This calls for the following objection : by nature the Balance indicator attributes egal and constant weights (+ 1 and - 1) to the (+) and (-) proportions. Now, for the reasons exposed in the introduction, we may expect these weights to be variable according to the rightness or wrongness of businessmen's expectations.

Therefore we prefer to define our forecasting indicator as follows :

let A_t^{t+n} (+) and A_t^{t+n} (-) be the weighted proportions of firms expecting at time t respectively an increase and a decrease in their production, <u>in the total number of firms having a definite opinion</u>. In other words, we only consider at this time the subset of all (+) and (-) answers, leaving the (=) aside for the time being.

We define the majority expectation A_t^M as :

$$A_t^M = (\text{sign}) \max (A_t^{t+n} (+), A_t^{t+n} (-)) \tag{10}$$

where (sign) is + when $A_t^{t+n} (+) \geq A_t^{t+n} (-)$ and - otherwise.

The minority expectation is then defined as :

$$a_t^m = (\text{sign}) (1 - A_t^M) \tag{11}$$

where the sign is (- 1) sign of A_t^M.

In a similar guise we may define a majority realisation for time t i.e.

$$R_t^M = (\text{sign}) \max (R_t (+), R_t (-)) \tag{12}$$

A problem of definition exists here however since for expectation the question is :

"In the course <u>of the following three months</u> and after adjustment for seasonal factors, do you expect your production

- to increase
- to remain about the same
- to decrease"

whereas for realisation the question is :

"Compared <u>to last month</u> and after adjustment for seasonal factors has your production

- increased
- remained about the same
- decreased".

In order to make the period compatible one has thus to replace the original realisation series by moving averages (with unit weights) over three successive months centered on the first month. This of course entails a risk of bias since a direct answer over the evolution for the last three months would probably differ from the moving average but we do not think it to be very important.

Should expectations in business survey be always exact forecasts one would observe :

$$R_t^M = A_{t-1}^M \tag{13}$$

Now of course it has been shown long ago (see e.g. Anderson (1951), Theil (1966)) that there is a systematic bias in expectations together with a stochastic error i.e. a relation of the kind :

$$R_t^M = \alpha + \beta\, A_{t-1}^M + \epsilon_t \tag{14}$$

And indeed when one runs these regressions, taking into account the auto-correlation caused by the overlapping of forecasting periods (4), the results do show that α is significantly different from zero and β is significantly different from one.

Beside, if our postulate is true, the relation should furthermore be written :

$$R_t^M = \alpha_t + \beta_t\, A_{t-1}^M + \gamma_t\, a_{t-1}^m + \epsilon_t \tag{15}$$

since, when the probability of error in the expectation formation process is great R_t^M will in fact more linked to the minority expectation a_{t-1}^m than to A_{t-1}^M. Hence the coefficients, β_t and γ_t, should be variable through time. The same is true for the systematic mean bias α.

We are now able to introduce our development about the Logit and Probit models since the easiest way to make α, β and γ variables is to multiply them by the probability of sucessful forecast, as derived from the objective indicators listed hereunder through the generalized Logit or Standard Probit

(4) Since firms give on a monthly basis a forecast for the next three months, one can expect the ϵ_t to show auto-correlation of first and second order with coefficients 2/3 and 1/3 respectively.

models.

The model to be estimated may be written as a two-equation system i.e. :

Generalized Logit model

$$(16)\quad \begin{cases} R_t^M = \alpha\,(1 - \hat{P}_t) + \beta\,[\hat{P}_t\, A^M_{t-1} + (1 - \hat{P}_t)\, a^m_{t-1}] + \epsilon_t \\ \hat{P}_t = [1 + \exp\,(- \sum_{k=1}^{K} Z_t^k\, \delta^k)]^{-\gamma} \end{cases} \qquad t = 1, \ldots, T$$

or Probit model

$$(17)\quad \begin{cases} R_t^M = \alpha\,(1 - \hat{P}_t) + \beta\,[\hat{P}_t\, A^M_{t-1} + (1 - \hat{P}_t)\, a^m_{t-1}] + \epsilon_t \\ \hat{P}_t = \dfrac{1}{(2\,\pi)^{1/2}} \displaystyle\int_{-\infty}^{\sum_{k=1}^{K} Z_t^k \delta^k} e^{-\frac{1}{2} u^{e}}\, du \end{cases} \qquad t = 1, \ldots, T$$

where $\hat{P}_t$ are the estimates of the probability of success as derived from the sample observed frequencies.

To be able to estimate the parameters δ^k in $\Sigma\, Z^k\, \delta^k$ and to compute for each period the probability of success of the expectations, it is necessary to define more precisely the objective criteria Z^k which are most likely to influence these probabilities.

Ideally, the explanatory variable matrix Z should include all the micro and macro bits of information that the respondents are likely to consider when they make their expectations.

In practice however, this would involve an untractable number of data series, even if we were able to solve the aggregation problem due to the sectoral nature of published data.

We will therefore postulate that part of the informational content of these economic environment variables can be represented by synthetic proxies, derived from the structure of the answers themselves, and in particular from "no-change" answers.

The first factor that we shall consider is an indecision factor, defined as the percentage of "no-change" answers :

$$I_t = A_t^{t+n} (=) \tag{18}$$

This factor is in itself an important proxy for the economic environment; from intuition (5) and empirical evidence, I_t increases near turning points in the business cycles, or in economic climates of uncertainty.
Since these occurences correspond to higher probability of error in forecasting, I_t should play a leading role in the construction of any success indicator of expectations.

A second factor which is likely to have a significant impact on the probabilities of success of expectations is what we shall call the "uncertainty weight" U_t (6) :

$$U_t = 1 - | A_t^{t+n} (+) - A_t^{t+n} (-) | \tag{19}$$

U_t will be equal to one, which corresponds to the maximum uncertainty, either when there are no "increase" nor "decrease" answers (i.e. all enterprises expect their production to remain constant), or when the proportion of enterprises who expect their production to increase is exactly the same as the percentage of enterprises who expect their production to decrease. The former case may be called maximum absolute uncertainty, the latter being a maximum relative uncertainty.
U_t will be equal to zero (minimum uncertainty) when all enterprises answer either that their production is going to increase, or that it will decrease ($A_t^{t+n} (+) = 1$ and $A_t^{t+n} (-) = 0$, or $A_t^{t+n} (+) = 0$ and $A_t^{t+n} (-) = 1$).

The introduction of the uncertainty factor into the realisation index enables us to take account of the fact that the subjective uncertainty introduced by the presence of "no-change" answers doesn't simply depend upon the amount of these answers, but also upon the distribution of the answers between (+), (-) or (=).

---

(5) "No-change" means that the rate of growth is included between two (variable) critical threshold. Since this indeference interval is liable to increase in period of greater uncertainty like those close to a turning point, it seems evident that the proportion of (=) answer will also grow during those periods.

(6) Defined graphically by Perrson (1972).

For instance, if we compare two distributions of answers D1 and D2, with :

	D1	D2
A_t^{t+n} (+)	0.2	0.1
A_t^{t+n} (=)	0.8	0.8
A_t^{t+n} (-)	0.0	0.1

I_t is equal to 0.8 in both cases, although it seems intuitively evident that the distribution (0.2, 0.8, 0.0) is more biased towards an "increase" realisation than the (0.1, 0.8, 0.1) distribution.

The next criteria which will be considered is more concrete, and represents the position in which the anticipator stands with respect to the last turning point in the business cycle.

Indeed, it appears that errors in expectations are maximal at both ends of the cycle phase, as shown by graph 1, where we plotted the evolution of probabilities of success of expectations, against a hypothetic business cycle. This overprojection of past trends is well known, and is liable to increase with the length, persistence and continuity of these economic phases. If we call 2m the length (in months) from point a to point b, the evolution of the probabilities of success of the expectations (all other things being equal) may be linked to the variable :

$$LC_t = \left(\frac{l_t - m}{2m}\right)^2 \qquad (20)$$

where l_t is the number of months separating period t from the last turning point (point b on the graph). Division by 2m has no meaning except as a normalisation factor.

The average half period 2m of the business cycle has been extracted from the 1961-1978 monthly industrial production index, through spectral analysis, after elimination of the trend and all seasonnal and stochastic elements.

Finally, we can also take into account the fact that the collection and publication of answers to business surveys is sufficiently quick for

Graph 1. Comparative evolution of a "pure" business cycle and of the probability of forecasting success.

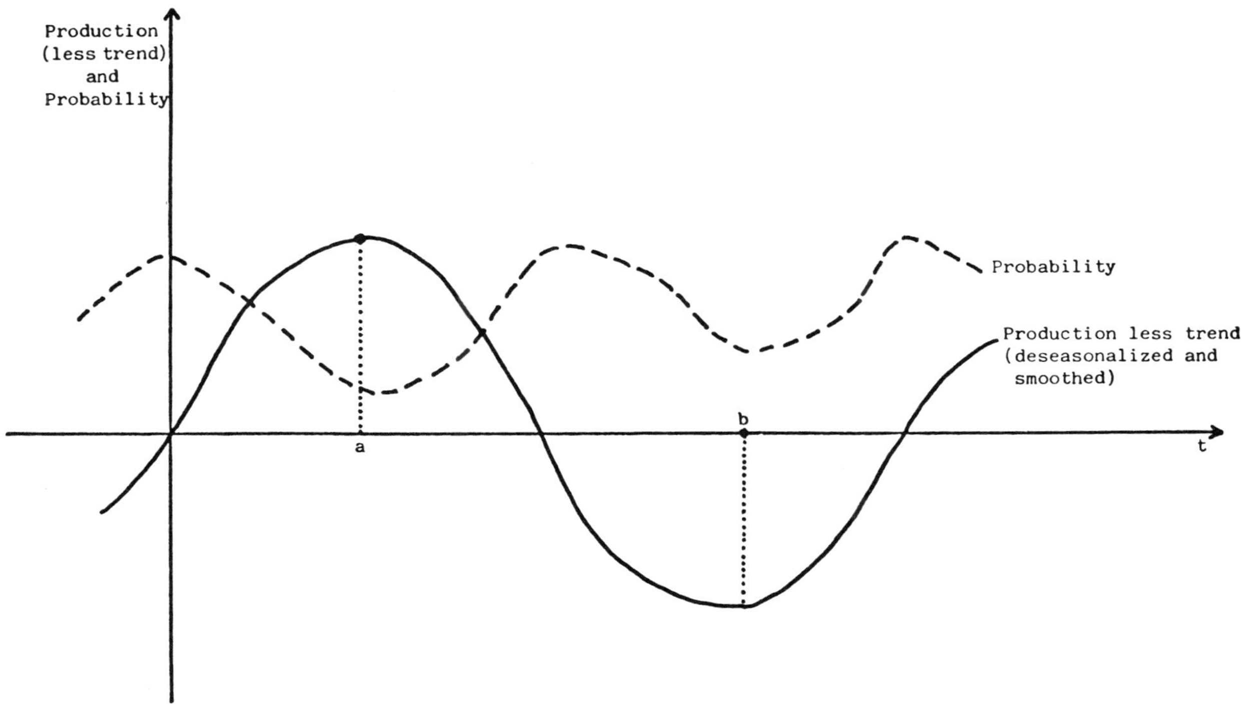

anticipators to be able to judge their performances, and eventually correct themselves.
In order to do so we introduced the prediction error of the preceding month among the explanatory variables of the realisation index R (Z_k, δ).
The prediction error is thus defined as :

$$CP_t = (R^M_{t-1} - A^M_{t-2}) \tag{21}$$

It remains now to choose the estimation technique for models (16) and (17) :

(i) since these models are a simultaneous set of two equations a joint estimation procedure is clearly needed;

(ii) beside, we know that residuals must be expected to show auto-correlation of first and second order;

(iii) finally both models are non linear in their P_t equation part.

For all these reasons we choose to estimate the system by Full-Information Maximum Likelihood, using the quadratic hill-climbing maximization algorithme as the most robust for the case (Eisenpress and Greenstadt (1966) and Goldfeld and Quandt (1972)).

The test that $\gamma = 1$ in model (16) will be done by likelihood-ratio procedures but, following Poirier (1980), we also used the Lagrange Multiplier (LM) testing procedure since it can be applied with information immediately available from the computation of the parameters by the standard computer programmes for Logit models.

All computations were done on a Control Data Cyber 170-750 computer under the FORTRAN V sub-system, using 15 significant decimal digit floating-point arithmetics, except for the extraction of eigenvalues where double precision (29 decimal digits) was used.

4. Empirical application

In order to test the validity of the approach we applied it to the Business survey data coming from the harmonized business survey data published by

Directorate General for Economic and Financial Affairs of the European Economic Commission.

The data we used are those related to the industrial production indices. We will simply remember here that the qualitative answers of the firms are collected monthly, weighted by the average turnover of each firm and aggregated first by sector and then by country.

When the estimation was done the available sample covered the period January 1969 to November 1979 i.e. 131 observations of which 128 only are usable owing to the differences in time coverage between the expectations and the realisations (see section 3, above).

Since harmonized data do only exist on that period for four countries, our sample is limited to Belgium, France, Germany and Italy.

This section will be subdivided into three parts. The first will present the maximum likelihood estimators together with their asymptotic standard errors. Goodness of fit is appreciated through a R^2-like measure i.e. the ratio of the explained variance to the total variance of the dependent variables. We will also show examples of the behaviour of the system around turning points in order to see whether or not our aim was fulfilled. Finally we will appreciate the forecasting power of the equations by dropping the last observations and predicting them with the reestimated system, using the root-mean-squared error (RMSE) as indicator. In order to see how the system behaves dynamically, we made the forecasting test over longer and longer periods i.e. we dropped successively the last one, the last two, etc... down to the last twelve observations. In that way any build-up of forecasting errors can be detected in the "chronological" evolution of the twelve RMSE statistics.

The second section will be devoted to some statistical inference using a set of hypothesis. First we tested the general acceptance of the whole model, without restrictions.

Next we tested the reduced model obtained by imposing symmetry for the logit distribution ($\gamma = 1$ in equation 16).

In parallel, we also tested the absence of bias in the forecasting process i.e. $\alpha = 0$ and $\beta = 1$ in equation 16.

Next, we tested the combined restrictions i.e. $\alpha = 0$, $\beta = 1$ and $\gamma = 1$.

Should $\alpha = 1$ be accepted then of course the probit model should be compared to the symmetric logit. In all cases we used the usual transformation of the likelihood ratio :

$$- r \log_e \lambda \simeq X_r^2 \qquad (22)$$

where :

$$\lambda = \frac{L (\theta_r, \theta_s)}{L (\theta)} \qquad (23)$$

with θ_r the r-components vector of constrained coefficients in the original set θ and L (.) the value of the likelihood function.

Finally section (c) deals with some comparisons with alternative methods and is followed by the conclusions.

(a) Estimation and forecasting results

(i) Estimated coefficients

Results for individual countries are summarized in table 1 hereunder in alphabetical order i.e. Belgium, France, Germany and Italy. Let us recall that at this stage the model tested is :

$$(16) \begin{cases} R_t^M = \alpha (1 - \hat{P}_t) + \beta [\hat{P}_t A_{t-1}^M + (1 - \hat{P}_t) a_{t-1}^m] + \epsilon_t \\ \hat{P}_t = [1 + \exp (- \sum_{k=0}^{4} Z_t^k \delta^k)]^{-\gamma} \end{cases}$$

We have thus eight parameters, i.e. α, β, γ, δ_0, δ_1, δ_2, δ_3, δ with δ_0 a constant term and the other four the coefficients of explanatory variables I_t, U_t, LC_t and CP_t, in that order. Asymptotic standard errors are given below the coefficients, between brackets.

Results proved extremely satisfactory since in all cases coefficients are significantly different from zero (except the constant term δ_0) and the general fit is quite good.

Table 1. Estimation results, four countries

Coefficients \ Countries	Belgium	France	Germany	Italy
$\hat{\alpha}$	- 0.106 (0.030)	- 0.028 (0.026)	- 0.213 (0.017)	- 0.253 (0.015)
$\hat{\beta}$	0.721 (0.058)	0.916 (0.044)	0.752 (0.051)	1.051 (0.049)
$\hat{\gamma}$	0.715 (0.079)	0.783 (0.085)	0.800 (0.081)	0.699 (0.100)
$\hat{\delta}_0$	1.152 (0.858)	0.998 (0.584)	1.081 (0.729)	1.211 (0.872)
$\hat{\delta}_1$	- 2.423 (0.910)	- 1.974 (0.575)	- 2.008 (0.547)	- 2.226 (0.951)
$\hat{\delta}_2$	- 1.985 (0.217)	- 2.427 (0.158)	- 2.473 (0.202)	- 2.575 (0.199)
$\hat{\delta}_3$	- 1.002 (0.185)	- 1.056 (0.128)	- 0.999 (0.105)	- 1.115 (0.153)
$\hat{\delta}_4$	+ 5.995 (0.166)	+ 6.097 (0.153)	+ 6.220 (0.146)	+ 5.823 (0.201)
$\sigma^2 \hat{y}/\sigma^2 y$ for R_t^M	0.919	0.928	0.986	0.907

Also, at first glance, leaving aside formal tests for section (t) below it does seem that expectations are biased $(\alpha \neq 0$ and/or $\beta \neq 1)$ except perhaps for France and that the hypothesis of symmetric distribution is not well suported.

Finally as a side exercise we also used the likelihood ratio for testing the relative importance of the explanatory variables in the determination of the explained sum of square. For all countries, the result was the following :

First, the autocorrective factor : large errors one period do entail an improvement in the quality of the expectation the next period;
Second, the uncertainty factor U_t;
Third, the position relative to the phase of the cycle
and fourth, the proportion of "no change" answers.

We should however point out that differences in relative position between these four factors are somewhat marginal : no variable may really be said to be significantly better than an other, all four are needed.

(ii) Dynamic behavior

If we now look towards the behavior of computed values around turning points we see the following facts :

Belgium : twelve sign reversals in R_t^M sample, eleven predicted, no incorrectly predicted.
The missed turning point is an isolated "minus" in the center of long series of "plusses" before and after (September 1973). The observed value is - 0.131, the computed $\hat{y}$ being 0.004, with a $\hat{P}_t$ of 0.587.

France : only four sign reversals in R_t^M sample (*), all predicted in the right quarter for the right period, none incorrectly predicted.

Germany : fifteen sign reversals in R_t^M sample, all are predicted at the right time for the right period, none are incorrectly predicted.

Italy : ten sign reversals in R_t^M sample, eight correctly predicted, two unpredicted, none incorrectly predicted.
The first missed sign reversal is located at the beginning of the sample (December 1969 - January 1970) where the behavior of the data is somewhat erratic (six sign reversals in the first two years i.e. 24 observations !). The observed values are - 0.123 and - 0.127, the computed $\hat{y}_s$ being 0.004 and 0.016. The corresponding $\hat{P}_t$ values are 0.531 and 0.532. The second missed turning point is, as in

(*) The French data show long sequences of "plus" followed by long sequences of "minus" signs whereas in the other three countries, small groups (2 or 3 observations) of plus (or minus) are often embedded in long sequences of minus (or plus).

Belgium, an isolated minus in the middle of a long sequence of plusses in December 1974 : the observed value is - 0.163 the computed one 0.002 with a $\hat{P}_t$ of 0.398.

Since the enumeration of long sequences of data are somewhat boring we will limit ourselves to two more specific examples, one for the best-fitting equations (Germany) the other for Italy, the lowest ($\hat{\sigma}^2\ \hat{y}/\hat{\sigma}^2\ y$) country.

For Germany we have for instance for the period October 1976 to April 1977 :

observed R_t^M : - 0.237 - 0.183 + 0.177 + 0.167 - 0.163 - 0.167 + 0.200
computed R_t^M : - 0.266 - 0.160 + 0.210 + 0.168 - 0.096 - 0.120 + 0.251

For Italy we have from June 1969 to February 1970 :

observed R_t^M : 0.127 - 0.133 - 0.133 + 0.143 + 0.147 + 0.133 - 0.123 - 0.127 + 0.130
computed R_t^M : 0.120 - 0.101 - 0.107 + 0.121 + 0.128 + 0.126 0.004 0.016 0.128

This in-sample capacity to follow sign variation needs however confirmation from out-of-sample tests. As explained at the beginning of this section we re-estimated the model over shorter and shorter samples in order to predict out of sample the missing observations. In all these tests, the absolute values of the coefficients did no vary by more than two to five percent with respect to the full-sample estimates.

The procedure was applied to the last twelve months of the sample giving thus twelve predictions on an increasing horizon, i.e. November 1979 predicted from October 1979 down to December 1978, January 1979, etc... to November 1979 predicted from October 1978. This gives us twelve RMSE, the average of which are 0.0173, 0.0161, 0.0155, 0.0190 for Belgium, France, Germany and Italy respectively, whereas the same concepts, when computed on the estimated residuals in the full sample exercise are in the same country order 0.0167, 0.0155, 0.0148, 0.0175. Their dynamic behaviour is given in table 2 hereunder.

No pathologic behavior seems in evidence in table 2. However above-average RMSE are more concentrated in the more-than-6-month-horizon period than in the less-than-6-month period but divergences between sub-means are certainly not striking except perhaps for Belgium.

Table 2. RMSE for increasing-horizon forecasts

Horizon \ Countries	Belgium	France	Germany	Italy
One month	0.0161	0.0160	0.0162	0.0185
Two months	0.0183	0.0152	0.0147	0.0182
Three months	0.0171	0.0146	0.0135	0.0200
Four months	0.0152	0.0143	0.0158	0.0187
Five months	0.0154	0.0162	0.0161	0.0182
Six months	0.0167	0.0172	0.0157	0.0187
Seven months	0.0167	0.0173	0.0150	0.0188
Eight months	0.0186	0.0150	0.0159	0.0174
Nine months	0.0182	0.0160	0.0156	0.0188
Ten months	0.0182	0.0173	0.0158	0.0184
Eleven months	0.0193	0.0168	0.0164	0.0204
Twelve months	0.0191	0.0167	0.0158	0.0198
Arithmetic average	0.0173	0.0161	0.0155	0.0190
First six average	0.0165	0.0155	0.0153	0.0187
Last six average	0.0181	0.0167	0.0157	0.0195

(b) Statistical inference

As could be expected for the estimation result, the X^2 test confirms the goodness of fit criteria and the information contained in the asymptotic standard errors since the null hypothesis $\bar{\theta} = 0$ with $\bar{\theta} = \{\alpha, \beta, \gamma, \delta_0, \delta_1, \delta_2, \delta_3, \delta_4\}$ is rejected at the 0.01 significance level. More specifically the critical value of X_8^2 is 20.090 whereas the computed test statistics from the likelihood ratios are 67.60, 92.46, 95.70 and 62.80 for Belgium, France, Germany and Italy.

The null hypothesis $\gamma = 1$ is also rejected at the 0.01 level for all countries, the computed values being 9.14, 10.51, 11.72 and 11.48 as against a significance level of 6.635. This leads to the rejection of either the symmetric logit or the probit models.

The absence of bias hypothesis $\alpha = 0$ and $\beta = 1$ is always rejected at the 0.05 level. However, for France, it has to be accepted at the 0.01 level. The critical values are 5.991 for five percent and 9.210 for one percent. For Belgium, Germany and Italy, the computed values are 13.25, 14.60 and 16.71 whereas for France it is 6.21.

Finally the combined hypothesis $\alpha = 0$, $\beta = 1$ and $\gamma = 1$ is rejected at the 0.01 level for all countries, but France where it is rejected at the 0.05 level. The critical levels are 11.345 for one percent and 7.815 for five percent and the computed levels are 11.880, 8.04, 13.64 and 14.63 in the usual country order.

(c) Comparison with other methods

The first question to be asked here is of course : "Is all that computational burden and complication really worthwhile ?". The answer is always a question of opinion but still it may be helped by some objective facts. The first alternative is of course a non-weighted approach. In our formulation, it would give :

$$R_t^M = A_{t-1}^M \tag{24}$$

or
$$R_t^M = a + b\, A_{t-1}^M + \epsilon_t \tag{25}$$

Results for equation (25) estimated by Generalized Least Squares are the following :

Belgium : $R_t^M = \underset{(0.010)}{0.153} + \underset{(0.053)}{0.700}\, A_{t-1}^M$ $\quad \bar{R}^2 = 0.748 \quad DW = 1.782$

France : $R_t^M = \underset{(0.011)}{0.046} + \underset{(0.070)}{1.688}\, A_{t-1}^M$ $\quad \bar{R}^2 = 0.822 \quad DW = 1.777$

Germany : $R_t^M = \underset{(0.066)}{0.0131} + \underset{(0.043)}{1.301}\, A_{t-1}^M$ $\quad \bar{R}^2 = 0.879 \quad DW = 1.604$

Italy : $R_t^M = \underset{(0.010)}{0.165} + \underset{(0.034)}{1.285}\, A_{t-1}^M$ $\quad \bar{R}^2 = 0.700 \quad DW = 1.875$

Although the adjustments are reasonnably good, it is already evident that the goodness of fit is lower than in our model (16).

Besides, the examination of the residuals do show the problem quoted before : sign reversals are predicted only with a lag of one to two months together with a number of incorrectly predicted sign reversals, a problem completely absent from the probabilistic approach. This amply confirm the problems encountered by other researchers when working with the balance between plus and minus or some other direct use of the business survey data as published.

We also made a comparison, this time at the forecasting level with non causal methods, according to the following methodology :

i) estimation of ARMA models for the majority realization R_t^M;
ii) use of this ARMA model for the forecasting of R_t^M on an increasing horizon from one to twelve months;
iii) computation of RMSE for these forecasts, to be compared with those of table 2.

Results are given in table 3 hereunder.

As can be seen from table 3 the application of non causal methods leads to larger RMSE than our own approach. The peculiar profile for Belgium and France is due to a sign reversal in the last nine and eight observations respectively (a sequence of minusses following a sequence of plusses). The ARMA models completely missed this sign reversal and from the eight-or-nine-to-twelve months horizon consistently predicted a wrong sign amount for the last eight or nine periods, which explains the considerable jump in the RMSE.

For Germany, there is no problem of that kind (all observations are minusses, correctly forecasted) but there is a significant increase in the RMSE when the forecasting horizon goes beyond six months. Finally, for Italy, the ecrease in the RMSE serie is due to the fact that the very last observation is consistently very badly predicted.

It does not seem therefore that ARMA methods might be a usefull alternative to our probabilistic scheme.

Table 3. RMSE for forecasts obtained with ARMA models

Horizon in months \ Countries	Belgium	France (ARMA 2,20)	Germany ARMA (1,9)	Italy ARMA (1,4)
1	0.048	0.057	0.036	0.234
2	0.045	0.031	0.034	0.173
3	0.054	0.035	0.046	0.163
4	0.058	0.023	0.056	0.158
5	0.060	0.032	0.048	0.157
6	0.075	0.052	0.061	0.136
7	0.071	0.068	0.107	0.121
8	0.069	0.043	0.093	0.109
9	0.056	0.406	0.087	0.104
10	0.415	0.403	0.088	0.098
11	0.375	0.380	0.097	0.095
12	0.327	0.370	0.111	0.106
Average	0.138	0.158	0.072	0.138
First six average	0.057	0.038	0.047	0.170
Last six average	0.219	0.278	0.097	0.106

5. Conclusions

Our probabilistic approach to the quantification of business survey data proved extremely satisfactory as far as the internal consistency of the data is concerned. In other words, a probability weighting of majority and minority expectations gives an "expectation" variable which anticipates effectively the corresponding realization data up to and including turning points.

It also shows that the implicit hypothesis of symmetry used, so to speak, as a matter of course in the rapidly expanding literature on discrete choice models may be misleading and should be tested.

We can see also that biases in the published expectation series are not only present as already proved but also variable with the phase of the business cycle and cannot therefore be properly represented by fixed coefficients in a standard regression analysis.

To conclude, we would thus say that, as far as the business data themselves are concerned, our method gives a way to relate expectations and realizations in a more efficient way. For prediction of quantitative data, results may vary from sector to sector or between kinds of goods, but where the correlation between business survey data and the evolution of the quantitative series is good, the introduction of expectation may improve significantly the quality of the forecast especially in the vicinity of turning points in the quantitative series which are as we all know the main pitfall of forecasting job.

Addendum to part one

Since the country coverage of the BUSY model includes the United Kingdom rather than Belgium, the UK Business Survey Data (BSD from now on) were also dealt with, with data provided from the BS data base of DG II.

Since results are completely in agreement with those described in the preceeding pages, we will present them without further comments.

UK expectations on industrial production (notations are the same as in table 1, page 19).

$\hat{\alpha}$	$\hat{\beta}$	$\hat{\gamma}$	$\hat{\delta}_0$	$\hat{\delta}_1$	$\hat{\delta}_2$	$\hat{\delta}_3$	$\hat{\delta}_4$	$\frac{\sigma^2_{\hat{y}}}{\sigma^2_y}$
0.168 (0.025)	0.864 (0.214)	0.806 (0.092)	1.111 (0.829)	- 1.847 (0.448)	- 2.603 (0.617)	- 1.024 (0.127)	+ 6.079 (0.140)	0.912

II. PRICE EXPECTATIONS EQUATION AND OTHER BSD EQUATIONS

As far as price expectation data are concerned, it proved impossible to apply the methodology described above. As they stay, Business Survey questions on prices only concern expectation about future price but no question about effective variation in the current period. It is therefore impossible to derive the RM figures needed for our logit approach.

../.

This leaves us two solutions :

(i) use the effective change observed in the "real world" price deflators as realization series.

(ii) work with the standard instrument used in other studies, i.e. the balance between plus and minus.

Since solution (i) would involve a mix-up of "internal" and "external" consistency with a risk of considerable bias in the estimated parametres, we choose solution (ii).

Our price expectation series are therefore the usual balances between (+) and (-) answers.

Our work is however not finished since we still have to deal with more-than-one-quarter-ahead forecasts. If the model is to be used for short term forecasting over four to six quarters we must of course provide for a way to "forecast" the expectations themselves both for prices and production. There are however strong logical objections against this. Indeed, one may argue that presumably the same economic behaviour determines both industrial production and industrial production expectations and that once we are out of the range of available expectations (i.e. one-quarter-ahead only), the forecasting of production expectations to forecast production might seem somewhat superfluous since a standard causal equation for industrial production might do just as well.

This argument certainly carries a considerable weight but it is based on the premice that the model should be causal. Now, it is well known that a forecasting model need not to be causal at all, the most extreme case being of course the Box-Jenkins and related approaches.

We believe therefore that, when what is needed is not the industrial production index "per se" but rather an expected production variable (to be used for the forecast of investment, labour demand, etc...) then it may be preferable to derive the expected values not from a pure mathematical derivation (as in rational expections, adaptative expectations, etc...) but rather from the single source of truly observed

../.

expectations we have i.e. the Business Survey Data. Therefore, the endogenous forecast of BSD together with other "real" variables in the model is not as illogical as it may seem at first glance.

The formulation used has been built in accordance with the principles quoted above, and mixes a time series approach with present and past values of standard quantitative variables.

More specifically, for the A(+) and A(-) series in industrial production, denoted hereunder for short AYP and AYM respectively, the regression is made on a distributed lag on past values of AYP and AYM together with the present and past values of GDP at constant prices. As a general rule, the lag distribution covers four quarters for BSD series, three to four for other variables. BSD data are in levels, GDP is in relative variation as approximated by first differences in the logarithme of GDP levels. For price expectations, the balance between (+) and (-) denoted APB is regressed upon its own past values together with present and lagged variations (first differences in logarithmes) of wages rates, prices and productivity.

This of course involves a serious risk of multicolinearity since the quantitative series on wages prices and productivity are all closely interlinked. The results should therefore be taken with caution when trying to detect the own-impact of the explanatory variables. For forecasting pruposes, however, provided that the degree of colinaerity remains stable through time, multicolinearity does not necessarily reduce the quality of the equation.

Results are given in the following tables. The differences in the levels of the coefficients when going from industrial production expectations to price expectations is due to the fact that in the latter case we are explaining a balance between two levels, with much wider variations than in the levels themselves. This also explains the sign pattern in the distributed lags.

../.

The test statistics are the usual one i.e. standard-errors of the coefficients and the associated t - statistics, the nominal and corrected values of R^2, the Lagrange Multiplier test for autocorrelation -(denoted by LM) and finally a stability test for the appreciation of forecasting performances.

Indeed since we emphasized the forecasting purpose of the BUSY model, the quality of the statistical adjustment as measured by R^2 is not enough. It is a well known fact that equations passing the usual test with flying colours may fail considerably in forecasting exercises, because their parameters are in fact unstable when estimated over different sub-periods.

We have therefore run a stability test (ST) using the following methodology:

(i) we dropped the last four quarters of the sample and reestimated the equation on the shortened series so obtained.

(ii) using the known values of the explanatory variables, we used the new equation to "forecast" the last four quarters dropped in stage (i).

(iii) we compared the forecasted values with the known outturn of the dependant variable, using the Chi-squarred stability test (*).

It should be pointed out that all the equations given here are indeed passing the stability test (at 5 %) whereas pure time series equations based on ARMA models are all showing inherent instability in the forecasting tests, except for Germany. The fundamental weakness of these methods in situations of <u>economic</u> instability does therefore seem to be confirmed.

(*) this test compares in fact the Root-Mean-squarred-Error of the forecast (out-of-sample-error) with the standard error of the estimated equation (in-sample error).

As a rule, the adjustment is better for production than for prices. In this field, a more sophisticated approach would probably give better results.

III - INTRODUCTION OF BUSINESS SURVEY DATA IN OTHER EQUATIONS

This chapter is but a glimpse of the structure of the final model. It deals with the introduction of Business Survey Data into selected econometric equations dealing with

- labour demand
- gross domestic fixed capital formation
- real wage rate

equations that are always critical in macro-models. Inventory investments were also analysed but inventory data are of very poor quality making the equations extremely unstable and the introduction of Business Survey Data seemed to worsen the situation.

1. Labour demand

The labour demand equations are straightforwards, variation in labour demand being determined by the variations in expected and effective levels of activity (with a distributed lag on the latter), together with expected and effective relative prices (real wages over real unit cost of capital), and with a negative time trend.

This formulation is compatible with the hypothesis of factor cost minimisation under a Cobb-Douglas production frontier and indeed, without specific constraints all country results are compatible with a Cobb-Douglas formulation with constant return to scale, as shown by the long-run elasticities given below, with perhaps the exception of Italy, where the implied capital share seems very high.

Formally, the long run equilibrium labour demand derived from a Cobb-Douglas production frontier (using * for equilibrium levels) is:

$$Y^* = A.\ K^a\ L^b\ e^{gt}$$

$$L^* = cst.\ Y^{*\frac{1}{a+b}}\ PR^{*-\frac{a}{a+b}}\ e^{-\frac{g}{a+b}t}$$

../..

Taking into account confidence intervals, the constant return condition a+b = 1 may be admitted from line (3) of the table. In that case, line 6 would give us a, the elasticity of capital in the production function.

Labour long-run elasticities with respect to production and relative prices

	F	G	I	UK
(1) Expected output (AY)	0.205	0.286	0.161	0.226
(2) Effective and past GDP	0.754	0.687	0.779	0.800
(3) Sum of (1) and (2)	0.959	0.973	0.940	1.026
(4) Expected relative price APR	-0.065	-0.088	-0.213	-0.036
(5) Effective and past relative price	-0.149	-0.153	-0.338	-0.116
(6) Sum of (4) and (5)	-0.214	-0.241	-0.551	-0.152

2. Gross Domestic Fixed Capital Formation

The capital demand equation is based on the same formulation as the labour demand function, in order to test any long run consistency in the respective evolutions of labour, capital and productivity compatible with the Cobb-Douglas hypothesis. Coefficients reproduce very long adjustment lags with a standard "inverted V" form in the GDP and relative price impact.

As always when working with capital stocks, R2 are very high. There is, however, a risk that very small forecasting errors on the stock may result in fairly large errors in the corresponding flow, i.e. investment in its National Account definition.

Capital Long run elasticities with respect to production and relative prices

	F	G	I	UK
(1) Expected output	0.094	0.275	0.246	0.142
(2) Effective and past GDP	0.500	0.681	0.753	0.643
(3) Sum of (1) and (2)	0.594	0.956	0.999	0.785
(4) Expected relative price	0.281	0.174	0.136	0.214
(5) Effective and past relative price	1.187	0.710	0.520	0.643
(6) Sum of (4) and (5)	1.468	0.884	0.656	0.857

The information given by the table is more mixed than for labour demand For Germany and Italy, the results (again given the combined standard deviations) are not incompatible with those formerly obtained and a joint estimation process with constraints on the coefficients across the equation would insure the uniqueness of the underlying production ~~front~~ frontier. For the United Kingdom, and above all for Germany, both tables are clearly in conflict and the Cobb-Doublas hypothesis should be rejected or at least more closely investigated.

3. Real wage rate

Average real wage per head is estimated as a function of average labour productivity both expected (as a bargaining power component) and realized (with a distributed lag), the unemployment rate acting as a delaying factor in the adjustment process between productivity increases and real wage increases.

The definition of expected productivity raises, however, a problem since expected output has to be combined with expected employment. Now, employment projections are available in the survey data on a bi-annual basis only. These data series had therefore to be interpolated into quarterly data and are therefore of a lesser quality than the output data. Results should therefore taken with some caution. Indeed, R^2 are lower than in the other relations and stability tests are closer to the limit. However the equations do show the desired steady- state properties, i.e. the long-run equilibrium elasticity between real wages and real labour productivity is equal to one.

../..

4. Comparative forecasting performances

Although the introduction of Business Survey Variable as a replacement for purely mathematical expectation processes does improve the quality of the equation in terms of goodness of fit and stability test there remains to see whether or not it improves the forecasting performances of the equations. We used the same technique as in chapter I and II i.e. out-of-sample forecasts based in this case on the period 1981-1 to 1982-3 (the latest quarterly data available when this paper was written).

The real wage, labour demand and capital demand equations were reestimated without Business Survey Data as expected variables, these being replaced by projections from ARIMA processes.

In order to obtain comparable magnitudes, the forecasting results were compared using the Theil U statistics i.e.

$$\sum_{i=1}^{n} (P_i - 0_i)^2 / \Sigma 0_i^2$$

where P_i = forecasted values

0_i = observed values

The results confirm that the econometric equation, plus survey is superior to the econometric equations plus pure "statistical" (ARIMA) expectations, with two exceptions; labour demand in Germany and capital demand in Italy.

U-Theil statistics, forecast vs. observations 1981-1 to 1982-3

		France	Germany	Italy	United Kingdom
Labour demand	without BSD*	0,187	0,269	0,163	0,260
	with BSD	0,166	0,299	0,155	0,251
Capital demand	without BSD	0,165	0,179	0,072	0,127
	with BSD	0,153	0,128	0,111	0,101
Real wages	without BSD	0,365	0,413	0,390	0,385
	with BSD	0,288	0,401	0,295	0,339

(*) BSD = Business Survey Data

without BSD = with BSD replaced by ARIMA projections.

General Conclusions

Despite the provisional character of our results, we believe that a more systematic use of Business Survey Data in macro-models should be of some benefit to their forecasting performance, even when predicting more than one quarter ahead. As a corrolary, a more systematic approach to Business Survey Data collection would also be important: at the present time, some series are available as realizations only, others as expectations only, but few are available in both modes. Considering the results of our generalised logit approach, the availability of most series both in expectations and in realisation form would be of great help for their efficient exploitation in macroeconomic forecasts.

o o o

Editorial remark:

Due to limited space the appendix (regressions 1-24) could not be included in this volume. Readers interested in these 12 pages are adviced to contact the author or the CIRET Office.

Adams, F.G. (1964), "Consumer attitudes, buying plans and purchases of durable goods: a principal component's time series approach", R.E.S.

Adams, F.G. (1965),"Prediction with consumer attitudes: the time series-cross section paradox", R.E.S.

Anderson, O. (1951), "Konjunkturtest und Statistik", Allgemeines Statistiches Archiv, vol. 35.

Boas, J. and Koerts, J. (1963), "A simulation approach to the problem of the relationship between business test data and conventional statistics", Report 6311, Research Center of CIRET, 22 March.

Box, G.E.P. and Jenkins, G.M..(1970), "Time series analysis, forecasting and control", Holden Day, San Francisco.

Cox, D.R. (1970), "The analysis of binary data", Methuen, London.

European Economic Commission (1967) "Principes et méthodes des enquêtes de conjoncture harmonisées dans la Communauté", Direction Générale des Affaires Economiques et Financières.

Eisner, R. (1971),"Longer term capital expenditures anticipations and sales expectations: a micro-economic analysis", Report to the 10th CIRET Conference, Brussels.

Friend, I. and Thomas, W. (1971), "The predictive ability of expectational variables in different types of econometric models", Report to the 10th CIRET Conference, Brussels.

Goldfeld, S.M. and Quandt, R.E. (1972), Non-Linear methods in Econometrics", North-Holland Publishing Co.

Haïtovsky, Y. and Treyz, G.E. (1971), "The informational value of anticipation data in macro-economic model forecasts", Report to the 10th CIRET Conference, Brussels.

König, H., Nerlove, M. and Oudiz, G. (1981) "Improving the quality of forecasts from anticipations data", Paper presented at the 15th CIRET Conference, Athens, September.

Lindlbauer, J.D. (1968), "Schätzung des Produktionsindex mit Hilfe von Ex-post- und ex-ante-Daten des Konjunkturtests", I.F.O., Institut für Wirtschaftsforschung, München.

Lonnqvist, 1. (1971), "The prediction power of quantitative investment forecasts as given in the Swedish investment survey", Report to the 10th CIRET Conference, Brussels.

Modigliani, F. and Cohen, K.J. (1961), "The role of anticipations and plans in the economy of the firm and their use in econometric analysis and forecasting", University of Illinois, Urbana.

Nerb, G. (1973), "Unternehmerische Antizipationen über den Bedarf an Arbeitskräften", Mitteilungen aus der Arbeitsmarkt und Berufsforschung, Kohhammer Verlag, Stuttgart.

Nerb, G. (1975), "Konjunkturprognose mit Hilfe von Urteilen und Erwartungen der Konsumenten und der Unternehmer". Dunker & Humblot, Berlin.

Poirier, D.J. (1980), "A Lagrange multiplier test for skewness in binary logit models", Economic Letters, Vol. 5.

Persson, B.A. (1977), "Balance series as true and false indicators of quantitative changes. Theory and practice", Report to the 13th CIRET Conference, München.

Prentice, R.L. (1976), "A generalization of the probit and logit methods for dose response curve", Biometrics, vol. 32.

Theil, H. (1958), "Economic forecast and policy", North-Holland Publishing Co., Amsterdam.

Theil, H. and Jochens, D.B. (1960), "Ein Überblick über einige Studien zur Analyse von Konjunkturtestdaten", I.F.O. Studien: Zeitschrift des I.F.O. Institut für Wirschaftsforschung, vol. VI, Dunker & Humblot, Berlin.

Tobin, J. (1955), "The application of multivariate probit analysis to economic survey data", Cowles Foundation Discussion Paper 1.

Van der Linden, E.J. (1977) "Principal component analyses with data from the E.E.C. - entrepreneurial and consumer surveys", Report to the 13th CIRET Conference, München.

Summary of the Discussion

G. Nerb
IFO-Institut für Wirtschaftsforschung
Munich

The concluding session was headed by C.F. Bergsten, Institute of International Economics in Washington D.C. The first two papers of this meeting dealt with methodological questions of business cycle forecasting. Thus, in their paper M. Baba, N. Namura and S. Tahara described the new design of an economic indicator system for Japan. The discussant V. Zarnowitz, University of Chicago, critisized that the choice of time series used was not based on theory or was, at least, insufficiently explained. This leaves it open to Koopman`s reproach of "measurement without theory". Besides, in the indicator system there should be a clearer distinction between real and nominal indicators.

The second methodological paper of this session was presented by A. Dramais, EC-Commission in Brussels, and dealth with the use of business survey data in econometric models. The discussant, M . J. Pyythiä, Bank of Finland, referred to the necessity of that internal consistence of entrepreneurial planning data, but emphasized the external consistence of the aggregated data. Mr. Dramais agreed and pointed out that business survey results "corrected" with the help of the methods presented by him, would be examined in an econometric forecasting model for their usefulness in forecasting. This second step on the investigation has not yet been completed however. The forecasting model "BUSY", being used in Brussels is still in the testing phase. Further experiences with the use of business survey data in a shortterm forecasting model will be reported at the next CIRET Conference.

The major item of the last conference session was an up-to-date economic forecast. Carl. P. Blackwell, International Monetary Fund in Washington D.C. presented an updated form of the "World economic Outlook" published by the IMF in June 1983. This was followed by statements by I. Dryden, OECD in Paris, and by G.H. Moore, Center for International Business Cycle Research at the Columbia University - Business School in New York. The concluding paper was given by

G. Nerb, Ifo Institute in Munich, who presented the latest results of the "Economic Survey International", carried out world-wide by the IFO Institute. All speakers agreed that the cyclical upswing had set in the industrialized countries, above all in North America, and that it would continue over the next 12 months. There was only some disagreement on the assessment of the economic prospects in France, whilst the OECD indicators and the ESI results indicated no imminent cyclical recovery in that country, the leading indicators presented by G.H. Moore already pointed to a cyclical upswing there, occuring in the course of the next few months. According to the IMF and the results of the ECONOMIC SURVEY INTERNATIONAL the economic recovery in the industrialized countries will have limited positive effects on the newly industrialized and developing countries in 1984. It will take a prolonged cyclical upswing to lead to a marked improvement in the newly industrialized and developing countries.

Contributed papers

R.A. BATCHELOR:
Expectations, Risks and Rates of Return in Western Europe: An Interim Report

K. CHANG/D. CHEN:
The Establishment and Application of the Integration System for Diagnosing and Forecasting the Business Cycle - Taiwan as a Case

G.J. DOORNBOS/W.F. van RAAIJ:
The Impact of Economic Conditions and Expectations on Household Saving

J. DRYDEN:
The OECD System of Leading Indicators

M. GERARD/G. MICHEL:
Investment Behaviour and Economic Indicators

W. GERSTENBERGER:
Forecasting Accuracy and Analytical Significance of Qualitative and Quantitative Plan Data

M. HEWER/J. PINKERTON:
The Westpac Banking Corporation/Confederation of Australian Industry Survey of Industrial Trends as a Short-term Qualitative Indicator

Å. HOLMEN:
Use of Tendency Survey Data in Forecasting a Preliminary Figure for the Swedish Retail Sales Index

T.-T. HSU:
Questionnaire Formulation for Business Tendency Surveys and its Usefulness on Business Cycle Analysis

W.J . de JONGE:
Changing Economic Conditions and Consumer Sentiment since World War II

J.S. LANDEFELD/E.P. SESKIN:
A Comparison of Anticipatory Surveys and Econometric Models in Forecasting U.S. Business Investment

J.D. LINDLBAUER/W.H. STRIGEL:
Some Comments on Ph.A. Klein's Paper: "Improving Forecasts with Survey Indicators - an Empirical Test"

This CIRET Study can be ordered with:

CIRET Office
C/O IFO Institute for Economic Research
P.O.Box 86 o4 6o

D- 8ooo Munich 86